D1329679

Arts and Aesthetics:
An Agenda for the Future

Based on a conference held at Aspen, Colorado, June 22-25, 1976.
Co-sponsored by CEMREL, Inc.,
and The Education Program of
The Aspen Institute for Humanistic Studies
with support from **The National Institute of Education**

Edited by **Stanley S. Madeja**

CEMREL, Inc., *St. Louis, Missouri*

Prepared by CEMREL, Inc., a private
nonprofit corporation supported in
part as an educational laboratory by
funds from the National Institute of
Education, Department of Health,
Education and Welfare. The opinions
expressed in this publication do not
necessarily reflect the position or
policy of the National Institute of
Education, and no official
endorsement should be inferred.

Library of Congress catalog card
number 77-75363
Manufactured in the
United States of America

CEMREL, Inc.
3120 59th Street
St. Louis, MO 63139

Acknowledgments

CEMREL would like to acknowledge The National Institute of Education for its support of the conference, and the Education Program of The Aspen Institute for Humanistic Studies for its co-sponsorship of the conference.

Conference Chairman

Stanley S. Madeja
Vice-President
CEMREL, Inc.
Director
Aesthetic Education Program

Conference Committee

Francis Keppel
Director
Education Program
Aspen Institute for Humanistic
　Studies

Sue Marsh
Administrative Assistant
CEMREL, Inc.

Nancy Pelz-Paget
Assistant Director
Aspen Institute for Humanistic
　Studies

Wade M. Robinson
President
CEMREL, Inc.

Mary Runge
Secretarial Supervisor
CEMREL, Inc.

Barbara Smith
Art Instructor
Aspen High School

Editorial Committee

Harry Broudy
Professor of Philosophy and
　Education Emeritus
University of Illinois at
　Urbana-Champaign

Stanley S. Madeja
Vice-President
CEMREL, Inc.
Director
Aesthetic Education Program

Annette Schroeder
Editor
CEMREL, Inc.

Sheila Onuska
Editor
CEMREL, Inc.

Mark Schubart
Director of Education
Lincoln Center for the Performing
　Arts

Table of Contents

"Art is that which is the most real, the most austere school of logic, and the last judgment."   *(Marcel Proust)*

"Art is art, and that is that!"   *(A Massachusetts Third-grader)*

"I must study war and politics so my children can study mathematics and philosophy so their children will have the right to study poetry, music and art."   *(John Adams)*

Stanley S. Madeja

Introduction

This yearbook is a record of the proceedings of a conference held June 22-26, 1976, at Aspen, Colorado, sponsored jointly by CEMREL, Inc., and the Education Program of the Aspen Institute for Humanistic Studies, and supported by the National Institute of Education (NIE). It is our hope that both the conference described below and yearbooks such as this will continue on an annual basis as forums for research ideas in the arts, aesthetics, and their place in educational enrichment of our nation.

Titled "The Arts and Aesthetics: An Agenda for the Future," the 1976 conference had a broad purpose: constructing a national agenda for research and development in the arts and education.

The year 1976 was a milestone year, marking the end of ten years since the passage of the Elementary and Secondary Education Act of 1965, the primary stimulus for federal support of research and development in education. There was a great deal of activity in that period related to the arts: the creation of the Arts and Humanities Program of the United States Office of Education (U.S.O.E.); the evolution of the educational laboratories—with CEMREL AND SWRL (Southwest Regional Laboratory) taking a major interest in research and development in the arts; the foundation of The National Endowment for The Arts and The National Endowment for The Humanities; and the initiation of major programs in the arts and education by such private foundations as the JDR 3rd Fund. In addition, the role of the arts in the community grew, with attendance at arts events and museums reaching an all-time high, while the numbers of performing groups in dance and theatre multiplied, and many state arts councils came into being and prospered.

All of these circumstances indicated a rich and fruitful ten years for the arts; and it seemed particularly important in 1976 to reflect on the progress of the decade as a starting point for determining research plans for the future.

Traditionally, the arts have been concerned with the creation of the art object or the development of the performance. The primary efforts in the arts and arts education over the last ten years have been devoted to bringing the artist and performance into a more prominent position in **1** the school and community. Research in the arts and aesthetics as they relate to education, however, has been a small part of the total national effort in the field. Hence the need for a symposium to highlight the continued need for research in the arts and aesthetics and to assist in setting a research agenda that would complement the growth of the arts in the communities and in the schools.

The Conference Design

In order to make the task of the conference a manageable one, the charge to the participants was limited to five specific questions that became the topics for the background papers that are published here and the substance of the discussions by the four seminar groups into which the conference participants were divided. The agenda for research would be developed from the answers to these five questions. The questions were as follows:

1. As we look ahead, what do we see as the major research questions in the arts and/or aesthetics?
2. What do we see as the rationale for conducting research on any one or more of these questions over the next ten years?
3. What effects, if any, do we expect research results to have on the general education of any student at any level?
4. What connections do these questions have to what has already been done in the field?
5. What should be the design for an institute for advanced studies in the arts and aesthetics?

Nearly one hundred people drawn from various groups and agencies attended the conference. The invited participants came from twenty-one states and the Province of Ontario; and they represented twenty-four institutions of higher learning, eight federal agencies (including one Canadian), and ten national cultural and arts organizations. There were participants from eight other arts-related organizations—educational laboratories, an educational television station, an arts association—as well as officials from state departments of education, art instructors in public schools, artists, and school administrators at the state and local levels.

The conference was divided into two types of sessions: general sessions where nationally recognized speakers provided a broad perspective on the problems of setting an agenda for research in the arts and aesthetics, and seminar sessions where an opportunity was provided for discussion and specific recommendations for action.

In the general sessions, the speakers, who represented different national constituencies, addressed themselves to the broad conference theme of setting an agenda for the future. Francis Keppel, the former Commissioner of Education, and currently Director of the Program on Education of the Aspen Institute for Humanistic Studies, presented his perspective on the federal government's role in educational research in general, and its contribution to the arts and aesthetics in particular.

David Rockefeller, Jr., presented his viewpoint as Chairman of the Associated Councils of the Arts and Chairman of the Arts, Education, and Americans Panel, which is studying the role of the arts in education. Harold Hodgkinson, Director of the National Institute of Education, offered information on how the NIE views research in education and how the arts might play a part in a national research effort. Margaret Bush Wilson, Chairman of the Board of the National Association for the Advancement of Colored People, gave her views on the relationship of the arts to minority groups, and on how research might contribute to a better cultural climate in the schools.

Throughout the conference, the seminar groups used the five questions plus the substance of the general sessions and the background papers as the framework for their discussions. In addition, each of the four seminars worked with a panel composed of some of the authors of background papers. The panel members acted as resource persons for the seminar, providing background information and a variety of viewpoints. The seminar groups were chaired by Nancy Pelz-Paget, Herbert J. Burgart, John J. Mahlmann, and Jack Morrison.

Seminar Reports

The seminar reports, which are summarized in this section, provide the substance for the research agenda, and contain the thinking of the participants on the content of the proposed research and on research methods and priorities. The reports are prepared by each group presented below.

Seminar One: Chairperson, Nancy Pelz-Paget

In Seminar One, the following categories were identified as crucial topics for research:

ACQUISITION AND DISSEMINATION OF BASELINE NORMATIVE AND/OR DESCRIPTIVE DATA. This data would include the collection of vital information so as to more intelligently and systematically plan for implementing arts education programs statewide and nationally, including the following activities:

1. Establish an ERIC system in the arts;
2. Review the compilation of existing research literature and its accessibility to the general public;
3. Take inventory of arts resources by reviewing teacher arts-learning centers; museums, universities, and other collaborative institutions; other arts support systems, such as parks and recreation departments; products of federal cultural programs; and community education efforts.

This data-collecting should create arts information networks that would identify arts programs, institutions, and key people working in arts research, both nationally and internationally.

BASIC RESEARCH IN THE ARTS AND AESTHETIC EDUCATION. The purpose of this basic research would be to build a philosophical foundation for the

arts and aesthetic education with the following objectives:
1. Improve instruction;
2. Provide information to help in systematically planning programs for arts learning, both expressive and appreciative;
3. Create a better understanding of the role of aesthetics in cultural and inter-cultural education in our pluralistic society;
4. Provide access from the arts to the other subject-matter disciplines.

This research should be conducted in the following areas:
1. Conduct studies in the philosophy of art through probing basic aesthetic concepts and developing aesthetic theory.
2. Research the development of aesthetic sensitivity, perception, and cognition through study of multi-sensory perceptual development and perceptual skills and their relation to reading, math, spatial learning, and other disciplines.
3. Study the effects of media and technology, aesthetic learning environments, and creative behavior and decision-making on perception and learning.
4. Research the effectiveness of specific teaching strategies in the arts for arts specialists, generalists, and members of the community; and study the effectiveness of new teaching resources in the arts and aesthetics on environmental design, architecture, psychology, technology, community, and parents.
5. Develop and test the conceptual basis for curriculum development in the arts, determining concepts central to integrated arts programs.
6. Investigate the relationship of culture to the arts in such questions as: How do we maintain or protect cultural aesthetics and heuristic values? Establish new ones?
7. Develop methods and tools in the arts to enable educators and others to measure the progress of arts learning by developing tests to measure such arts-learning tasks as creativity and divergent thinking, the art work produced (the product), and aesthetic judgments.
8. Design implementation models as mechanisms for massive implementation of arts programs at all levels of development for all people. This could be accomplished through the establishment of arts and aesthetic centers in every school (including universities) and other institutions most ready for change. Concomitant programs in research funneled through or controlled (facilitated) by a central unit (Institute for the Study of Arts and Aesthetics) or set of units should also be set up. *(See Figure 1.)*

Seminar Two: Chairperson, Herbert J. Burgart
    Seminar Two reported three critical recommendations derived from several days of sharing both the import and the prospect of the future of

Figure 1

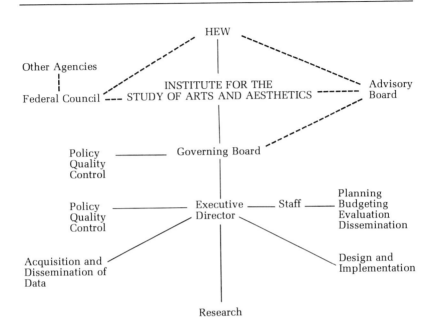

research in the arts and aesthetics. Throughout the discussions, it was evident that, while the participants all came from quite different backgrounds, experiences, and environments, and while they represented diverse constituencies, they nonetheless found an uncommon amount of agreement in matters of direct and long-lasting concern relative to the charge before them. Surely there were disagreements in semantics, but the general timbre was one of cooperation and of valuable professional sensitivity to the several larger issues beyond their own parochial interests. Another pleasurable realization was that each individual could submerge, for the time and the task at hand, his or her more insular and particularized interests in order to arrive at what can best be described as an "ecumenical" concern for the future of research in the arts.

CONSIDERATIONS FOR A RESEARCH INSTITUTE IN THE ARTS. In no particular order of priority, three clear and precise research needs to be met by an institute were voiced by Seminar Two: the need for the establishment of a national focus relative to research into fundamental issues surrounding the arts experience from the point of view of both the maker and the perceiver; the need for the establishment of a central clearinghouse for the gathering, collation, interpretation, analysis, retrieval, publication, and dissemination of arts research on a national/international scale; and the need for an arts-practitioner service that would provide in-service teacher programs, workshops, match-making/problem-solving services — all on a continuing-education basis.

A NATIONAL RESEARCH FOCUS FOR THE ARTS. Nowhere is there less evidence of nor greater need for substantial investment in the arts than in the area of research in the arts. Presently, research is fragmented, couched in the particular and often parochial interests of individual researchers, removed from a forum of common programmatic exchange of developments, and too often concerned with less than substantive issues. Why the arts in particular find themselves in this position is debatable but irrelevant at this time. That the problem exists is reason enough to address the issues through the establishment of a national research focus.

Realizing that the amount of funding for the establishment of such a national research focus in the arts would be necessarily limited, Seminar Two set forth some recommendations as to early priorities in this effort:

1. Research should address actual situations of making and perceiving the arts, of environmental effects on the arts, of educational/institutional interactions, or whatever actual arts situation exists.
2. Insofar as possible, research should be undertaken non-intrusively.
3. Research should be basic and descriptive rather than experimental, whenever and wherever possible;
4. Research should be microscopic rather than macroscopic in nature, developing a closer proximity to the arts phenomena;
5. Research should address the roles of both the maker and the perceiver as active participants and contributors to the arts experience;
6. Research should emphasize the long-term developmental profile of individual needs and abilities relative to making and perceiving in the arts, while at the same time recognizing the need for cross-sectional studies in support of longitudinal emphases;
7. Research should involve the several arts but should not presume, without some logical or empirical grounds, that findings may be generalized from one art form to another. Emphasis should be placed on issues and concepts that may yield broader understanding, application, and insight for all arts experiences;
8. Research should emanate from a programmatic base, which should find its direction through the multiple service needs of the varied constituencies of the arts practitioner.

A NATIONAL CLEARINGHOUSE FOR RESEARCH IN THE ARTS. Perhaps the greatest problem facing the arts practitioner at all levels today, is the relative waste of research effort when there is little or no emphasis on the pragmatic interpretation or application of research findings. Another critical issue for the arts practitioner is the lack of a central information source from which to draw relative to past and present research. Here, computer cross-referencing would be of invaluable service to the arts.

Annotated bibliographies, area and field analyses, comparative studies, longitudinal updating, and similar operations would provide a common and proven source base; eliminate duplicative efforts; and, at the same time, provide valuable research insights into the establishment of national research goals.

Finally, the problem of publication/dissemination of research findings and applications must be addressed resolutely. Through a concerted arts effort, common research methodologies, language, and interpretative formats may be established, without negating the unique differences within each art form. A central publishing focus for research in the arts could combine the existing thrust of individual arts voices into a national thrust, again reflecting the centrality of the arts, one to the other.

A NATIONAL ARTS-PRACTITIONER SERVICE. While there actually is some overlap between this and the two previous concepts, it was felt that an arts-practitioner service should be emphasized as a separate entity to bring home the need for a national focus on practitioner needs, not all of which are evident in the aforementioned proposals. First, some attention must be given the identification of practitioner needs. Many arts practitioners do not have the technical research background to be able to form reasonable or answerable questions. In-service programs/ consultants/workshops should be an integral arm of the arts-practitioner service, not so much on a "one-to-one" basis, which may be quite inefficient, but providing for a "resource-matching" function that could be very efficient and productive. In a sense, the arts-practitioner service follows logically after the "clearinghouse" function, which, in turn, is a practical function of the research effort recommended.

GOVERNANCE OF A RESEARCH INSTITUTE FOR THE ARTS. Given the three considerations as to function, certain conclusions as to governance of a national institute for research become natural mandates: that there be established an arts-practitioner constituent advisory group having the responsibility for initial goal-setting, periodic review, and ultimate evaluation of program substance; and that a "staff" research capability be established covering the three recommended functions of the institute.

OTHER MISCELLANEOUS CONSIDERATIONS. The following are other considerations discussed in Seminar Two:

1. The institute should recognize the breadth and complexity of its many constituencies: teachers at all levels, public taste-makers, politicians and policy-makers at all levels, professional organizations in the arts, and artists.
2. The institute should be insulated against fruitless overlap of its research and service delivery responsibilities with those of already established agencies. Here the intention is to emphasize the need for cooperation and sharing of efforts in an obviously fragmented arts thrust without setting up mutually exclusive preserves.

3. A "visiting fellows" program may well be established that could enhance the three primary functions of the institute. Fellows may be drawn from a variety of sources for a variety of reasons. Eminent research scholars, graduate-student research assistants, computer programmers, philosophers, authors, and so on, may each uniquely represent the national thrust of the institute and its goals.

4. Whenever and wherever possible, research efforts should be confined to existing settings rather than be allowed to create arbitrary experimental environments.

5. The institute should establish clear and precise communication links between and among practitioners of the arts for the purpose of enhancing the evident centrality of their needs, interests, and yields.

6. Because the participants of Seminar Two felt that they, as a group, were only beginning to approach a level of understanding, they expressed the need for a second similar meeting—representing the varied constituencies of the present conference—wherein shared recommendations could be prioritized and set in a more precise order.

PARTICULAR RESEARCH TOPICS OF INTEREST. Seminar Two proposed the following questions that might be investigated through research:

1. What are the maturational, cultural, psycho-motor, cognitive, and creative factors that facilitate learning in the arts?

2. How do the arts relate to each other as well as to other non-art areas?

3. How can we identify, evaluate, and enhance effective methods of teaching in the arts?

4. How can we best provide for the opportunity of the arts experience outside the classroom setting?

5. What is the impact of cultural/social significance derived from the arts experience?

6. How can we enhance an "arts accountability" and, in effect, direct it into becoming a more positive force in our society?

7. What are the current evaluative instruments available in the arts? What are the alternatives and potential alternatives to existing measurement instruments?

8. Will the optimal development of one's perceptual apparatus result in an increased appetite for "quality" arts, both from the point of view of the maker as well as the perceiver?

9. What physiological research findings have application to the arts experience? What physiological research must be undertaken in order to establish a fundamental base for understanding the arts experience? What current investigations into brain functions have meaning for the arts or for arts research?

10. What perceptual studies have application to the arts experience?

What research in human perception must be undertaken in order to establish a fundamental base for understanding the arts experience? For understanding the arts teaching/learning experience?

11. Can the professional artist function as an effective educator?

Seminar Three: Chairperson, John Mahlmann

Seminar Three participants reported their findings as a list of priority questions for research in the arts and aesthetic education. These questions comprise their agenda for research. The questions are as follows:

1. What are the educational benefits in terms of human competencies and attitudes that may be derived from comprehensive arts-in-education programs?
2. What are the social, political, and economic impediments to effective arts education in the schools? For example, how do we persuade school board members with limited background and understanding of the arts, of the value and worth of arts in education?
3. What contributions can comparative aesthetics make to the understanding of human nature and human culture?
4. What are the developmental patterns (stages) of human growth in aesthetic sensibilities?
5. How do changes in teaching and learning of arts in the education of every child strengthen the role of the arts in kindergarten through grade twelve?
6. What is the status of the arts in American public education, kindergarten through grade twelve?
7. What contributions can the arts make to increasing student motivation in schools?
8. What and where are exemplary programs in the arts and aesthetic education, and what makes them so?
9. How can we develop programs to prepare arts educators to be effective administrators of arts programs?
10. How do human beings learn about and through the arts, and how can instruction make such learning more effective?
11. What is the content of basic and sequential programs in the arts in the context of the regular classroom?
12. What are the effects of selected media images on value formation?
13. To what extent is the creation and appreciation of art a cognitive process?
14. What are the benefits of school-centered curriculum development?
15. Can evaluation instruments and procedures be designed that will facilitate the teaching of the arts and disclose artistic forms of learning and experience?

16. Can experience in the arts increase students' understanding in reading and math?

Figure 2 shows the structure of an institute for arts in education that would strive, among its other objectives, to improve general education in the schools by encouraging the teaching of all the arts to all the students. (See Figure 2).

Seminar Four: Chairperson, Jack Morrison

The report of this seminar was structured as follows: Each member of the group was asked to present two basic ideas or concepts fundamental to the arts and aesthetic education. A discussion was then held to evaluate each presentation. A subcommittee of the group took this material and organized it into the following four categories:

1. Research into Aesthetic Education
2. Research into Interdisciplinary Education
3. Research into Evaluation
4. Research Methods

Figure 3 shows the organization of these four categories and outlines the topics considered within each of them.

Next, the subcommittee of the group took the categories and organized them into five issues, each of which contained the "factored" ideas existing in the original charts. The five issues are as follows:

1. Nature of the phenomena of arts and aesthetic education.
2. Nature of learning in the arts and aesthetic education.
3. Nature of delivery in the arts and aesthetic education.
4. Nature of evaluation/assessment in the arts and aesthetic education.
5. Nature of the impact of the arts and aesthetic education.

The lists of research topics and research examples in each category are suggestive rather than definitive; and, in many instances, an item could be listed in more than one place.

1. TOPICS FOR RESEARCH IN THE NATURE OF THE PHENOMENA OF ARTS AND AESTHETIC EDUCATION: aesthetic experience, aesthetic response, identification of basic aesthetic skills, opportunities, interdisciplinary concerns, theory constructions, epistemology, and values.

- *Research examples:*
  - What constitutes aesthetic responsiveness to music?
  - What is the basis for aesthetic responsiveness to music and the basis for musical perception?
  - What is the influence of aptitude and maturation on musical responsiveness and perception?
  - How does achievement of performance skills, listening skills, and skill in analyzing compositional devices and stylistic characteristics affect the development of music responsiveness and perception?
  - What is the nature of the aesthetic experience and what does it add to the individual's life?

Figure 2

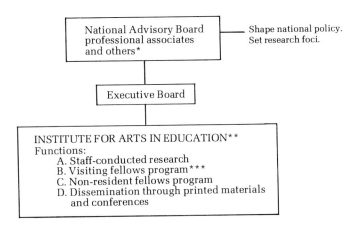

*State departments of education, school districts, cultural institutions, legislators, artists, federal agencies interested in arts and education and so on.

**NIE should solicit RFPs for limited competition from the field for institute.

***Artists, practitioners, scholars.

- What are the implications of the variety of views of what constitutes artistic knowledge? In each case, how do we achieve this knowledge? How do we learn about what we know? And how do we learn better?
- Inquiries in human experiencing and the "aesthetic" (generated toward theory-building—construct or synthesis—a scholarly eclecticism).
- Basic descriptive research into teaching and learning aims and purposes.
- Investigation of the child's ability to do aesthetic inquiry.

Further research inquiries. Inquiries into "experiencing" that recognize the possibility of the aesthetic as a phenomenon of human potential not exclusively within the domain of the arts; to attempt to establish a relationship between an understanding of experience—behaviors, perception, awareness—and our understanding of the arts. These correlated ways of knowing could better delineate the means to education for the aesthetic, that is, the determining of environmental conditions conducive to the aesthetic and hence allowing a better comprehension of the phenomenon itself as it relates to teaching and learning.

Inquiry could be in the arts and aesthetics, as well as in sociology, psychology, anthropology, philosophy, parapsychology, psychopathology, neurophysiology, social biology, biofeedback, psychocybernetics,

Figure 3

Research into Aesthetic Education	Research into Interdisciplinary Education	Research into Evaluation	Research Methods

Values	Psychology
	  Learner
	  Developmental stages
	  Etc., etc., etc.
		Learner
		  Affective,
		  Cognitive, etc.
			Selection of designs appropriate for problem-solving

Response	Sociology
	  Ecology (eco-systems)
	  Delivery systems
		Teacher	Unique designs (methods) for each art problem

Experience	Aesthetics
	  Value systems
	  Value education
		Community	Multi-cultural concerns

Society (multi-cultural)	Curriculum/Instruction	Instruments	Interdisciplinary concerns
Ecology	Biology	Curriculum	Delivery systems
Arts	Epistemology	Strategies	Staff development

Curriculum/Instruction	Multi-cultural concerns	Interdisciplinary
		  Synaesthesia
		  Chromaesthesia
		  Intersense modalities	

Evaluation	Arts	Multi-cultural concerns	
Epistemology		Delivery systems	
Aesthetics			
Interdisciplinary concerns			
Higher Education			
In-service/Pre-service			
Staff Development			

and so on. (This is an umbrella area that presumes a variety of interdisciplinary research.)

An institute such as the one described later in this report should provide the "luxury" of specialized, small-sample, longitudinal studies of behaviors from a sociological-phenomenological point of view (e.g., Munson, "Joey: An Inquiry in Enrichment and Affect," 1973-76, ongoing). These studies of individuals and small groups within context and their particular milieus (e.g., Tally's Corner) are often biographical and can be revealing of the affect of such phenomena as we call the aesthetic. However, they are time consuming, extended, and, because of their specific focus and sample size, not traditionally fundable/feasible in the current education-research mode.

To prescribe what the child ought to do (perform, achieve) entails the belief that the child *can* do "x"; but, it does not follow that what the child *can* do, he or she *ought* to do. We do not know what the case is with regard to the abilities of children to do aesthetic inquiry.

Problems in teaching basic aesthetic skills of response to art need to be identified; e.g., discerning and describing components and relations of works of art, and interpreting and assessing works of art.

2. TOPICS FOR RESEARCH INTO THE NATURE OF LEARNING IN ARTS AND AESTHETIC EDUCATION: development levels, learning environments, and biological, psychological, sociological, philosophical, multi-cultural, and cross-cultural considerations.

• *Research examples:*
  • What is the relationship of the arts to basic skills?
  • What are the entry levels for curriculum in aesthetics?
  • Are there developmental stages in adult aesthetic learning that are comparable to those of children? What socioeconomic factors, family factors, and demographic factors affect adults' aesthetic learning?
  • What applications to aesthetic learning are there in the recent research on hemispheric specialization of the brain?
  • What is the effect of the learning environment on aesthetic education?
  • What is the relationship between aesthetic education and general education (cognition, retention, etc.)?
  • What are the affective stages of development that parallel Piaget's cognitive stages?
  • Psycho-historiographies (Henry Murray's concept) by artist-teachers, teachers, principals, and so on, who have had significant careers in the arts.
  • Research into the nature of learning and experiencing in the arts and aesthetic education.
  • What types or experiences in formal education and in society will develop in the individual both artistic and critical skills and, in addition, the will to continue personal development beyond formal training?

- Development of a strong research base concerned with the major contributions of non-European cultures to the art cultures of the world in order to provide accurate baseline information for developing the complete history of the arts for this and future generations.

3. TOPICS FOR RESEARCH INTO THE NATURE OF DELIVERING THE ARTS AND AESTHETIC EDUCATION in the areas of teaching, staff development, pre-service and in-service training, multi-cultural concerns, institutional means, information-gatherings and funding.

- *Research examples:*
  - Given that arts/arts education occurs both within the school and in the community, basic research should address itself to aesthetic education that occurs in the schools.
  - How can teachers be encouraged to get involved with aesthetic education?
  - How can we maximize opportunities for aesthetic learning throughout the life-span?
  - How can results of research be effectively translated, interpreted, and communicated to the constituency for practical use?
  - Identify effective methods of staff development in the arts for boards of education, superintendents, coordinators, supervisors, principals, teachers, and develop ways of disseminating and diffusing those methods.
  - How are opportunities for the individual maximized?
  - How do various social agencies intervene between audiences and artists?

4. TOPICS FOR RESEARCH INTO THE NATURE OF ASSESSING/EVALUATING THE ARTS AND AESTHETIC EDUCATION through individual assessment, program assessment, and development of methodologies.

- *Research examples:*
  - How to develop evaluation systems that take both skills and will into account as they develop the individual.
  - Research in evaluation in terms of assessing individual progress, assessing program progress, and developing methodologies.
  - Research on how can we tap the resources of the external offerings (community centers, media) so that there can be some meaningful cooperation in educational programming.

5. TOPICS FOR RESEARCH INTO THE IMPACT OF THE ARTS AND AESTHETIC EDUCATION: short-term and long-term; different experiences, maturation, multi-cultural concerns; and on various populations, on values, and on thinking abilities.

- *Research examples:*
  - Does early aesthetic experience affect values and personality at mid-life? If so, what are the implications for society?
  - What are the research methods that derive specifically from the arts themselves (drama, music, art, dance, etc.) rather than fı other disciplines (e.g., psychology, social psychology, ethnology,

on the one hand, or history analysis, etc., on the other)?

- Research on the effect and impact of aesthetic education on the development of human values.

BASIC INSTITUTE FOR ADVANCED STUDIES. In addition, Seminar Four recommends that a center be created to carry on research in the arts and aesthetic education. While research into immediate needs of the field should be initially emphasized, Seminar Four recommends that an appropriate balance between basic and applied research be maintained.

Towards these ends, Seminar Four recommends that a policy body be created, composed of relevant discipline specialists. The policy group will be drawn from the entire constituency of arts organizations, arts support organizations, educators, artists, educational institutions, educational support groups, and leaders from the lay public.

Research Issues

A number of issues focusing on policy and methods of research emerged from the conference and affected the formulation of the research agenda.

The conference also strongly advocated support for the basic research needed for continued expansion of the knowledge base in the arts and aesthetic education. There was a great deal of concern among participants that basic research of all types be continued and be upgraded in quality, and that opportunities for this type of research be expanded. While there is a need for applied and practical studies relating to the teaching of arts and aesthetics at every level, there is still a critical shortage of the scholarly inquiry that, over time, provides the theoretical voice for the field. The knowledge base needs to be expanded, and that knowledge needs to be in the hands of the practitioner. Scholars who would like to pursue historical or empirical study in or about the arts should have opportunities to gain support for their work. Increased support for basic research projects initiated by individuals or institutions in the field was deemed critical by the conference participants since there has been little opportunity for basic research funding at national or state levels for at least five years. The conference participants agreed that this concern should not be neglected or set aside.

Related to the issue of support for basic research is the question of the modes of inquiry for research in the arts and aesthetic education. This concern emerged because of the continuing emphasis and reliance on technology to generate data for research. Research in the arts and aesthetics should not be limited to the manipulation of data; it should include all the domains of inquiry, analysis, and method as they relate to the arts and aesthetic education. A number of conference participants were concerned that the empiricists would take over arts research. They argued the need to maintain a balance between empirical types of studies and those that were more anthropological, sociological, or historical in approach.

The general advocacy for basic research was tempered by the concern that there was a break in the flow of information between researcher and audience. The ultimate audience for information derived from research in education is made up of teachers and, by extension, other individuals responsible for instruction. At present, they are not getting the information they need or want. Persons representing the teacher and the classroom point of view at the conference had a needs-oriented perception of research. Their position was very clear: Any research conducted in the arts or aesthetics that is applicable to education should connect directly with the student and the teacher in the classroom, and with the administrator in the school. They argued vehemently that school-based research, or applied research, ought to have the highest priority in any agenda for the future.

The distance between the teacher and other school-based personnel, and the "researcher" from agencies outside the school is a problem not only for arts research but for any research carried on in schools; and there are many reasons for this. Schools present many obstacles to conducting research; it is far easier to conduct studies outside the classroom.

Furthermore, the arts are not priority areas for school research; research issues related to student achievement in basic skills are of far more interest to the schools. At the same time, the arts community does not have a large cadre of trained researchers who can work in schools. The result of this situation is the very small amount of research activity in the arts initiated by either school personnel or outside researchers.

Conference participants agreed on the critical need to initiate more school-based studies whose outcome would be the improvement of arts instruction. Both those representing the schools and the researchers acknowledged the need to work together to this end; and, although the conference assisted in developing some links between the groups, the mechanism for further cooperative efforts still need to be created. There was agreement that there should be more cooperation between the researcher and the classroom practitioner in the arts, and that studies having direct implications for the improvement of arts instruction in the schools should be carried out. As a result, it was strongly recommended that further investigation of the areas for cooperation between schools and research should have a prominent place on any future agenda for the arts and aesthetics.

Another major issue that evolved from conference discussions was the varying quantities of research in some areas of arts education. In reviewing the discussions and the papers, it became evident that more research was being initiated in visual arts and music education than in theatre or dance education. Visual arts and music have had a long tradition of research, while theatre and dance are just now beginning to build their research history. There are two different factors hindering the growth of research activity in these disciplines. While there is only a small group of researchers trained to conduct research in the arts in general, the number of those trained in or interested in theatre or dance research is far smaller. Very few individuals in the fields of theatre or dance are trained to initiate, design, and implement research studies.

Secondly, research has not traditionally been a part of the body of knowledge in theater or dance education, at least partly because these programs have not been as strong a part of the school curriculum. This is a problem that art and music faced and solved earlier in this century; theatre and dance are now moving to correct it. Improving the climate and capabilities for research in theatre and dance was, therefore, a major concern at the conference.

The role of the artist in research was another theme that developed during the conference. Should the artist be the researcher, or should the artist be the subject of research? Some of the arguments over these questions evolved from differing perceptions of what constitutes research in the arts. The term "researcher" was used in many discussions to mean "an individual possessing a particular scholarly background and special training." The artist was rarely considered a "researcher." Traditionally, the artist, the arts object, and the arts experience are the phenomena to be investigated. The researcher investigates the way artists work, the objects and performances they create, the effects of the arts on the society, and the audience's response to arts objects and events. The researcher, once removed from the creative act and the created object, studies its properties, makes generalizations, and determines theoretical and pedagogical applications. This conception of research as a strictly academic or professional pursuit does not allow for what many conference participants saw as a major part of the role of the artist—the investigation of problems within their area of interest.

The artist as researcher investigates a process, a technique, a creative problem—probing all the elements and components of that problem in order to solve it. For example, the sculptor conducts a controlled study of various methods of casting bronze, or a painter studies the possibilities of a new epoxy material, or a technical director experiments with lighting techniques. These activities can all be considered research. They add to the body of knowledge in the field, they contribute to the development of the artist, and they enhance the teaching of the arts. Without playing a semantic game, but using these terms to illustrate the issue, it became evident that, in the minds of most of the conference participants, the "artist" could conduct "research" in the arts and aesthetics, although the means might differ from more clinical approaches. Accordingly, the artist is not to be confined to being the subject of research. Both groups—researchers and artist/researchers—must work to make their contributions applicable to the concerns of education.

The conference participants were also particularly aware of the need to provide the results of research in the arts and aesthetics to the classroom, the school, and the whole field. At present, there is no single source of statistical data such as, for example, the number of arts teachers now in the schools, the number of student enrollments in the arts, the number of credit hours allocated to the arts, and the amount of dollars spent on the arts in various categories. This type of information can be collected through a centralized agency for use as raw baseline data for setting long-range research priorities. The conference participants saw the need for a simple method of collecting this kind of information, and for a simple process of disseminating it to all constituencies within the arts field.

Also, there is no separate clearinghouse for the arts and aesthetic education within the present ERIC system. Studies relating to these areas are buried in other subject areas or are not entered into the system at all. The need to establish a clearinghouse for the arts and aesthetic education was a dominant issue throughout the seminar discussions. Mechanisms for storage and dissemination of information were outlined in the seminar reports.

Related to all of the conference discussions was the question of how research priorities should be set and by whom: Should the researcher supported by public monies be free to investigate any topic? Should research topics be targeted for the national welfare, with support going to persons who are knowledgeable about or willing to work on these problems? In the past, research topics have been chosen by individuals and not on the basis of any kind of national agenda. Research and development priorities concentrating talent and resources on the solution of major problems in the arts have not been articulated. The need to set these priorities was continually raised at the conference. The participants felt that the future of the field required a more coordinated approach to research. Their specific recommendations as to the priorities and contents of the agenda for the future are contained in the following paragraphs.

The Research Agenda

We were able to categorize eight primary areas of research for an agenda. These areas are drawn from the seminar reports, the general sessions, and the conference discussions. They are as follows:

1. TESTING AND REVISING THEORIES OF AESTHETIC DEVELOPMENT IN STU-DENTS. This area of research would concern itself with how aesthetic education and aesthetic learning contribute to general learning and enhance the overall growth and development of the student. Further, this research will examine the relationship between aesthetic response in the sensory modes—aural, visual, auditory, kinetic, and olfactory— and its relationship to cognitive functions. In the area of developmental psychology, research is needed to determine how the child develops aesthetically and to define descriptors for aesthetic development that will provide some generalizable criteria for categorizing aesthetic response. Answers are needed to such questions as: Are there structural properties of aesthetic development, and can they be discerned? Does aesthetic development relate to any existing developmental theories? Is

it hierarchical or linear? Does growth in aesthetic development contribute to cognition?

2. OPTIMIZING THE LEARNING EXPERIENCE WITHIN THE SCHOOLS THROUGH AESTHETIC EDUCATION AND THE ARTS. This research would include: design and development of aesthetic learning environments that enhance the total instructional process; design of experimental facilities to explore the effects of environmental conditions on aesthetic learning and cognition; examination of the aesthetics of media and technology and their effect on learning and teaching; investigation of the effects of arts and aesthetic education programs on general learning; investigation of ways to enhance arts instruction in schools, and to improve teacher training in the arts and aesthetics; answering the questions: How do the arts relate to other areas of knowledge, and how can we transmit the knowledge to the practitioner?

3. INVESTIGATING THE RELATIONSHIP OF CULTURAL VALUES TO AESTHETIC LEARNING. Research in this area would focus on how cultural biases affect visual, auditory, and kinetic concept formation; how various cultural conditions may affect general learning in mathematics, reading, and the arts; and how the aesthetic values of a culture affect the learning of basic skills.

4. IMPROVEMENT OF EVALUATION IN THE ARTS AND AESTHETICS. This area of research would focus on the development of new testing methods and instruments for assessing aesthetic learning; the development of generalizable instruments across all grade levels for assessing student achievement; and the development of diagnostic instruments for use by teachers and school systems in planning and assessing school projects and programs in arts and aesthetics.

5. PREPARATION OF AN EDUCATIONAL POLICY IN THE ARTS AND AESTHETICS FOR THE PUBLIC SCHOOLS. Studies in this area would investigate the value systems now operating in the schools to reveal how aesthetic learning and arts education might fit into those systems. Research would highlight roadblocks that prevent the installation of aesthetic education and arts programs in the schools. Studies to determine what data to collect and how to collect it would be included as part of this area. Answers must be provided to such policy questions as how the accelerating pace of community involvement in the arts will affect school policy.

6. ESTABLISHMENT OF A MECHANISM FOR DATA COLLECTION IN THE ARTS AND AESTHETIC EDUCATION THAT WILL RELATE TO EXISTING SYSTEMS SUCH AS THE NATIONAL CENTER FOR EDUCATION STATISTICS IN THE EDUCATION DIVISION OF THE DEPARTMENT OF HEALTH, EDUCATION, AND WELFARE. The identification and standardization of methods for collecting data will permit more accurate identification of future needs in the field. In addition, this information will allow a more precise and systematic assessment of the needs of the field. In addition, the U.S.O.E. should support, within its network of ERIC Clearinghouses, an ERIC Clearinghouse concentrating on the arts and aesthetic education. This would

compensate for the current lack of such a central information source and would facilitate ongoing research. The clearinghouse would aid in wider distribution, dissemination, and usage of research information.

7. CREATION OF A NATIONAL CENTER FOR RESEARCH IN THE ARTS AND AESTHETICS. Such a center would concentrate the resources and talents available and direct them to the larger issues facing arts education in our schools. This would involve a permanent organizational structure such as an institute or center capable of coordinating research and of providing a mechanism for scholars at all levels to conduct basic research in the arts and aesthetic education. Such a center for research would define priorities for the field as a whole and would enable scholars to carry out short-term research projects. The research program would act as a broker between and a catalyst for the scholars, resources, and institutions in the field, and the academic and school communities.

The eight research areas defined above are not necessarily listed in the order of their priority. Taken together they represent the agenda for the future for research in the arts and aesthetics in relation to education.

I

Speeches from the
General Sessions

In order to give the research agenda the broadest source for topics, the four speakers who addressed the general sessions of the Aspen Conference were asked to address themselves to the needs or trends in research in the arts and aesthetics. Each speaker brought a different perspective. **Francis Keppel,** as a former Commissioner of the United States Office of Education, described what he termed "trend lines" in education. He noted in his remarks that, even though interest in the arts in our American society has been increasing since the sixties, population, teachers, research funding, and basic skills have all been decreasing in education. Nor is there much change for the better in relations between artists and educators, or among specialities in the arts. Research is needed, **Keppel** said, to form public policy on and to define the role of the government in the arts and education, to develop teacher training in the arts, to assess the arts resources in the community and the impact of media, to determine the place of arts in "basics" education, and to unify all factions toward the setting of research priorities in the arts that are advantageous to all.

Harold L. Hodgkinson, who spoke next, is Director of the National Institute of Education—the federal-government agency whose responsibility it is to design and implement a national program in educational research and development. The National Institute of Education is a relatively new agency, created in 1972, that is still seeking ways to interact with the research community. **Hodgkinson** outlines program areas the agency has defined for research and development: basic skills (including aesthetic education); career education, awareness, and access; educational equity (including desegregation studies); women's studies; education and the law; and bilingual education. The NIE studies educational trends (such as the recent competency-based emphasis) and current problems in education (such as population decline), and then supports projects, labs, and centers that do research and development to fill needs as they become evident. The NIE also explores educational delivery systems to disseminate materials and reorganize people's access to education. He indicated that the NIE believes the arts to be indispensable and advocates alliances between artists, teachers, schools, and researchers in order to improve the quality of education and life for the average American by means of effective programs in the arts.

David Rockfeller, Jr., who has been an activist in cultural organizations and on the professional staff of performing arts groups, described his present role as Chairman of the Arts, Education, and Americans Panel, which is studying the state of the arts in education in public schools. He noted in his remarks that recommendations arising from the study should be made to the power structure of public schools, and should address the role of all the arts in the context of public schools. **Rockefeller** pointed out the need to strengthen teacher training in

23

the arts; to expand the existing arts programs to include other areas such as dance, theater, media; to improve the planning process to include each individual school; and to enhance the interaction between the arts in schools and the arts in the community. To facilitate these and other recommendations, research is needed in such areas as perception; creativity; the arts as related to other learning; and the arts as related to the handicapped and other "special populations"; and the evaluation of student progress and of arts programs. Further, he sees the necessity of translating all the data into workable contexts for arts programs in the schools.

Margaret Bush Wilson sounded a warning note about the inclusion of minorities in any agenda for arts research. She noted that, in our multicultural country, persons from a huge variety of minority groups need to be involved in all facets of American life lest their special contributions be lost to us. Opportunities need to be made available to develop talents and promote accomplishment for all the varieties of people. We dare not overlook existing problems resulting from the decreasing involvement of people in the productive processes in our country as we plan an agenda for the future of arts and aesthetic education. **Wilson** asked the question: Can our country sustain a climate of equality of opportunity when educated and unskilled people alike are being systematically excluded both from learning and from working? In 200 years, the descendants of multi-faceted groups of people have created this mighty nation, and have weathered some very difficult times. But, she concluded, we can lose all we have built if we don't search for lasting solutions to some of our society's most urgent problems. She challenged the participants to provide some of the needed equipment.

Francis Keppel

The Arts and Education Today as Compared to the Sixties

Stanley Madeja has asked me, as an ex-Washington-bureaucrat, to compare the situation in the arts and education in the mid-1960s to what I think is going on today. He has also been unwise enough to let me make a few remarks about forming public policy in this area.

First, as to the comparison — it is what might be called the "Rip Van Winkle task." Compared to a decade ago, I find a higher level of *both* action *and* dissatisfaction with the arts and education situation.

Let me refer to trend lines — lines that seem to be going up, going down, and staying the same. First, *going up*: There seems to be far more activity in the arts in the society — stimulated by private, federal, and state funds — than in education. In the last decade, arts activity in society included the following growths:

- the number of professional dance companies with budgets over $100,000 has risen from fewer than ten to fifty;
- resident, nonprofit, professional theater has grown from thirty to fifty;
- community arts councils from 100 to 1,200;
- state appropriations rose from $1.7 million to $55 million;
- Harold Horowitz reports that the United States artist labor force now exceeds 1 million, and in 1975 grew 5.5 percent;
- The National Endowment for the Arts grew from $2.5 million to $74 million;
- bachelor degrees in fine arts have more than doubled;
- undergraduate enrollments in the arts in recent years have been increasing from 12 percent to 23 percent a year.

No wonder the arts organizations in this country are referred to, in one of the reports you have before you, as "a growth industry." This seems to me a major change within a decade. Let me emphasize its importance. In the long run, education is profoundly affected by external forces in society. If the arts take a larger part in the nation's life, eventually they will take a large part in the educational institutions. Our job is to help in the process.

FRANCIS KEPPEL *is Director of the Program of Education of the Aspen Institute for Humanistic Studies.*

But there are obviously serious troubles. The early 1960s were a time of hope and optimism about the importance of education in the society. Far more was promised than was wise. While the words "lack of confidence" may be too strong, they may not be far off the mark in describing today's educational mood. The public is, in fact, less doubting than the educators themselves. Therefore, not only are we faced with dealing with the attitudes of others, we have to face our own attitudes.

What are some of the discouraging trends? The lines going down in the past decade include the following:

- The population, ages five to thirteen, has gone down 4 percent in the last decade and will drop another 11 percent in the next decade. It will drop 15 percent in ages fourteen to seventeen.
- The Office of Education estimates that there will be a drop of 9 percent in secondary teachers in the next decade.
- Though hard data seems to be lacking, we are all hearing more and more reports of a reduction in the number of arts teachers in the schools.
- Research funds available for studying education in the arts, according to CEMREL, Inc., have been reducing in the last four years.
- The reports from the National Assessment on Educational Progress show the opposite of progress in reading, writing, and science — and the understandable public reaction is emphasis on the basics.
- The report of an official of the federal government itself emphasizes an even greater lack of coordinated policy for the arts and education.

Compared to the activities in the arts, therefore, "Rip Van Winkle" has to report the opposite of a growth industry.

But some things stay the same. As several of the papers before you make clear, we still lack basic data on the arts in education in the schools. As Elliot Eisner wrote, "studies . . . of the arts in American schools have only rarely been undertaken. I refer here to statistical descriptions of important dimensions of the field. . . . We do not know," he goes on, "whether enrollment in the arts has changed significantly since, say, 1970. . . ." And apparently we still have only a few standardized test instruments available, even though more and more states — rightly or wrongly — are demanding data on an annual basis of how well the schools are doing. I can assure you, as a veteran witness wriggling before legislative committees, life is miserable without data. Without it, your friends on the committees can't help you.

Perhaps you will forgive me as an outsider for both noting and reporting on another similarity over the last decade. In general, I do not sense much change in the attitudes of artists toward educators, or vice versa. There seems to be a continuing uncertainty (should I say lack of trust?) in the relationship, even though there is far more interaction than there was a decade ago because of cooperative programs. Nor does there seem to be a substantial change in the relations between the several specialties within the world of the arts in education, which in the 1960s were scrambling for their place in the sun. I hope that I am wrong.

So much for the trend lines, up, down, and the same. What inferences can one draw? Let me emphasize that I am neither researcher, nor artist, nor teacher, but rather someone who has been asked to look at this situation and comment from the point of view of forming public policy. I am not competent to propose the research strategies that you are being asked to develop. I can only suggest some approaches to their development.

First, at a time when educational institutions are in the situation of having to manage decline, they need allies and sources of help. The growth of arts in thousands of communities suggests a source *both* for help in teaching students *and* in teacher in-service education. The next decade is no time to let old troubles block future collaboration. At this conference, we should not consider schools and colleges themselves the primary education instrument in the arts, but rather recognize the role of the immediate community and the vast impact of television. To me this implies that the approach to a research strategy should not be limited to the formal schooling process.

Second, perhaps the word "research" in its *purest* meaning does not include the kind of nuts-and-bolts, regular collection of statistical data that I mentioned earlier. If so, I hope that you will not be "pure" in your research. Those who are interested in the arts and in research in arts and education, and want to help, simply have to know what is going on.

Third, remembering the overstatements and overclaims of the 1960s, let us beware of promising too much or using good arguments in the wrong way. One example of what seems to me the right approach is in Morris Weitz's paper, with regard to research problems that are "just tractable enough." Another example is in the area of arguing for the arts in schools on the grounds that they help to teach the so-called "basics." How far should one go? My own strong preference is to place the major emphasis on the arts as a necessary part of human education and argue the case on those grounds primarily. Let me remind you of Elliot Eisner's words on this matter in the section of his paper subtitled, "Studies of the Non-Artistic Consequences of Work in the Arts."

My last point may seem mundane, if not positively political. The community concerned with arts and education is in too tight a spot — if "Rip Van Winkle" is right — to allow the onrushing events to split it into factions. The need seems to be, rather, to get together, to seek allies, to take part actively in developing public policy, and to seek a more clearly defined role for federal and state governments. It is surely the case that quarreling factions will not create conditions conducive to support within education or government. Can we not agree that we have much to learn, that priorities are essential, and that there is strength in unity to urge the setting of those priorities? I hope so.

Harold L. Hodgkinson

Arts in the Future: A Pragmatic Analysis

I'm very sorry that I can't be with you today* in what's obviously going to be a very exciting conference, but I will be in other parts of the world. I'd much rather be in your part of the world just because I know it fairly well, and it is indeed a marvelous place to do what you're doing. I would like to talk for about a half an hour today — granted it is a somewhat dull "talking-head" format, but we'll try to liven it up a bit — about the arts in the future, a pragmatic analysis.

One of the things you might be interested in knowing about is NIE's activities in the area of the arts. I'm very happy and proud to be associated with CEMREL, one of the laboratories and centers that is funded by NIE, in the establishment of a teacher center at the John F. Kennedy Center for the Performing Arts in Washington, D. C. That center is now about to become a going concern, and we are all very pleased and proud of it.

The second is a decision that was made by me just yesterday, and that is that we will, as part of the Institute's efforts, develop a series of cooperative, special relationships with a fair number of institutions. And one of the first seven special relationships to be approved will be a center for the arts, humanities, and aesthetic education. It is our hope that the center can get underway in the very near future. It will emphasize the things NIE has special competence in, that is, research, evaluation, and the development of prototypes in education. We are particularly interested in programs of in-service teacher education because we know that the current teaching force is roughly the group that will be with us for the next decade. It is one of the few opportunities that we have had in American life to upgrade by a considerable margin the quality of the average teacher in the American school. So these two activities, I think, are some indication of the Institute's commitment to the arts and to education.

I'd like to talk to you briefly this afternoon about our heritage in terms of what's gotten us where we are as it relates to the arts; secondly,

---

HAROLD L. HODGKINSON is Director of the National Institute of Education.
*This speech was presented via videotape.

where we are in the arts at present; and a few concepts about where we might be going as far as the future in the arts is concerned.

First of all, let me just tell you one or two brief things about the role of educational research and development in the United States. The government provides most of the money for educational research, development, dissemination, and evaluation. Indeed, the government provides about $511 million of that total. The states come up with about $40 million, and local communities produce about $4 million. The foundations produce $57 million. About eleven foundations provide 85 percent of that money, and then independent sources account for $5 million. Thus the total amount from all sources in the United States for educational research, development, dissemination, and evaluation is about $617 million. That may sound like a lot of money to you; but, if you think of the fact that the total American investment in education runs about $116 billion — not million, but billion — you can see that we're spending a little less that one-half of one percent on finding out what works, what didn't work, and why.

If you look at agriculture, you'll find that between 3.6 percent and 4 percent of their total goes into finding out what works and why. In medicine, the figure is somewhere between four percent and eight percent, depending upon whose numbers you count and whose numbers you trust.

We are, then, I think, underfunded in terms of the amount of money that we as a nation have put into educational research and development. It's an enormous undertaking in terms of its total size. One hundred and sixteen billion dollars is nothing to be sneezed at. We do, however, need to know far more about what works and why.

The National Institute of Education was established by Congress to do just that. Our mission is to improve the quality of education in the United States through research and development. It's the only agency that has *that* as its lead title. There are, however, about thirty federal agencies that do work of this sort, and part of our job is to try to establish some coordination with other federal agencies and with other granting sources that are interested in the same kind of thing we're interested in.

The National Institute has six specific program areas. They are probably familiar to you. We do work in the basic skills and, incidentally, we consider our program in aesthetic education to be part of the basic skills program. We do a lot of work in education and work, relating career awareness and career preparation to career access. We are very interested in the issues of education equity and do work in desegregation studies, in women's studies, in education and the law (which is a rapidly increasing field), and in bilingual studies. We have a program called "School Capacity for Problem Solving," which begins with the notion that there is within every school building a large number of people with great talents and that those talents have never been successfully put forward. So that program emphasizes the notion that we should capitalize on the talents that are currently within schools rather than relying entirely on our outside experts who will come in, tell teachers what they should be doing, and then leave on the next plane.

In addition, the finance and productivity part of our operation runs the ATS-6 satellite program, which is one of the world's largest educational satellite delivery systems; and, in general, is concerned with the issues of the delivery and the financing of education at every level, from kindergarten through graduate school. We also fund, through that part of our program, the University of Mid-America, which is the only university in the country that crosses state lines. As you know, that is a fairly difficult thing to pull off.

So the program areas where NIE has been committed are those we think provide more effective ways to organize than using student age as a cutoff criterion; and we have chosen to organize programmatically.

We currently fund seventeen regional laboratories and centers that do research, development, and dissemination dealing with curriculum and other matters involved in the public schools. The seventeen labs and centers form one of the major sources of competent, professional work within the field of education research and development.

Let me now tell you just a little bit about the heritage out of which, I think, we begin. If you look back at the history of education in this country, you find that there are two outstanding examples of interesting laws, and they were both passed early in our heritage — one in 1642, and the other in 1647. These are referred to as the "Old Deluder Laws"; and they are so called because at that particular time in our history, Satan was seen as the "Old Deluder." It was assumed that, if one was not able to read or write or keep oneself busy at all times, Satan would be there, and we know how it would end from that point on.

Thus, from the beginning of our nation, we have had a feeling that somehow play is wrong. The devil has work for idle hands to do. And because the arts appear to be "playing," there is a sort of *ergo* in many people's minds that the arts are, therefore, inappropriate as part of an educational system. This is not exactly a new idea. John Calvin wrote about it in the *Institutes of Christian Religion;* and, indeed, if you go back to Plato's and Socrates' time, you find a great deal of discussion about whether Doric or Lydian music is best for soldiers, and if soft, romantic music would make a soldier less willing to fight. So the issue of play as being inappropriate in a school setting — that is, education is serious and play is not — is, I think, something that has given us a lot of difficulty in our American educational system.

Indeed, even zoologically you will find that play is the primary learning mechanism for most species. And, if you look at animals playing, you will find that they are quite serious. If they make mistakes once, they seldom make them twice. It's a very effective learning environment. In addition, if you will look at young children playing with various artistic materials, you tend to find total absorption, total dedication, and quite often a high awareness of competence when achieved.

One of the things that's beginning to emerge from several projects that we're supporting — including one called "Project Zero," which is producing a particularly fascinating set of data — is that, if one has an early experience in the arts, it's likely that one's ability to read competently may be improved. So there's some possibility, then, that in education as in the natural sciences, one finds certain accidental combinations that may turn out to be very beneficial in the long run. If you have a chance to see the CEMREL film *How Does a Rainbow Feel?*, you will see a number of children engaged in some very disciplined and rigorous activity that might be called play, but I think it is more appropriately called artistic expression.

Let's look now for just a minute at what's happening in terms of how the American educational system has developed. There are three primary stages through which the educational system has progressed. The first deals with an aristocratic system. If you want dates, you can talk about 1860 to 1920. During this period, who you were determined whether you got into college or not, not aptitudes or any kind of measure of performance. One went to Harvard for one reason only, and that was to meet other young people who went to Harvard; because, when you became president of the bank, the person who had the room next to you would probably be the lawyer who you would need in order to make more money as the president of the bank. In that particular period, the gentleman's "C," which was quite common at Harvard and Yale, was a sort of symptom of the students' utter derogation of faculty values. It was the notion that one should do well but not too well, because that would suggest that one was trying too hard.

In the meritocratic period, on the other hand — 1930-1960, let's say — we had large numbers of people who sought access to education as the primary mode for success. It was through the educational system that they would achieve their goals. There was an enormous emphasis, particularly in the fifties, on testing and rejecting. The point of the test might well be to reject twenty students and accept one. During the fifties, if you went to the dean of a small college — a good one — and asked him or her how good the institution was, one likely response would be the number of students who were rejected and not allowed to attend the institution. At the time, it seemed reasonable; now it seems an odd performance-measure of an institution to say that it was good because it was able to reject a larger number of people than any other institution of its type.

During the meritocratic period, we spent a lot of time developing aptitude tests, and aptitude tests are peculiar in that they are not directly subject to public domain. If you were told that you got a 590 verbal score on the Scholastic Aptitude Test, there isn't much you can do about that to check it out. Nobody has ever heard, smelled, felt, or touched an aptitude. Aptitudes are not public-domain criteria.

As we enter the egalitarian phase — and one difficulty is that many faculty members are still in the meritocratic phase while school boards and state legislatures are quite often moving us in an egalitarian direction — we have a decline in the numbers who are seeking education, a diversity of ways people can attain what they call success, and a far greater belief in educating everybody throughout their lives. Indeed, one occasionally hears reference in Washington to "Educare," being the educational equivalent of Medicare, meaning that the state owes the citizen the right to as much education as the citizen wants or can easily tolerate. If that sounds like a new and exciting idea, you can find it first in educational writing in the plan for education for the state of Virginia, written several hundred years ago by Thomas Jefferson.

There is a lack of interest today in aptitude testing, but far more interest in proficiency or competency testing. Half the states in the Union now have, or have under consideration, legislation that will establish minimal competency levels for the attainment of a high-school diploma. In addition, many school boards are making the decision that, unless you can reach a certain level of competency in the sixth grade, for example, you will not be able to pass to the seventh grade. So, we are clearly in a stage where accountability is being revised, and the aptitude-test notion of accountability is giving way to a series of performance indicators that will allow anybody to virtually walk in off the street, demonstrate the competencies he or she possesses, and get the appropriate reward.

That, then, is a brief historical accounting of how we got where we

Figure 1

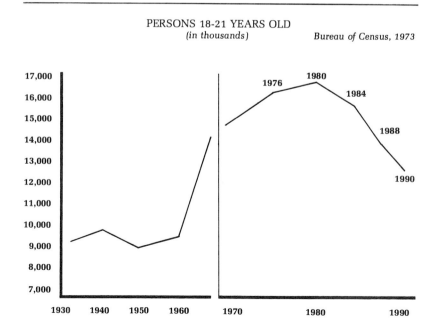

PERSONS 18-21 YEARS OLD
(in thousands)   *Bureau of Census, 1973*

are in our educational system and of some Calvinistic perspectives that have always occupied us in the American schools.

Now let's look for a few things about the present. First of all, there are some very interesting population shifts that have taken place just in the last few years; and it's important, I think, that we realize the implications of these shifts for education. Indeed, one question we have to ask today is: "Why are there so many people who are interested in lifelong learning and in working more with adults?" As the chart (Figure 1) indicates, one of the reasons this is happening is that we're about to run out of eighteen-year-olds. This chart indicates the number of people in the eighteen to twenty-one age cohort as one moves up from 1975 to 1980 at the top of the peak, and then on down to 1990; and, as you can see, in 1980 there is a remarkable downturn in the number of conventional college-aged students. This downturn is not something new, after all. This is not a projection. These cohorts are here; they were born some twenty to thirty years ago. They are around and, unless the human gestation period changes drastically, these numbers aren't going to shift much either. That population decline has run straight through the elementary schools of this country. It has decimated a few of them: Many of them have had 800 students one year, 200 students the next year. We have learned a little bit about how to mothball schools, a little bit about how to mothball faculty, but it's not an easy task. So there is in the educational system, then, an inability to learn from the previous population shifts that have taken place. The high schools get that trend this fall, as a matter of fact. It will run for four years and, after that, it will then begin to decimate the colleges. My prediction is that, as this trend appears, each educational level will treat that phenomenon as if it were brand new and will not be able to learn much from what has happened in the past.

In addition to the population problem itself, there is another aspect that I think is worth pointing out. This data comes from the Office of Management and Budgets, so you know that it's right. The top line of Figure 2 indicates the number of white eighteen-year-olds; and, as you can see, in 1980, there is that same spectacular downturn that I mentioned. The middle line indicates the number of black eighteen-year-olds; and, as you can see, the line holds remarkably steady, and the bottom line indicates the fraction of black eighteen-year-olds going up in this data from about 12 percent to 18 percent during those years. Now, this is a particularly important phenomenon for the educational system, because it suggests that a larger cohort of the available youth — and that's a declining number as you recall — will come from minority-group backgrounds. They also will be coming from lower socioeconomic backgrounds. These are two groups that characteristically have not done terribly well in the educational system. Thus, we have to be very concerned with how we're going to treat this particular set of phenomena.

Another dimension that's quite important has to do with the courts

Figure 2

18-YEAR-OLDS BY RACE — 1965 - 1985

(OMB – Social Indicators, 1973.)

and the impact the courts are having through the legal decisions they are making that affect the credentialing function of education. The most important of these decisions that I can think of is *Griggs v. Duke Power*. In this particular case, the court said that an educational credential cannot be used to reject individuals as candidates for jobs unless it can be shown that those who possess a certain credential do the job better than those who do not possess the credential. Generally, with the Bachelor of Arts degree or with a high-school diploma that has been a very tough case to prove. Indeed, Mr. Griggs wanted to be a maintenance man for the Duke Power Company, and he was told that he didn't have a high enough score on a personality inventory and didn't have the appropriate educational credential. Mr. Griggs, who happened to be black, wondered if maybe there were some other reasons why he was being rejected from the position and therefore took the case all the way to the Supreme Court and won.

So the educational system is now in a new ballgame. That is, according to *Griggs*, when decisions about hiring are made, a candidate's credentials must be at least matchable to the occupations using those credentials. That's a very important distinction.

Related to that is how we came out of the meritocracy. You will recall that, earlier on, I mentioned the three stages of education and that we were moving somewhat away from the meritocratic perspective toward something that could be called egalitarianism. Let me now mention how we get at the concept of merit in a slightly different way. Figure 3 shows a group of twenty-six second-grade students who happen to be in a Utah classroom. This is not a national survey, but it is astonishing how well the data support what one can get nationally.

Figure 3

MULTIPLE TALENT SCORES OF 26 SECOND-GRADE STUDENTS

Students	Academic	Creativity	Planning	Communicating	Fore-casting	Decision-Making
1	++	+	—	0	0	0
2	++	+	—	0	—	—
3	++	—	0	+	—	—
4	++	—	0	0	0	0
5	++	—	—	0	0	0
6	++	—	—	0	0	0
7	++	—	0	0	—	—
8	+	++	+	++	+	0
9	+	++	+	+	0	0
10	+	0	++	0	+	+
11	+	+	+	++	0	0
12	+	+	0	0	+	++
13	+	++	0	+	0	0
14	+	—	—	—	0	—
15	0	+	—	++	—	0
16	0	++	+	+	0	0
17	0	—	—	++	0	0
18	—	++	+	+	0	0
19	—	++	0	0	0	—
20	—	++	—	0	0	0
21	—	++	—	0	—	—
22	—	+	++	0	0	—
23	—	—	0	++	0	0
24	—	0	0	—	+	++
25	—	—	0	0	+	+
26	—	—	—	—	—	++

Legend: ++ = Highest; + = Above Average; 0 = Average; — = Below Average

(From Beverly Lloyd's project for a master's degree, College of Education, University of Utah.)

These students are arranged according to their academic achievement. Now let's look first at the column marked "academic." The double "x's" mean the highest ranking possible. In other words, if we take this school's assessment of this group of twenty-six young people, we find that there are seven good ones (these will go to four-year selective institutions); there are seven less good (they will probably go to relatively mediocre institutions without any national reputation); there are three even less good, and they will probably go to community colleges, if they go at all; and in the last nine we have the "scum of the earth." That is, the educational system is saying these are the rejects, the people without talent, because of the fact that, according to academic standards, they didn't have it.

But now it's interesting to look at that same group of twenty-six second-grade students along some other dimensions. We could add five or six more to this. I just picked two that are interesting. One is tests of creativity—and there are now reasonably good and reliable tests of creativity, which turns out to be testable and teachable; and another dimension is decision-making. But first of all, notice that our high academics don't do very well on creativity. They are actually the second lowest group. The group that was reasonably good in academics turns out to be reasonably bad on creativity measures. The group that was next to the lowest also isn't terribly high; but notice that the lowest group of academic performers turns out to be the highest group in creativity. In fact, Getzels and Jackson, in their research on the relationship between creativity and intelligence, pointed out that particular factor. That may be one reason why many people in the arts have been somewhat uneasy about getting too closely allied to the educational system: We don't have a direct relationship between merit, as defined in the classroom, and merit in terms of its utility for creative people.

In addition, if you will look at the decision-making column in Figure 3, you find that, again, there is a curious reversal. The best decision-makers in this class are about five children who are the lowest in academic aptitude and achievement. And, after chairing faculty meetings at colleges and universities for twelve years, the truth of that lack of correlation bursts upon me with a certain magnitude. If you put into a room two hundred people who are trained to see dichotomies and ambiguities and difficulties where everybody else sees simple truth and ask them to arrive at a decision, you've got problems on your hands.

So here, then, we have a nice example, I think, of how different the educational version of merit may be from some other kinds of talents, equally testable, equally teachable, and perhaps equally desirable to American life, if they could be developed.

That, then, is one problem we have with the assessment of merit. In addition, we are having some difficulties that very likely would interest all of you; difficulties in establishing a competency-based approach to education. If we look at some of the problems with aptitudes and grades, we find some very interesting difficulties. I think all of us have assumed that the straight "A" student goes on to become the straight "A" person — however you wish to define "straight 'A' person." But, as a matter of fact, the results are quite the opposite.

David McClelland, who is not a wild-eyed radical but a professor of psychology at Harvard University and a former president of the American Psychological Association, looked at all of the existing studies that try to relate aptitude tests to grades in college, and he discovered some very interesting things. First of all, aptitude tests do predict college grades pretty well; but then, when people leave college and enter what some students refer to as the "afterlife" — the world of work and home and so forth — the predictability of that whole set drops to near zero. (There is one exception: the AT&T study, which I won't go into at this time because it has its own special problems.)

What McClelland found, then, was that it was not the straight "A" student in law school who went on to become the most distinguished or important member of the bar. Nor was it the most highly graded student in medical school who went on to have the most successful career in medicine. There is, then, an astonishing lack of relationship between grades in college and success in later life. If you want to define success in later life in terms of philanthropy, political interest, travel, arts-related interests, leisure—any of those activities that we normally assume are related to the quality of life—you will find they are not related to grades in college. That is something for us to think about.

A final problem with where we are in the educational system at present has to do with our interest in competency, and we have some particular problems to deal with there. Let's take, for example, a very simple competency: being able to maintain a motor car. This is something that many of us are interested in. What follows is a committee version of what would happen if you began to develop criteria for being able to change a tire.

One of the things you have to do occasionally as a car owner is to change tires. You immediately run into some interesting questions. (As I said, probably the first mistake was to give this to a committee). First, what if you are driving your neighbor's car and the tire goes flat; do you have to know how to change your neighbor's tires? How about changing truck tires and bike tires and motorcycle tires? Second, how about using equipment? You know, these days if you get a tire changed at a garage, it is put on mechanically with an air wrench, and that's so powerful you can't get the tire off with the hand wrench they give you when you buy your car. Third, how about repairing leaks in tires? Do you want to do that, or should you put on the spare even if it's flat, as fifteen thousand Americans do every year? And, fourth — the committee decided this is where the issue really reached its peak — how much time you are going to give the competent tire-changer to change his or her tire? A pit crew at Indianapolis takes about two seconds; the average weekender takes about thirty-five minutes, if there is no coronary involved. Somewhere between those two extremes the committee felt they had to make a decision on competence, based upon the length of time it took somebody to perform the task. Indeed, when we think about educationally measured competence, one of our difficulties is that we think almost all the time about putting a stopwatch on people, assuming that the quicker they learn something, the better. There is a lot of reason to think that that's not necessarily true.

Among other things the committee came up with were: How about reverse threads? On European cars, for example, if you put the nuts on clockwise on one side of the car and clockwise on the other side, you strip the threads, and that's a $140 repair job. Furthermore, do you want people to know about wheel weights and what happens when they fly off? And do you want them to know that, if they take the right-hand radial and put it on the left-hand side of the car, they have a good chance of killing themselves? These are, then, a few of the issues raised in what was originally a very simple exercise: How do you establish competence in tire changing?

It's my feeling that, as far as certain evaluation problems of competency are concerned, we are moving quite far along the trail, and that we have not moved terribly far in certain other areas. If you think about evaluation, there are only three questions we really have to ask. The first is the criterion question, and this is where a lot of people in the arts get nervous. What are the things we want people to do? This relates also to faculty members. What do we consider a good faculty member to be? What kinds of skills do we want that person to maintain? Or, at the program level, what is a good program in the performing arts? What is a good program in aesthetic appreciation? There are other issues of that sort. In my opinion, we are getting much better on the criterion questions in America. Through the public-domain exercise I mentioned earlier, we are beginning to develop criteria that most people can understand. Criteria are getting simpler. Criteria are getting more visible, so that you know when you're in the presence of them and when you're not.

The second question we have to ask is the standards question. Remember in the tire-changing example, this is where everybody got hung up. How high a level of performance do we require? How much is enough? This is the place, I think, where most efforts in competency-based education are having a lot of difficulty right now. The technique question, much to our surprise, is virtually null and void. That is, if you know what it is that you want to have produced, either in student behavior, attitudes, values or whatever, there is probably a logical, reasonable, and even useful way to test for that behavior. There are a large number of new evaluation devices in constant use today, including games, simulations, and many other kinds of techniques, which lead us to believe that the technique question is, indeed, behind us.

So, when you think about evaluation, it's a fairly simple problem, conceptually. There are three kinds of things. There is the criterion question: What do we want people to do? There is the standards question: How well do they have to do it before we give them some kind of merit badge? And there is the technique question: How do we know that they are doing the things that we thought they were doing? I think we are getting better on criteria. We don't know much about what standards are appropriate; we are still playing magic numbers far too often. However, I think the technique question is pretty well solved.

Now a brief look at the future. Most important for the consideration of this conference is something I mentioned earlier: that the American population is going to age rather rapidly in the next few years. There is no satisfactory evidence I have seen to indicate that the downturn in birth rates is beginning to reverse itself. It probably will sometime, just because such trends tend not to continue forever; but, at the moment, we cannot be assured of a larger birth cohort in the immediate future. This means, then, that businesses and the rest of the society will be gearing themselves towards selling more things to older people and towards a market structure that will be made up predominantly of those over eighteen.

That the general population age is going to increase rather strikingly seems to me to have important implications for the arts for all people. Now when we think about adults, we might want to look at some of the kinds of educational needs those adults are indicating they have. Figure 4 gives some recent data you might find interesting. It is from a survey

Figure 4

EDUCATION-RELATED EFFECTS

Vocational guidance	*very inadequate for* *88% males, 75% females.*
Quality of teaching	*Males: good & bad impacts even;* *Females: more good than bad.*
Personal support & *counseling*	*for 33% of all sample, this was* *"critical need."*

(John C. Flanagan, AIR)

done in the state of California by the Field Poll organization on the Californian's desire to do different kinds of things. Some of you may not think Californians are typical, and I would be willing to concur with your judgment if you wish; but it's interesting to note that although a lot of people would like to take a course, there are some other competencies people are very interested in and other skills they would like to develop that are not directly related to the educational system.

For example, according to the data in Figure 4, about thirty-three percent of those surveyed simply want some assessment of their personal competencies in order to assess their personal growth. They don't want to do this so they can go back to college; they simply want to find out how good they are at things. Twenty-eight percent want tests of strengths and weaknesses in specific skills and subjects. And most interesting to me was that twenty percent of the adult population expressed in face-to-face interview some need for personal counseling. That suggests, then, that many adults—one-fifth of the population of California—have a need for somebody who can help them think through their future and make a better set of decisions based on what they would like in terms of quality of life.

It seems important to me that adults are telling us things they need that are not necessarily congruent with the existing educational system. It is my opinion that in the very near future we may begin developing an entirely different kind of educational delivery system using some new devices. First of all, where do adults congregate? Well, in churches, museums, various kinds of concert halls, waiting rooms, hospitals — places like that. Those are places that could benefit from the use of certain kinds of literature and the development of people with multiple competencies, not only to work there, but also to talk to adults about their various needs. Then we could move toward development of diagnostic centers that adults would find useful for making up their minds about what new things they would like to do; centers that could refer the adults to outside agencies, if that seemed to be needed.

That's one model. There are a number of others being talked about. One could think seriously about a matter of alternative delivery systems to bring various kinds of education to people when they need it and, in a very personalized way, help them define their educational goals much more clearly. Right now, we in this country make the assumption that first you go to school, then you go to work, and then you retire and have leisure time. This notion is almost totally fallacious because people are going to school throughout their lives, they are working throughout most of their lives, and they are also having a larger component of leisure throughout their lives. So the older model, based on linearity, is no longer with us.

Let me conclude this portion of our little talk with a metaphor. I don't know what time it is for you, but it is after lunch here, and this is a particularly appropriate metaphor for me because I haven't eaten yet. If you want to think about a delivery system for education, you need to visualize a standard cafeteria model. It doesn't seem to be particularly interesting; it's just there. But, if you think about it in systems terms, it is a linear, one-way, bounded system. You come in at the left, you go by items in a certain order, and you go out at the right. But, if you get to meat and decide you really want two vegetables instead of one, try going back in that line and see if you don't get some scowls, a little jostling, maybe some people asking you, "What's the matter? Don't you know how to behave in a cafeteria line?"

The cafeteria setup forces you past a series of items laid out according to someone else's notion of a proper order. But think about a scrambled-access cafeteria, which is in use in about thirty thousand institutions in the country. This is a model wherein you are free, once you get into the arena, to move from any one of those specialized feeding stations to any other; and you determine not only what items you want, but the sequence you take them in. To me, this model is particularly important, because it represents a new kind of access, and because it is about fifteen percent more efficient than the ordered model. That is, you can get fifteen percent more people through the scrambled cafeteria than you can through the traditional one. When this particular set of data about the efficiency of the scrambled set was presented to cafeteria managers, their response, I thought, was quite interesting. Almost to a person they said: "It's immoral." When asked what they meant by that, the responses were usually loud and clear. They would then refer to the traditional model and say: "What you don't realize about this model is that we deliberately put desserts at the end of the line. We force people to go by things that are good for them, so that they will fill up their trays with those things, and then they will have time for only one dessert when they get to the end." On the other hand, they said, "If you look at the other model here, you'll see that if you give people that much freedom, obviously they will take nothing but desserts."

Well, of course, if you look at what people do take in that scrambled-access model, they don't take any more desserts at all. They take just about the same things people have always taken. But when I thought about it, it seemed interesting to me that cafeteria managers could be so misguided and so misinformed about human selection processes.

And then I looked at the traditional model again, and I thought of every registrar in every college I've known and the primary sets of values that seem to run colleges and universities. And as I looked at this model, I thought of freshman, sophomore, junior, senior. If you take a semester out in your junior year, it means that you've committed some major crime — that your girlfriend is in some sort of trouble or you're out on a drug rap or something — because otherwise, you go right straight through. And I also thought of instructor, assistant professor, associate professor, and full professor. And I thought of English 101, English 201, English 301, and English 401. You can't take English 401 unless you've taken English 301, often for no particularly good reason.

Thus, most of the educational system at present is organized around the traditional cafeteria model; most of the educational system of the future, in my opinion, is organized around the second cafeteria model. And, if in the second model you consider those feeding stations to be schools, colleges, theaters, museums, old people's homes, newspapers, a number of agencies, churches with an educational program, and medical institutions, you will then discover a very different view of the educational system. It is that view I would like to leave with you this afternoon; because, in my opinion, that is the view of the educational system wherein we will finally have to come to some terms with the role of the arts.

Figure 5

SOME HYPOTHETICAL LEARNING CURVES & FORGETTING

(From Drumheller)

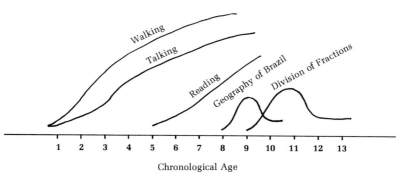

Chronological Age

Nor is there any question in my mind that the arts are indispensable to almost any human being. We have some particular kinds of problems that relate to the arts in learning that I think are worth pointing out at this particular time because of a hunch I have that is not yet backed up with very many facts, but that I would like to present to you now. When we think about learning, we don't think very much about forgetting. There are thousands of studies of learning; maybe eight studies of forgetting. I am more interested in the problem of forgetting, because I cannot remember my three children's birth dates, even though I can remember 200 items in a bibliography without any trouble at all.

In *Figure 5* are some hypothetical learning curves that I think you might find interesting. Generally, when we learn to walk, we keep on. Nobody punishes us for it, and it's sort of a good thing to do. Similarly, when we learn to talk, we keep on talking. Some people even have an exponential curve that would just explode off the top of the chart. And for reading, when we learn to read, we generally keep on. But consider for a minute the geography of Brazil. When we were all about nine or ten years old, we were experts on the geography of Brazil. We knew the rivers, the tributaries, the imports, the exports, the capital city, the climate. We knew everything there was to know about the geography of Brazil. I would be willing to wager we could take a short test this afternoon, but I think you'll agree with me that the knowledge of Brazil's geography disappeared about as quickly as it was acquired. Similarly with the division of fractions — you learned it fast and you forgot it just about as quickly. That leaves us with a new set of questions about the educational system: How long do we expect people to retain various kinds of materials? Are there goals for retention that might be made part of the public's demands for the educational system? And, indeed, are the arts retained for longer periods of time than other kinds of instruction?

It is my conviction, based on absolutely no facts whatsoever, that when one does get involved with the arts, one is involved in a deeply human way. Thus, it is quite likely, if not a logical certainty, that learning in the arts, especially if it actively involves the individual, has a very large chance indeed of being retained by that individual throughout a great deal of his or her life.

Why do I think the arts are so indispensable? First of all, they have been very important to me; and, secondly, I believe there are some new things emerging from the area of socio-biology, which are contained in a short, beautiful book that I recommend you read: *The Lives of a Cell,* by Lewis Thomas. In the book, Thomas talks about how other forms of life, in addition to human beings, create "art." I find it most fascinating. I guess my own personal conviction is that music is the basic art; and that when the first cave man painted the first picture on the wall of the cave, he was probably humming to himself a song that his tribe had learned three or four hundred years earlier.

In closing, let me read a couple of things from Thomas's book that I think make it clear why the arts are so indispensable — not only important to human beings, but perhaps to other species as well. Thomas is preoccupied with termites for reasons I don't quite understand, but the analogies, I think, are quite interesting:

> Termites are even more extraordinary in the way they seem to accumulate intelligence as they gather together. Two or three termites in a chamber will begin to pick up pellets and move them from place to place, but nothing comes of it. Nothing is built. But as more join in, they seem to reach a critical mass, a quorum, and the thinking begins. They place pellets atop pellets, then throw up columns and beautiful symmetrical arches, and the crystalline architecture of vaulted chambers is created. It is not known how they communicate with each other. How the chains of termites building one column know when to turn toward the crew on the adjacent column, or how, when the time comes, they manage the flawless joining of the arches. The stimuli that set them off at the outset, building collectively instead of shifting things about, may be pheromones released when they reached committee size. They react as if alarmed. They become agitated, excited, and then they begin working, like artists.

The second thing that preoccupies Thomas is the use of music by other animals. Let me read what I think is a beautiful description of what whales do:

> There are, of course, other ways to account for the songs of whales. They might be simple, down-to-earth statements about

navigation or sources of food or limits of territory. But the proof is not in, and until it is shown that these long, convoluted, insistent melodies, repeated by different singers with ornamentations of their own, are the means of sending through several hundred miles of undersea such ordinary information as "whale here," I will believe otherwise.

Now and again in the intervals between songs, the whales have been seen to breach, leaping clear out of the sea and landing on their backs, awash in the turbulence of their beating flippers. Perhaps they are pleased by the way the piece went, or perhaps it is celebration at hearing one's own song returning after circumnavigation. Whatever it is, it has the look of jubilation.

I suppose that my extraterrestrial visitor might puzzle over my records in much the same way on first listening. The *Fourteenth Quartet,* for example, might mean for him a communication announcing "Beethoven here," answered after passage through an undersea of time and submerged currents of human thought by another long signal a century later that says "Bartok here."

If, indeed, then, there is some relationship between the katydid's ability to rub its legs together and produce certain kinds of vibrations and the ability of humans to produce music, it may well be that it is as normal and natural for human beings to play the *Air for "G" String* on a Stradivarius as it is for the katydid to do what the katydid does.

We are, then, through socio-biology, I think, in an interesting phase of the relationship between what is unique about the human species and what is not. And I would urge you to think sometime about the particularly fascinating problem of the need to communicate through what we consider to be artistic domains in other species besides the human.

It is very clear to me that the arts are indispensable genetically. I think if you put people off by themselves, you will after a certain time find them singing, dancing, and doing creative and artistic things, because people have a need to do them. The questions of how well they do them, and the role of the professional and the amateur, is, I presume, what your conference is all about. I've tried to provide a setting for what I think the future might hold, and some numbers and data — which, I realize, may be out of place at a conference on the arts. It might help you as you think through your problem, however.

There is clearly a need for an alliance of some sort between artists, teachers, schools, people who are doing research and development, and all the other people who work, in order to improve the quality of education for the average American. This is not an easy task. We know that we must have absolute excellence from the performers; and we also know that the average citizen has the right to certain kinds of enjoyment and improvement of the quality of life.

Your job, it seems to me, is to begin thinking about a range of issues that in my mind relate to meritocracy versus egalitarianism and how we can most effectively begin programs in the arts — both for performers and for active members of the audience — that will stimulate and enrich the lives of the American people. At the moment, I can't think of a more important agenda for you to think about, and I certainly wish you the best of luck and hope that the conference is a success. Thank you for letting me be with you today via videotape.

David Rockfeller, Jr.

The State of Arts Education in American Public Schools

I speak to you in a strange posture today—I'm reminded of H. G. Wells's story *The Invisible Man;* because, in a sense, I'm being asked to describe that "invisible man" to you, to unwrap him; and the invisible man really is a report that our panel owes to the public in 1977. But I do want to stress at the beginning that what I'm going to say is not going to be a preview of the report because, in fact, the recommendations have not been made, although the directions have certainly been charted. What I will say today will suggest what I personally feel and will also attempt to describe how the panel viewed its task, because the things we have ultimately chosen *not* to study were areas that were too complex, or the research was not far enough along — *not* because we thought they were unimportant. Just a few comments about the background of this study, which is national in its scope — it is not worldwide. The parent agency is the American Council for the Arts in Education, and we are a child of it; we are nationally funded, with a rather unusual variety of funders. The Office of Education, the National Endowment for the Arts, private foundations and corporate foundations have backed us, each in significant measure. We are a panel of twenty-five from Maine to Hawaii. We are artists, educators, people with a television background, journalists, and representatives of labor, the Congress, city government, business, and others. We are apparently upwardly mobile. And I say that because we, in trying to get a school superintendent, ended up with a college president; in trying to get a representative of a state department of education, ended up with a lucrative outside consultant in the field; and, in trying to get a congresswoman, may end up with a Senator.

The six panel meetings have been held in New York, Memphis, Los Angeles, and the Twin Cities (Minneapolis-St. Paul); and, in each of these places, we have tried to absorb the particular qualities of the area. Each of the meetings has been three days long. The panel has listened to volumes of testimony by expert witnesses, and the staff has produced

DAVID ROCKEFELLER, JR., *is Chairman of the Arts, Education, and Americans Panel, and Chairman of the Associated Councils of the Arts.*

reams of paper. I should also say that we've had considerable help from many of you in this room, and I apologize if I'm going over territory you are already very familiar with. In addition to the four panelists here today, there are four of you who have appeared as witnesses before us; there are four of you who have helped us in the planning stage of the entire study effort; and there are seventeen others whom I or the staff have visited personally.

Who is the audience for this report? That was one of the questions we first asked and a question that, to some extent, we're still asking. The audience is potentially vast — it is a national report. Some people liken it to a "white paper" such as they produce in England. As we set our camera on the audience target, we have tried to adjust it for maximum depth of field to reach, on the one hand, the general population — especially parents and particularly those parents who are active in parent-teacher associations and on local school boards. Yet, at the same time, we hope to provide at least airplane reading for the educational philosophers, aestheticians, and those with a more academic interest in the subject. But, primarily, our focus will be on the power system of public schools — the principals, superintendents, and teachers (both the specialists and the generalists), state departments of education, state school boards, state legislatures, and finally the national agencies and the Congress.

The subject of the report, as I already suggested in the last section, is the state of arts education in America's public schools — we're talking about *arts* education, we're talking about *this* nation, we're talking about *schools,* and we're talking about *publicly funded* schools.

A year ago, as we were looking at arts education throughout the entire nation, we somewhat hungrily thought we could take on the whole universe; and we knew that arts education is not restricted to schools. (In fact some of the very best programs may occur outside the schools.) But, in looking at what we could reasonably do in a short period of time, we decided to focus on public schools. There were two reasons for this: First, the great preponderance of Americans have passed through public schools and, whether we like it or not, will probably continue to do so. The second reason relates directly to the subject of this conference — the quantum of available knowledge in the field. We may not know much about the six-year-old or the adolescent, but we know less about the arts and the infant, the arts and the elderly, the arts and the mentally ill, the arts and the incarcerated, and so on. If we could have written this report in 1985 not 1975, I hope, however, we would have vastly expanded its scope.

The other areas wherein we wish we had much more information include the interplay and function of the two hemispheres of the brain, the neurological foundations of the art experience, developmental psychology and early arts training, the arts and learning disabilities, the arts and mental disorders, the arts and antisocial behavior. The list is very long indeed, and we've had to accept the fact that there is much that is not known. I agree with what Frank Keppel said yesterday: We should not bite off more than we can chew; and we should not overclaim for the arts. But it is 1976, not 1986, and we're writing about the arts and the average public-school child from age six to age seventeen. There will also be important sections on higher education and community-based programs and resources, but primarily as those two areas relate back to the functioning of schools.

Now, what general areas of recommendations are we considering? As I said, the recommendations have not been formulated, but I can give you a feeling for the panel's principal areas of interest: The first is the question of teacher preparation. It's not news to you that the next decade will probably find something like 90 percent of today's teachers with us throughout that decade. Turnover is likely to be very much dampened by the drop in school population. In many sections of the country, we see cutbacks on specialists and many of these are art specialists. The "back to basics" movement reinforces this trend; although I think most of us here, if we were to define "basics," would be certain to include the arts. But that is not the popular understanding of the word "basics"; so one essential question we face is: are we talking about training teachers to deal with arts as a discrete subject, or about classroom teachers, or about social studies teachers, or about our projected success in developing a new cadre of arts teachers? If we are talking about developing new art teachers, at whose expense?

The second general area of panel concern is that the definition of the arts should be expanded beyond music and art. Here again one runs into tremendous difficulties in terms of training; because, in order to expand beyond music and art, you need teachers who have some familiarity with those other art forms, and positions in music and art themselves are in peril. Third is the need to combine the direct, creative experience with learning from the creative work of others.

Fourth, there is a focus on the individual school, both as the primary functioning unit of arts education and as the environment wherein the arts can become part of the total planning process. I think that too few school administrators or teachers have recognized the simple fact that the school is itself an environment with a potential for change.

Then, fifth, there is a multi-faceted area of recommendation (and I understand my co-panelist Frank Keppel spoke eloquently on this subject yesterday), namely, the thorough employment by schools of the resources outside of the school building proper but close at hand in the community. What are these resources? There are many; and the first one that comes to mind is artists. But the question of how artists can be integrated into the educational process is not at all a simple one: For example, what kind of preparation should an artist have to become an educator? Can all artists be good teachers? How can the artist be helped to interact with the teacher and school administrators? Should artists take on some of the housekeeping duties that teachers do? What about the accreditation of artists?

The second community resource is its arts institutions. Here again, there are many questions that can be raised: Who should initiate an arts program? Is it up to the school or the arts institution to say, "We'd like to buy a piece of what you can offer"? No matter who takes the initiative, who pays for the buses? Where does the experience take place?

The third resource is parents. After all, who has more vested interest in the future of the schools? Particularly among the younger parents, there is a growing interest in taking more active roles in the schools, and I think this can be capitalized upon.

Fourth, there are volunteer agencies and their members. Fifth—and this is a very broad area and hard to define—there are community-funded social and cultural agencies. Sixth, there are municipal agencies: departments of parks and recreation, city-planning departments, and so forth. Seventh, there are the materials of the immediate environment, the immediate community, whether we're talking about industrial castoffs or materials available through retail outlets. Eighth, an often neglected resource is nature itself. Ninth, there are the local colleges and universities, whether they have a teacher-training component; whether they're involved in a professional training of artists, whether they offer performance space and equipment that could be more widely used by the schools; whether some of their personnel can become instructors. These institutions of higher education often represent tremendously under-utilized local resources.

Tenth, there are organizations with a strong cultural history, and private organizations that have active arts traditions. These organizations, often minority-based, have a kind of a vitality and linkage with specific cultural forms that are not appreciated by schools. Finally, there is the media, including both local television, video and film within the classroom structure.

What are the primary areas wherein the panel perceives a need for further research? The first area involves the question of how man perceives in the first place, and what the nature of a creative act is. Then, how can that ability to perceive and that ability to create be enhanced through the educational process?

The second area is how arts learning relates to the entire fabric of education; and I've isolated three different levels at which I think we need to consider their relationship. The first concerns how the arts relate to particular skills such as reading and math.

The second level is how the arts relate to more generalized skills such as memorizing and sequencing, which bridge many different courses of study. Then, the third level is how the arts relate to even more abstract human qualities such as motivation, self-discipline, empathy, and so on. This is a controversial area, and I think the controversy relates to our sense that to argue for the arts other than on their own basis is to demean them. My own point of view is somewhat different; to argue for them on multiple bases is to give them one more chance to succeed.

A third area for further research is the special power of the nonverbal arts for the very young, for those afflicted with certain types of mental disorders such as autism, for the antisocial, and for victims of strokes and other physically immobilizing diseases.

Fourth, a totally different type of research: How can we better identify programs that are already working? How do we isolate the component parts that contribute to the success of these programs? And, the most difficult question: How do we translate these findings into useful information for other systems? For instance, is the "super teacher" a necessary component of a successful arts program? Can you prepackage a school like a new town? These are just a few of the questions suggested.

Fifth, what are the particular qualities of the arts that can be useful to what I call "special populations," or the "isolated and the impeded"? The "isolated" would include prisoners, members of cultural ghettos, and non-English-speaking Americans. Those whose facilities are "impeded" may be residents of a hospital for mental or physical problems, residents of a nursing home, or children with special learning problems. Then, there is the "gifted child," who may be equally isolated in the sense of needing special care and attention.

Sixth, we need far better evaluative tools. I have a deep belief in the power of intuitive discovery, but the public demands more than that. Finally, we need to know more about the effect of the media on the perception of the children and about the potential creative uses of the media in education.

To conclude, having unfurled the gauze from our protagonists, I'll spool it up, leaving you with only a memory image of its form. But, I would stress that anything that sounded here like a real recommendation was merely my personal opinion; and any similarity to these remarks and the ultimate report of the panel will either be the result of happenstance or coercion.

Margaret Bush Wilson

The Arts and the Minorities

I'm not very good at telling funny stories, but I do like gentle, irreverent wit—and I have been the object of some of it since I have been elected chairman of the board of the NAACP. The most recent of these was an introduction that the former dean of my law school gave me when I went to speak to a group in Westchester County, New York. After the usual introductory amenities, he said, "Ladies and gentlemen, I'm very happy to present the big mama of NAACP!"

Yesterday, the speakers carefully defined and delineated aspects of past, present, and future trends that have bearing on your deliberations here. As I see it, my approach will come from yet a different perspective. Quite persistently since my arrival and as I have thought about what I wanted to say to you, I have been reminded of a compelling vignette that ostensibly occurred in a large, central-city third-grade classroom during those halcyon days of what I call the "big FD days." We speak of the "big D" for Dallas, but the "big FD days" are the "big federal dollar days." This was a school with a funded artist-in-residence; and, on this particular day, the artist was visiting a third-grade class where the youngsters were in the midst of an art experience. They were given all kinds of materials — paints, crayons, clay, easels and what not. One youngster grabbed a handful of colored crayons — reds and oranges and yellows — and went to one of the easels and began vigorously stroking the paper on the easel with his crayons. The artist stopped, observed him for a few moments and finally said quietly, "What is it?" Without pausing or glancing in the direction of the artist, the youngster replied, "It's a house on fire." After a moment, the artist persisted, "But I don't see any house." And the youngster replied firmly, "I know; it's covered by the flames."

In a sense I have the uneasy feeling that, figuratively speaking, in this conference we have been sitting and planning for a house that is on fire. The difficulty is that, while the flames are visible, I do not believe they are burning any of us in this room. But the phenomenon of fire

MARGARET BUSH WILSON is Chairman, National Board of Directors of The National Association for the Advancement of Colored People (NAACP).

carries an urgency to sound the alarm, to set the engines rolling, to douse the flames before they roar out of control and engulf us all.

This "house" is, of course, some 200 years old. It is built on very sound foundations, but it is not fireproof. Its four corners are firmly supported by a quartet of documents that embrace some very high principles and undergird a unique system of government.

But it is not the *house*, with its Declaration of Independence, its Northwest Ordinance, its Bill of Rights, or its Constitution about which I wish to speak; rather I would speak about the *flames* that, in my judgment, may threaten its survival. Two weeks ago, in a Missouri town called Joplin, the city council was wrestling with an extremely sensitive issue — whether or not to rename their main street, called Broadway, for a deceased native son who had been a poet. The poet happened to be a black man, and some forty years ago, he happened to write a poem — a protest poem if you please — that some citizens of the little city of Joplin viewed as inimical to the best interests of American society. The poet's name was Langston Hughes; and, in the city council meeting that night, there was a packed house and considerable debate about the wisdom and the possibilities of renaming Broadway Boulevard for Langston Hughes. I'm happy to report that the council finally voted in favor of the issue and did, in fact, rename the street for this distinguished poet. But, as I thought about the incident, it occurred to me that for one Langston Hughes, who now is commemorated by his own community for his contributions both as an artist, as a poet, and as a person concerned about this country, there have been innumerable artists in this country from other groups and ethnic backgrounds who either have been ignored or forgotten, and whose heritage and tradition have been lost to us. Therefore, it gets to be rather crucial that somehow we have a perception of the need and urgency in these deliberations and indeed in every area where we are involved; not only to understand this multi-cultural country we are a part of, but to do more than that—to make a studied effort to involve and make a part of what we're doing persons from all these various groups who have talents for the work that lies ahead. I emphasize that point because I think we have reached a rather fascinating period in the history of this country when more and more we're going to be seeing and hearing those who feel that they have not been recognized become increasingly vocal about their frustrations and their concerns.

Indeed, the civil rights movement is no longer just about the rights of black Americans, it's a multi-faceted movement. It's about native Americans. Spanish-surnamed Americans. Mexican-Americans, the old, the young, the handicapped, the convicted, homosexuals and heterosexuals, and even one group that's not a minority at all but finds the civil rights tactics useful and uses them to advocate vigorously — and that's that great group called *women*. This, it seems to me, makes for an entirely different ballgame than the one in which many of us have been working over the years.

I wandered into a bookstore the other day and there was a section on ethnic contributions. I continue to be amazed at the number of books, pamphlets, and polemics about black Americans, for example, that are written by "experts" who are not black Americans at all. I get a little weary of these "experts," and I am beginning to believe that we must be very conscious of the fact that it's difficult to be an expert about this very fascinating area of our society unless one is involved and a part of those who make it up. On that bookshelf, I did find a very fascinating little paperback. It is written by another Margaret, who really should be up here speaking in my place. Her name is Margaret Just Butcher. She is an educator and a writer and has done some fascinating things in the course of her career, including serving on the board of education of the District of Columbia and as an educational consultant to the NAACP in its legal defense structure. But what makes this book so fascinating is that it is a book Margaret Just Butcher wrote out of love for and commitment to a man who had dedicated his life to compiling some accurate information and facts about the contributions of our greatest minority in this country. Dr. Alain Locke of Howard University died leaving seventy-five pounds of collected materials about the Negro in American culture unfinished and incomplete. Margaret Just Butcher took those seventy-five pounds of materials and spent a considerable part of her time organizing, editing, and then publishing them so that today there is available this splendid volume which, in a very real and meaningful way, is a compendium of the contributions of African-Americans to American culture.

The Negro in American Culture, by Margaret Just Butcher, belongs on every bookshelf that is set aside for the proper understanding of American history. I mention this too because I continue to have some concern about my friends and colleagues who persistently tell me they find it difficult to locate competent people in minority groups to work with them on various phases of their projects. Now I can concede that there may be some basis for this in terms of having no large pool of competence to draw from, but I would suggest to you that behind this lies the real challenge that it seems to me a group like this must be quietly conscious of all the time. We need to ask ourselves: How do we create the pools of competence and skills, and how do we go about discovering and developing the kinds of talents we need for what we have to do? And the answer is simple: We make the opportunities available early on. It is this disposition on the part of some to persist in excluding from opportunity those with talent that constitutes one of the most intense flames threatening this house of ours. It is in the area of lack of opportunity that it seems to me there is a challenge to meet.

I read carefully Stan Madeja's paper, and he makes a persuasive case for research in the arts and technology. Our nation has, in fact, the most highly developed combination of wealth and technology and the largest cadre of scientists and scholars in the world. Dr. Broadus Butler, in a very perceptive article in the May issue of the NAACP's *Crisis* magazine, has a comment I want to share with you. He said:

> We have the scientific and the technological destructive capacity to obliterate virtually all human life as we now know it upon the earth. Yet we do not have full control of either its use or proliferation. That capability combined with a 200 year curse of racism is now further exacerbated by our high level of tolerance for crime, libertinism and both political and private corruption. These, more than any external power or force are the major threats to the fabric of this nation.

Then Dr. Butler put his finger on what in his judgment will be the ultimate third-century contest in America. He said, "It will be between man and technology."

That brings me to the next and perhaps most disturbing flame that it seems to me we are confronting today: the urgent problems relating to our urban communities and the human predicament in our society. There is a new kind of tension abroad in this land. It involves the affluent as well as the poor. It involves the skilled as well as the unskilled. It results from the decreasing involvement of human beings in the productive processes of this country. Insecurity, uncertainty, and unemployment are almost as serious among some of those who are trained and educated as among those who are not. This is an interesting new phenomenon in our society that we in this room must be concerned about as we talk about and plan an agenda for the arts and aesthetic education.

Indeed, it seems to me that the pressing and urgent question that must be asked and answered is: Can this great country of ours sustain a climate of equality of opportunity for human beings when more and more of us face systematic exclusion from dignity both psychologically, in the learning process, and economically, in the lack of work? There is cause for alarm in the trend that now encourages resigned acceptance of unemployment rates in this country of between seven and ten percent, and three times that rate among some of our minorities.

We are here to plan and project an agenda for the future in the arts and aesthetic education—

when some forty percent of all the black children in this country are concentrated in the urban schools of about twenty cities, and —

when the violence in some of those schools has reached crisis proportions, and—

when there is no stated public policy or national commitment about meeting the needs of our cities and these children . . .

I have mentioned these facts and highlighted them, not to dampen your deliberations or to discourage your sincere efforts, but to emphasize that the context of these times is sufficiently compelling to merit your best thinking, free of parochial interests.

Your discussions here are tied to the allocation of scarce resources, and it is in the self-interest of us all that those resources have the best and highest impact for good.

While I have been quite serious, I have to confess that I am not really pessimistic about the future. Indeed, I think this is a rather exciting time in which to be alive; and there are a couple of reasons why I'm optimistic.

The first is that this is fascinating country, peopled by persons who come from varying backgrounds; and all of us are immigrants or the descendants of immigrants — except the FBI. I know you think I'm talking about the Federal Bureau of Investigation. The fact is, I'm talking about full-blood Indians. There may be one FBI here. The rest of us, you know, came from someplace else.

The other thing I know is that we all came from very modest backgrounds; we're so-called "common folk." I say this without real fear of contradiction because I know something about the history of this country. It was peopled by the discontents and the malcontents and the rejects of Europe, the captured and unwary of Africa, the disheartened and discouraged of Ireland, the starving and the poor of Asia, and I could go on and on. Yet, in 200 years, the descendants of this multifaceted group of people from all these various backgrounds have built and created this mighty nation. We have also created a new kind of aristocracy — it is an aristocracy of character, competence, and accomplishment.

The other thing that impresses me about us is that we are somehow mature enough to have weathered some rather dramatic times in the last few years, and I'm inclined to think that not many other countries on the face of the earth could have done as well. It is a great tribute, for example, that we managed on a certain day in August, 1974, to make a quiet, almost unobtrusive transition of power involving the most powerful office in the world without a single bullet being fired, without a single troop being mobilized and, indeed, if you were not at your television sets, with no real indication that a momentous event was taking place in our society. To me these are manifestations not only of great maturity, but of the potential for greatness. What now lies ahead is not too certain, but it will be a challenge to all of us and it may very well make the difference between whether we survive as a civilization or lose our way.

I started my remarks by talking about fire and I'd like to close by referring to the same element. Last fall, I just happened in midday to have reason to go back to my home. When I walked in the house, which was then not occupied by anyone, I immediately smelled smoke — pervasive and compelling enough for me to be concerned. I went about the entire house looking for the source of this smoke and potential fire. I could not find anything on fire. Finally, in a kind of desperation, I went to the telephone and called the fire department. I decided to be restrained and quite calm because there really wasn't a fire that I could detect, and I said to the fireman who answered the phone, "I'm calling from my residence at such-and-such an address; and, while I don't see any sign of a fire, there is a distinct odor of smoke."

I will always remember the brusque and forthright response of the fireman who answered my call: "Lady, if you have a problem, we will send the equipment."

Perhaps, this is an appropriate note on which to end these remarks, because I have been reviewing with you some urgent problems in our society. It is you, and people like you, who can help in devising some lasting solutions and I hope, therefore, you too are willing to provide the equipment.

II

Surveys and History of Research in the Arts and Aesthetics

This section gives a historical perspective on research and development in the arts and aesthetics through historical reviews of research and status reports of arts research in government agencies and arts organizations. The disciplines in the arts—mainly art and music—provide the major resource for historical studies, with dance and theater being comparatively new to this enterprise.

Harlan Hoffa, in his paper, describes the history of the idea of research in the arts and aesthetics—particularly on the national level—as being brief and rocky. Following World War II, research in the arts emerged from several postwar factors, including a panicky reform of science education that eventually affected other fields; a new research orientation within arts education that developed, in part, out of influences imported by European scholars and researchers; and, finally, a new mandate for federal support of the arts that evolved in the Kennedy administration. **Hoffa** goes on to point out that research in arts education blossomed in the sixties and withered in the seventies, but a workable research program revolving largely around the concept of a national research and development center still seems possible. Most of the capable researchers are still active, the institutional bases have expanded into educational laboratories, and the vexing arts-education questions have persisted and expanded as the arts assume a more important role in the lives of all Americans. The history of research in arts education is closely tied to recent political history, but the idea prevails and calls for a new and carefully prescribed relationship between the leadership of the federal arts establishment and the leadership of the federal educational establishment to benefit arts education in the future.

Charles Leonhard, Richard Colwell, and **D. Jack Davis** provide historical surveys of research activity in music and art. The studies described go back some one hundred years, pointing to the long tradition of educational research in these disciplines.

In their article, **Leonhard** and **Colwell** describe the difficulty of subjecting an art form to scientific research, even though considerable research has been done in music and music education in this century. Research studies have concentrated on problems in music teaching and learning, development, and maturation; musical training; musical attitudes and appreciation; music perception and psychoacoustics; automated learning in music; musical creativity; and psychological theory in music education. They compiled an extensive reference list of these studies; and they propose that the direction of future research in music education should concentrate on the nature and development of musical responsiveness and perception. They advocate that all research efforts be designed to establish a sound and comprehensive theory of music education—done with continuity, with adequate funding on long-term bases, and by a corps of professional music researchers.

Davis does a comprehensive review of research in arts and art education. He notes that published research in the visual arts and art education began before the turn of the century, and has experienced a phenomenal growth of interest since 1950, perhaps because research evidence was needed to substantiate the profuse generalizations and beliefs that grew with the rapid development of this field. Also, the development of graduate-level art and art education, increased interest by professional organizations, and increased financial support aided research activity. The eight major categories of arts-education research **Davis** defines include studies relating to color vision and color preference, to drawing or graphic ability, to picture preference and appreciation, to tests and measurements, to the study and teaching of art, to art and personality, to creative ability, and to the therapeutic values of art. All published research, keyed to these categories, is listed in his extensive bibliography. He advocates that future research relative to art education deal with basic problems that will improve the quality of art instruction; such areas as: the content(s) of the visual arts and aesthetic experience, how learning in the arts takes place, the inducement or stimulation of learning in the arts, evaluation of learning and experiencing in the arts, and the impact of art instructional programs and efforts.

Gil Lazier and **Alma Hawkins** review the current status of theater arts and dance. According to **Lazier,** the principal dilemma of theatre research is that the *essence* of art is inexpressible and cannot be analyzed directly. He indicates that several techniques, however, make it possible for arts behavioral research to get closer to this essence and its effect on the rest of life: training the artist in scientific methodology, using a research-team approach (pooling the specialities of artist-researcher, social-scientist, education-learning theorist, and design-statistics expert), disseminating the best information in the simplest language to the people who can make

the best use of it, using videotaping technology to record the behavior of both performer and audience, and using the methods of content analysis (or other models from the social sciences) to yield useful data. **Lazier** states that future research priorities in theatre must focus on studies concerning children's theatrical experiences (as doers and observers); the participational experience of art; and the simplest, most basic questions using uncluttered research methods. Also, these studies should be made by researchers with a mastery of the tools of scientific inquiry, working in the most natural environment. And these studies must yield results that can be generalized to the largest possible universe.

Alma Hawkins reports the need for research in selected areas of dance. She states that, since dance has only recently been established as an art-education discipline and grown substantially as a performing art, it is therefore, important that research programs be undertaken to further the understanding of dance as an aesthetic experience and to improve the teaching-learning process in dance. **Hawkins** maintains that research in dance needs to address the creative growth process of the learner in dance, both in perceiving and in performing; and the development of the body instrument that will serve the aesthetic needs of the performer-choreographer. Dance research would also enrich the work already done in aesthetic education.

Linda Fosburg, Harold Horowitz, and **Martin Engel** all provide an overview of research trends, priorities, and needs from the viewpoint of arts organizations and government agencies concerned about the arts.

Linda Fosburg defines the place and function of community and state arts councils in the new arts and education alliances. New and experimental arts-education programs—such as Artists-in-Schools Project (AIS), Cultural Enrichment Program (CEP), and Cultural Voucher Program (CVP)—all need quality control, administration, and evaluation—a role that could be filled by arts councils functioning as the interested but uninvolved third party. Other functions that arts councils could perform include political advocacy for both the arts community and the educational community, program development using arts and other resources outside the school (such as public television), environmental design, magnet-school programs, and so on. Advocate, evaluator, administrator seem the most likely roles for arts councils to assume: maximizing the impact of funds, minimizing conflicts, helping in the development of future programs, and facilitating the operation of existing programs in arts education. **Fosburg** states that research could uncover the specific areas where the arts councils could be most effective and could provide means for quality control.

Harold Horowitz outlines the program of the Research Division of the National Endowment for the Arts in its first year. He indicates that this new division of the NEA has responsibility for planning and coordinating the research efforts of the Arts Endowment, and the monitoring and evaluating of supported research projects, conducted primarily through contracts or grants to qualified research organizations or individuals. The Research Division staff is concerned more with problem definition and research management than with doing the actual research in its three major areas of interest: arts and cultural institutions, the condition of artists, and the provision of arts and cultural services to the consumer. The current (or pending) research activities he describes include audience studies, and program-support studies in such areas as state art agencies; census studies of artists (possibly put into a rapid and convenient data retrieval system) and business establishments for the performing arts and other amusement and recreational services; economic studies on the arts and cultural institutions as well as consumer

demands in the arts; planning studies for national studies of the craft arts, and of arts and cultural programming on radio and television; and a pilot study concerning symphony orchestra musicians and directors.

Martin Engel has developed a plan for a federal policy for the arts in education directed toward those federal agencies concerned with arts and humanities education. These agencies need to pool their funds, capabilities, and commitment and develop a comprehensive federal program of effective research and development, dissemination, and evaluation in arts and humanities education. **Engel** advocates a cooperative federal policy, generated by systematic planning and based on research data, that is designed to organize and administer the diversity of programs necessary to effect the improvement of the content, methods, and integral role of the arts and humanities in education. He goes on to say that cooperative efforts by educators, researchers, artists, administrators, and government agencies can bring about the integration of the arts, aesthetics, and humanities in the total educational enterprise. Applied research, development, evaluation, and dissemination is needed at every stage of the educative process and in each subject area that is part of the arts and humanities in the educational matrix: theory and concept base, instruction and pedagogy, curriculum, management and administration, evaluation, facilities and environment, home/school/community linkages, funding and implementation, and institutional coordination. The resulting program must be designed to infuse the arts into all aspects of the curriculum at all levels as a means of enhancing and improving the quality and quantity of aesthetic education and of expanding the use of arts for cognitive and affective learning experiences in the total school curriculum.

Harlan Hoffa

The History of the Idea

Before research can exist as a fact, it must exist as an idea and, for better or worse, it is not an idea that has grown naturally out of artistic traditions or processes. The arts, the sciences, and the humanities have evolved idiosyncratic modes of inquiry, each unique to their needs and purposes. In science these are called research; in the humanities, scholarship; and in the arts, creative performance and production. These modes of inquiry do not always prevail within disciplines but for most practical purposes, they do describe the differing ways scientists and humanists and artists work; deviations from these established patterns, though not uncommon, usually appear as aberrations. Among these aberrations is the idea that issues affecting the arts in educational settings might be researchable, or that the findings of such research could influence teaching or learning in the visual, performing, and literary arts.

A second aberration is the nature of activity that arts educators themselves define as research. While scientists—even social and behavioral scientists—stick to carefully defined and prescribed procedures in their research—the so-called "scientific method"—arts educators tend to be more catholic in what they will accept under that rubric. Any consideration of the history of research and development in arts education must, therefore, take these factors into account: first, that research as a mode of inquiry in the arts is thought to be a strange notion; and, second, that arts educators engage in research activities on their own terms rather than those of scientific purists. To ignore the first of these facts is to deny that very real differences exist between the artistic and the scientific modes of inquiry, but to ignore the second is to deny that bridges can be—and, indeed, have been—built between these modalities without violating the integrity of either.

The Early Years
Prior to World War II, research was a foreign concept to most arts

HARLAN HOFFA *is Head, Division of Art and Music Education at Pennsylvania State University.*

educators and it was foreign in both senses of the word. It was foreign, first, in that most research done by arts educators prior to that time had been conducted in Europe; and, second, it was foreign in that few arts educators in this country understood its application to their disciplines, and fewer still were skilled research methodologists. This is not to suggest that educational research in the arts was entirely unknown before the mid-1940s; or that art, music, theatre, dance, literature, and film have developed evenly since that date. It is safe to say, however, that most research done before those dates was scattered and had little impact on the practice of arts education. Starting about 1950, several influences were joined which, in combination, provoked major changes in the professions. The first of these was the installation of relocated European arts educators in influential positions in several American universities, of whom Viktor Lowenfeld was, perhaps, a classic example. He brought a research orientation to the doctoral program at Penn State that was unique to the field, and he instilled in his students the traditions and skills of objective inquiry he had learned in his native Vienna. The second factor was the passage of the Cooperative Research Act in 1954, which provided federal support for research throughout the educational community, and which enabled many educators to undertake large-scale research projects for the first time. The arts did not benefit appreciably from the early years of this program, but it had the effect of stimulating a research climate that was to permeate even those fields not its immediate beneficiaries. Finally, the Sputnik scare of the same era generated reforms in science education that were, eventually, to have an influence upon disciplines far removed from math and physics, including the arts.

In spite of one or two privately sponsored efforts, such as the Carnegie-supported Owatonna Project in Minnesota; a cluster of arts-measurement projects, such as that conducted by Meirs and Seashore; and a few incursions into the arts by psychologists, such as Alschuler and Hatwick or Harris and Goodenough, it is safe to say that little was conducted by, or in behalf of, art educators in the years before or immediately following World War II. By 1949, however, the Eastern Arts Association (later to beome the Eastern Region of the National Art Education Association) had published its first *Research Bulletin,* followed by annual issues each year until it was absorbed in 1958 by NAEA's journal of research and issues, *Studies in Art Education.* The pattern of research reporting is similar in music education and comparable, though at somewhat later dates, in dance and theatre education; and it is evident from these publications that most of the research in arts education done in this country before 1950 was conducted irregularly and was without significant influence on the profession at large.

The Feds and the Arts

It would appear that the government did not recognize that the arts existed in American schools until after World War II; for, though the

U.S. Office of Education was established in 1867, it was not until 1949 that a position was created in that agency to attend to them. The first person appointed to this position was Arne Randall. His job description said, in effect, that he was to keep in touch with what was happening in all of the arts at all levels of education; and, in addition, he was to maintain liaison with every manner of arts institution—museums, professional associations, arts councils, and performing groups. Randall was expected to accomplish all of this with no program money to bring people together and no travel funds to permit on-site visitations. It is, therefore, not surprising that neither he nor his successors, Ralph Beelke and Mayo Bryce, were to significantly affect the professions from their bunkers deep within the Washington bureaucracy. It might be noted, parenthetically, that the effect of Randall, Beelke and Bryce upon the federal establishment in the 1950s is almost identical to that of Harold Arberg, Martin Engel, and John Kerr a quarter-century later, in spite of intervening events, and for some of the same reasons — isolation, an absence of program money, and disinterest in arts education on the part of higher officialdom. Lest the lack of consequences from the Randall-Beelke-Bryce period blind us completely, however, one simple truth must be credited to them. They established and maintained a toehold for the arts in the U.S. Office of Education and, though they rarely prevailed, they did at least survive, and so did their line in the table of organization.

It might be unfair, though not intentionally misleading, to isolate the Office of Education in this regard — as if that agency alone, among all of those in government, was deaf, dumb, and blind to the arts. Government, like the schools, is a better *mirror* of social values than it is a *molder* of them; and, if the arts have come in second, tenth, or one hundred and fourteenth in governmental priorities, it is probably because that is where they lie in the priorities of the voting citizenry. Nor is the situation unique to our times. In 1431, Lucas Moser inscribed a tabernacle with the words: "Cry aloud, Art, and mourn bitterly for no one desires you. Alas. Alas." And he was not the first artist to feel the pinch and the pain of meagre patronage — nor the last. Alas. Alas.

America's roots in Puritanism, in combination with its tilt toward a frontier that remained unconquered for 250 years, have produced a value system that has treated the arts as if they were useless at best, or sinful at worst. August Heckscher, in his report, *The Arts and the National Government*, noted that "government in the United States has not in the past showed consistent concern for the state of the arts"; and, though he pointed out that statesmen in the formative period of the republic "possessed a clear realization that the forms of art reflected the inner ideals of the social order," he also noted that "this awareness was dimmed during the period of westward expansion and industrial progress." During the early years of the twentieth century, the government, according to Heckscher, was more positively inclined toward the arts; but, until 1933, public policy seemed to be more a matter of showcasing the arts or of setting up fancifully titled commissions than of giving direct support to artists, arts education, or arts institutions.

It was not until 1933 that Franklin Roosevelt initiated the WPA Federal Art Project, a public works project that was intended to employ the ten thousand artists who were estimated to be among the 15 million then unemployed. Francis O'Connor's monograph, *Federal Art Patronage 1933 to 1943*, provides a detailed chronology of this first governmental effort to support artists directly and, according to him, it was a uniquely successful program that "gave to the artists of America more than mere financial security — it gave them a sense of professional dignity and historical purpose." The merits of the WPA Federal Art Project are all the more notable as we now emerge from the worst economic depression since that of the 1930s; and, in its way, the National Endowment for the Arts has replicated the WPA program by employing artists in hard economic times through the Artist-in-Schools Program. Though the WPA program produced murals for public buildings across the land, while the Endowment placed artists in public schools across the land, each program employed artists on direct federal grants (although with a time lag of more than forty years); and, in this sense at least, they are comparable. One might only hope that the kids will turn out as well as the post office walls. The real meaning of the WPA Federal Art Project—and perhaps the Artist-in-Schools Program as well—is not that artists were recognized by the government as an economically depressed minority requiring special attention; but, instead, that the arts were recognized by the government as a national resource to be sustained and developed. Cynics might say that the meaning is even more basic than that; namely, that the arts were recognized by the government at all.

The most dramatic change in governmental policy toward the arts took place in the years between the WPA Art Project and the Artist-in-Schools Program, however. During the presidency of John Kennedy, the state of the arts in American life became, for the first time, a matter of public policy rather than a presidential hobbyhorse. During these years, Arthur M. Schlesinger described the arts as "close to the national purpose." In March of 1962, President Kennedy appointed August Heckscher as his Special Consultant on the Arts (the first in White House history) and Heckscher's report, *The Arts and the National Government*, led to the establishment of a separate program within the U.S. Office of Education that was to pioneer the use of federal funds for educational research in the arts. In this sense, the Heckscher report is perhaps the single pivotal document in the history of research in arts education. This report, only thirty-five pages long, touched upon programs of information-gathering in the arts; legislative responsibilities; advisory activities; the governmental role in acquiring works of art; federal design standards; the cultural heritage; taxation policies affecting the arts; a national foundation for the arts; and, not incidentally, upon education, training, and research in the arts. His recommendations on education and educational research were as follows:

It is recommended that further consideration be given to increasing the share of the Federal Government's support to education which is concerned with the arts and the humanities. This should include the same type of across-the-board assistance now given to modern languages, mathematics, and science; for example, facilities and equipment, teacher training, teaching techniques and materials, scholarship and fellowship programs. The predominant emphasis given to science and engineering implies a distortion of resources and values which is disturbing the academic profession throughout the country.

Late in Heckscher's tenure as Special Consultant on the Arts (March, 1962 to May, 1963), President Kennedy made another nomination that was to have far-reaching consequences for education in general and for art education in particular. Upon the resignation of Sterling McMurrin as the U.S. Commissioner of Education, Kennedy asked Francis Keppel to assume this important post in his administration. Keppel had been the dean of Harvard University's Graduate School of Education and, as such, earned a well-deserved reputation as a capable and innovative educational administrator. His appointment was particularly significant to arts education because he was in a key position to implement some of August Heckscher's recommendations pertaining to the Office of Education; and, more importantly, he was inclined by temperament and his own earlier experiences as a sculptor to do so. Shortly after his appointment, he named Kathryn Bloom as head of a new arts unit in the Office of Education, which was eventually to become the Arts and Humanities Program. Subsequently, he followed the precedent President Kennedy had set with Heckscher's appointment by naming Miss Bloom as his Special Advisor on the Arts and Humanities.

Keppel's appointment of Kathryn Bloom proved to be far more than a *pro forma* nod in the general direction of the arts; and his unflinching support of her, publicly and privately, immeasurably strengthened her hand in building a strong arts component in the staid old Office of Education. By virtue of this special relationship to the Office of the Commissioner, she was able to slice through the bureaucratic morass that would otherwise surely have stifled her efforts to make the Arts and Humanities Program a significant force in the Office of Education.

The chronology of these events is complex; but, whatever the specific relationships might have been during the early 1960s, it is evident that a great deal of ferment was taking place regarding the role of the government in arts education. It can never be known with absolute certainty if Keppel's decision to upgrade the Office of Education's responsibilities for the arts was an independent judgment or if it grew out of the Heckscher report — or perhaps even the unpublished Cater report. Nor can his decision to appoint a special advisor on the arts and humanities be directly related to, or isolated from, President Kennedy's prior appointment of Heckscher to a comparable post. The roles of

McMurrin and Harold Cater (as his consultant on the arts) appear to be minimal, at least on the surface, for neither had the charisma nor the power of personality that characterized others who succeeded them. Yet, a few inescapable facts nag at this easy judgment. The Cultural Affairs Branch was established in August, 1962, only a month before McMurrin's resignation; but it did happen, nevertheless, during his tenure as Commissioner. His last-minute appointment of Harold Cater at that same time could be interpreted to mean that he was trying to assure continued attention to arts education even after his own departure; and Cater, though a historian with no publication record in the arts, continued to represent the only significant federal presence in arts education until Kathryn Bloom's appointment. It is difficult to believe that Cater's tenure was without consequence, but the record shows none and his report was, unexplainably, never published. Strange!

Within a year after Kathryn Bloom's 1963 appointment as Director of the new Arts and Humanities Program in the Office of Education, rhetoric ended and action began. A staff of seven professional arts educators were recruited and $700,000 in educational-research funds was allocated specifically for the arts; and, also for the first time, arts educators were assured that their research proposals would be reviewed and monitored by their professional peers. The complete chronology of these events is contained elsewhere (Hoffa, 1970); but, for these purposes, suffice it to say that, from 1963 until 1968, the Arts and Humanities Program was actively engaged in a program of research support for arts educators, ranging from basic research to research training and from research dissemination to the support of a series of conferences under the "developmental activities" authority of the Co-op Research Program.

Science, Technology, and the Arts

At about the same time that the Office of Education established its Arts and Humanities Program, one of the strangest events in the history of arts education was shaping up in the office of the President's Science Advisory Committee. This blue-ribbon committee had been instrumental in reforming science education in the 1950s. It had, in fact, established its own Panel on Education Research and Development, which worked enthusiastically with the National Science Foundation and somewhat grudgingly with the Office of Education in pursuit of that objective. In 1963, however, this panel, which had neither the mandate nor the expertise to do so, took upon itself the task of reforming art and music education in the same way it had remade science education in preceding years.

The President's Science Advisory Committee was chaired by the Special Assistant to the President for Science and Technology, and it was supported by full-time staff members who carried out the daily work of maintaining the committee's program. The committee itself, with the exception of the chairman, were part-time consultants, however, and they were convened only as their services were required. The business of this committee was complex and far-ranging; and, in order to assure equitable attention to all areas of their concern, a series of sub-committees were established. One of these sub-committees, called panels, was the Panel on Educational Research and Development, chaired by Jerrold Zacharias, of the Massachusetts Institute of Technology. The committee, particularly its chairman and a staff associate named Joseph Turner, were centrally involved in the first research conference in music education and also in the first such conference in art education. These conferences, at Yale in 1963 and at New York University in 1964, respectively, set the precedent for many succeeding seminars and conferences; and, for this reason if no other, the role of the Panel on Educational Research and Development warrants attention.

As previously mentioned, the first research conference in any of the arts that was supported by the Cooperative Research Program was the 1963 Yale Seminar on Music Education. This conference preceded Kathryn Bloom's appointment by about a month; it followed Keppel's confirmation by only three months; it was separated from Heckscher's resignation by only three weeks; and it came almost at the middle of Cater's eighteen-month tenure in the Office of Education. None of these persons is shown on the list of conferees or observers, however; and only Harold Arberg, who was then the music education specialist for the Office of Education, participated in the conference, though it was supported entirely by Office of Education funds.

The explanation for this anomaly seems to be that, though the Office of Education provided the funds, it was only peripherally involved in the actual planning of conference activities. Kathryn Bloom, for example, has written that the ". . . interest of the Panel on Educational Research and Development—which advises the Commissioner of Education, the Director of the National Science Foundation, and the White House Advisor on Science and Technology—was responsible for the Yale Seminar on Music Education. . . ." This judgment is confirmed in *Innovation and Experiment in Education*, a progress report of the panel, which reported that early discussions of the panel lead to questioning "the lack of balance in federal assistance to the arts as compared to science and . . . the question of whether curriculum reform as it developed in science education could be applied to the arts." It continues to say that the "panel decided to urge an appropriate group to start a project and it chose music as the place to begin."

Joseph Turner acknowledged in an interview that he was responsible for the initial meetings leading to the Yale Seminar, primarily through his personal acquaintance with Lionel Nowak of Bennington College's Music Department. It is interesting that, according to Turner, there were no music educators on the Steering Committee for the Yale Seminar; and that the panel, whose primary responsibility, expertise, and authority was in science and technology rather than the arts, was "the source of names" for that seminar. In defense of the panel, however, it must be noted that they represented many diverse viewpoints, including those of James Allen, who was eventually to become President Nixon's first Commissioner of Education; Jerome Bruner, of Harvard's Center for Cognitive Studies; Fred Burkhardt, of ACLS (American Council of Learned Societies); Ralph Flynt, from the Office of Education's Bureau of Research; Sister Jacqueline Grennan, then of Webster College; Sterling McMurrin, the former Commissioner of Education; and Ralph Tyler, who had served for two years as the Chairman of the Cooperative Research Advisory Committee. There were no acknowledged representatives of the arts on the panel, however; and it seems likely that outside consultants were called upon to identify participants for the Yale Seminar.

The first art education seminar was held some fifteen months after the Yale meeting; and, though Zacharias, Turner, and Sister Jacqueline were once again involved and very much in evidence, their control over the conference program and the participant list had been sharply curtailed by developments within the Office of Education. The panel had provided planning money for each of these conferences, though Office of Education funds were used for all of the direct conference costs; and, needless to say, both agencies sought to have the dominant voice in determining how their funds were spent. By the time the New York University conference jelled, Kathryn Bloom was firmly in control of the new Arts and Humanities Branch, however, and her influence was unmistakable and resolute. The Arts and Humanities Branch had, by then, been shifted out of the Division of Library Services and Continuing Education and into the Division of Educational Research; and because this unit administered the Cooperative Research Act (through which the seminar was supported), a direct line of authority and control was in effect between this new unit in the Office of Education and the few research projects in the arts that were then being supported—including the New York University seminar in art education.

The import of the Science Advisory Panel's incursion into the arts (in addition to the example of unmitigated gall it demonstrated) is that the model for science education reform became the model for arts education reform as well, with an emphasis upon curriculum development (note the CEMREL program) and upon modeling learning behavior after that of working professionals in the field (note the Artist-in-the-Schools Program). Other choices might have been made at the outset, had it not been for examples of science education; but even the generous benefits of hindsight cannot now tell us whether the results would have been better. They would almost surely have been different, however.

Between 1968 and the present, the Arts and Humanities Program (AHP) has changed its functions, its personnel, and its purposes; and, in the process, it entirely abdicated research support as a mission. During the same period of time, however, a number of other programs relating to research in arts education have been initiated, some of which are lineal descendents of USOE/AHP activities, while others have been conducted by individuals who were affiliated, in one way or another, with its programs. These include a host of Title I and Title III programs of the Elementary and Secondary Education Act (see the Kern and the Eddy reports); CEMREL's Aesthetic Education Program, which is supported by the National Institute of Education; the Advanced Placement Program, now directed by Educational Testing Services; educational television programming in art, under the auspices of the National Center for Instructional Television; the JDR 3rd Fund's Arts in General Education Program; the Artist-in-the-Schools Program of the National Endowment for the Arts; the Alliance for Arts Education of the Kennedy Center for the Performing Arts; the arts component of the National Assessment of Educational Progress; and a persistent trickle of research projects that are supported by foundations and by university research agencies, if at all.

In spite of the vitality of these events, however, (at least when compared with the situation prior to the mid-1960s) no national program of research in arts education now exists to enable educators in the visual, performing, or literary arts to identify significant researchable issues, to conduct a program for their resolution, to marshal the necessary resources, and to get about the business of improving arts education through the sort of coordinated research that a national research and development center would provide.

In *The Guns of August*, Barbara Tuchman described 1914 as a watershed year, after which "the great words and beliefs . . . could never be restored"; and, in a similar vein, 1968 represents such a time for researchers in arts education. A series of events, some of which affected arts educators directly and others only indirectly, took place at that time and, for better or worse, many of the "great words and beliefs" that existed, however briefly, before 1968 were forever beyond recall by the end of that year. The year 1968 was a period of unrest on campuses and in cities, of riots at political conventions, of a debilitating and demoralizing war in Southeast Asia and, finally, in November, of an election that was to result in wholesale federal retreat from involvement in social issues — including education. It was also, not coincidentally, the year that saw the end of the Arts and Humanities Program in the Office of Education as an influential force for arts education. This was due, in part, to the resignation of more than half of the professional staff, including Kathryn Bloom (after a year divided between Washington and New York), Stanley Madeja, Richard Grove, and Irving Brown; and, in equal measure, to the effective end of both program funds and the special relationship that had previously existed between the Arts and Humanities Program and the Office of the Commissioner. At the same time, however, new programs at CEMREL and the JDR 3rd Fund came into being under the direction of Madeja and Bloom respectively; the National Endowment for the Arts was rapidly establishing its identity as *the* federal font for support of the arts (though neither then nor now for arts education); and the research posture of the Office of Education was slowly shifting from field initiation to Request for Proposals (RFP's) involving federally targeted priorities.

In short, after 1968, nothing was quite the same as it had been before. International events affected national attitudes and these new attitudes provoked traumatic events across the entire spectrum of American life. Declining confidence in government, in its turn, affected federal domestic programs of every sort, including educational research; and it affected especially educational research in the arts where the precedents were meagre and where the vulnerability was, therefore, greatest. At the same time, it is doubtful that CEMREL's Aesthetic Education Program or the JDR 3rd Fund Program, which emphasized "all the arts for all the children," could or would have developed as they did in the 1970s except for the fault line in our national history that was 1968. With all due regard to CEMREL and JDR 3rd, however, neither have sought the opportunities for field-generated research that went before; and, in the trade-offs of 1968, corporate activity in arts education (as elsewhere) clearly prevailed while individual effort and initiative were wiped out almost completely.

The R and D Idea

The concept of a national research and development center in the arts was first proposed in 1965 by Manuel Barkan, of Ohio State, though the roots of the idea are complex and not easily traceable to any single source. The Barkan proposal developed directly out of a conference held at The Pennsylvania State University in September of that year. The proposal was intended to maintain the flow of ideas he and others had then found stimulating, provocative, and sorely needed. His proposal noted that ". . . the current status of art education reveals confused perceptions of, and inadequate solutions to, curricular and instructional problems . . . frequent ambiguities, troublesome contradictions and all too many discontinuities between ends and means." He wrote of the paucity of theoretical support for much educational practice in arts education, of piecemeal curriculum revision, and of the inability of individual teachers, schools or school systems to alter "current orthodoxies" guiding such instruction. He, therefore, proposed a Center for Arts Education Curriculum Development that "could focus the energies of the number of experts required to attack the ramifications of the problem," and that would "thus spearhead a mutually supportive program which might well transform the processes of art(s) education in American schools."

For a variety of reasons — none bearing upon Barkan's premises but, instead, upon the administrative complexity he had proposed — his proposal was disapproved by the Research and Development Program at the Office of Education; but, fortunately, the concepts his proposal contained did not die with the rejection. They were reframed, restated, and revitalized in early 1967, at the Whitney Museum Conference, and became the foundation for CEMREL's Aesthetic Education Program.

Though Barkan's original hope that such a center would "transform the processes of art(s) education in American schools" has not been realized through CEMREL's program, its influence on art, music, theatre, dance, and film education in many school systems across the land is both obvious and laudable. Regardless of the successes of CEMREL's Aesthetic Education Program, however, it is evident to many arts educators, to concerned educational philosophers and theoreticians, and to behavioral scientists who are concerned with the arts in education, that the development of instructional materials, however sophisticated and imaginative they might be, is insufficient to the task of reforming arts education in the nation's schools. Many of the flaws and frailties that Barkan noted a decade ago still plague arts education because basic research dealing with the field is either scattered or nonexistent, and because development activities have often been supported without adequate theoretical and conceptual foundations. In the absence of a center for advanced study in the field, which could provide both a data source and a center for scholarly activity in aesthetic education, this unfortunate situation seems likely to continue.

Recession

Barkan's ill-fated proposal and his subsequent work on the guidelines for the CEMREL program reflected an attitude toward scholarship that has not often prevailed in arts education, and an attitude that is seemingly at odds with past and present governmental policy toward educational research. At the outset, the Cooperative Research Program (through which most federally supported research in education was conducted) offered six more-or-less distinct options to its applicants ranging from developmental activities to basic research, from curriculum development to dissemination, and from training to the establishment of large-scale research and development centers. In actuality, however, most research in the early years was "project" research, in which an individual worked on a problem of his or her choosing under the auspices of an educational institution of one sort or another. The problem with this approach quickly became obvious, for it was a scatter-gun attack that made coordination impossible and implementation of findings spotty and often ineffective as well. In our effort to solve these problems, changes were made in the program to favor programmatic research, wherein research priorities were established and proposals were judged in accordance with these mandates; but, here too, the problems were manifold: limited wisdom in setting the priorities; unpredictable shifts in their emphasis; and a total disregard for untargeted issues, regardless of their credibility beyond the Washington establishment. Moreover, recent administrations have shown little interest in supporting basic research of any kind, whether in education or elsewhere, and have concentrated on such areas as "career education" and "competency-based education" instead, on the assumption that they better represent the "real" needs of the schools.

The Barkan proposal obviously flew in the face of this history whether during the times that favored project research (his was programmatic) or during the times favoring targeted research on "real" problems (his was not tied to the same set of realities many others saw); and sad to say, his proposal was, indeed, flawed. It was an administrative nightmare involving the departments of art, music, theatre, and dance at five widely scattered universities. But, even more critical than that, it was presented at a time when, in the language of PL 80-10, a "national system of regional education laboratories" was under consideration, and when proposals for university-based research and development centers were, therefore, not well-received. In addition, it proposed a scope of work having no precedent; and it offered no guarantees that he, or anyone else lacking research-management experience, could weld it into a unified whole. By the time of the Whitney Museum Conference in early 1967, however, a national system of educational laboratories had been established, the Central Midwestern Regional Educational Laboratory (CEMREL, Inc.), in St. Louis, had demonstrated an interest in the arts as a program area, and Barkan, having recovered from the pique of having his earlier proposal disapproved, agreed to work with CEMREL's director, Wade Robinson, on the development of a new proposal. Several options were explored in discussions between Robinson, Barkan, and Jim Gillis of the laboratory program staff, including, according to Harry Kelly, a revival of the original R and D center concept, a "lodging" of the program with a lab and/or a university, a consortium of labs or, finally, a new national laboratory devoted exclusively to the arts. The compromise that was eventually worked out divided the aesthetic education program into two phases; the first was to be conducted at Ohio State and the second at CEMREL. In effect, CEMREL subcontracted the development of program guidelines to Ohio State while maintaining its own proprietary interests; and, though this was to prove less than ideal for either Barkan or Robinson, it was, nevertheless, a workable compromise between two individuals who had equally strong claims to the program.

At that moment, the time seemed righter than ever before (or perhaps since) for the establishment of the Research and Development Center in Arts Education. Indeed, the potency of those ideas has prevailed through the current decade, in spite of every manner of domestic and international travail. It is interesting to speculate on what might have happened had CEMREL become the hoped-for R and D Center.

The fact remains, however, that activity in the arts has become a national "growth industry" and that many of the educational programs generated ten years and four administrations ago have continued into the present, despite a declining school population and economic and political decisions in Washington that have adversely affected educational programming. At the same time, and in some ways because of this continued federal attention to the arts and to education, however, a paradox has developed that operates to the disadvantage of educational research in the arts. With the establishment of the National Arts and Humanities Foundation on one hand and of the National Institute for Education on the other, the federal support for research in arts education that existed during the 1963-68 period, under the auspices of the Arts and Humanities Program of the U.S. Office of Education, has "dropped into the cracks." The Foundation, with its mandate for the support of artists and arts institutions, has neither the capability for nor evident interest in supporting educational research. And NIE, though it has continued to support educational development in the arts through CEMREL and one or two other programs, has not attended to the arts as an area of high priority, nor has it established a policy to guide its efforts in the arts. As a result, arts educators with the capability and the motivation to do research have no place to turn for support or for the mutual exchange of knowledge and information. Moreover, with increased community arts activity, a large number of problems with no answers has been added to those previously identified and, as yet, untended. A 1970 analysis of research conferences in the visual arts (Hoffa, 1970) identified four clusters of recommendations for further research—none of them yet attended to—which related to teacher education, to interdisciplinary cooperation, to increasing student contact with bona fide art objects or producing artists, and finally to filmmaking and other processes whereby visual images can be reproduced, transported, isolated, or compared for educational purposes. Similar analyses have not been undertaken for the other arts but, because the patterns of their development have been comparable, their needs are probably not very different. In short, the needs are there, well-known, and awaiting only the attention of the professional community.

Sharing and Pairing

An additional factor that also has limited research opportunities for arts educators since 1968 is federal "revenue sharing" and related policies. On the surface, revenue sharing is intended to return tax dollars to the states, which each state can then use for its own purposes rather than for those mandated by Washington. The rhetoric is familiar — "returning government to the people," "debloating Washington's bureaucracy," "block grants in place of categorical programs" — but the underlying political purpose seems clearly to be the dismantling of social programs that came into being in the early to mid-1960s, including many in education. The long-term effects of this federal policy are difficult to evaluate, but some of the consequences are clear — even from this perspective. First, it means that educational programs of a national scope are increasingly difficult to undertake. Second, it means that fifty (often petty) bureaucracies at the state level have been added to the ponderous, unwieldy, and unresponsive federal bureaucracy. And, third, it means that many, if not most, of the innovation-minded professional people who came into government during the Kennedy-Johnson years have resigned, leaving the Washington bureaucracy even more firmly in the hands of career bureaucrats. Each of these, in its own way, has had its obvious effect upon the opportunities for educational research in the arts, especially insofar as large-scale programmatic research is concerned. Its immediate effect, however, was to eviscerate the Arts and Humanities Program in the Office of Education, which, for a few brief years, had provided the only research support that arts educators had ever known. No state department of education or state arts council has used its "shared revenue" to support educational research in the arts, nor has the National Endowment for the Arts or the National Institute of Education, in spite of their mandate to do so. In short, "revenue sharing" and other policies nominally intended to decentralize the control of social programs, have succeeded only in diluting many of them out of existence—including, unfortunately, research in arts education. We might legitimately wonder what the effect of such policies would be if they were applied to defense, commerce, agriculture, or any of the other untouchable monoliths of the government.

Potpourri

Because the history of research in arts education covers a relatively brief period, current events (or those nearly current) assume an importance that would be unseemly under other circumstances. Among these events are recent status studies of the arts in American life, publications bearing upon educational research in the arts, research training for arts educators, and, finally, the Artist-in-the-Schools Project — the only major federal program in arts education now in existence.

The New York Story

The most comprehensive survey of public attitudes toward the arts that has been done in recent years is titled *Arts and People,* and it may well serve as a model for similar studies in other places or at other times. This 1973 survey was conducted for the American Council for the Arts in Education (ACAE) by (an affiliate of Louis Harris and Associates) the National Research Center for the Arts, with support from the New York State Council on the Arts. It was limited to New York State; but, within that parameter, it was exceedingly thorough—with chapters on attitudes toward the arts, education in the arts, artistic activity of New York residents, attendance, preferences, background, access to cultural activities, and the funding of the arts in the state. Its one hundred pages of text and one hundred pages of tables provide the reader with some surprising insights into public attitudes toward the arts, and should be required reading for all political figures and governmental officials. It notes, for example, that two thirds of the adult population in New York State consider the lack of cultural facilities to be a major concern "in company with far more publicized problems such as crime, inadequate housing and so on." According to these figures, an arts plank might well be built into every political platform, without its seeming at all frivolous or inconsequential.

It is interesting to note, however, that this survey was conducted by a public-opinion survey organization and not by the ACAE itself, which suggests that one or more factors may be operating to affect research in arts education. The first of these is that the research orientation of arts educators may be geared too much to academic questions and too little to those of more general concern; the second is that public opinion surveys require resources that specialized firms alone can provide; and the third is that ACAE did not choose, inexplicably, to utilize resources from within the professions it presumes to represent.

Endowment Research

A second research thrust of this sort was announced in February of 1976 by the National Endowment for the Arts that "intends to support research in nine project categories to improve the accomplishment of agency goals." These nine categories relate to economic data on the arts, studies of arts personnel, cultural programming on radio and TV, regional studies and the like; and they are clearly data-gathering activities similar to the ACAE study in New York State, in contrast to those of a more academic nature that might be undertaken in an arts education "think tank," as now envisioned. The interesting element in this move by the Endowment is that proposals are being solicited from outside the agency (though admittedly for internal purposes), and it is tempting to wonder if the Endowment's Research Division may not soon extend its program to accommodate needs external to those of the agency.

The Data Game

In 1963, the National Education Association published their research monograph, *Music and Art in the Public Schools,* containing exhaustive data on enrollments, staffing patterns, and facilities for instruction in art and music in elementary and secondary education. These data are now grossly out-of-date; but the model that the study provides could and should be used to replicate it, and possibly to expand it to include theatre, dance, and film, and to extend its range into higher education as well. Because the National Art Education Association and the Music Educators National Conference have both disaffiliated with NEA, however, and because NEA has itself changed its professional orientation in recent years, it is unlikely that a replication could be undertaken through the NEA Research Division. A more reasonable expectation might be for the "DAM'T group (the four professional associations in dance, art, music, and theatre education) to approach NIE for funding, and to pursue the study using the resources of their own research-trained membership.

Publications and Such

Since its founding in 1966, the *Journal of Aesthetic Education* has been the only scholarly journal to address itself exclusively to theoretical issues involving the arts in education. The several professional associations each publish research periodicals (in which doctoral-thesis reports predominate); and several other journals such as *Arts and Society* and the *Journal of Aesthetics and Art Criticism* publish occasional articles or even whole issues relating to education in the arts. Finally, in regard to research dissemination, many of the articles bearing most directly upon teaching and learning in the arts appear in research journals that are read primarily by behavioral scientists. Such journals occasionally publish articles on creativity, perception, or similar topics that bear directly or indirectly upon issues concerning arts educators—but few are aware of the existence of these journals. There is not now, nor has there ever been, a periodicals index relating to research in arts education; nor do the arts and humanities represent an area presently covered by an ERIC center. In 1967, a request for proposals for an ERIC center in the arts and humanities was published, but to little avail since only two proposals were received and neither was then deemed satisfactory. The need persists, however; and it, too, is one that might be incorporated into an R and D center in arts education.

The Training Question

The training of educational researchers, including those in arts education, has traditionally been conducted in university settings and this pattern continues today, most particularly at the doctoral level. But such entry-level research training is often the last opportunity available to arts educators to upgrade or maintain research skills, due to the current lack of research support funds. As was previously noted, research in arts education was transformed in the immediate postwar years by European scholars who had immigrated to American universities, where they, in turn, educated a new generation of research-oriented arts educators. These new arts educators entered the profession with research capabilities that were quite sophisticated; and, for those who graduated in the salad years of the mid-sixties and were able to obtain federal funds to support further research, it seemed as though a new day in arts education was surely aborning. That particular balloon was shot down over Southeast Asia in the late 1960s and over the Mideast oilfields a few years later, however, and a full generation of frustrated researchers in arts education was left holding an empty and deflated bag. The result of that frustration has been a marked decline in their research interests, a shrinkage of research output, a pervasive cynicism regarding the federal role in supporting both the arts and education, and an atrophying of hard-earned research skills. In some ways, the situation in this regard is worse than it has been in the pre-war period when there was no research consciousness whatsoever in arts education; and it was not unlike the frustrated expectations of minority groups in the same period. Research training, except in the sciences, has rarely benefited from federal funds, and there is no direct relationship between the decline of such support for educational research as a whole and for the university programs that educate most young professionals in the arts. Indirectly, however, there is a clear sense of futility involved in receiving such training when, after graduation, little opportunity appears to exist for applying the skills so acquired. In addition to this attitudinal problem, however, research training depends, in a large measure, upon research that was previously conducted and, equally important, upon systems of access to this research. A national center for the storage and retrieval of such data would benefit research training very significantly, and such a resource would be of inestimable value to institutions engaged in educating the next generation of arts educators.

Opportunities — Going and Gone

A variety of federally supported programs affecting arts education have surfaced in the past decade; some of them have offered opportunities for research that were never realized. Titles I and III of the 1965 Elementary and Secondary Education Act represent such programs that are now beyond recall, as does IMPACT; but the Endowment's Artist-in-Schools (AIS) Program remains very much alive and its research possibilities remain almost entirely untapped. In 1973, however, Michael Straight, the Associate Director of the National Arts Endowment, approached Elliot Eisner during the NAEA convention in San Diego regarding an evaluation of the AIS Program—in effect, a research study of its means and ends. The study never took place, though Eisner did publish a rather negative article about the program in *Art Education* about a year later, which succeeded only in further alienating AIS personnel from professional art educators—as their 1975 conference report, *Extending the Dream,* clearly indicates.

Eisner's article was not, of course, the sole cause of alienation between AIS and the art education establishment, but it is the item many AIS people have pointed to as an illustration of the intransigence of the professional art-education community toward artists in schools. The real reasons, however, are much more basic. First, there has been a very real fear among some art educators that the AIS program might jeopardize the jobs of the regularly employed and certified art teachers — a fear that, incidentally, seems entirely without foundation. Secondly, there is a certain jealousy among art educators about the role that artists-in-residence are allowed to play in schools — roles these teachers feel they could have played equally well, had they been allowed to operate in accordance with their self-image as artist-teachers. Thirdly, there has been an undeniable arrogance on the part of some AIS folks about art education — an arrogance often compounded by a blind naivité as well. One of the tacit assumptions underlying the AIS Program is that art teachers are not adequately educating children in the arts and that professional artists are better able to do so. This criticism has, of course, angered many art teachers because they felt it unwarranted (if not inaccurate), and that it came from a group of *auslanders* who neither understood nor were obliged to deal with the daily pettifogging routine of the classroom that is part and parcel of every teacher's life. Such problems are, in large measure, attitudinal; but they have also emerged out of a genuine ignorance that research could do much to alleviate. And they seem destined to continue until overcome by contravening factual data.

It was announced in late 1975, however, that "the first large-scale study of AIS" will be conducted under the auspices of the Western States Art Foundation. It is obvious that Joseph Wheeler, the project director, has proven more tractable than Eisner because he indicated that "the results will document and describe rather than make recommendations or pass judgments" and that his study will be "descriptive rather than prescriptive." This thought was reinforced by the study coordinator, Morgan Johnson, who was reported to have cautioned that "all of our results will have to be taken with a pound of salt." A pound of salt may be preferable to a grain of salt, but that remark seems revealing, in any case. Moreover, it contrasts vividly with a comment by Thomas Bergin, who said, "we must assess what happens to the students . . . discern what is good, detect what is bad, and change our strategies in the light of these findings." Obviously, Joseph Wheeler and Thomas Bergin have different expectations for the study, and it will be interesting to see who will prevail.

A second area of concern bearing upon the Artist-in-Schools Program is in what it reveals about the relationship between the Endowment and USOE — two presumably independent agencies of government. The Artist-in-Schools Program has been supported, in part, by funds transferred from the Office of Education to the Endowment; but the control of the program appears to be entirely in the hands of the Arts Endowment. And it is noteworthy that moneys appropriated to one agency should be transferred to another, with no evidence of control over the program they support. One might legitimately wonder whether the same one million dollars that was transferred in 1972-73 might, in the long run, have been better invested in educational research; but we shall never know. No one thought to ask. One million would, however, go a long way toward the establishment of a national research and development center for arts education.

Summing Up

In summary, the history of the research idea in arts education is brief. It emerged out of several unrelated postwar factors including a panicky reform of science education that eventually affected other fields; a new research orientation within arts education that developed, in part, out of influences imported by European scholars and researchers before and after the war; and, finally, a new mandate for federal support of the arts that evolved in the Kennedy Administration. Research in arts education blossomed very rapidly in the 1960s and withered almost as quickly in the 1970s; but, as long as hope springs eternal, a workable research program in arts education still seems possible. Most of the researchers who have been educated in the past two decades are still active in their profession; the institutional bases, once limited to a few universities, have now expanded into educational laboratories as well; and the questions vexing arts education have persisted and, indeed, have expanded as the arts assume a more important role in the lives of all Americans. The history of ideas teaches us, however, that ideas do not, in and of themselves, alter events. Events are altered by ideas only to the extent that they coincide at a given moment with the energy and the will to put them into effect. And, in this sense, the history of research in arts education bears more than a passing relationship to recent political history.

In a review of the work of Woodward and Bernstein for *Saturday Review*, Max Lerner assessed their essentially journalistic efforts by the criteria of historical scholarship and, in so doing, noted that the "craft of history is always in need of rebarbarization by the energies of talented amateurs, lest it come under the dictatorship of the mandarins." The craft of research in arts education may also benefit from "rebarbarization," but Lerner's comment raises the additional question of who the "amateur" is and who the "mandarin" is. Current events suggest that federal policies affecting the support of such research are being dictated by the "amateurs" — whether those of NIE who know not of the arts, or those of the Endowment who know not of education—and that professional arts educators (presumably the "mandarins" in this frame of reference) are without an effective voice in these affairs. Rebarbarization by amateurs may, indeed, inject new energy into a field; but, as Lerner himself would surely agree, it is no substitute for the sustained growth and development that can be provided uniquely well by the scholars within a discipline.

A Recommendation

The need that this brief history of research in arts education confirms, therefore, is for a new and carefully prescribed relationship between the leadership of the federal arts establishment and that of the federal education establishment; a relationship that, while recognizing their obvious authority and their presumed expertise within specialization will also honor the distinctive research and development interests of arts educators, who are in some ways a part of each community and in other ways a part of neither.

Clearly, that is not now the case.

University Park, Pennsylvania
June 1976

BIBLIOGRAPHY

Art Objectives: National Assessment of Education Progress. Ann Arbor, Michigan, 1971.

Arts and the People: A Survey of Public Attitudes and Participation in the Arts and Culture in New York State. New York: American Council for the Arts in Education, Inc., 1973.

Arts Impact: Curriculum For Change. Final Report, Interdisciplinary Model Programs in the Arts for Children and Teachers. University Park, Pennsylvania: Pennsylvania State University, March 1973.

The Arts: An Instructional Guide for a Course in the Arts in the Secondary Schools. Working paper, Division of Arts and Humanities, Bureau of Curriculum Services. Harrisburg, Pennsylvania: Pennsylvania Department of Education, reprinted, 1973.

Barkan, Manuel. *Planning Project for Research and Development Center for Curriculum and Teaching Materials for Aesthetic Education.* Columbus, Ohio: The Ohio State University Research Foundation, December 1, 1965.

Bloom, Kathryn. "The Arts for Every Child." *Toward an Aesthetic Education.* Washington, D. C.: Music Educators National Conference, 1971.

Comprehensive Arts Planning. New York: Ad Hoc Coalition of States for the Arts in Education, coordinated by The JDR 3rd Fund, October 1975.

Conference on Aesthetic Education. New York: Whitney Museum, January 1967.

Current Issues, Problems and Concerns in Curriculum Development: A Report and Set of Recommendations. Washington, D. C.: National Institute of Education, U.S. Department of Health, Education and Welfare, January 15, 1976.

Eddy, Junius. *A Review of Projects in the Arts Supported by ESEA's Title III: A Report to the Ford Foundation.* August 1970.

Eddy, Junius. *A Review of Federal Programs Supporting the Arts in Education: A Report to the Ford Foundation,* May 1970.

Eisner, Elliot. "Is the Artist-in-the-Schools Program Effective?" *Art Education.* Washington, D. C.: National Art Education Association, February 1974.

Extending the Dream: A Report of the 1975 Artists-in-Schools National Conference, July 16-18, 1975. South Bend, Indiana: Center for Continuing Education, University of Notre Dame, 1975.

Gault, Judith. *Federal Funds and Services for the Arts.* Washington, D. C.: U.S. Government Printing Office, 1967.

Heckscher, August. *The Arts and the National Government: Report to the President.* Washington, D. C.: U.S. Government Printing Office, 1963.

Hoffa, Harlan E. *An Analysis of Recent Research Conferences in Art Education.* Bloomington, Indiana: Indiana University Foundation, December 1970.

Kelly, Harry. *A Brief History of the Aesthetic Education Program to September 1969.* Unpublished paper. St. Louis, Missouri: CEMREL, Inc., 1970.

Kern, Evan J. *Pace and the Arts: A Survey of Title III Projects, January 1966 to July 1967.* St. Louis, Missouri: CEMREL, Inc., 1968.

Music and Art in the Public Schools. Research Monograph. Washington, D. C.: National Education Association, August 1963.

O'Connor, Francis V. *Federal Art Patronage, 1933-1943.* College Park, Maryland: University of Maryland, 1966.

Program Announcement, 1975-1976. Washington, D. C.: National Endowment for the Humanities.

Research Division Program Solicitation. Washington, D. C.: National Endowment for the Arts, February 4, 1976.

Charles Leonhard and Richard J. Colwell

Research in Music Education

We begin this report by citing two of the basic problems confronting research in music as an art and in music education. The most basic problem, and the most troubling to many musicians, lies in the essential conflict between the nature of art and the nature of science, between artistic behavior and scientific behavior. Art represents a unique way of doing; science, a unique way of knowing. The product of art is an object; the product of science is an idea.

Research must be well-controlled and objective, but art is by its very nature free and subjective. Reducing an art to the degree of simplicity necessary for research may result in the loss of the essence of the art.

This conflict is, however, resolvable if both researchers and musicians arrive at an understanding of the relationship between science and art. A scientific approach to art involves "a search for a reliable idea for dependable knowledge regarding the nature of the art object, the nature of artistic activity and the nature of art experience."[1] The researcher establishes hypotheses concerning art and either verifies or negates them by obtaining verifiable knowledge in which he or she can place a high degree of confidence.

A second problem lies in the limited number of researchers who are knowledgeable in both the art of music and the scientific method, and who sustain their research effort over a significant period of time. The bulk of research in music and music education is done for doctoral dissertations, and the dissertation too frequently represents the single research effort of a lifetime.

This problem, too, is solvable and, indeed, progress in overcoming it has been made in recent years. Its solution lies in the early identification of musicians with a scientific bent and the development of their musical and research competence through a well-planned program of undergraduate and graduate study that includes continuing authentic research experience. An essential corollary has to do with the provision of

CHARLES LEONHARD is Professor of Music and RICHARD J. COLWELL is Professor of Music Education in the School of Music at the University of Illinois at Urbana-Champaign.

financial support for music researchers by universities and other funding agencies.

Having identified these two problems, we proceed to review music-education research of the past decade and to establish a rationale for conducting research during the next ten years by formulating what we view as the major broad questions that research should focus on.

Background

The work of Carl Seashore at the University of Iowa in the first third of the twentieth century stands as a landmark in the history of research in the psychology of music. He carried on his work in the measurement of musical aptitude[2] with a degree of thoroughness and scientific rigor unique in his time and enviable today.

Although Bingham,[3] shortly after the turn of the century, had written a theoretical paper on melody and its functions, and the British psychologists Lowery[4,5,6] and Mainwaring[7,8] had initiated research on music concepts such as cadences and phrasing, their work had little significant impact. Seashore's elements approach to musical aptitude, however, appealed to researchers: elegant research designs could be set up; sophisticated statistical techniques could be used; and a variety of interesting laboratory hardware could be incorporated. Researchers who tried to deal with larger musical entities or those more closely related to real music, on the other hand, produced fuzzy and inconclusive results.

Seashore dominated the psychology of music field during the second and third decades of the century. His students used his aptitude measures in both long- and short-range studies, but none saw fit to extend or refine the work of the master. Other researchers developed similar measures that were generally inferior to Seashore's.

A continuing controversy arose between Seashore[9] and Mursell,[10] who gained prominence in music education in the late thirties. Mursell criticized the Seashore *Measures of Musical Talent* for their atomistic conception of musicality and aptitude and their mechanistic approach to measurement. Mursell became the most influential authority in music education — the only productive market for aptitude tests — and his powerful opposition to the use of tests constructed on the Seashore model served to stifle further research in aptitude testing. With the departure of Seashore from the scene, an unfortunate hiatus in research in the psychology of music occurred and lasted until mid-century.

The 1950s saw a resurgence of interest in the psychology of music and in a broader field of research encompassing many aspects of music teaching and learning. While the reasons for this resurgence are not clear, the sudden growth of doctoral programs in music education was certainly a factor, along with the great strides in research design and statistics achieved by researchers in psychology and education. The resurgence was signaled by a growing interest in research on the part of the Music Educators National Conference. A group of doctoral advisors began to organize sessions on research at meetings of the Conference and, in 1953, initiated the publication of the *Journal of Research in Music Education* by the Conference.

The resurgence was solidified by the publication of the *Musical Aptitude Profile,* [11] developed by Edwin Gordon at the University of Iowa. On Gordon's initiative, the University of Iowa reinstituted publication of *Studies in the Psychology of Music* — a publication that had brought the bulk of Seashore's work into print but had been dormant since Volume IV, published in 1936. Volume V, published in 1967, was devoted to studies investigating various aspects of the *Musical Aptitude Profile.* The series continued through Volume X, but suspended publication for a second time in 1975, subsequent to Gordon's departure from the University of Iowa.

Achievement testing in music received considerable impetus as the result of the publication of the Colwell *Music Achievement Tests* [12] in 1967. This battery of tests represented the first effort to base a standardized music achievement test on behavioral objectives established for a school music series. MAT has been widely used in research studies to secure data on the musical achievement of research subjects ranging from elementary-school pupils to college music majors.

Several publications in the United States and abroad have made significant contributions to research in music education and the psychology of music. The University of Illinois sponsors the *Bulletin of the Council for Research in Music Education,* which began operation with its first issue in 1963, and has published forty-six issues to date. A series of conferences on the status of music education research organized by Arnold Bentley at Reading, England, resulted in the biannual publication, *Psychology of Music,* the first volume of which appeared in January, 1973. The University of Paris supported the publication of *Scientific Aesthetics (Sciences de L'Art)* beginning in 1965; the 1974 issues were devoted exclusively to the psychology of music. The famous Staatliches Institut für Musikforschung Preussischer Kulturbesitz initiated its yearbook in the 1970s.

Two organizations have spurred interest in research: the Music Education Research Council of the Music Educators National Conference and the Research Commission of the International Society for Music Education, which held its first meeting in 1968, and has held biennial meetings since that time at various places around the world.

Finally, the passage of the Elementary and Secondary Education Act by the United States Congress in 1962 must be credited with contributing profoundly to music research activity. It resulted in the identification of competent researchers and spawned a breadth of research effort never before conceived.

Four recent texts in the field merit mention. The first of these, *The Psychology of Musical Ability,* [13] (1968) by Rosamund Shuter, appeared too early to reflect the renewed activity in the psychology of music. The second edition of Paul Farnsworth's *The Social Psychology of Music* [14] (1969), was updated to include as much as possible of the work then current, but was basically the same book as that published originally in 1958. *The Psychology of Music Teaching*,[15] by Edwin Gordon (1971), presented a solid rationale for Gordon's own reasearch. Two excellent chapters, one on tonal learning and one on rhythmic learning, provide researchers with many clues for work in musical learning. Finally, a book by Erik Franklin, *Music Education, Psychology and Method*[16] (1972), attempts to combine the psychology of music with method. Though it deals with such areas as perception, test psychology, developmental psychology, and learning, as well as music education, it reports no original research and only a minimum of the research of others.

Funded Research

Most of the large-scale research sponsored in the 1960s by the U.S. Office of Education under the Elementary and Secondary Education Act was not concerned with controlled inquiry into fundamental problems of musical learning. It was, on the other hand, designed to develop new curriculum materials and innovative approaches to musical learning. Many of the materials produced were superior to those in prior existence; some were based upon improved, more carefully thought-out goals; but without any follow-up in the form of systematic evaluation, and without any long-term commitment from the schools for which they were developed, their effect was ephemeral.

Interest in the production of new teaching materials received a powerful impetus from the Yale Seminar on Music Education of 1964. Although the participants in the Seminar were not, for the most part, interested in doing research themselves, they stimulated widespread ferment by their outspoken and penetrating criticism of the status of music education. This criticism, together with the general dissatisfaction with public-school education at that time, resulted in at least sixty-five major projects in music education and numerous smaller endeavors funded by grants from regional offices. Among the undertakings that had some long-range effects was Reimer's General Music Curriculum,[17] which resulted not only in an influential final report but in a new technique for teaching music appreciation. Reimer carefully differentiates between aesthetic perception and aesthetic reaction. He sees music as a means for exploring human feelings and establishes levels of difficulty for exploration in continually more sophisticated settings. His study offered evidence of the successful use of certain pedagogical arrangements of materials, most notably the use of the "exemplar" approach wherein extensive use is made of a few selections that are returned to again and again in cyclical fashion, with greater understanding and deeper perception expected from the student upon each return. At the college level, Reimer's ideas have been incorporated into a music appreciation text,[18] and at the public school level into a music series for grades one through eight.[19]

A second influential project funded by the U.S.O.E. was the string project of Paul Rolland.[20] Rolland and his colleagues developed a method of teaching strings that represents an American adaptation of the Suzuki method. A wealth of teaching materials was produced[21,22] including films, records, methods books, drill materials, and some minor hardware, which continue to be widely used. Workshops held in Great Britain as well as the United States have demonstrated the teaching method and introduced the materials to teachers. Two other government-funded projects resulted in published materials: Gordon Hardy's repertory for grades kindergarten through six[23] is designed for classroom use, and for vocal and instrumental ensembles. It is an impressive collection of nearly 230 short vocal and 53 short instrumental compositions, categorized by period from pre-Renaissance to contemporary and folk music. It offers no pedagogical arrangement nor a "method"; the value of the publications resides in the nature of the compositions; high musical worth, varied stylistic representation, brief and simple enough for elementary-school children. Among the U.S.O.E. grants, the Manhattanville Project[24] of Ronald B. Thomas attracted the most publicity and received the greatest attention due to its radical departure from traditional modes of school music instruction. Through numerous demonstrations at conventions and workshops, the Manhattanville scheme has had a genuine impact on the procedures and goals for music at every educational level, though its complete adoption has occurred in only a limited number of situations. Briefly, the method approaches music instruction through improvisation, composition, and experimentation, and emphasizes the use of contemporary sounds and compositional devices.

Unfortunately, no data are available on which to base objective judgments of the educational merits of any of these materials and methods. They can be appraised as interesting, or musical, or provocative, or some other value-weighted adjective, but not in terms of actual results compared with the results of using other materials and methods. Music education curricula have yet to face the standards imposed upon curricula in other subject-matter areas.

Several status studies resulted from federal grants. Three of these may be mentioned as giving some indication of children's behavior and achievement with regard to selected musical concepts and elements: Petzold's study of the auditory perception of elementary school children,[25] Andrews' and Deihl's exploration into children's musical concepts,[26] and the study by Zimmerman and Secrest of the ways children organize musical sounds.[27] Although Heller and Campbell's study of the auditory characteristics of musical performance[28] has some elements of a status study, it is one of the few studies that provided useful basic research data and some clues to the perceptual process.

Systematic, long-term research into musical learning is only possible with government support. Two research organizations in the United States have received their support from federal monies. These are the CEMREL Aesthetic Education Program, with which readers of this paper are already familiar, and SWRL (Southwestern Regional Laboratories) Educational Research and Development Laboratory. The rationale for the research at SWRL is contained in a working paper by Williams and Carlsen, dated 1974.[29] Their concern is primarily with children's listening skills. Emphasizing skills related to melodic, harmonic, and rhythmic perception, the research has been concentrated on how children identify melody in terms of motion and shape, motivic expansion, and formal organization. Some studies have had to be as basic as determining the extent to which children can identify the direction of melodic intervals — up, down, or same pitch. The effect of timbre and loudness variation on the child's perception of melodic interval motion is studied. Also investigated for these kindergarten through grade-two children is the effect of their initial proficiency levels and response mode training. This work uses the SWRL audio laboratory with a programmable pitch generator, earphones, and visual stimuli presented by a programmable slide projector. It may be thus categorized as basic research rather than applied research. The psychoacoustical aspects are illustrated by one of the findings: When a timbre shift is made from triangle wave on the first tone to square wave on the second, a child's ability to identify melodic direction is affected.

Worthy of mention is the activity in the scientific aspects of aesthetic education being conducted at the University of Toronto under the direction of D. E. Berlyne. A report of this work is contained in his latest book, dated 1974.[30]

Research on Music Teaching and Learning

This section contains a brief summary of the findings of recent research in various aspects of music teaching and learning. These aspects will be presented as: method, developmental or maturational studies, the effect of training, attitudes, perception, automated learning, creativity, psychological theories, and aptitude. Taken together, they form a fairly complete picture of the present status of research.

A large number of curriculum studies completed as doctoral dissertations have established that the application of different methods does not affect learning. On the surface, this is a surprising finding, for an author's method profits from the halo effect and novelty, and possibly as well from some bias on the part of study participants. This finding is, however, consistent for different age levels, for different media, and for researchers at different institutions.

Siemens (1969)[31] compared the Orff method with traditional methods of teaching and reported attitudinal differences in favor of Orff but knowledge advantages in favor of the traditional methods with other musical learning equivalent. Other studies that resulted in no differences are: Ruth Keraus (1973), Suzuki violin instruction;[32] Zumbrunn (1969), 20th-Century Art Music;[33] Klemish (1968), music reading using a vocabulary of tonal patterns;[34] Goewey (1969), use of line scores in listening;[35] Palmer (1974), a comparison of Kodaly and Gordon syllables for music reading;[36] Lowe (1973), violin tone quality: long bow- and short bow-stroke;[37] and Ware (1968), music appreciation, three organizational plans.[38] The Ware study raises some interesting questions for teacher education. The three plans used were (1) music taught by the classroom teacher, (2) music taught by the music specialist, and (3) music taught by both types of teachers. Measurement by the *Oregon Test of Musical Discrimination* revealed no difference among the three plans. Test developers confirm the finding; classes taught by classroom teachers perform as well or better on tests than those taught by music specialists, markedly so in the lower elementary grades.

One study of methods of teaching preschool children attained similar results. Greenberg, studying the Hawaii curriculum project's preschool program (1974), found no differences in the results of his curriculum and the traditional program.[39]

Petters (1974)[40] rated two groups of students on expressive phrasing in performance after a nine-month period during which one group participated in decision-making processes about musical performance and the other group was given all performance directions by the conductor. When evaluated by Hoffren's *A Test of Expressive Phrasing in Music* and rated by three judges on the basis of recorded performances, the first group showed no difference from the second. McDaniels' study (1974)[41] tested fourth-grade pupils using three of the Colwell *Music Achievement Tests* and found an advantage only in the area of pitch for students taught by the Kodaly method (as exemplified in *Threshold to Music*) over students taught by the traditional method (using *Making Music Your Own.*) Perhaps these efforts have been futile because the tests lacked curricular validity; perhaps because the diversity already present within one class was greater than the difference that would result from the teaching method — diversity springing from environmental, aptitudinal, or other factors; perhaps because no consideration was given to the role of maturation; or perhaps because the goals were too ambitious for the time limits of the study.

Research on Development and Maturation

Paul Michel, of the D.D.R. (German Democratic Republic), is making a significant contribution to the music education profession with some basic research and some well-informed speculation. Charged by law with developing an effective music curriculum for all East German children, he is making an effort to find the optimum conditions for musical development. One goal is to find realistic upper limits of achievement for each age without imposing excessive and injurious demands upon children. He rejects the "artificial" stages of Piaget and any "fatalistic nativistic determination of musical aptitude." He further refutes the ideas of Revesz that the first year is of little importance; rather his research indicates that the first six months represent the period in which a child learns to hear. Two different timbres can be distinguished by the age of two to three months, pitches can be distinguished by the second half of the first year, and the child can begin to sing a few notes with the mother by the end of the first year of life. By the time he or she enters school, the student has developed the ability to hear and listen to major and minor modes.[42] Michel's research places in doubt the belief that children go through a pentatonic stage of development. With the exposure that children have to varied sound sources at home and school, and from television, radio, and cinema, they use the triad for their creative activities. Each child will develop if engaged in the proper activities, but the teacher must offer the right learnings at the right time. For language training, the child is language sensitive at ages three to five, during which period he or she learns in a reproductive-imitative manner. For the development of vocal and auditory abilities, it appears to Michel that the peak period encompasses the fifth and sixth years.[43]

Almost all of the developmental and maturational studies in the Western World dealing with musical elements or musical concepts use as subjects very young children, eight and below. Such studies are numerous, but none has provided a satisfactory solution to the problem of separating the factors of maturation and education. In view of the inadequate quality of musical experience provided in the primary grades in many schools, which often represents recreation more than instruction, we may venture the surmise that increased achievement is largely the result of maturation. Interpretation of the results of maturational studies is further complicated by the fact that little exploration has been done to ascertain what should be taught at any age level, or what skills and concepts are needed before the appropriate learning can take place. Most of the research dealing with the relationship between age level and skill is focused on the earliest age at which the skill (concept) can be learned, rather than on the age after which the skill is increasingly difficult to acquire. Age levels for musical reponsiveness have not been investigated; we know that children react to music almost from birth, but the reaction may not have any of the elements of musical responsiveness. Further, attempts at early musical training for skill may bring negative learning as well as, or in lieu of, positive learning. Again, some learnings achieved at great expenditure of effort for one age may come about naturally at a later age. The paucity of research literature prevents us from drawing any conclusions in these areas. Research in the 1930s by Jersild and Bienstock,[44,45,46] Moorhead and Pond[47] and recently that of Robert Smith[48] provide the principal data base for the results of longitudinal work for children of any age.

Moorhead and Pond studied young children, two to six years of age, from 1937 to 1944. They concluded that children can be taught to read and write music at this age. Jersild and Bienstock studied children two to five years of age. Over a period of three years, children improved only slightly in rhythmic responsiveness but did improve in their ability to sing. Smith's work over a ten-year period has emphasized the importance of early musical experiences for later development.

A skill area that has fascinated musical researchers is that of perfect pitch. Following Michel's dictum of teaching the right thing at the right time, Sergeant's ex *post facto* study[49] of the development of perfect pitch in 1500 musicians attempted to determine whether a relationship exists between the age of initial music instruction and the possession of perfect pitch. His results indicate a rather linear progression based on the age of first instruction. Those whose musical study began at the age of two to four usually had perfect pitch; more than ninety percent of Sergeant's sample fit into this category. Those whose study began as late as age twelve to fourteen possessed perfect pitch in only five percent of the cases. This study, like many nonexperimental efforts, is plagued by the impossibility of determining causation. The capacity for perfect pitch may in most of the cases studied be part of a complex of talents that led to early music study. Once again we reiterate, as did Kwalwasser, that training attracts the talented.

Over the course of the last seventy-five years, some experimental studies have attempted to teach perfect pitch. For the strict behaviorist it is necessary that perfect pitch be teachable and learnable. Limited success has been reported, usually with very small samples. With the plethora of musicians in this world who would like to develop perfect pitch in themselves and their students, we can safely conclude that no widely successful method has yet been found for any age level, else we would have heard the great news sung out, on a perfect A-440, of

A number of studies have dealt with aural perception and/or discrimination at various age levels. Seashore believed that the pure elements of ability would not improve with practice or maturity, but his selection of the elements as well as his findings regarding their stability are still open to question. Among Seashore's pure elements are pitch, loudness, timbre, and rhythm. The following studies include one or more of these elements. Spencer[50] tested eighty students between the ages of two-and-one-half and six years, and concluded that the ability to match pitch and the ability to rhyme did not improve with age during the years the study was concerned with. Bridges[51] studied harmonic discrimination in children in kindergarten through the third grade, and states that children possess this ability in varying degrees both within and between grade levels, but that at the kindergarten level the instance of this ability may well be the result of chance.

Thackeray (reported 1973)[52] believes that children develop a harmonic sense before age nine. They can discriminate between a single tone and a chord. It is much more difficult, however, for them to tell if a chord heard is repeated in a sequence of chords, or if the harmony remains identical for a repeated melody. Working with children from grades two through eight, Schultz (1969)[53] evaluated responses to melody, rhythm, tempo, instrumental timbre, mode, and key change. He found steady improvement in ability with a plateau at grades five to seven; conservation of melody was the most difficult of the tasks in his study, recognition of key change next most difficult. This study begins where most studies cease — at the age level (approximately eight years) where conservation occurs — and was not concerned with the pre-operational stages that Piaget assigns to the earlier years. Another study dealing with conservation is that of Lawes (1971)[54] who tested children at kindergarten, second, fourth, and sixth grades for conservation of pitch patterns in rhythmic transformation. He concludes that no special stages exist; that children improve by grade level. Laverty (1969),[55] using measures from the Andrews and Diehl *Battery of Musical Concept Measures* with children in grades three, five, and seven, found that ability to discriminate pitch, duration, and loudness increased between the third and the fifth grades, but that seventh graders were no more proficient in discriminating than fifth graders. The influence of a host of variables upon perception is illustrated by the work of Hermanson (1971),[56] who explored the effects of timbre on pitch perception and acuity with young children. She found the pitch acuity of third graders superior to that of kindergarten pupils. She also concluded that singing with a woman's voice produced more pitch stability than singing with another child's voice, piano, or an oscillator. Interestingly, singing with the piano produced the poorest pitch acuity. The work of McDonald (1970)[57] was an effort to determine the effect of socioeconomic class on the development of musical concepts. She found that middle-class students could handle concepts more easily than lower-class students, due, perhaps, to a significant relationship between mental age and the formation of musical concepts. She found identification of pitch the most difficult, discrimination of loudness the easiest.

In a well-designed study, Dittemore (reported 1970)[58] explored development of pupil achievement in a well-structured music program. He concluded that, at first grade, musical capabilities are developed for minor mode, duple and triple meter; at second grade for major mode, dorian mode, mixed meter, round and counter-melody; at third grade, unusual meter and two-part music. His research on the concepts of non-tonal music and three-part music was inconclusive. Compared with the findings in other studies cited, Dittemore plainly shows the influence of a well-structured educational program in music. For all the developmental studies, the element of training and experience enters in; in the research to be discussed below, training is the focus of the studies.

Research on Training

Success with training has been reported primarily by the behaviorists. Greer and his associates at Teachers College have reported (1973)[59] a number of studies that achieved moderate success, as long as the correct responses were associated with high teacher approval. One study[60] reported significant improvement in vocal intonation when the behavior was reinforced, with the type of music used being unimportant. Another study at Teachers College[61] found that the greater the number of approvals, the more the ability to match pitch improved. They concluded that more rigorous programs would result in increased achievement.

Another Greer study (reported 1974)[62] provides evidence that the period from third to fourth grade is a pivotal one for the formation of musical taste, thus reinforcing Petzold's conclusion that this is an important period for the acquisition of other musical behaviors as well. Foley (1974),[63] in a well-designed research study with second-grade children, achieved some success in improving the ability of children to conserve tonal and rhythmic patterns through training. The developmental aspect intrudes, however; her students were at the age when conservation is thought to occur, and her success compared with the control group may be explained by readiness or near-readiness for training. The conclusions of Taebel (reported 1974)[64] regarding the effects of instruction on children's conceptual abilities raise some interesting questions about the Piagetian theory. Taebel found large individual differences within grade levels, often larger than those between grade levels, suggesting that factors beyond simple maturation are at work, though age seems to be the major single factor. He found that ability to hear dynamic differences is greater in children than ability to hear pitch differences. Confirming the work of Petzold, he found little change between single grade levels, and minimal growth between first and second grades. The Britisher Sam Taylor (1973)[65] studied children aged seven to eleven. He found that for ability to perceive melody, rhythm, and harmony, age rather than training made a consistent difference except in the case of rhythm, which did not improve between the ages of ten and eleven. Training seemed to have relatively little effect on perception of musical elements, on ability to discriminate which piece was error-free, or on preference for types of music. Similarly, McCarthy (1969)[66] found that scores on a perception test did not improve as the number of years of participation in musical organizations increased. Kuhn and Gates reported (1974)[67] that tempo perception as measured by clapping performance does not improve with age or experience; first and second graders are as competent as college undergraduates. A slowing of the tempo is more readily perceived than a speeding up. A change of pulse is easier to identify than is continuation of the same pulse. This study, like many others reported in this article, must be accepted only tentatively because the research was conducted on a small scale. Kuhn and Gates themselves advise caution in interpreting the results, due to the limited number of subjects and the wide variance found at each grade level. A perspective on these studies may be gained from the work reported by Piper and Shoemaker (1973).[68] Their investigation indicates that *without* any training kindergarten pupils can distinguish between same and different phrases, identify gross features of melodic contour such as ascending and descending lines, distinguish between accompanied and unaccompanied music, distinguish between fast and slow pulse, and distinguish between loud and soft dynamic levels. The above list is a close approximation of those objectives often given for the first three grades, objectives used to compare the various methods of instruction. Romenek's study (reported 1974)[69] tends to reinforce the findings of

Piper and Shoemaker. Working with a self-instructional program for preschool children in singing, listening, performing, and moving to music, she found that the children had a well-developed concept of loudness but were much weaker in pitch and duration. She suggests that instructional activities do not result in learning to the extent that teachers believe they do.

With the exception of the work of Greer and his associates, the studies just discussed deal with the effects of training in musical perception. They indicate that training as it is presently offered makes little difference in musical perception. Research into training for musical skills, however, results in a mixed picture. Contributing to the negative data regarding instruction is the study made by Groves (1965).[70] He found no difference in the ability to synchronize body movements with rhythmic stimuli between children who had undergone rhythmic training and those who had not. His conclusions, based on a posttest, were that age and maturation are greater factors than instruction, and that native ability is more influential than home environment. One study indicates that training does improve certain aspects of singing performance. Madsen, Wolfe and Madsen (reported 1969)[71] were able to improve the performance of uncertain singers by use of reinforcement as a teaching technique and the descending scale as teaching material. Training can improve the reading ability and the intonation of beginning wind instrumentalists, according to two studies. Macknight (reported 1975)[72] used syllables for pitch and a consistent mnemonic device such as Gordon's system of rhythm syllables to improve reading ability. Miles (reported 1972)[73] improved the intonation of beginning wind instrumentalists by the technique of beat elimination; 75 of his 118 subjects succeeded in eliminating the beat in tuning.

Research on Attitudes

In the area of attitude and appreciation, research findings are, similarly, largely negative. Schukert and McDonald (reported 1968)[74] attempted to modify the musical preferences of four- and six-year-olds; and, though they were partially successful, their data for change were not statistically significant. Duerksen, (reported 1968)[75] working at the other end of the educational ladder, had similar results with college students, finding that both preference and ability levels change little between high school and college. He asks these disturbing questions: "Why is there little average change with increasing class level? Is the only discrimination a college music major learns [that of] a better liking for rock-and-roll?" Several studies reveal the lack of positive results for appreciation at the elementary-school level. Oberdin (reported 1967)[76] used notation to assist fifth-grade students in remembering thematic material, but without success. Two studies by Nolin, several years apart, (reported 1967[77] and 1973[78]) indicate that music educators may not only be failing to improve appreciation of music and attitude towards music, but may indeed be fostering negative attitudes. His results in both studies are almost identical to those of an earlier study by Broquist (1961)[79] in which positive attitude toward the study and appreciation of music appeared to decline with age. Wragg (1974)[80] reported a similar decline in interest between elementary and secondary school.

Research on Perception and Psychoacoustics

Two rather significant research endeavors offer sizeable data on perception in music, and perhaps provide some future directions. Heller and Campbell, working at the University of Connecticut, argue that music is a formal system derived from the structural component of natural language. Their belief is that we must understand the elementary aspects of musical patterning (such as the child's conservation rules) before we can understand musical behavior and conduct research in this area. They argue that we need a theoretical model of musical perception, that basic model building and testing are presently needed which, when accomplished, can lead to structural and functional models that can be tested. Based on their present work, they suggest that musical patterning depends upon implicit formal operations; that is, aesthetic response is the result of a cognitive, intellectual process. There is a relationship between musical perception and musical intelligence; basic problem-solving is the same in music as in other areas. Their matrix suggests that the human being can respond to music from auditory or notational stimuli, and to the macro or micro elements — macro elements being the formal elements that presently have symbols and micro elements including the interpretive aspects of music such as stress, change of timbre, and so forth. As music is a natural language, we should expect form to take precedence over content (reported 1976).[81] One of their component studies was an effort to identify and classify the significant perceptual parameters of musical performance. They have developed hardware for use in learning what acoustical factors are important to the subjective response of a musically perceptive listener (1971).[82]

A doctoral dissertation by Divenyi (1970)[83] consisted of research into the rhythmic perception of two-note "melodies." Divenyi used pure sound rather than music; by using broad-band white noise, he was able to hold constant the power of the tonal signal and the power of noise. He concluded that the discrimination of time intervals is influenced by absolute and relative attributes of the tone's frequency, range, absolute distance, and whether it is ascending or descending relative to the prior tone. His research led him to believe that the human being has two separate perceptual processes, one for intervals shorter than .6 second and one for those over .6 second. The findings help to explain other research wherein discrimination has not improved over time or with training; for he concludes that the interference of tonal frequencies in the discrimination of time intervals, delimited by short tones, is an authentic sensory phenomenon and is not readily influenced by learning. Such a conclusion leads one to ask whether musicians have made any serious efforts to identify the sensory aspects of responsiveness or perception that do not lend themselves to training.

Divenyi further believes that perceived rhythm is a function of the melodic intervals (page 132) and that musically rhythmic melody, per se, is not physically rhythmic. In other words, absolute metrical regularity in any given melody may well make the listening experience unmusical. In support of his conclusions, he cites his finding that perfect melodic intervals need more time (agogic inflection) to be perceived as rhythmic. Melodies of low dynamic level need considerable articulation to escape from an apparent lack of rhythm, a phenomenon that is also true of melodies in the high register. Thus, at least for our culture, melodic-rhythmic perceptual interaction is a phenomenon inherent to hearing and independent of learning or of cultural factors. (To conjecture as to the nature of this interaction for other cultures is pointless; different patterns of interaction may exist, or the phenomenon may be consistent across cultures.)

This information throws some light on the findings of Rupert Thackeray (reported 1969),[84] who attempted to discover a common factor of ability. He found some relationship, but that between rhythmic performance, rhythmic perception, and movement was not high. He nevertheless still posits a commonness between music and dance (reported 1969[85] and 1972[86]). Any common factors probably pertain to the relationship of dance to pitched music rather than to any common rhythmic factor in dance, athletics, and music. Thackeray does confirm the research of Kuhn and Moore[67] that the ability to maintain a steady tempo increases little with age.

The larger area of perception as it overlaps into psychoacoustics has received attention from numerous researchers in the past decade. An excellent summary of the status of research in this area is provided by Juan Roederer.[87] Although much of the research does not pertain to musical responsiveness, there are aspects of the field of psychoacoustics that hold potential enlightenment for the musician who wishes to understand more fully the nature of the musical response. The following list touches briefly upon the studies pertinent to music.

The complexity of tuning was demonstrated by Swaffield (reported 1974)[88] in a study that found tuning to be dependent upon timbre, intensity, duration, and relative frequency. Although we continue to equate pitch with frequency, in common-sense layman's terms, Leonard (1967)[89] demonstrated that pitch discrimination was affected by register, intensity, timbre, duration, context, and interstimulus time interval. Greer, whose studies usually focus on a practical problem, in working with instrumentalists, assessed the effects that different timbres have on a subject's ability to match pitch (1970).[90] Haack (reported 1975)[91] and Stephenson (1971)[92] have investigated the influence of loudness upon musical perception; Branning (1967)[93] and Sisson (1969)[94] studied tuning preferences using various ratios including just intonation, Pythagorean, and equal temperament. Other studies include Oddo's (1971)[95] research into the relationship between pure and complex tones and pitch and loudness; Vorce's (1964)[96] exploration of the effect of simultaneous stimulus on vocal pitch accuracy; Linger's (1966)[97] experimentation with durational notation, and Williams' work (1973)[98] in retention of pitch sequence. The complexity of musical perception is illustrated by the diversity of these pieces of work. Although the quantity of information contributed from any single study is minute in comparison to the immensity of our ignorance, the amount of activity in the field of perception will surely produce results we will find useful in teaching for musical responsiveness.

One might speculate the music researchers have concentrated their efforts on the wrong elements of musicality. For example, the importance of a factor that is termed musical cognition is pointed up by the research of McLeish. The basic study was completed some twenty-five years ago but was not reported until after it was replicated in 1965. From a careful factor analysis of the Seashore, Wing, and Oregon tests, McLeish concludes that the important factors of musicality are not those usually identified as pitch, duration, timbre, etc.; but there is a single important factor of musical cognition, the ability to recognize and understand the nature of changes in musical or quasi-musical materials. Elements of musical cognition perhaps consist of musical memory, pitch discrimination, and ability to analyze chords.[99] Sergeant and Roche[100] and Sergeant and Thatcher[101] hint that they agree that musical cognition is critical in musical responsiveness but that it does not stand alone due to a relationship with intelligence. Neither by itself is satisfactory, but in combination, they suggest we have the beginnings of an understanding of one of the key elements of musicality.

Research on Automated Learning

In any review of significant research over the past decade, automated learning legitimately requires a place. Walter Ihrke is in many senses a real pioneer in this phase of exploration and innovation. One of his earlier articles appeared in the Spring 1963 *Journal of Research in Music Education* and other articles appeared around the same time in the *Bulletin of the Council for Research in Music Education*. Before others had given automation much serious consideration relative to musical learning, Ihrke suggested that one of its real advantages would be in forcing educators to take a new look at what needs to be taught, and the sequence of presentation. He further suggested that to compare automated training with that offered by the traditional teacher approach may hold little profit because the human approach has not been every effective. Researchers into automated learning, however, tend to make just this comparison, since no other type of comparison is possible unless it be with a second form of automation. Dean (1971)[102] used an autoinstructional device with fourth-grade students and found that learning music symbols and terms, as well as general music achievement, was higher than that resulting from the traditional music-class approach. Three studies, typical of programmed learning studies produced indecisive results: Michels (1972),[103] Oakes (1973)[104] and Rives (reported 1970)[105] found no significant differences between self-instruction (with or without hardware) and the traditional approach in situations ranging from third grade to college level. A study or programmed learning that produced positive results for the programmed activity is that of Norton (1973).[106]

The most sophisticated hardware system, PLATO, resides at the University of Illinois. Two studies done there are designed to exploit the capabilities of the computer. Done by Peters (1973)[107] and Placek (1972),[108] they establish the fact that the computer is a feasible tool for teaching musical learnings. Whether such findings will result in general use of the computer for this purpose is a question that has yet to be answered. A number of other computer-assisted instruction (CAI) programs have been devised by researchers working in places as varied as Buffalo, New York; Salt Lake City, Utah; Kansas City, Missouri; and Evanston, Illinois. These deal with such phases of learning as: music theory (Hulfish, 1969),[109] sightsinging (Thompson, 1973),[110] general music (Von Feldt),[111] and the sight-reading of rhythm (Mortenson).[112]

The invaluable nature of the computer as a bibliographic aid to researchers is just beginning to be recognized, with three of our major storehouses of information established around the United States. In addition to Datrix, ERIC, and the social sciences index, the system being built at the University of Georgia is expected to contain an exhaustive coverage of music (Edwards and Douglas, 1972).[113] Presently, however, there are a number of good summaries found in publications of the past few years that offer the opportunity for qualitative judgment. These will be listed towards the end of this article.

Research on Creativity

The area of creativity, which seems such a fertile field for research, has been all but totally neglected in the past few years. Two studies deserve mention, both of them larger in scope than the bulk of those included in this article. Kyme (1967),[114] supported by government funds, explored the contribution of musical composition to the development of musicality in junior high school. He found the traditional instrumental program the most universally effective in developing musicality; composition was more effective as a tool at the higher socioeconomic levels than elsewhere throughout the social spectrum. An attempt to evaluate objectively the effect of the Comprehensive Musicianship Program was made by Boyle and Radocy (reported 1973).[119] They identified thirteen outstanding and representative teachers for this project. Criterion-referenced tests were constructed for each teacher depending upon her or his objectives for the CMP program. The Music Achievement Tests of Colwell were selected as the standardized tests to provide baseline data. Students within the CMP did show improvement as measured by the criterion-referenced tests, and MAT, but the researchers were forced to ask, in summary, whether the objectives of the program and/or the testing tools were too difficult; whether the teaching was of poor quality; whether their evaluative procedures in some manner prevented accurate measurement of criterion attainment. Achievement fell far short of what seemed to be reasonable goals. The study confirms once again how little we really know about the factors entering into musical learning. It points up the futility of developing new methods without first answering the basic questions about musical response, musical learning, and music teaching, and the further question of accurate evaluation in these areas.

Research on Psychological Theory

In 1963, it was suggested by Leonhard[116] that music educators attempt to apply psychological theories as a means of finding more successful teaching insights. The earliest such study was that by Pflederer (1963),[117] who took the Piagetian principle of conservation and applied it to responses children made to a set of musical tasks. The study was an influential one; Pflederer expanded the project into the federally funded work with Secrest, already mentioned.[27] A number of other pieces of research on conservation followed; (most of them have been referred to earlier.) Boswell (1969)[118] turned to Bruner's theory of mental growth and applied it to beginning instrumentalists, formulating from the theory teaching strategies by which basic musical concepts could be systematically taught. Bruner continues to be explored by music educators, but his suggestions are not rigorously followed. Boswell derived five strictures from Bruner: (1) the development of musical concepts is based upon the utilization of a generic coding system; (2) the optimum sequence must progress in a manner consistent with the course of cognitive growth; (3) meaningful verbal cues should be given in classifying stimulus patterns; (4) experiences should be provided that alert students to sameness under changed conditions; and (5) guidance should be given the learner to explore concordance and discordance among the modes of representation.

Other psychologists whose ideas have been applied to aspects of musical learning are Ausubel (Hieronymus, 1967)[119] and Maslow (Harvey, 1974).[120] Harvey's study focused on correlating Maslow's concept of self-actualization with creative teaching. He concludes that we need to investigate teacher personality more carefully, insure a student-centered program with more creativity throughout, and develop an aesthetic foundation for teacher education. Although Skinner has not been, as such, the subject of music education research, his ideas have found wide applicability with the behaviorists, who represent a large and influential segment in music education. A good example of the use of Skinnerian shaping procedures in music education is found in Cobes' (1969)[121] use of conditioning to improve uncertain singers. The work of Greer and his associates and of Madsen mentioned earlier in this article represent the application of Skinnerian techniques.[59,60,61,71]

A valuable summary of several theories is contained in the Katz work (1972),[122] *The Arts as a Vehicle for the Exploration of Personal Concerns.* Investigating the work of William James, Abraham Maslow, Carl Rogers, and Clark Mouspakas, he concludes that an acute objective perceptual faculty may be one possible key to helping the adolescent acquire a unique and satisfying personal identity, and to help him better understand himself, others, and the relationship between the two. Katz cites Erik Erikson and David Elkind to support a curriculum based on experiences in perception for the adolescent. He tests his curriculum and draws implications for teacher education, offering the conclusion that art is accessible to secondary-school students. A comparison of his seemingly positive conclusions with the negative ones of Duerksen[75] (who limited his study to music rather than the arts) might be revealing.

A project with as many philosophical as psychological roots is the Harvard Project Zero, directed by V. A. Howard (reported 1970).[123] A long-term endeavor, its purpose is, first, to analyze and classify the types of symbol systems and symbolic reference that are characteristic of different art forms. The second phase is to conduct experimental study of the skills and abilities required for the manipulation of art symbols; and, third, to determine methods of nurturing and training those abilities. When the project comes to maturity, it will have much to offer music education as well as to education in the various other arts.

One of the more serious researchers is Edwin Gordon, of the University of Buffalo. Gordon is concerned with the teaching and learning of tonal and rhythmic concepts. In order to investigate these aspects of musicality, he has developed a music aptitude test and six levels of a music achievement test. In the work of his students these instruments have been used and scrutinized, providing us with one of the better data bases for speculating on the future.

Gordon has pointed up the importance of aptitude in his longitudinal study of musical achievement of disadvantaged students.[124] He found that disadvantaged children with talent can succeed in spite of their background and the quality of the schools they attend, if identified and given a chance. In fact, they do as well as advantaged students with the same talent. He is arguing for the importance of providing training to those who can profit from it.

His work and that of DeYarman[125] continue to attest to the early stabilizing of aptitude. DeYarman holds on good evidence that aptitude is stabilized by the age of six and that the level of musical aptitude is not influenced by early school exposure to music.

The ability to improvise is not musicality, *per se,* as defined by Gordon, but involves other factors that are equally or more important. Gordon's *Musical Aptitude Profile* was not successful in discriminating in the area of improvisation.[126]

The studies of the validity of the aptitude test are fairly well known, including Gordon's own longitudinal study.[127]

Several studies have been conducted on the *Iowa Tests of Musical Literacy* (ITML), with James Mohatt's the most definitive with respect to validity. Working with eighth-grade students, he obtained satisfactory results for the validity of the battery, except for aural perception of rhythmic concepts. The study of rhythm was a troublesome one for Gordon in developing the aptitude tests, and remains a difficult task for all researchers.

Using the ITML, DeYarman[128] and Miller,[129] in separate studies, investigated the effect of instruction on achievement test scores. Confirming the general thrust of this article on how little we know about the effect of instruction, they used music with mixed meter with kindergarten and first-grade children, and nontonal and modal songs with first-grade students. In general, these students did as well as students more conventionally trained, but there were almost no significant differences between experimental and control groups. They conclude that we can use these materials without confusing young students. Miller did find that excessive exposure to nontonal music (one-third of instruction time) probably inhibits a child's ability to sing tonal songs. Although not disagreeing with their conclusions, we conclude that maturation and aptitude remain larger factors than instruction.

Gordon's present project is an attempt to establish levels of difficulty of tonal and rhythmic patterns. These findings will be used in developing sequences of instruction.

This article would be incomplete without a list of the summaries of recent research that can be found in various publications. The list includes: Lehman,[130] Zimmerman,[131] Benner,[132] Duerksen,[133] Rainbow,[134] Gonzo,[135] Turrentine,[136] Klemish,[137] Schwadron,[138] Jellison,[139] Whybrew,[140] Deihl and Partchey,[141] Schneider,[142] and Colwell.[143] Examination of the titles of these articles will reveal that some are specialized lists and some are general and that much overlapping occurs, but enough information is offered to furnish a fairly complete guide to the field as it looks today.

Direction for the Future

Having selectively reviewed research of the past ten years, we proceed with an attempt to establish a rationale for the conduct of research in music education during the next ten years.

Major Research Questions

These questions have been formulated to provide a focus for research pertinent to the establishment of music education as a partner in an overall program of aesthetic education. The questions do not encompass research into the history of music, the development of musical style, or other topics in the realm of musicology. They are concerned with the nature of musical responsiveness and perception and the means of developing them. They point toward basic research, the results of which may later be applied to music teaching and learning:

    1. What is music as art?

    2. What constitutes aesthetic responsiveness to music?

3. How does aesthetic responsiveness to music relate to aesthetic responsiveness to other arts?
4. What is the basis for aesthetic responsiveness to music?
5. What is the basis for musical perception?
6. What is the influence of aptitude on the development of musical responsiveness and perception?
7. What is the influence of maturation on the development of musical responsiveness and perception?
8. To what extent can a growth gradient be established for the development of musical responsiveness and perception?
9. How can aptitude for musical responsiveness and perception be measured?
10. How can achievement in musical responsiveness and perception be measured?
11. How does achievement of performance skills, listening skills, and skill in analyzing compositional devices and stylistic characteristics affect the development of musical responsiveness and perception?
12. What types of experience with music contribute to the development of musical responsiveness and perception?

It appears obvious that a program designed to find answers to questions such as these requires the collaboration of philosophers and scientists. Aesthetic theories represent potential sources of hypotheses pertinent to answering the first three questions. The hypotheses derived from aesthetic theory must be tested by the scientist and, if verified in the laboratory, can provide direction for research into the remaining questions.

We close by establishing conditions that would make feasible research into such questions as these.

First, the research effort in music education must be focused on basic research designed to verify hypotheses and to establish a sound and comprehensive theory of music education. The present unsubstantial character of all aspects of the music program other than performance is largely due to hasty, enthusiastic, but often misguided efforts to apply unsubstantiated theory to practice.

Second, the research must exhibit the quality of continuity possible only in an ongoing program with a group of researchers involved. SWRL and Gordon's program at the University of Buffalo exhibit this characteristic to an extent, but additional centers are needed. A few major universities with large doctoral programs and competent research personnel are in a position to establish such a program contingent on the availability of funds, and it would be feasible to establish consortiums of two or more universities having significant resources for research. The function of CEMREL could be altered to serve as a coordinating agency for a group of individual researchers working in their own institutions.

Third, a program of basic research requires consistent and dependable funding. Commitment of funds for a minimum of three years is essential. Short-term commitments inevitably lead to trivial results, due both to pressure on the researcher to show quick results and the fact that it is next to impossible for a researcher to gain real relief from administrative and teaching assignments on a short-term basis.

Fourth, it is essential that a corps of professional researchers be developed; and such personnel can be supplied only when there is a reasonable prospect of a continuing demand for their expertise. Currently, there is a little motivation for a music-education faculty member to develop research competence and become involved in ongoing research since it is apparent that he or she will be evaluated on his or her performance in supervising student teachers, conducting a band, or administering instructional programs. It must be emphasized, however, that doctoral programs in this country have, over the past few years, produced an impressive cadre of competent researchers who have the potential for becoming members of a professional research corps. Financial support is the essential ingredient that is missing.

Urbana, Illinois
May 1976

FOOTNOTES

[1]Max Schoen, "Psychological Problems in Musical Art," *Journal of Research in Music Education*, Vol. 3, No. 1 (Spring 1955).

[2]C. E. Seashore, *Seashore Measures of Musical Talent* (New York: Columbia Phonograph Company, 1919).

[3]W. V. D. Bingham, "Studies in Melody," *Psychological Monographs Whole* #50 (1910).

[4]H. Lowery, "Cadence and Phrase Tests in Music," *British Journal of Psychology*, Vol. 17 (1926).

[5]H. Lowery, "Fundamental Considerations in the Study of Musical Ability," *Journal of Educational Psychology*, Vol. 20 (1929).

[6]H. Lowery, "On the Integrative Theory of Musical Talent," *Journal of Musicology*, Vol. II (1940).

[7]James Mainwaring, "Psychological Factors in the Teaching of Music," *British Journal of Educational Psychology*, Vol. 21 (1951).

[8]James Mainwaring, "Experiments on the Analysis of Cognitive Processes Involved in Musical Ability and in Music Education," *British Journal of Educational Psychology*, Vol. 1 (1931).

[9]C. E. Seashore, "The Psychology of Music: XI," *Music Educators Journal*, Vol. 24 (December 1937).

[10]James L. Mursell, "What About Music Tests," *Music Educators Journal*, Vol. 24 (November 1937).

[11]Edwin Gordon, *Musical Aptitude Profile* (Boston: Houghton Mifflin Company, 1965).

[12]Richard J. Colwell, *Music Achievement Tests, I, II, III and IV* (Chicago: Follett Educational Corporation, 1967, 1970).

[13]Rosamund Shuter, *The Psychology of Musical Ability* (London: Methuen and Company, Ltd., 1968).

[14]Paul Farnsworth, *The Social Psychology of Music*, 2nd ed. (Ames, Iowa: The University of Iowa Press, 1969).

[15]Edwin Gordon, *The Psychology of Music Teaching* (Englewood Cliffs, New Jersey: Prentice-Hall, 1971).

[16]Erik Franklin, *Music Education, Psychology and Method* (London: George G. Harrap and Company, Ltd., 1972).

[17]Bennett Reimer, *Development and Trial in a Junior and Senior High School of a Two Year Curriculum in General Music* (Washington, D. C.: U. S. Office of Education Project 5-0257, 1967).

[18]Bennett Reimer and Ed Evans, *The Experience of Music* (Englewood Cliffs, New Jersey: Prentice-Hall, 1972).

[19]Elizabeth Crook, Bennett Reimer, David Walker, *Silver Burdett Music* (Morristown, New Jersey: Silver Burdett Company, 1974-75).

[20]Paul Rolland, *Development and Trial of a Two Year Program of String Instruction* (Washington, D. C.: U.S. Office of Education Project 5-1182, 1971).

[21]Paul Rolland, *Prelude to String Playing* (Oyster Bay, New York: Boosey and Hawkes, 1972).

[22]Paul Rolland and Marla Mutschler, *The Teaching of Action in String Playing* (Urbana, Illinois: String Research Associates, 1974).

[23]Gordon Hardy, *Julliard Repertory Library* (Cincinnati, Ohio: Canyon Press, 1970).

[24]Ronald Thomas, *Manhattanville Music Curriculum Project* (Washington, D. C.: U. S. Office of Education Project 6-1999, 1970).

[25]Robert Petzold, *Auditory Perception of Musical Sounds by Children in the First Six Grades* (Washington, D. C.: U.S. Office of Education Project 5-0202, 1965).

[26]Frances Andrews and Ned Deihl, *Development of a Technique for Identifying Elementary School Children's Musical Concepts* (Washington, D. C.: U.S. Office of Education Project 5-0233, 1967).

[27]Marilyn Zimmermann and Lee Secrest, *How Children Conceptually Organize Musical Sound* (Washington, D. C.: U.S. Office of Education Project 5-0256, 1968).

[28]Jack Heller and Warren Campbell, *Computer Analysis of the Auditory Characteristics of Musical Performance* (Washington, D. C.: U.S. Office of Education Project 9-0546, 1972).

[29]David B. Williams and James Carlsen, *A Programmatic, Long-term Plan for Child Psycho-musicology* (Los Alamitos, California: SWRL Educational Research and Development, 1974).

[30]D. E. Berlyne, ed., *Studies in the New Experimental Aesthetics; Steps Toward An Objective Psychology of Aesthetic Appreciation* (Washington, D. C.: Hemisphere Publishing Company, 1974, distributed by John Wiley).

[31]Margaret T. Siemens, "A Comparison of Orff and Traditional Instructional Methods in Music," *Journal of Research in Music Education*, Vol. 17, No. 3 (Fall 1969).

[32]Ruth Keraus, *An Achievement Study of Private and Class Suzuki Violin Instruction*, Dr. Diss., University of Rochester, 1973.

[33]Karen L. F. Zumbrunn, *A Listening Program in 20th-Century Art Music for Junior High School Students*, Dr. Diss., University of California, 1969.

[34]Janice Klemish, *A Comparative Study of Two Methods of Teaching Music Reading to First Grade Children by Developing a Vocabulary of Tonal Patterns*, Dr. Diss., University of Wisconsin, 1968.

[35]Gordon Ira Goewey, *An Experimental Study of the Effectiveness of the Melodic Line Score Approach to Music Listening in Developing Musical Literacy in Gen-

eral College Students, Dr. Diss., Boston University, 1969.

[36]Mary Henderson Palmer, *The Relative Effectiveness of the Richards and the Gordon Approaches to Rhythm Reading for Fourth Grade Children*, Dr. Diss., University of Illinois, 1974.

[37]Harold Lowe, *A Study of the Tone Quality of Beginning Violin Students Using the Long Bow Stroke Approach as Compared to the Short Bow Approach*, Dr. Diss., Ball State University, 1973.

[38]Robert Livingston Ware, *A Study of the Relative Effectiveness of Three Organizational Plans of Music Instruction in Developing Appreciation for Music in the Elementary Grades*, Dr. Diss. University of Oregon, 1968.

[39]Marvin Greenberg, "The Development and Evaluation of a Preschool Music Curriculum for Preschool and Headstart Children," *Psychology of Music*, Vol. 2, No. 1 (January 1974).

[40]Robert Bruce Petters, *How Student Participation in Decision Making Processes About Musical Performance Affects their Perception and Performance of Expressive Phrasing*, Dr. Diss., University of Michigan, 1974.

[41]Marvin Albert McDaniel, *A Comparison of Music Achievement Test Scores of Fourth Grade Students Taught by Two Different Methods — Kodaly Threshhold to Music and Traditional (MMYO)*, Dr. Diss., Louisiana State University and Agriculture and Mechanical College, 1974.

[42]S. Bimberg, *Untersuchunger über die Hör- und Singefähigkeit in Dur und Moll*, Dr. Diss., University of Halle, 1953.

[43]Paul Michel, "The Optimum Development of Musical Abilities in the First Years of Life," *Psychology of Music*, Vol. 1, No. 2 (June 1973).

[44]Arthur Jersild and Sylvia Bienstock, "Development of Rhythm in Young Children," *Child Development Monographs*, Vol. 22 (1933).

[45]Arthur Jersild and Sylvia Bienstock, "A Study of the Development of Children's Ability to Sing," *Journal of Educational Psychology*, Vol. 25, No. 7 (1934).

[46]Arthur Jersild and Sylvia Bienstock, "The Influence of Training on the Vocal Ability of Three-Year-Old Children," *Child Development*, Vol. 2 (1931).

[47]Gladys Moorhead and Donald Pond, *Music of Young Children*, No. 1 *Chant* (1941); No. 2 *General Observations* (1942), No. 3 *Musical Notation* (1944) (Santa Barbara, California: Pillsbury Foundation for Advancement of Music Education).

[48]Robert B. Smith, "The Effect of Group Vocal Training on the Singing Ability of Nursery School Children," *Journal of Research in Music Education*, Vol. 11, No. 2 (Fall 1963).

[49]Desmond Sergeant, "Experimental Investigation of Absolute Pitch," *Journal of Research in Music Education*, Vol. 17, No. 1 (September 1969).

[50]Ellen Spencer, *An Investigation of the Maturation of Various Factors of Auditory Perception in Preschool Children*, Dr. Diss., Northwestern University, 1958.

[51]Virginia Ann Bridges, *An Exploratory Study of the Harmonic Discrimination Ability of Children in Kindergarten through Grade Three in Two Selected Schools*, Dr. Diss., Ohio State University, 1965.

[52]Rupert Thackeray, "Tests of Harmonic Perception," *Psychology of Music*, Vol. 1, No. 2 (June 1973).

[53]Stephen W. Schultz, *A Study of Children's Ability to Respond to Elements of Music*, Dr. Diss., Northwestern University, 1969.

[54]William Frederick Lawes, *The Detection of Invariant Pitch Patterns over Rhythmic Transformation by Elementary School Children: A Preliminary Study of the Application of Differentiation Theory to Musical Perception*, Dr. Diss., University of Iowa, 1971.

[55]Grace Laverty, *The Development of Children's Concepts of Pitch, Duration,*

and Loudness as a Function of Grade Level, Dr. Diss., Pennsylvania State University, 1969.

[56]Luella Hermanson, *An Investigation of the Effects of Timbre on Simultaneous Vocal Pitch Acuity of Young Children,* Dr. Diss. Teachers College, Columbia University, 1971.

[57]Dorothy Taylor McDonald, *The Identification of Elementary School Children's Musical Concepts as a Function of Environment,* Dr. Diss., Ohio State University, 1970.

[58]Edgar Dittemore, "An Investigation of Some Musical Capabilities of Elementary School Students," *Studies in the Psychology of Music,* Volume 6, *Experimental Research in the Psychology of Music,* ed. Edwin Gordon (Iowa City: University of Iowa Press, 1970).

[59]R. Douglas Greer, Laura Dorow, and Suzanne Hanser, "Music Discrimination Training and the Music Selection Behavior of Nursery and Primary Level Children," *Bulletin of the Council for Research in Music Education,* No. 35 (Winter 1973).

[60]R. Douglas Greer, Andrew Randall, Craig Timberlake, "The Discriminate Use of Music Listening as a Contingency for Improvement in Vocal Pitch Acuity and Attending Behavior," *Bulletin of the Council for Research in Music Education,* No. 26 (1971).

[61]Suzanne Hanser, *The Effect of Peer Approval and Disapproval on Pitch Matching Performance and Group Behavior,* Dr. Diss., Columbia University, 1975.

[62]R. Douglas Greer, Laura Dorow, Andrew Randall, "Music Listening Preferences of Elementary School Children," *Journal of Research in Music Education,* Vol. 22, No. 4 (Winter 1974).

[63]Elspeth Foley, *The Effects of Training in Conservation of Tonal and Rhythmic Patterns on Second Grade Children,* Dr. Diss., University of Iowa, 1974.

[64]Donald Taebel, "The Effect of Various Instructional Modes on Children's Performance of Music Concept Tasks," *Journal of Research in Music Education,* Vol. 22, No. 3 (Fall 1974).

[65]Sam Taylor, *Musical Development of Children Aged Seven to Eleven,* Dr. Diss., University of Southhampton, 1969.

[66]Kevin McCarthy, *Effects of Participation in School Music Performance Organizations on the Ability to Perceive Aesthetic Elements in Recorded Music,* Dr. Diss., Case-Western Reserve University, 1969.

[67]Terry L. Kuhn, "Discrimination of Modulated Beat Tempos by Professional Musicians," *Journal of Research in Music Education,* Vol. 22, No. 4 (Winter 1974).

[68]Richard M. Piper and David M. Shoemaker, "Formative Evaluation of a Kindergarten Music Program Based on Behavioral Objectives," *Journal of Research in Music Education,* Vol. 21, No. 2 (Summer 1973), page 145.

[69]Mary Romenek, "A Self-Instructional Program for Musical Concept Development in Preschool Children," *Journal of Research in Music Education,* Vol. 22, No. 2 (Summer 1974).

[70]William Groves, *Rhythmic Training and its Relationship to the Synchronization of Motor Rhythmic Responses,* Dr. Diss., University of Arkansas, 1965.

[71]Clifford K. Madsen, David E. Wolfe, Charles Madsen, "The Effect of Reinforcement and Directional Scalar Methodology on Intonational Improvement," *Bulletin of the Council for Research in Music Education,* No. 18 (1969).

[72]Carol Macknight, "Music Reading Ability of Beginning Wind Instrumentalists after Melodic Instruction," *Journal of Research in Music Education,* Vol. 23, No. 1 (Spring 1975).

[73]Edgar Miles, "Beat Elimination as a Means of Teaching Intonation to Begin-

ning Wind Instrumentalists," *Journal of Research in Music Education*, Vol. 20, No. 2 (Winter 1972).

[74]Robert F. Schukert and Ruth L. McDonald, "An Attempt to Modify the Musical Preferences of Preschool Children," *Journal of Research in Music Education*, Vol. 16, No. 1 (Spring 1968).

[75]George Duerksen, "A Study of the Relationship Between the Perception of Musical Processes and the Enjoyment of Music," *Bulletin of the Council for Research in Music Education*, No. 12 (Winter 1968).

[76]Helen E. Oberdin, "The Use of Notated Examples in Fifth Grade Music Appreciation Classes," *Journal of Research in Music Education*, Vol. 15, No. 4 (Winter 1967).

[77]Wallace Nolin, *A Study of the Attitudes of Selected Fifth and Sixth Grade Students Toward Their School Music Program*, unpublished report, University of Akron, 1967.

[78]Wallace H. Nolin, "Attitudinal Growth Patterns Toward Elementary School Music Experiences," *Journal of Research in Music Education*, Vol. 21, No. 2 (Summer 1973).

[79]Oliver Broquist, *A Survey of the Attitudes of 2594 Wisconsin Elementary School Pupils Toward Their Learning Experiences in Music*, Dr. Diss., University of Wisconsin, 1961.

[80]Dorothy Wragg, "An Investigation into Some Factors Affecting the Carryover of Music Interest and Involvement During the Transition Period Between Primary and Secondary Education," *Psychology of Music*, Vol. 2, No. 1 (1974).

[81]Jack Heller and Warren Campbell, *Models of Language and Intellect in Music Research, Music Education for Tomorrow's Society* (Jamestown, Rhode Island: GAMT Press, 1976).

[82]Jack Heller and Warren C. Campbell, "Music Performance Analysis," *Bulletin of the Council for Research in Music Education*, No. 24 (Spring 1971).

[83]Pierre Laszlo Divenyi, *The Rhythmic Perception of Micro-melodies; Detectability by Human Observers of a Time Increment Between Sinusoidal Pulses of Two Different Successive Frequencies*, Dr. Diss., University of Washington, 1970.

[84]Rupert Thackeray, "Rhythmic Abilities and their Measurement," *Journal of Research in Music Education*, Vol. XVII, No. 1 (Spring 1969).

[85]Rupert Thackeray, "An Investigation into Rhythmic Abilities," *Music Education Research Papers*, No. 4 (London: Novello and Company, Ltd., 1969).

[86]Rupert Thackeray, "Rhythmic Abilities in Children," *Music Education Research Papers*, No. 5 (London: Novello and Company, Ltd., 1972).

[87]Juan Roedderer, *Introduction to the Physics and Psychophysics of Music*, 2nd ed. (Heidelberg Science Library, English Universities Press, Springer Verlag, 1975).

[88]William Robert Swaffield, "Effect of Melodic Parameters on Ability to Make Fine Tuning Responses in Context," *Journal of Research in Music Education*, Vol. 22, No. 4 (Winter 1974).

[89]Nels Leonard, Jr., *The Effect of Certain Intrinsic and Contextual Characteristics of the Tone Stimulus on Pitch Discrimination*, Dr. Diss., West Virginia University, 1967.

[90]R. Douglas Greer, "The Effect of Timbre on Brass Wind Notation," *Studies in the Psychology of Music*, Vol. 6, *Experimental Research in the Psychology of Music*, ed. Edwin Gordon (Iowa City: University of Iowa Press, 1970).

[91]Paul Haack, "The Influence of Loudness on the Discrimination of Musical Sound Factors," *Journal of Research in Music Education*, Vol. 23, No. 1 (Spring 1975).

[92]Robert A. Stephenson, *A Comparison of Judgments of the Loudness of Certain Musical Textures*, Dr. Diss., Indiana University, 1971.

[93]Howell Pierce Branning, *Audition Preferences of Trained and Untrained Ears on Hearing Melodic and Harmonic Intervals when Tuned in Just Intonation or Pythagorean Ratios*, Dr. Diss., University of Texas, 1967.

[94]Jack Ulness Sisson, *Pitch Preference Determination, A Comparative Study of Tuning Preferences of Musicians from the Major Performing Areas with Reference to Just Intonation, Pythagorean Tuning, and Equal Temperament*, Dr. Diss., University of Oklahoma, 1969.

[95]Vincent Oddo, *Pure and Complex Tone Equal Contours for Pitch and Loudness*, Dr. Diss., Indiana University, 1971.

[96]Fred Vorce, *The Effect of Simultaneous Stimulus on Vocal Pitch Accuracy*, Dr. Diss., The Florida State University, 1964.

[97]Bernard Linger, *An Experimental Study of Durational Notation*, Dr. Diss., The Florida State University, 1966.

[98]David B. Williams, *Short Term Retention of Pitch Sequence*, Dr. Diss., University of Washington, 1973.

[99]John McLeish, "Musical Cognition," *Music Education Research Papers, No. 2* (London: Novello and Company Ltd., 1968).

[100]Desmond Sergeant and Sheila Roche, "Perceptual Shifts in the Auditory Information Processing of Young Children," *Psychology of Music*, Vol. 1, No. 2, (1973).

[101]Desmond Sergeant and Gilliam Thatcher, "Intelligence, Social Status and Musical Abilities," *Psychology of Music*, Vol. 2, No. 2 (1974).

[102]Roger A. Dean, *The Effect of an Adjunct Autoinstructional Device on the Learning of Music Symbols and Terms and on General Music Achievement of Fourth Grade Students*, Dr. Diss., University of Oregon, 1971.

[103]Walter Michels, *A Visual-aural Self-instructional Program in Pitch Error Detection for Student Choral Conductors*, Dr. Diss., North Texas State University, 1972.

[104]Rodney Oakes, *An Investigation of a Self-directed Approach to Classroom Music in Grades Three Through Eight in an Alternative School*, Dr. Diss., University of Southern California, 1973.

[105]James Rives, "A Comparative Study of Traditional and Programmed Methods for Developing Music Listening Skills in the Fifth Grade," *Journal of Research in Music Education*, Vol. 18, No. 2 (Summer 1970).

[106]Mary Ann Norton, *The Development of Selected Musical Concepts Through the Use of Individualized Fixed Pace Instructional Program*, Dr. Diss., Boston University, 1973.

[107]George D. Peters, *The Feasibility of Computer-assisted Instruction for Instrumental Music*, Dr. Diss., University of Illinois, 1974.

[108]Robert W. Placek, *Design and Trial of a Computer-assisted Lesson in Rhythm*, Dr. Diss., University of Illinois, 1972.

[109]William R. Hulfish, *A Comparison of Response Sensitive and Response Insensitive Decision Rules in Presenting Learning Materials in Music Theory by Computer-assisted Instruction*, Dr. Diss., State University of New York at Buffalo, 1969.

[110]Edgar Thompson, *Sightsinging Constant Rhythm Phrases: A Computer-assisted Instructional System*, Dr. Diss., University of Utah, 1973.

[111]James Von Feldt, *Computer-assisted Instruction in the Public School General Music Class: A Comparative Study*, Dr. Diss., University of Missouri at Kansas City, 1971.

[112]Glen Mortenson, *The Development and Use of Computerized Procedures for Scoring Sight Reading of Rhythm to Compare the Effectiveness of Metric and*

Representational Notation with Conventional Notation, Dr. Diss., Northwestern University, 1970.

[113]John S. Edwards and Charles Douglas, "Model Computer-assisted Information Retrieval System in Music Education," *Journal of Research in Music Education*, Vol. 20, No. 4 (Winter 1972).

[114]George Kyme, *A Study of the Development of Musicality in the Junior High School and the Contribution of Musical Composition to this Development* (Washington, D. C.: U.S. Office of Education Project 5-0427, 1967).

[115]J. David Boyle and Rudolf E. Radocy, "Evaluation of Instructional Objectives in Comprehensive Musicianship," *Bulletin of the Council for Research in Music Education*, No. 32 (Spring 1973).

[116]Charles Leonhard, "Newer Concepts in Learning Theory as They Apply to Music Education," *Bulletin of the Council for Research in Music Education*, No. 1 (1963).

[117]Marilyn Pflederer, *The Responses of Children to Musical Tasks Embodying Piaget's Principles of Conservation*, Dr. Diss., University of Illinois, 1963.

[118]Jacquelyn Boswell, *An Application of Bruner's Theory of Mental Growth to the Teaching of Musical Concepts in Beginning Instrumental Music*, Dr. Diss., University of Illinois, 1969.

[119]Nora Gretchen Hieronymus, *Meaningful Reception Learning and Secondary School General Music*, Dr. Diss., University of Illinois, 1967.

[120]Arthur Harvey, *Abraham Maslow: Implications for the Development of Creative Music Educators*, Dr. Diss., Temple University, 1974.

[121]Cathy Jean Cobes, *The Conditioning of a Pitch Response Using Uncertain Singers*, Dr. Diss., Pennsylvania State University, 1969.

[122]Theodore Katz, *The Arts as a Vehicle for the Exploration of Personal Concerns*, Dr. Diss., Harvard University, 1972.

[123]V. A. Howard, "Harvard Project Zero: A Fresh Look at Art Education," *Bulletin of the Council for Research in Music Education*, No. 21 (Summer 1970).

[124]Edwin Gordon, "Fourth and Fifth Year Final Results of a Longitudinal Study of the Musical Achievement of Culturally Disadvantaged Students," *Studies in the Psychology of Music*, Vol. 10, *Experimental Research in the Psychology of Music*, ed. Edwin Gordon (Iowa City: University of Iowa Press, 1975).

[125]Robert DeYarman, "An Investigation of the Stability of Musical Aptitude Among Primary Age Children," *Studies in the Psychology of Music*, Vol. 10, *Experimental Research in the Psychology of Music*, ed. Edwin Gordon (Iowa City: University of Iowa Press, 1975).

[126]Joseph J. Briscuso, "A Study of Ability in Spontaneous and Prepared Jazz Improvisation Among Students Who Possess Different Levels of Musical Aptitude," *Studies in the Psychology of Music*, Vol. 9, *Experimental Research in the Psychology of Music*, ed. Edwin Gordon (Iowa City: University of Iowa Press, 1974).

[127]Edwin Gordon, "A Three Year Longitudinal Predictive Validity Study of the Musical Aptitude Profile," *Studies in the Psychology of Music*, Vol. 15, *Experimental Research in the Psychology of Music*, ed. Edwin Gordon (Iowa City: University of Iowa Press, 1967).

[128]Robert DeYarman, "An Experimental Analysis of the Development of Rhythmic and Tonal Capabilities of Kindergarten and First Grade Children," *Studies in the Psychology of Music*, Vol. 8, *Experimental Research in the Psychology of Music*, ed. Edwin Gordon (Iowa City: University of Iowa Press, 1972).

[129]Philip H. Miller, "An Experimental Analysis of the Development of Tonal Capabilities of First Grade Children," *Studies in the Psychology of Music*, Vol.

10, *Experimental Research in the Psychology of Music,* ed. Edwin Gordon (Iowa City: University of Iowa Press, 1975).

[130]Paul Lehman, "The Predictive Measurement of Musical Success," *Journal of Research in Music Education,* Vol. 17, No. 1 (Spring 1969).

[131]Marilyn Zimmerman, *Musical Characteristics of Children* (Washington, D. C.: Music Educators National Conference, 1971).

[132]Charles Benner, *Teaching Performing Groups* (Washington, D. C.: Music Educators National Conference, 1972).

[133]George Duerksen, *Teaching Instrumental Music* (Washington, D. C.: Music Educators National Conference, 1972).

[134]Edward Rainbow, "Instrumental Music: Recent Research and Considerations for Future Investigations," *Bulletin of the Council for Research in Music Education,* No. 33 (Summer 1973).

[135]Carroll Gonzo, "Research in Choral Music: A Perspective," *Bulletin of the Council for Research in Music Education,* No. 33 (Summer 1973).

[136]Edgar Turrentine, "Historical Research in Music Education," *Bulletin of the Council for Research in Music Education,* No. 33 (Summer 1973).

[137]Janice Klemish, "A Review of Recent Research in Elementary Music Education," *Bulletin of the Council for Research in Music Education,* No. 34 (Fall 1973).

[138]Abraham Schwadron, "Philosophy in Music Education: State of the Research," *Bulletin of the Council for Research in Music Education,* No. 34 (Fall 1973).

[139]Judith Jellison, "The Frequency and General Mode of Inquiry of Research in Music Therapy, 1952-1972," *Bulletin of the Council for Research in Music Education,* No. 35 (Winter 1973).

[140]William Whybrew, "Research in Evaluation in Music Education," *Bulletin of the Council for Research in Music Education,* No. 35 (Winter 1973).

[141]Ned Deihl and Kenneth Partchey, "Status of Research: Educational Technology in Music Education," *Bulletin of the Council for Research in Music Education,* No. 35 (Winter 1973).

[142]Erwin Schneider, "Music Education," *Encyclopedia of Educational Research,* 4th ed. (London: Macmillan Company, 1969).

[143]Richard Colwell, "The Present State of Research in Music Education," *Studies in Music,* No. 7 (1973).

D. Jack Davis

Research Trends in Art and Art Education: 1883-1972

Research activity has become increasingly important in the field of art and art education during recent years. Because visual artists are relative newcomers to the field of research, they have been somewhat slow in communicating research results and in developing professional organs for the dissemination of research in the visual arts and in visual arts education. It was not until the Fall of 1959 that the National Art Education Association (NAEA) published the first volume of *Studies in Art Education*, a journal of issues and research in art education. Prior to that time, three yearbooks (fifth, seventh, and ninth) of the NAEA had been devoted to research in the field (1954, 1956, 1959). Although art educators were rather slow in launching into the field of research, a thorough review of general research literature reveals that in the past there have been many investigations in such related fields as psychology and sociology. Since visual artists have become more and more involved in systematic research, it has become increasingly important to know what has been researched by those in the field, as well as by those in related areas. Yet, there has been no readily available resource that provides collective information concerning research endeavors in the field of art and art education. In that interest, it is the purpose of this paper to examine and discuss trends in research in art and art education through 1972.

At the outset, it seems appropriate and necessary to establish a working definition for "research" or the general concept that guided the efforts to survey the literature and compile a comprehensive bibliography. Needless to say, "research" is not an easy term to define; it is often misused and misunderstood. Although the scientific method of inquiry was first applied in the physical sciences, it has also become useful in the study of human behavior. The most commonly used types or classifications of educational research are: (1) historical research, which describes *what was* by "investigating, recording, analyzing, and interpreting the events of the past for the purpose of discovering generalizations

D. JACK DAVIS *is Professor of Art and Chairman of the Department of Art at North Texas State University. He is also Senior Editor of* Studies in Art Education.

that are helpful in understanding the present and in predicting the future"; (2) descriptive research, which attempts to describe *what is* by describing, recording, analyzing, and interpreting "the present nature, composition, or processes of phenomena"; (3) experimental research, which "describes *what will be* when certain factors are carefully controlled" (Best, 1959, page 12).

In order to examine and discuss trends in research in art and art education, it is imperative to establish a broad statement of principle that encompasses all of the many types and levels of research, and that provides a common base for integration and an opportunity for each type or level to make a contribution to knowledge in accordance with its respective possibilities and limitations. In such a survey, it is not of concern whether any one type or level of research is better, more sophisticated, or more respectable than another. Rather, a broad, general framework or concept of research is needed if a comprehensive examination of research trends in the visual arts is to be made. Such a perspective encompasses research as including all forms of scholarly work that is aimed at discovering new knowledge or at making creative interpretations, organizations, or applications of this knowledge. Therefore, research may involve experiments in the laboratory, clinic, or classroom, requiring considerable apparatus and equipment; or it may be abstract and theoretical, demanding new facilities beyond paper and pencil (Hastie, 1959).

Research activity has become increasingly important in the field of education during recent years. As a vital and integral part of the larger field of education, art education has also experienced a phenomenal growth of interest in research, especially since 1950. A survey and examination of the research literature relating to art and art education reveals some interesting facts and trends. Although the past thirty-five years has been the period of the most vigorous activity in research relating to the visual arts, scientific experiments of interest to artists and art educators were carried on prior to these years.

Three separate surveys and analyses of the published research in art and art education provide the bases for the analyses presented in this paper. In 1940, Mary Strange, then a graduate student at Baylor University, compiled from available resources a bibliography of scientific investigations relating to art. She identified and abstracted 163 studies, dating from 1883. Due to this writer's interest in her project, he pursued the continuing and developing research trends in the visual arts by compiling and categorizing scientific investigations relating to art since 1940. The first effort concerned itself with the period between 1940 and 1960 (Davis, 1961), and the second effort examined the period between 1961 and 1972 (Davis, Footnote 1). Three hundred and eighty-one studies were identified and abstracted as a result of these two efforts. In examining these separate efforts both independently and collectively, it is readily apparent from a quantitative point of view that publication of research activity in art and art education has accelerated at a rapid pace

Table 1

PUBLISHED RESEARCH RELATED TO
ART AND ART EDUCATION, 1883-1972

Time Span	No. of Published Manuscripts	% of Total Manuscripts
1883 - 1939 (57 years)	163	29.96
1940 - 1972 (33 years)	381	70.04
	544	100%

since 1883, when G. Stanley Hall published *The Contents of Children's Minds on Entering School*. Compared to the 163 published studies that Strange identified during the fifty-seven-year period between 1883 and 1939, the thirty-three-year period between 1940 and 1972 yielded 381 published studies — an increase of approximately 135 percent in approximately one-half as much time. (See *Table 1.*)

Thus, the increased volume of published research is readily apparent. There are some very obvious reasons why we have experienced such phenomenal activity and growth in art-education research. The most obvious reason is perhaps related to the rapid development of the field, and the realization that research evidence is necessary to substantiate the generalizations and beliefs expounded rather profusely in the literature. "By the 1940s the field of art education had developed to the point that research was necessary if continued growth was to be made" (Davis, 1967, page 13). Closely allied to this is the rapid growth of graduate education in art and art education. As F. M. Logan points out:

> By the middle fifties, the younger art education people were, for the most part, holders of doctoral degrees in education. Their work begun as art students was often difficult to continue on a productive level, and their status in graduate school and as young college faculty members was achieved on the basis of study and research potential seen in their graduate degree work. There was no longer much likelihood that they would compete as producing artists with their studio colleagues. They turned instead to the tasks of university research, modeled on school of education samples (1975, pages 8-9).

A third reason for rapid growth of research activity is the attention given research by the professional organizations. A fourth motivating factor was the increased financial support through the federal government and private foundations, particularly during the 1960s.

Looking beyond the sheer quantity of the published research, it is interesting to note the trends and patterns of the research efforts. The 163 studies identified and categorized by Strange (1940) were sorted into four major categories. The categories were as follows:

1. Studies relating to color vision and color preference;
2. Studies relating to drawing or graphic ability;
3. Investigations of picture preference and appreciation;
4. Tests and measurements in the field of art.

Between 1940 and 1972, the 381 studies identified were categorized into eight categories (Davis, 1961: Davis, Footnote 1). The four categories added were the following:

5. Investigations relating to the study and teaching of art;
6. Studies relating to art and the personality;
7. Investigations relating to creative ability;
8. Therapeutic values of art.

For a more thorough examination of the trends and the relative emphasis each received, it is necessary to examine each of the eight categories separately. *Table 2* presents the number of studies sorted into

Table 2

CATEGORIES OF RESEARCH
IDENTIFIED BETWEEN 1883-1972

Category	No. of Studies In Category*	% of Total
1. Studies relating to color vision and color preference	75	13.5
2. Studies relating to drawing or graphic ability	115	20.7
3. Investigations of picture preference and appreciation	79	14.2
4. Tests and measurements in the field of art	74	13.3
5. Investigations relating to the study and teaching of art	112	20.1
6. Studies relating to art and the personality	30	5.4
7. Investigations relating to creative ability	46	8.3
8. Therapeutic values of art	24	4.3
9. Uncategorized	1	.2

*Twelve studies are listed in two categories.

556

each of the eight categories and the percentage of the total those studies represent.

An examination of *Table 2* reveals that studies relating to drawing and graphic ability have received the most research interest over the years, with 115 (or 20.7%) of the published research studies (No. 2). "A great deal of work has been done in studying the developmental patterns of children in relation to their drawing and graphic ability. Interest has also been shown in the effect of various factors such as socioeconomic status and different motivational devices upon drawing and graphic ability. Considerable interest is also expressed in comparing the drawings produced by abnormal children and those produced by normal children" (Davis, 1967, page 14). In more recent years, concern has focused upon approaches to teaching drawing and relationships that exist between drawings and various learning styles, creativity, self-concept, and the like. Some attention has also been given to an examination of such things as spatial concepts and body proportions expressed in drawings, as well as to comparisions of drawings made using various media.

Receiving almost equal attention with 112 (or 20.1 percent) of the published research are investigations related to the study and teaching of art (No. 5). These studies have focused upon pedagogical considerations and delivery systems for the visual arts. Much of the work has been descriptive in nature and has provided valuable and much-needed base-line data for various aspects of the art-education field. While much of the research in this area has been directed toward providing a data base for immediate decision-making and projection, some efforts have also been concerned with the long-range effect of educational efforts in the arts. Of particular interest in this area is the body of research dealing with teaching methodologies in the visual arts. While this has been a growing area of interest, the studies in this important area reflect a major problem that has confronted many research efforts in the visual arts, i.e., the identification of relevant research problems and the proper utilization of research methodologies for dealing with these problems. Too often the research program has been adapted to fit known methodologies and assessment devices, rather than developing or adapting research methodologies to fit the real problem at hand.

While these two areas of research endeavor have accounted for approximately 41 percent of the total published research, three other areas, receiving almost equal emphasis, account for another 41 percent of the published research, as shown in *Table 2*. They are (1) studies relating to color vision and color preference, (3) investigations of picture preference and appreciation, and (4) investigations relating to tests and measurements in the field of art.

The research relating to color vision and color preference "is dominated by studies of color sensitivity and color preferences and seems to be of primary concern to people outside the field of art education, especially psychologists. Investigations have been made in such areas as color and form reaction as a basis of interpersonal relationships, color combinations as indices to personality traits, and abstraction of form and color as a function of the stimulus object." (Davis, 1967, page 14.)

Within these three areas, the area of research relating to picture preference and appreciation has been concerned with the nature of a general factor in aesthetic perception. Efforts have also been made to determine children's preferences for traditional and modern pictures, as well as the influence of various factors such as prestige and age upon picture preferences and the ability to appreciate.

Research related to tests and measurements in art has been an area of rather interesting activity. Between 1920 and 1940, standardized tests in art enjoyed a great deal of popularity. As early as 1912, Thorndike's *Drawing Scale* was published in an attempt to standardize evaluation and set up criteria for judgment. This was followed by the *Kline-Carey Measuring Scale for Freehand Drawing* in 1922, the *Providence Drawing Scale* in 1928, and others. Aside from the early interest in drawing scales, standardized measurements also appeared in relation to art aptitudes and art appreciation. These early tests were hindered by the fact that there were no working definitions of the factors which were being measured. Fundamental factors such as art appreciation and art aptitude were not adequately investigated and delineated before attempts were made to measure these factors. The usefulness of these tests was further crippled by the lack of use of established statistical methods in constructing and validating the instruments. The result was that many of the tests measured things which they were not constructed to measure and did not measure factors which they were intended to measure.

In general, a lack of interest has prevailed in the last twenty-five years in the field of art measurement. Since 1940, some attempts have been made to revise the existing tests and to create new ones; however, the research literature has been virtually void of any concentrated or serious efforts in this area. By contrast, efforts of art educators in testing and measurement during the 1950s and 1960s were devoted to the testing and measurement of creativity or creative thinking abilities. This work was not, by any means, limited to art education; rather some of the most basic and extensive work has been conducted outside the field of art education by psychologists, educational psychologists, and others. (Davis, 1967, page 14.)

Dr. J. P. Guilford's presidential address to the American Psychological Association in 1950, wherein he outlined his interests and proposed research program in creativity, stimulated work in this area. His address and subsequent research provided the basic groundwork upon which measurements of creative thinking have been built. These efforts were extended by the work of many others, including Getzels and Jackson, Taylor, and Torrance. In 1964, Torrance identified at least seventeen groups (most on university campuses), in the United States who indicated a sustained interest in creativity research that had the potential of accumulating knowledge concerning creative thinking and creative behavior.

Although individuals outside the field of art education led the way in this most important area of measurement, art educators have not been totally unaware and uninterested. At least one major research center — The Pennsylvania State University — has been largely devoted to efforts to measure creative thinking similar to those identified by Guilford. Brittain scanned the literature on creativity and composed a test of thirty-six sections to cover seventeen qualities which he had abstracted. The results of his research indicated that eight of the thirty-six sections clearly differentiated a more creative from a less creative group as judged by an art faculty. Guilford, working under a grant on aptitudes of high-level talent, used a factor analytical approach to determine whether or not there were stable criteria which significantly measured creativity in the exact and applied sciences. He started with thirty-five tests and found that eight factors emerged. A comparison of the two studies reveals that six criteria were named identically, one was in content alike, while one in the Brittain study appeared to differ. Upon the basis of similarities noted in these two studies, further research was carried on by Beittel at The Pennsylvania State University in an effort to correlate four tests by Brittain. The results of Beittel's work further supported the position that creativeness, whether applied in the arts or in the sciences, has common attributes. (Davis, 1967, pages 14-15.)

In contrast to early attempts at the development of measuring devices in art, the attempts to measure creative-thinking abilities were based on a more solid foundation. A more scientific approach was established, with concerted efforts made to determine what kind of mental operations are involved in creative thinking before attempts were made to measure it. Yet, there is a definite need for continued thinking and experimentation with means of measuring the creative-thinking abilities, especially artistic creative-thinking abilities.

Most recently, efforts have been made to measure such factors as aesthetic sensitivity and perception. Attempts have also been made in developing objective scales for evaluating art work.

Under a grant from the U.S. Office of Education, Rouse developed and validated a descriptive scale for the measurement of art products. In further work along this line, Lewis and Mussen reported on the development of an instrument for evaluating children's artistic creativity. In another effort to objectively evaluate children's drawings Eisner developed a scale for assessing representation of space. Aside from the drawing scales, the literature reveals other efforts to develop measurement devices in the visual arts. Flick put together a battery of ten assessment devices to measure visual/haptic attitude, while Beittel and Burkhart developed a number of instruments in relation to their studies of spontaneous, divergent, and academic strategies. More recently, we have experienced the work of Eisner in assessing art attitudes, art information, and the ability to analyze works of art, as well as Wilson's work in designing an instrument to elicit language describing an individual's method of perceiving and evaluating paintings and what the individual perceived in the paintings. . . .

The progress is encouraging, but we still have much to achieve in this area, especially when we reflect upon Eisner's calculations in relation to tests in print. Out of the 2,126 tests listed, he determined that only 1.4 percent (29) are in the five arts with only 10 in the visual arts. Three of the 10 were constructed in the 1920s and 1930s. (Davis, 1971, page 9.)

While some studies have been made in this area, research related to tests and measurements in art has not received the sustained attention it deserves and demands, especially in the age of accountability.

The remaining eighteen percent of the published research can be put into three categories: (6) studies relating to art and the personality (5.4%); (7) investigations relating to creative ability, which comprises 8.3 percent of the published research; and (8) research relating to the therapeutic values of art (4.3%).

Based upon the review of available research literature, one of the most pressing needs in the field is the accumulation of bodies of research knowledge that address issues and areas of concern in the field. Achievement of this goal necessitates consideration of several factors. First of all, we must identify our most pressing areas of concern and the related researchable problems. This is a task demanding the best thinking of all aspects of our field — researchers, teacher educators, artists, aestheticians, and classroom teachers. These concerns must constantly reflect the problems and issues of our time, and even project in a futuristic way to the extent that this is possible. The identified areas of concern need not remain constant, although they may. Certainly the specific research problems must reflect the issues before us. Considering the available published research literature in art and art education, as well as the task that confronts the art educator in the last quarter of this century, it appears that there are at least five areas of concern that the art-education researcher must consider in the future.

First, we must deal with the content(s) of the visual arts and the aesthetic experience. We must investigate and amass both knowledge and experience as they relate to art education. This area of research concern involves close cooperation with researchers in related areas of our discipline — art historians, designers, studio artists, aestheticians, and the like. While most of the content is known and simply needs interpreting for educational purposes in the arts, there are obvious gaps in our knowledge. There is still much knowledge to be amassed. We have not dealt with even some of the most basic content problems in our area. For example, there has been little systematic thought given to the characteristics of the creative product that students are supposedly producing on a daily basis in our art classrooms. When we move beyond the most generalized quantitative level, the literature reveals little that is of assistance to the practitioner or the learner. To be effective in curriculum building and implementation, it appears that we must at least be able to provide some insight into the critical properties of the creative product. An equally dramatic void is in research relating to the new technology and its implications for teaching art. We know very little about this technology and its capabilities and possibilities as an expressive device or as an aesthetic influence. Researchers dealing with content must constantly be expanding, updating, and exploring to provide us with the necessary information and experience for a relevant program in art education.

To utilize the results of research dealing with the content(s) of art and the aesthetic experience, we must also consider how learning in the arts takes place. In addition to examining the research data in the related fields of psychology and education and making creative interpretations of their findings, we must know all that it is possible to know about the nature of the learner involved in creative artistic expression and response. The opportunities for research in this area are great, but the complexities of dealing with the real issues are staggering. For example, we know very little about sensory learning as it is related to the visual arts. For years we have been tossing around, at a philosophical level, whether or not it is possible for a child to deal with more than one sense modality at a time. Research has provided us no guidance, not even any explorations. New insights and findings in medical and psychological research are constantly posing new possibilities for the educator, specifically the art educator. For example, the investigations into the hemispheres of the brain pose some interesting questions for us.

In addition to knowing more about the learner, we must also examine the nature of the learning environment and how it assists or deters meaningful learning in the visual arts. Because of the unique and specific consideration in such areas, these are tasks that can best be done by researchers in art education. We must not be content to let others deal exclusively with these concerns. Cooperative or team research efforts in this area may hold the solution. Such approaches pose some interesting possibilities for the art-education researcher.

A third area in need of a research base deals with the inducement or stimulation of learning in the arts. It is not enough to know how learning occurs in the individual and what environments are most conducive. We must also devise and examine alternative delivery systems in the arts. Individualized learning, self-paced learning, interdisciplinary curricula, modular curricula, community-based arts programs, and the like provide fruitful and needed areas of research investigation for art educators. We cannot limit our thinking and our research efforts to traditional modes of providing instruction in the arts. We must think beyond the classroom and the child as being our only concerns. In-creased leisure time for adults and increased life spans, for example, challenge our thinking for delivering the arts to people.

A fourth area of research interest, and one demanding futuristic thinking is that of evaluation, or determining if the learning and ex-periencing takes place and to what extent it does. We need to be able to assess, to the degree possible, individualized learning and progress in the arts as well as program effectiveness. We must deal with both criteria and methodology issues for both short- and long-range efforts. We must not limit our thinking to traditional modes of assessment. Rather, we must devise new approaches that are compatable with new kinds of learning and experiencing in the visual arts. An area of specific concern in relation to assessment is that of data-gathering devices for research efforts.

A fifth research area concerns the impact of art instructional pro-grams and efforts. We must constantly be concerned with whether or not the educational experiences have an impact, particularly over a long-range period of time. Research efforts in this area must deal with short-range descriptive studies that provide a data base for immediate decision-making and projection. More importantly, research in this area must deal with the long-range effect of educational efforts in the arts—how they affect values and how they improve the quality of life.

Within each of these broad areas of research interest are numerous specific and researchable problems, some examples of which have been suggested. We must articulate these research questions so that they focus directly upon relevant issues and concerns, and yield the output that will build the much-needed bodies of research data for all aspects of the field. We cannot overlook the need for careful articulation of the research questions, as has apparently been done in the existing research relating to art and art education.

Even more critical is the need to avoid, at all costs, the manipulation and distortion of the real research questions in order to make them fit known research methodologies. To deal with the critical questions in art and art education, we must devise appropriate methodologies for the questions we ask. This is a research effort of its own and an important one. Because research questions have been manipulated to fit the re-search methodologies that art-education researchers have learned from other disciplines, too much of the research data we have is of questiona-ble value. In dealing with this problem, we must not get caught up in professional pressures that cause us to sacrifice our real concerns.

Likewise, we must not let false notions about building research repu-tations force us into research models employing complex and rigorous methodologies that elude the real issues in the field. Basic descriptive data are most often a necessary prelude to experimental efforts. Such a data base is embarrassingly absent from too many areas of concern in the field of art and art education. This absence is exemplified well in an example used earlier — the characteristics of creative products. In examining this area in some detail (Davis, 1973, Footnote 2), it appears that we have attempted to become too sophisticated too quickly. In so doing, we have achieved little that is actually useful for instructional purposes. To move beyond the generalized quantitative level of research reported in this area demands some extensive preliminary descriptive research in specific areas or disciplines. As is the case with many areas of concern, it seems that we have been working backwards by trying to generalize without sufficient knowledge for generalization. We can no longer afford the luxury of simply doing research exercises in the arts. Our research must count; and it must count toward the accumulation of a body of research knowledge that will guide our efforts in delivering quality instruction in art, which will ultimately improve the quality of life for every individual who comes under our guidance and tutelage.

Denton, Texas
June 1976

FOOTNOTES

[1]D. J. Davis, "Bibliographies of Research Relating to Art and Art Education, 1883-1972," (Unpublished manuscript, 1973). (Available from D. J. Davis, P. O. Box 5098, N. T. Station, Denton, TX 76203.)
[2]D. J. Davis, "Characteristics of the Creative Product," *Needed Research on Creativity: A Special Report of the USOE-sponsored Grant Study: Critical Appraisal of Research in the Personality-Emotions-Motivation Domain*, ed. S. B. Sells. Ft. Worth, Texas: Institute of Behavioral Research, Texas Christian University, 1973.

BIBLIOGRAPHY

Barkan, M., ed. *Research in Art Education*. Fifth Yearbook of The National Art Education Association. Kutztown, Pennsylvania: NAEA, 1954.

Barkan, M., ed. *Research in Art Education*. Seventh Yearbook of The National Art Education Association. Kutztown, Pennsylvania: NAEA, 1956.

Best, J. W. *Research in Education*, Englewood Cliffs, New Jersey: Prentice-Hall, Inc., 1959.

Davis, D. J. "A Summary of Scientific Investigations Relating To Art, 1940-1960." Unpublished Masters Thesis, Baylor University, 1961.

Davis, D. J. "Research Trends in Art and Art Education." *Art Education* Vol. 20, No. 7 (1967), pages 12-16.

Davis, D. J. "Research in Art Education: An Overview." *Art Education*, Vol. 24, No. 5 (1971), pages 7-11.

Hall, G. S. "The Contents of Children's Minds on Entering School." *Princeton Review*, Vol. 11 (1883), pages 249-272.

Hastie, W. R. "Introduction." *Research in Art Education*, ed. W. R. Hastie. Ninth Yearbook of The National Art Education Association. Kutztown, Pennsylvania: NAEA, pages vi-ix.

Hausman, J., ed. *Research in Art Education*. Ninth Yearbook of The National Art Education Association, Kutztown, Pennsylvania: NAEA, 1959.

Logan, F. M. "Update '75, Growth in American Art Education." *Studies in Art Education*, Vol. 17, No. 1 (1975), pages 7-16.

Strange, M. "A Summary of Scientific Investigations Relating to Art." Unpublished Masters Thesis, Baylor University, 1940.

Bibliography

---

*Descriptive and Experimental Research in Art and Art Education
Compiled by D. Jack Davis*

The bibliography, resulting from the review of the literature, has proven to be a valuable tool in continuing research efforts in art and art education and is presented here as a basic research tool. Not only is it a useful resource in reviewing related literature, but it is potentially helpful in establishing research trends in the field and pointing up the pressing need for the accumulation of bodies of research knowledge in the visual arts.

The bibliography is alphabetical and may be further interrogated in relation to the eight major categories of research endeavor that have been established by the coded number in parentheses appearing to the left of each bibliographic entry. This number indicates inclusion in the corresponding categories of research listed below. (It should be noted that some entries are coded to more than one category.)

(1) Studies relating to color vision and color preference;
(2) Studies concerning drawing and drawing or graphic ability;
(3) Investigations of picture preference and appreciation;
(4) Tests and measurements in the field of art;
(5) Investigations relating to the study and teaching of art;
(6) Studies relating to art and the personality;
(7) Investigations relating to creative ability;
(8) Studies relating to the therapeutic values of art.

(8) Albee, G. W., and R. M. Hamlin. "An Investigation of the Reliability and Validity of Judgments of Adjustment Inferred from Drawings." *Journal of Clinical Psychology,* Vol. 5 (1949), pages 389-392.

(8) Albee, G. W., and R. M. Hamlin. "Judgments of Adjustment from Drawings: The Applicability of Adjustment of Rating Scale Methods." *Journal of Clinical Psychology,* Vol. 6 (1950), pages 363-365.

(6) Alschuler, R. H., and L. A. Hattwick. *Painting and Personality,* 2 vols. Chicago: University of Chicago Press, 1947.

(2) Ames, L. B. "Free Drawing and Completion Drawing: A Comparative Study of Preschool Children." *Pedagogical Seminary and Journal of Genetic Psychology,* Vol. 56 (1945), pages 161-165.

(2) Ames, L. B., and G. Arnold. "The Development of Directionality in Drawing." *Pedagogical Seminary and Journal of Genetic Psychology*, Vol. 68 (1946), pages 45-61.

(2) Anastasi, A., and J. P. Foley, Jr. "An Analysis of Spontaneous Artistic Productions by the Abnormal." *Journal of General Psychology*, Vol. 28 (1943), pages 297-313.

(2) Anastasi, A., and J. P. Foley, Jr. "An Experimental Study of the Drawing Behavior of Adult Psychotics in Comparison with that of a Normal Control Group." *Journal of Experimental Psychology*, Vol. 34 (1944), pages 169-194.

(4) Anastasi, Anne, and C. E. Schaefer. "The Franck Drawing Completion Test as a Measure of Creativity." *Journal of Genetic Psychology*, Vol. 119 (1971), pages 3-12.

(6) Andersen, I., and R. Munroe. "Personality Factors Involved in Student Concentration on Creative Painting and Commercial Arts." *Rorschach Research Exchange*, Vol. 12 (1948), pages 141-154.

(3) (7) Anderson, F. E. "Aesthetic Sensitivity, Dogmatism, and the Eisner Art Inventories," *Studies in Art Education*, Vol. 12, No. 2 (1971), pages 49-55.

(3) (5) Anderson, F. E. "Aesthetic Sensitivity, Previous Art Experiences, and Participation in the Scholastic Art Awards." *Studies in Art Education*, Vol. 10, No. 3 (1969), pages 4-13.

(4) Anderson, R. G. "A Modification of the McAdory Art Test." *Journal of Consulting Psychology*, Vol. 12 (1948), pages 280-281.

(7) Anwar, M. P., and I. L. Child. "Personality and Esthetic Sensitivity in an Islamic Culture." *Journal of Social Psychology*, Vol. 87, No. 1 (1972), pages 21-28.

(1) Arlitt, A., and S. Buckner. "A Study of Color Preference in White and Negro Three-Year-Olds." *Proceedings of the Thirty-fifth Annual Meeting of the American Psychological Association* (1925), pages 190-198.

(8) Arlow, J. A., and A. Kadis. "Finger Painting in the Psychotherapy of Children." *American Journal of Orthopsychiatry*, No. 16 (1946), pages 134-146.

(7) Armstrong, C. "Art Product Characteristics of Elementary Education Majors Measuring High in Flexibility." *Studies in Art Education*, Vol. 13, No. 3 (1972), pages 43-61.

(3) Ausubel, D. P., F. Dewitt, B. Golden, and S. H. Schpoont. "Prestige Suggestion in Children's Art Preferences." *Journal of Genetic Psychology*, Vol. 89 (1956), pages 85-93.

(2) Ayer, F. C. "Present Status of Drawing With Respect to Scientific Investigation." *The Eighteenth Yearbook of the National Society for the Study of Education*, Part II, (1925).

(2) Ayer, F. C. *The Psychology of Drawing*. Baltimore: Warwick and York, 1916, pages 157-169.

(2) Badri, M. B. "Use of Figure Drawing in Measuring the Goodenough Quotient of Culturally Deprived Sudanese Children." *Journal of Psychology*, Vol. 59 (1965), pages 333-334.

(4) Badri, M. B., and W. Dennis. "Human Figure Drawings in Relation to the Modernization in Sudan." *Journal of Psychology*, Vol. 58 (1964), pages 421-425.

(1) Baldwin, E. T., and L. I. Stecher. *The Psychology of the Pre-School Child*. New York: D. Appleton and Co., 1926, pages 123-130.

(1) Baldwin, M. M. *Mental Development of the Child and the Race*. New York: The Macmillan Co., 1911, pages 253-262.

(2) Ballard, P. B. "What Children Like to Draw." *Journal of Experimental*

Pedagogy, Vol. 1 (1912), pages 185-197.

(1) Bamberger, F. E. "The Effect of the Physical Make-Up of A Book Upon Children's Choices." *Johns Hopkins University Studies in Education*, No. 4 (1922).

(7) Barkan, M., and J. Hausman. "Two Pilot Studies with the Purpose of Clarifying Hypotheses for Research into Creative Behavior." *Research in Art Education*, ed. M. Barkan. Seventh Yearbook of the National Art Education Association, a department of the National Education Association. Kutztown, Pennsylvania: State Teachers College, 1956, pages 126-146.

(5) Barkan, M., J. Hausman, and C. Howlett. "Current Supply and Placement of Art Teachers." *Research in Art Education*, ed. M. Barkan. Fifth Yearbook of the National Art Education, a department of the National Education Association. Kutztown, Pennsylvania: State Teachers College, 1954, pages 20-27.

(2) Barnes, E. "A Study on Children's Drawings." *Pedagogical Seminary*, Vol. 455, No. 2 (1893), page 463.

(2) Barnhart, E. N. "Developing Stages in Compositional Construction in Children's Drawing." *Journal of Experimental Education*, Vol. 11 (1942), pages 156-184.

(4) Barrett, D. M. "Aptitude and Interest Patterns of Art Majors in a Liberal Arts College." *Journal of Applied Psychology*, Vol. 29 (1945), pages 483-492.

(1) Barrett, D. M., and E. B. Eaton. "Preference for Color or Tint and Some Related Personality Data." *Journal of Personality*, Vol. 15 (1947), pages 222-232.

(4) Barrett, H. O. "An Examination of Certain Standardized Art Tests to Determine Their Relation to Classroom Achievement and to Intelligence." *Journal of Educational Research*, Vol. 42 (1949), pages 398-400.

(4) Barrett, H. O. "Sex Differences in Art Ability." *Journal of Educational Research*, Vol. 43 (1950), pages 391-393.

(6) Barron, F. "Personality Style and Perceptual Choices." *Journal of Personality*, Vol. 20 (1952), pages 385-401.

(6) Barron, F. "Some Personality Correlates of Independence of Judgment." *Journal of Personality*, Vol. 21 (1953), pages 287-297.

(6) Barron, F. "Some Relationships Between Originality and Style of Personality." *American Psychologist*, Vol. 9 (1954), page 326.

(7) Barron, F. "The Disposition Toward Originality." *Journal of Abnormal and Social Psychology*, Vol. 51 (1955), pages 478-485.

(4) Barron, F., and G. S. Welsh. "Artistic Perception as a Possible Factor in Personality Style: Its Measurement by a Figure Preference Test." *Journal of Psychology*, Vol. 33 (1952), pages 199-203.

(6) Barry, H., III. "Relationships Between Child Training and the Pictorial Arts." *Journal of Abnormal and Social Psychology*, Vol. 54 (1957), pages 380-383.

(1) Bateman, W. G. "The Naming of Color by Children." *Pedagogical Seminary*, Vol. 22 (1915), pages 469-486.

(2) Beach, V., and M. H. Bressler. "Phases in the Development of Children's Painting." *Journal of Experimental Education*, Vol. 13 (1944), pages 1-4.

(2) Beck, W. *Self Development in Drawing*. New York: G. P. Putnam's Sons, 1928.

(4) Beckham, A. S. "A Study of Social Background and Art Aptitude of Superior Negro Children." *Journal of Applied Psychology*, Vol. 26 (1942), pages 777-784.

(5) Beelke, R. G. "A Study of Certification Requirements for Teachers of Art in the United States." *Research in Art Education*, ed. M. Barkan. Fifth Yearbook

of the National Art Education Association, a department of the National Education Association, Kutztown, Pennsylvania: State Teachers College, 1954, pages 28-77.

(3) (4) Beittel, K. R. "Experimental Studies of the Aesthetic Attitudes of College Students." *Research in Art Education*, ed. M. Barkan, Seventh Yearbook of the National Art Education Association, a department of the National Education Association. Kutztown, Pennsylvania: State Teachers College, 1956, pages 47-61.

(2) (5) Beittel, K. R. "Manipulation of Learning Set and Feedback in the Teaching of Drawing," *Studies in Art Education*, Vol. 10, No. 1 (1968), pages 17-32.

(7) Beittel, K. R., and W. L. Brittain. "Analysis of Levels of Creative Performances in the Visual Arts." *Journal of Aesthetic and Art Criticism*, Vol. 19 (1960), pages 83-90.

(5) Beittel, K. R., and R. C. Burkhart. "Strategies of Spontaneous, Divergent, and Academic Art Students." *Studies in Art Education*, Vol. 5, No. 1 (1963), pages 20-41.

(4) Beittel, K., and V. Lowenfeld. "Interdisciplinary Criteria in the Arts and Sciences: A Progress Report." *Research in Art Education*, ed. W. R. Hastie. Ninth Yearbook of the National Art Education Association, a department of the National Education Association. Kutztown, Pennsylvania: State Teachers College, 1959, pages 35-44.

(5) Beittel, K. R., E. L. Matill, Herbert J. Burgart, Robert C. Buckhart, Clarence Kincaid, Robert Steward, Research Associates. "The Effect of a 'Depth' vs. a 'Breadth' Method of Art Instruction at the Ninth Grade Level." *Studies in Art Education*, Vol. 3, No. 1 (1961), pages 75-87.

(8) Bender, L., and J. A. Montague. "Psychotherapy Through Art in a Negro Child." *College Art Journal*, Vol. 7 (1947), pages 12-16.

(8) Bender, L., and J. Rapport. "Animal Drawings of Children." *American Journal of Orthopsychiatry*, Vol. 14 (1944), pages 521-527.

(8) Bender, L., and W. Q. Wolfson. "The Nautical Theme in the Art and Fantasy of Children." *American Journal of Orthopsychiatry*, Vol. 13 (1943), pages 462-467.

(2) Bennett, V. D. C. "Combinations of Figure Drawing Characteristics Related to the Drawer's Self-Concept." *Journal of Projection Techniques and Personality Assessment*, Vol. 30 (1966), pages 192-196.

(3) Berliner, A. "Aesthetic Judgment of School Children." *Journal of Applied Psychology*, Vol. 2 (1918), pages 229-242.

(8) Berman, A. B., A. A. Klein, and A. Lippman. "Human Figure Drawing as a Projective Technique." *Journal of General Psychology*, Vol. 45 (1951), pages 57-70.

(3) Bernberg, R. E., "Prestige Suggestion in Art as Communication." *Journal of Social Psychology*, Vol. 38 (1953), pages 23-30.

(5) Bernheim, G. D. "Dimensionality of Differential Criteria in the Art Product: an Empirical Study," *Studies in Art Education*, Vol. 6, No. 1 (1964), pages 31-48.

(2) Berrien, F. K. "A Study of the Drawings of Abnormal Children." *Journal of Educational Psychology*, Vol. 26 (1935), pages 143-150.

(8) Bettleheim, B. "Schizophrenic Art: A Case Study." *Scientific American*, Vol. 186 (1952), pages 30-34.

(5) Bettelheim, B. "What Students Think About Art." *General Education in the Humanities*, ed. H. Baker. Washington: American Council on Education, 1947.

(3) Bevan, W., Jr., and G. Seeland. "An Exploration of the Influence of Personal

Relevance Upon Statements of Aesthetic Preference." *Acta Psychologica*, Vol. 9, No. 4 (1953), pages 274-287.

(4) Bieliauskas, V. J., and R. B. Bristow. "The Effect of Formal Art Training Upon the Quantitative Scores of the H-T-P." *Journal of Clinical Psychology*, Vol. 15 (1959), pages 57-59.

(3) Birney, R. C., and J. P. Houston. "The Effects of Creativity, Norm Distance, and Instructions on Social Influence." *Journal of Personality*, Vol. 29 (1966), pages 294-302.

(2) Blum, L. H., and A. Dragositz. "Finger Painting: The Developmental Aspects." *Child Development*, Vol. 18 (1947), pages 88-105.

(5) Bolton, S. L. "An Introductory Study of Art as Creative Learning for the Rural Culturally Disadvantaged." *Studies in Art Education*, Vol. 10, No. 2 (1969), pages 50-56.

(6) Borg, W. R. "Personality Characteristics of a Group of College Art Students." *Journal of Educational Psychology*, Vol. 43 (1952), pages 149-156.

(6) Borg, W. R. "Some Factors Relating to Art School Success." *Journal of Educational Research*, Vol. 43 (1950), pages 376-384.

(5) Borg, W. R. "Study of the Relationship Between General Intelligence and Success in Art College." *Journal of Educational Psychology*, Vol. 40 (1949), pages 434-440.

(3) Bottorf, E. A. "A Study Comparing Two Methods of Developing Art Appreciation with College Students." *Journal of Educational Psychology*, Vol. 38 (1947), pages 17-44.

(3) Boudreau, J. C., and W. A. Woods. "Design Complexity as Determiner of Visual Attention Among Artists and Non-Artists." *Journal of Applied Psychology*, Vol. 34 (1950), pages 355-362.

(4) Boyer, R., and C. Wilson. "Use of the Easel Age Scale to Evaluate Crayon Drawings." *Elementary School Journal*, Vol. 59 (1959), pages 228-232.

(1) Bradford, E. J. A. "Notes on Relation and Aesthetic Value of the Perception Types in Color Appreciation." *American Journal of Psychology*, Vol. 24 (1913), page 544.

(8) Brick, M. "Mental Hygiene Value of Children's Art Work." *American Journal of Orthopsychiatry*, Vol. 14 (1944), pages 136-146.

(3) Brimmer, J., R. H. Knapp, and M. White. "Educational Level, Class Status, and Aesthetic Preferences." *Journal of Social Psychology*, Vol. 50 (1959), pages 277-284.

(6) Bradley, W. R. "A Preliminary Study of the Effect of Verbalization and Personality Orientation on Art Quality." *Studies in Art Education*, Vol. 9, No. 2 (1968), pages 31-37.

(4) Brittain, W. L. "An Experiment Toward Measuring Creativity." *Research in Art Education*, ed. M. Barkan. Seventh Yearbook of the National Art Education Association, a department of the National Education Association. Kutztown, Pennsylvania: State Teachers College, 1956, pages 39-46.

(5) Brittain, W. L. "An Exploratory Investigation of Early Adolescent Expression in Art." *Studies in Art Education*, Vol. 9, No. 2 (1968), pages 5-12.

(5) Brittain, W. L.. "Some Exploratory Studies of the Art of Preschool Children." *Studies in Art Education*, Vol. 10, No. 3 (1969), pages 14-24.

(7) Brittain, W. L., and K. R. Beittel. "Analyses of Levels of Creative Performances in the Visual Arts." *Journal of Aesthetics and Art Criticism*, Vol. 19 (1960), pages 83-90.

(7) Brittain, W. L., and K. R. Beittel. "A Study of Some Tests of Creativity in Relationship to Performances in the Visual Arts." *Studies in Art Education*, Vol. 2, No. 2 (1961), pages 54-65.

(4) Brooks, F. D. "The Relative Accuracy of Ratings Assigned With and Without the Use of Drawing Scales." *School and Society,* Vol. 27 (1928), pages 518-520.

(5) Brouch, V. M. "An Experimental Study of the Effect of Synchronized Slide-Tape Learning Experiences on the Tempera Paintings of Third and Fourth Grade Children." *Studies in Art Education,* Vol. 12, No. 3 (1971), pages 31-42.

(2) Brown, E. E. "Notes on Children's Drawings." *University of California Studies,* Vol. 2, No. 2 (1897), pages 1-77.

(5) Bryan, A. I. "Grades, Intelligence, and Personality of Art School Freshmen." *Journal of Educational Psychology,* Vol. 33 (1942), pages 50-64.

(4) (5) Bryant, A. R., and L. B. Schwan. "Art and the Mentally Retarded Child." *Studies in Art Education,* Vol. 12, No. 3 (1971), pages 50-63.

(3) Buermeyer, L. "An Experiment in Education." *Nation,* Vol. 120 (1925), pages 442-444.

(6) Burgart, H. J. "Art in Higher Education: The Relationship of Art Experience to Personality, General Creativity, and Aesthetic Performance." *Studies in Art Education,* Vol. 2, No. 2 (1961), pages 14-35.

(7) Burkhart, R. C. "Analysis of Individuality of Art Expression at the Senior High School Level." *Research in Art Education,* ed. W. R. Hastie. Ninth Yearbook of the National Art Education Association, a department of the National Education Association. Kutztown, Pennsylvania: State Teachers College, 1959, pages 90-97.

(6) Burkhart, R. C. "The Creativity-Personality Continuum Based on Spontaneity and Deliberateness in Art." *Studies in Art Education,* Vol. 2, No. 1 (1960), pages 43-65.

(6) Burkhart, R. C. "The Interrelationship of Separate Criteria for Creativity in Art and Student Teaching to Form Personality Factors." *Studies in Art Education,* Vol. 3, No. 1 (1961), pages 18-38.

(6) Burns, R. "Some Correlations of Design with Personality." *Research in Art Education,* ed. W. R. Hastie. Ninth Yearbook of the National Art Education Association, a department of the National Education Association. Kutztown, Pennsylvania: State Teachers College, 1959, pages 125-130.

(4) Burt, C. "Mental and Scholastic Tests." *Report of London County Council.* London, England: 1921.

(8) Bychowski, G. "The Rebirth of a Woman: A Psychoanalytic Study of Artistic Expression and Sublimation." *Psychoanalytic Review,* Vol. 34 (1947), pages 32-57.

(4) Cain, T. "The Objective Measurement of Accuracy in Drawings." *American Journal of Psychology,* Vol. 56 (1943), pages 32-53.

(3) Calkins, M. W. "An Attempted Experiment in Psychological Aesthetics." *Psychological Review,* Vol. 7 (1900), pages 580-591.

(1) Campbell, I. G. "A Study of the Fitness of Color Combinations, in Duple and in Triple Rhythm, to Line Designs." *Journal of Experimental Psychology,* Vol. 30 (1942), pages 311-325.

(3) Campbell-Fisher, I. G. "An Experiment on the Expressiveness of Shell and Textile Montages." *Journal of Experimental Psychology,* Vol. 40 (1950), pages 523-526.

(5) Carter, B. "Artistic Development and Auditory Sensitivity: An Initial Study." *Art Education Bulletin,* Vol. 14 (1957), pages 28-29.

(5) Carter, M. R., and W. H. Fox. "Art in the Elementary Schools of Indiana." *Bulletin of the School of Education, Indiana University,* Vol. 26 (1950), pages 1-82.

(5) Castrup, J., E. Ain, and R. Scott. "Art Skills of Pre-School Children." *Studies in Art Education*, Vol. 13, No. 3 (1972), pages 62-69.

(6) Cattell, R. B. "Personality Traits Associated With Abilities: I. With Intelligence and Drawing Ability." *Educational and Psychological Measurement*, Vol. 5 (1945), pages 131-146.

(3) Cattell, J., J. Clascock, and M. F. Washburn. "Experiments on a Possible Test of Aesthetic Judgment of Pictures." *American Journal of Psychology*, Vol. 29 (1918), pages 333-336.

(3) Child, I. L. "The Experts and the Bridge of Judgment that Crosses Every Cultural Gap." *Psychology Today*, Vol. 2, No. 7 (1968), pages 24-29.

(4) Child, I. L. "Observations on the Meaning of Some Measures of Esthetic Sensitivity." *Journal of Psychology*, Vol. 57 (1964), pages 49-64.

(6) Child, I. L. "Personality Correlates of Esthetic Judgment in College Students." *Journal of Personality*, Vol. 33 (1965), pages 476-511.

(3) Child, I. L. "Personal Performance as an Expression of Aesthetic Sensitivity." *Journal of Personality*, Vol. 30 (1966), pages 469-512.

(3) Child, I. L., and L. Siroto. "Balswele and American Aesthetic Evaluation Compared." *Ethnology*, Vol. 4 (1965), pages 349-360.

(2) Childs, H. G. "Measurement of the Drawing Ability of 2,177 Children in Indiana City School Systems by a Supplemented Thorndike Scale." *Journal of Educational Society,* Vol. 6 (1915), pages 391-408.

(5) Chipley, D. R., and S. M. Chipley. "Structural Criteria for Textbook Evaluation in Art Education." *Studies in Art Education*, Vol. 11, No. 3 (1970), pages 61-65.

(3) Christensen, E. O., and T. Karowski. "A Test for Art Appreciation." *Journal of Education Psychology*, Vol. 17 (1926), pages 187-194.

(2) Clark, A. B. "Children's Attitude Toward Perspective Problems." *Stanford University Studies in Education*, Vol. 1 (1897), pages 283-294.

(2) Clark, J. S. "Some Observations on Children's Drawings." *Educational Review*, Vol. 13 (1897), pages 76-82.

(7) Clark, P. M., and H. L. Mirels. "Fluency as a Pervasive Element in the Measurement of Creativity." *Journal of Educational Measurement*, Vol. 7, No. 2 (1970), pages 83-86.

(5) Clements, R. D. "Art Student-Teacher Questioning." *Studies in Art Education*, Vol. 6, No. 1 (1964), pages 14-19.

(4) Cohen, J. "The Use of Objective Criteria in the Measure of Drawing Ability." *Pedagogical Seminary*, Vol. 27 (1920), pages 137-151.

(3) Cole, J. *Psychology of Elementary School Subjects.* New York: Farrar and Rinehart, 1934, pages 270-290.

(3) Comalli, P. E., Jr. "Studies in Physiognomic Perception: VI. Differential Effects of Directional Dynamics of Pictured Objects on Real and Apparent Motion in Artists and Chemists." *Journal of Psychology*, Vol. 49 (1960), pages 99-109.

(1) Cook, W. M. "Ability of Children in Color Discrimination." *Child Development*, Vol. 2 (1931), pages 303-320.

(2) Cooke, E. "Art Teaching and Child Nature." *Journal of Education*, 1885-1886.

(1) Conley, H., and R. Staples. "The Use of Color in the Finger Paintings of Young Children." *Child Development*, Vol. 20 (1949), pages 201-212.

(1) Corcoran, A. L. "Children's Responses to Color Stimuli." *Research in Art Education*, ed. M. Barkan. Seventh Yearbook of the National Art Education Association, a department of the National Education Association. Kutztown, Pennsylvania: State Teachers College, 1956, pages 84-95.

(1) Corcoran, A. L. "Color Usage in Nursery School Painting." *Child Development*, Vol. 25 (1954), pages 107-113.

(2) Coyle, F. A., Jr., and R. Eisenman. "Santa Claus Drawings by Negro and White Children." *Journal of Social Psychology*, Vol. 80 (1970), pages 201-205.

(4) Crannell, C. W. "The Validity of Certain Measures of Art Appreciation in Relation to a Drawing Task." *Journal of Psychology*, Vol. 35 (1953), pages 131-142.

(2) Crawford, C. C., and M. A. Malin. "An Experiment With Three Ways of Teaching Water Color Painting." *Elementary School Journal*, Vol. 36 (1935), pages 40-43.

(7) Csikszentmihalyi, M., and J. W. Getzels. "Concern for Discovery: An Attitudinal Component of Creative Production." *Journal of Personality*, Vol. 38, No. 1 (1970), pages 91-105.

(7) Csikszentmihalyi, M., and J. W. Getzels. "Discovery-Oriented Behavior and the Originality of Creative Products: A Study With Artists." *Journal of Personality and Social Psychology*, Vol. 19, No. 1 (1971), pages 47-52.

(4) Damrin, D. E., and W. E. Martin. "An Analysis of the Reliability and Factorial Composition of Ratings of Children's Drawings." *Child Development*, Vol. 22 (1951), pages 133-144.

(5) Danielson, P. I. "Selected Teacher Characteristics of Art Student Teachers." *Studies in Art Education*, Vol. 12, No. 2 (1971), pages 42-48.

(1) Dashiell, J. F. "Children's Sense of Harmonies in Colors and Tones." *Journal of Experimental Psychology*, Vol. 2 (1917), pages 466-475.

(3) Dattman, P. E., W. C. Shipley, and B. A. Steele. "The Influence of Size on Preference for Rectangular Proportion in Children and Adults." *Journal of Experimental Psychology*, Vol. 37 (1947), pages 333-336.

(3) Davis, C. A. "A Study of Controlled Attention to Aesthetic Qualities in Works of Art by Ninth-Grade Students of Differing Socioeconomic Environments." *Studies in Art Education*, Vol. 3, No. 10 (1969), pages 49-62.

(5) Davis, D. J. "The Effects of Depth and Breadth Methods of Art Instruction Upon Creative Thinking, Art Attitudes, and Aesthetic Quality of Art Products in Beginning College Art Students." *Studies in Art Education*, Vol. 10, No. 2 (1969), pages 27-40.

(5) Davis, D. J., and E. P. Torrance. "How Favorable Are the Values of Art Education to the Creative Person?" *Studies in Art Education*, Vol. 6, No. 2 (1965), pages 42-53.

(5) Day, M. D. "The Compatibility of Art History and Studio Art Activity in the Junior High School Art Program." *Studies in Art Education*, Vol. 10, No. 2 (1969), pages 57-65.

(4) Dennis, W. "Goodenough Scores, Art Experience, and Modernization." *Journal of Social Psychology*, Vol. 68, No. 2 (1966), pages 211-228.

(2) Dennis, W. "The Human Figure Drawings of Bedouins." *Journal of Social Psychology*, Vol. 52 (1960), pages 209-219.

(4) Dennis, W. "The Performance of Hopi Children on the Goodenough Draw-a-Man Test." *Journal of Comparative Psychology*, Vol. 34 (1942), pages 341-348.

(2) Dennis, W., and E. Raskin. "Further Evidence Concerning the Effect of Handwriting Habits Upon the Location of Drawings." *Journal of Consulting Psychology*, Vol. 24 (1960), pages 548-599.

(2) Dennis, W., and A. Uras. "The Religious Content of Human Figure Drawings Made by Nuns." *Journal of Psychology*, Vol. 61 (1965), pages 263-266.

(5) Diamond, F. R. "The Effectiveness of a Children's Workshop in the Creative

Arts in Forwarding Personal and Intellectual Development." *Studies in Art Education*, Vol. 11, No. 1 (1969), pages 52-60.

(3) Dietrich, G. L., and C. W. Hunnicut. "Art Content Preferred by Primary Grade Children." *Elementary School Journal*, Vol. 68 (1948), pages 557-559.

(5) Diffily, J. "Course Requirements for Prospective Teachers of Art, 1941-1962: A Comparison." *Studies in Art Education*, Vol. 4, No. 2 (1963), pages 52-58.

(4) Dimmick, F. L. "The Inter-Society Color Council Color Aptitude Test." *Journal of Optical Society of America*, Vol. 32 (1942), page 745.

(1) Dobbie, W. J. "Experiments With School Children in Color Combinations." *University of Toronto Studies, Psychological Series*, Vol. 7 (1900), pages 251-267.

(5) Doerter, J. "Influences of College Art Instructors Upon Their Students' Painting Styles." *Studies in Art Education*, Vol. 7, No. 2 (1966), pages 46-53.

(1) Dorcus, R. M. "Color Preferences and Color Associations." *Pedagogical Seminary*, Vol. 33 (1926), pages 399-434.

(5) Douglas, N. K., and J. B. Schwartz. "Increasing Awareness of Art Ideas of Young Children Through Guided Experiences With Ceramics." *Studies in Art Education*, Vol. 8, No. 2 (1967), pages 2-9.

(4) Dreffin, W. B., and C. G. Wrenn. "Spatial Relations Ability and Other Characteristics of Art Laboratory Students." *Journal of Applied Psychology*, Vol. 32 (1948), pages 601-605.

(2) Dubin, E. R. "The Effect of Training on the Tempo of Development of Graphic Representation in Preschool Children." *Journal of Experimental Education*, Vol. 15 (1946), pages 166-173.

(7) Eiduson, B. T. "Artist and Nonartist: A Comparative Study." *Journal of Personality*, Vol. 26 (1958), pages 13-28.

(7) Eindhoven, J. E., and W. E. Vinacke. "Creative Processes in Painting." *Journal of General Psychology*, Vol. 47 (1952), pages 139-164.

(2) Eisenman, R., and J. Smith. "Moral Judgment and Effect in Human Figure Drawings." *Perceptual and Motor Skills*, Vol. 23 (1966), pages 951-954.

(7) Eisner, E. "A Typology of Creativity in the Visual Arts." *Studies in Art Education*, Vol. 4, No. 1 (1963), pages 11-22.

(7) Eisner, E. W. "Children's Creativity in Art: A Study of Types." *American Educational Research Journal*, Vol. 2 (1965), pages 125-136.

(5) Eisner, E. W. "Curriculum Making for the Wee Folk: Stanford University's Kettering Project." *Studies in Art Education*, Vol. 9, No. 3 (1968), pages 45-56.

(5) Eisner, E. W. "The Development of Information and Attitude Toward Art at the Secondary and College Levels." *Studies in Art Education*, Vol. 8, No. 1 (1966), pages 43-58.

(2) Eisner, E. W. "The Drawings of the Disadvantaged: A Comparative Study." *Studies in Art Education*, Vol. 11, No. 1 (1969), pages 5-19.

(6) Elkisch, P. "Children's Drawings in a Projective Technique." *Psychological Monographs*, Vol. 58, No. 1 (1945), pages 1-31.

(1) Ellis, H. "The Psychology of Red." *Popular Science Monthly*, Vol. 57 (1900), pages 365-375.

(1) Ellis, H. "The Psychology of Yellow." *Popular Science Monthly*, Vol. 68 (1906), pages 456-463.

(2) Ellsworth, F. F. "Elements of Form in the Free Paintings of Nursery School Children." *Journal of General Psychology*, Vol. 20 (1939), pages 487-501.

(2) Eng, H. *Psychology of Children's Drawings*. New York: Harcourt Brace, 1931.

(2) England, A. O. "A Psychological Study of Children's Drawings: Comparison of Public School, Retarded, Institutionalized and Delinquent Children's Drawings." *American Journal of Orthopsychiatry*, Vol. 13 (1943), pages 525-530.

(8) England, A. O. "Non-structured Approach to the Study of Childhood Fears." *Journal of Clinical Psychology*, Vol. 2 (1946), pages 364-368.

(1) Eysenck, H. J. "A Critical and Experimental Study of Colour Preferences." *American Journal of Psychology*, Vol. 54 (1941), pages 385-394.

(3) Eysenck, H. J. "The General Factor in Aesthetic Judgments." *British Journal of Psychology*, Vol. 31 (1940), pages 94-102.

(3) Eysenck, H. J., and S. Iwasaki. "Cultural Reactivity in Aesthetic Judgments: A Empirical Study." *Perceptual and Motor Skills*, Vol. 32, No. 3 (1971), pages 817-818.

(7) Farley, F. H., and M. T. Dionne. "Value Orientations of Sensation-Seekers." *Perceptual and Motor Skills*, Vol. 34, No. 2 (1972), pages 509-510.

(3) Farley, F. H., and P. M. Dowling. "Aesthetic Preference in Adolescents as a Function of Race and Visual Complexity." *Studies in Art Education*, Vol. 13, No. 2 (1972), pages 23-26.

(3) Farnsworth, P. R., and S. Misumi. "Further Data on Suggestion in Pictures." *American Journal of Psychology*, Vol. 43 (1931), page 632.

(2) Farnum, R. B. *Present Status of Drawing and Art in the Elementary and Secondary Schools of the United States.* United States Bureau of Education Bulletin No. 13, 1914.

(3) Feasey, L. "Some Experiments on Aesthetics." *British Journal of Psychology*, Vol. 12 (1921), pages 253-271.

(4) Fehl, P. P. "Tests of Taste." *College Art Journal*, Vol. 12 (1953), pages 232-248.

(1) Fernberger, S. W. "Notes on the Affective Values of Color." *American Journal of Psychology*, Vol. 25 (1914), page 448.

(1) Finisinger, J. E., and J. Reusch. "The Relation of the Rorschach Color Response to the Use of Color in Drawings." *Psychosomatic Medicine*, Vol. 3 (1941), pages 370-388.

(7) Fisichelli, V. R., and L. Welch. "The Ability of College Art Majors to Recombine Ideas in Creative Thinking." *Journal of Applied Psychology*, Vol. 31 (1947), pages 278-282.

(4) Flick, P. B. "Ten Tests of the Visual Haptic Aptitude." *Studies in Art Education*, Vol. 4, No. 2 (1963), pages 24-34.

(5) Force, L. S. "An Experimental Study to Examine the Response of Sixth-Grade Students to Programmed Instruction in Art Designed to Correspond to Selected Ability Trait Variables." *Studies in Art Education*, Vol. 11, No. 2 (1970), pages 37-50.

(3) Ford, C. S., et al. "Some Transcultural Comparisons of Aesthetic Judgment." *Journal of Social Psychology*, Vol. 68 (1966), pages 19-26.

(5) Frost, F. H. "Design Decisions After College as Related to Education in Art." *Studies in Art Education*, Vol. 4, No. 1 (1962), pages 46-55.

(5) Frankston, L. "Some Explorations of the Effect of Creative Visual Art Experience Upon the Poetry Writing Quality of Eighth Grade Students." *Studies in Art Education*, Vol. 5, No. 1 (1963), pages 42-59.

(5) Frankston, L. "Effects of Two Programs and Two Methods of Teaching Upon the Quality of Art Products of Adolescents." "*Studies in Art Education*, Vol. 7, No. 2 (1966), pages 23-32.

(5) Freas, S. J. "Gee! You Can Learn Right Off the Wall." *Art Education Bulletin*,

Vol. 15 (1958), pages 25-26.

(2) Freeman, F. N. *The Psychology of the Common Branches.* New York: Houghton Mifflin Co., 1926, pages 34-66.

(3) French, J. E. "Children's Preferences for Abstract Designs of Varied Structural Organization." *Elementary School Journal,* Vol. 56 (1956), pages 202-209.

(3) French, J. E. "Children's Preferences for Pictures of Varied Complexity of Pictorial Pattern." *Elementary School Journal,* Vol. 53 (1952), pages 90-95.

(2) Freyberger, R. M. "Differences in the Creative Drawings of Children of Varying Ethnic and Socio-Economic Backgrounds in Pennsylvania Based on Samplings of Grades One Through Six." *Research in Art Education,* ed. M. Barkan. Seventh Yearbook of the National Art Education Association, a department of the National Education Association. Kutztown, Pennsylvania: State Teachers College, 1956, pages 115-125.

(6) Gahm, R. C., and Michael A. Wallach. "Personality Functions of Graphic Construction and Expansiveness." *Journal of Personality,* Vol. 28 (1960), pages 73-88.

(5) Gaitskell, C. D., and M. R. Gaitskell. *Art Education for Slow Learners.* Peoria, Illinois: Charles A. Bennett Co., 1953.

(5) Gaitskell, C. D., and M. R. Gaitskell. *Art Education in the Kindergarten.* Peoria, Illinois: Charles A. Bennett Co., 1952.

(3) Gardner, H. "Children's Sensitivity to Painting Styles." *Child Development,* Vol. 41 (1970), pages 813-821.

(3) Gardner, H. and J. Gardner. "Developmental Trends in Sensitivity to Painting Style and Subject Matter." *Studies in Art Education,* Vol. 12, No. 1 (1970) pages 11-16.

(1) Garth, T. R. "A Color Preference Scale for 1,000 White Children." *Journal of Experimental Psychology,* Vol. 7 (1924), pages 233-241.

(1) Garth, T. R. "Color Preferences of 559 Full Blood Indians." *Journal of Experimental Psychology,* Vol. 5 (1922), pages 392-418.

(1) Garth, T. R., and J. R. Collado. "The Color Preferences of Philipino Children." *Journal of Comparative Psychology,* Vol. 9 (1929), pages 397-404.

(1) Garth, T. R., and P. P. Porter. "The Color Preferences of 1,032 Young Children." *American Journal of Psychology,* Vol. 46 (1934), pages 448-451.

(5) Gayne, C., Jr. "Art Education in Minnesota." *Design,* Vol. 49 (1947), pages 12-13.

(2) Gayne, C. A., W. R. Hastie, C. J. Hoyt, M. M. Page, C. L. Stankard, and P. R. Wendt. "A Comparison of Two Methods of Instruction in Beginning Drawing." *Journal of Experimental Education,* Vol. 20 (1952), pages 265-279.

(2) Geck, F. J. "The Effectiveness of Adding Kinesthetic to Visual and Auditory Perception in the Teaching of Drawing." *Journal of Educational Research,* Vol. 41 (1947), pages 97-101.

(5) Gemignani, B. P. "The Gifted Child in Art." *Research in Art Education,* ed. M. Barkan. Seventh Yearbook of the National Art Education Association, a department of the National Education Association. Kutztown, Pennsylvania: State Teachers College, 1956, pages 8-17.

(1) Gesche, I. "The Color Preferences of 1,152 Mexican Children." *Journal of Comparative Psychology,* Vol. 7 (1927), pages 297-311.

(2) Gesell, A. L. *The Mental Growth of the Pre-School Child.* New York: The Macmillan Co., 1925.

(7) Getzels, J. W., and M. Csikszentmihalyi. "The Value-Orientations of Art Students as Determinants of Artistic Specialization and Creative Performance." *Studies in Art Education,* Vol. 10, No. 1 (1968), pages 5-16.

(5) Goldwater, R. J. "The Teaching of Art in the Colleges of the United States." *College Art Journal,* Vol. 2 (1943), pages 3-31.

(2) Goodenough, F. L. "A New Approach to the Measurement of the Intelligence of Young Children." *Pedagogical Seminary,* Vol. 33 (1926), pages 185-211.

(2) (4) Goodenough, F. L. *Measurement of Intelligence by Drawings.* Chicago: World Book Co., 1928.

(2) Goodenough, F. L. "Racial Differences in the Intelligence of School Children." *Journal of Experimental Psychology,* Vol. 9 (1926), pages 388-397.

(2) Goodenough, F. L. "Studies in Psychology of Children's Drawings." *Psychological Bulletin,* Vol. 25 (1928), pages 272-283.

(1) Goodenough, F. L., and C. R. Brian. "Relative Potency of Color and Form Perception at Various Ages." *Journal of Experimental Psychology,* Vol. 12 (1929), pages 197-213.

(3) Gordon, D. A. "Individual Differences in the Evaluation of Art and the Nature of Art Standards." *Journal of Educational Research,* Vol. 50 (1956), pages 17-30.

(3) Gordon, D. A. "The Artistic Excellence of Oil Paintings, As Judged by Experts and Laymen." *Journal of Educational Research,* Vol. 48 (1955), pages 579-588.

(5) Gordon, H. C., R. E. Hubbard, and E. W. McDaid, "Comparative Expenditures of Art Supplies in Typical School Systems." *Research in Art Education,* ed. M. Barkan. Fifth Yearbook of the National Art Education Association, a department of the National Education Association. Kutztown, Pennsylvania: State Teachers College, 1954, pages 13-19.

(3) Gordon, K. "A Study of Aesthetic Judgments." *Journal of Experimental Psychology,* Vol. 6 (1923), pages 36-43.

(1) Gordon, K. "Aesthetics of Simple Color Arrangements." *Psychological Review,* Vol. 19 (1912), pages 352-303.

(1) Granger, G. W. "An Experimental Study of Colour Harmony." *Journal of General Psychology,* Vol. 52 (1955), pages 21-35.

(1) Granger, G. W. "An Experimental Study of Colour Preferences." *Journal of General Psychology,* Vol. 52 (1955), pages 3-20.

(4) Graves, M. *The Art of Color and Design.* New York: McGraw-Hill Book Company, Inc., 1951.

(4) Graves, M. "What Is Your I.Q. in Design?" *Art Instructor,* Vol. 3, No. 4 (1939), pages 11-14.

(5) Gray, W. "Graduate Art Education Programs in the Western Arts Association Area." *Western Arts Association Bulletin,* Vol. 39 (1955), pages 5-24.

(4) Greene, H. A., and A. N. Jorgensen. *The Use and Interpretation of Elementary School Tests.* New York: Longmans, Green and Co., 1936, pages 460-468.

(5) Grossman, M. "Art Attitudes and Teaching Behavior." *Studies in Art Education,* Vol. 12, No. 3 (1971), pages 64-66.

(2) Grossman, M. "Perceptual Style, Creativity, and Various Drawing Abilities." *Studies in Art Education,* Vol. 11, No. 2 (1970), pages 51-54.

(1) Guilford, J. P., and P. C. Smith. "A System of Color Preferences." *American Journal of Psychology,* Vol. 72 (1959), pages 487-502.

(4) Guilford, J. P., et al. "A Factor Analytic Study of Creative Thinking, I. Hypotheses and Description of Tests." *Reports from the Psychological Laboratory,* No. 4. Los Angeles: University of Southern California, 1951.

(4) Guilford, J. P., et al. "A Factor Analytic Study of Creative Thinking, II. Administration of Tests and Analysis of Results." *Reports from the Psychological Laboratory,* No. 8. Los Angeles: University of Southern California, 1952.

(4) Gunn, C. E. "Art Ability of Junior High School Pupils in a Cosmopolitan Community." *School Review*, Vol. 45 (1937), pages 769-775.

(3) Gunthorp, J. M. "Aesthetic Maturity." *Pedagogical Seminary and Journal of Genetic Psychology*, Vol. 58 (1940), pages 207-210.

(5) Hager, W. E., and E. Ziegfeld. "Course Requirements for Teachers of Art in Fifty Institutions." *Art In American Life and Education*. Fortieth Yearbook of the National Society for the Study of Education. Bloomington, Illinois: Public School Publishing Co., 1941, pages 735-743.

(2) Hall, G. S. *Educational Problems*. New York: D. Appleton Co., 1911, pages 493-554.

(2) Hall, G. S. *Some Aspects of Child Life and Education*. Boston: Ginn and Company, 1914.

(2) Hall, G. S. "The Contents of Children's Minds." *Princeton Review*, Vol. 11, No. 249 (1883), page 272.

(4) Hall, L. P., and L. M. Ladriere. "A Comparative Study of Diagnostic Potential and Efficiency of Six Scoring Systems Applied to Children's Figure Drawing." *Psychology in the Schools*, Vol. 7 (1970), pages 244-247.

(6) Hammer, E. F. "An Exploratory Investigation of the Personalities of Creative Adolescent Art Students." *Studies in Art Education*, Vol. 1, No. 2 (1960), pages 42-72.

(7) Hammer, E. F. "Creativity and Feminine Ingredients in Young Male Artists." *Perceptual and Motor Skills*, Vol. 19, No. 2 (1964), page 414.

(6) Hammer, E. F. "Personality Patterns in Young Creative Artists." *Adolescence*, Vol. 1, No. 4 (1966), pages 327-350.

(5) Hardiman, G. W., and J. J. Johnson. "Analysis of Motivational Stimulus Structure: An Exploratory Study." *Studies in Art Education*, Vol. 7, No. 2 (1966), pages 14-22.

(5) Hastie, R. "Current Opinions Concerning Best Practices in Art for the Elementary Schools and for Elementary School Teacher Preparation." *Research in Art Education*, ed. M. Barkan. Fifth Yearbook of the National Art Education Association, a department of the National Education Association. Kutztown, Pennsylvania: State Teachers College, 1954, pages 78-113.

(5) Hastie, R., and D. Templeton. "Profile of Art in the Secondary Schools: Report of a National Survey." *Art Education*, Vol. 17, No. 5 (1964), pages 5-9.

(2) Hausman, J. J. "Children's Art Work and Their Sociometric Status." *Research in Art Education*, ed. M. Barkan. Fifth Yearbook of the National Art Education Association, a department of the National Education Association. Kutztown, Pennsylvania: State Teachers College, 1954, pages 131-151.

(7) Helson, R. "Personality of Women With Imaginative and Artistic Interests: The Role of Masculinity, Originality and Other Characteristics in Their Creativity." *Journal of Personality*, Vol. 34, No. 1 (1966), pages 1-25.

(7) Hendrickson, P. R. "Non-Verbal Manipulation and Creativeness in Art." *Studies in Art Education*, Vol. 5, No. 1 (1963), pages 60-70.

(4) Henton, R. W. "Faft: An Evaluation Technique in Furniture Arrangement." *Studies in Art Education*, Vol. 13, No. 2 (1972), pages 44-45.

(2) Herberholz, D. W. "An Experimental Study to Determine the Effect of Modeling on the Drawing of the Human Figure by Second Grade Children." *Research in Art Education*, ed. W. R. Hastie, Ninth Yearbook of the National Art Education Association, a department of the National Education Association. Kutztown, Pennsylvania: State Teachers College, 1959, pages 65-69.

(2) Herrick, M. A. "Children's Drawings." *Pedagogical Seminary*, Vol. 3 (1893), pages 338-339.

(5) Heussenstamm, F. K. "On the Education of Architects: A Study of Fourth

Year Students at the University of Southern California." *Studies in Art Education,* Vol. 12, No. 3, pages 43-49.

(2) Hicks, M. D. "Art in Early Education." *Pedagogical Seminary,* Vol. 2 (1893), pages 463-466.

(2) Hildreth, G. *The Child Mind in Evolution: A Study of Developmental Sequences in Drawing.* New York: King's Crown Press, 1941.

(2) Hildreth, G. "The Simplification Tendency in Reproducing Designs." *Pedagogical Seminary and Journal of Genetic Psychology,* Vol. 54 (1944), pages 329-333.

(1) Hildreth, G. H. "Color and Picture Choices of Young Children." *Pedagogical Seminary and Journal of Genetic Psychology,* Vol. 49 (1936), pages 427-435.

(2) Hinrichs, W. E. "The Goodenough Drawing in Relation to Delinquency and Problem Behavior." *Archives of Psychology* (1935), pages 627-633.

(1) Hirohashi, B. "Some Experiments on Beauty of Color." Japanese *Journal of Psychology,* Vol. 9 (1926), pages 406-432. After *Psychological Abstracts,* No. 2 (1928), pages 608-609.

(4) Hoffa, H. E. "The Relationship of Art Experience to Conformity." *Studies in Art Education,* Vol. 1, No. 2 (1960), pages 35-41.

(5) Hogg, J. C., and H. J. McWhinnie. "A Pilot Research in Aesthetic Education." *Studies in Art Education,* Vol. 9, No. 2 (1968), pages 52-59.

(1) Holden, W. A., and K. K. Bossee. "Order of Development of Color Perception and Color Preference in the Child." *Archives of Opthalmology,* (1900), pages 261-278.

(7) Holland, J. L. "Some Limitations of Teacher Ratings as Predictors of Creativity." *Journal of Educational Psychology,* Vol. 50 (1959), pages 219-223.

(2) Hollingsworth, L. S. *The Gifted Children.* New York: The Macmillan Company, 1926, pages 209-210.

(2) Hollingsworth, L. S. *Special Talents and Defects.* New York: The Macmillan Company, 1923.

(2) Hollingsworth, L. S. *Psychology of Subnormal Children.* New York: The Macmillan Company, 1920, pages 183-184.

(1) Honkavaara, S. "The Color and Form Reaction as a Basis of Interpersonal Relationships." *Journal of Psychology,* Vol. 46 (1958), pages 33-38.

(4) Horn, C. A., and L. F. Smith. "The Horn Art Aptitude Inventory." *Journal of Applied Psychology,* Vol. 29 (1945), pages 350-355.

(5) Horn, G. F. "Art and the Under-Achiever; A Study." *Art Education,* Vol. 17 (1964), pages 10-14.

(5) Howlett, C. S. "An Analysis of Art Curriculums in Terms of the Developmental Needs of Youth." *Research in Art Education,* ed. W. R. Hastie. Ninth Yearbook of the National Art Education Association, a department of the National Education Association. Kutztown, Pennsylvania: State Teachers College, 1959, pages 142-152.

(1) Huang, I. "Abstraction of Form and Color as a Function of the Stimulus Object." *Pedagogical Seminary and Journal of Genetic Psychology,* Vol. 56 (1945), pages 59-62.

(3) Hudson, W. "Pictorial Depth Perception in Sub-Cultural Groups in Africa." *Journal of Social Psychology,* Vol. 52 (1960), pages 183-208.

(2) Hurlock, E. B. "The Spontaneous Drawings of Adolescents." *Pedagogical Seminary and Journal of Genetic Psychology,* Vol. 63 (1943), pages 141-156.

(5) Hurst, R., J. Schwartz, and H. Sutton. "A Study of Some Values Held by Students in Courses in Teacher Education in Art." *Research in Art Education,* ed. M. Barkan. Seventh Yearbook of the National Art Education Association, a department of the National Education Association. Kutztown, Pennsylvania:

State Teachers College, 1956, pages 28-38.

(7) Israeli, N. "Social Interaction in Creation and Criticism in the Fine Arts." *Journal of Social Psychology,* Vol. 35 (1953), pages 73-89.

(3) Iwao, S. and I. L. Child. "Comparison of Esthetic Judgments by American Experts and by Japanese Potters." *Journal of Social Psychology,* Vol. 68, No. 1 (1966), pages 27-33.

(5) Janes, H. E. "Conceptual Modes of Children in Responding to Art Objects." *Studies in Art Education,* Vol. 11, No. 3 (1970), pages 52-60.

(1) Jastrow, J. "The Popular Aesthetics of Color." *Popular Science Monthly,* Vol. 54 (1897), page 361.

(2) Jenson, B. T. "Left-Right Orientation in Profile Drawing." *American Journal of Psychology,* Vol. 65 (1952), pages 80-83.

(2) Jones, C. A. "Relationships Between Creative Drawing of Sixth Grade Children." *Studies in Art Education,* Vol. 3, No. 2 (1963), pages 34-43.

(5) Jones, L. H., Jr. "Student and Teacher Interaction During Evaluative Dialogues in Art." *Art Education,* Vol. 18, No. 4 (1965), pages 13-15.

(5) Kannegieter, R. B. "The Effects of A Learning Program in Activity Upon the Visual Perception of Shape." *Studies in Art Education,* Vol. 12, No. 2 (1971), pages 18-27.

(3) Katz, E. "Motion Pictures in Art Education." *Education,* Vol. 55 (1934), pages 197-201.

(3) Katz, E. "Testing Preferences with 2″ x 2″ Slides." *Educational Screen,* Vol. 21 (1942), page 301.

(1) Katz, S. A., and F. S. Breed. "The Color Preferences of Children." *Journal of Applied Psychology,* Vol. 6 (1922), pages 255-266.

(5) Kendrick, D. "A Dilemma Concerning the Compatibility Between Creative and Arithmetical Measurements." *Studies in Art Education,* Vol. 8, No. 2 (1967), pages 37-45.

(5) Kendrick, D. "The Influence of Teacher Motivation and Non-Motivation on the Overall Aesthetic Quality of the 'Whole' and the 'Parts' of Cut-Paper Art Products." *Studies in Art Education,* Vol. 3, No. 2 (1962), pages 52-63.

(5) Kensler, G. L. "Effects of Perceptual Training and Modes of Perceiving Upon Individual Differences in Ability to Learn Perspective Drawing." *Studies in Art Education,* Vol. 7, No. 1 (1965), pages 34-41.

(4) Kieselbach, A. G. "An Experimental Study in the Development of an Instrument to Measure Aesthetic Perception." *Research in Art Education,* ed. M. Barkan. Seventh Yearbook of the National Art Education Association, a department of the National Education Association. Kutztown, Pennsylvania: State Teachers College, 1956, pages 62-73.

(7) Kincaid, C. E. "The Determination and Description of Various Creative Attributes of Children." *Studies in Art Education,* Vol. 2, No. 2 (1961), pages 45-53.

(4) Kinget, G. M. *The Drawing-Completion Test.* A Projective Technique for the Investigation of Personality. New York: Grune and Stratton, Inc., 1952.

(3) Klein, S. P. "A Description of Points of View in Esthetic Judgments in Terms of Similarity Dimensions." *Studies in Art Education,* Vol. 10, No. 1 (1968), pages 33-42.

(3) Klein, S. P., and R. W. Skager. "Spontaneity vs. Deliberateness as a Dimension of Esthetic Judgment." *Perceptual and Motor Skills,* Vol. 25, No. 1 (1967), pages 161-168.

(4) Kline, L. W., and G. Carey. "A Measuring Scale for Freehand Drawing." *Johns Hopkins University Studies in Education,* No. 5. Baltimore: The Johns Hopkins Press, 1922.

(4) Kline, L. W., and G. Carey. "A Measuring Scale for Drawing." *Johns Hopkins University Studies in Education*, No. 5a. Baltimore: The Johns Hopkins Press, 1923.

(3) Knapp, R. H., and A. Wulff. "Preferences for Abstract and Representational Art." *Journal of Social Psychology*, Vol. 60, No. 2 (1963), pages 255-262.

(4) Knauber, A. J. "Testing for Art Ability." *Education*, Vol. 56 (1935), pages 219-223.

(4) Knauber, A. J. "The Construction and Standardization of the Knauber Art Tests." *Education*, Vol. 56 (1935), pages 219-223.

(2) Koppitz, E. A. "A Comparison of Pencil and Crayon Drawings of Young Children." *Journal of Clinical Psychology*, Vol. 21 (1965), pages 191-194.

(2) Koppitz, E. M. "Teacher's Attitude and Children's Performance on the Bender Gestalt Test and Human Figure Drawings." *Journal of Clinical Psychology*, Vol. 16 (1960), pages 204-208.

(5) Krippner, S., and R. Blickenstaff. "The Development of Self-Concept as Part of an Arts Workshop for the Gifted." *Gifted Child Quarterly*, Vol. 14, No. 3 (1970), pages 163-166.

(5) Lanier, V. "The Status of Current Objectives in Art Education." *Research in Art Education*, ed. M. Barkan. Fifth Yearbook of the National Art Education Association, a department of the National Education Association. Kutztown, Pennsylvania: State Teachers College, 1954, pages 114-130.

(2) Lansing, K. M. "Effect of Class Size and Room Size Upon the Creative Drawings of Fifth Grade Children." *Research in Art Education*, ed. W. R. Hastie. Ninth Yearbook of the National Art Education Association, a department of the National Education Association. Kutztown, Pennsylvania: State Teachers College, 1959, pages 70-74.

(4) (5) Lansing, K. M. "Intelligence and Art Ability." *Studies in Art Education*, Vol. 1, No. 2 (1960), pages 73-84.

(4) Lark-Horovitz, B. "Comparison of Subjective and Objective Judgments of Children's Drawings." *Journal of Experimental Education*, Vol. 10 (1942), pages 153-165.

(2) Lark-Horovitz, B. "Interlinkage of Sensory Memories in Relation to Training in Drawing." *Pedagogical Seminary and Journal of Genetic Psychology*, Vol. 49 (1936), pages 69-89.

(3) Lark-Horovitz, B. "On Art Appreciation for Children: Preferences of Picture Subjects in General. *Journal of Educational Research*, Vol. 31 (1937), pages 118-137.

(2) Lark-Horovitz, B. "On Learning Abilities of Children as Recorded in a Drawing Experiment: I. Subject Matter." *Journal of Experimental Education*, Vol. 9 (1941), pages 332-345.

(2) Lark-Horovitz, B. "On Learning Abilities of Children as Recorded in a Drawing Experiment: Aesthetic and Representational Qualities." *Journal of Experimental Education*, Vol. 9 (1941), pages 346-360.

(2) Lark-Horovitz, B., and J. Norton. "Children's Art Abilities: The Interrelations and Factorial Structure of Ten Characteristics." *Child Development*, Vol. 31 (1960), pages 453-462.

(2) Leggitt, D. "A Comparison of Abilities in Cursive and Manuscript Writing and in Creative Art." *School Review*, Vol. 49 (1941), pages 48-56.

(2) Lehman, H. C. "Environmental Influence Upon Drawing 'Just for Fun'." *School Arts Magazine*, Vol. 27 (1927), pages 3-7.

(2) Leightner, M. A., and R. M. Patterson. "A Comparative Study of Spontaneous Paintings of Normal and Mentally Deficient Children of the Same Mental Age." *American Journal of Mental Deficiency*, Vol. 48 (1944), pages 345-353.

(4) Lewerenz, A. S. *A Test of Fundamental Abilities in Visual Art.* Los Angeles: Research Service Company, 1928.

(4) Lewerenz, A. S. "I.Q. and Ability in Art." *School and Society,* Vol. 27 (1928), pages 489-490.

(4) Lewerenz, A. S. "Sex Differences on Ability Tests in Art." *Journal of Educational Psychology,* Vol. 19 (1928), pages 629-635.

(3) Lewis, F. H. "Development of Artistic Appreciation." *Psychological Bulletin,* Vol. 31 (November 1934), page 679.

(2) Lewis, H. P. "Developmental Stages in Children's Representation of Spatial Relations in Drawings." *Studies in Art Education,* Vol. 3, No. 2 (1962), pages 69-76.

(2) (3) Lewis, H. P. "Spatial Representation in Drawing as a Correlate of Development and a Basis for Picture Preference." *Journal of Genetic Psychology,* Vol. 102, No. 1, (1963), pages 95-107.

(2) Lewis, H. P., and N. Livson. "Correlates of Developmental Level of Spatial Representation in Children's Drawings." *Studies in Art Education,* Vol. 8, No. 2 (1967), pages 46-57.

(4) Lewis, H. P., and P. H. Mussen. "The Development of an Instrument for Evaluating Children's Artistic Creativity." *Studies in Art Education,* Vol. 10, No. 3 (1969), pages 25-48.

(5) Lienard, M. "What is the Relationship of Children's Satisfaction With Their Art Products to Improvement in Art?" *Studies in Art Education,* Vol. 3, No. 1 (1961), pages 55-65.

(1) Lignon, E. M. "A Genetic Study in Color Naming and Word Reading." *American Journal of Psychology,* Vol. 44 (1930), pages 103-122.

(5) Lindauer, M. S. "Effects of Clues in Perceiving the 'Good Figure'." *Perceptual and Motor Skills,* Vol. 30, No. 2 (1970), page 588.

(6) Linderman, E. W. "The Relation of Art Picture Judgment to Judge Personality." *Studies in Art Education,* Vol. 3, No. 2 (1962), pages 46-51.

(5) Lissim, S. "Art Education for Adults." *College Art Journal,* Vol. 8 (1949), pages 288-292.

(5) Lockhart, B. C. "Parental Understanding of School Art Programs and Its Relationship to Certain School Supervisory Practices in Art Education." *Research in Art Education,* ed. M. Barkan. Seventh Yearbook of the National Art Education Association, a department of the National Education Association. Kutztown, Pennsylvania: State Teachers College, 1956, pages 96-102.

(5) Loughram, B. B. "Survey Concerning the Role and Function of the Art Specialist as Supervisor." *Research in Art Education,* ed. W. R. Hastie. Ninth Yearbook of the National Art Education Association, a department of the National Education Association. Kutztown, Pennsylvania: State Teachers College, 1959, pages 137-141.

(6) Loursenso, S. V., J. Greenberg, and H. H. Davidson. "Personality Characteristics Revealed in Drawings of Deprived Children Who Differ in School Achievement." *Journal of Educational Research,* Vol. 59, No. 2 (1965), pages 63-67.

(2) Lovano, J. J. "The Relation of Conceptual Styles and Mode of Perception to Graphic Expression." *Studies in Art Education,* Vol. 11, No. 3 (1970), pages 39-51.

(7) Lowenfeld, V. *The Nature of Creative Activity.* London: Rontledge and Kegan Paul, Ltd., 1952.

(4) Lowenfeld, V. "Tests for Visual and Haptical Aptitude." *American Journal of Psychology,* Vol. 58 (1945), pages 100-111.

(3) Luchins, A. S. "Social Influences on Perception of Complex Drawings." *Jour-*

nal of Social Psychology, Vol. 21 (1945), pages 257-275.

(3) Lucio, W. H., and C. D. Mead. "Investigation of Children's Preferences for Modern Pictures." *Elementary School Journal*, Vol. 39 (1939), pages 678-689.

(1) Luckeisch, M. "A Note on Color Preference." *American Journal of Psychology*, Vol. 27 (1916), pages 251-255.

(2) Lukens, H. T. "A Study of Children's Drawings in the Early Years." *Pedagogical Seminary*, No. 4 (1896), pages 79-110.

(4) Mac Gregor, R. "The Development and Validation of a Perceptual Index for Utilization in the Teaching of Art." *Studies in Art Education*, Vol. 13, No. 2 (1972), pages 11-18.

(7) Machler, B., and F. C. Shontz. "Life Style and Creativity: An Empirical Investigation." *Perceptual and Motor Skills*, Vol. 20 (1965), pages 873-896.

(6) Machover, K. *Personality Projection in the Drawing of Figure*. Springfield, Illinois: Charles C. Thomas, 1949.

(7) Mackler, B., and J. Y. Spotts. "Characteristics of Responses to Tests of Creativity: A Second Look." *Perceptual and Motor Skills*, Vol. 21, No. 2 (1965), pages 595-599.

(5) Madeja, S. S. "The Effects of Divergent and Convergent Emphasis in Art Instruction on Students of High and Low Ability." *Studies in Art Education*, Vol. 8, No. 2 (1967), pages 10-20.

(2) Maitland, L. "What Children Draw to Please Themselves." *Inland Educator*, Vol. 7 (1895), page 87.

(1) Major, D. R. "On the Single Sense Impressions." *American Journal of Psychology*, Vol. 7 (1895), pages 51-77.

(2) Manson, J. B. "The Drawings of Pamela Bianca." *International Studio*, Vol. 68 (1919), pages 21-25.

(2) Manuel, H. T. "Talent in Drawing." *School and Home Educational Monograph*, No. 3. Bloomington, Illinois: Public School Publishing Co., 1919.

(2) Manzella, David. "The Effect of Hypnotically Induced Change in the Self-Image on Drawing Ability." *Studies in Art Education*, Vol. 4, No. 2 (1963), pages 59-67.

(5) Manzella, D. B. "The Teaching of Art in the Colleges of the United States." *College Art Journal*, Vol. 15 (1956), pages 241-251.

(8) Margolis, M. F. "A Comparative Study of Figure Drawings at Three Points in Therapy." *Rorschach Research Exchange and Journal of Projective Techniques*, Vol. 12, No. 2 (1948), pages 94-105.

(1) Marsden, R. E. "A Study of the Early Color Sense." *Psychological Review*, Vol. 10 (1903), pages 37-47, 299-300.

(2) Martin, A. W., and A. J. Weir. "A Comparative Study of Drawings Made by Various Clinical Groups." *Journal of Mental Science*, Vol. 97 (1951), pages 532-544.

(5) Masley, A. "The Place of Art in a High School Subject Matter Preference Scale as Determined by Some College Architectural Majors." *Studies in Art Education*, Vol. 3, No. 2 (1962), pages 77-84.

(3) Maslow, A. H., and N. L. Mintz. "Effects of Esthetic Surroundings: I. Initial Effects of Three Esthetic Conditions Upon Perceiving Energy and Well-being in Faces." *Journal of Psychology*, Vol. 41 (1956), pages 247-254.

(3) McAdory, M. *The Construction and Validation of an Art Test*. Contributions to Education, No. 383. New York: Teachers College, Columbia University, 1929.

(2) (4) McCarty, S. A. *Children's Drawings*. Baltimore: Williams and Wilkins Company, 1924.

(1) McDougall, W. "An Investigation of the Colour Sense of Two Infants." *British Journal of Psychology*, Vol. 2 (1908), pages 338-352.

(5) McFee, J. K. "A Study of Perception-Delineation: Its Implications for Art Education." *Research in Art Education*, ed. W. R. Hastie. Ninth Yearbook of the National Art Education Association, a department of the National Education Association. Kutztown, Pennsylvania: State Teachers College, 1959, pages 9-14.

(5) McFee, J. K. "Children and Cities: An Exploratory Study of Urban- Middle- and Low-Income Neighborhood Children's Responses in Studying the City." *Studies in Art Education*, Vol. 1 (1971), pages 50-63.

(8) McIntosh, J. R., and R. W. Pickford. "Some Clinical and Artistic Aspects of a Child's Drawings." *British Journal of Medical Psychology*, Vol. 19 (1943), pages 342-362.

(5) McVitty, L. F. "An Experimental Study on Various Methods in Art Motivation at the Fifth Grade Level." *Research in Art Education*, ed. M. Barkan. Seventh Yearbook of the National Art Education Association, a department of the National Education Association. Kutztown, Pennsylvania: State Teachers College, 1956, pages 74-83.

(5) McWhinnie, H. J. "Effects of a Learning Experience Upon the Preference for Complexity and Asymmetry." *The Journal of Experimental Education*, Vol. 35 (1966), pages 56-62.

(4) McWhinnie, H. J. "A Note on Methodology in Using Children's Figure Drawing to Assess Racial and Cultural Differences." *Studies in Art Education*, Vol. 13, No. 2 (1972), pages 30-33.

(7) McWhinnie, H. J. "Some Relationships Between Creativity and Perception in Fourth Grade Children." *Actd Psychologica Amsterdam*, Vol. 31, No. 2 (1969), pages 169-175.

(5) McWhinnie, H. J. "A Third Study of the Effects of Learning Experience Upon Preference for Complexity-Asymmetry in Fourth, Fifth, and Sixth Grade Children." *California Journal of Educational Research*, Vol. 21, No. 2 (1970), pages 216-225.

(2) McWhinnie, H. J., and V. Lascarides-Morgan. "A Correlational Study of Perceptual Behavior and Perceptual Learning in Four and Five Year Old Children." *Scientia Paedogogica Experimentalis*, Vol. 8, No. 1 (1971), pages 38-61.

(7) Mednick, S. A., and J. P. Houston. "Creativity and the Need for Novelty." *Journal of Abnormal and Social Psychology*, Vol. 66 (1963), pages 137-141.

(3) Meier, N. C. "A Measure of Art Talent." *University of Iowa Studies*, Psychological Monograph, No. 39 (1928), pages 184-188.

(3) Meier, N. C. "Aesthetic Judgment as Measure of Art Talent." *University of Iowa Studies*, Vol. 7, No. 19 (1926).

(4) Meier, N. C. "Art Ability Without Instruction or Environmental Background: Case Study of Loran Lockhart." *Studies in Psychology of Art: II*, No. 1. Whole Number 213. Princeton, New Jersey: Psychological Review Company, 1936, pages 155-163.

(4) Meier, N. C. "Diagnosis in Art." *Educational Diagnosis*. Thirty-fourth Yearbook, National Education Society for Study of Education. Bloomington, Illinois: Public School Publishing Company, 1935, pages 463-476.

(3) Meier, N. C. "Special Artistic Talent." *Psychological Bulletin*, Vol. 25 (1928), pages 265-271.

(3) Meier, N. C., and C. E. Seashore. *The Meier-Seashore Art Judgment Test*. Iowa City: Bureau of Educational Research and Service, Extension Division, University of Iowa, 1929.

(3) (4) Mellinger, B. E. *Children's Interests in Pictures.* New York: Bureau of Publications, Teachers College, Columbia University, 1932.

(4) Mellone, M. A. "A Factorial Study of Picture Tests for Young Children." *British Journal of Psychology,* Vol. 35 (1944), pages 9-16.

(1) Mercer, F. M. "Color Preferences of 1006 Negroes." *Journal of Comparative Psychology,* Vol. 5 (1925), pages 109-146.

(5) Metzger, W. "The Influence of Aesthetic Examples." *Education of Vision,* ed. G. Kepes. New York: George Braziller, 1965, pages 16-26.

(7) Michael, J. "Effect of Award, Adult Standard, and Peer Standard Upon the Creativeness in Art of High School Pupils." *Research in Art Education,* ed. W. R. Hastie. Ninth Yearbook of the National Art Education Association, a department of the National Education Association. Kutztown, Pennsylvania: State Teachers College, 1959, pages 98-104.

(1) Michaels, G. M. "Color Preferences According to Age." *American Journal of Psychology,* Vol. 35 (1924), pages 79-87.

(5) Miles, J. B. "An Analysis of Relationship Between Experiences in Correlated Courses in Art, Music, and Modern Dance, and Certain Behavioral Changes Related to Aesthetic Experiences." *Studies in Art Education,* Vol. 4, No. 1 (1963), pages 34-45.

(3) Miller, W. A. "The Picture Choices of Primary-Grade Children." *Elementary School Journal,* Vol. 37 (1936), pages 273-282.

(3) Miller, W. A. "What Children See in Pictures." *Elementary School Journal,* Vol. 39 (1938), pages 280-288.

(3) Mintz, N. L. "Effects of Esthetic Surroundings: II. Prolonged and Repeated Experience in a 'Beautiful' and an 'Ugly' Room." *Journal of Psychology,* Vol. 4 (1956), pages 459-466.

(5) Mitchell, C. "A Study of Relationships Between Attitudes About Art Experience and Behavior in Art Activities." *Research in Art Education,* ed. W. R. Hastie. Ninth Yearbook of the National Art Education Association, a department of the National Education Association. Kutztown, Pennsylvania: State Teachers College, 1959, pages 105-111.

(5) Mitchell, E. L., and J. B. Smith. "Curriculum Investigations — Art." *Review of Educational Research,* Vol. 7 (1937), pages 128-130, 189-191.

(5) Mittler, G. "Efforts to Secure Congruent and Incongruent Modifications of Attitude Toward Works of Art." *Studies in Art Education,* Vol. 13, No. 2 (1972), pages 58-70.

(8) Modell, A. H. "Changes in Human Figure Drawings by Patients Who Recover from Regressed States." *American Journal of Orthopsychiatry,* Vol. 21 (1951), pages 584-596.

(8) Modell, A. H., and H. A. Potter. "Human Figure Drawing of Patients with Arterial Hypertension, Peptic Ulcer, and Bronchial Asthma." *Psychosomatic Medicine,* Vol. 11 (1949), pages 282-292.

(7) Mohan, M. and R. K. Gupta. "Interaction of Physical Environmental Cues With Creativity and Intelligence." *Proceedings of the Annual Convention of the American Psychological Association,* Vol. 7, No. 2 (1972), pages 513-514.

(1) Monroe, W. S. "Color Sense of Young Children." *Paidologist,* Vol. 9 (1907), pages 7-10.

(1) Mooney, R. L., and H. L. Sherman. "The Problem of Color in Teaching Drawing." *College Art Journal,* Vol. 6 (1946), pages 106-114.

(2) Mott, S. M. "Muscular Activity and Aid in Concept Formation." *Child Development,* Vol. 16 (1945), pages 97-109.

(2) Mott, S. M. "The Development of Concepts." *Pedagogical Seminary,* Vol. 48 (1936), pages 199-214.

(3) Munsinger, H., and W. Kessen. "Uncertainty, Structure and Preference." *Psychological Monographs: General and Applied*, Vol. 78, No. 9 (1964), page 24.

(6) Munsterberg, E., and P. H. Mussen. "The Personality Structures of Art Students." *Journal of Personality*, Vol. 21 (1953), pages 457-466.

(1) Myers, C. S. "Some Observations on the Development of the Colour Sense." *British Journal of Psychology*, Vol. 21 (1908), pages 353-362.

(1) Nagel, W. A. "Observations on the Color Sense of a Child." *Journal of Comparative Neurology and Psychology*, Vol. 16 (1906), pages 217-230.

(6) Napoli, P. J. "Finger Painting and Personality Diagnosis." *Genetic Psychology Monographs*, Vol. 34 (1946), pages 129-230.

(2) Nash, H., and D. B. Harris. "Body Proportions in Children's Drawings of a Man." *Journal of Genetic Psychology*, Vol. 117 (1970), pages 85-90.

(5) National Education Association, Research Division. "Art Instruction in the Public Schools." *NEA Research Bulletin*, Vol. 41 (1963), pages 90-93.

(8) Naumburg, M. "Children's Art Expression and War." *Nervous Child*, Vol. 2 (1943), pages 360-373.

(8) Naumburg, M. *Schizophrenic Art: Its Meaning in Psychotherapy.* New York: Grune and Stratton, Inc., 1950.

(8) Naumburg, M. "Studies of the 'Free' Art Expression of Behavior Problem Children and Adolescents as a Means of Diagnosis and Therapy." *Nervous and Mental Disease Monograph Series*, No. 71. New York: Collidge Foundation, 1947.

(2) (5) Nelson, T. M., and M. E. Flannery. "Instructions in Drawing Techniques as a Means of Utilizing Drawing Potential of Six and Seven Year Olds." *Studies in Art Education*, Vol. 8, No. 2 (1967), pages 58-65.

(3) Nelson, T. M., and G. A. MacDonald. "Lateral Organization, Perceived Depth and Title Preference in Pictures." *Perceptual and Motor Skills*, Vol. 33, No. 3 (1971), pages 983-986.

(5) Neperud, R. W. "An Experimental Study of Visual Elements, Selected Art Instruction Methods, and Drawing Development at the Fifth-Grade Level." *Studies in Art Education*, Vol. 7, No. 2 (1966), pages 3-13.

(5) Neperud, R. W. "Towards a Structure of Meaning in the Visual Arts; A Three-Mode Factor Analysis of Non-Art College Student Responses to Selected Art Forms." *Studies in Art Education*, Vol. 12, No. 1 (1970), pages 40-49.

(5) Newton, R. "Elementary School Art Experiences Remembered by Students of Elementary Education." *Research in Art Education*, ed. M. Barkan. Seventh Yearbook of the National Art Education Association, a department of the National Education Association. Kutztown, Pennsylvania: State Teachers College, 1956, pages 18-27.

(3) Nidorf, L. J., and A. H. Argabrite. "Aesthetic Communication: Mediating Organismic Variables." *Journal of General Psychology*, Vol. 82, No. 2 (1970), pages 179-193.

(3) Niles, H. R. "Aesthetic Appreciation and Intelligence." *School Arts Magazine*, Vol. 23 (1924), pages 608-612.

(4) Noller, P. A., and A. Weider. "A Normative Study of Human Drawings for Children." *American Psychologist*, Vol. 5 (1950), pages 319-320.

(5) Nyquist, F. V. *Art Education in the Elementary Schools.* Baltimore: Warwick and York, 1929.

(4) Oakley, C. A. "Drawings of a Man by Adolescents." *British Journal of Psychology*, Vol. 31 (1940), pages 37-60.

(2) Oakley, C. A. "Interpretation of Children's Drawings." *British Journal of*

Psychology, Vol. 21 (1931), pages 256-270.

(8) Orzehowski, J. J. "A Pilot Study Involving Art Education for Emotionally Disturbed Youth." *Research in Art Education,* ed. W. R. Hastie. Ninth Yearbook of the National Art Education Association, a department of the National Education Association. Kutztown, Pennsylvania: State Teachers College, 1959, pages 168-173.

(4) Osborne, J. W., and F. H. Farley. "The Relationship Between Aesthetic Preference and Visual Complexity in Abstract Art." *Psychonomic Science,* Vol. 19, No. 2, pages 69-70.

(2) O'Shea, M. V. *Mental Development and Education.* New York: The Macmillan Company, 1921, pages 110-114.

(2) O'Shea, M. V. "Some Aspects of Drawing." *Educational Review,* Vol. 14 (1897), pages 263-284.

(7) Owen, C. "An Investigation of Creative Potential at the Junior High Level." *Studies in Art Education,* Vol. 3, No. 2 (1962), pages 16-33.

(3) Pan, S. "Study in Esthetic Judgment: The Influence of Familiarity." *Psychological Abstract,* Vol. 10, No. 2134 (1936), page 233.

(7) Pappas, G. "An Analysis of the Process of Beginning and Developing Works of Art." *Research in Art Education,* ed. W. R. Hastie. Ninth Yearbook of the National Art Education Association, a department of the National Education Association. Kutztown, Pennsylvania: State Teachers College, 1959, pages 119-124.

(5) Parker, W. A. "Statistics on College Art Teachers." *College Art Journal,* Vol. 14 (1955), pages 263-269.

(5) Parkhurst, H. "What Kind of Art Teacher Do Children Like Best?" *Art Education Today, 1949-1950.* New York: Teachers College, Columbia University, 1950, pages 25-34.

(3) Patrick, C. "Different Responses Produced by Good and Poor Art." *Journal of General Psychology,* Vol. 34 (1946), pages 79-96.

(2) Paulsson, J. "The Creative Element in Art." *Scandinavian Science Review,* Vol. 2 (1923), pages 111-173.

(2) Peck, L. "An Experiment With Drawing in Relation to the Prediction of School Success." *Journal of Applied Psychology,* Vol. 20 (1936), pages 16-43.

(3) Peel, E. A. "On Identifying Aesthetic Types." *British Journal of Psychology,* Vol. 35 (1945), pages 61-69.

(4) Perry, H. T., and E. T. Prothro. "Group Differences in Performance on the Meier Art Test." *Journal of Applied Psychology,* Vol. 34 (1950), pages 96-97.

(8) Phillips, E., and E. Stromberg. "A Comparative Study of Finger-Painting Performance in Detention Home and High School Pupils." *Journal of Psychology,* Vol. 26 (1948), pages 507-515.

(4) Pikunas, J., and H. Carberry. "Standardization of the Graphoscopic Scale: The Content of Children's Drawings." *Journal of Clinical Psychology,* Vol. 17, No. 3 (1961), pages 297-301.

(5) Plummer, G. S. "The Summer Workshop for High School Students on the University Campus; An Attempt at Evaluation." *Studies in Art Education,* Vol. 13, No. 2 (1972), pages 51-57.

(6) Prados, M. "Rorschach Studies on Artists — Painters. I. Quantitative Analysis." *Rorshach Research Exchange,* Vol. 8 (1944), pages 178-183.

(5) Preston, E. E. "A Survey of Time Allotments for Art in the Public Schools of the Middle West." *Record of the Conventions at St. Louis and Milwaukee,* Department of Art Education Bulletin, Vol. 6 (1940). Washington, D. C.: National Education Association, pages 95-104.

(1) Preyer, W. *The Mind of the Child.* New York: D. Appleton Company, 1903, pages 6-22.

(4) Printer, R., and H. A. Toops. "A Drawing Completion Test." *Journal of Applied Psychology,* Vol. 2 (1918), pages 164-173.

(1) Putnam, A. H. "Notes." *Pedagogical Seminary,* Vol. 2 (1893), page 331.

(2) Putney, W. W. "Creative Drawings of Stutters." *Research in Art Education,* ed. W. R. Hastie. Ninth Yearbook of the National Art Education Association, a Department of the National Education Association. Kutztown, Pennsylvania: State Teachers College, 1959, pages 161-167.

(3) Pyron, B. "Rejection of Avant-Garde Art and the Need for Simple Order." *Journal of Psychology,* Vol. 63 (1966), pages 159-178.

(5) Qualley, C. A. "A Comparison of Spontaneous and Divergent Strategies to Historical Analyses of Style." *Studies in Art Education,* Vol. 12, No. 1 (1970), pages 17-24.

(2) Rand, G., and S. Wapner. "Graphic Representations of a Motivated Act: An Ontogenetic Study." *Studies in Art Education,* Vol. 12, No. 1 (1970), pages 25-30.

(2) Rankin, P. T. "Diagnosis, and Remedial Instruction in Creativeness." *Educational Diagnosis,* Thirty-fourth Yearbook, National Society for the Study of Education. Bloomington, Illinois: Public School Publishing Co., 1935, pages 478-498.

(1) Reavis, W. C. "The Interests of Children of Primary and Intermediate Grades in the Use of Color." *School Arts Magazine,* Vol. 19 (1920), pages 573-577.

(1) Reed, J. D. "A Note on Reaction Time as a Test of Color Discrimination." *Journal of Experimental Psychology,* Vol. 39 (1949), pages 118-121.

(6) Rees, M. E., and M. Goldman. "Some Relationships Between Creativity and Personality." *Journal Genetic Psychology,* Vol. 65 (1961), pages 145-161.

(5) Rennels, M. R. "Two Methods of Teaching Spatial Tasks to Disadvantaged Negroes." *Studies in Art Education,* Vol. 11, No. 1 (1969), pages 44-51.

(2) Ricci, C. "The Art of Little Children." *Pedagogical Seminary,* Vol. 3 (1894), pages 302-307.

(1) Riffenburgh, G. H. "Responses to Color Combinations as Indices of Personality Traits." *Journal of General Psychology,* Vol. 41 (1959), pages 317-322.

(1) Riker, O. M. *Color Preferences of Elementary School Children.* M.A. Thesis on file in the University of Wisconsin Library. Summarized in the Third Yearbook, National Education Association, 1925.

(1) Rivers, W. H. R. "Observations on the Senses of the Todas." *British Journal of Psychology,* Vol. 1 (1905), pages 321-396.

(1) Rivers, W. H. R. "Primitive Color Vision." *Popular Science Monthly,* Vol. 54 (1901), pages 41-58.

(5) Robinson, J. P., and P. Landon. "Labeling and Imagining Aids to Memory." *Child Development,* Vol. 42, No. 2 (1971), pages 641-644.

(7) Roe, A. "Alcohol and Creative Work. Part I. Painters." *Quarterly Journal of Studies on Alcohol,* Vol. 6 (1946), pages 415-467.

(7) Roe, A. "Artists and Their Work." *Journal of Personality,* Vol. 15 (1946), pages 1-40.

(6) Roe, A. "Painting and Personality." *Rorschach Research Exchange,* Vol. 10 (1946), pages 86-100.

(5) Rogers, D. W. "Visual Expression: A Creative Advantage of the Disadvantaged." *Gifted Child Quarterly,* Vol. 12, No. 2 (1968), pages 110-114.

(5) Rose, H. C. "Directions in Junior High School Art Education: A Pilot Survey of City Junior High School Art Programs." *Research in Art Education,* ed. W.

R. Hastie. Ninth Yearbook of the National Art Education Association, a Department of the National Art Education Association. Kutztown, Pennsylvania: State Teachers College, 1959, pages 131-136.

(4) Rosen, J. C. "The Barron-Welsh Art Scale as a Predictor of Originality and Level of Ability Among Artists." *Journal of Applied Psychology*, Vol. 39 (1955), pages 366-367.

(3) Roubertoux, P., M. Carlier, and J. Chaguiboff. "Preference for Non-Objective Art: Personal and Psychosocial Determiners." *British Journal of Psychology*, Vol. 62, No. 1 (1971), pages 105-110.

(2) Rouse, M. J. "A New Look at an Old Theory: A Comparison of Lowenfeld's 'Haptic-Visual' Theory with Witkin's Perceptual Theory." *Studies in Art Education*, Vol. 7, No. 1 (1965), pages 42-55.

(5) Rouse, M. J., and G. Hubbard. "Structured Curriculum in Art for the Classroom Teacher: Giving Order to Disorder." *Studies in Art Education*, Vol. 11, No. 2 (1970), pages 14-26.

(8) Royal, R. E. "Drawing Characteristics of Neurotic Patients Using a Drawing-of-a-Man-and-a-Woman Technique." *Journal of Clinical Psychology*, Vol. 5 (1949), pages 392-395.

(7) Russell, I., and B. Waugaman. "A Study of the Effect of Workbook Copy Experiences on the Creative Concepts of Children." *Research Bulletin*, Vol. 3 (1952). Eastern Arts Association, pages 5-11.

(7) Russell, I. M. "Relationships Between Certain Aspects of Creative Expression and Reading Development." *Research in Art Education*, ed. M. Barkan. Seventh Yearbook of the National Art Education Association, a department of the National Education Association. Kutztown, Pennsylvania: State Teachers College, 1956, pages 103-114.

(4) Russell, R. W. "The Spontaneous and Instructed Drawings of Zuni Children." *Journal of Comparative Psychology*, Vol. 35 (1943), pages 11-15.

(1) Salkind, N. "Realistic Use of Color by Children." *Studies in Art Education*, Vol. 3, No. 3 (1972), pages 38-42.

(2) Salome, R. A. "A Comparative Analysis of Kindergarten Children's Drawings in Crayon and Colored Pencil." *Studies in Art Education*, Vol. 8, No. 2 (1967), pages 21-36.

(5) Salome, R. A. "The Effects of Perceptual Training Upon the Two-Dimensional Drawings of Children." *Studies in Art Education*, Vol. 7, No. 1 (1965), pages 18-33.

(5) Salome, R. A., and D. Reeves. "Two Pilot Investigations of Perceptual Training of Four-and-Five-Year-Old Kindergarten Children." *Studies in Art Education*, Vol. 13, No. 2 (1972), pages 3-10.

(2) Sargent, W. *Fine and Industrial Arts in the Elementary School.* New York: Ginn and Company, 1918. (Reported in Instruction in Art in United States Bureau of Education, No. 43, 1918).

(2) Sargent, W. "Problems in the Experimental Pedagogy of Drawing." *Journal of Educational Psychology*, Vol. 3 (1912), pages 264-276.

(2) Sargent, W., and E. Miller. *How Children Learn to Draw.* Boston: Ginn and Company, 1916.

(7) Schaefer-Simmern, H. *The Unfolding of Artistic Activity.* Berkeley: University of California Press, 1948.

(8) Schaefer-Simmern, H. "Therapeutic Implications of Artistic Activity: A Case Study." *American Journal of Mental Deficiency*, Vol. 49 (1944) pages 185-196.

(4) Schmidl-Waehner, T. "Formal Criteria for the Analysis of Children's

Drawings." *American Journal of Orthopsychiatry*, Vol. 12 (1942), pages 95-103.

(2) Schmidl-Waehner, T. "Interpretation of Spontaneous Drawings and Paintings." *Genetic Psychology Monographs*, Vol. 33 (1946), pages 3-70.

(2) Schnall, M. "Children's Drawings and Reasons for Anticipating Progressive Changes in Successive Stimuli." *Perceptual and Motor Skills*, Vol. 32, No. 3 (1971), pages 783-786.

(2) Sherman, H. L. "The Eye in the Arts." *Educational Research Bulletin*, Vol. 23, pages 1-6. Columbus, Ohio: Ohio State University, 1944.

(5) Sherman, L. B. "An Experiment in Teaching Method in Art." *Research in Art Education*, ed. W. R. Hastie. Ninth Yearbook of the National Art Education Association, a department of the National Education Association. Kutztown, Pennsylvania: State Teachers College, 1959, pages 75-82.

(1) Shinn, M. W. "Development of the Sense in Childhood." *University of California Studies in Education*, Vol. 4, No. 2 (1907).

(1) Shinn, M. W. "Notes on the Development of a Child." *University of California Studies*, Vol. 1 (1897).

(5) Silverman, R. H., R. Hoepfner, and M. Hendricks. "Developing and Evaluating Art Curricula for Disadvantaged Youth." *Studies in Art Education*, Vol. II, No. 1 (1969), pages 20-33.

(7) Singer, D. L., and M. B. Whiton. "Ideational Creativity and Expressive Aspects of Human Figure Drawing in Kindergarten-Age Children." *Developmental Psychology*, Vol. 4, No. 3 (1971), pages 366-369.

(5) Slapo, D. "The Effect of Problem-Solving Training on the Creative Art Work of Sixth Grade Students." *Graduate Research in Education and Related Disciplines*, Vol. 4, No. 2 (1969), pages 42-62.

(3) Slettehaugh, T. "Difference in Reactions of Children in Various Levels of Development to Three-dimensional Abstract Ceramic Forms." *Art Education Bulletin*, Vol. 15 (1958), pages 22-23.

(2) Slockhover, M. Z. "Experiments on Dimensional and Figural Problems in the Clay and Pencil Reproductions of Line Figures by Young Children: I. Dimension." *Pedagogical Seminary and Journal of Genetic Psychology*, Vol. 49 (1946), pages 57-75.

(2) Slockhover, M. Z. "Experiments on Dimensional and Figural Problems in the Clay and Pencil Reproductions of Line Figures by Young Children: II. Shape." *Pedagogical Seminary and Journal of Genetic Psychology*, Vol. 69 (1946), pages 77-95.

(1) Smith, H. C. "Age Differences in Color Discrimination." *Journal of General Psychology*, Vol. 29 (1943), pages 191-226.

(4) Smith, I. M. "Validity of Tests of Spatial Ability as Predictors of Success on Technical Courses." *British Journal of Educational Psychology*, Vol. 30 (1960), pages 138-145.

(5) Smith, M. E., and E. Ziegfeld. *Art for Daily Living: The Story of the Owatonna Art Education Project*. Minneapolis: University of Minnesota Press, 1944.

(3) Speer, R. K. "Measurement of Appreciation in Poetry, Prose, and Art." *Studies in Appreciation*. New York: Bureau of Publications, Teachers College, Columbia University, 1929.

(6) Spiaggia, M. "Investigation of the Personality Traits of Art Students." *Educational and Psychological Measurement*, Vol. 10 (1950), pages 285-293.

(2) Spoerl, D. T. "Drawing Ability of Mentally Retarded Children." *Pedagogical Seminary and Journal of Genetic Psychology*, Vol. 57 (1940), pages 259-277.

(6) Spoerl, D. T. "Personality and Drawing in Retarded Children." *Character and Personality*, Vol. 8 (1940), pages 227-239.

(7) Spotts, J. V., and B. Mackler. "Relationships of Field-Department and Field-Independent Cognitive Styles to Creative Test Performance." *Perceptual and Motor Skills,* Vol. 24, No. 1 (1967), pages 239-268.

(4) Springbett, B. M. "The Semantic Differential and Meaning in Non-Objective Art." *Perceptual and Motor Skills,* Vol. 10 (1960), pages 231-240.

(8) Springer, N. N. "A Study of the Drawings of Maladjusted and Adjusted Children." *Pedagogical Seminary and Journal of Genetic Psychology,* Vol. 58 (1941), pages 131-138.

(1) Staples, R. "Color Vision and Color Preferences in Infancy and Childhood." *Psychological Bulletin,* Vol. 28 (1931), pages 297-308.

(1) Staples, R. "Responses of Infants to Color." *Journal of Experimental Psychology,* Vol. 15 (1932), pages 119-141.

(6) Stringer, P. "A Comparison of the Self-Images of Art and Architectural Students." *Studies in Art Education,* Vol. 9, No. 1 (1967), pages 33-49.

(5) Stumbo, H. W. "Changes in Meaning That Follow Phenomenological Analysis." *Studies in Art Education,* Vol. 12, No. 1 (1970), pages 50-60.

(1) Stutsman, R. *A Scale of Mental Tests for Pre-School Children.* Ph.D. Diss., Department of Psychology, University of Chicago, 1928, pages 175-178.

(3) Sullivan, M. "A Study of the Preferences of Elementary Children for the Pictures Used in the Pennsylvania State Course of Study." *Art Education Bulletin,* Vol. 14 (1957), pages 33-36.

(2) Sully, J. "Children's Drawings, The Young Draftsman." *Popular Science Monthly,* Vol. 48 (1896), pages 533-546.

(2) Sully, J. *Studies in Childhood.* New York: D. Appleton Company, 1908, pages 331-398.

(7) Taylor, R. E., and R. Eisenman. "Perception and Production of Complexity by Creative Art Students." *Journal of Psychology,* Vol. 57, No. 1 (1964), pages 239-242.

(2) Taylor, W. S. "A Note on Cultural Determination of Free Drawings." *Character and Personality,* Vol. 13 (1944), pages 30-36.

(5) Thirion, A. M. "An Experimental Study of Spatial Representations in 3 to 6 Year Old Children." *Scientia Paedogogica Experimentalis,* Vol. 6, No. 1 (1969), pages 121-183.

(3) Thompson, G. C. "The Effect of Chronological Age on Aesthetic Preferences for Rectangles of Different Proportions." *Journal of Experimental Psychology,* Vol. 36 (1946), pages 50-58.

(4) Thorndike, E. L. "A Scale for General Merit of Children's Drawings." *Teachers College Bulletin,* Fifteenth Series, No. 6 (1923).

(3) Thorndike, E. L. "Individual Differences in Judgment of the Beauty of Simple Forms." *Psychological Review,* Vol. 24 (1917), pages 147-153.

(3) Thorndike, E. L. "Tests of Aesthetic Appreciation." *Journal of Educational Psychology,* Vol. 7 (1916), pages 509-523.

(4) Thorndike, E. L. "The Measurement of Achievement in Drawing." *Teachers College Record,* Vol. 14 (1913), pages 345-383.

(4) Tiebout, C., and Meier, N. C. "Artistic Ability and General Intelligence." *Studies in Psychology of Art,* Vol. 2. University of Iowa Studies in Psychology, No. 19, *Psychological Monographs,* Vol. 48, No. 1 (1936), pages 95-125.

(5) Tighe, T. J. "Concept Formation and Art: Further Evidence on the Applicability of Walk's Technique." *Psychonomic Science,* Vol. 12, No. 8 (1968), pages 363-364.

(3) Todd, J. "Preferences of Children for Modern and Older Paintings." *Elementary School Journal,* Vol. 44 (1943), pages 223-231.

(7) Torrance, E. P. "Predictive Validity of 'Bonus' Scoring for Combinations on Repeated Figure Tests of Creative Thinking." *Journal of Psychology*, Vol. 81, No. 1 (1972), pages 167-171.

(7) Torrance, E. P. "Tendency to Produce Unusual Visual Perspective as a Predictor of Creative Achievement." *Perceptual and Motor Skills*, Vol. 34, No. 3 (1972), pages 911-915.

(1) Tracy, F., and J. Stimpel. *Psychology of Childhood*. Boston: D. C. Heath, 1909, pages 11-19.

(7) Trowbridge, N. "Creativity in Children in the Field of Art: Criterion Development Study." *Studies in Art Education*, Vol. 9, No. 1 (1967), pages 2-17.

(7) Trowbridge, N. and D. C. Charles. "Creativity in Art Students." *Journal of Genetic Psychology*, Vol. 109, No. 2 (1966), pages 281-289.

(1) Tucker, A. W. "Observations on the Color Vision of School Children." *British Journal of Psychology*, Vol. 4 (1911), pages 33-43.

(2) Uhlin, D. M. "Relationships of Adolescent Physical Development to Art Expression." *Studies in Art Education*, Vol. 3, No. 2 (1962), pages 64-68.

(1) Valentine, C. W. "The Colour Perception and Colour Preference of an Infant." *British Journal of Psychology*, Vol. 6 (1914), pages 363-386.

(4) Varnum, W. H. "Opportunities in the Art Field and a Selective Art Aptitude Test." *Record of the Conventions at St. Louis and Milwaukee*, Department of Art Education Bulletin, Vol. 6 (1940). Washington, D. C.: National Education Association pages 182-185.

(5) Walk, Richard D. "Concept Formation and Art: Basic Experiment and Controls." *Psychonomic Science*, Vol. 9, No. 4 (1967), pages 237-238.

(5) Walton, W. "Academic Movement in Art." *Scribner's Magazine*, Vol. 38 (1905), page 637.

(1) Washburn, M. F. "A Note on the Affective Value of Color." *American Journal of Psychology*, Vol. 22 (1911), page 114.

(1) Washburn, M. F., and S. L. Grose. "The Voluntary Control of Likes and Dislikes: The Effect of an Attempt to Change the Affective Value of Colors." *American Journal of Psychology*, Vol. 32 (1921), page 284.

(1) Washburn, M. F., M. T. McDonald, and D. Van Alstyne. "Voluntarily Controlled Likes and Dislikes of Color Combinations." *American Journal of Psychology*, Vol. 33 (1922), page 426.

(3) Waymack, E. H., and G. Hendrickson. "Children's Reactions as a Basis for Teaching Picture Appreciation." *Elementary School Journal*, Vol. 33 (1932), pages 268-276.

(2) Weglein, D. E. "The Correlation of Abilities of High School Pupils." *Johns Hopkins Studies in Education*, No. 1 (1917).

(4) Welch, L. "Recombination of Ideas in Creative Thinking." *Journal of Applied Psychology*, Vol. 30 (1946), pages 638-643.

(2) White, H. D. "The Use of Graphic Representation in Learning and Problem Solving at the College Level." *Journal of Educational Research*, Vol. 48 (1953), pages 35-43.

(2) Whitford, W. G. "Functional Approach to Art Education in the Elementary School." *Elementary School Journal*, Vol. 36 (1936), pages 674-681.

(2) Whitford, W. G. "An Empirical Study of Pupil Ability in Public School Art Courses." *Elementary School Journal*, Vol. 20 (1919), pages 33-46, 95-105.

(2) Whitford, W. G. *An Introduction to Art Education*. New York: D. Appleton and Company, 1929.

(1) Whitford, W. G. "An Investigation to Determine the Correct Art Concepts of

Tone for Teaching Purposes." *North Central Association Quarterly*, Vol. 8 (1934), pages 444-453.

(5) Whiting, M. R. "An Investigation of Art in the Teaching Procedures in Various High School Subjects." *Record of the Conventions at St. Louis and Milwaukee*, Department of Art Education Bulletin, Vol. 6 (1940). Washington, D. C.: National Education Association, pages 45-55.

(5) Wiggin, R. G. "Art Activities for Mentally Handicapped Children." *Studies in Art Education*, Vol. 3, No. 1 (1960), pages 88-102.

(5) Willard, G. D. "An Experimental Study of Techniques of Instruction Which Attempt to Promote the Growth of Adaptive and Spontaneous Flexibility in Senior High Art Students." *Art Education Bulletin*, Vol. 14 (1957), pages 37-40.

(3) Williams, F. "An Investigation of Children's Preferences for Pictures." *Elementary School Journal*, Vol. 25 (1924), pages 119-126.

(3) Wilson, B. G. "An Experimental Study Designed to Alter Fifth and Sixth Grade Students' Perception of Paintings." *Studies in Art Education*, Vol. 8, No. 1 (1966), pages 33-42.

(5) Wilson, B. G. "Relationships Among Art Teachers', Art Critics' and Historians', and Non-Art-Trained Individual's Statements About *Guernica*." *Studies in Art Education*, Vol. 12, No. 1 (1970), pages 31-39.

(3) (5) Wilson, B. "The Relationship Between Years of Art Training and the Use of Aesthetic Judgmental Criteria Among High School Students." *Studies in Art Education*, Vol. 13, No. 2 (1972), pages 34-43.

(1) Winch, W. H. "Colour Preferences of School Children." *British Journal of Psychology*, Vol. 3 (1909), pages 42-65.

(2) Wischner, G. J., and A. E. Goss. "Pictorial Representations of Situations Involving Threat." *Journal of Clinical Psychology*, Vol. 16 (1960), pages 196-200.

(1) Woelfel, F. C. "An Adaptation of the Ishihara Test for Use with Children of the Pre-School Age." *Child Development*, Vol. 1 (1930), pages 144-151.

(1) Wolfe, H. K. "On the Color Vocabulary of Children." *University of Nebraska Studies*, Vol. 1 (July 1890), pages 205-234.

(2) Wood, M. G. "Some Uses of Primitive Art in the Teaching of Young Children." *Teachers College Record*, Vol. 24 (1923), pages 49-59.

(5) Woods, Walter A. "The Role of Language Handicap in the Development of Artistic Interest." *Journal of Consulting Psychology*, Vol. 12 (July 1948), pages 240-245.

(1) Wooley, H. T. "Some Experiments on the Color Perception of an Infant and Their Interpretation." *Psychological Review*, Vol. 16 (1919), pages 363-376.

(1) Yokoyama, M. "Affective Tendency as Conditioned by Form and Color." *American Journal of Psychology*, Vol. 32 (1921), page 81.

Gil Lazier

Scientific Research in Theatre

This paper concerns the state of measurement research within the art of the theatre. It presents an opinion of the assets and liabilities of this approach to the understanding of the art. It poses basic questions to be studied, discusses current conditions in the field, sets some priorites, and offers some models.

I. Some Essentials

The principal dilemma of theatre research is that the *essence* of art is inexpressible. It is unquantifiable. It is beyond reason. It is the peak experience of Maslow, the sublime of Longinus, the goal of mysticism. It cannot be analyzed directly.

At the same time, this inexpressible essence may be the most important ingredient of life, that most direct route to Wonder, that thing that makes all else interesting, that clearest human imitation of the spark of consciousness. Even though its core is beyond conception, there are dimensions that approach the soul of art — outer manifestations leading to it — that can and must be submitted to rational inquiry. Thus, any meaningful research pursuit in the arts must somehow relate to two foundational questions: (1) *How does one get closer, more directly, more fully, more quickly to this essence, with less error and waste?* (2) *What effect does closeness to this essence have on the rest of life?*

From the most theoretical, subjective, speculative kind of thinking to the most empirical, objective, systematic of efforts, the researcher must hold onto these questions. Whether we're dealing with the dramatic improvisations of functionally illiterate students in a classroom in the South Bronx or the arts curriculum of the elementary system in the entire state of Pennsylvania, whether we're organizing the pre-professional MFA actor-training program at a theatre in Sarasota or trying to discover an effective text for the Introduction to Theatre course at FSU, whether we're trying to prepare a workable rehearsal schedule

GIL LAZIER *is Professor of Theatre and Director of the Graduate Program in the School of Theatre at The Florida State University.*

for a production of *The Glass Menagerie* or attempting to understand phenomenological criticism in a graduate seminar — these questions remain the same: How can we get to that maximum payoff of art that gives us pleasure beyond even our thoughts, the experience that is antecedent to analysis? What does that experience do to us?

It probably seems strange for one who has developed some reputation in evolving behavioral, empirical research techniques in the theatre to begin this paper on such a transcendental note. But at the basis of my work in recent years is a personal attempt to express what it is about my own art form that is so important to my life. I assume that if I can get closer to explaining that essence of art for myself, I can be more accurate in my research priorities.

I was standing in the stage-left wings of a ballroom at the San Francisco Hilton during one of the activities of the Acting Center I had organized for the 1972 American Theatre Association Convention. It was around ten in the morning. There was a hard and direct beam of light aimed at the center of the dark stage and in it, circled in white, was Mamyko, a Japanese mime from the American Conservatory Theatre. She was performing a piece of her own invention to depict a *haiku* poem just read to the audience. The presentation lasted no more than a minute.

She was alone—no props, no sound. It was a simple, pure combination of precise movements—abstract, flowing, sculpting the empty space. It was extraordinary. I had never seen anything like it in my life. Tears welled in my eyes; time stopped. The endless procession of thought faded. I relaxed. There was just her creation and no labels to place on it. That experience stayed with me. It's there now. It provided instantaneously a new frame of reference, a new model, a new piece of reality for me—one that demanded nothing in return except my need to assimilate it, to relate it to other things. It gave me a direct energy that penetrated my general resistance to the new.

The mind looked at that experience as it was abating and whispered: "There it is again. That's what it's all about. Remember it!" And I say now, four years after that one-minute mime at the San Francisco Hilton, that Mamyko's work at that place at that time, grasped by my perceptors in whatever state they happened to be at that moment, is a condensed example of the basis of arts research. Whatever process is attached to that essence will flourish. It can be used to teach, to heal, to expand, to purify. As I relate these images and ideas, I realize that such statements are usually considered affirmations of faith, unresearchable, inappropriate to behaviorism. They are the domain of the philosopher, not the empiricist, who is practical, material.

In my own work, however, this base of the peak experiences in art is what keeps me honest (when I remember it deeply enough), for it offers the fundamental reference point from which to judge the value of my own and others' research endeavors. I can enjoy the "game playing" of skilled researching and can appreciate a project that handles the rules with ingenuity and sophistication. But at the same time, I know that such work is often self-indulgent and even wasteful, especially during an era wherein "accountability" is the rule and there simply isn't enough support available to condone anything but the most practical of efforts. Thus, the most significant arts research for me is that which offers rigorously systematic information, according to the latest methods and technology, about the joy that the best of artistic endeavors can offer us and the effect it has on other things we do. Amazing technological breakthroughs have occurred in recent years that make the systematic analysis of the natural art experience more possible and judgments of norms in art more accurate. As long as we don't get too carried away with the hardware we are using, we can harness it to do the job more efficiently than ever before.

Unfortunately, we are not living in an age and society where the pursuit of the arts experience is a touchstone to progress. In our world, art is something most people worry about when they wish to demonstrate to others that they are cultured. It is something that is taught our children after they are instructed in the "essentials." It is something that is supported by public and private agencies often with leftover money, with tax write-offs, with token endowments. Consequently, in the back of the minds of many of us who really care about the arts is that energy-draining, frustrating realization that we have to sell what we do to people who do not care to buy, and that what should be accepted as one of the most important activities of people is not wanted very much anymore.

This is a situation that the arts behavioral researcher can help correct by functioning as a professional salesman of sorts. The behavioral researcher sells through skill at providing objective data, through mastery of techniques for measurement and prediction. If the researcher is good at it he or she can legitimately demonstrate through numbers the value of something that should be self-evident. The researcher can offer hard data to justify the worth of an activity that should need no justification other than itself. At the same time, the researcher can provide important information to the artist and teacher about those dimensions of the arts process that are generalizable.

There are many dangers in the applications of the empirical method to art. It is reductive and can deal efficiently only with its own labels. It necessitates a conversion process whereby the real is stripped down and intermittently observed, the observations are labeled, the labels are coded, the codes are grouped, the groups are compared, and relationships are inferred in terms of probabilities. This system has a beauty and clarity of its own. It is efficient and, within its own rules, is very honest. But as each of these steps is taken, the path often leads away from the natural toward the artificial. Considerable energy must be expended to remain at every step as close to the real, the authentic as possible. Otherwise, the empirical approach degenerates to an intricate exercise in the manipulation of jargon and numbers.

Researchers owe it to themselves and to the art form they are studying to resist the hazards of the method selected for study. Inept studies do great damage if they are published and accepted as the rule. Frequently, those who know the method don't know the arts and vice versa. But, even with such liabilities, the scientific approach can contribute a great deal to an understanding of the two principal questions presented earlier, and to the selling of the arts experience to our society.

II. Research Strategy in Theatre

Research Training

I consider myself first a theatre artist, a stage director, and second a teacher-researcher. I learned research methodology relatively late in my formative training and only after I had considerable experience on the stage. I had no research courses *per se* in undergraduate school, no direct methodology instruction except in the methods of acting and directing in front of a real audience. Some theory courses were scattered here and there that occasionally generated some interest, but these were exceptions. The feel of conducting a systematic investigation and reporting it according to refined conventions was almost totally foreign to me. Friends in psychology and math were taking statistics and design courses as juniors and seniors; I was relieved that I didn't have to go through that. I was spending my days in performance classes and my evenings in rehearsal, for the most part, and had little time or interest in other things.

When I got into graduate school and had to write a thesis that qualified as an original research activity with generalizable conclusions, I had no idea what to do. Research, for me, was an activity that had some connection with reconstructing past events and searching for patterns in plays. In my second graduate year, I was fortunate to be introduced to empirical methodology by an expert and was spoon-fed through an experimental thesis study. I learned much about the techniques through doing, but "research" was still an awesome word with an intimidating mystique to it. It had little intrinsic worth but was endured in order to obtain the degree. At the same time, however, some glimmer of the purpose of research as a method of providing answers to significant questions was coming through by osmosis.

It was not until I had been in the field a few years after receiving the Ph.D. that the potential contributions of solid research occurred to me, and only after I became part of a research team. Now, after some ten years of in-service training in running graduate research programs in theatre, I realize that my personal educational experiences in theatre are the rule. For the most part, the people conducting theatre research today, writing grant proposals, acting as agency consultants, running graduate programs, publishing articles, come from pretty much the background that I did. And our students today are going through pretty much the same experiences.

Further, in theatre most graduate students pursuing a doctorate drop out before degree-granting, and those who do understand research well enough to get through the dissertation seldom do any more of it. There are only a handful of reliably productive, empirical theatre researchers in the field today who are genuinely equipped to counsel the researchers of tomorrow. On the optimistic side, there are more than there were ten years ago, and their projects and publications are more relevant to students, audiences, and artists. But widespread impact on the field has yet to be made by the theatre researcher.

I doubt seriously that much theatre research would be done at all if it were not necessary to getting the doctorate or considered by university administrators as evidence of productivity. The theatre practitioner looks at everything he or she does as a kind of experimentation that deals intuitively with norms and predictions. That kind of experimentation attracted him or her to the theatre in the first place. The other kind, the one that deals with variable relationships, factors, confidence levels, and often defines worth in terms of numbers, is not natural to the inclinations of the typical, competent, sensitive theatre artist. It is often antithetical.

On the other hand, for truly productive behavioral research to occur in the theatre, it must be supervised by the artist-researcher — the project director or principal investigator whose training is first in theatre and second in research methods. An experiential background in theatre is mandatory. Evidence of artistic accomplishment as practitioner or theorist is crucial. Under those circumstances, the one running the project knows the problem deeply and intimately and has the right background to hold onto questions important to the field. If it were the other way around, a raft of interesting methodological work could be done with very little relevance to those two questions of essence and effect presented earlier. The problem in our field is that there are very few who can combine the principal knowledge of the insides of the art with the scientific method. Even though this is the case, *future theatre research should be directed principally by the artist-researcher who can demonstrate a mature understanding of his or her field first, and a grasp of the fundamentals of scientific methodology second.*

The Team Approach

The research team is the most workable model for systematic theatre study. In it, there is a minimum of three senior staff: the director who is the artist-researcher referred to above, the social-science specialist (psychologist, sociologist, education-learning theorist, curriculum expert), and the design-statistics expert. Each member of the team must know enough about the others' fields to converse intelligently in the language of that discipline. Each, however, is independently responsible for his specialized contribution to the project in all phases from preliminary theorizing to design to execution to data analysis to write-up. Each could have junior researchers (graduate students, if the project is contracted through a university) who are responsible for specific tasks and who also interact with all others on all levels and in all project phases.

This team approach generates an excitement and momentum that can lend vitality to the process of conducting research. It further presents a model very familiar and comfortable to the theatre artist, who is used to preparing productions for audiences. In the theatre, the director does not design the sets, lights, costumes himself, if he can help it. The director hopes for specialist-artists who will lend their creative skills to evolve a production concept that realizes the script. The director should not be expected to be an expert in lighting design or set construction, although he or she must know enough about them to coordinate successfully the creative energies of the production team. The final product, the show itself, must present a *gestalt*, a unified entity built from all constituent contributions of the various specialists whose work has been appropriately orchestrated to serve the play. This is a direct analog to the team function in theatre research.

In our doctoral program in theatre at Florida State, we have attempted to use this model whenever appropriate to dissertation projects. It has produced a horizontal training situation rather than the usual vertical doctoral dissertation experience where the student becomes the autonomous, self-sufficient expert in a significant but narrow area of inquiry. We turn out few specialists. Rather, many of our students are busy taking courses in computer usage, educational psychology, and research methods in diverse fields. They are badgering graduate students in other areas to serve as consultants on their projects. Their results, while not always lasting contributions to posterity, are usually relevant and practical. And they are not isolated from the current research issues and techniques of other fields.

Few theatre researchers know enough about the subtleties of statistical method or the latest computer packages to make the best choices without help anyway. Further, they must solicit professional assistance from the social scientist who knows the dimensions of his or her field. But if the research is aimed at the theatrical experience, if the search is for more substantive information about that gift the theatre can bestow and its impact on life, then the theatre specialist should direct the work. He or she should keep the team as close to the natural as possible in order to provide answers that are related to key questions rather than to interesting methods.

Disseminating Findings

I recently presented a paper on a program concerning empirical research at the Southeastern Theatre Conference in Memphis. I spoke on the history and applications of a content-analysis technique developed for the study of dramatic improvisations. Counting the panel of four, there were about a dozen people in the room and three of those were my students.

This situation can be explained in part by the fact that many other performance-oriented panels were going on simultaneously at a regional conference in a geographic area that is not known particularly for interest in systematic arts research. Such low attendance, however, is typical; it demonstrates that *most theatre arts teachers and practitioners do not understand and are not interested in research* enough to attend panels on it if there are other things to do.

Even on the national-conference level, panels on theatre research are attended mainly by researchers. They are often self-serving sessions wherein individuals present technical papers to other individuals who are interested in presenting technical papers. Certainly the high-level exchange of research techniques and findings among scientists is essential to any field of inquiry. But the people for whom much of the research is done, the artists and teachers who can benefit from rigorous, scientific study and who can put the findings to direct and practical use, do not usually get the message.

A similar problem exists with published research materials. In my field, there are certain journals that publish technical studies and others that appeal to a popular readership. Seldom do the twain meet. My major research reports have been published in *Speech Monographs, Quarterly Journal of Speech,* and *Empirical Research in Theatre.* The first two are not really arts publications but rather are sponsored by the Speech Communication Association of America. They are quarterlies of quality but do not have a wide readership of those people who are teachers and practitioners of theatre. The last publication is relatively new, published usually once a year, very specialized, with a very small readership. Other journals, *Speech Teacher, Educational Theatre Journal, Children's Theatre Review, Secondary School Theatre Journal,* for example, publish empirical research articles infrequently for a variety of reasons related to editorial policy, lack of quality material available, and readership interest.

One of the major rationales for this condition (which is not unique to theatre) is that reporting behavioral research necessitates a technical language in order to present information with accuracy. Such writing in turn demands a mastery of the language on the part of the reader. To the enlightened, research style is a shortcut to understanding; to the uninitiated, it is incomprehensible.

Thus we encounter a basic problem in the entire field of arts measurement research: The most relevant of findings, the most beneficial work, the most significant breakthroughs in arts research can be buried in technical journals and hidden in panel presentations, so that it is never put into practice by the teacher and artist. Some attempts to aid in the dissemination of practical findings have helped. ERIC, CEMREL, and the JDR 3rd publications[1] for example, have improved the situation somewhat, but this difficulty is overwhelming in its proportions. *Some kind of delivery system is needed to get the best information in accurate but understandable form to the people who can get the most mileage out of it.* This need must be given careful attention over the next decade.

The situation calls for an arts organ, beautifully packaged, highly publicized, nationally distributed, which includes research information on all arts areas. Articles should be based upon the most rigorous and useful research studies reported in technical journals, rewritten to be understood by the widest possible readership of artists and teachers. Although I am very apprehensive of the dangers of hard-sell popularizing and oversimplification that can so easily distort and overstate, I am advocating a combination *Reader's Digest/Psychology Today* of the arts. Somehow the best arts research of the future must be delivered properly.

III. Future Research in Theatre

In the period between January, 1965, and May, 1975, seventy-nine measurement studies directly related to theatre were reported in the form of journal articles, masters' theses, doctoral dissertations, and conference papers.[2] These projects may be divided broadly into two categories: those that analyze the relationship of variables *within* the theatrical universe (such as the Miller and Bahs study, which attempts to discover how a stage director's preconceived expectations of a character influences actors' performances),[3] and those that attempt to demonstrate the relationship between some dimension of the theatrical experience and something *outside* of it (such as the Koenig and Seamon study, which correlates scores on a cognitive complexity test with ratings of acting ability).[4] A large majority of these studies are of the former type.

There seem to be few trends in the focus of this research. Topics vary tremendously. An individual researcher pursues an investigation through one or two projects; then the work seems to evaporate. Occasionally, a method generates enough interest to be used in a few studies, but then it disappears. About the only broad topic that has emerged over the last ten years with enough regularity to constitute any trend of interest concerns the effect of the theatrical experience upon children. Thirteen of the seventy-nine theatre measurement projects involve children. Most of these may be classified in the "outside" category mentioned above.

It is unfortunate that more follow-up has not occurred in theatre measurement studies in the last decade. But at least some hint of a concerted effort is indicated by the concern for the effect of the dramatic experience upon the child. We must build upon this interest in the next ten years. This is not to say that systematic inquiry into the theatre should be restricted to its effects upon populations under the age of twelve. But if we are faced with funding priorities at a time when there is very little money for arts research, we must be selective. Funds should go to projects for children if only on the grounds that the child of today is the art maker and appreciator of tomorrow. Related to those two basic research questions presented at the outset of this paper, *we must find efficient ways of providing the deepest artistic enjoyment for our children on the widest scale and must study how this experience shapes them.* This research should be conducted by a team and reported in a form that is understandable and available to the largest possible readership.

Before we can study with assurance how the art experience affects other processes, we must know more about how it works within itself. This is especially true of research devoted to the theatre and youngsters. And yet most studies in this area have not been inside the dramatic context because of the pressure from outside for accountability. In order to justify drama training as a regular curricular activity for children, researchers have devoted themselves to demonstrating its value within the larger educational context. This means that its worth must be measured in the observable effect it has upon other things. Experience with theatre must be viewed as an independent variable that brings about changes in such dependent variables as reading proficiency or "socialization" or "communication."

This classic research model is the rule in arts measurement studies, but it is problematic for two crucial reasons. First, it forces the artist-researcher to define the yield of the arts experience *not in itself as a thing to be desired for the pure joy of it,* but rather only as it becomes a tool for achieving other goals. More important, *not enough systematic information is available about the theatrical experience per se to permit much sophistication in considering it as cause for change in other areas of human behavior.* This situation suggests the need for a great deal of of internal research to be done within the art form itself before its implications in a larger educational context can be reliably ascertained.

In practice, this situation often manifests itself in the following ways. A doctoral student in creative dramatics (improvisational drama with the child as participant) is looking for a dissertation topic that will help justify the value of his or her specialization, offer hard data, and provide a more active research experience than writing a history or critical analysis of literature. The student struggles through some courses in design, statistics, and educational theory; then realizes after a while that he or she has to design an experiment that treats creative dramatics as one variable, as a presumed cause for some significant change in the behavior of the children to whom this one variable is introduced. The student learns about controls, sampling, generalizing; chooses the area of change to be studied and looks for tests for it. Creative dramatics — a complex, multi-varied universe it itself; an interactional matrix of Gordian intricacy — is simply labeled the independent variable and left at that — *even though little systematic information about it is available in the first place.* No wonder most studies of this nature provide results of little significance. The fact is that we must devote much more energy to finding out how creative dramatics works; to discovering effective and ineffective instructional techniques; and to ascertaining which background factors influence relationships within it. We must do this first or the results of our work relating it to other things will be invalid.

Consider also studies that attempt to demonstrate the effects of children's audience experiences on other things. Meticulous work is done on research design and testing. Factors that could influence the targeted relationship are carefully filtered out and controlled. Great attention is paid to all details except one: *the performance itself.* I have seen it happen more than once; the show presented to the kids who are being tested to see if their audience experience influences other behaviors is undramatic and boring. How could it motivate anything but the urge to avoid this kind of experience in the future? Whether or not it is all that awful by critical standards, the fact remains that we have little scientific information about how variables *within* the universe of performance affect children of different backgrounds. The state of systematic and generalizable knowledge in our field is primitive. We have no business dealing with anything but basics.

Given, then, that our work should be centered on children's behavior within the theatrical set, it might be useful to consider such activity in two categories that view the child: (1) as *doer* or active participant, and (2) as *observer* or audience. In both cases, in order to provide the basic information needed, *considerable effort should be devoted to developing unobtrusive, systematic observation techniques.* We must develop ways of collecting information about the child as doer and observer that will not destroy the reality of the experience. Some attempts have already been made to find ways of doing this, but they have been sporadic and frequently unsuccessful.

My own work over the past eight years provides an illustration of the attempt to evolve a systematic observation procedure for the research category of the child as active participant. It also demonstrates how much help the arts researcher can receive from parallel work in the social sciences.

In 1968, I met Professor Brian Sutton-Smith, head of the Developmental Psychology program at Teachers College, Columbia University, and an expert in the field of children's play activities and games. We met principally because of Brian's interest in spontaneous dramatic play activities of children and my recognition that improvisations had become a very important element, not only in creative dramatics and children's theatre, but also in adult actor training. We were both working at Columbia with graduate students interested in behavioral research methods and theatre; thus we decided to involve ourselves and our students as a research team to investigate improvisation and its effects.

A literature search disclosed an almost total lack of systematic, observational data on improvisations, even though claims had been made concerning behavior norms and positive effects of the experience on both child development and actor training. We felt strongly that, before the growth implications of this subject matter could be studied with accuracy, some systematic account of what people do naturally while involved in an improvisational situation was essential. Once a method was developed to discover the natural behavior patterns of the improvisation, we could begin to construct a realistic picture of age and sex norms, for example, and could thus ascertain empirically whether textbook and teacher expectations had anything at all to do with real behavior. Further, we could begin to correlate improvisation norms not only with organismic variables but also with test scores on other measures like creativity tests.

We decided to start by watching real-life improvisations in creative dramatics classes instructed according to the most widely used format and techniques. Our goal was to take as much time as necessary with our observations so that an inventory of dramatic behaviors could evolve naturally, based on authentic behavior rather than on some *a priori*, theoretical opinions. An exhaustive list of variables was sought that could be collapsed into factors later. Fortunately, the university provided a space that was ideal to our needs. Fifteen of us in a sound-proofed area could observe classes through one-way mirrors and listen via microphones and speakers. We could chat during our observation sessions, argue about terminology, reinforce or dispute opinions while actually observing the behaviors in question without contaminating them. This phase of our project took almost one year.

In order to evolve categories of actual, observable behavior that could be spotted and counted with accuracy and then compared with other, relatively hard measures of the same system, around fifty variables were eventually reduced to eight categories that have been used in all our studies to date.[5] An efficient means for preserving actual improvisations by children was needed, a way of recording this behavior so that it could be coded accurately according to our categories. Thus we began to experiment with videotaping.

While evolving the instrument, we also were concerned with the question of uniform kinds of behavior samples to be analyzed. A scenario for the videotaped improvisations was created that gave subjects the opportunity to exhibit an adequate variety of the types of behaviors characteristically presented by improvisors. In this case, we went to the literature of creative drama and improvisation to find theoretical models for our task. Most texts suggest an inductive progression leading from very simple, individual improvisational tasks to more complex; and eventually to full-story dramatization, or "polished" improvs. They further imply that a fundamental skill to be mastered — one that by definition separates dramatic behavior from other activities — is the ability to react to something imaginary as if it exists. It is believed that, as long as this active reaction to, and use of, imaginary elements is present, the event is dramatic. And, as long as the activity is not completely programmed — if the tasks permit spontaneous behavior— then the event is improvisational. From these theoretical guidelines we developed improvisational premises presented uniformly to hundreds of children over the past seven years, from which we have been able to provide the field with some meaningful information.

As we became more involved in this project, we discovered that our line of research paralleled that of an entire school of social inquiry called *content analysis,* defined by Paisley as "a phase of information-processing in which communication content is transformed, through objective and systematic application of categorization rules, into data that can be summarized and compared."[6] We began to think of our work as a dimension of the scientific analysis of communication messages. A review of content-analysis literature revealed a large body of theory dating back to the turn of the century[7] marked by an influx of activities over a twenty-year period ending in the mid-1950s. Such researchers as Harold Lasswell, Irving Janis, Bernard Berelson, and Abraham Kaplan contributed greatly to the form of the discipline during this time. Now content analysis is being used extensively in sociology, anthropology, general communications, and political science;[8] it provides an extensive methodological bibliography, including an entire quarterly; and it offers computer programs and scanning techniques designed specifically for its use.[9]

The parallels between our work and the content-analysis discipline are immediately evident. First, the normative data of improvisational dramatic behavior we sought could be found only through the systematic behavioral analysis of the improvisation itself. In 1952, Berelson defined content analysis as a "research technique for the objective, systematic and quantitative description of the manifest content of communication."[10] Second, the basic methods of content analysis require a progressive sub-categorization procedure of the communication sample; *i.e.,* dividing the message into categories (major subsets), then defining the recording unit (segment of content to be placed in a given category), and finally affixing the system of enumeration or method of associating numbers with units in categories. Our work necessitated isomorphic analyses of the improvisation by recording it on videotape, dividing it into eight categories, defining units within each, and selecting the manner for coding these units numerically. Most important, content-analysis theory has clearly articulated the potentials and limits of inference-making and has provided models directly applicable to the use of the "Inventory of Dramatic Behavior" — the name we eventually gave our instrument. The content-analysis approach has been beneficial to our work. It might be of value to researchers interested in similar questions in other arts areas.

In sum, I have suggested that research priorities must focus on studies within the theatrical universe concerning children's experiences as doers or observers. Further, methods for the unobtrusive and systematic observation of natural behavior are badly needed in order to provide information antecedent to evaluating the effects of the dramatic experience upon other aspects of existence. Useful models from the social sciences can contribute meaningfully to this task.

IV. Some Final Considerations

It might be helpful to condense some of the main ideas of this paper into a few basic criteria for evaluating research grants in theatre over the next ten years. These guidelines might also apply to arts proposals in general. In this context, the following five qualities should be looked for.

Relevance to the Arts Experience

The farther away from the actual participational experience of art, the more artificial the project is. Look for studies that directly incorporate the arts experience as the primary focus of research. In a field like theatre and children, it is wise to look for projects that study relationships within the experience itself. Empirical technique tends to pull researchers away from art toward less-variable contexts; it tends to impose its limitations upon the thing to be studied. Consequently, evaluate projects on their relevance to the artistic activity first and foremost.

Simplicity

The simplest, most basic questions should be asked and the most uncluttered methodologies employed in research. Often, in the attempt to answer a simple question, a Rube Goldberg design is constructed that in turn necessitates a set of overly complicated statistical adjustments. Equally as often, researchers become enamored with methods that force them to fashion baroque research questions. The best research in the arts is very simple in statement. It always gets complex in the execution anyway. Therefore, look for proposals that read simply and deal with basic questions.

Mastery of Tools of Scientific Inquiry

A research proposal in the arts must instill in the reader confidence that the researchers have command of the values and techniques of their method. This comes not only from a past record of accomplishments in the *vitae* of the researchers, but also from the research statement itself. Traditional social-scientific criteria of objectivity, systematization, and generalizability are always pertinent to proposals — even the softest, narrowest case studies — for they protect the project from inaccuracy and bias. Projects in the arts often require special skill and understanding of research technique because of the nature of the subject area itself and the difficulty of applying empirical procedures to it. This is one reason that the research team model discussed earlier is a workable approach since it combines subject and method expertise in the working unit. However this problem is approached, the proposal must evidence a comprehensive grasp of the assets and liabilities of the methods employed. In studies that attempt to generate methods, this requirement is even more crucial if only because others are likely to use these tools in later work.

Naturalness of Context

Whatever the subject and method, the environment wherein the measurements are made must be as close to real life as possible. Often it is necessary to include an initial laboratory phase that permits more precise controls before the field study sequence. But it must be remembered, especially in arts research, that the more artificial the environment, the less applicable the findings.

I have seen too many empirical theatre studies in which this principle was not considered vigorously enough. Thus the contexts of the projects were so contaminated by gadgets or so removed from the usual, natural, authentic arts situations that applicabilities to real-life environments were tenuous at best. As a rule, audience analysis studies should be conducted in the usual audience environment; studies of performers should be made in a natural performance area, whatever that may be. If it is impossible to do this because of measurement procedures, alteration of the natural contexts should be made most grudgingly.

Cautious Generalizability

Obviously, proposals must be justified upon their applicability to the largest possible section of humanity. The results must generalize to the largest possible universe. On the other hand, the pressures of accountability often force researchers to attempt to generalize past the level of knowledge of their subject. They either try to relate findings to an audience larger than is appropriate or to demonstrate relationships to areas too far removed from the major focus of inquiry. As mentioned earlier, I advocate a relatively conservative point of view that values more careful, basic, "closer-to-home" research that is more generalizable to *intra-* than *inter*relationships, at least at this point in the development of the science of art. In considering the generalizability of a proposal, the limitations of existing knowledge must be weighed against the attempts to provide information relevant to the largest possible context.

In closing, I am once again reminded of Mamyko and my experience with her in San Francisco. Her gift to me calls to mind other moments when a touch of peace entered my life through art. I see Alfred Lunt's ritual assassination in Peter Brook's production of *The Visit*. I recall the magic of Brook's *Marat/Sade* with those bizarre steel-blue and gray-tinted tableaux set on deep-brown, rough-hewn wooden planks against the white tile walls. I remember the faces of children watching a show at FSU possessed with such total concentration that there is no tension, no conflict; all is direct and spontaneous for a tiny moment of their lives. I am convinced, once again, that the purpose of arts research is to approach an understanding of these moments and what they do to us.

An incompatibility has often been argued between art and science. There is some cause for the artist to view the scientist with suspicion when methods for analysis contaminate the reality of art or findings miss the appropriate issues of the arts experience. These mistakes have happened in theatre research as much if not more than in other areas of arts study. But, if we believe that systematic tools of inquiry have steadily improved, and the careful applications of them to the appropriate dimensions of art can lead us more efficiently to that essence beyond even thought, then we have an obligation to pursue scientific research in the arts with vigor. We have an obligation to every artist, every teacher of art, every person who is touched in any way by the arts experience. At the same time, we have an obligation to understand the limits and pitfalls of our approach.

P. D. Ouspensky, a scientist (abstract mathematics) and a philosopher of tremendous scope and impact, was a man who, like Einstein, could perceive the compatibility of art and science on the highest level of thought. In *A New Model of the Universe,* he states:

> Art is based on emotional understanding, on the feeling of the Unknown which lies behind the visible and the tangible, and on creative power, the power, that is, to reconstruct in visible or audible forms the artist's sensations, feelings, visions and moods, and especially a certain fugitive sensation, which is in fact the feeling of the harmonious interconnection and oneness of *everything* and the feeling of the "soul" of things and phenomena. Like science and philosophy, art is a definite *way of knowledge.* The artist, in creating, learns much that he did not know before. But an art which does not reveal mysteries, which does not lead to the sphere of the Unknown, does not yield new knowledge, is a parody of art, and still more often it is not even a parody, but simply a commerce or an industry.[11]

The best scientific research in theatre uses one "way of knowledge" to help us understand another. It makes it easier for artist and audience to learn. It helps artist and audience to share "the mysteries of the Unknown," and "the feeling of the oneness of everything."

Tallahassee, Florida
May 1976

FOOTNOTES

[1]See *Final Report, Educational Laboratory Theatre Project, 1966-1970,* 4 vols. (St. Louis, Missouri: CEMREL, Inc., 1970); and Robert Stake, ed., *Evaluating the Arts in Education* (Columbus, Ohio: Charles E. Merrill Publishing Co., 1975).

[2]Extracted from three unpublished bibliographies: "Bibliography of Empirical Research in Theatre to April, 1971," prepared by George Gunkle, San Fernando Valley College, for the Empirical Research Interest Group of the American Theatre Association; "Addendum" to the aforementioned bibliography, updated by Gunkle to September, 1971; and "Empirical Research in Theatre: A Checklist

of Bibliographical References," prepared by Antoinette V. Zabaldo, Florida State University, as an update to the Gunkle bibliographies.

[3]Keith A. Miller and Clarence W. Bahs, "Director Expectancy and Actor Effectiveness," *Empirical Research in Theatre,* Vol. 4, No. 1 (Summer 1974), pages 60-74.

[4]Fredrick Koenig and Jerral Seamon, "Cognitive Styles and Dramatic Acting Ability," *Perceptual and Motor Skills,* Vol. 36, No. 2 (April 1973), pages 561-62.

[5]See Gil Lazier and Brian Sutton-Smith, "Assessment of Role Induction and Role Involvement in Creative Drama (abstract)," *Research in Education* (October 1970); Gil Lazier, Brian Sutton-Smith, and Douglas A. Zahn, "A Systematic Analysis of Developmental Differences in Dramatic Improvisational Behavior," *Speech Monographs,* Vol. 38, No. 3 (1971), pages 155-65; Gil Lazier, Brian Sutton-Smith, E. Joseph Karioth, and Douglas A. Zahn, "The Inventory of Dramatic Behavior: A Content Analysis Technique for Creative Dramatics," a monograph published by Florida State University through HEW funds (1-D-063) for the 1972 ASSITEJ International Congress (36 pages); Gil Lazier, Douglas A. Zahn, and E. Joseph Karioth, "Dramatic Behavior Norms of Florida Children," *Empirical Research in Theatre,* Vol. 3, No. 1 (1973), pages 41-70; Brian Sutton-Smith, Gil Lazier, and Douglas A. Zahn, "Developmental Stages in Dramatic Improvisation," *American Psychological Association Proceedings,* Vol. 79 (1971), pages 421-23; and Brian Sutton-Smith and Gil Lazier, "Psychology and Drama," *Empirical Research in Theatre,* Vol. 1, No. 1, (1971), pages 38-47.

[6]Cited in Ole R. Holsti, *Content Analysis for the Social Sciences and Humanities* (Menlo Park, California: Addison-Wesley Publishing Co., Inc., 1969), page 3.

[7]See F. E. Barcus, "Communications Content: Analysis of the Research, 1900-1958." Unpublished Ph.D. Diss., University of Illinois, 1959.

[8]Holsti, page 21, explains that these three disciplines account for seventy-five percent of all empirical studies in content analysis: sociology-anthropology 27.7%, communications 25.9%, and political science 21.5%.

[9]Programs currently in wide use are included as part of the "General Inquirer" system originally developed at the Laboratory for Social Relations at Harvard.

[10]Bernard Berelson, *Content Analysis in Communication Research* (Glencoe, Illinois: Free Press, 1952), page 18.

[11]P. D. Ouspensky, *A New Model of the Universe* (New York: Vintage Books, 1971), page 33.

Alma Hawkins

Exploration of the Need for Research in Selected Areas of Dance

Research in dance, both experimental and experiential, that contributes to new understandings and the scholarly literature has been limited. One explanation for the lack of scholarly work may well be the fact that only recently has dance been recognized as a discipline in higher education. Not until 1962, when UCLA established a separate department of dance with B.A. and M.A. degree programs, did this discipline have an opportunity to develop along with the other arts.

During recent years, as other departments of dance have been established, the primary concern of leaders has been to develop degree programs that would implement the body of knowledge and allow dance to develop as a performing art. After a decade of this kind of growth, it is important that we now embark on significant research programs that will further understandings about the aesthetic nature of dance and provide an important literature in various areas of the body of knowledge. Such work would enhance our understanding of dance, provide much needed scholarly literature for graduate study, and eventually bring about qualitative changes in the teaching-learning situation at all levels.

Though research is needed in many areas of dance, such as definitive studies in the history of dance, written or visual recording of dance, and kinesiological foundations, I want to discuss two areas of research that are specifically related to the teaching-learning situation. They are concerned with the following:

1. the creative growth of the learner in dance;
2. the development of the body instrument that serves the aesthetic needs of performer-choreographer.

I believe that fuller understanding in these two areas would encourage us to provide teaching-learning environments that would make use of an aesthetic and holistic approach to dance.

ALMA HAWKINS is Chairman of the Department of Dance at the University of California at Los Angeles.

Part 1. Research Concerned with Creative Growth in Dance

A dance work (piece of choreography) presents an externalization or objectification of experience. The progress of choreographing involves the bringing together and transforming of experience into a meaningful entity. The creative process depends on getting in touch with, releasing, and nourishing inner responses in the organism.

We need to know more about the nature of this process. A variety of studies present evidence that the human organism is equipped with two ways of responding and processing information, which really means two ways of "knowing." Research by Sperry, Ornstein, Tart and others suggest that the two hemispheres of the brain serve us in different ways. It is believed that the left hemisphere uses what is referred to as the rational, logical approach and processes information in a linear fashion using language as its means of communication. The right hemisphere is identified with the intuitive, a-rational mode of consciousness and processes information in an holistic manner using a nonverbal means of communication. It appears that the right hemisphere is concerned especially with spatial, qualitative, and movement aspects of experience.

Though the process of responding and acting seems to involve both hemispheres, it is believed that each hemisphere functions as dominant in certain kinds of experience. I believe that an understanding of the two modes of consciousness has real relevance for dance. It would seem that the right hemisphere is deeply involved in the intuitive, imaginative, holistic approach we associate with dance and the arts.

In the early stages of choreographing, the time when the image is evolving and developing, it appears that the organism is using the right hemisphere more than the left. During this period, the choreographer is primarily concerned with abstracting aesthetic qualities, responding with spontaneity and imagination. From this process comes the transforming of experience and the forming of a new entity.

The professional artist is not usually concerned with the nature of this process, but the individual who is responsible for providing the learning environment for dance as a creative experience needs to understand how the organism functions in this kind of a process.

How does one facilitate experiences that make available the inner resources and nourish the creative growth of the individual? How does one assist the student in learning to cut off temporarily his outer orientation, attend to inner sensations, and allow the felt process to take over and guide the selecting and forming of aesthetic elements?

So much of our teaching of choreography has been guided by one of two points of view. One view holds that a good technical preparation enables one to choreograph. Another view supports the idea that creative development comes through sequential problem-solving experiences. Often the teaching process relies upon a highly verbal approach. The creative problem is explained verbally and students are expected to proceed with their work. Frequently, there is little preparation that facilitates "experiencing" at the felt level nor is there understanding of the developmental nature of the learning process that would deepen and enrich the "inner experiencing"—sensory awareness, spontaneity, and imagination.

I believe that the learning process concerned with responding and creating in dance can and should contribute to aesthetic understandings, ability to process information in an intuitive manner, and growth in creating forms that reflect felt life.

I am suggesting that we need in-depth study of this aspect of dance so that the teaching-learning process can be guided by conceptual understandings instead of imitation or trial-and-error procedures.

Research Project I
1. Bring together knowledge that is available in these areas:
   a. the nature of creativity;
   b. the creative process;
   c. two modes of consciousness (brain research);
   d. a metaphor approach to processing information.
2. Clarify the implications of available knowledge for the teaching-learning process in dance.
3. Develop guidelines for learning experiences that include the following:
   a. essential ingredients in the process:
   b. developmental stages in growth.
4. Conduct field research, utilizing the concepts and guidelines established in items 1, 2, and 3.
5. Carry out experimental studies for different age levels; primary grades, middle grades, secondary-school grades and college level.

Questions That Need Answers
Research needs to address itself to such questions as: How does the teacher accomplish the following?
1. Facilitate the movement experiences that enable the learner to increase sensory awareness to external and internal stimuli, to learn to "listen" to inner sensations, to allow movement to be motivated by felt responses, to respond with spontaneity, and to sustain the imaginative process that leads to a synthesis of experience?
2. Adapt concepts and experiencing so that they are appropriate to different development levels?
3. Incorporate conceptual understandings related to aesthetic elements and formed within an "experiential" approach that utilizes the holistic mode of consciousness?
4. Use the verbal process for purposes of reflecting upon and evaluating works so that the creative atmosphere and the creative

work is enhanced. How can we avoid the judgmental aspects of the linear process that stifle the sense of freedom and spontaneity?

Research Project II

Conduct longitudinal studies in kindergarten through grade twelve in the forming process in dance (composition) in order to do the following:

1. Identify the forming characteristics for each age level;
2. Clarify the innate tendency and the unfolding process in dance.

At the present time, our understanding of the developmental tendency in the creative growth process in forming dances depends entirely upon our teaching experience. We do not have longitudinal studies such as those available in the visual arts (Kellogg, Schaeffer-Simmern, Arnheim) that reveal form characteristics at different age levels.

We need studies that would provide an understanding of what to expect at different growth periods. From this knowledge could come guidelines that would help the teacher provide appropriate and meaningful experiences in creative work.

No doubt the "forming process" in dance has a relationship to the individual's development in perceiving and integrating experiences. But how are these levels of perception and integration reflected in dance? For example, our experience suggests that first dance studies tend to be short and symmetrical in nature; attempts to make a longer study usually result in repetition of movement with little concern for transition. Only later is one able to differentiate and develop the movement patterns.

How helpful it would be to have research that reveals the natural growth tendencies! Teachers could provide appropriate sequencing of creative experiences and would not expect certain levels of competency in composition until the learner had passed through natural growth stages in perceiving and performing.

Part II. Research Concerned with the Development of the Body Instrument

Traditionally, we have tended to think of "technique" as a means of preparing an individual for dancing. In many teaching situations, the learner is presented with specific and varied movement patterns that are thought to contribute to his or her dance competence. A common practice is to demonstrate the "technique" for students to observe and then to try. In this approach, the teacher provides a model that the students attempt to emulate. Corrections are made and the learner tries to make appropriate adjustments in his or her movement.

This method represents an "external" approach to learning. The student tries to "put the movement on his or her body." It is true that after extensive practice, some individuals become beautiful performers; but it is also true that many individuals never get beyond moving in a mechanical, contrived manner that lacks an aesthetic quality.

For the past several years, many students and teachers have had a strong motivation, almost a compulsion, to achieve technical excellence — sometimes without much concern for other aspects of dance. No doubt this desire is related to the current emphasis in our society on technical achievement, as well as the dancer's awareness of the specific need for a competent instrument.

Striving for excellence is a worthy goal, but it would seem that the "striving" should be in a context that relates the movement study to the holistic experience of dance as an expressive art. Movement has potential to be a powerful expressive medium yet we often see classes and concerts where the performance of dancers never rises above a mechanical way of moving. The body may reveal accuracy, but little in the way of aesthetic quality.

There is another approach used by some teachers that directs the learner's attention to "inner experiencing." This way of working aims at heightening kinesthetic awareness. The movement study is concerned with concepts and movement explorations that are acquired through a "discovery" process rather than through imitation. The discovery approach seems to result in understandings that have greater transfer value. Also, this way of working incorporates self-directed responses and spontaneity that seem to relate to and prepare for creative work.

At the present time, the approaches to technical competence vary widely. Often the methods are eclectic, not related very closely to conceptual understandings nor to aesthetic use of movement. I believe that it is possible for us today to make our teaching of dance more effective. The teaching-learning situation in movement study, "technique," should be guided by the best information available. Knowledge does exist in various disciplines that has significant implications for the teaching-learning situation in dance. We need to become aware of this knowledge and its implication. I believe that this kind of study would make it possible for the learner to do the following:

1. develop greater competency in less time;
2. discover the aesthetic quality of movement as an inherent part of technical study;
3. perceive a meaningful relationship between the technical study and the creative, expressive aspects of dance.

Research Project III

1. Bring together knowledge and experience from various disciplines, such as:
   a. scientific study of movement;
   b. perception and the learning process;
   c. creativity;
   d. personal experiences of artist-performers — choreographers and artist-teachers.
2. Clarify the essential ingredients required for the development of

technical competence. Consider the needs related to the following:
 a. the body instrument;
 b. movement skills;
 c. creative use of aesthetic elements in movement study (energy, space, time).
3. Identify the types of experiences needed to achieve the goals in movement competence while keeping in mind the concern for quality and self-directed growth.
4. Identify the physiological and kinesiological concepts and principles that relate to the study of movement and the development of effective performance.
5. Develop guidelines for experiences designed to further the sequential development of movement competence in various areas including these:
 a. awareness of the body-self as an entity with a sense of center, balance, and harmonious relationship of body parts;
 b. understanding of the aesthetic elements and skill in patterning movement that makes effective use of range and variety;
 c. awareness of movement possibilities and skill in performance using approaches that give emphasis to kinesthetic awareness and discovery through self-directed responses and aesthetic use of movement;
 d. building stamina that enables one to achieve the above goals.
6. Conduct field research using the concepts and guidelines established. Include experiential studies for each age level: primary grades, middle grades, secondary-school grades, and college.

Research Project IV

Study the use of videotaping as a means for self-perception in the development of movement skills, and for self-direction in changing movement patterns in relation to understandings and principles.

Comment

The research projects described in this statement will require leadership that has experience and awareness of the broad scope of knowledge relating to the dance process.

One aspect of the project might be a working conference that brings together highly select people from related disciplines as well as dance.

I believe the result of the research projects described in this paper could enhance our understanding of dance as aesthetic experience, clarify concepts that could give direction to the teaching-learning process, and provide depth understandings that could enrich the previous work done in aesthetic education.

Los Angeles, California
June 1976

Linda Fosburg

Arts Councils and Arts Education

Each arts education program that exists adds a new facet to the prism that makes up the field. There seem to be as many definitions to the term "arts education" as there are people who define it. To some it is the exposure of as many children as possible to arts experiences of all kinds within the basic classroom curriculum. To as many others, it is the discrete experience of making art. Still others see the crux of the matter as the presence of an artist in the classroom, imparting his or her particular magic to the children who inevitably must add a dimension to their own perception of his or her art. There are those who advocate the use of cultural institutions for educational programs — either for children or for those who come to the arts as children, the non-culture consumer. And there are those who would foster the pure development of aesthetic or sensory literacy — the supporters of affective learning devoted to whichever available programs may be useful in that elusive and delicate task. Whatever else this diversity of interpretation means, it assures even a casual observer that arts education is a popular, if controversial, issue. Some at closer range might consider arts education as the new darling of the arts industry these days, a new source of money for arts projects with the unimpeachable purpose of enriching the country's youth.

Where in this puzzle of new arts and education alliances do community and state arts councils fit? And more important, how can arts agencies at the state and local levels be most effective in this complex endeavor? Effectiveness in this field for arts councils is in itself a tangled web, dealing less with the tangible product orientation of developing an arts program for a school or the curriculum for a classroom and more with the less-easily measured tasks of raising consciousness, mediating, evaluating, identifying resources, and working between the various constituents. Such a function dovetails with the goals of the other components—the artists, the educators, the institutions—of trying to assure that the constituencies represented are

170   LINDA FOSBURG *is a Consultant to the Associated Councils of the Arts.*

best served; but the emphasis from the arts council perspective must be the overview of the management and administration of the programs.

The paradox for these managers is to become involved enough to be sensitive advocates for the needs and desires of the constituents and, at the same time, to retain an objectivity and perspective that will permit them to discharge such management tasks as development of quality-control criteria, evaluation mechanisms, and allocation of funds. A look at the current situation indicates this dual need. All over the country, in a variety of ways, arts education programs are burgeoning. The energy and diversity of these many programs give substance to the claim made in the unprecedented 1975 public-opinion survey of the arts, *Americans and the Arts,* prepared for Associated Councils of the Arts by the National Research Center of the Arts, and quoted as follows:

> The public feels strongly that cultural opportunities are important for children. Moreover, the public endorses the presentation of the arts and creative activities in the core curriculum, alongside the basics of the educational system. . . . The public also recognizes the importance of an interplay between what happens in the schools and what is available in the community at large, and favors more exposure across the board to cultural events for children.

This desire seems to have been followed by the widespread creation of programs. Perhaps the most dramatic example of a newly developed education program bringing money to the arts and bringing arts programs to millions of children, many of whom have previously not been reached by the arts, is the Artists-in-the-Schools (AIS) Project, funded by the National Endowment for the Arts and administered by state arts agencies across the country. The value of this program, while still evaluated in purely educational terms, has been attested to anecdotally by those who have been involved at arts agencies, in the school system, and, best of all, by the children themselves. One dancer said of his experience in schools: "We feel that we belong there, and we are nourished by the experience." One administrator speaks of a child who was touched by an AIS Program: "This child was in the habit of coming to school two or three days a week, just putting in time. Then we had a sculptor—a guest artist. We gave the child a clump of clay and you would not believe it. The child has really found himself and he has not missed a day of school since." In 1975, the Artists-in-the-Schools Program made available more than $3.5 million, which funded some five thousand programs. This money produced potentially another $3.5 million from local sources, public and private, so that the maximum made available because of this program was $7 million—a substantial sum for a single program in the arts universe. The National Research Center of the Arts tells us that, in 1974, Artists-in-the-Schools accounted for a plurality of 25 percent of project expenditures made to the state arts agencies themselves and 36 percent of funds to schools and school systems. But consider these figures against the $6 billion or so that were allocated in the same year just through the Office of Education.

This kind of reality points toward what must be a continuing dilemma in arts education projects: The arts dollar is but a drop in the bucket in education dollars. How can arts councils with their own scarce resources maximize the effect of the programs and establish the arts as valid pursuits for schoolchildren? One of the keys, attested to by many who have worked with AIS programs and with other programs involving educational systems, is to establish a working relationship with state education departments and local boards of education — by finding political leadership as well as responsive rank-and-file teachers and serving as an organizational voice for arts interests. Functioning between the arts and the schools must take place in a substantive way, with arts councils as advocates at both state and local levels. In terms of effectiveness, channeling funds is the least of their problems. The role must be broader and more commanding than fiscal caretaker. A variety of "ifs" were enumerated in recent congressional testimony by participants about the AIS programs; a list of these articulate the substantive need to be filled:

> If a strong, national effort is mounted to establish the arts as an essential, valid area of learning . . . , if financial support is available . . . , if the quality of the arts remains the first priority . . . , if the public is kept satisfied about the program's worth . . . , if we are effectively organized on all levels and conscious of our direction . . . , if artists are enabled to remain artists, and paid well enough . . . , if the program keeps its goals clear . . . , if we avoid tying up with boards of education . . . , if it continues in the present direction, keeping the focus not just on artists but on the arts, which belong to all the people.

Another approach pointing out a different set of challenges is the Cultural Enrichment Program (CEP) in Washington State, funded by the state legislature for $1,111,000 during the last fiscal year. It is one of the significant outgrowths of a Title III project, quietly picked up by the state in the wake of Title III. It has grown during these past seven years from a small regional program to a statewide offering serving 305 school districts, delivering arts services and rigorously evaluating its own effectiveness as it goes, through the use of written objectives and criteria, classroom preparation weeks in advance of the arts experience itself, and complemented by evaluation forms sent to each teacher after the arts experience. This program has refined its evaluative techniques so far as to have discovered that using the letterhead of the State Superintendent of Schools for the evaluation forms elicits more frank and useful answers than using its own letterhead does. This program has developed an evaluative mechanism. But, if the scant amount of hard data gathered nationwide for evaluation purposes is any indication of the need in arts education programs, here is a challenge to arts councils for those specialized management skills that would develop a broadly useful model. A creditable job of devising perhaps just such an item is currently underway by the Western States Arts Foundation to evaluate the impact of the program from the point of view of teacher, arts administrator, and student. It is an acknowledged fact that, save for this exceptional case, councils have been remiss in developing credible methods for establishment of criteria for evaluation. In fact, no data have been gathered, to our knowledge, about the skills or training in skills of this kind possessed by those who are currently administering arts programs. A few years ago, a singular study funded by the New York State Council on the Arts examined the internal evaluation mechanism of the arts education projects funded by that agency and revealed, not only a widespread misconception within the staff about the amount of money they were allocating with such contracts, but also a stubborn and alarmed resistance by the decision-makers at the agency to such a revealing examination of their own weakness in this area. Another effort was made by a course at the Harvard Business School within the past year to study the evaluation techniques used by arts councils to evaluate all kinds of their own programs. Through questionnaires circulated to several arts agencies, it was revealed that no evaluation mechanisms of any kind had been set up at any of the agencies. On the other hand, some of the active arts education programs, like the AIS and the CEP, have recognized from the outset that evaluation and quality control are two of the critical factors in continued success. In addition, there is the political reality that data can be useful as a fund-raising tool among local or state private sources, as well as in the public arena in competing for tax dollars from education budgets and from other government departments.

The Cultural Voucher Program (CVP) in New York City, funded largely through a demonstration grant from HEW and supplemented with money from the New York State Council on the Arts, has seen already — although it is still in the early days of its life — the potential significance of vouchers in providing services to traditional non-culture users and in decentralizing the allocation of public funds. Such allocation would direct money away from the traditional consumers of arts funds — such as large, urban institutions — and redirect it to areas where there are few cultural programs existing. While this whole situation may seem remote to the arts education field, in fact arts education programs could provide fundable entities. But an astute manager would be needed to bring all the parts of such a situation together successfully.

The Cultural Voucher Program provides a model of the kind of program that might work. Through a careful selection of museums on the one hand and community organizations on the other, this program has already demonstrated significant innovation in offerings of quality for the newly developing constituency (such as making films on drug addiction, learning professional museum skills in order to hang their own shows, etc.) and in developing the constituency itself. Given a good choice of community organizations coupled with adequate salary stipends and program funds, a cultural voucher program — really a gift certificate for community organizations redeemable at the selected institutions — can reach potentially hundreds of thousands of non-culture users in a way denied to traditional educational programs of museums or to program-development-oriented voucher programs. This could mean adding a new dimension of public accountability by arts programs. This program, in contrast to the AIS and the CEP, does not deal with the traditional educational organizations nor with traditional education programs of cultural institutions at all, in recognition of the fact that the target group of community organizations has consistently received severely limited services from these educational organizations and programs. But the success of CVP, as informally evaluated in its early stages by one of its administrators, will depend on the third-party role played by the administrative component. This role is to work out details of the relationship between the community organizations and the institutions, helping the users themselves to develop programs suitable for their needs. This charge parallels the still sometimes uneasy alliance between the arts community and the educational community that prevails in the AIS program and points to a likely role for the arts councils to play. The administrators of the CVP, in fact, look forward to its management's becoming a continuing arts council function after this initial demonstration project is over.

Still another type of arts education program blending the innovative use of institutions with the penetration of the traditional educational system is the Cultural Education Collaborative (CEC) in Massachusetts, a large-scale attempt to pass new legislation that would create funds for a projected alliance between schools and cultural institutions. In the intentionally non-technical language the Collaborative uses to explain the bill to potential supporters, "Schools don't have animals, actors, dancers, or collections of paintings. Zoos, theaters, dance groups, and museums do. This act will make these things available to all the schools across the state." Since support of cultural institutions has long been a major concern of arts councils, an act such as this would be a natural one for arts council support and management. This program, as now conceived, would concentrate on intensive months of preparation for exposure through class curricula to programs at institutions, on the development of new programs at the institutions that are suited to the needs and interests of the students, on the purchase of these educational services by the schools, and on intensive follow-up also through the classroom curricula. This proposed legislation constitutes a high-level effort to remove the traditional visit to a cultural institution from the vacuum in which it often occurs and transform it into a total aesthetic experience for the user. The typical cultural visit has been cynically and provocatively described by some as no more valuable than a way of putting school buses to use; a program bringing more benefit to the transportation constituency than to the cultural one. The CEC points again, as have the other programs examined so far, to the need for expanded and improved communication between the arts and the education constituencies. One of the answers this pilot project has found is to deal with collaboratives of school districts that exist in any state. The administrator of CEC joins many arts administrators who feel strongly that arts education projects of all kinds must be administered from the arts side; with utmost sensitivity to the educational *constituency's* priorities and needs, to be sure, but with emphasis on the artistic quality that the arts people can provide. It is strongly felt by some arts administrators, in conjunction with this point, that quality control criteria be established and maintained by the arts community, and that the arts councils would be likely agencies to perform these functions.

The management and political advocacy skills required just for these existing programs alone are legion, and they do not begin to deal with the scope of arts education programs that might exist. Given the growing professionalism in the field of arts management, the development of these highly specialized skills should be incorporated into the preparation of arts administrators. Such skills as quantitative analysis, decision analysis, cost-benefit analysis, survey research, and linear programming would be necessary in order to provide the tools for development of criteria and evaluation methods. Extra-academic groundwork has already been done in management areas, such as the development of nonprofit accounting procedures, described in ACA's publication, *Financial Management of the Arts.*

Concomitant to this training must be the efficient and economical use of these skills by the arts councils. They might look to "modular management" as a solution: installing and removing management components to deal with given issues as they become germane. This might range from working with education departments to developing quality-control criteria. If ongoing management in an area seemed appropriate, fitting it into the structure of a council would be most economical and effective to determine once it had been part of the council's operation in this *ad hoc* relationship. In certain cases, an arts education generalist might become a long-term staff member to supervise the various arts education programs and personnel, and to identify and serve evolving needs for management modules.

Good management has always meant a large dose of good politics. Many arts councils have always played a political role, thrust as they are into the annual competition for funds from their state or local governments, not to mention their willingness to function as advocates for arts-related legislation locally, statewide, and federally. This function as political advocate could easily expand in a systematic way to include a specialized advocacy in arts education. Just finding and dealing with the responsive leadership in a given education department could be a full-time job for somebody. And doing just that might be crucial to the effective functioning of an arts program, as some of the existing programs have already discovered. The Cultural Enrichment Program in Washington State, because it started regionally and quite informally with a small amount of money, was able to pick out a single representative from each of the more than 300 school districts involved. And because of this clear line of communication, it has been able to cut through a major bureaucracy.

Arts councils could perform a mediator's role, not only between the arts community and the education community or any other group served (like the community organizations in New York City that form the constituency of the Cultural Voucher Program and consist of such diverse non-culture users as a group of prison inmates and ex-offenders, an Hellenic-American group, and a collection of senior citizens organizations in Queens), but even within the arts community itself. A controversy is growing between the value of arts education programs as a source of support for artists and as a source of enrichment of children. Such conflicts could be eliminated through adequate communication. And this function the arts council — the involved yet objective third party — might provide.

Advocate, evaluator, administrator — such seem to be the likely roles for arts councils to assume. Serving these functions, a council would surely have found a significant role to play in maximizing the impact of small amounts of money and in minimizing conflicts. At the same time, councils could help in the development of future programs as well as facilitating the operation of existing ones. Think only of the role that television, even public television, has never played in sensory education, or even less-elusive arts experiences. When pressured by the cognitive gaps in preschool learning, public television came up with innovative children's programming, such as the shows produced by the Children's Television Workshop. Yet these shows themselves are of questionable value in reaching the hard-to-reach. Some halting steps have been taken by the programs of National Instructional Television Service in the development of their *Images and Things* series and the *Inside Out* series; and much more could be done through such a network as the community arts councils, investigating and perhaps even generating funds with their public television stations, especially in the larger cities. Similarly, there might be a whole unexplored world in the home-instruction materials, as curriculum development becomes increasingly sophisticated.

Still another area is environmental design. Such government agencies as Redevelopment Authorities could become actively involved in design schemes, and possibly could provide additional sources of revenue for program development. To plan for expansion into such areas, an arts council would be a likely strategist. *Citygames*, a book prepared by the Children's Museum of Boston for the Boston 200, the Bicentennial agency of the city, provides a worthy model to follow, along with the Discovery Project, an architectural experiment being carried out in a public high school in Cambridge, Massachusetts.

In addition, we must not overlook the role of arts education projects as possible crisis-intervention solutions in racially troubled areas. The magnet-school programs being tried in Boston and other cities, based on the principle of matching predominantly white schools with schools in black areas because of the high quality of the education being offered there — an attempt to have quality outweigh racial strife — have been a focus for the Cultural Education Collaborative programs and have been mutually beneficial to the Collaborative and to racial harmony.

Even the blatantly political goal of putting arts representatives, perhaps arts council chairmen or executive directors, on the state education boards or on other strategic public boards, might be a suitable function for an arts council to assume as the plot thickens between the arts and education communities.

This matrix of concerns gives rise to an identifiable group of questions about potentially valuable research areas relating to the role of state and community arts councils in arts education.

1. What is the ideal structural relationship between arts councils (both state and community), state departments of education, local school boards, and other related organizations and agencies that would enable all sides to do what they do best in arts education programs?
2. What are the most appropriate funding and decision-making responsibilities of the arts community and the education community, given the imbalance of fiscal resources?
3. How can arts councils economically and efficiently use specialized management skills for effective administration and evaluation of arts education programs?
4. How does an arts council develop criteria that consider both high-quality programming and the needs of the users?
5. How can research and development for arts education projects occur within councils, given their limited operating funds?
6. On the assumption that it is different in kind from other council activities, what are the pros and cons of arts councils seeking legislative provision for arts education?
7. What is the most workable organizational nexus between arts councils, the education system, and television to make the most effective use of television for arts education programs?

New York, New York
June 1976

Harold Horowitz

The Research Division of the National Endowment for the Arts: Background and Highlights of the First Year

Background

On September 3, 1964, Congress established the National Council on the Arts to make recommendations on matters relating to the cultural development of the nation. The following year, the National Foundation on the Arts and Humanities was created as an independent federal agency in the executive branch. The Arts Endowment and its sister agency, the National Endowment for the Humanities are components of the National Foundation on the Arts and Humanities. They received their first appropriations of program funds for fiscal year 1966. The two endowments formulate their own programs and policies while sharing certain administrative staff. This paper is concerned with the Research Division of the Arts Endowment that began its activities in April, 1975.

The Research Division is now a little more than one year old, but the history of research at the Arts Endowment begins with the first year, 1966, when four contracts were made for the conduct of policy-related research. One of these was made to Stanford Research Institute for a study of the feasibility of establishing an American Film Institute. Other contracts provided for a study by Robert R. Nathan Associates of the feasibility of establishing a National Institute of Design, a study by the Association of American Dance Companies of the services provided by existing arts organizations and the development of a guide for improving personnel and performing facilities in dance, and a study by Julian Euell of the role of the arts in the education of the poor.

Research continued to be supported under contracts since 1966 on many subjects of concern to the agency and the fields it serves. To date, the largest contract for a study was awarded in fiscal year 1972 to the National Research Center of the Arts for a national survey of museums. The results of the survey have been published in several volumes. One is addressed to a technical audience of research workers and profession-

HAROLD HOROWITZ *is Director of Research for the National Endowment for the Arts.*

als in the museum field; a second volume is aimed at a more general readership. They present the most comprehensive description of the nation's art, history, science, and combined-subject museums that has been put together.

In addition to research supported under contract like the examples that have been cited, many of the Arts Endowment's programs have supported research projects by means of grants to provide services to their fields and the Arts Endowment's Special Projects Program has provided grant support for research projects of general concern to the agency or that cross over many fields. Examples of such projects are: a grant by the Education Program to the American Council for the Arts in Education for a study of the role of the arts in general education; a grant by the Museum Program to the American Association of Museums for the development of a manual of standardized accounting procedures; and a grant by the Special Projects Program to the Council on Foundations, Inc., to collect information on economic conditions of a representative group of arts and cultural institutions on a semiannual basis during 1975-6.

Establishment of the Research Division

A broad study of the management and administrative services in the Arts Endowment was conducted in 1974, leading to the establishment of a new post of Assistant Chairman for Management and several divisions — Budget, Planning, Evaluation, and Research — to provide a focus for these types of activities that had gradually grown in importance in the operations of the agency. The establishment of a Research Division became effective at the end of April, 1975, when the first full-time professional research staff reported for duty. The Research Division was given responsibility for planning and coordinating the research efforts of the Arts Endowment, and the monitoring and evaluation of supported research projects. The individual programs of the Arts Endowment continue to support research projects by means of grants that are in service to their fields. The Research Division, however, is gradually assuming the responsibility for research concerned with broad policy issues. To this end, a substantial amount of the time during the first year has been devoted to planning activities to determine the first projects that should be supported.

The general management plan for the Research Division is to conduct most of its work through contracts to research organizations, universities, and other qualified individuals or organizations rather than by means of its own staff. This approach recognizes the limited staff size of the Division and provides flexibility because highly qualified individuals can be found with the special skills necessary for particular problems under contracts, while the staff is concerned more with problem definition and management of the research. The project plan that is now being followed recognizes three major areas of interest. They concern arts and cultural institutions, the condition of artists, and the provision of arts and cultural services to the consumer. Priorities were established so that some projects might be initiated in fiscal year 1976. The machinery has been set in motion for the selection of research contractors through a competitive proposal procedure using a program solicitation form of advertisement. This process has been in operation since last November; and, at the time this paper is being prepared, competitive proposals have been received by the Research Division for nine projects. *Table 1* lists the subjects and the status of the awards for these projects.

A major study of the fifty-five state and jurisdictional art agencies had been initiated by the Arts Endowment prior to the establishment of the Research Division and has been assigned to it for management. The division is also participating in the management of several other projects that were initiated before April, 1976, by the programs.

Highlights of Current Research Division Activities

Study of the State Arts Agencies

A descriptive survey of the fifty-five state and jurisdictional arts agencies was initiated in 1974 and is being conducted for the Arts Endowment through a contract with the National Research Center of the Arts. The state arts agencies came into existence after 1960, the year of the funding of the New York State Council on the Arts as a temporary commission. The New York State Council was made a permanent agency in 1965. The Missouri State Council on the Arts was created as a governor's committee in 1962, and received agency status in 1965. Within the following decade, all fifty states and the District of Columbia, Puerto Rico, American Samoa, Guam, and the Virgin Islands established arts agencies. In fiscal year 1974, the base year for study in our project, the project expenditures of these agencies in the states and territories was $34,553,000. The fifty-five agencies' funds included $8,250,000 as bloc grants from the program funds of the National Endowment for the Arts, which were $46,025,000. The study of these agencies used four questionnaires. One of them is a very extensive opinion questionnaire administered by a field interviewer to the directors of the fifty-five agencies. Three of the questionnaires were completed by the staffs of state arts agencies. These questionnaires provide financial data, staff data for both the employees and the governing boards or councils, and detailed project data. A very large body of data was collected by means of these survey instruments, and the process of data assembly and report preparation is nearly completed. We expect to receive the final reports from the contractor this summer and will then set into motion the preparation of a summary report that can be given wide distribution.

Census Studies

The Research Division is working on several projects with data generated by the Bureau of the Census. The goals of these projects are to

Table 1

PROGRESS REPORT — RESEARCH DIVISION PROGRAM SOLICITATION

1. **Feasibility Study for an Economic Data Program on the Condition of Arts and Cultural Institutions**

   Due Date for Proposals: April 6, 1976
   Number of Proposals Received: Nine
   Review Group Meeting: May 5, 1976
   Number of Proposals Recommended for Award: One
   Status of Award: Selected proposal now in negotiation process to clarify questions raised at the review meeting.

2. **Model Study for an Economic Data Program on the Condition of Arts and Cultural Institutions**

   Due Date for Proposals: April 6, 1976
   Number of Proposals Received: Nine
   Review Group Meeting: May 6, 1976
   Number of Proposals Recommended for Award: Two
   Status of Award: Selected proposals now in negotiation process to clarify questions raised at the review meeting.

3. **Consumer Demand Analysis for Arts and Cultural Services for the South**

   Due Date for Proposals: May 4, 1976
   Number of Proposals Received: Twenty-three
   Review Group Meeting: To be scheduled

4. **Analysis of Economic Impacts of Arts Activities and Cultural Institutions on Their Communities**

   Due Date for Proposals: May 4, 1976
   Number of Proposals Received: Forty-one
   Review Group Meeting: To be scheduled

5. **Planning Study for a National Survey of the Craft Arts**

   Due Date for Proposals: March 9, 1976
   Number of Proposals Received: Eleven
   Review Group Meeting: March 25, 1976
   Number of Proposals Recommended for Award: One
   Status for Award: Selected proposal now in Grants Office for contract preparation.

6. **Planning Study for a National Survey of Arts and Cultural Programming on Commercial and Public Radio and Television**

   Due Date for Proposals: March 9, 1976
   Number of Proposals Received: Sixteen
   Review Group Meeting: March 24, 1976
   Number of Proposals Recommended for Award: One
   Status of Award: Selected proposal now in Grants Office for contract preparation.

7. **Critical Review and Evaluation of Audience Studies of Museums and Performing Arts Organizations**

   Due Date for Proposals: May 4, 1976
   Number of Proposals Received: Eleven
   Review Group Meeting: To be scheduled

Table 1, continued

8. **Pilot Study of Education, Training, and Careers of Symphony Orchestra Musicians**

Due Date for Proposals: April 6, 1976
Number of Proposals Received: Fourteen
Review Group Meeting: April 28, 1976
Number of Proposals Recommended for Award: One
Status of Award: Selected proposal now in negotiation process to clarify
questions raised at the review meeting.

9. **Estimate of Needs for Musical Directors and Managing Directors for American
Orchestras**

Due Date for Proposals: April 6, 1976
Number of Proposals Received: Six
Review Group Meeting: April 29, 1976
Number of Proposals Recommended for Award: One
Status of Award: Selected proposal now in negotiation process to clarify
questions raised at the review meeting.

make census data about artists and about arts and cultural institutions more accessible to the field, to conduct special studies that may be helpful to the Arts Endowment and the National Council on the Arts in the consideration of policy issues, and to work toward the improvement of data being collected by the Bureau of the Census, with the 1980 Census of Population and the 1977 Census of Business as the immediate targets.

More than 885,000 persons reported themselves employed as writers, artists, and entertainers, architects, and college and university teachers of art, drama, and music in the 1970 Census of Population. The same detailed data that was collected about every American was, of course, collected about these individuals. A selection of this information has been published by the Bureau of the Census in its occupational data series. One step in our studies has been to extract and compile some of the published data about artists. Several of these tables of particular interest at the Aspen Conference are included as part of this paper. *Table 2* summarizes certain social and economic characteristics of the experienced artist labor force by occupation and sex for 1970. *Table 3* shows the age of the artist labor force by occupation and sex in 1970. This interesting table provides information on the age distribution of artists in each of the occupations and provides an indication of their positions within their career spans. It may be useful for estimating rates of replacement necessary to maintain the same size artist labor force. *Table 4* shows the years of school completed by artists. *Table 5* shows the distribution of artists by the classes of wage and salary worker, self-employed worker, and unpaid family worker. *Table 6* provides a useful statistic on the artists not counted in the labor force in 1970, but who were last employed in their artistic occupation within the preceding decade.

Table 2

SUMMARY OF SOCIAL AND ECONOMIC CHARACTERISTICS OF THE EXPERIENCED CIVILIAN LABOR FORCE BY DETAILED OCCUPATION AND SEX: 1970

United States

	Both sexes	Male					Female				
		Total	Median earnings (dollars)	Median weeks worked	Median school years completed	Median age	Total	Median earnings (dollars)	Median weeks worked	Median school years completed	Median age
Total, 16 years old and over	80 071 130	49 536 472	7 620	50+	12.3	40.1	30 534 658	3 646	50+	12.4	39.3
Professional, technical, and kindred workers	11 666 966	6 992 250	10 617	50+	16.3	37.7	4 674 716	6 030	50+	16.1	37.7
Architects	57 081	54 948	13 188	50+	17.0	40.7	2 133	6 995	50+	17.0	36.8
Teachers, college and university	496 412	354 671	11 248	50+	17+	36.5	141 741	6 220	43.6	17+	35.9
Art, drama, and music	30 654	19 992	10 735	48.6	14.1	38.2	10 662	5 242	42.0	14.1	39.8
Writers, artists, and entertainers	797 574	554 123	9 430	50+	14.1	37.1	243 451	4 170	50.0	14.1	35.8
Actors	14 140	8 213	6 816	37.9	14.5	35.1	5 927	5 021	28.5	13.8	34.8
Athletes and kindred workers	52 985	37 998	6 273	50+	12.9	30.1	14 987	1 650	38.7	12.9	27.9
Authors	26 004	18 069	10 823	50+	15.9	40.9	7 935	5 451	50+	16.2	42.8
Dancers	6 924	1 271	4 421	42.7	12.9	29.0	5 653	3 469	36.9	12.3	23.7
Designers	112 325	85 243	11 155	50+	14.1	37.5	27 082	5 461	50+	13.7	36.1
Editors and reporters	152 984	91 501	10 618	50+	16.2	39.1	61 483	5 530	50+	15.7	35.8
Musicians and composers	96 537	63 677	4 668	45.0	12.9	28.9	32 860	1 395	44.2	13.6	37.5
Painters and sculptors	107 476	67 917	9 454	50+	13.7	39.3	39 559	3 946	49.2	13.9	35.8
Photographers	65 960	56 526	8 551	50+	12.7	39.6	9 434	3 655	50+	12.6	38.5
Public relations men and publicity writers	75 852	55 698	11 713	50+	15.9	42.0	20 154	2 153	50+	14.7	39.8
Radio and television announcers	22 296	20 873	6 974	50+	13.8	28.3	1 423	2 963	50+	13.4	37.9
Writers, artists, and entertainers, n.e.c.	64 091	47 137	9 350	50+	14.0	37.8	16 954	4 490	48.3	13.5	36.8

Source: Table 1, Bureau of the Census, Census of Population: 1970 Subject Reports, Final Report PC(2)-7A, Occupational Characteristics.

Table 3

AGE OF THE EXPERIENCED CIVILIAN LABOR

United States	16 and 17 years	18 and 19 years	20 to 24 years	25 to 29 years	30 to 34 years
Male experienced civilian labor force	1 367 099	1 916 309	5 341 703	5 856 814	5 144 449
Professional, technical, and kindred workers	22 965	78 315	749 860	1 168 416	985 549
Architects	87	111	2 806	7 592	8 248
Teachers, college and university	313	3 029	33 749	64 498	59 874
Art, drama, and music	50	112	1 017	3 886	2 863
Writers, artists, and entertainers	7 826	17 918	72 707	81 204	71 195
Actors	122	329	1 180	1 218	1 246
Athletes and kindred workers	1 557	2 879	8 285	6 232	4 317
Authors	–	41	1 264	2 260	2 469
Dancers	53	–	354	283	186
Designers	99	541	7 569	14 683	13 655
Editors and reporters	546	1 700	10 071	13 268	11 868
Musicians and composers	3 326	6 009	15 597	8 940	6 378
Painters and sculptors	278	916	7 486	9 763	8 489
Photographers	435	2 002	6 456	7 319	6 392
Public relations men and publicity writers	60	410	3 719	6 578	7 175
Radio and television announcers	676	1 657	5 290	4 232	2 774
Writers, artists, and entertainers, n.e.c.	674	1 434	5 436	6 428	6 246
Female experienced civilian labor force	844 935	1 697 124	4 660 022	3 099 895	2 604 807
Professional, technical, and kindred workers	21 068	69 307	800 423	719 163	480 716
Architects	–	–	254	243	262
Teachers, college and university	260	4 276	22 257	24 585	16 856
Art, drama, and music	–	280	1 192	1 823	1 057
Writers, artists, and entertainers	4 358	9 364	44 678	34 407	25 488
Actors	70	233	1 089	1 076	517
Athletes and kindred workers	1 117	1 704	3 623	1 822	1 370
Authors	55	40	608	927	1 093
Dancers	162	671	2 663	1 246	461
Designers	204	436	5 600	3 735	2 987
Editors and reporters	369	1 336	11 168	10 281	6 726
Musicians and composers	1 714	2 063	3 977	3 393	3 610
Painters and sculptors	187	1 272	8 511	5 385	3 835
Photographers	113	564	1 632	1 267	651
Public relations men and publicity writers	9	373	3 009	2 819	2 136
Radio and television announcers	62	43	318	65	138
Writers, artists, and entertainers, n.e.c.	296	629	2 480	2 391	1 964

Source: Table 3, Bureau of the Census, Census of Population: 1970 Subject Reports, Final Report PC(2)-7A, Occupational Characteristics.

An especially important use that has been made of census data is the study just completed of *Employment and Unemployment of Artists: 1970-1975.* This study is a response to requests from Congress for information about unemployment of artists. The report contains data on the unemployment and employment of artists comparable with the widely used Bureau of Labor Statistics data for the total United States population. The data for 1970 is from the 1970 Census of Population. The data for subsequent years is from annualized monthly averages from the monthly Current Population Studies conducted for the Bureau of Labor Statistics by the Bureau of the Census. The Bureau of Labor

FORCE BY DETAILED OCCUPATION AND SEX: 1970

35 to 39 years	40 to 44 years	45 to 49 years	50 to 54 years	55 to 59 years	60 to 62 years	63 to 64 years	65 to 69 years	70 years and over
4 998 280	**5 434 567**	**5 392 193**	**4 854 341**	**4 158 370**	**1 985 750**	**982 840**	**1 223 703**	**880 054**
899 763	831 479	751 637	552 662	417 616	200 260	101 617	129 722	102 389
7 476	8 446	7 535	4 127	3 189	1 901	859	1 450	1 121
51 749	41 754	35 768	23 372	17 544	8 501	4 546	6 750	3 224
3 260	2 577	2 305	1 648	1 102	373	229	337	233
62 018	62 546	55 255	42 826	35 153	16 116	8 488	11 205	9 666
1 133	918	587	586	198	263	127	245	61
2 781	2 860	2 491	1 909	1 910	852	651	692	582
2 429	3 061	1 902	1 844	1 162	648	37	361	591
129	124	63	17	--	17	--	45	--
12 035	10 585	9 228	6 106	4 972	2 363	1 051	1 297	1 059
10 121	10 621	10 131	7 769	5 797	3 264	1 909	2 326	2 110
4 549	4 328	3 317	3 268	3 294	1 487	757	1 255	1 172
8 189	8 586	7 802	5 992	4 600	1 873	1 088	1 676	1 179
6 108	6 838	6 316	5 125	4 809	1 764	1 008	983	971
6 864	7 507	7 398	5 375	5 079	2 105	1 161	1 257	1 010
1 795	1 694	1 191	720	449	170	83	112	30
5 885	5 424	4 829	4 115	2 883	1 310	616	956	901
2 770 874	3 213 933	3 327 997	3 003 311	2 484 339	1 134 735	536 056	667 040	489 590
457 823	483 650	455 881	404 361	352 759	179 247	87 818	98 161	64 339
407	237	115	150	223	84	--	82	76
15 496	14 881	14 048	9 992	7 758	4 396	1 990	3 275	1 671
1 015	1 236	1 187	858	859	403	157	387	208
22 692	25 980	23 300	18 375	13 902	6 520	3 497	5 523	5 367
628	545	583	380	328	171	122	105	80
1 549	1 265	1 011	681	426	146	83	87	103
694	975	828	939	569	258	208	343	398
263	66	20	59	22	--	--	20	--
2 595	3 400	2 408	2 235	1 632	687	239	537	387
5 478	5 676	6 040	4 685	4 043	1 887	1 113	1 309	1 372
3 281	3 438	2 555	2 090	2 156	1 297	631	1 270	1 385
3 527	4 914	3 930	3 303	1 884	846	473	750	742
699	1 097	1 120	820	589	341	97	283	161
1 814	2 335	2 637	2 096	1 440	496	318	342	330
149	208	199	38	39	39	18	89	18
2 015	2 061	1 969	1 049	774	352	195	388	391

Statistics released to the National Endowment for the Arts detailed data on artists' occupations for 1971 to 1975 that has not been made available through its regular publications.

The most striking observation from the examination of employment and unemployment data for artists' occupations is the increase in the total work force that has occurred in recent years. In 1975, the total experienced writers, artists, and entertainers labor force grew at a rate of 8.1 percent. Artist unemployment follows the general trend of United States population and, in 1975, was substantially greater than in 1974. *Table 7* compares the percent of unemployment for selected artists'

Table 4

YEARS OF SCHOOL COMPLETED BY THE

United States	Total	Elementary		
		Less than 5	5 to 7	8
Male, 16 years old and over	49 536 472	1 582 564	3 637 294	4 796 031
Professional, technical, and kindred workers	6 992 250	17 381	39 900	73 164
Architects	54 948	206	377	658
Teachers, college and university	354 671	206	382	730
Art, drama, and music	19 992	16	22	43
Writers, artists, and entertainers	554 123	2 191	6 676	11 385
Actors	8 213	20	182	91
Athletes and kindred workers	37 998	406	1 360	1 820
Authors	18 069	21	–	128
Dancers	1 271	–	38	–
Designers	85 243	299	874	1 571
Editors and reporters	91 501	42	211	569
Musicians and composers	63 677	489	1 228	2 409
Painters and sculptors	67 917	254	742	1 229
Photographers	56 526	98	810	1 847
Public relations men and publicity writers	55 698	67	378	577
Radio and television announcers	20 873	22	19	123
Writers, artists, and entertainers, n.e.c.	47 137	473	834	1 021
Female, 16 years old and over	30 534 658	617 889	1 542 402	2 199 245
Professional, technical, and kindred workers	4 674 716	13 958	23 259	47 122
Architects	2 133	44		8
Teachers, college and university	141 741	137	243	363
Art, drama, and music	10 662	53	–	17
Writers, artists, and entertainers	243 451	910	1 501	3 967
Actors	5 927	–	20	108
Athletes and kindred workers	14 987	41	100	282
Authors	7 935	18	44	–
Dancers	5 653	22	85	281
Designers	27 082	150	300	569
Editors and reporters	61 483	87	157	491
Musicians and composers	32 860	165	176	586
Painters and sculptors	39 559	96	226	671
Photographers	9 434	24	89	322
Public relations men and publicity writers	20 154	47	61	212
Radio and television announcers	1 423	–	–	–
Writers, artists, and entertainers, n.e.c.	16 954	260	243	445

Source: Table 5, Bureau of the Census, Census of Population: 1970 Subject Reports, Final Report PC(2)-7A, Occupational Characteristics.

occupations in 1974 and 1975. In 1975, the percent of unemployment increased for most of the selected occupations and was substantially greater than for all professional, technical, and kindred workers. The increase or decrease in the percent of unemployment between 1974 and 1975 must be interpreted with caution in the light of the statistical problems associated with the sample and detailed in the report. Table 8 compares the percent of unemployment for writers, artists, and enter-

EXPERIENCED CIVILIAN LABOR FORCE BY DETAILED OCCUPATION AND SEX: 1970

| Years of school completed | | | | | Median school years completed | Percent completed 4 years of high school or more | Percent completed 4 years of college or more |
| High school | | College | | | | | |
1 to 3	4	1 to 3	4	5 or more			
10 631 063	15 631 490	6 418 736	3 539 792	3 299 502	12.3	58.3	13.8
297 419	1 178 610	1 338 434	1 651 817	2 395 525	16 3	93 9	57.9
1 434	4 796	6 615	12 019	28 843	17.0	95.1	74.4
1 542	7 429	16 835	26 895	300 652	17 +	99 2	92.4
91	486	1 165	1 491	16 678	17 +	99.1	90 9
51 805	147 198	157 011	109 143	68 714	14.1	87.0	32.1
690	1 847	2 542	1 768	1 073	14.5	88.0	34.6
6 136	10 778	10 794	4 496	2 208	12.9	74.4	17.6
585	3 024	5 421	4 841	4 049	15.9	95.9	49.2
245	394	299	199	96	12.9	77.7	23.2
5 931	24 100	26 590	15 194	10 684	14.1	89.8	30.4
3 238	14 467	22 127	32 212	18 635	16.2	95.6	55.6
12 195	17 658	17 895	5 476	6 327	12.9	74.4	18.5
5 359	21 930	20 051	12 305	6 047	13.7	88.8	27.0
8 339	23 658	15 424	4 594	1 756	12.7	80.4	11.2
2 394	11 259	13 623	18 320	9 080	15.9	93.9	49.2
1 527	6 314	8 956	2 779	1 133	13.8	91.9	18.7
5 166	11 769	13 289	6 959	7 626	14.0	84.1	30.9
6 381 722	12 449 111	4 114 831	2 088 367	1 141 091	12.4	64.8	10.6
226 824	912 800	961 731	1 534 077	954 945	16.1	93.3	53.2
74	280	160	481	1 086	17.0	94.1	73.5
1 632	7 577	14 374	24 678	92 737	17 +	98.3	82.8
36	589	1 288	1 897	6 782	17 +	99 0	81 4
22 692	68 592	65 294	58 188	22 307	14.1	88.1	33.1
414	1 858	2 060	1 112	355	13.8	90.9	24.8
2 885	4 657	4 403	1 732	887	12.9	77.9	17.5
175	1 131	1 964	2 715	1 888	16.2	97.0	58.0
1 745	2 382	870	226	42	12 3	62.3	4.7
2 806	7 940	7 282	6 162	1 873	13.7	85.9	29.7
3 110	13 497	14 658	22 250	7 233	15.7	93.7	48.0
4 161	9 479	9 289	5 857	3 147	13.6	84.5	27.4
2 641	12 301	12 844	7 904	2 876	13.9	90.8	27.3
1 627	4 634	1 618	892	228	12.6	78.1	11.9
1 285	5 066	5 851	5 831	1 801	14.7	92.0	37.9
123	541	369	231	159	13.4	91.4	27.4
1 720	5 106	4 086	3 276	1 818	13.5	84.3	30.0

tainers with that of all professional, technical, and kindred workers for the period 1970 to 1975, and is greater by two to two-and-one-half times. Data on the growth of the artistic labor force for the 1970 to 1976 period is presented in *Table 9* and varies from 2.9 percent to 13.6 percent. *Figure 1* illustrates graphically the rise in this labor force during the period and the changes in the subgroups of the unemployed and the employed. The report contains substantially greater detail and

Table 5

CLASS OF

United States

	Total
Male, 16 years old and over	**47 730 661**
Architects	54 194
Teachers, college and university	352 429
Art, drama, and music	19 859
Writers, artists, and entertainers	531 785
Actors	5 567
Athletes and kindred workers	36 115
Authors	17 322
Dancers	1 005
Designers	83 227
Editors and reporters	89 008
Musicians and composers	58 528
Painters and sculptors	65 934
Photographers	55 147
Public relations men and publicity writers	54 638
Radio and television announcers	20 361
Writers, artists, and entertainers, n.e.c	44 933
Female, 16 years old and over	**29 074 510**
Architects	2 090
Teachers, college and university	139 278
Art, drama, and music	10 526
Writers, artists, and entertainers	229 309
Actors	3 855
Athletes and kindred workers	14 051
Authors	7 611
Dancers	4 901
Designers	25 603
Editors and reporters	59 104
Musicians and composers	31 496
Painters and sculptors	37 459
Photographers	8 803
Public relations men and publicity writers	19 229
Radio and television announcers	1 344
Writers, artists, and entertainers, n.e.c	15 853

Source: Table 43, Bureau of the Census, Census of Population: 1970 Subject Reports, Final Report PC(2)-7A, Occupational Characteristics.

many additional tables that can't be described even briefly in this paper.

Some additional observations that may be made from this data are that the United States artist labor force now exceeds one million individuals and has been growing very rapidly. The overall rate of 6.7 percent for 1970-1976 would indicate a doubling of the artist labor force if continued for about eleven years. There are very great differences in unemployment in the artistic occupations. Unemployment is most

WORKER OF EMPLOYED PERSONS BY DETAILED OCCUPATION AND SEX: 1970

| Wage and salary workers | | | | | | Self-employed workers | Unpaid family workers |
| Private wage and salary workers | | Government workers | | | | | |
Total	Employee of own corporation	Total	Federal	State	Local		
35 975 960	**970 970**	**6 711 592**	**2 190 565**	**1 617 682**	**2 903 345**	**4 918 213**	**124 896**
30 740	3 404	6 717	3 477	1 760	1 480	16 716	21
117 971	–	234 458	3 861	201 041	29 556	–	–
7 051	–	12 808	81	10 697	2 030	–	–
396 625	13 776	47 090	20 568	17 108	9 414	86 762	1 308
4 527	80	349	68	131	150	691	–
24 027	784	4 951	397	1 775	2 779	6 947	190
9 739	247	1 836	1 510	267	59	5 645	102
943	–	21	–	21	–	41	–
72 491	3 275	3 797	1 583	1 681	533	6 873	66
76 545	1 836	7 613	4 289	2 676	648	4 695	155
39 612	1 107	1 524	268	533	723	17 175	217
42 782	1 969	4 020	2 353	1 017	650	18 968	164
32 844	2 015	7 966	4 191	2 765	1 010	14 281	56
44 219	1 476	7 812	2 470	3 471	1 871	2 523	84
19 194	126	949	324	440	185	218	–
29 702	861	6 252	3 115	2 331	806	8 705	274
22 018 704	**168 915**	**5 676 267**	**1 087 794**	**1 431 626**	**3 156 847**	**1 088 072**	**291 467**
1 339	79	176	64	60	52	526	49
49 620	–	89 658	2 141	70 724	16 793	–	–
4 497	–	6 029	74	4 837	1 118	–	–
171 000	2 928	21 076	7 367	7 524	6 185	35 360	1 873
3 086	–	486	110	230	146	262	21
9 715	96	2 273	99	274	1 900	1 832	231
2 947	274	979	539	334	106	3 524	161
4 552	–	60	24	36	–	289	–
20 524	718	611	147	298	166	4 275	193
50 437	409	6 039	3 329	2 267	443	2 445	183
25 372	107	1 768	226	538	1 004	4 298	58
22 336	625	2 771	805	1 354	612	11 903	449
5 681	186	777	367	327	83	2 083	262
15 072	329	3 160	875	1 088	1 197	851	146
1 130	–	105	–	87	18	109	–
10 148	184	2 047	846	691	510	3 489	169

severe among actors, ranging from a high of 47.4 percent recorded in both 1971 and 1974, to a low of 33.4 percent recorded in 1970. The percent of unemployment of actors in 1975 was 35 percent, close to the low of 33.4 percent in 1970, and in contrast to unemployment among the other artistic occupations as the only one showing a decrease in 1975. Dancers are second in percent of unemployment, ranging from a low of 14.5 percent in 1970 to a high of 30 percent in 1971. However,

Table 6

EMPLOYED, EXPERIENCED UNEMPLOYED, NOT IN LABOR FORCE, BUT WORKED 1960 TO 1970, BY DETAILED OCCUPATION AND SEX: 1970

United States	Male				Female			
	Experienced civilian labor force			Not in labor force, last worked 1960 to 1970	Experienced civilian labor force			Not in labor force, last worked 1960 to 1970
	Total	Employed	Experienced unemployed		Total	Employed	Experienced unemployed	
Total, 16 years old and over	**49 536 472**	**47 730 661**	**1 805 811**	**9 308 386**	**30 534 658**	**29 074 510**	**1 460 148**	**17 461 616**
Architects	54 948	54 194	754	4 908	2 133	2 090	43	790
Teachers, college and university	354 671	352 429	2 242	29 845	141 741	139 278	2 463	44 691
Art, drama, and music	19 992	19 859	133	966	10 662	10 526	136	3 357
Writers, artists, and entertainers	554 123	531 785	22 338	75 307	243 451	229 309	14 142	125 215
Actors	8 213	5 567	2 646	3 141	5 927	3 855	2 072	5 814
Athletes and kindred workers	37 998	36 115	1 883	15 697	14 987	14 051	936	18 078
Authors	18 069	17 322	747	2 181	7 935	7 611	324	3 328
Dancers	1 271	1 005	266	403	5 653	4 901	752	4 733
Designers	85 243	83 227	2 016	6 049	27 082	25 603	1 479	12 466
Editors and reporters	91 501	89 008	2 493	8 828	61 483	59 104	2 379	25 255
Musicians and composers	63 677	58 528	5 149	12 508	32 860	31 496	1 364	14 999
Painters and sculptors	67 917	65 934	1 983	6 310	39 559	37 459	2 100	17 587
Photographers	56 526	55 147	1 379	6 493	9 434	8 803	631	4 704
Public relations men and publicity writers	55 698	54 638	1 060	5 536	20 154	19 229	925	8 470
Radio and television announcers	20 873	20 361	512	1 702	1 423	1 344	79	887
Writers, artists, and entertainers, n.e.c	47 137	44 933	2 204	6 459	16 954	15 853	1 101	8 894

Source: Table 51, Bureau of the Census, Census of Population: 1970 Subject Reports, Final Report PC(2)-7A, Occupational Characteristics.

Table 7

COMPARISON OF UNEMPLOYMENT FOR SELECTED
OCCUPATIONS WITH ALL PROFESSIONAL,
TECHNICAL AND KINDRED WORKERS: 1974 and 1975

	1974	1975	Change
All Professional, Technical & Kindred Workers	2.3%	3.2%	+.9%
Architects	2.7%	5.4%	+2.7%
Actors	47.4%	35.0%	−12.4%
Authors	2.1%	4.3%	+2.2%
Dancers	*	*	*
Designers	2.3%	7.4%	+5.1%
Musicians & Composers	4.1%	7.9%	+3.8%
Painters & Sculptors	3.2%	5.8%	+2.6%
Photographers	3.8%	6.2%	+2.4%

*Data base is too small to provide a meaningful estimate.
Source: Unpublished data furnished by the Bureau of Labor Statistics.

Table 8

COMPARISON OF UNEMPLOYMENT FOR WRITERS, ARTISTS,
AND ENTERTAINERS WITH ALL PROFESSIONAL,
TECHNICAL AND KINDRED WORKERS: 1970 - 1975

	%Unemployment Writers, Artists & Entertainers	%Unemployment All Professional, Technical and Kindred Workers
1970[1]	4.6%	1.8%
1971[2]	7.1%	2.9%
1972[2]	5.6%	2.4%
1973[2]	4.8%	2.2%
1974[2]	4.8%	2.3%
1975[2]	7.4%	3.2%

[1]Table 51. U.S. Bureau of the Census, Census of Population: 1970 Subject Reports, Final Report PC(2)-7A. Occupational Characteristics.
[2]Unpublished data furnished by the Bureau of Labor Statistics.

Table 9

TOTAL WRITERS, ARTISTS AND ENTERTAINERS,
GROWTH OF LABOR FORCE AND UNEMPLOYMENT: 1970 - 1976

Year	Total Labor Force	Growth Rate From Previous Year	Number Unem- ployed	% Unem- ployed	Standard Error of % Unem- ployment
1970[1]	797,574	—	36,480	4.6%	.1%
1971[2]	906,000	13.6%	60,000	6.6%	.5%
1972[2]	947,000	4.5%	50,000	5.3%	.4%
1973[2]	974,000	2.9%	45,000	4.6%	.4%
1974[2]	1,048,000	7.6%	48,000	4.6%	.4%
1975[2]	1,133,000	8.1%	78,000	6.9%	.5%
1976[2]	1,178,000	4.0%	79,000	6.7%	.4%

[1]*Table 51, U.S. Bureau of the Census. Census of Population: 1970 Subject Reports, Final Report PC(2)-7A, Occupational Characteristics.*
[2]*Unpublished data furnished by the Bureau of Labor Statistics.*

the data on the unemployment of dancers is considered unreliable except for the census year 1970; and comparisons with other occupations should be made cautiously. This is because of the relatively small number of dancers and the difficulty of obtaining satisfactory data for this occupational group in the monthly Current Population Studies.

The data published by the Bureau of the Census for 1970 is a limited selection. A sample of the complete 1970 census questionnaires is available as the Public Use Sample. This is published in the form of sixty-six magnetic tapes intended for use in automatic data processing equipment to permit the users to construct tabulations of data of their own choosing and in formats particularly suited for the intended purpose. The Research Division is now preparing to have all of the data about persons in artistic occupations and their households consolidated from the sixty-six magnetic tapes onto a single tape to make possible rapid and convenient retrieval of information in the cross-tabulations we believe will be most helpful. Several preliminary studies on the possibilities of doing this have been completed by our staff and through the use of a consulting organization — Data Use and Access Laboratories. The Arts Endowment is now contracting with this

Figure 1

TOTAL WRITERS, ARTISTS, AND ENTERTAINERS LABOR FORCE,
EMPLOYED AND UNEMPLOYED: 1970 - 1975

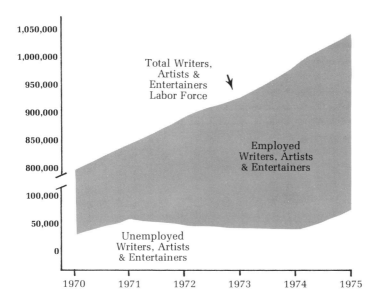

Source: Table 9

organization to produce the extract tape and then to use this for a series of new studies. Among the first subjects of the studies are the determination of the geographic location of artists, the differences in distribution of artists in various locations of the United States compared to the national norm, and a study of migration of artists. This is possible because of data on location of residence that was collected in the 1970 census for both 1965 and 1970. The results of these studies should be interesting in themselves and will provide valuable comparisons when data becomes available from the 1980 census.

Data from the 1972 Census of Business has also been studied by the Research Division during the past year. The Bureau of the Census conducts a census of United States business establishments at five-year intervals. The last was conducted in 1972, and it will be repeated in 1977. Business establishments are classified into several hundred "kinds of business." Among the basic data collected and published for each classification of business is the total number of establishments and the total amount of operating receipts. Breakdowns of this basic data are provided by geographic region, state, county, standard metropolitan statistical area, and city. A substantial amount of time has been required in learning how to use this information source and to understand its limitations. To illustrate this, business establishments are classified into kinds of business by their major source of receipts. As an example, operating receipts of university-related performing arts groups may be included under colleges and universities and excluded from the Census of Business coverage for the performing arts. Also, only establishments with payroll are included, so volunteer groups are excluded. The effect of these exclusions on total receipts is probably small, but most likely causes a significant understatement of the number of establishments. Another limitation is that establishments with tax-exempt status are permitted by law to elect not to pay FICA payroll taxes; and, in the cases where this is done, they are not included in the census. We have learned

Table 10

AMUSEMENT AND RECREATION SERVICES
ESTABLISHMENTS WITH PAYROLL, TOTAL U.S. (1972)

	Number of Establishments	$ Receipts (millions)
Total Amusement & Recreation Services	66,064	$12,660.1
A. Motion Picture & Television Production, Distribution, Services	4,962	2,939.6
B. Motion Picture Theaters	11,670	1,815.9
C. Producers, Orchestras, Entertainers	7,383	1,027.7
1. Classical Music & Dance Groups	389	85.5
2. Music Groups Except Classical, Other Entertainment including Variety	4,811	407.5
3. Producers of Legitimate Theater	934	277.2
4. Theatrical Services (inc. Ticket Agencies, Equipment Rentals)	1,249	257.5
D. Bowling Alleys, Billiards, Pool	9,048	1,142.3
E. Dance Halls, Studios, Schools	2,370	89.5
F. Professional Sports	537	515.9
G. Racing Operations	2,196	1,007.9
H. Golf Courses, Membership Sports & Recreation Clubs	11,868	1,855.9
I. Amusement Parks, Carnivals, Circuses, Fairs, Other	16,030	2,268.9

Source: U.S. Department of Commerce, Bureau of the Census, Census of Business: 1972
Census of Selected Services Industries: Area Statistics, U.S. Summary, Table 3.

that some orchestras, opera companies, and dance organizations elect this option. Generally, the organizations that do not pay FICA taxes have budgets below $100,000 and would not make a major impact on the aggregate value of receipts that is reported. Virtually all professional theatre groups are included because Actors' Equity requires payment of FICA payroll taxes in its contracts. As a result, the data in *Tables 10, 11, 12, 13,* and *14* based on the Census of Business data for 1972 may show some underreporting of the number of classical music and dance groups. The underreporting of receipts is probably small, and we have checked this by noting that the aggregate receipts for this group compares closely with the estimate by the Ford Foundation in Finances of the Performing Arts for the total operating receipts for all such nonprofit organizations with expenditures above $20,000 per year in 1970 and 1971.

The Census of Business data makes it possible for us to compare the size of the classical music and dance and legitimate theatre "types of business" with other types of amusement and recreation service business in terms of the national aggregates shown on *Table 10* and also in terms of regional and state distributions. (The latter data is not shown in the tables appearing in this paper but is available.) *Tables 11* and *12* provide information on the regional distribution of theatre and classical music and dance in terms of percent of total United States population, percent of total United States establishments, percent of total receipts, and dollar receipts per capita. *Table 13* shows how New York City theatre comprises half of the United States total of receipts in this field. These receipts are generated by a fourth of the United States legitimate theatre establishments. The dominance of New York City is much less in classical music and dance than in theatre. Finally, *Table 14* illustrates the concentration of theatre, classical music, and dance combined in comparison to several measures of United States urbanization.

Economic Studies

A substantial program of economic studies on the arts and cultural institutions as well as on consumer demand will be initiated shortly. Proposals for such research projects are now being processed. These proposals were received in response to the Research Division Program Solicitation that was described in an earlier part of this paper. Under consideration is the establishment of a data series to measure the economic conditions of museums (including art, history, science, and combinations of these) and nonprofit performing organizations. For theatre, both profit and nonprofit organizations are to be considered in the data series. In the near future, we plan to initiate a feasibility study of alternatives for the establishment of this data series. Four tasks will be included in this analysis. First, a comparative analysis of the various economic data series that have been started in the past for the United States arts and cultural institutions. Examples include: the Ford Foundation, Finances of the Performing Arts; Census of Business; and the an-

Table 11

REGIONAL DISTRIBUTION OF ESTABLISHMENTS
WITH PAYROLL AND RECEIPTS
PRODUCERS OF LEGITIMATE THEATER

Region	% of Total U.S. Pop.	% of Total U.S. Establishments	% of Total U.S. Receipts	$ Receipts Per Capita
New England	5.8	7.2	n.a.	n.a.
Mid-Atlantic	18.3	34.6	56.0	$4.17
East North Central	19.8	12.3	10.9	.75
West North Central	8.0	5.1	n.a.	n.a
South Atlantic	15.1	10.0	4.9	.44
East South Central	6.3	3.7	1.4	.30
West South Central	9.5	5.7	4.9	.71
Mountain	4.1	6.0	2.6	.86
Pacific	13.1	15.3	11.9	1.24
Total	**100.0**	**100.0**	**100.0**	
Base for Percentage	(203.2 mil.)	(934)	($277.2 mil.)	

Source: *U.S. Department of Commerce, Bureau of the Census, Census of Business:* 1972
Census of Selected Services Industries: Area Statistics, U.S. Summary, *Table 3.*

nual data-collection programs of the arts service organizations. Several
of these series are continuing at the present time. These data series will
be compared for the items of data being collected, problems of data collection, methods of operation and management, methods of data dissemination, access of the public to information, utilization of data, and
costs. The second task will be to evaluate the difficulties, cost of collection, and quality of each type of data in relation to experience in the
utilization of the data and the benefits that have been gained. The third
task will be an assessment of the data items that are desired by the National Endowment for the Arts staff, National Council on the Arts members, service organizations, and other potential users of data on the
economic conditions of arts and cultural institutions. Consideration of
the experience in the utilization and benefits of data items that have
been collected for economic data series started in the past will be balanced against these needs definitions. Finally, the fourth task is to prepare recommendations on the data items that appear to be most valuable

Table 12

REGIONAL DISTRIBUTION OF ESTABLISHMENTS WITH PAYROLL AND
RECEIPTS
CLASSICAL MUSIC & DANCE GROUPS

Region	% of Total U.S. Pop.	% of Total U.S. Establishments	% of Total U.S. Receipts	$ Receipts Per Capita
New England	5.8	5.1	5.4	$ .39
Mid-Atlantic	18.3	23.3	38.1	.88
East North Central	19.8	14.4	17.0	.36
West North Central	8.0	8.2	5.7	.30
South Atlantic	15.1	10.3	9.1	.25
East South Central	6.3	6.4	2.0	.13
West South Central	9.5	6.9	3.8	.17
Mountain	4.1	4.6	1.7	.18
Pacific	13.1	20.6	17.1	.55
Total	**100.0**	**100.0**	**100.0**	
Base for Percentage	(203.2 mil.)	(389)	($85.5 mil.)	

Source: *U.S. Department of Commerce, Bureau of the Census, Census of Business:* 1972 Census of Selected Services Industries: Area Statistics, U.S. Summary, *Table 3.*

and readily useable. In addition to the feasibility study, we plan to support research for the development of models that will project future conditions helpful for planning purposes. The model development research will use techniques of economic analysis to construct models combining general economic condition factors and indices with factors descriptive of the economic conditions of arts and cultural institutions.

In the consumer-demand analysis area, many research projects are anticipated over the coming years. For our first study, the subject of consumer demand for arts and cultural services in the South has been selected, and we expect to support a research project that will consider both nonmarket or life-style factors and market factors such as prices of alternative opportunities for this region of the United States. We also anticipate supporting research on the economic impact of arts activities and cultural institutions on their communities through one or more projects that may be concerned with a state, a region within a state, a standard metropolitan statistical area, or a city or town. Of primary interest

Table 13

SELECTED DISTRIBUTION OF ESTABLISHMENTS WITH PAYROLL AND RECEIPTS
MID-ATLANTIC & PACIFIC REGIONS, 1972

	% of Total U.S. Pop.	Producers of Legitimate Theater		Classical Music & Dance Groups	
		% of Total U.S. Establishments	% of Total U.S. $ Receipts	% of Total U.S. Establishments	% of Total U.S. $ Receipts
Mid-Atlantic Region	18.3	34.5	56.0	23.4	38.1
New York State	9.0	30.1	52.8	17.0	28.7
New York SMSA	5.7	26.9	49.5	13.6	25.9
New York City	3.9	25.7	49.2	12.3	25.4
Pacific Region	13.1	15.3	11.9	20.6	17.1
California State	9.8	12.5	11.0	15.7	13.9
Los Angeles SMSA	3.5	7.2	7.9	7.2	7.6
Los Angeles City	1.4	4.0	6.5	3.3	6.2
San Francisco SMSA	1.5	2.5	1.5	3.6	5.3
San Francisco City	.3	1.1	1.2	2.0	5.0

Source: *U.S. Department of Commerce, Bureau of the Census, Census of Business: 1972 Census of Selected Services Industries: Area Statistics,* U.S. Summary, *Table 3.*

Table 14

REGIONAL DISTRIBUTIONS: THEATER, CLASSICAL MUSIC AND DANCE COMBINED:
COMPARISON TO TOTAL AMUSEMENT & RECREATION SERVICES AND URBAN CONCENTRATION

	% of Total U.S. Pop. (1970)	% of Total U.S. "Urbanized" Pop. (1970)	% of Total U.S. Pop. in cities over 200,000 Size (1970)	Producers of Legitimate Theater, Classical Music & Dance Groups Combined		Total Amusement & Recreation Services
				% of Total U.S. Establishments	% of Total U.S. $ Receipts	% of Total U.S. $ Receipts
New England	5.8	6.3	1.5	6.7	n.a.	4.4
Mid-Atlantic	18.3	23.1	27.5	31.3	51.8	24.6
New York City	3.9	6.7	18.1	21.8	43.6	13.7
East North Central	19.8	20.8	19.4	12.9	12.3	15.4
West North Central	8.0	5.8	6.2	6.0	n.a.	5.4
South Atlantic	15.1	12.1	10.0	10.1	5.9	12.9
East South Central	6.3	3.5	4.0	4.5	1.5	2.8
West South Central	9.5	8.5	12.0	6.0	4.7	5.6
Mountain	4.1	3.5	3.7	5.6	2.4	6.4
Pacific	13.1	16.4	15.8	16.9	13.1	22.4
Total	100.0	100.0	100.0	100.0	100.0	100.0
Base for Percentages	(203.2 mil.)	(118.4 mil.)	(43.5 mil.)	(1,323)	($362.7 mil.)	($12,660.1 mil.)

Source: U.S. Department of Commerce, Bureau of the Census, Census of Business, 1972 Census of Selected Services Industries: Area Statistics, U.S. Summary, Table 3, New York, Table 4, 1970 Census of Population, Characteristics, VI, Part A, Tables 16, 28 (section 1).

are employment of human resources, utilization of physical resources, and effects on income and production levels.

Audience Studies

Many audience studies have been conducted of individual arts and cultural institutions, primarily museums, theatres, and symphonies. Our first project in this area will be a critical review and evaluation of the studies that have been conducted in the past and will include a systematic collection and selection of studies, followed by their analysis and evaluation with respect to technical quality, utility for policy-making, and potential for standardization of procedures.

Program Support

The individual programs of the Arts Endowment continue to support research projects as services to their field, in the manner they have in the past. However, the Research Division is now assisting with the problem-defining, planning, and monitoring of the projects. In addition, the Research Division will be able to support a certain number of projects for the programs. At present, the Division is in the process of developing contracts to conduct four projects on behalf of the programs.

A PLANNING STUDY FOR A NATIONAL STUDY OF THE CRAFT ARTS. This study will be a step toward a national survey on behalf of the Crafts Program. The planning study is needed to define the scope of the future national study and estimate the necessary costs and resources that will be required. It has the objectives of collecting information from a number of sources, and of preparing a systematic classification of United States crafts with estimates of the numbers of individuals and organizations in each classification group so that recommendations can be developed on approaches, methods, and costs for surveying each of these elements of the field. All United States craft activities will be considered in the planning study including individual craftsmen, crafts organizations, craft material supply houses, craft equipment manufacturers, craft schools, university and college art departments, public agencies, craft sales galleries and other sales outlets, and other significant components of the craft field.

A PLANNING STUDY FOR A NATIONAL SURVEY OF ARTS AND CULTURAL PROGRAMMING ON COMMERCIAL AND PUBLIC RADIO AND TELEVISION. This study will probe into a number of questions of terminology and taxonomy to provide guidance for the planning of the subsequent survey on behalf of the Public Media Program. Among the kinds of information that we must obtain are an understanding of how the phrase "arts and cultural programming" is understood by key executives in the commercial and public radio and television industries. We also need to know what terminology is used to describe the categories of broadcasting activity that includes significant programming about areas of interest to the Arts Endowment including the subjects of literature (fiction and poetry), drama, film and video as art forms, dance, music (classical, jazz, and folk), the visual arts (painting, sculpture, and craft arts), and architecture and environmental arts.

A PILOT STUDY OF EDUCATION, TRAINING, AND CAREERS OF SYMPHONY ORCHESTRA MUSICIANS; AND ESTIMATE OF NEEDS FOR MUSICAL DIRECTORS AND MANAGING DIRECTORS FOR AMERICAN ORCHESTRAS. These are two projects now in the process of development on behalf of the Music Program. The first project is a systematic review of the educational history and training of the professional musicians currently performing with the major, metropolitan, and community symphony orchestras in the United States. This study aims at providing an evaluation of the impact of historic educational and training experiences on the career achievements of symphony orchestra musicians. The second project will develop an estimate of the numbers of musical directors and managing directors needed for American orchestras. The results of this research will be utilized to determine the appropriate level of effort at which the currently supported program for young conductors should be continued in the future. This program is now jointly supported by the National Endowment for the Arts and the Exxon Corporation. At present, this program provides for nine conductorships. They are with the National Symphony Orchestra, Atlanta Symphony Orchestra, Milwaukee Symphony Orchestra, Pittsburgh Symphony Orchestra, St. Paul Chamber Orchestra, Los Angeles Philharmonic Orchestra, St. Louis Symphony Orchestra, Texas Opera Theatre, and the San Diego Symphony Orchestra.

The preceding summary of soon-to-be-started economic studies, audience studies, and program-support studies does not include the names of the research organizations that will do the work or specific project details. This paper is being written at the time when proposals for the research have been received and are in the evaluation process. The selection of proposals to be recommended for awards, the processing of awards, and initiation of the projects is in process now. Several of the research projects will have been started at the time of the Aspen Conference where this paper was presented.

Washington, D. C.
May 1976

Martin Engel

Toward a Federal Policy
for the Arts in Education

Background

In much the same way that it is impossible to legislate a single education policy for the decentralized school system of the United States, it is
equally unlikely that a single unifying policy can be developed that will
apply forcefully to the various federal agencies concerned with education in the arts and humanities. A number of such agencies are involved
in the support of education programs in this area; among them, the National Endowment for the Arts, the National Endowment for the
Humanities, the U.S. Office of Education, and the National Institute of
Education (NIE). For lack of a coordinative effort, each agency has been
going its own way, with its own agenda. A cursory overview of their
activities can be a useful point of departure for a discussion of policy.

Public Law 209, amended in 1973, authorized the National Endowment for the Humanities to "develop and encourage the pursuit of a
national policy for the promotion of progress and scholarship in the
Humanities. . . ." That legislation also provides that the Endowment
"strengthen the research and teaching potential in the Humanities. . . ."
With such a legislative charge to improve education in the humanities,
the Endowment supports curriculum development activities, but with
major emphasis upon post-secondary education. It also supports workshops for schoolteachers of the various humanities subjects, strengthening their skills in content areas. Although the education budget of
the Endowment is considerable (it is even argued that all of it is
education-targeted), much of the expenditure is directed toward post-
secondary-school settings and relatively little is provided for education
improvement in the nation's elementary and high schools. The research
is traditional, and appropriate to humanistic scholarship. However,
because it is neither empirical, clinical, or scientific, there is no way of
knowing whether a new curriculum, in-service training program, or any
other treatment is actually effective. In other words, the Endowment

MARTIN ENGEL is Advisor for Arts and Humanities for the National Institute
of Education.

emphasis is upon the humanities as a body of knowledge and a literature rather than as an educational process.

The National Endowment for the Arts initially supported an education program that placed poets of professional standing into the classroom. It was—and presumably continues to be—a highly effective program because not only does the poet work with all the youngsters in the classroom but in concert with the teacher as well. Furthermore, the mode of discourse, though aesthetic, is verbal, and this is a language with preliminary commonality among all participants. With the transfer of funds from the U.S. Office of Education in 1969, and continuing several years thereafter, the Poet-in-the-Schools Program was expanded to become the Artists-in-Schools Program. That the Endowment for the Arts should enter the educational arena is rather remarkable, inasmuch as the enabling legislation, Public Law 209, emphasizes artistic and cultural projects and productions or professional standards, but makes no reference to education. Section 5, paragraph C, point 3 states that the Chairman of the Endowment will provide support for "projects and productions that will encourage and assist artists and enable them to achieve wider distribution of their works, to work in residence at an educational or cultural institution, or to achieve standards of professional excellence." Thus, the legislative intent is to provide residency programs for artists, and indeed, the Artists-in-Schools Program does just this. While the program is eminently successful in the fulfillment of its mandate to place artists in residence in the schools, as an educational program it has generated considerable doubt among a growing number of constituencies. Though evaluation activities are underway, no satisfactory answer has yet been provided regarding the question of learner outcomes. The statistical analysis of attitudes and testimonials falls short of the needs for a thorough and independent evaluation. Biased evaluators with strong commitments to the program under review cannot provide the professional objectivity such evaluation requires.

The problem becomes distinct as one reviews the programs of the various agencies. No educational design exists. There has been no educational planning; there is no educational policy; there is no educational evaluation. Indeed, it would seem somewhat strange that the major educational agency in the federal government, U.S.O.E., would transfer its funds to a non-educational agency for the purpose of supporting education. The federal model of facilitating education in the arts in the schools has now been set in concrete by the National Endowment for the Arts. That model is based on the process of bringing a practicing artist or team of performers, not teachers, "off the street," so to speak, into a school for a limited period of time. Unless a great deal more structuring at the front and back ends of that activity is introduced, the results, while highly visible as modes of intervention, can yield very little in terms of learner outcomes when observed from the point of view that there are new sets of students every year and that we are talking about *all* 51 million students, not just a self-selecting few. This paper is concerned with that structuring — the educational design — of the learning process in the schools.

The U. S. Office of Education pioneered the federal role in the arts in education; but, since 1970, has provided no funds or program in that area. The Arts and Humanities Branch in the Bureau of Reseach was reduced to one professional with the function of advisor to the Commissioner rather than as administrator of a funding program. During its peak years, the Arts and Humanities Branch invested about $2 million per year, creating significant development in arts education. Since then, the Office of Education has emulated the Endowment for the Arts model in its education programs.

The Alliance for Arts in Education is the Kennedy Center Education Program, which is funded by the Office of Education and creates a second network in the states, parallel to the state arts councils, and multiplies bureaucracies of administrators. The purpose is to bring educators and artists together in some kind of working relationship. Presently, this is more normative than descriptive of the program. In addition, the Office of Education, through its Emergency School Aid Act, supports performing arts groups in some kind of conjunction with schools; but again the emphasis is upon the performing arts group, rather than upon an educational design that has a life expectancy longer than the particular funded program.

This last point is the most crucial one in describing the various activities of the several federal agencies supporting the arts and humanities. The support is focused upon particular artists and performers, not upon programs. No serious training takes place regarding the interaction of the adults and their students. No curriculum is made explicit and relatively permanent. No learner outcomes are determined to ascertain the value, success, or failure of the treatment. When the funds stop, the program stops. Merely bringing artists and children together in a school setting (or out of school, for that matter) is not education in the arts and humanities.

With the mandate to further education in the United States, the National Institute of Education (NIE) has developed several priority areas to focus its resources on. "Basic skills" is one such area, stressing the acquisition of learning skills in the manipulation of verbal and mathematical cognitive discourse. This means more than reading, however; it means understanding.

The mission of the agency, then, is to identify and create proven effective programs in education that facilitate the development of learning skills among the nation's 51 million school children. It means that the agency will support the techniques of systematic research and development to facilitate the work of the schools. However, NIE is not yet in a position to assume the burden of activities "dropped" when the Arts and Humanities Branch ended its efforts over six years ago. This agency needs a policy generated by systematic planning and an organizational capacity to administer the diversity of programs necessary to effect the improvement of education in the arts and humanities.

One final organizational unit might be mentioned in the context of the federal role in the arts in education. The Federal Interagency Committee for Education (FICE) is made up of representatives from all agencies involved in education and includes a subcommittee for arts and humanities, which, in its several-year history, has not yet assumed responsibility for the generation of a broad policy that would have application to all the concerned agencies, nor has it explored those policy considerations that might persuade the several member agencies to regard their own efforts in the field of arts in education in a more comprehensive and systematic way. The history of the federal government, at least since 1965, in the field of research and development in the arts and humanities has been discussed by several authors (Hoffa, Eddy, Engel); and the general conclusions point to not merely the need for greater financial commitments to the area of the arts in education, but to more systematic and thought-through programs, based upon carefully considered policy issues and designed to achieve positive learner effects.

The degree of interest, nationally, is approaching a critical mass. A number of foundations and other organizations are focusing their efforts in this area. However, there is little solid intellectual research and development foundation and, therefore, most of the effort is improvisatory, exhortatory, and produces more heat than light. Entirely too much is left to the ineffable magic of the arts to teach themselves! The need is greatest at the basic research end of the spectrum. All areas — theory/concept, instruction, curriculum evaluation, and dissemination — must be based upon a meaningful and disciplined inquiry. Solution of policy research problems, clarification, taxonomies, definitions, and the like, must precede other work since so much confusion exists.

Furthermore, the more basic issue of interrelationship between the affective and the cognitive-verbal domains is becoming of greater and greater concern. We now realize that to ignore the affective is to study only half the problem in the cognitive areas.

The Cognitive Aspects of Arts Education

Given that the mission of NIE is research and development in basic skills such as reading and mathematics, why should that agency engage in such peripheral and affective areas ("frills") as the arts and humanities?

Perhaps some fragments from a discussion by two empirical experimenters at the Harvard Graduate School of Education will indicate that not only are the arts and the humanities significant motivators for student participation in the total educational context—creating enabling conditions—but that education in the arts and humanities is much more:

> an emerging consensus suggests that skills involved in such areas bear strong analogies to skills utilized in more traditional subject matters; that any division between cognition (reason) and affect

(feeling) is artifical and ill-motivated; . . . that certain of the arts bear strong analogies with certain of the sciences; that the capacity to read and produce symbols is central in both of the "two cultures"; and that any curriculum which focuses exclusively on the sciences or on "discursive language" is neglecting significant proportions of the mind, and, equally, of the human brain. . . .

There are striking findings emerging in a number of laboratories and research centers which have completely revised traditional notions about the structure of knowledge. . . . Any such claim must be understood against the meaning of "cognitive." Cognition refers to the act of knowing — to the exercise of knowledge. Knowledge, in turn, involves not only propositional knowledge about things, but the know-how concerning how to accomplish them. Also, knowledge may be overt and explicit, or covert and tacit. With these extensions in mind, the obvious misgivings that cognition involves solely linguistic, discursive sorts of knowledge is set aside. (David Perkins and Howard Gardner, Project Zero, 1976.)

In short, the arts and humanities have traditionally been taught in the schools as an enrichment of the basic curriculum, as ancillary to the core of knowledge and skills acquisition, and therefore as expendable frills. However, recent research suggests that the arts and humanities constitute the discipline or process as well as the body of knowledge of nonverbal cognition. Studies of aphasics have produced new insights into brain functions. We now know about the classic example of the brain-damaged patient who cannot recite (speak) verbal information but can *sing* the words. Another case cannot read the letters "D-I-X" as "dicks" but can translate them as the Roman numerals "509." Such research findings constitute clues to brain functioning that have profound significance for education — an education that must incorporate a much more prominent dose of perceptual and sensory training in the arts, as well as values education through the humanities and through aesthetic education.

That the arts, if not the humanities, are receiving more serious consideration in the planning of the National Institute of Education is apparent in language that is presently under consideration for inclusion in the FY (fiscal year) 1978 program plans of the Basic Skills Group, one of five groups formed around the Institute's problem-solving priorities. That language, which at this writing is not yet officially endorsed, is, nonetheless, actively discussed at all agency levels. Its relevance to the arts in learning, growth, and development is sufficient to justify its inclusion in this presentation, in its entirety:

Basic Skills Group

Strategy #9: Basic Skills in the Arts and Humanities

The principal focus of the Basis Skills Group is on the domains of reading, writing and mathematics. A concentration of NIE funds and energies on these three disciplines bring to them an emphasis which has and will continue to produce progress in the development of our knowledge about verbal and mathematical learning and teaching. At the same time, there are other important areas of learning which are not presently included in the domains of literacy and mathematics, but nonetheless are of high significance in the growth and development of responsible and mature adults. Among these are the competencies usually associated with the arts and humanities and the way that they are learned and taught.

Knowledge of and ability in the arts and humanities clearly include disciplines in which value formation and other aspects of affect combine with cognition, such as the creation and appreciation of the Arts, the study and comprehension of literature, philosophy and history, moral and ethical issues, and creativity as intrinsic to human growth and development. These disciplines could very well have profound impact upon the more basic skills of reading comprehension and writing; that is, verbal expression.

While it is not the intention of the Basic Skills Group to make a major new commitment to these areas in FY '78, the fact is that ongoing activities relevant to these areas will continue to be supported in FY '78. Coherence and increased demand requires that the arts and humanities be recognized as distinct from literacy and mathematics, yet basic to the total academic curriculum. Furthermore, learning and teaching in these areas includes abilities which are truly fundamental to critical societal functioning. The capacity to receive and express verbal information within the cultural context, and to have competence in mathematical thinking demands a more comprehensive understanding of modes of human symbolization. In this larger sense, Basic Skills are coping, or survival skills in an increasingly complex society. Thus, reading must be understood as human literacy among *all* modes of expression and communication essential to personal and social well-being.

There are two reasons why these areas must be retained as a focus — albeit small — within the Basic Skills Group:

1. While there is a growing sense that it exists, the interrelationship among the affective and cognitive/verbal domains is unclear. We believe that to ignore affective outcomes is to study only part of the problem in the cognitive areas.
2. These affectively imbued, higher-order cognitive skills are considered, by growing sectors of our society, to be of equal or greater importance than our present conception of reading, writing and mathematics.

Consistent with the above reasons, NIE has been committing over 2 million dollars per year in research and development in the arts, humanities and other affective-dominant disciplines. For example, we have supported the development of a K-7 curriculum in aesthetic education for the general classroom complete with a teacher training curriculum for pre- and in-service training, as well as an art and music, K-3, curriculum. In addition, we have supported a research group which has taken as its special concern the theoretical foundations of learning in non-verbal cognitive domains, such as various modes of symbolization and metaphor, seeking avenues toward enhanced practice in the classroom. In FY '77 we intend to initiate a planning effort in moral/citizenship education. Curricular products and concepts papers in this area are presently being generated as the consequence of an FY '76 contract.

As with the present emphasis upon certain cognitive skills, our interest in the area of affective and higher-order cognitive outcomes cross-cuts the Basic Skills Group. Of interest to the Adequacy Groups for example, are the Court and Legislative mandates related to non-cognitive outcomes. Both the Learning and Teaching Divisions are concerned with the acquisition of valuation, attitudes and ability, such as motivation, altruisim and decision-making, the effects of the instructional process on non-cognitive outcomes, and the possibilities of tradeoffs among various emphases within the classroom. And of course measurement of affective outcomes is a major problem. Further, most major programs which are seemingly concerned only with cognitive outcomes (such as the Beginning Teacher Evaluation Study), also include a battery of non-cognitive measures in the design, recognizing the importance of the integration of the cognitive with the affective as Basic Skills.

The point must be made again that the preceding words are not yet, and (God forbid) might never be, integrated into the program plans of NIE. Nonetheless, the fact that preliminary draft versions are being circulated for discussion provides a modest ray of hope.

What is being argued in this paper involves a much more rigorous approach to the integration of the arts and education as fundamental to the learning process than has previously operated in the schools. The performance approach, which is the basis of most art or music education in the classroom, seeks to develop manipulative skills; but what is or is not, in fact, learned by the student tends to remain unknown and unsought. Remarkably little systematic thought has been applied to the arts in an educational setting. What research has been conducted in the field has yielded little more than final reports that sit on the shelves of the funding agencies. As Nuthall states it, regarding research in open education: "It must be obvious to the critical reader that what is missing from many of the reported studies is the sense of direction and contolled orderliness which can only be provided by adequate theory . . ." (Nuthall, 1968).

An even more compelling argument for an adequate theory of instruction generated by research and policy development is offered by

Glaser (1976). He contends that there are four components necessary for an operational theory of instruction:

1. analysis of the competence, the state of knowledge and skill to be achieved;
2. description of the initial state with which learning begins;
3. conditions that can be implemented to bring about change from the initial state of the learner to the state described as competence; and
4. assessment procedures for determining the immediate and long-range outcomes of the condition that are put into effect to implement change from the initial state of competence to further development.

Glaser elaborates on the second component by stating that: "descriptive theory (research knowledge) of some kind is a necessary prerequisite for prescriptive theory (theory of instruction) if the design procedures we (in education) use in the design of instruction are to be at all like the procedures used in other professions." Stated in the most direct terms, we might say that we ought to know what we are doing before we go ahead and do it! It is only a small exaggeration to point out that in the field of education in the arts, we don't know very much about what we are doing.

One final caveat is offered here to suggest that present program support for education in the arts, of which the bringing of artists into schools is the leading example, suffers certain shortcomings. In his famous *Theory of Instruction,* Jerome Bruner says the following: "The type of supporting research that permits one to assess how well one is succeeding in the management of relevant instructional variables requires a constant and close collaboration of teacher, subject-matter specialist, and psychologist." I would embellish Bruner's condition by adding that both developmental and cognitive psychologists are essential to development in the instructional process.

The Fields in which Research Is Called For

There are three levels of consideration in the field of arts and humanities requiring the systematic study that research and development can bring to the improvement of education in that field:

THE ARTS AND HUMANITIES AS TRADITIONAL SUBJECT MATTER. In the schools that means the art and music specialists and their respective curricula. While it is unclear how the level of education is to be enhanced, that improvement is necessary goes almost without saying. Career development in the arts, knowledge acquisition, or at least an amateur's level of performance is, or should be, an obligatory part of every school's curriculum in the visual arts, music, theatre, dance, and the humanities, so that those with the predisposition and the talent can enjoy the opportunity of development in that direction.

NEW INTERDISCIPLINARY AREAS, SUCH AS AESTHETICS AND HUMANITIES CORE PROGRAMS. Recent development efforts have enlarged the school's offerings in the arts and traditional humanities (history, literature, etc.) with interdisciplinary or reconceptualized disciplines that seek to permeate the basic academic subject areas. In many cases, such efforts are exhortative and prescriptive rather than adequately predicated upon solid theoretical and pedagogical grounds. New disciplines or restructuring of old and compartmentalized subject areas require epistemological underpinnings than are now not adequately provided.

THE THIRD AREA HAS ALREADY BEEN ALLUDED TO IN THIS DISCUSSION AS HIGHER-ORDER COGNITIVE LEARNING. This recent area of research and development crosses cognitive and affective lines, and sees the human organism as a nonverbal (as well as verbal) symbol-maker, metaphor user, perceiver and creator of patterns and structures that constitute at once an integrated model of reality and a mode of discourse.

It is to be understood that the three areas above are not mutually exclusive, nor do they invite a rank ordering. They are, in fact, considered to be part of a whole, each incomplete without the understanding and educational implementation of the other. Given these strictures, it becomes possible to outline the tasks necessary to conduct research and development in the arts in education:

1. Study the state-of-the-art in the field of arts and humanities education; that is, collect baseline data about present school utilization (dollars, personnel, etc.) and conduct comparative studies with other advanced nations in the area of education in the arts and humanities. The last serious, comprehensive, statistical study of arts and music in the schools of the United States was published in 1963. There has been some recent updating, and elementary school enrollments are believed to have increased 41 percent since that last large study. While many colleges and universities offer a program in the arts and in the humanities, ranging from Germanic traditionalism and scholarship to recent interdisciplinary and thematic approaches, the elementary and secondary schools suffer from a serious neglect in those same subject areas. We assume the art and music education in the nation's schools are less than satisfactory. Similarly the humanities are usually tacked on as enrichment to social studies or English curricula. The fact is, we don't really know the quality or level of effort. What, then, do we expect from research?

2. Through research and development, we expect to bring the educational technology to a state comparable with that of reading.

3. Through research we expect to explore the relatively new frontier of basic cognitive/affective learning, as these two separate areas inform each other and work conjointly.

4. Through research, development, and dissemination, we expect to increase the effectiveness of all the components of education in the arts and humanities in the schools.

There is a significant shift presently taking place in educational research that recognizes the complexity and interdependence of the many components of the education process. Thus, the traditional research procedure that operates solely by the molecular analysis of one element as the subject of study is gradually giving way to the ethnographic observation of the total integral phenomenon of the classroom or the school. Curriculum development of "teacher-proof" materials, injected into the system after the completion of the packages, is being replaced by emphasis upon practitioner-created curricula and the integration of teacher training with curriculum development. Recognition is being given to the fact that teaching cannot be mechanically separated from what is to be taught. Indeed, there are many dimensions of the educative process requiring closer and more systematic analysis in order to better understand the individual elements and how they fit into the total, organic whole of the system.

The research and development program in the arts in education should take into account, in a vertically integrated way, all of the following:

- concept and theory formulation
- policy research, data and survey collection
- analysis of the field, statistical analysis
- basic research in such areas as nonverbal cognition
- applied research in natural settings
- ethnographic studies of a variety of treatments
- development of processes and materials for students, teachers and parents, administrators
- evaluation design and development
- dissemination, installation, information diffusion
- market, consumer linkages with research and development community
- funding strategy development, foundation and other resource coordination
- advocacy and public information
- personnel development

We need to organize the presently fragmentary and random activities that purport to improve the teaching of the arts in the schools, in a fashion that can be structured along three dimensions. These three dimensions are integrated into a matrix cube. See *Figure 1*.

The first dimension of the matrix cube lists the major activites usually subsumed under the rubric of arts and humanities. There are professional organizations representing the teaching profession in each of these areas. There is a literature and there are publications specifically for each of these sections. When the activity is primarily theoretical, focusing upon theory, criticism, analysis, and history, then that activity falls more properly into the humanities. When the activity is primarily performance and production, it becomes an art. This is not the proper place to trace the development of the humanities from the medieval trivium and quadrivium, nor is it appropriate to explicate the distinc-

Figure 1

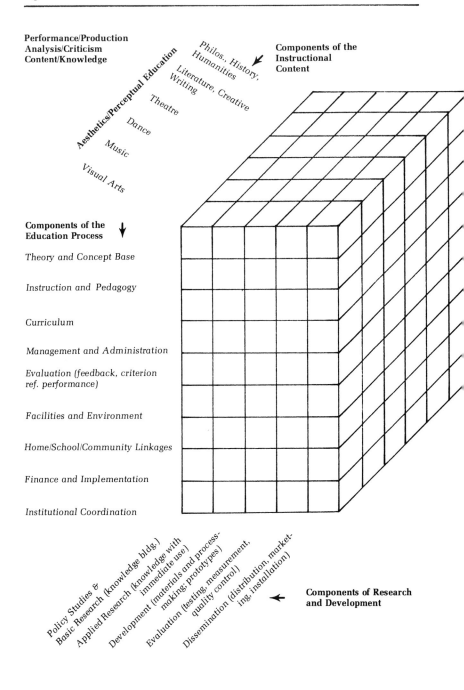

Performance/Production
Analysis/Criticism
Content/Knowledge

Aesthetics/Perceptual Education
Philos., History, Humanities
Literature, Creative Writing
Theatre
Dance
Music
Visual Arts

Components of the
Instructional
Content

**Components of the
Education Process**

Theory and Concept Base

Instruction and Pedagogy

Curriculum

Management and Administration

Evaluation (feedback, criterion
ref. performance)

Facilities and Environment

Home/School/Community Linkages

Finance and Implementation

Institutional Coordination

Policy Studies & Basic Research (knowledge bldg.)
Applied Research (knowledge with immediate use)
Development (materials and process-making; prototypes)
Evaluation (testing, measurement, quality control)
Dissemination (distribution, market-ing, installation)

**Components of Research
and Development**

tions among the arts and humanities beyond those already made between the two National Endowments. For purposes of a research and
development policy, let it suffice to specify the program area to be limited, along the dimensions of content, to:

1. The visual arts, including painting, graphics, sculpture, architecture, photography, cinema; and such practical arts as environmental design and urban planning, insofar as their focus is primarily
   aesthetic;
2. Music, including composition, performance, and musicology;
3. Dance;
4. Theatre;
5. Literature and creative writing, as distinct from those language
   arts stressing functional literacy and practical skills development;
6. The traditional humanities, such as history, philosophy, and
   theology, as distinct from social science and those subjects pursued for practical rather than intellectual values;
7. Aesthetic education as a distinct subject, incorporating appreciation, analysis and criticism, taste, sensory, and perceptual awareness, and skills. Aesthetic education would also incorporate the
   above-listed six areas. Aesthetic education would include art as
   well as non-art. Non-art would include the artificial, man-made
   world as well as natural phenomena. The three major dimensions
   of the aesthetic experience include the sensory surface (that is, the
   immediacy of experience of the senses apart from the meaning of
   the phenomenon); the formal, structural, or compositional elements of the phenomenon as revealed through analysis; and, finally, the content, the meaning, or symbolic aspects of the experience, which are parallel to the act of reading comprehension and
   related to it (Broudy, 1972).

The components of the education process constitute the second dimension of the matrix cube:

THEORY AND CONCEPT BASE. This means that there must be a rational and defensible foundation, rooted in philosophy and psychology,
that justifies any one or all of the activities listed in the first dimension.
The issue under consideration as policy here is the area of overlap between the arts and humanities on the one hand and the education process on the other. Therefore, theories must be developed that are appropriate to both aspects. For example, there are many theories of
aesthetics, which itself is a subdivision of philosophy. But there are very
few theories of aesthetic *education*, and there are as yet none that have
been tested and proven in the implementation of a program based upon
such a theory. By the same token, most educational theories are too
mechanistic for the teaching of the arts.

INSTRUCTION AND PEDAGOGY. Assuming that significant improvement in education is attained only when all the necessary change pieces
are in place, it is desirable to consider instructional improvement in the
context of a solid theoretical foundation as well as a well-designed cur-

riculum. Indeed, it seems likely that curriculum and delivery systems ought to be designed simultaneously. For purposes of analysis, however, instructional processes have been selected as a separate category. The primary emphasis should be on teaching research. Teaching, I believe, is the single most critical variable; yet, it has been the weakest link in the educational chain. Most long-range projections point to the need for massive in-service training programs.

CURRICULUM. A study is needed identifying all existing curriculum materials and packages, distinguishing between systems and single events, and multi-media materials and texts. It may well be that curriculum has received too much attention in relationship to the other aspects of the educational system. More important than the curriculum itself may be the process of development, where and how it is conducted, and how it is utilized. Furthermore, the usual exclusive association between curriculum and schools may be too limiting, and thought should be given to a consideration of out-of-school curricula, such as for home use.

MANAGEMENT AND ADMINISTRATION. Because the arts lack the political base available to the basic skills in the schools, they lack the administrative commitment that could bring them into the core of the school program. The JDR 3rd Fund has made such administrative commitment its major goal in furthering its program, "All the Arts for Every Child." Coalitions of states and cities constitute the cutting edge of their agenda.

While over half of the states have included the arts and humanities in their basic educational-goal statements, that aspect of the curriculum is still relegated to the fringes of the program and the school budget. Additionally, the management of organizations established to further the arts has turned it into a vast, fragmented network of state and local bureaucracies, each vying for limited funds, and competing with the school system at the state and local level for federal and foundation support.

EVALUATION. One of the reasons that the arts and humanities have not attained a more central place in the school curriculum is the lack of adequate evidence that such a program can make a difference in student learning. A number of researchers have been working in the area of "soft" evaluation (Torrance, Barron, Stake), but none has yet developed adequate and universally satisfactory measures of student performance in the creative areas. More recent developments in student and teacher evaluation could have an even more significant impact upon the arts and humanities education field; that is, on efforts in measures of performance-based education and criterion-referenced evaluation.

FACILITIES AND ENVIRONMENT. Usually neglected as an area either irrelevant to education or not susceptible to intervention from the instructional community, facilities and environment have recently become recognized as having significant educational impact. Several projects have generated research designs that take the physical environment into effect. It may be as important as the psychological environment of which it is a part. One possible outcome of research in this area may be that school buildings are not necessarily the best places to conduct an education in the arts. Such findings would impinge significantly upon the other elements of this dimension.

HOME/SCHOOL/COMMUNITY LINKAGES. As research in developmental psychology more and more suggests the importance of home and community, educational research and development must take that factor into account. On the one hand, school budgets are stretched to the breaking point; and the arts, as special services, are lowest on the priority list and are therefore, most expendable. The burden of responsibility for education in the arts and humanities must, consequently, be spread more widely. On the other hand, the community already serves as a major educational resource in a variety of areas — the arts are among the most prominent. The Expansion Arts division of the National Endowment for the Arts has facilitated community arts growth and its educational potential. However, the Endowment is not equipped or mandated to make the educational aspects of these programs systematically functional. Their educational impact is, therefore, a matter of chance. These two factors join to provide a major task for NIE in the creation of linkages among home, school, and community.

FUNDING AND IMPLEMENTATION. Just as the Finance and Productivity Group of NIE is looking at the problem of fiscal support for the school system, a similar examination is necessary for an understanding of costs and dollar needs in the area of the arts and humanities. Processes of installation, implementation, and sustenance of arts and humanities programs are a major problem in education during times of economic retrenchment.

INSTITUTIONAL COORDINATION. Coordination is necessary among state and local school administrations and their divisions of arts and humanities supervision and their respective roles. These include professional arts organizations and the professional arts education organizations, the foundations, the colleges of art, and the colleges of education. The distribution of functions and the coordination of resource allocation for equitability among the arts is needed, but not to the disadvantage of the arts education community. All these issues demand calm, professional investigation, devoid of the petty political maneuvering that now animates some of these organizations.

The third dimension of the matrix pertains to the research and development process itself. While certain approaches in research and development may, at one one time or another, become more useful, yield more significant results, or be more appropriate to one area of concern than another, it becomes clear that *all* approaches must be considered and integrated to obtain a comprehensive picture. That is the message of the matrix. All three dimensions must be subject to rigorous, systematic and professional inquiry and development at the same time in order to achieve the critical mass necessary to impact the schooling process in the arts.

The first element in the research and development process confronts the large picture, the macro-goals, and critical policy issues. Policy is a course of action predicated upon certain principles. Such principles can be derived from a comprehensive study of an issue that yields a number of action alternatives. They are also derived from empirical research, psychology, and philosophy. Without an informing set of principles, any policy lacks a rationale and intellectual legitimacy. Too many pieces of funding legislation are created devoid of explicit principles. Too many agencies function with one set of policies that conceal another divergent, underlying set of policies. Thus, vague educational principles distract from political realities. Needs assessments, resource assessments, task analyses, and other modes of disciplined inquiry constitute the necessary first cut at research. Sophisticated statistical methodology, secondary analysis, and psychometrics have their place in empirical studies that seek to increase the verifiability of knowledge. However, there are other modes of obtaining reliable knowledge (as distinct from data or information). Such more clinical and subjective observational techniques will come to play a larger role in educational research, and appropriately so. The other elements of the research and development process—*applied research,* meaning knowledge with immediate applicability; *development,* which refers to processes as well as products; *evaluation,* which incorporates testing and all forms of measurement and other judgement formation; and *dissemination,* getting the knowledge out into the field—all these processes must be employed at *every* stage of the educative process and in each of the subject areas that constitute the arts and humanities in education.

The implementation of such a comprehensive research and development matrix calls for massive institutional capability. This will not be possible so long as the funding organizations, the government, school systems, and the foundations do not communicate and plan with each other. It will not be possible so long as the receiving organizations, the research companies, the institutes, the labs and centers, and the various independent researchers in the universities and the school systems do not participate in a vast information network of the kind that has been so essential to the evolution of scientific and technological research and development.

The initial step in priority-setting for creating policy in arts and aesthetic education is the installation of a far more effective communication system. Every project should incorporate dissemination as a line item. A national network for information, newsletters, planning conferences, and publication is a first-order activity. There has been too much "territorial defense," "turf-building," and empire protection among both the funders and the implementers; too much political maneuvering, too many hidden agendas, too much propaganda and self-serving rhetoric. There has been too little admission of failure or expression of doubt, too little sharing of problems, too little willingness to function cooperatively among what are now competing constituencies. And, above all, there has been too little professional and intellectual honesty and rigor.

The second priority is closely tied to the first. There is considerable talent and activity in research and development distributed across the United States, in colleges and universities, research institutions, school systems, and school support organizations. For lack of coordination, and centralized analysis and review, the same or similar proposals are being written simultaneously on both coasts, and the same or similar support institutions, such as Humanities Institutes or Arts Education Research Institutes, are being established competitively at the same moment. I say competitively due to the struggle to obtain what are clearly very limited resources for the creation of such institutions. The proliferation of such "centers" will consume the bulk of the resources in administrative and managerial costs, create new and expanded bureaucracies, and provide handsome offices for well-travelled organization men. Thus, those resources will not be available for substantive work in the broad and demanding array of areas previously identified in the matrix.

We need to know what we are doing when we conduct education in the arts. However, there are those who would prefer not to base their activities upon a rational policy model, but instead respond to or create political pressures that obviate any efforts to create a professionally respectable, intellectually honest knowledge base.

The next most pressing area of work in this field is the gathering of information about the present state of the arts. We know next to nothing about the raw baseline data: How many teachers? What are they doing? What are the costs? What are the outcomes of the present levels of effort? How many students? What are the longitudinal effects of present modes of intervention? Etc. Such data collection should be the basis of policy research. Like the blind men and the elephant, no one seems to have a complete overview of the situation. Indeed, the situation may be far worse or far better than is commonly supposed. What is the present level of competence among teachers of music or visual art or theatre in the schools? How many teachers are there who are duly certified and what have been the criteria for their certification? Unless that data base is created, any research and development work will be like groping in the dark. One may stumble upon something good, but it is too chancy and not a cost-effective way to proceed.

The list of priorities can be reconstituted in any of a number of ways, but certainly among the first three points is the need for determining a universally acceptable language of mission, purpose, and goals for education in the arts. While there can be little disagreement that such language ought to include the enhancement of student development in the six areas that Lowenfeld identified so long ago — emotional, physical, perceptual, social, aesthetic, and creative—far greater specificity is called for.

Criteria for making arts in education programs acceptable to national standards have been incorporated in the *Federal Register* (vol. 40, no. 126) in seven points, which bear repeating here. While these points

cannot fulfill the need for a federal policy in arts and humanities education, they do mandate a set of conditions not yet fully realized in the
programs of *any* agency. A research program that takes this important
but vague language and gives it operational meaning has yet to be developed. Such a program should use these seven points as guides, if not
as objectives:

1. The program must be designed to encourage the development
   in students of aesthetic awareness in the arts, and to foster
   self-actualization and the development of communicative skills
   through movement, sound, visual images, and verbal usage;
2. The program must be designed to involve all the students in
   the school or schools served. (The program may serve one or
   more schools in a single school district or, in case of joint applications, in several school districts);
3. The program must be designed to involve each student in appreciation, enjoyment, understanding, creation, participation,
   and evaluation with respect to the arts;
4. The program must be designed to involve students at all grade
   levels in the school or schools served;
5. The program must address the spectrum of major art forms, including dance, music, drama, and the visual arts;
6. The program must be designed to infuse the arts into all aspects
   of the school curriculum as a means of enhancing and improving the quality and quantity of aesthetic education offered in
   the school and of expanding the use of the arts for cognitive
   and affective learning experiences in the total school curriculum; and
7. The program must integrate all the major art forms into the
   regular educational program of the school or schools served, as
   distinguished from treating them on an extracurricular or
   peripheral basis.

Summary

To encapsulate the several points suggested in this rambling discourse:
The piecemeal approach to education in the arts in unsatisfactory. The
intuitive casting together of varieties of artists with student populations
on the assumption that good, educational things will happen is also
unsatisfactory. A comprehensive federal program can and should be
developed and pooled among the various funding agencies, each
contributing its substantive capability and commitment as well as its
dollars. The approach must be coordinated so that standing committees
of representatives will meet constantly to share their respective
agencies' agendas. Research and development must be supported and the
many pieces more effectively integrated to attain some degree of
progress. That education is a complex enterprise consisting of many
components must be understood as the basis for an integrated program
of research and development embracing all activities, from concept and

theory building on one end of the spectrum to dissemination and the measurement of learner outcomes on the other end. Not only is education, as it is conducted in the schools, a highly complex set of activities and processes, but the research and development system is equally diverse—with the impact of various philosophies and psychologies to serve as the intellectual foundations for empirical analysis, as well as an organic and humanistic synthesis leading to more effective learning in the arts and humanities, and more universal availability of education to facilitate such learning.

There has been an unreasonable mutual hostility among a variety of constituencies. Artists have little use for educators or teachers of the arts. Teachers see the artist as totally self-serving and irresponsible. Educational research has been viewed (and perhaps rightly so) for many years as a worthless counting of grains of sand on the beach, accumulating data that no one cares about and that have no value to the teacher in the classroom. However, educational research has become a great deal more than this. It has become a systematic and serious activity with potentially important consequences to the student in the schools. At its best, it is disciplined inquiry, comprehensive, and intellectually thorough and honest. It elevates, or can elevate, education from random success by one or two talented teachers, to a process that will attain positive results with more students in many kinds of educational settings under diverse conditions. It can do so when it looks at education in the larger, interactive perspective that is becoming the hallmark of good research. The arts, aesthetic education, and the humanities have been neglected by the larger educational community because it has been unable to see the importance of the humanistic disciplines as *disciplines* in the total educational enterprise. It will be the mission of the educational research and development community to provide light in order to make that vision possible and universally available.

Washington, D. C.
June 1976

Methodological Issues
in the Arts and Aesthetics

This section deals with the methodological issues of research. As mentioned in the introduction, these issues concern procedures and philosophic stances that should be used in designing a research agenda. Each of the authors in this section points to the need for research in one or more topics, but also supports a method for accomplishing it.

Morris Weitz argues for less reliance on the scientific mode of inquiry, and says that research does not have to be scientific, nor does science own research. He goes on to say that creation is not the same as research, it need not involve research, nor can artistic creation even be scientifically researched. Research on the arts or in aesthetics, therefore, would be most effective in the area of actual response to art and the aesthetic. Research as theory building and testing should be supported and should concentrate on psychological problems such as the genesis of the aesthetic in the development of the child. This, according to **Weitz**, constitutes the only way to a science of aesthetic education.

Eugene Kaelin and **David Ecker** look toward teacher education and university-based research as the method for accomplishing our goals in aesthetic education. They describe an aesthetic-education program that would promote the growth of the "whole child." The child's responses to its total environment—the goal of all education—can be achieved through aesthetic education. According to **Kaelin** and **Ecker,** informed aesthetic perception would cause the whole person to focus on a single experience and, through this, the unique experience of self. Since no "subject" is separate from the experience of the child, aesthetic education could serve to integrate everything taught in the public schools. Such a comprehensive education program will require university training of fully self-experiencing teachers of this interdisciplinary program, as well as curriculum development to infuse the arts into the total school environment. Thus, what future basic experimental research and development in aesthetic education requires is nothing less than a fully conceptualized and empirically grounded picture of human potential for aesthetic inquiry. To achieve the ends of a fully comprehensive education program when budgets are limited, universities will have to be the leaders in innovative research, development, training, and whatever else is required.

Arthur Wells Foshay poses key questions for curriculum research to answer, and describes areas in other domains of knowledge we can draw on for information for curriculum development in the arts and aesthetics. In order to develop a curriculum, these questions must be addressed: *Who* is to encounter *what, why, how,* in what *circumstances,* under what *governance,* at what *cost?* Descriptive research in philosophy, social psychology, learning psychology, anthropology, and political science can find answers to these problem questions. However, **Foshay** says that multi-disciplinary research should be avoided in order to benefit from each discipline's distinct point of view. Such descriptive research will eventually yield classification systems that can be used in the design of studies in the arts and in aesthetic education.

Harry Broudy describes the basis for the variety of reactions to a concept of aesthetic education. He states that groups interested in aesthetic education share an intent to educate in a variety of the arts, a hope that aesthetic education will achieve a solid position in the public-school curriculum, and a belief that aesthetic education is possible and desirable for the total school population. **Broudy** goes on to say that there is less agreement among the advocates of aesthetic education on the degree of its link with extra-aesthetic—moral, political, economic, religious, civic—values; the integration of aesthetic education with other fields of instruction; and the aesthetic and education theories behind the objectives and approaches to aesthetic education. He advocates extensive research and development activity to ameliorate many of the maladies preventing progress in aesthetic education; providing that communication of findings can be made available through a central, unifying agency.

Morris Weitz

Research on the Arts and in Aesthetics: Some Pitfalls, Some Possibilities

It is a common assumption that research dominates and unites all the sciences and, consequently, can serve as the defining condition of respectability for all disciplines. This assumption and ideal, pushed to its extreme, not only renders aesthetics suspect but, more important, does less than justice to the differences among the sciences. Research is hardly the defining characteristic, for example, of pure mathematics — traditionally the hardest of the hard sciences — for there are no theories or hypotheses in mathematics that are arrived at either by induction from observations of data or that are projected as conjectures submitted for refutation. Thus, in the sense, debatable as it is, in which physics, from Galileo to Einstein and beyond, can be characterized as primarily a research discipline — that is, a mixture of theory and experiment, always in relation to data or phenomena that cry out for explanation — neither pure mathematics nor some of the social sciences, such as history, engage in research. Theory, testing of theories, experiment, and consequent confirmation and information, are simply out of place here.

Our problem, however, is not "What is science?" or "What counts as a science?", but rather "What is or counts as research?" Is it restricted to the model of the physical sciences, the model of theory and experiment?

While it is true, I think, that some of the recognized sciences, such as chemistry, astronomy, and biology, aspire to the ideal of research or a research program in which the formulation and testing of theories are dominant; and that some of the putative sciences, such as psychology, anthropology, sociology, and even history, recognize and pursue this ideal, there are disciplines that engage in research without, at the same time, centering on such formulations and testings of theories. These disciplines, which encompass the humanities and philosophy, including aesthetics, may not be scientific in their deviation from the model of theory-building and testing, but they are nevertheless committed to research.

Science without theory and experiment may be a misnomer, though mathematics would demur. But research without theory and experiment

MORRIS WEITZ *is Professor of Philosophy at Brandeis University.*

is no misnomer, unless such research is legislated away by scientists, who would then themselves misname by unduly restricting the reference of "research" to what they do.

Historians, for example, engage in research. They delve into archives, search out documents in valiant efforts to uncover long-forgotten facts about the past. In probing the past or in writing up their findings and in telling their stories about their chosen bits, small or large, about the past, they may seek generalizations; they may even employ causal laws of one sort or another, but they need not — indeed they had better not — aim at the formulation of a theory, for that way lies those philosophies of history, such as Augustinianism, Marxism, or Freudianism. so roundly rejected by working historians. At most, historians may offer interpretations or explanations of the phenomena they are concerned with, in which hypotheses are proffered and historical evidence is marshaled to support these hypotheses. Perhaps these interpretations are sufficiently similar to the formulation and testing of theories to validate history as *scientific,* if not as a science; however, history and historical research may begin and end with the marshaling of facts without converting these facts into evidence for any hypothesis. In science, the discovery of uninterpreted data — that is, phenomena that present themselves, as it were, quite accidentally, therefore independently, of the formulation and testing of theories — is outside the mainstream of the hypothetical-deductive method, although it may, if a happy accident, lead to further theories. But in history, the discovery of data, prompted or not by a hypothesis — a hunch — may be the very point of the research.

The meticulous assembling of facts for its own sake is, thus, a kind of research. That it is castigated as pointless unless it is an integral part of a research program of theory formulation and testing is itself pointless, since it rules out the importance of the discovery of facts and the crucial authentication of documents.

What, next, of philosophy and, in particular, of aesthetics? Neither, it seems to me, is a science. Nor are they scientific, except in the putatively analogous sense in which some great philosophers and aestheticians have conceived them: as the statement of true theories or ontological, epistemological, moral, or aesthetic hypotheses that can be confirmed by experience, if not by experiment. But that philosophy is scientific in the first sense of a true theory is rejected by those very philosophers who promote philosophy as true theory, and dissociate such theory from the fallible theories of science. And that philosophy is scientific in the second sense of the formulation of hypotheses, to be confirmed by experience, is repudiated by those philosophers (and scientists) who claim that it is precisely the untestability of philosophical theories that precludes their being scientific at all and therefore makes them rightly castigatable as meaningless because unverifiable in any sense.

Without indulging in this fundamental debate about the nature of philosophy and whether or not it is science, scientific, allied to science, or downright unscientific, there is at least one aspect of philosophy, both traditional and contemporary, that emphasizes the conceptual character of philosophy — that philosophy is essentially the probing and clarification of the concepts we employ in thinking and talking about the world. Philosophy, according to this conviction, deals with concepts, not things; with thoughts, not facts. Philosophy, then, is not science; it is not scientific. But since it probes, describes, clarifies, or analyzes the way or ways we think and talk about things, it too is a kind of research: into concepts, their nature and roles in human life. Philosophy's primary aim is to assemble reminders of the ordinary ways that we use certain concepts. Its derivative aim is to resolve those problems that rest on conceptual muddles and not on confused facts. That the concept of art or the word "art" is not employed as a concept or term to describe and evaluate works of art under a set of *definitive* conditions or criteria is a paradigm of this kind of conception of philosophy. Such a logical investigation is a claim about a concept, not about art. Is it, as a philosophical claim, a putative result of research, even if it is not the formulation and testing of a theory or an assemblage and authentication of facts? Perhaps it is closer to the creation (rather than research) that one finds in pure mathematics. But it does not resemble the creation of art; and, because it does not, perhaps we ought to allow it as a form of research: an inquiry into concepts, without theories as hypotheses submitted for experimental refutation, and without searches into hitherto lost facts. Having devoted much of the last two decades or so to this sort of logical probing of the conceptual life, I am most reluctant to call these endeavors anything other than a kind of research. I wish it were a species of artistic creation. I am delighted that it is not a form of the theory-building and testing of the scientist. It is a probing, a digging, into how we think and talk; it does uncover, it does clarify and explain. So why is it not research? Of course it *is*.

Science, then, does not *own* research. Research is not necessarily scientific either. Nor is it the same as creation; nor must creation involve any kind of research, including the scientific, that some have misleadingly called "problem-solving," in an ingenious effort to render scientific the creative process of the artist, but with the result that it perverts both creation and science. Here, then, are some of the pitfalls I flagged in the title. What, now, about the possibilities of research on the arts and in aesthetics?

If I am right in distinguishing between creation and research, then it is a mistake to talk about research *in* the arts, at least as this is confined to artistic creation. I do not know what artistic creation is; nor does anyone else, as all definitions and attempts at definition, with all their failures, both yesterday and today, attest. Consequently, that the creation of a work of art is the doing of a piece of research or even includes some research, in any of the acceptable senses of "research," is at best egregious and at worst false. And to pose the possibility of an extensive research program in the full-scale sense of the formulation and testing of theories about art creation — firmly rooted in psychological, physical, and sociological laws, though mind-boggling in itself — would have to consign research in the arts to established areas of already ongoing scientific disciplines. I do not for one moment wish to suggest that such a program is not ideal or even feasible — it is certainly as ideal and feasible as the search for a general theory of human behavior and action. Rather, I would suggest that such a program cannot be restricted to artistic creation since it must include the whole class of human activity, of which artistic creation is a species, as adamant perhaps as any of the other species.

Traditionally, aesthetics has distinguished four sets of problems: (1) What is artistic creation? (2) What is a work of art? (3) What is aesthetic experience or the distinctive response to art or beauty? (4) What is the function of art?

I am suspicious of all these questions. I do not think, to begin with the first, that there is a definitional answer to "What is artistic creation?"; and I think that there is no extant or forthcoming scientific answer that would provide the requisite overall hypothesis or theory about human behavior, as well as the specific hypothesis or theory about artistic activity. However, though the definitional approach is, I think, conceptually self-contradictory, since the concept of creativity is not amenable to any real definition, the scientific is not self-contradictory; consequently, there is no reason why we should stop seeking an answer. The only bit of advice I can offer here is that if scientific research—theory-building and testing—is to be carried on in this area, we must begin not with testable theories about artistic creation but with the questions we need to ask and to answer. What are these questions about the role of research in the arts and, in particular, in artistic creation, that we want to ask and to answer? I have yet to hear a clear and askable set of them.

About the second question of traditional aesthetics — What is a work of art? — there is the same vast array of claims and generalizations about the common denominators of art and their differentia from each other, along with accompanying wholesale definitions of art or music or painting or poetry, and so on. However one assesses these claims, generalizations, and theories or real definitions, there is little, if any, place for research as science or as the scientific method conceives theory; and there is almost nothing but research as conceptual probing and clarification in regards to the real definitions of art, whether traditional or recent ones. Thus, "What are the discernible features of works of art?" and "What defines a work of art?"—however we rank these questions — belong, as they traditionally have, to criticism and philosophy. I see no opening here for scientific research to move in.

What about response to art or to the aesthetic? Here, too, we have traditionally been treated to a medley or amalgam of factual and normative theories: how people do respond and vary in their responses to the same work or different works, within the same or in different cultures; as against how they ought to respond, once the nature of art or the beautiful is noted and offered as a desiderated value. The normative programs and recommendations, from Plato to Tolstoy and beyond, suggest the very opposite of research in any of its senses since they constitute pure philosophy as normative argument or conceptual closure. The factual claims and generalizations, on the other hand, about responders to art, like the analogous theses about the creators of art, do invite all sorts of questions that are relevant to the theory formulation and testing we associate with psychology and sociology. Here, too, there are wholesale questions, such as, Why do human beings respond as they do to works of art "x," "y," or "z," or to the properties "a," "b," or "c" of "x," "y," or "z"? Why do we see certain patterns as we do, hear certain sounds as we do, and so on? If Freudianism seems to have led the day in regard to a psychology of art creation, *gestaltism* seems to remain the leading theoretical model for the theories and experiments of the factual problems that converge on the aesthetic problem of response to art and the aesthetic in the world. Rudolf Arnheim *(Art and Visual Perception)* and E. H. Gombrich *(Art and Illusion)*, among others, have been singularly successful in applying already worked-out theoretical models to certain questions about responses, especially to visual art. Leonard Meyer *(Music, the Arts and Ideas)* also has applied an already independently established scientific theory or research program to our appreciation of music as he attempts to explain our experience and attribution of style or styles to compositions by utilizing certain fertile hypotheses within the general framework of information theory.

Thus, if there is such a thing as research or the possibility of a research program on the arts or in aesthetics, it is my conviction, which I submit for consideration, that it is precisely in this area of actual response to art and the aesthetic that progress can be hoped for and achieved. "Why do certain individuals create art?" seems too intractable; "Why do we respond as we do to art or to the aesthetic in nature, and in general and in particular?" seems just tractable enough.

As I conceive such a research program, it would eschew sociology, with its amassing of data, most of it statistical, and concentrate instead on the psychological problems invested in this congeries of problems. For the truth is, if only we would admit it, that we already know a great deal, mostly by our (sad) observations about the dearth of aesthetic responses among those whom I have called, in other contexts, the "under-perceivers." What we know nothing about is the genesis of the aesthetic in the growth of the child. Jean Piaget, in some classic studies, and now Jerome Bruner and his associates have invested a lifetime of research into the cognitive growth of the child. Why not, at this present time, the same full-scale inquiry into the genesis of the aesthetic in the child; and before the non-aesthetic, or the rejection of, or indifference to the aesthetic takes over? For there is a distinction, however difficult and debatable it is, between the sensory, cognitive, emotive, and aesthetic;

and psychology can proceed in a scientifically theoretical search for the origins and development of the aesthetic without getting bogged down in the struggle for a precise and strict definition of the aesthetic. Of course, it may very well be that there is no aesthetic genesis, as there is the cognitive development, in the child. Maybe the aesthetic is a wholly trained, cultivated, imposed-upon experience. *But we ought to find out.* If the aesthetic in the child can be ascertained and secured, and in such a manner as will allow us not only to explain but to predict, that discovery would be as important as anything forthcoming in aesthetic education, since the embodied theories of such a discovery could serve as established, scientific guidelines for the reinforcement of the aesthetic. This would enable us, as devotees of aesthetic education, to obviate or foreclose on the prevalent and massive contamination of the natural sense of the aesthetic in our society by adults. I do not know if what I am asking of psychology and of aesthetic research is coincident with what Thomas Kuhn *(The Structure of Scientific Revolutions)* characterizes as a revolution in science or not. But what is clear, at least to me, is that what he calls "normal science"—the working within established paradigms—will leave aesthetic research where it is now: the Cinderella sister of both psychology and aesthetics.

To sum up: there are various kinds of research, each as valuable and legitimate as the others. Each has application to the arts and to aesthetics. Search or re-search into facts or the authentication of data is one form. It is, I have said, best left to critics and historians of art; it needs no special research aid from any funding agency to be set up for this purpose, though it needs more than it receives to achieve its highest and noblest ends. So, too, with the second form of research on the arts and in aesthetics: conceptual inquiry. Philosophy does it; and it will continue to do it well or poorly without any new financial help, but with an increase of present support. It is only the third form — research as theory building and testing — that deserves new and aggressive support. Properly conceived and manned, such research could turn to — and as things pitifully are, not re-turn to — the basis, if not the *raison d'être*, of aesthetic education: the genesis of the aesthetic in the development of the child. That way, and only that way, beckons the road to a *science* of aesthetic education.

Waltham, Massachusetts
May 1976

Eugene F. Kaelin and David W. Ecker

The Institutional Prospects of Aesthetic Education

Until passage of the Elementary and Secondary Education Act of 1965, the history of related arts programs in the public schools had been largely a rag-tailed affair. The kite was made, but it wouldn't fly. Courses in "general music" and "general art" were taught, mostly in junior high school, but accomplished little by way of integrating those arts into the students' total programs. Music teachers taught courses in chorus or band for the students with a special interest in the subject, and even attempted to introduce programs of "music appreciation" as a peripheral subject open to the choice of all the students. Because the (graphic) art teacher benefitted by a group of children who had all passed through an earlier stage wherein they used pencils and crayons to draw things they saw about them—the better to coordinate their powers of perceiving with the habitual responses appropriate to the concepts they had inherited willy-nilly along with the language of their parents—the art classes were frequently designed to exploit the growing motor skills of the students: drawing became the "coordination of the hand and the eye." This is a powerful skill indeed, but one too easily bent to a strictly utilitarian purpose. Arguments grew up around the distinction between process-oriented and product-oriented models for training the young in the skills of art.[1] Meanwhile, out in the field, in extreme cases even the drawing was lost, since the aim of the training was the development of motor skills; and the art class became an exercise in the crafts, where students were supplied with two pieces of leather to be made into wallets by threading them through preset holes. There was no Picasso in the classroom because teachers had no Picasso in their experience. If there had been, of course, parents would have been equally as dismayed by what might have been brought home as they were by those symbolically empty wallets. The school is an expression of a given society; it will produce what that society wants. If the society sees art as a means for developing motor skills, that is what

EUGENE F. KAELIN *is Chairman of the Department of Philosophy at The Florida State University.* DAVID W. ECKER *is Professor of Art Education at New York University.*   **229** it will get from its schools; if it sees art as craftsmanship, then it should not be astonished that the schools provide it with leather craft and knick-knack shelves. What is there to be appreciated in art anyway?

Put in this way, the problem may seem unsolvable. Students received no art in the schools because their teachers lacked the experience, and the teachers lacked the experience because they received no art in their schools. But history has always refused to recognize unsolvable problems. Although it is true that the schools express the values of a society, the values of that society are amenable to change. Lest we be criticized for talking in abstractions, let it be said that a society is composed of both people and institutions. People we think we know something about; our institutions often baffle us. People think and institutions don't; that is why it is of some importance to have educational administrators who are capable of drawing thought out of the people whose work they administer. In a democratic society, administrators cannot think for their teachers. The institution is itself only a codifiable system of human behavioral patterns set up to promulgate a specific human value. The value promulgated by the church as an institution, for example, is community; of the school, human development. What was lacking in this stage of our historical account, then, was a recognition that art itself is an independent social institution — one that exists to allow the free expression and communication of aesthetic values, defined roughly as the experience of the qualities of human experience for the sake of those qualities.[2] The problem confronting the people thinking for and within our educational institutions was to devise a curriculum that would enable teachers and students to pursue the values of the aesthetic institution within the confines of the public schools.

The model for such an institution was clearly enough understood to contain the activity of artists and of critics. Now it has become commonplace to hear of art education on the model of the artist; the aim of such an education is to produce self-conscious artists.[3] And there arose proponents of the other view, objecting to the narrowness of the former, which takes the work of the practicing critic as its model:[4] not the making, but the informed judgment of works of art is the aim of aesthetic education. What relates the two sorts of activities, of course, is the common attitude of aesthetic judgment; but that question is now and may always remain moot within the scope of our knowledge concerning aesthetic experiences. At the university level, of course, both models have long been employed — in literature, in art and in music; and more recently in architecture, dance, and theater. Is it possible to bring the benefits of aesthetic education to the children of our public schools? The answer to such a question would seem to depend upon the strength of our expectations. In the classroom we may find fledgling artists, but few self-conscious creators of aesthetic experiences; some students who talk about their work, but few self-conscious critics. Something like what the artist does and something like what the critic does is, however, a necessary part of aesthetic education.

Perhaps the greatest impetus towards aesthetic education was created by professional societies, such as the National Art Education Association, the Music Teachers' National Association, the International Society of Music Education, the National Association for the Physical Education of College Women (for the dance), and the like, which were dedicated to the development of skills for the teachers of the teachers of the particular arts. And, as more teachers took their ranks within the schools, these organizations prospered with growing numbers of members, each imbued with the aims of a professional education in the arts. As their expertise grew, classes became more proficient centers of aesthetic education. School band and choral groups began producing music for the sake of the experience of the music; on some level, at least, art teachers could expand their curricula to include true art appreciation; and dance instructors could teach their medium as a means of creative expression.

The educational influence was healthy. Colleges of education took their responsibilities seriously, and the results began to trickle down into the public schools. That was the situation confronted by the Elementary and Secondary Education Act of 1965.

The colleges were producing teachers of the various arts, and all district school systems worth their salt had at least one program in arts instruction. But the movement, if such it may be called, became stultified by its very success. Departments of music and departments of dance, art, and theater tended to pursue the aims of their own particular art form. This situation still exists today, and constitutes one of the chief obstacles to developing a truly comprehensive arts program in the public schools.

Answers to such questions as why this, rather than another art program were phrased in terms of platitudes no thinking person of the general society was prepared to accept: "I don't know" (which is honest enough); or, "It's the nice or right thing to do"; or, "If you don't have something like this, you're just not cultured." The professionals were dedicated to teaching their medium as an end of instructional purposes, while parents and school boards began to ask the all-important questions of means: For example, what are you educating for when you use the various art media as the means of public school instruction? What aspect, if any, of the child's personality is being developed by increasing that child's responsiveness to the qualities of his or her experiences? Indeed, such questions as these posed the possibility of creating a new area of academic concern. When it was discovered that each of the arts served an overarching purpose, and that each of them could be used to develop that purpose in unique ways, the concept of aesthetic education became a compelling necessity.[5] In higher education, the University of Illinois instituted a program, under the direction of Harry Broudy, that began producing specialists within the field; and the federal government began its subsidization of the aesthetic education program to further implement the innovative idea. A good portion of that subsidization was awarded to the Central Midwestern Regional Educational Laboratory (CEMREL), Inc., of St. Ann, Missouri. The Illinois experiment was a phenomenon of the fifties, while the CEMREL experience was generated in the middle sixties.

The CEMREL Model

Within the last ten years. CEMREL's program in aesthetic education has gone through two exhaustive phases. The first was a joint venture between the Ohio State University and CEMREL, Inc., and headed by Manuel Barkan. The project had taken its impetus from a *Seminar in Art Education for Research and Curriculum Development*,[6] a report on the seminar on that topic held on the campus of the Pennsylvania State University in 1965 (Edward L. Mattil, project director). The task was to implement the change from the narrower concerns with art education to building a curriculum in aesthetic education. August Hecksher had already made his report to the President (John F. Kennedy) on the statement of national goals for the next decade, in which education in the arts was given prominent mention.[7] The times were ripe, the money was available, and the idea conceived. Professor Barkan mobilized a staff to design the guidelines for curriculum development in aesthetic education. The guidelines were published in February of 1970;[8] the work had been completed in December of 1969.

The guidelines were what must be called a conditional success. They allowed the Director of Phase II (Stanley Madeja) to collect a staff of curriculum writers with special training in one of the arts, introduce them to the aims of aesthetic education, and set them to work producing "program packages" through which these aims may be achieved in the classrooms of kindergarten through twelve. However, where the virtue of guidelines is to be short and incisive, CEMREL's guidelines were long and merely suggestive. Someone has already said that guidelines are written to be ignored, and these are no exception. The curriculum writers quickly learned that once the general aims of aesthetic education were understood, they could rely on their own intuitions and experience, counting on the feedback from hothouse and field trials to correct their errors of judgment. Quite literally, the curriculum writers became experts at what they did by doing it, sometimes with the help of the guidelines; but, lately, to a larger and larger degree, without that help. Up until the last review by the National Institute of Education, they had succeeded in producing curriculum packages for aesthetic education in grades kindergarten through seven, most of which are available from a publisher.

While the guidelines of Phase I were being prepared for publication, CEMREL had published its own account of its program plan; it appeared as *Basic Program Plan, Aesthetic Education* (1969, revised 1970).[9] In that document we read:

> The guidelines represent the first attempt to clarify and articulate
> a theoretical base for aesthetic education, to bring scholars from

many fields to discuss and make decisions about aesthetic education and to determine its relative importance, and, finally to give
direction to those who think aesthetic education is important
enough to be included in the school's curriculum. Such foundations are necessary for the development of sound and acceptable
curricula which are intended to be disseminated nationwide.[10]

The original guidelines did provide the foundations; curriculum packages were developed, used, and evaluated; and we now face the problem of the nationwide dissemination. It is interesting to note in passing,
however, that this same document succeeds in reducing the original
guidelines of 617 pages to a four-page appendix, entitled: "Suggestions
for preparing content outlines in aesthetic education for the primary
level."[11]

If the original guidelines were only conditionally successful — one
would need a special course in aesthetic education at the present level
of development even to read them intelligently — the program packages
of Phase II have yet to prove themselves in nationwide use. In the mean-
time, in the face of the nationwide economic recession, funds are becoming scarcer, and some school boards are finding the commercially
produced packages a heavy burden on limited budgets. Indeed, criticisms of the program have ranged from the high cost of procuring the
materials to a lack of teachers to use them effectively.

CEMREL is aware that its curriculum packages must depend for their
effectiveness on the interest and knowledgeability of public-school
teachers; so, as a kind of stopgap operation, is currently engaged,
through its Teacher Training Centers, in the training of teachers who
must use the materials. In the most recent review of the program it was
pointed out that, without specially trained teachers to introduce the
comprehensive aesthetic education program into the schools, no curriculum packages, however well-designed, will be an effective instrument to attain the goals now projected into the elementary and secondary schools' programs. And so, institutions of higher learning must be
inveigled into producing the teachers of aesthetic education — in a
specialized "Triple-T" program to be undertaken by graduate schools of
education. But the enormity of this task only becomes more obvious
when we realize that no graduate specialties in the field are now available to prospective teachers of the teachers; and that, until there are, few
qualified teachers will be produced for the public schools. In the next
ten years of research and development, that should be one of our primary aims.

Where are we now? If one of the reviewers of the program is correct,
that "CEMREL *is* aesthetic education in this country; it has the field to
itself," there is no point in beginning a new project that would replace
the last ten years' research and development for which the federal government has already spent millions of dollars. Although it may be coun-
terproductive to look back over our shoulders for an understanding of
the limitations of our success, it certainly is not without point to look

for the causes of our present condition. Why, for example, did Phase I end with guidelines that are too massive? And what will come of an effort of this size and scope when the proposed curriculum is evaluated by the public schools?[12]

The massiveness of the guidelines is perhaps the easiest to understand. Professor Barkan and his colleagues surveyed the literature available in philosophical and psychological aesthetics, literary and art criticism of all stripes, and the many manifestos of artists and schools of art. The aim was to keep from loading the program toward a particular point of view. And, given this base, the thesaurus of concepts and the sample list of "curriculum sentences" based thereon swelled to a quasi-infinity.

The authors of this paper tried to provide a more manageable grasp of the range of relevant aesthetic inquiry in two different attempts.

The first was completed with the help of the CEMREL staff. It surveyed the range of relevant disciplines, including experimental psychology, analytical philosophy, and contemporary phenomenological analysis.[13] And, more recently, the authors of the present essay have presented a sketch of the scope of aesthetic inquiry to the readers of the yearbook of the National Society for the Study of Education.[14] The title of the essay is suggestive: "The Limits of Aesthetic Inquiry: A Guide to Educational Research." There is no need in the present place to repeat that demonstration; it suffices to state that the explanatory "ladder" therein produced provides an adequate means of evaluating the relevance of aesthetic discourse. The methodological tool used to construct the ladder is the logical theory of language levels — a technique that could replace the one used to construct CEMREL's guidelines. And, in the second instance, it provides the framework for *a curriculum* in aesthetic education: both a list of the means to make operational the aims of aesthetic education, and a tool for measuring the success of the operation. The authors' claim is simple: Determine the possible scope of aesthetic knowledge — the five levels of inquiry noted — and you have a definition of the possibilities for aesthetic education. And it will be the structure of that knowledge that is to guide our curriculum development.

The Goals of Aesthetic Education

Aesthetic education should be conceived as an independent field of instruction, not as a replacement for courses in the general humanities, or in art, music, dance, and the like, whose purpose is to develop the specific human capacities served in the pursuit of the various artistic media. On the contrary, aesthetic education should be structured so as to use the particular specialities of the various art media to fulfill an educational aim not currently served in such courses. In spite of the growing number of courses in the particular arts, our school children are still being deprived of the essential good a workable curriculum in aesthetic education could provide. The particular arts are merely controlled examples of what might be done for students whose attention is drawn to the conditions of having aesthetic experiences in the various media. It's the responsiveness to aesthetic quality that provides the end of aesthetic education, and not greater skill in the performance within, or the "appreciation" of, a particular art form. As John Dewey would put it, every experience recognizable as an experience is pervaded by aesthetic quality.[15]

In aesthetic education, one can achieve what has been set as the goal of all education: the growth of the "whole child" through its reponses to its total environment. But only in aesthetic education is the whole child implicated in the educative process; as only in informed aesthetic perception are the centers of sense, affectivity, conceptualization, and imagination brought to focus in a single experience. Nowhere else, indeed, can one have such a clear notion of the experiencing self. The purpose of designing curriculum packages in aesthetic education is to allow teachers to come into contact with such an experiencing self — all the more reason to have knowledgeable teachers out in the field. These teachers must be able to work in more than one art form, and in such a way as to educate the child in its wholeness, rather than to teach a given subject. In this field there is no "subject" separate from the experiences of the child.[16] When these teachers have succeeded in institutionalizing the aims of the program by operationalizing the generating concepts of relevant aesthetic discourse, we shall have succeeded in introducing a new area into the public school curriculum: aesthetic education, that may take its place with the current staples — mathematical skills; language skills; the natural, the life, and the social sciences.

But we will have achieved more than that; for, when it is done correctly, aesthetic education should be able to do something no other of these staple disciplines may even approach. Besides a program that would integrate all the instruction in the various arts media, aesthetic education may serve to integrate all the materials taught in the public schools: mathematics, as the symmetry and proportion of perceptual forms; the linguistic skills of communication, as literary art; the chemical and physical properties of arts materials, as sources of expressive media; the natural selection of the life sciences, as the production of enduring forms; and the science of society, as insight into the growing cultures of diverse peoples, each an expression of the aesthetic values of social groups sensitized in the same way to a common environment. And that is about as comprehensive as an educational result may become.

The Role of the University

As in the past, no amount of discussion by philosophers of art and aesthetic education will determine what the schools will actually do. The CEMREL program was funded on the assumptions of the sixties. Given the national goals laid down by the Hecksher commission, the federal monies were available to bring us where we are. If we consult the *Federal Register*,[17] we can easily find what sorts of arts program the federal government is now prepared to support. There are seven points describing the kinds of goals that will be favorably considered:

1. The program must be designed to encourage the development in students of aesthetic awareness in the arts and to foster self-actualization and the development of communicative skills through movement, sound, visual images and verbal usage;

2. The program must be designed to involve all the students in the school or schools served. (The program may serve one or more schools in a single school district or (in the case of joint applications) in several school districts);

3. The program must be designed to involve each student in appreciation, enjoyment, understanding, creation, participation, and evaluation with respect to the arts;

4. The program must be designed to involve students at all grade levels in the school or schools served;

5. The program must address the spectrum of major art forms including dance, music, drama, and the visual arts;

6. The program must be designed to infuse the arts into all aspects of the school curriculum as a means of enhancing and improving the quality and quantity of aesthetic education offered in the school and of expanding the use of the arts for cognitive and affective learning experiences in the total school curriculum; and

7. The program must integrate all the major art forms into the regular educational program of the schools served, as distinguished from treating them on an extra-curricular or peripheral basis.

A careful reading of these points indicates that the NIE and other federal educational agencies have been instructed to begin funding projects in a *comprehensive education program* — just that sort of program we have been outlining as the future development of the CEMREL idea.

But ideas need institutionalization, and CEMREL will not be funded to teach the teachers of aesthetic education. That is where the universities must enter the picture. There are already two distinct strands of university endeavor for teaching such teachers. The first is composed of philosophers and psychologists trained in the special field of aesthetics, a generalized field of inquiry into the nature of aesthetic objects and experiences. Here we may find the conceptual base. The other is composed of educators in the particular arts media. Both strands, taken together, offer what we are looking for: the conceptual foundation and the means of conceptual operationalization. Our beginnings, then, must be interdisciplinary.

The same law now on the books prescribes how the universities are to use these resources; by providing the following:

1. In-service training for such programs for administrators, regular classroom teachers and specialized teachers in the arts; . . .

2. Curriculum development to infuse the arts into the total school environment.[18]

Here too a message lies buried, if only our educational administrators may be prodded to dig for it. What seems to be articulated within this law is the admonition to organize our resources and to take on the job.

Lastly, should we do so, there is a further benefit for the universities themselves. When an aesthetic education program of a comprehensive nature has become operational in the public schools, there will be a need for a new specialization of study within graduate schools of education as the development of the area of aesthetic education and its evaluation in particular contexts provide previously inexistent sets of data for empirical educational inquiry. Eventually, then, the program in graduate schools of training the teachers of aesthetic education will lose its interdisciplinary character to become the independent field of inquiry the original aesthetic-education program was initially designed to be.

An Agenda for Research and Development
How, then, should the university organize its resources? The short answer is: quite differently from the way it has in the past. The longer answer will take more space.

The support of basic research and development within the disciplines represented in the university has been a traditional function of the university. It is to be hoped this support will continue. Yet the very conception of what is basic in the arts and education changes radically, given the generic notion that one achieves an aesthetic education by means of one's own aesthetic inquiry, and a commitment to the idea that a teacher must in the first instance be educated in his or her wholeness, i.e., become a fully experiencing self. Since the domain of aesthetic inquiry is limited only by what humans are capable of experiencing, a fully developed, comprehensive aesthetic education program — whether for teachers or for children — must necessarily cut across all traditional subject-matter areas, so long as these areas are utilized for their means value in the aesthetic education context. Before declaring its independence from its sister "disciplines," the initial program should be as realistically interdisciplinary within the present university structure as it is possible to make it.

In any sound educational innovation, research logically precedes development; so we shall draw out the requirements for such a program in that order.

In our judgment, top priority should be given to research designed to uncover the abilities of children to engage in aesthetic inquiry at all levels. But, specifically, we propose that children's talk about the arts be analyzed in terms of each of the levels of inquiry mentioned earlier. Our framework, or taxonomy of the domain, "catches up" talk at the levels of criticism, meta-criticism, theory, and meta-theory — all of which find their ultimate referents in the first level, identified as the "creation and appreciation of objects or events"; this first level being the experiential ground for any "higher" inquiry. There is an urgent need for such studies, since the model for teaching and learning in aesthetic education apparently will be derived increasingly from the example of the critic. Critical activities, it has been argued, would bridge the gap between studio activities and the higher levels of inquiry educators say they want in aesthetic education programs.

Unfortunately, curriculum-builders around the country have been going about their business by prescribing objectives in terms of what students *ought to do* in each grade, virtually in the absence of empirical evidence of what teachers and students *can do* in aesthetic inquiry. Yet "ought" still implies "can." Although Lowenfeld,[19] Kellogg,[20] Gardner,[21] and others have provided developmental analyses of children's art, there has been no systematic study of children's talk about art. Our argument is that, without such basic information, arts educators are in a position neither to prescribe nor to justify educational objectives that are performance-based. The widespread behavioral approach, consisting of operationally defining objectives by specifying the desired "terminal behaviors" of students, is certainly premature, if not simply wrong-headed.[22]

Curriculum-building, like any other human project, does involve planning; and planning involves choices. A curriculum plan is the result of decisions to work toward some objectives at the expense of others equally possible. At this point it is not idle to recite an intuitively obvious maxim: What is the case is possible. The purpose of the research we are proposing is to obtain a general description of what *is* the case, and therefore what *can be* the case, with regard to performance of aesthetic inquiry at the four levels in typical classrooms and art rooms, as well as in exemplary arts programs.

The procedure might consist of the following steps: A national sample of classrooms (grades two, four, six, eight, ten, twelve) is taken, and exemplary arts programs identified; videotape recordings are made when arts activities take place; recordings are transcribed and the situations within which inquiry is conducted are described; "units of discourse" are analyzed to determine quantitative and qualitative distribution of aesthetic inquiry between and across grades. Not only have curriculum-makers devised curricula in the absence of this kind of information; so, too, have researchers themselves tended to select isolated concepts for experimentation, reporting how they have altered children's perceptions of paintings, how children can be sensitized to visual objects, and the like. Thus, what future basic experimental research—as well as sound curriculum development—in aesthetic education requires is nothing less than a fully conceptualized and empirically grounded picture of human potential for aesthetic inquiry.

With something less than the "big picture," however, there is evidence that some progress has been made in some public-school systems. Video- and audiotapes of classroom situations have been analyzed, in which aesthetic inquiry at the levels of theory and meta-theory has been of a startling quality, even as low as the fourth and fifth grades.[23] At the college level, both authors have had their own courses in criticism and aesthetics completely recorded, and, in one case, fully transcribed for analysis. Moreover, for the past ten years, we have made use of recordings of classes in which visiting artists, critics, and student-teachers were inquiring with their students into the problems of art and art criticism. While most of these research efforts were informal and undertaken for immediately practical purposes (e.g., the supervision of student-teachers), the evidence is sufficient to indicate what formal research might yield.

The potential for comprehensive aesthetic education programs was also in evidence. In those schools where it was recognized that aesthetic inquiry can be prompted not only by experiences in art, music, literature, film, dance, and theater, but also from critical reflection upon the communications media, sports, recreation, industry, city planning, the environment — indeed, the quality of one's personal and social life — the number and kinds of professionals participating inevitably increased. Teachers, supervisors, and administrators representing the fields of English, social studies, home economics, physical education, and industrial arts have joined forces with art and music specialists in direct proportion to the degree that they perceived a common interest.[24] Can their counterparts in academic university departments — the professors of home economics, for example — find the concept of aesthetic education sufficiently interesting to join with the professors of arts and arts education in developing a teacher-training program with such a focus? In our view, this is a pivotal question. So let us elaborate upon the example.

The briefest glance at the textbooks, instructional materials, and journals in the field of home economics reveals an aesthetic component that is not reducible to nutrition or health, food technology, home management, child care, or consumer education — as vital as these topics are in preparing students to cope with modern life. We are referring to such areas of study as clothing construction and design, interior design, architectural planning, home furnishings, and even family entertaining. University courses may now be found with the titles of "Art in the Home," "The Study of Foods as an Aesthetic Experience," and "Cultural Understanding through Foods," aesthetic inquiry by yet another name.

Interest in the arts among home economists in apparent. Consider the fact that an entire issue of *Illinois Teacher of Home Economics,* an important publication in the field, was given over to "Unified Arts Programs Including Home Economics."[25] One home economics teacher described a team-teaching approach in her junior high school involving the art and industrial arts teachers. Flexible modular scheduling of students allowed for blocking of courses and varying the length of class periods. Another article told of a "dinner theater" production of *Char-*

ley's Aunt in the high-school cafeteria, which brought together students and teachers of the Entertaining with Foods, Actor's Studio, and Stagecraft classes in a joint venture.

The University Program

To move from the basis of common interests to a functioning program of studies will require similar cooperative efforts at the university level. The following steps are projected:

1. An interdepartmental commission is constituted to review all present courses in all departments with regard to their potential for providing students with an aesthetic education. Gaps are noted, and new course offerings devised where required. Each course ultimately contributing to the aesthetic education program is administratively assigned to one of the participating departments, while the program itself is assigned to one department or division. The focus of these courses would be on the aesthetic foundations of the arts.
2. New courses for administrators, curriculum specialists, teachers in the field, and student-teachers are created, which focus on the administrative, curricular, and instructional problems associated with the development of aesthetic education programs, kindergarten through grade twelve.
3. With the aid of participating state departments of education, laboratory situations and participating public school systems are designated for placement of student-teachers and teams of specialists. Initial integration of aesthetic inquiry with other areas of the total school program should occur in these situations by means of trial units of instruction and curriculum innovation. The focus of attention is on the aesthetic foundations of education.
4. Workshops and summer institutes are organized to provide a task force of inside and outside specialists, scholars, and researchers not available during the regular academic and school year. The task force focuses on a special project; e.g., specifying and designing evaluative instruments for a specific school system.
5. Supervision, test and measurement, and overall evaluation of the aesthetic education program is the joint responsibility of the institutions involved. The chief purpose of evaluation is to provide justification for all future modifications in the program.

The present needs of professionals in visual art, music, dance, film, drama, industrial arts, and home economics programs are real enough; yet a re-thinking of traditional roles is required if aesthetic education is to "infuse the arts into the total school environment."

Assuming that the professional, administrative, and political difficulties in initiating such a program can be overcome, the overriding problem, in our view, will be to strike a balance between research and development. The danger is that participants, whether professors, school personnel, or state departments of education, may tend to define the program in terms of the current needs as perceived by the arts specialists who have traditionally had separate roles in the university and in the public school system. The effect would be to reduce the program to a service function, while neglecting the new constituency, i.e., elementary classroom teachers and school administrators, who must share the burden of implementing the program.

To achieve the ends of a truly comprehensive education program at a time when budgets are severely limited, universities will have to show a willingness to innovate and to extend their flexibility of adjustment to meet society's needs in a way never before demanded of them. Here we have no Sputniks, no NDEA; but then, perhaps, it is time for universities to prove they can handle the job alone — within the parameters of their currently existing resources. The challenge is ours to meet.

Tallahassee, Florida
and
New York, New York
May 1976

FOOTNOTES

[1] See also the authors' "Aesthetics in Public School Art Teaching," *College Art Journal,* Vol. 17 (Summer 1958), pages 382-91.

[2] See also the working definition of "aesthetic experience" in *Curriculum Development for Aesthetic Education: Guidelines* (St. Ann, Missouri: CEMREL, Inc., 1970), page 7.

[3] Irving Kaufman, "Art Cannot be Reduced to Ideas," *Curriculum Theory Network,* Vol. 4, Nos. 2-3 (1974), pages 124-39.

[4] David W. Ecker, "Teaching Art Criticism as Aesthetic Inquiry," *Curriculum Theory Network,* Vol. 4, Nos. 2-3 (1974), pages 112-23.

[5] See also *Basic Program Plan: Aesthetic Education,* revised version (St. Ann, Missouri: CEMREL, Inc., 1970), pages 3-8.

[6] United States Office of Education Cooperative Research Project No. V-002 (University Park, Pennsylvania: Pennsylvania State University, 1966).

[7] August Hecksher, "The Quality of American Culture," in the *Report to the President's Commission on National Goals* (Englewood Cliffs, New Jersey: Prentice-Hall, Inc., 1960), pages 127-34, 145-46.

[8] Manuel Barkan, et al., *Guidelines: Curriculum Development in Aesthetic Education* (St. Ann, Missouri: CEMREL, Inc., 1970).

[9] (St. Ann, Missouri: CEMREL, Inc., 1970).

[10] Ibid., pages 30-31.

[11] Ibid., pages 127-30.

[12] A curriculum design and handbook for aesthetic education will be published in Fall 1976 by CEMREL, Inc.

[13] David W. Ecker, et al., "Aesthetic Inquiry," *Review of Educational Research,* No. 39 (December 1969), pages 577-92.

[14] David W. Ecker and Eugene F. Kaelin, "The Limits of Aesthetic Inquiry," *Philosophical Redirection of Educational Research,* Lawrence G. Thomas, ed.

(Chicago: University of Chicago Press, 1972), pages 258-86.

[15] See also his "Qualitative Thought," *Philosophy and Civilization* (New York: Minton, Balch & Co., 1931), pages 93-116.

[16] See John Dewey, *The Child and the Curriculum*, published with *The School and Society*, with an introduction by Leonard Carmichael (Chicago: Phoenix Books, The University of Chicago Press, n.d. Original edition, 1902), pages 3-31.

[17] "Proposed Program Criteria for Arts Education," Office of Education, Department of Health, Education and Welfare, *Federal Register*, Vol. 40, No. 126 (Monday, June 30, 1975), pages 27486-491.

[18] Ibid., page 27488.

[19] Viktor Lowenfeld, *Creative and Mental Growth* (New York: Macmillan, 1957).

[20] Rhoda Kellogg, *Analyzing Children's Art* (Palo Alto, California: National Press Books, 1969).

[21] Howard Gardner, *The Arts and Human Development* (New York: John Wiley and Sons, 1973).

[22] See David W. Ecker, "How to Think in Other Categories; The Problem of Alternative Conceptions of Aesthetic Education," *The Journal of Aesthetic Education*, Vol. 4, No. 2 (April 1970), pages 21-36.

[23] See David W. Ecker, "Analyzing Children's Talk about Art," *The Journal of Aesthetic Education*, Vol. 7, No. 1 (January 1973), pages 58-73.

[24] Enlarging the area of common interest appears to be essential for a successful program. This has been our experience in working with various school systems, e.g., the Unified Arts Program of the Brookline (Mass.) Public Schools, and the Art Curriculum Task Force of West Chester Area School District (Pa.).

[25] *Illinois Teacher of Home Economics*, Vol. 18, No. 1 (September-October 1974).

Arthur W. Foshay

Inquiry into Aesthetics Education for Curriculum-Making

In order for research to have an effect on the actual curriculum offerings in schools, it must address the necessities for curriculum decision-making. Here, we shall consider briefly what these necessities are, and then ask ourselves what lines of inquiry into aesthetic education they imply.

To me, there appear to be seven parts to a decision concerning the curriculum. Ignore one of them and the decision won't stick, or perhaps won't be made. Recent curriculum development efforts have failed repeatedly because of such oversights.

The seven parts to a curriculum decision may be stated as a question: *Who* is to encounter *what, why, how,* in what *circumstances,* under what *governance,* at what *cost?*

Who refers to the proposed student. What kind of person is he or she? What is the nature of the student's development as it pertains to the proposed curriculum? What of his or her environment? Relevant interests? Fears? Hopes? Abilities? Where is the student developmentally? *Who* includes all those matters — the whole host of them — that have been found to pertain to students' attempts to learn.

What refers to the content, or what I prefer to call the object-matter (i.e., what shall be the objects of the student's attention?). Most curriculum proposals, and especially those proposed by amateurs both from within and without the ranks of the educationists, consist of a list of topics, or perhaps materials, and little more. Such lists are useful as one of seven parts of a curriculum proposal, but are of little use by themselves. Since the days of the Progressives, it has been common to temper the list of materials or objects or topics with some consideration of who is to encounter them, though lists lacking such consideration continue to appear, chiefly from university sources.

Why refers to the ends to be sought — the goals, or (in a more restricted sense) the objectives. It is interesting that attention has not been given to the goals, or purposes, of educational endeavors during recent

ARTHUR W. FOSHAY *is Professor of Education Emeritus at Teachers College, Columbia University.*

years. During the period of rapid development of education as a self-conscious field, roughly from 1890 to 1940 or 1950, extensive attention was given to the purposes of education. There was a series of highly influential committee and commission documents, ending on a sour note with the final publication of the Educational Policies Commission, *The Central Purpose of American Education,* which turned out to be a narrow intellectualism. Perhaps this final document in what has been an outstanding succession of statements portended what was to happen during the next two decades when serious discussion of purposes has almost ceased and a narrow intellectualism has indeed become dominant. Meanwhile, the students have rebelled against the apparent (to them) irrelevance of much of what is offered; and the secondary schools especially are in a shambles. To leave the question "why?" to take care of itself is to risk meaninglessness in the subject-matter offerings. We have taken the risk and we are paying the price. In general, the purposes of the subjects now offered are social in character (as were those of the Progressive Era) or they are personal in character (as the unstated purposes of some current experimental offerings such as Confluent Education), or they are both (but there do not appear to be programs that seriously confront the problem of having it both ways). The study of purposes is difficult and sometimes frustrating, but it is essential.

How refers to learning methods to be carried on by students. Mind, we do not speak of teaching methods, since a teaching method is best understood as a proposed learning method. How shall students go about learning what is to be confronted? Why should they do it? The unity of purpose and technique is only now beginning to be talked about, with renewed attention to the so-called "latent curriculum" — that which is implied by the learning methods proposed to students by teachers. In the arts, for example, the latent curriculum may be the implication that the arts are only for the talented, or that one should pursue the arts only as a reward for having completed the more serious (that is, conventionally academic) parts of one's work. What is the most productive way for a given student to undertake learning about object-matter? The question was examined by the learning psychologists during the twenties and thirties; but then the psychology of school subjects fell out of fashion, and consistent research has not been devoted to it until recently, when the still-new field of aptitude-treatment interaction began to emerge. If the question of how different students are to undertake learning activities is left out of a curriculum decision, no action is possible.

The *circumstances* in which learning is to take place have only recently begun to receive consistent attention, usually under the rubric of "learning environments." We know more than we are using in the field, if one takes the environment, or the circumstances, to include both the physical arrangements and the social climate wherein activities take place. Most of what is now being discussed has to do with physical environments — if a classroom shall be more like a studio or more like a lecture hall, for example, or if activities outside the school building should be frequent. The old studies of social atmosphere should have kept us from such partial considerations, but in our a-historical educational times, they haven't. In some experimental schools, the social environment as a force is being reinvented under new names; but, for example, the social-environmental meanings of competition for grades or test scores, of cooperation, of emotional supportiveness or lack of it have not been thought of. What does it mean, for example again, to display a student's work in the arts? To fail to display it? What is the actual impact of a studio setting or a formal setting on students? Does the setting fit the purposes? Forget the deliberate arrangement of the circumstances wherein learning is to take place, and the curriculum decision risks losing its quality.

The *governance* over content selection controls much of the meaning to be taken from the content. It was apparent to the Progressives that students should be involved in the process of curriculum-making, and there was a substantial literature written on the cooperative curriculum planning among students and teachers. What one plans is one's own, and the personal meaning of the experience is enhanced by such planning. The large curriculum projects of the fifties and sixties have generally overlooked this imperative, with the result that many a teacher sees them as "canned" or "packaged." That is why it is so unfortunate that the Aesthetic Education Program chose to call its materials "packages."

Ideally, the governance over the curriculum is shared with students. That is not the same as suggesting that it be left to the students to determine. Obviously, society, and society's surrogate, the teacher, have a controlling voice in such decisions, at least at the level of policy. In general, it would seem wise to leave the details of sequence and method to be determined jointly by students and teachers.

Such considerations seem particularly important in the field of aesthetics, since there is reason to doubt that a broad social base exists for support of aesthetics in the schools. Lacking such a base, students and art teachers are both vulnerable (to budget cuts) and are cut off, for example, from such current anxieties as the "back to basics" movement. It is interesting that, left to themselves in some of the alternative schools, the first and most prominent curricular activities students undertake are in the arts, especially music and the visual arts. There is little question about their sense of what is first in importance. But society, which also takes part in governance, does not share their judgment about priorities.

Governance governs not only acts, but meanings, as was said above. What one takes away from an experience is in major part a matter of to whom one feels accountable. "Who cares?" is a central question. It is rewarding to be praised by a significant other — be it parent, peer, or official. That's why some people distort their efforts to get a good press, and the press is part of the governance. It's rewarding to receive acclaim from the whole community. That's why marching bands take up an inordinately large part of the music program in some high schools. Governance, then, is not only a matter of directing the efforts of one's self and others, it is also a matter of basic social reward for one's efforts. Forget it, and the curriculum decision will wither and die.

Cost is often overlooked by curriculum developers as they begin their efforts, but it cannot be overlooked at the receiving end. Cost includes not only money, but time and talent. There is no use in installing a curriculum if there isn't time for it; and, even if there is, it will be aborted if the staff cannot carry it out sensitively.

Of all the elements of cost, staff training or staff competency is most often overlooked or underestimated. Since there is no such thing as "teacher-proof" materials (the naiveté of those in the early sixties who talked such nonsense continues to be astonishing), the questions of training and re-training the staff has to be given major consideration. Otherwise, the curriculum decision simply won't hold.

Some Research Considerations

The approach to curriculum-making discussed above raises a very large number of questions, some suitable for behavioral science research, some (such as *why*) lending themselves to philosophical treatment; some to practical, multi-faceted action research. Of the many questions, I shall discuss seven to illustrate where the approach leads.

1. Arising from the question "who?" is the need for a detailed account of aesthetic development among growing young people. The studies of child development in the past have been fruitful sources of curriculum content and the arrangement of experience. Since the fifties, with the revival of interest in Piaget, considerable influence has shown itself in the developmental aspects of cognitive growth, especially in the fields of science and mathematics.

   Alas, except for the beginnings showing in Project Zero, little or nothing has been done in the field of aesthetic development since the early work of Thomas Munro and Victor Lowenfeld in the visual arts. A whole program of work in the development of aesthetic responses among the young is available. What of the development of role-taking from dramatic play onward? What of the development of movement for aesthetic purposes, as distinguished from motor development? Music teachers "know" a good deal about how children may learn to perform, but the efforts in the Aesthetic Education Program reflect no coherent theory of such development, since none appears to exist. Perhaps, in this field, the studies of the development of the visually and aurally handicapped would be helpful.

   Similarly, the arts as social enterprises are worth studying. If one of the central purposes of aesthetic activity is to communicate, and since most aesthetic undertakings in school are in a social context, it should repay the efforts of the researchers to learn more about how children regard one another during aesthetic attempts. Teachers "know" that children imitate each other. Some of them try to avoid it. Perhaps they shouldn't. No one knows.

2. Studies of the perceptual process should yield information on *what* to offer. How do growing young people see? hear? feel? imagine? Aside from some speculation on the "ear-oriented" and the "eye-oriented," little is known about the perceptual processes; at least, little of use in making curriculum decisions. Again, help might come from examination of the research on the perceptually handicapped.

3. The social context of aesthetic education has not been examined. The *why* of aesthetic education is to be answered in part by such social considerations.

Several areas for systematic study arise from such social considerations. Among others, the question of the relationship between "high" culture and "low" culture, or between the popular arts and the serious arts, as Broudy calls it, requires examination. For some of us, remembering childhood, popular arts seem to offer access to serious arts. One way to gain access to Bach is through good jazz. Children gain a kind of access to serious visual arts through childish experimentation with visual media at the elementary school level. We should ask systematically if poster art, or cartoons, are a means of access to serious arts. We haven't even asked whether the popular arts ought to be considered in this way.

Meanwhile, in the United States especially, the popular arts dominate our sensibility, and they show no signs of becoming deeper or more sophisticated than they have been. Support for the serious arts is deplorably poor; it has been pointed out that only 10 percent of our people have access to serious dance, theater, music, or museums, since they are concentrated in the largest population centers. To change this requires public subsidy, and we show no signs of producing such subsidy on a scale to match the problem. There is only one Aspen Conference. There ought to be fifty.

Research into aesthetic experience would begin in the discipline of philosophy and continue into politics and social psychology before it became an empirical affair in the domain of the learning psychologists and the evaluators. The great public question is, "What does one gain from aesthetic experience?" As things stand, the great majority of our people haven't the slightest idea.

4. With respect to the *how* of aesthetic curriculum efforts, much has been done, but there is much more to do. Most teachers in the aesthetic fields are convinced, as learning theory would say they ought to be, that the basic experience in the arts is an active affair — a matter of doing art. What of that form of doing that consists of contemplating the work of others? Amateur musicians make ex-

cellent audiences for professional musicians, and the growth of the recording industry suggests that the audience for good music is large. But the audience for live theater has not been growing nearly so fast, nor has the audience for serious visual art, nor dance, nor serious film. All show growth, and the educators and professionals are quick to notice it, but the growth is still not massive. Serious art continues to be an elite affair. Aesthetic education in the public schools cannot, by definition, be elite.

An area for systematic study, therefore, is the relationship between doing and appreciating. We are flying blind in this area now, trusting that somehow doing contributes to the depth of aesthetic awareness, but not considering what kind of doing is related to what kind of appreciation. What is needed is knowledge that would guide a teacher in the selection of media and the direction of children's perceptual processes (see #2, above).

The Miller-Dollard model of learning is suggestive of lines of research in aesthetic education. Briefly, the model declares four requirements for learning:

a. There has to be a drive, or motive. The learner has to *want* something.
b. There has to be a cue, or a stimulus. The learner has to *notice* something.
c. There has to be a response. The learner has to *do* something.
d. There has to be a reward, or an observable consequence. The learner has to *get* something.

Taken together, these requirements are suggestive of the nature of school encounters with aesthetic experience. They need to fit one another. What the student gets for his or her efforts should bear a close relationship to what he or she wanted in the first place. The nature of the cue should bear a relationship to the student's development (see #1, above). What the student does should be related to both the motive and the consequence, or reward, that accrues to him or her. What is required, if research into these matters is to be pursued, is classroom experimentation, in the context of evaluative tools that make it possible to gather evidence concerning how the four requirements are met, individually and as they interact.

5. In what *circumstances* should aesthetic education take place? Practice with respect to this question is casual and opportunistic. In general, an attempt is made to create something like a studio environment for the arts — art rooms, music rooms, gymnasiums, auditoriums — and the assumption appears to be that the best environment for learning the arts is a workroom appropriate to the art in question. Beyond this, there are occasional visits from artists and field trips to places of cultural interest. All of these manipulations of the environment have been undertaken out of common sense. The actual impact of such environments on students

has not been studied, and practice suffers accordingly.

To study the effects of environments on students, it would be necessary to begin in a simple-minded way, by asking students what they noticed, how they felt in the various environments where they worked during the school day and after it, and what their expectations were, given various environments. Such interviewing would be followed by systematic observation of students in environments. More subtle experimentation with environments might then be undertaken. Such research would begin from scratch. Very little is known now in this field.

6. The matter of *governance* has to do with who makes curriculum decisions; and especially it pertains to the participation of students in such decision-making. In addition, however, and overlooked as a matter of governance, is the question of the place of the arts in life. Aside from laments over the deplorable state of the public landscape, especially along the highways, we have not attended to this matter. The way the arts function in one's life will determine the place they are given. Our talk to the students and to the larger public in this arena is confused and ambiguous. It could be improved, if close observation of the aesthetic behavior of ordinary people were undertaken. What, in fact, is the state of public taste? What does the taste consist of? What could it be (not what ought it to be), given the constraints of the life experience of ordinary folk and the requirements for living?

The questions raised by this consideration would require the attention both of philosophers and social scientists, to the end that the basic nature of the place of the arts in life be declared, and the actual state of the arts in life be described. As things stand, the matter appears to be in the hands of commercial entertainers (such as TV producers) and advertising people.

7. We turn to the matter of *cost*. It is a matter of common sense that the monetary cost of an aesthetics program must be taken into account. It is a little less obvious that the cost in time to develop an adequate staff should also be studied. As things stand, we squeeze out time for staff training with little or no knowledge of how much time different kinds of staff people require. One does not hear of cost-benefit studies in in-service training for aesthetic education—or, indeed, for anything else. How much time ought students to have in aesthetic education? Again, we fight for all the time we can get, but we don't know how much we need.

A Comment on Research Procedures

As has been mentioned, research on aesthetic education requires that the disciplines of philosophy, social psychology, learning psychology, and political science all be involved. It is to be hoped that the snare of multi-disciplinary research will be avoided. The members of these disciplines have distinct ways of approaching reality, and each must be given full freedom to proceed in ways true to the disciplines, separately.

However, a plan of the kind described above may guide such efforts. The plan is actually a grid of grids. The seven parts of a curriculum decision described here all interact. At every point where they meet, an array of questions about both the component in question and its interaction with all the other components is raised.

To avoid the enormous complexity produced by the many disciplines and the grid of grids, it would be desirable that early attention be given to the larger plan, and later attention to its components. Such a large plan could function as a guide to a program of research.

The research itself probably needs to proceed on a very simple, rather detailed basis. We are not a science, since we lack organizing theories. We are at a natural history stage of our own development, which is to say that what is needed now is careful, replicable observation of the phenomena we wish to study. It follows that the research needs to be simple in concept — basically, what is required is not explanatory research, but descriptive research. What such research will yield is, eventually, classification systems that can be used in the design of experiments. It is possible that the most useful discipline in this endeavor will be, not psychology, but anthropology — though the work of the developmental psychologists has been of enormous value to curriculum-makers in the past, and it may continue so.

Rowe, Massachusetts
June 1976

Harry S. Broudy

Some Reactions to a Concept of Aesthetic Education

No consensus on the meaning or the usage of the term "aesthetic education" being discernible, what follows refers pretty much to my own
concept of it. Nevertheless, it is possible to make a few generalizations
on the reactions toward the concept by various groups that in one way
or another have shown an interest in it.

1. They share an intent to educate in more than one of the arts and
   therewith a belief that the several arts have some common features
   that can be used to give structure to a program of aesthetic education.
2. They share a hope that aesthetic education will achieve a solid
   position (a required subject) in the curriculum of the public
   schools, a status it has not achieved through existing programs in
   arts education.
3. They share a belief that aesthetic education is possible and desirable for the total school population and need not be restricted to
   pupils with special talent.
4. There is less agreement among the advocates of aesthetic education on the degree to which it should be linked with extra-
   aesthetic — moral, political, economic, religious, civic — values.
   The lack of agreement would extend to the use of aesthetic materials for facilitating the teaching of other subjects and the integration of aesthetic education with other fields of instruction.
5. The least agreement is to be found in the aesthetic and educational
   theories by which the objectives of and approaches to aesthetic
   education are explicated and justified.

I shall comment briefly on some particular reactions of arts
educators, classroom teachers not trained in the arts, artists and other
members of the arts establishment, aestheticians, interested laypeople,
and representatives of the school constituencies (school board members,
parents).

HARRY S. BROUDY *is Professor of Philosophy and Education Emeritus at the
University of Illinois at Urbana – Champaign.*

Arts Educators

Among arts educators I include art supervisors, teachers of arts in the secondary schools, and college faculty members engaged in training arts educators. They agree that something should be done to improve the curricula and the methods of teaching in music, the visual arts, and such other arts as may be taught in their school systems. They tend to pattern their curricula and methods on the studio training of professionals or talented amateurs. Depending on their ideology, they are more or less permissive about technical standards of performance.

Many arts educators believe that performance training in the arts will also produce the only sort of appreciation of art that amounts to anything. They use two kinds of criteria to evaluate programs. One is that the course or program "turns the students on," that is, the course attracts students. Courses with this power to attract are often described as exciting and liberating. The other criterion is that there be a product of the course — a band concert, an art exhibition, a play. Both students and public are impressed by such products, and thereby help to gain and maintain political and financial support for the program.

Arts educators, although often interested in media other than their own, are hesitant about working on teams that purport to give instruction in related arts programs or broad field-humanities courses. The reaction to aesthetic education from this quarter is not so much hostile as cautiously skeptical. Hospitality to the concept is tied to the hope that it will help the standard arts program without threatening it.

Classroom Teachers

Classroom teachers who have to teach art and music in the elementary grades have mixed reactions to the various aspects of aesthetic education. First, they welcome anything that can be used to methodize teaching, but they especially appreciate method in the teaching of the arts, because they feel that lack of artistic talent disqualifies them from doing anything but follow the directions of the supervisor. In my own version of aesthetic education, it is possible for anyone to learn to scan a work of art — in any medium — for its sensory, formal, technical, and expressive properties. Classroom teachers, once they have learned to do this scanning, acquire confidence in teaching these skills to the pupil.

Second, classroom teachers favor aesthetic education's emphasis on the skills of impression rather than on those of expression. When the doing of art is undertaken as part of aesthetic education, it is subsidiary to developing the skills of impression. Accordingly, in aesthetic education (my version) the demand for technical proficiency — in performance, not in perception — is relaxed. This relieves the teacher and the pupil from the embarrassment of having classwork criticized adversely by a skill-oriented supervisor. Many classroom teachers like this leniency with respect to technical standards because it sanctions the messing around with clay, paint, and other materials — activities that afford a welcome relief from the more structured cognitive studies.

Third, classroom teachers are less comfortable with what I have sometimes called "the principle of phenomenological objectivity." This argues that properties attributed to the aesthetic object be perceived as being locatable in the object rather than in the perceiving subject, regardless of their *psychological* and *ontological* status. Teachers, on the contrary, tend to think of the work of art as a trigger to set off all sorts of associations, to release pent-up feelings, and to produce insight into values and sentiments. Although they grant that aesthetic objects yield pleasure of a sort when they are "pretty" or "beautiful," they do not generally subscribe to the doctrine of a special aesthetic pleasure nor to D. W. Gotshalk's definition of an aesthetic object as one that is intrinsically interesting to perception. Accordingly, when classroom teachers are advised not to begin the study of a work of art by asking the pupils to tell a story about it, or to tell how it makes them feel, or of what it reminds them, they demur, for this is the customary way of getting the child "interested" in any learning task.

Not only does this injunction run counter to the teachers' professed commitment to the complete subjectivity of the aesthetic judgment, but also to their conviction that the values of aesthetic experience lie in extra-aesthetic activities. This view is not without support in the theories of art, but I have found that when it is used as the starting point in the aesthetic encounter, the encounter never gets back to the distinctively aesthetic mode of experience. Nothing is more difficult to explicate than the difference between an emotional experience as a glandular psychological event and the "portrayal" of that emotion in some artistic form; between the anger aroused by frustration and the anger "recalled in tranquility" in a work of art. But then this is one of the most elusive differences in all of aesthetic theory.

Friends of the Arts

Laypeople devoted to the arts include art lovers, friends of museums, supporters of musical organizations, members of arts councils, and art patrons of all kinds. They devote time, energy, and money to the arts and would like to develop a strong public for them. They agree pretty much that if first-rate orchestras, theater companies, dance groups, and art exhibitions were made available to the general public, the citizenry would be "hooked" for life. If aesthetic education means anything at all to them, it is to send the Chicago Symphony on tour to the hinterlands or to bus several thousand children into Chicago to hear a concert by that orchestra. Artists in residence at the public schools and exposure of public school children to fine art seem to them to be the only sensible approach in aesthetic education.

The interested layperson places a good deal of value on becoming sophisticated about art. He or she reads criticism, keeps abreast of art news, knows what and who are "in," and can talk about art and artists. He or she does what persons who take appreciation courses in art hope they will be able to do — to take the first steps toward connoisseurship in taste and judgment.

Artists and Critics

Neither practicing artists nor professional critics react with enthusiasm to the notion of aesthetic education. The former are primarily interested in producing works of art and not in talking about them or teaching anybody anything. Some are articulate about the meaning of art and the politics of art, but not necessarily about the way in which they themselves create works of art. They tend to talk to or at each other rather than to the public in general or to young pupils in public schools.

Professional critics, on the contrary, are articulate enough, but address a readership that is already privy to the activities, persons, and the language of the art world. Both artists and critics would like the general public to patronize the arts more generously, especially the serious arts, but are not quite sure that aesthetic education carried on in schools can do much to bring this about. Like the interested layperson, they prefer to rely on exposure to good works of art rather than on the efforts of school teachers or even art supervisors.

Aestheticians

One might expect that aestheticians would be interested in aesthetic education. Many are, as is witnessed by the number of articles on the subject that have found their way into the columns of *The Journal of Aesthetic Education*. The following names come to mind, but the list is far from complete: Thomas Munro, D. W. Gotshalk, Richard Peltz, F. E. Sparshott, Monroe C. Beardsley, L. A. Reid, Harold Osborne, E. F. Kaelin, George Linden, Albert William Levi, Allan Shields, Alexander Sesonske, and Iredell Jenkins. But there can be a wide gulf between formal aesthetics and aesthetic education. Aesthetic education needs a theory of aesthetic experience, the aesthetic object, the nature and purpose of art, and, indeed, knowledge about all of the topics that are treated in courses in aesthetics or the philosophy of art. Unfortunately, personnel in the teaching of the arts and general classroom teachers have little formal background in aesthetics or the philosophy of art. Few have ever taken a course in aesthetics; indeed, not every philosophy department offers courses in this field. Conversely, aestheticians are not always interested in the public schools and how their theoretical gambits are related to what happens there. Furthermore, classroom teachers are likely to be allergic to theory.

It is especially difficult to make the connection between aesthetic education and the kind of aesthetic writing that is concerned primarily with the discourse about aesthetics, "meta-aesthetics." The logical properties of aesthetic judgments and definitions are not themselves aesthetic objects. This is not to say that speaking precisely is not important to aesthetic education. On the contrary, if one is to distinguish aesthetic experience from other kinds, if one is to defend one attitude toward the aesthetic object rather than another, then discussions of definitions and criteria for usage cannot be avoided. But, whereas in formal aesthetics this can go on as an end in itself without engaging in concrete transactions with particular aesthetic objects, this cannot be the case in aesthetic education. Accordingly, aesthetic theory has to be given educational relevance, a task that is not quite the same as generating either aesthetic or educational theory.

School Constituencies

Laypeople connected with the public schools who might be involved in establishing and supporting aesthetic education include, first of all, the parents, after them the members of school boards, and after them citizens and writers who, from time to time, editorialize on education in general and on the local schools in particular. More peripheral but nonetheless influential are organizations of taxpayers and vigilante groups representing the various interests that would like to have the school get the young started on the right roads to their respective ideologies and utopias.

Parents, by and large, would like their children to savor the finer things in life, among them enjoyment of the arts. Millions are spent on musical instruments, dancing lessons, and on other art instruction available to children after school. As between reading and art in the curriculum, no doubt they would choose the former, but quite rightly they do not understand why it has to be one or the other. Yet, so long as the arts program is performance-oriented, art will be regarded as a luxury and reading as a necessity. Aesthetic education in the broader sense is more likely to be accepted as a necessity by parents to whom it is explained, perhaps because it promises to give their children the confidence with respect to the fine arts that they themselves often lack.

Boards of education are not hostile to aesthetic education if the funds are available for it. But unless they understand the difference between aesthetic education programs and the conventional courses in the arts, they too will regard them as desirable luxuries rather than as educational basics. As to making the distinction comprehensible to school board members, I have often wondered what a good painter or composer collaborating with a good critic in analyzing a work of art at a school board meeting would do for aesthetic education. The confidence that aesthetic education can contribute to the individual's encounter with the arts is something that laypeople prize. The layperson can excuse her- or himself for lack of proficiency in artistic expression but not for deficiencies in artistic appreciation. Aesthetic education as the development of "literacy" in the arts can be "sold" to the public.

Strategic to the arguments for or against aesthetic education is the relation of aesthetic experience to extra-aesthetic value. The layperson knows that art has something to do with emotion, that emotion has much to do with preferences, and that preferences have almost everything to do with choices and actions. He or she knows also that totalitarian societies, as well as advertising agencies, use art to persuade the public to feel and act in certain ways. And while the American citizen may not approve of indoctrination on behalf of totalitarian ideologies and values, he or she is not always averse to using these aesthetic resources to indoctrinate the school population in behalf of the "right" values. The artist who declares her- or himself independent of the value commitments of the community and claims autonomy for art may be tolerated by the community but will not be enthusiastically supported by it.

I agree with the layperson that aesthetic images are very powerful social forces, and that the mass media exploit this power unmercifully and often irresponsibly. But I try to discourage the use of the arts or aesthetic education to inculcate ideologies and values, even those congenial to the democratic ethos.

This is not an easy position to maintain, because the aesthetic values are only one type of human values; and, intrinsic and genuine though their satisfaction may be, their importance for life as a whole lies in their relation to other forms of activity and satisfaction. Yet, there is a difference between works of art that use themes of great human import as a vehicle for aesthetic creativity and works that justify their claims to artistic merit because they deal with great human themes. The great tragedies of Shakespeare and some of the current soap operas use the same themes, but we do not attribute the same artistic merit to both on that account. Pedagogically, one might defend selecting works of art for study that have great extra-aesthetic import as well as artistic merit, but I doubt that we would wish to exclude from study those works that do not have such obvious extra-aesthetic import; nor would we wish the aesthetic response to be judged solely in terms of extra-aesthetic effects. It is of utmost importance to maintain this distinction, but only teachers knowing their way around aesthetic education can tread these fine lines with confidence.

It has been asked by laypeople interested in the schools why, with so much popular art available to the public, school time and budget need to be expended on aesthetic education. I have replied that proper aesthetic perception — i.e., perceiving in the manner of the artist and critic — provides the individual with a filter that separates the aesthetic properties from the adventitious freight that may have been loaded on their backs. Just as critical thinking is a defense against indoctrination by poor thinking, and good science is a corrective of popular science, so trained aesthetic perception is a defense against the naive responses to images. In other words, I try to make the case for the formal cultivation of aesthetic experience on the same grounds one might put forward for the cultivation of our cognitive powers. Unfortunately, self-cultivation in any mode of experience is difficult to "sell" to anyone who really needs to be sold.

To persuade the layperson that aesthetic experience is not confined to museums and concert halls, I have tried to point out that it pervades everyday life; that we rely upon appearances in the quality of voice, clothing, demeanor, and our physical surroundings for cues to a wide range of theoretical and practical judgments. Great art enhances the quality of life, but the appearance of any object viewed aesthetically may also enhance or demean it. Of the numerous obligations to our fellowmen, improving the aesthetic quality of their environment is not the least important; and human bodies, speech, houses, and landscapes are among the most intrusive and ubiquitous components of that environment.

Reasons for Resistance

Among the reasons for resistance to the notion of aesthetic education are the following:

In the first place, some of the difficulty with the concept of aesthetic education can be traced to unfamiliarity with the vocabulary and concepts of formal aesthetics. In the absence of a more or less standard terminology in this field, it is difficult to be understood or to avoid being misunderstood.

Second, there seems to be no middle ground between creating art of one kind or another on the one hand, and appreciating it on the other. In both, the right wingers insist on standards and the left wingers glory in subjectivity. Those who venture to suggest a middle ground will be beaten over the head by militants on both flanks.

Third, the scope of aesthetic education is too broad for some and too narrow for others. It is too broad for those who want it confined to one art. It is too narrow for teachers who want to use the arts for illustrating social studies, for therapy, and for value education.

Fourth, I find some lay- and schoolpeople not a little shocked by the proposal that aesthetic education should be a central part of the required curriculum from kindergarten through grade twelve. I, in turn, am not a little shocked that those who take the aesthetic dimension of life seriously should settle for anything less.

Fifth, there is some misapprehension about aesthetic education threatening the conventional performance and appreciation courses. While some proponents of aesthetic education may have such sinister intentions, most do not. On the contrary, they see aesthetic education as a form of aesthetic literacy in every art for everyone, and the work in the individual arts as elective opportunities for those who want competence in them.

Last but not least is the widespread doctrinal — if not actual — commitment to the relativity and subjectivity of the aesthetic response and the aesthetic judgment. Whatever the philosophical dimensions of the problem may be, it is unrealistic, as far as formal schooling is concerned, to ask for time and public money for activities that cannot be improved by instruction — activities in which improvement is taken to be a meaningless notion.

Aesthetic Education in the Future

What about the future? I do not anticipate any sudden or substantial alteration in the situations outlined above. But there are factors within the culture that warrant continuing the effort in behalf of aesthetic education. Of these, the most important is the role of the aesthetic image in all phases of life. The image or appearance becomes the operative datum for judgment when other data — factual and scientifically refined — are no longer available in usable form for the layperson, even the educated and socially concerned layperson. The basis of trust has shifted from truth to credibility, and credibility is more a matter of the persuasiveness of images than of the truth value of propositions.

We have come full circle, so to speak, from the reliance by early people on aesthetic clues for gauging the benign and threatening aspect of their environment because no more reliable clues were available, to our own time, when we rely on aesthetic clues because scientific ones, even when available, are beyond our comprehension.

Images are no more reliable indices of the nature of things than they ever were; yet so much of our lives turns not on what is true about objects but on what is true about subjects (persons), that a finer sensitivity to the import of images may give to aesthetic clues a special kind of truth value.

My own preference, as indicated earlier, is not to rely on art to produce moral and intellectual excellence; albeit, at a deeper metaphysical level, the good, true, and beautiful may have closer relationships than the asepsis of logical discourse permits us to assert. Educationally, it is sufficient to argue for aesthetic education because imaginative perception and perceptive imagination are uniquely human powers and, as such, need to be cultivated by all members of the school population.

The future might hold greater promise if even a small portion of the effort and resources that are devoted to the study of other phases of education could be directed to the problems of aesthetic education. Another paper (see Hoffa) prepared for this conference recounts the history of research and development activity in this field and indicates the need and possibility of further scholarly work.

Research in Aesthetic Education

Research in aesthetic education suffers from the layperson's general distrust of academics and from the aversion of the artist to intellectual analysis of creative work. Furthermore, scholarship in aesthetic education draws on the resources of many disciplines, and these involve discrete disciplinary guilds and diverse modes of inquiry. Finally, there is no guarantee that the findings of the scholars will reach the teachers and administrators of aesthetic education programs. In short, the idea of scholarship in the domain of the arts and aesthetic education is not easy to "sell"; different strands of inquiry are difficult to integrate, and dissemination of the results to the field presents problems.

Perhaps a few observations, albeit already familiar to most of us, about the ambivalence of the public to the academic syndrome are in order. The symptoms constituting the syndrome are narrowness, abstruseness, long-windedness, aridity, a strange jargon, and a general fussiness. This syndrome alienates many persons because the symptoms betoken real fragmentation, abstraction from the existential flow, and the multiple woes and joys in which it envelops the concrete individual. The technical language of the academician strikes the layperson as a wall erected to shut him or her out; and yet the layperson must regard the scholar as an intercessionary with powers and mysteries that may dwell behind that wall. Nevertheless, without this narrowness of specialization and some of its unlovely consequences, the scholar could not contribute to the world his or her unique product and knowledge, nor could he or she practice his or her unique virtue—an unqualified loyalty to the search for truth. When norms and standards are having such a rough time of it, the rigorous adherence of the academician to the canons of inquiry as legitimated by his or her guild is one of the few things that does abide. And this guild loyalty to the value and method of truth is about the only basis we have for authority that is not hopelessly arbitrary or authoritarian.

Among the maladies aesthetic education suffers from, two can be ameliorated by scholarship: glib, almost irresponsible, relativism and conceptual anarchy. Inasmuch as these maladies are often regarded as signs of blooming health, it is necessary to distinguish between warranted and mindless relativism on the one hand, and between warranted and chaotic conceptual diversity on the other. Scholarship warrants relativism on the basis of evidence for or against certain generalizations. Glib relativism in the aesthetic domain grows out of ignorance and assuages the guilt that such ignorance may engender. The dispensation from having to give reasons for one's likings and dislikings in art granted by rampant relativism is a welcome excuse for not removing that ignorance.

The second malady is amply illustrated by the responses of the various constituencies to aesthetic education. Examining the list of difficulties listed above, one is struck by how many of them can be traced to diversity in the definitions of aesthetic experience, art, the aesthetic object, and attitude. The goals of art education also cover a wide spectrum of opinion. Distinctions that are of utmost importance to some theoreticians are dismissed by others as denoting zero difference. As for the practitioners, which distinctions they make or take seriously is anybody's guess; and, yet, what they do in the classroom or in designing a curriculum depends on the categorial schema chosen.

The two kinds of infirmities point to a broad construal of research and scholarship in this field. Research that arrives at warranted assertions about fact will help reduce unwarranted relativism, but it may do little to bring order into categorial chaos, and vice versa.

Clearly the study needed for the second malady is not the correlation of behavioral variables nor is it a search for causal generalizations. The scholarship needed is largely in the field of formal aesthetics and the philosophy of art. If consensus is out of the question, scholarship can at least disclose the main issues, the main arguments, and, one might hope, their educational consequences.

This kind of analytical study — which, by the way, has a corresponding role in the study of educational problems — is basic not only in logic but in the order of research as well. For, suppose that a psychologist investigates the origins of the aesthetic response and finds them in the turmoil of childhood. It still tells us nothing about the nature and structure of the work of art as phenomenologically present to consciousness. Every discipline is necessarily reductionist. It must, perforce, impose on the phenomenon its own categorial stencil — the biological, psychological, political, physiological, etc.—in order to do its thing, so to speak. The stencil inevitably eliminates some aspects and dimensions of primary concern to other disciplines.

Accordingly, aesthetics, philosophy of art, and theories of criticism set the ground rules for other inquiries into the transaction with aesthetic objects, natural or contrived for that purpose. For example, the aesthetician might reasonably argue that, if the psychologist presents subjects with paintings and then records their reminiscences associated with them, he or she is investigating something of interest to the psychologist but not the aesthetic experience. Why an experience has the character it, in fact, has is not substitutable for that character. However, given agreement on what that character is, finding out what brings it about or impedes its coming to be, can be of the greatest pedagogical importance. In other words, psychologists, sociologists, anthropologists, and other academicians should do their own thing with the aesthetic experience by their own methods, applying their own distinctive stencils to it. This is all to the good, so long as they do not slip into the fallacy of substituting for the aesthetic experience itself what they do with that experience or with the characterization of it. How to bring about whatever it is aesthetic education wishes to bring about, is not a definition of what is to be brought about.

There is scarcely an academic discipline that cannot undertake research and study of some sort of aesthetic education, but much of it will be dissipated and undercut, if, as is now the case, there is no unifying agency that can identify scholars interested in the field; that can help find support for such scholars; and that can insure communication among them and with the larger public of artists, art educators, and others interested in aesthetic education in one form or another.

No such central agency exists in this country. Although no little study is being devoted to the field, much of it is known to limited coteries; and often members of one coterie are unknown to members of another. We need an annual stocktaking of research among the scholars themselves. The report of such stocktaking could constitute the beginning of an authoritative, but not authoritarian, corpus of study on aesthetic education — something that could be of inestimable value to other researchers, to arts educators, and to those who have the opportunity and responsibility for inaugurating and sustaining programs of aesthetic education.

Such an institute would be a signal to the academic community and the public that what has been peripheral to the educational enterprise has moved closer to its center.

Urbana, Illinois
April 1976

IV

Researchable Problems in the Arts and Aesthetics

This final section defines researchable topics for the research agenda. The topics, although diverse, do group themselves under the larger headings described in the introduction: aesthetic development, optimizing learning in the schools, cultural studies, evaluation studies, and policy research. The authors may emphasize one or all of these topics in their papers, but their charge was to define topics in their area of expertise within the arts and aesthetics and to give some rationale for their consideration.

Howard Gardner and **David Perkins, R. A. Smith** and **C. M. Smith,** in part or all of their papers, describe research activities in the area of testing and of revising theories of development.

Howard Gardner, from the perspective of a developmental psychologist investigating human symbolic competence (Project Zero), proposes that the arts and arts education share many aspects with other forms of knowledge; and a research agenda should investigate *how* the arts are special and *which* aspects are shared with other domains. Human knowing centers about the use of symbols, and the science of artistic knowledge studies how symbols are learned and utilized in the creation and perception of art objects. **Gardner** contends that research could pursue further such lines as the relationship of arts training to skills of central importance in the sciences, or verbal and nonverbal patterning in interaction with various media. The sum total of these researches should clarify which aspects of artistic skills are shared with general cognitive development, and which seem special to the arts; which findings have special aesthetic implications and which will be most apparent when plotted within the broader range of symbolic activities.

David Perkins views talk as being a fundamental educational and acculturational force in our perception and understanding of the arts, and education uses talk for just that purpose. Designing education programs in the arts, then, demands exploring the weak and strong points of talk about art, as well as the possibilities of talk and the practicing of good talk. **Perkins** contends that scholarly discussion of art has its own value apart from the experience of art itself, just as in other disciplines; and certainly can serve to enlighten, enrich, and expand artistic experience and aesthetic development.

Ralph A. Smith and **C. M. Smith** outline a schema of aesthetic perception. They contend that aesthetic education will be successful when students know where to look for aesthetic value and how to realize it—and these are teachable skills. Further, people with the appropriate skills for perception as well as for aesthetic discourse should be able to reach a consensus on the value of a particular aesthetic experience through the application of relevant critical concepts and critical discourse. They look toward research to determine *which* perceptual and critical skills and concepts to teach

263

when in the course of aesthetic education.

Studies having their end results in the improvement of classroom practices and the optimizing of learning are the main concern of many of the papers, particularly **Kathryn Bloom's** and **Anne Taylor's.**

Kathryn Bloom, through her program at the JDR 3rd Fund's Arts in Education Program, is working for the establishment of comprehensive arts in education programs that make all the arts integral to the basic education of all students in all schools. Since the arts are part and parcel of society and life, they are also integral to the total pattern of education. And, she maintains, as children become totally involved in the arts, attitudes and motivation toward other subjects improve, thus helping them learn the "basics" more readily. The arts, then, become useful tools for improving the environment and the quality of life for each child. **Bloom** contends that such approaches as interdisciplinary studies, support of the arts for their own intrinsic value, use of community arts resources, and special programs for special students can be developed in concert; and if they include all the arts, and are designed for students at all grade levels from kindergarten through high school, a comprehensive arts in education program can be the outcome. She advocates research that helps to implement educational change to this end, and that improves teacher training, curriculum development, evaluation of programs, and dissemination of findings.

Anne Taylor sees research in and about aesthetic learning environments as the key to improving instruction. She contends that today's classrooms may be somewhat improved pragmatically, but the relatively untapped potential of school environments as learning tools for children has been largely ignored by architects, educators, and parents—resulting in student apathy or in increasing violence towards school buildings. Classrooms that conceive of the learning and teaching environment as a single system demanding total participation of both student and teacher are needed. **Taylor** points out that research has already shown that the aesthetic learning environment can be a work of art in and of itself; and can be designed, engineered, and provisioned to act as a learning tool in and of itself. The process of designing new learning environments should be a synergistic effort among architects, curriculum coordinators, community artists, cultural specialists, parents, children, and other community planners, using data supplied by environmental research.

George Anselevicius outlines the need for research on the environment and its effects on education in order to improve the education of architects—the designers of objects. He contends that, in our frantic search for quality of life and community yet individuality, Americans struggle against bureaucratic controls, exploit and pollute the physical environment (natural and man-made), grasp at materialism and technology, and destroy each other in the process. From **Anselevicius'** point of view as an architect, some solutions could be found in creating a new man-made environment of visual quality, social vitality, and opportunity. Research could determine the controls (safety, health, historic preservation, highway networks, sewer systems, etc.) that are needed for the well-being of all, while preserving a maximum of aesthetic freedom, variety, and vitality, as well as determining the kind of education that future architects should have.

John W. Cataldo sees that the inevitable acceleration of technology has created a need to form new research alliances, and to develop strategies of response wherein change and collaboration with technology are part of the learning processes, particularly in arts education. **Cataldo** states that the nomenclature and taxonomy of art and science have become mutually applicable to descriptions of visual technologies, mechanisms, and processes. Eventually, technology and mass media will become subject to, and subject of, an improved social and aesthetic research. He contends that this research should improve learning systems developed on the basis of existing sophisticated technologies already far in advance of the emerging nontraditional learning and arts curricula, and the emerging group of dedicated techno-process artists.

Stanley S. Madeja states that, as an agenda of research and development in arts and aesthetics over the next decade, we should select to improve instruction on the basis of national priorities and limits of resources, concentrating our efforts on solving such major problems as evaluation in the arts and aesthetics, and the relationship of the arts and aesthetics to technology. In evaluation in an arts instructional program, two approaches are proposed for further research and development: one concerns using descriptive techniques for evaluating the effectiveness of an arts and aesthetics program; the other concerns developing a diagnostic instrument to assess student progress in the arts and in aesthetic judgments. In arts and technology, research could determine the vast potential that all the technological advancements of this century have in arts and aesthetic education: One approach would be to create a "sense laboratory" for the investigation of aesthetic perception; another approach would be to research the aesthetics of television itself.

Samella Lewis expresses some of the concerns as **Margaret Bush Wilson** about representing our minorities in research. **Lewis** states that, though it is difficult to generalize about all minority groups, it is true that the dominant culture in the United States does not provide sufficient outlet for the talents and energies of minority peoples. From the perspective of the Afro-American heritage, it is vital to develop a strong research base showing the major contributions of non-European cultures to the art of all the world; research done by members of minority groups that demonstrates the value that uniqueness and differences have to society. Research needs to open avenues of change in our limited, biased system through a more complete education of and expanded opportunities for each individual through the arts and humanities.

Lionel Landry makes a similar case for Asia. He states that multicultural education can be most ideally conveyed through the arts; the crystallization of Asian societies, values, aesthetic canons, ethics and norms of behavior, and so on, is in its arts. Experimental education projects have shown that experiencing Asian arts *does* communicate to American students an understanding of Asian cultures, histories, and peoples. In our multicultural American society, we have the resources, the funds, the expertise, and the responsibility to research Asian arts and replace inadequate texts with multi-media materials using the arts and humanities as powerful instruments for comprehension and appreciation of Asian life and world view—if we expect to improve transcultural communication and maintain peaceful relations with almost two thirds of the world's population.

In the concluding paper, **Elliot Eisner** deals with a broad range of topics for a research agenda. He contends that this agenda of studies should include: survey research in the educational context and the quality of arts teaching and arts curriculum in schools (educational criticism); development and assessment of new approaches to evaluating artistic learning and experience; investigation of the extent and the ways that work in the arts affects competencies in other academic fields, and developmental studies in artistic learning.

Howard Gardner

Sifting the Special from the Shared: Notes Toward an Agenda for Research in Arts Education*

An Agenda and its Assumptions

In these notes, I shall dwell neither on the need for research in arts education, nor on the inadequacies of past efforts. Instead, proceeding from my own perspective as a developmental psychologist investigating human symbolic competence, I shall sketch out an agenda for research. Were it executed, such research should increase our understanding of artistic knowledge; suggest the optimal means for fostering central skills; provide leads for initiating and evaluating programs; and pinpoint the relationship between artistic and other forms of knowledge.

This seemingly innocuous opening paragraph has housed a slew of tacit assumptions. I have presumed that statements can be made not only about single art forms, but also concerning the family of pursuits called the arts. I have asserted the relevance of developmental psychology. Tacitly, therefore, I have called, first, for a definition of the "end state" of artistic competence; second, for an outline of developmental stages culminating in such competence. I have highlighted skill in the use of symbols, thereby reflecting a belief that artistic competence involves the ability to create and to decode various symbolic vehicles.

Other presuppositions lurk above. A cognitive bias underlies the recurrent use of the phrase "artistic knowledge" as well as the reference to other forms of knowledge. A high premium on basic research motivates the claim that understanding of artistic knowledge must precede and inform programs drafted specifically to achieve aesthetic-educational goals. Finally, efforts to relate to one another artistic and

HOWARD GARDNER is Co-Director of Project Zero at Harvard University and a Clinical Investigator at the Boston Veterans Administration Hospital.

*Preparation of this paper was supported in part by the Spencer Foundation, the National Institute of Education (Grant G-00-3-0169), and the National Institute of Neurological Diseases and Stroke (NS 11408-04). Helpful comments on an earlier draft were provided by Jen Silverman and Ellen Winner.

other forms of knowledge have been situated at the center of the proposed agenda.

In my view—and here I allude briefly to the sins of the past— previous efforts have suffered from one of the following defects. In one common approach, the arts have been viewed as an area entirely separate, requiring particulate tools of analysis, research approaches, pedagogical procedures, and the like. This "separatist" point of view implies that lessons and procedures associated with other forms of knowledge are irrelevant. The other assumption, equally vocal, though heard in different circles, finds nothing special characteristic of the arts: This aspect of life yields its secrets via the same analyses used in other lines of inquiry. This "nihilistic" point of view further implies that, once completely understood, the whole area now designated as *aesthetics* or *artistic research* will dissolve.

I wish to confront directly this intellectually unpalatable set of alternatives. I believe that many aspects of the arts are shared with other forms of knowledge; any attempt to divorce the arts completely from other areas is as self-defeating as it is wrong-headed. I believe with equal conviction that certain mental skills, attitudes, and forms of symbol use are especially characteristic of, and focally important in, the arts. Not only will our ultimate understanding of the arts depend upon tracing with greater precision these connections and boundaries, but the possibilities of a firm integration of aesthetic education into the general curriculum will also depend upon a deeper understanding of *how* the arts are special, and *which* of their aspects are shared with other domains. In other words, the payoffs of sifting the special from the shared will be both conceptual and practical.

To justify such "sifting" is one thing; to effect it quite another. In my own work as a researcher at Harvard Project Zero,[1] I have helped to draft a general approach to this congeries of questions. At the same time, I have launched specific programs of research in the hope of illuminating the issues addressed here. In what follows, I will sketch the general program; cite some examples from work we have done and work we plan to execute; touch on possible deficits or omissions from the agenda; and mention certain educational implications that follow from its implementation.

Research Strategy

Given an assumption that the arts entail a way of knowing the world—as a creator as well as a perceiver—it becomes necessary to offer a preliminary taxonomy of different forms of knowledge. Of the numerous ways this issue might be attacked, we have ourselves focused upon a delineation of different kinds of symbols, symbolic relations, and systems of symbols.[2] Our contention, stated baldly, is that human knowing centers about the use of symbols—elements that represent (or denote) other elements, or, upon occasion, themselves.[3] Human knowing entails the creation and "reading" of words, pictures, diagrams, musical patterns, numbers, codes, and the like. It is the task of cognitive psychology to delineate the different skills needed for dealing with various symbolic systems.[4]

Certain symbols (e. g., pictures) are featured primarily in the arts; other (e. g., numbers) figure primarily outside the arts. Yet other symbols—such as words—function equally in aesthetic and non-aesthetic domains. Overall, we have found it useful to view the arts as activities that primarily employ symbols of a certain type in certain kinds of ways. For instance, I am using words here in a non-aesthetic way, simply to convey some concepts and arguments. Other words could readily be substituted. But should words be used to call attention to themselves—highlighting figures of speech, alliteration, assonance, irony, and the like—then these symbols are being employed in an aesthetic fashion. The science of artistic knowledge studies how symbols are learned and utilized in the creation and perception of art objects.[5]

A useful point of departure for such an endeavor is an articulated notion of adult competence in a symbolic medium: the skills entailed in using words, pictures, lines, or notes in a compelling and aesthetically effective manner. Initial clues derive from common sense and from general observation; more precise understandings come from the study of proficient practitioners, as well as from contrasting those who are highly proficient with those who are still novices.[6]

Once such a comparison has been initiated, a developmental analysis is underway. One searches for steps, or stages, en route to competence—steps that may, but need not, parallel changes associated with age. In most cases, the administration of identical tasks to subjects of different ages and degrees of competence will uncover the normal development of skill in a given symbolic medium. Relevant individual differences also emerge from intensive study of the phases of symbol mastery.

Once an "end-state" has been mapped out, and a working picture of the preceding developmental stages has been sketched, an educationally tinged lens becomes appropriate. For, at this point, one can ask what steps might aid an individual in achieving more sophisticated and comprehensive skills. The goal here should not be to "speed up" attainment of competence, but rather to make available to an individual the fullest set of examples, problems, and themes for which he will be searching at a particular stage in development. Access to a treasure-trove of materials should enable him to attain the next stage in the fullest, most flexible, and most meaningful fashion. Various candidate methods of training or sensitizing can be proposed: Which work, how widely, and if they should be employed at one or another time are empirical questions. Admittedly, it is far easier to conjure up training methods than to test them. But, in any case, the comparison of competing regimes should follow the tentative plotting of a normal developmental trajectory.

The whole enterprise of studying artistic knowledge is studded with value judgments. To begin with, one must decide which aspects of symbolization are worthy of study; which are of lesser importance. Then, after a developmental sequence has been clarified, and various training approaches have been assayed, one must again ask: *Should* one be training this set of capacities? Is training best left to the initiative of the individual, to his or her teacher, or to some outside agency? Need an individual possess such a skill in order to thrive in our society? Such value decisions are by no means limited to the aesthetic domain; indeed, they prove endemic to all education. Yet, just because the arts are widely viewed as a value-laden domain, and because most observers will have strong opinions about which artistic facet should (and should not) be trained, these issues must be confronted with special sobriety in the arts.

Lines of Investigation

Cross-Sectional Studies of Central Artistic Skills

Having sketched out our general plan of attack, let me indicate in some detail a few of the areas we have probed. A major program of research has focused on capacities judged of importance across various art forms. One specific line of study has investigated the ability to detect the styles of artists in various media; another has focused upon the ability to create and appreciate metaphors—more generally, on the capacity to perform metaphoric operations in different domains.

Rather than sketch out the specific findings that have emerged in each area,[7] let me instead touch upon some common themes. To begin with, we have had to abandon the widespread assumption that children are naturally "in tune with" and capable of "reading" the art objects of their culture. It is, in fact, the case that style and metaphor sensitivity are not available in young children. Indeed, in the middle years of childhood (around the ages of eight or nine) children prove to be extremely literal-minded.[8] They reject figures of speech that cut across domains (a color can't be loud; a heart can't be heavy);[9] they dislike paintings that deviate from the strictly representational.[10] Here, then, lurk obstacles to artistic understanding that must be confronted by art educators.

Our developmental perspective not only points up an area of potential difficulty for children, it also suggests when prudent intervention can help. In our own studies, we have found that children at about the fifth-grade level—age ten or so—can benefit markedly from a brief program of instruction in the concepts of style and metaphor.[11] The regimes are hardly elaborate: Children merely participate in exercises (or games) for twenty minutes a week over a period of two months. Yet the dividends are impressive: Significant increases in sensitivity are found in nearly every child. Moreover, the steps of growth in both areas prove remarkably similar.[12] In each case, the child must first be weaned away from literalism; a stage ensues where the child flails about in search of an alternative way of organizing experience; next, some verbal formulas are learned but inappropriately applied; after more groping, a central dimension of the relevant concept is grasped (e.g., the clue of texture in style discrimination;[13] the notion of category boundary in metaphoric understanding[14]); and, finally, the child becomes able to draw upon a variety of dimensions or factors as he or she conceptualizes anew in the artistic realm.

Two codas to this line of research are worth noting. First of all—and this finding should cheer those who must justify art education in terms of something else—training in the arts proves integrally related to skills of central importance in the sciences. For instance, subjects trained to sort paintings by style prove better able to recognize which portions of an electron micrograph come from the same biological specimens.[15] This intimate relationship between aesthetic and scientific capacities also cuts in the reverse direction. Thus, subjects trained to classify together animals coming from "closely related" species prove better able than control subjects to sort abstract works of art by style.[16] And, in a similar, though less dramatic fashion, subjects trained to adopt the role of an ethologist—to enter the "life-environment" of various creatures—are more successful than control subjects at producing effective metaphors.[17]

Finally, in some related work with brain-damaged patients, we have found that successful decoding of artistic symbols correlates with the preservation of specific brain structures. Thus, as one example, sensitivity to painting styles seems dependent upon an intact right hemisphere.[18] Sensitivity to linguistic metaphor, on the other hand, is linked to two critical areas of the brain. Specifically, the ability to appreciate the context in which a metaphor is appropriate requires a preserved right hemisphere; the ability to explicate (or paraphrase) a metaphor requires intactness of the left hemisphere.[19] Though we cannot pursue this digression further, such a neuropsychological approach holds promise of defining with some biological certitude how skills coalesce and are organized in the human cognitive arsenal.[20]

In these cross-sectional studies, we have barely sampled a few of many candidate central artistic capacities. Currently on our drawing boards are studies probing the criticism of works of art; knowledge of the levels of reality and fantasy that can be captured in artistic works; sensitivity to composition or overall structure in artistic media; and several others as well. Following the research strategy sketched above, we hope in each case to sketch out principal developmental stages; identify pivotal modes for training intervention; pinpoint relationships between these skills as practiced in art and as embodied in other areas of knowledge; and secure information on the way such skills may be organized in the central nervous system.

I should hasten to add that we scarcely hold a monopoly on such studies. For instance, Jeanne Bamberger,[21] a member of Project Zero currently at M.I.T., and Peter Wolff,[22] at Harvard Medical School, are conducting important research on the nature of various musical capacities as well as on their relation to diverse cognitive domains, ranging from mathematics to reading. Related studies are underway in the developmental psychology of literature and visual art forms.[23] The sum total of these researches should clarify which aspects of these artistic skills are shared with general cognitive development, which seem special to the Muses.

Much can be learned from cross-sectional and from brief training studies; indeed, given current funding practices, these are practically the only kinds of studies that researchers have the opportunity to undertake. Yet, to yield a firm understanding of a phenomenon, there is no substitute for intensive case studies, carried out over a number of years by a skilled research team.

A Longitudinal Study of Early Symbolization

With Dennie Wolf,[24] we are currently engaged in an intensive longitudinal study of early symbolization in five firstborn infants. Working with children as young as eight months of age, we have been tracing initial efforts at representing meaning in six media: language, symbolic play, two-dimensional depiction (e. g., drawing), three-dimensional depiction (e. g., construction with clay), music, and gesture. The children are observed daily by their parents, seen weekly by our team of researchers, exposed on a regular basis to a large set of symbolic and cognitive measures, and videotaped for more intensive analysis several times each year. The study is a massive undertaking and our impressions after two years are still preliminary. Yet it is already patently clear that our understanding of human symbolization will be significantly enriched as a result of this study.

Perhaps it will suffice here to mention the questions we have posed and the initial picture that is emerging. To begin with, we are seeking to determine whether symbolic development is basically of a piece. Does progress in one medium immediately redound to other symbolic media; or is the course of symbolization more irregular, with advances in certain media occurring apart from the level of symbolization in others? Our initial impression is that certain cognitive milestones—for example, the attainment of object permanence[25]—have widespread and immediate sequelae. However, these consequences are not felt with equivalent strength across media. Specifically, alteration in the level of symbolic play and of language follow closely upon the attainment of object permanence; analogous milestones do not occur until much later in the realms of two- and three-dimensional depiction.

A second concern centers about the regularity of progress within each symbolic medium. The rate at which children progress, and the degree of engagement they exhibit toward each medium differ widely; moreover, children often favor different media. Nonetheless, to the extent that progress occurs within a medium, it seems to occur in much the same form and order across children. In other words, ordinal developmental scales[26] are the rule in the domain of symbolic development.

A third point of focus is the relationship between symbolic development and the larger culture. We find a close interplay between symbolization and other domains of importance, for instance, the child's relationship to other people. Of special interest is an apparent shift of the child's relation to symbols at about two-and-one-half years of age. Before that time, children are allowed to make what they will of symbols, with parents intervening only to clarify or aid. Thereafter, however, the child is increasingly expected to interpret and utilize symbolism in the manner embraced by the culture. At this time, the child's involvement with text and television undergoes a fundamental change—the child is now expected to interpret these vehicles in the way that other individuals do.

Our final enigma is the nature and extent of individual differences among children. As already suggested, our five subjects differ enormously from one another. While many of the variations were expected, one way in which they differ was not. Certain youngsters (including ones not "enrolled" in our study) adopt in their symbolic activity the stance of a *patterner.* They are intrigued by visual and other static configurations; they attend to overall *gestalten;* they are interested in formal properties of objects or scenes accessible in a single moment of time. Other subjects, whom we have called *dramatists,* have a flair for media that unfolds over time; they are much more riveted by semantic content; they are more comfortable with, and often seek out interpersonal situations; and they are likely to assimilate events to a story context or to happenings in their own lives.

Were this difference merely a rehearsal of the verbal/nonverbal distinction found in intelligence tests, or merely a reflection of preferences for different media, it would be of only marginal interest. What has fascinated us is that these approaches—or ways of knowing the world—predict with surprising acuteness how specific children will interact with diverse materials. Presented with a set of blocks, for instance, patterners will predictably, and almost compulsively, stack them up in a balanced and visually appealing structure; dramatists will grab the same blocks, immediately name them, and proceed to act out a story with the block-characters. Similar differences have been observed in other kinds of puzzles, tasks, and interpersonal contexts. Nor do these differences reduce to sheer imitations of parents. Rather, we have the impression that discrete processing paths are being tapped and that their evocation requires little environmental stimulation. Indeed, in a speculative vein, we hypothesize that these approaches to symbolization may reflect different neurological proclivities, and hence, the activation of different parts of the brain.

Between the cross-sectional study of specific artistic abilities, and the longitudinal study of early symbolization, we have traversed a wide territory. Ultimately, results from these two investigative paths will have to brought into contact with one another so that a single view of symbolization can be obtained. We have already begun this rapprochement in a limited way by administering some tasks drawn from different media to school-age children. Moreover, we hope to revisit these older children on an annual basis so that their changing patterns of symbol use can be monitored.

Our preliminary impression is that the individual differences so manifest among younger children can still be discerned; and that precocity with one medium in no way dictates precocity with others. Yet, overall, the individual differences may become somewhat muted with age, as each child acquires at least a modicum of proficiency with each symbolic medium. Somewhat less happily, it also appears to be the general rule that *only* minimal proficiency is acquired; third-grade children seem "content" to be adequate in all media rather than scintillating in any. Indeed, ongoing data analysis suggests a high point of originality and "flavorfulness" in the artistic creations of first graders. At this time, the testing situation is no longer strange and intimidating to the child, yet patterns of normalization and schooling have not become so firmly entrenched that unusual expressive approaches have been foreclosed.

In focusing on the range of symbolization, we may appear to have abandoned our interest in artistic knowledge in favor of "straight" cognitive-developmental psychology. Indeed, our data can be examined without any reference to the aesthetic domain. Yet, given our original motivations for undertaking these studies, we are pondering these findings for their aesthetic implications. For instance, we want to know whether patterners and dramatists approach the arts in different ways, gain different experiences from them, favor different media, and might benefit from different training regimes. By the same token, we wish to determine how the high point in creativity that seems to emerge in first grade reverberates across the artistic realm; and whether or not steps can be taken to preserve the focal features of this "golden age." Yet, consistent with our goal of sifting the special from the shared, we feel that the particular genius of artistic knowledge will be most apparent if its place can be plotted within the broader range of symbolic activities.

Limitations

Even if the relevance of our research to aesthetic education is conceded, it is patent that many areas have been neglected. Some are simply beyond our research skill: For instance, the phenomenological experience of the individual involved in the arts is clearly crucial, but we know of no way of studying it. An individual's affective responses are also crucial, but we are equally ignorant of how to study affect. And we have a further stricture to offer. While affective involvement clearly permeates aesthetic experience, it is never an independent component. Rather, affective responses can be appropriate only to the extent that they reflect knowledge of the work. Accordingly, a focus on cognition of the work should be primary. Knowing how to apprehend a work may not in itself be sufficient to produce appropriate affect (or any affect at all); but unless the work can somehow be apprehended (and this means knowing how to "read" the words in a poem, the forms in a painting, or the tonal sequence in compositions), any talk of affective responses is ill-conceived or meaningless. If an individual experiences a "high" for a reason unrelated to the content or form of the work, this response is devoid of aesthetic relevance.

In addition to these broad issues, we are also ignoring many other more focused questions. We have said little about individuals' artistic preferences and how they change over time; attitudes toward the arts; children's conceptualizations; differences among sexes, social classes, ethnic groups, different cultures, and the like. We do not minimize these questions; indeed, we have ourselves researched several of them. Yet, in our view, such questions are best approached after a broad picture of symbolization in the arts has been limned. And so we prefer for the most part to suspend inquiries on these questions until essential spadework on symbolization has been consummated. Naturally, other researchers will hold other priorities; and this pluralism is beneficent.

Let me reformulate this point: In my view, research on aesthetic education has yet to come of age. To be sure, there are important studies and competent researchers. But as yet there is neither an experimental paradigm nor a theoretical framework that has been widely accepted. The marrow of the field is missing. Our wager is that the crucial character of artistic knowledge and education will most clearly emerge if the arts are seen as a symbol-using endeavor, calling for certain kinds of cognitive skills. And so, we have elected to devote our efforts to an investigation of the nature and developmental course of these symbolic capacities. We trust that chips of more immediate relevance to artistic education in the classroom may then fall into place.

Might our inquiry miss what is special about the arts? This outcome is possible, of course, but we remain cautiously optimistic. If certain features of the arts are indeed special, they should emerge clearly from the kind of broad-based inquiry that we are proposing. And should they emerge under such conditions, their uniqueness will be more firmly established than if it has simply been asserted.

Implications for Education and Evaluation in the Arts

Rather than being charted in a vacuum, programs of arts education should always be conceived with an eye toward the other domains of knowledge. Up to now, art educators and the rest of the educational establishment have been at loggerheads, each eager to preserve its domain against the onslaughts of the other. Yet, once it has been recognized that all knowledge involves symbolization, and that no slot in the brain or the mind is labelled "all art here" or "no art permitted," then the essential artificiality of these camps will become evident.

Indeed, such a raising of consciousness has already become apparent in certain quarters. If, however, the arts are to assume their appropriate place as girders of the house of education (rather than as an elaborate surrounding filigree), then these insights have also to enter the awareness of principals, administrators, parents, school boards, and most important of all, classroom teachers. Since many of these individuals are themselves highly ambivalent about the role of the arts, equally insecure about their own aesthetic capacities, efforts to promote the cause of the arts are likely to be viewed with suspicion. Yet if the case can be made that the arts are ways of knowing the world, and that they are uniquely suited to convey certain kinds of information, then perhaps some of the misgivings will dissolve and the place of the arts within education can be solidified.

Even as this view of the arts may prove suggestive to the general educational community, I hope it will prove helpful to those of us concerned with arts education. I believe that many of the problems we have encountered in implementing and evaluating programs in aesthetic education have reflected our own uncertainty about just how the arts relate to other areas of knowledge. If they are wholly special, must they not be taught and evaluated in special ways? And if they are just like everything else, why develop special means for teaching them? By charting the boundaries between the special and the shared, it should become possible to devise programs that speak more directly to the rest of the curriculum; that fit within the range of skills being developed by students; and that allow for procedures of evaluation that are at once reliable and comprehensive, yet also flexible enough to accommodate to the special genius of the arts. Many would applaud this vision. It is the special burden—and opportunity—of arts researchers to bring it to life.

Boston, Massachusetts
May 1976

FOOTNOTES

[1] For an introduction to the work of Harvard Project Zero, cf. V. Howard, "Harvard Project Zero: A Fresh Look at Art Education," *Journal of Aesthetic Education*, Vol. 5 (1971), pages 67-74; D. Perkins, "Probing Artistic Process: A Progress Report from Harvard Project Zero," *Journal of Aesthetic Education*, Vol. 8, No. 3, pages 33-57; H. Gardner, "Promising Paths to Artistic Knowledge," *Journal of Aesthetic Education*, Vol. 10 (1976), pages 201-207.

[2] H. Gardner, V. Howard, and D. Perkins, "Symbol Systems: A Philosophical, Psychological, and Educational Investigation," *Media and Symbols: The Forms of Expression, Communication, and Education*, ed. D. Olson (Chicago: University of Chicago Press, 1974), pages 27-56.

[3] N. Goodman, *Languages of Art* (Indianapolis: Bobbs-Merrill, 1968).

[4] Gardner, et al., 1974, op. cit.

[5] D. Perkins, and B. Leondar, *The Arts and Cognition* (Baltimore: Johns Hopkins University Press, 1977).

[6] D. Perkins, "A Better Word: Studies of Poetry Editing," *The Arts and Cognition*, ed. D. Perkins, and B. Leondar (Baltimore: Johns Hopkins University Press, 1977).

[7]For a review of this research, cf. H. Gardner, "Style Sensitivity in Children," *Human Development*, Vol. 15 (1972), pages 325-338; E. Winner, A. Rosenstiel, and H. Gardner, "The Development of Metaphoric Understanding," *Developmental Psychology*, Vol. 12 (1976), pages 289-297; J. Silverman, E. Winner, and H. Gardner, "On Going Beyond the Literal: The Development of Sensitivity to Artistic Symbols," *Semiotica*, (1976, in press).

[8]Cf. J. Silverman, E. Winner, and H. Gardner, "On Going Beyond the Literal: The Development of Sensitivity to Artistic Symbols," *Semiotica*, (1976, in press): H. Gardner, *The Arts and Human Development* (New York: Wiley, 1973); D. Wolf, and H. Gardner, "Beyond Playing or Polishing: The Development of Artistry," *Arts Exemplar Models*, ed. J. Hausman (1976, in press).

[9]H. Gardner, E. Winner, M. Kircher, and D. Perkins, "Children's Metaphoric Productions and Preferences," *Journal of Child Language*, Vol. 2 (1975), pages 125-141; E. Winner, A. Rosenstiel, and H. Gardner, "The Development of Metaphoric Understanding," *Developmental Psychology*, Vol. 12 (1976), pages 289-297.

[10]H. Gardner, "The Development of Sensitivity to Figural and Stylistic Aspects of Paintings," *British Journal of Psychology*, Vol. 63 (1972), pages 605-615; H. Gardner, "Style Sensitivity in Children," *Human Development*, Vol. 15 (1972), pages 325-338.

[11]H. Gardner, "The Development of Sensitivity to Figural and Stylistic Aspects of Paintings," *British Journal of Psychology*, Vol. 63 (1972), pages 605-615; J. Silverman, E. Winner, A. Rosenstiel, and H. Gardner, "On Training Sensitivity to Painting Styles," *Perception*, Vol. 4 (1975), pages 373-384; J. Silverman, E. Winner, and II. Gardner, "On Going Beyond the Literal: The Development of Sensitivity to Artistic Symbols," *Semiotica*, (1976, in press).

[12]J. Silverman, E. Winner, and H. Gardner, "On Going Beyond the Literal: The Development of Sensitivity to Artistic Symbols," *Semiotica*, (1976, in press).

[13]H. Gardner, "The Development of Sensitivity of Figural and Stylistic Aspects of Paintings," *British Journal of Psychology*, Vol. 63 (1972), pages 605-615; H. Gardner, "On Figure and Texture in Aesthetic Perception," *British Journal of Aesthetics*, Vol. 12 (1972), pages 40-59.

[14]J. Silverman, E. Winner, and H. Gardner, "On Going Beyond the Literal: The Development of Sensitivity to Artistic Symbols," *Semiotica*, (1976, in press).

[15]H. Gardner, "The Development of Sensitivity of Figural and Stylistic Aspects of Paintings," *British Journal of Psychology*, Vol. 63 (1972), pages 605-615.

[16]J. Silverman, E. Winner, A. Rosenstiel, and H. Gardner, "On Training Sensitivity to Painting Styles," *Perception*, Vol. 4 (1975), pages 373-384.

[17]E. Winner, "Training Children's Metaphoric Sensitivity," (Unpublished research, 1975).

[18]H. Gardner, "Artistic Capacities in Aphasia," (Paper presented at the Academy of Aphasia, Vancouver, British Columbia, October 1975).

[19]H. Gardner, "Promising Paths to Knowledge," *Journal of Aesthetic Education* (1976).

[20]H. Gardner, *The Shattered Mind* (New York: Knopf, 1975); H. Gardner, "Brain Damage: A Gateway to the Mind," *Saturday Review*, August 9, 1975.

[21]J. Bamberger, "In Search of a Tune," *The Arts and Cognition*, ed. D. Perkins, and B. Leondar (Baltimore: Johns Hopkins University Press, 1977).

[22]Cf. I. Hurwitz, P. H. Wolff, B. Bortnick, and K. Kokas, "The Effects of Kodaly Music Instruction on Cognitive Task Performance and Academic Achievement of First Grade Children," *Journal of Learning Disabilities*, Vol. 8 (1975), pages 167-174.

[23]Cf. B. Sutton-Smith, "The Importance of the Storytaker: An Investigation of the

Imaginative Life," *The Urban Review*, Vol. 8 (1975), pages 82-95; J. Goodnow, S. Friedman, "Orientation in Children's Human Figure Drawings: An Aspect of Graphic Language," *Developmental Psychology*, Vol. 7 (1972), pages 10-16; N. Smith, "Developmental Origins of Graphic Symbolization in the Paintings of Children Three to Five," (Unpublished doctoral dissertation, Harvard University, 1972).

[24]H. Gardner, D. Wolf, and A. Smith, "Artistic Symbols in Early Childhood," *New York University Education Quarterly*, Vol. 6 (1975), pages 13-21; D. Wolf, J. Silverman, A. Smith, A. K. Rosenstiel, J. Shotwell, and H. Gardner, *Symbolization in Early Childhood*, (Annual report to the Spencer Foundation, Chicago, 1975).

[25]J. Piaget, *The Construction of Reality in the Child* (New York: Basic Books, 1954).

[26]I. Uzgiris, and J. McV. Hunt, *Scales of Infant Psychological Development* (Urbana, Illinois: University of Illinois Press, 1975); L. Kohlberg, "Stage and Sequence: The Cognitive-Developmental Approach to Socialization," *Handbook of Socialization Theory and Research*, ed. D. Goslin (New York: Rand McNally, 1969).

David Perkins

Talk About Art*

Clothespin names a theme and series of works conceived by artist Claes Oldenburg. Graphic images and sculptures display, in varying sizes and transformations, clothespins standing on end. There is something about most of these clothespins that many viewers never notice: Each can be seen as a couple embracing. Oldenburg himself sanctions the reading (Walker Art Center, 1975, pages 63-64). Simply telling a viewer about this has always epitomized for me what talk about art can do. The message is clear and direct: "Regard this as a couple embracing." The viewer looks and sees. One sentence wields leverage far beyond its bare content, remaking the work.

Despite such glad circumstances, the role of talk about art is challenged continually. Meaningful talk is doubted to be possible at all: By what standards do we discourse on the merit of works? With what words can we section the shades of emotion the arts can deliver? When rationally well-founded, talk threatens emotional ruin; the dry dissection of words withers the happy panoply of perception. Such chatter might be dismissed as naive. But perhaps its innocence rests less in positing problems than in presuming what those problems are. Perhaps talk that is good talk—clear, comprehensive, insightful—offers a valuable guide to perception. But not all talk is good—in fact much of it is very bad—and the ways it is bad invite inquiry. If talk can make

DAVID PERKINS is Co-Director of Project Zero, Harvard University.

*The writing and research for this paper were undertaken at Project Zero, Harvard Graduate School of Education, operating under support from National Institute of Education Grant G-003-0169 and the Spencer Foundation. The opinions expressed do not necessarily reflect the position or policy of the Aspen Conference or the supporting agencies, and no official endorsement should be inferred.

The title of this article is adapted from the course "Verbalizing About Art," offered at the Massachusetts College of Art. Diana Korzenik, Chairperson of the Education Division at the College, and member of project Zero, conceived the course as part of the required graduate curriculum and found several faculty members to offer it. Though I know only a little about how the course has been handled, I was impressed by the idea and the need, and Ms. Korzenik's example set me thinking along the lines developed here.

mischief as well as magic in guiding our perceptions, the ways that the best and the worst can happen require charting.

This enterprise raises questions reaching beyond the arts as such. In one way or another, most talk concerns things perceived or to be perceived; and much of what we preceive makes its way into words. In examining talk about art, one inevitably probes the general relations between word and experience. But the arts offer an especially good context wherein to do just that. There, fine points of perception and understanding urge continual discussion and debate. Discourse often enjoys the presence of the stimulus itself, rather than proceeding after the fact. Like circumstances do occur—in medical diagnosis or biological observation, for instance. But the arts are handier, and perhaps most thoroughly exercise those thin threads of convention and construction that bind language to experience.

However general the underlying issue, its exploration means much to the practice of the arts in our culture. We think of artistic experiences as isolated—something between the artist and his or her evolving product, or between the audience and the work. But, in fact, all our intercourse with art occurs in an elaborate frame of discourse about art. Of course "talk" here spans lecture or dialogue, spoken or written. Critics talk, professors talk, artists talk, friends talk. They talk about meaning, value, motivation, technique, style, significance. They talk about music, painting, dance, film, literature, sculpture. They talk about the fine and popular arts, and about aesthetic dimensions of everyday life—food, clothing, living and working spaces, furniture, automobiles. One even suspects that those decrying talk about art do quite a lot more talking than they acknowledge or even realize.

In all likelihood, then, talk amounts to a fundamental educational and acculturational force in our perception and understanding of art. At least, formal and informal education tries through and through to use talk for just that purpose. If talk can serve this purpose well, it would be well to know how talk can best do so. If not, it's about time that were firmly established and other tactics sought. Planning for education in the arts demands comprehending the weak and strong points of talk about art. That comprehension will be gained through distinguishing the possibility from the practice of good talk.

Denying some popular and scholarly positions, the following section will hold that language provides sufficient vocabulary, reach, subtlety, and expression to speak significantly about the arts. A later section will argue that much talk about art is objective and testable, despite a seeming relativity of standards. These discussions can hardly settle such classic issues, or even review them comprehensively; and, indeed, for many they are not even issues, but matters taken for granted. Nevertheless, at least a perspective can be offered.

But if the possibility of talk urges optimism, the practice does not. Most of this essay reviews informal and formal investigations of talk as actually accomplished. Explored are such matters as comprehensiveness, the giving of reasons for judgments, problems of dialogue such as talking past one another, emotional problems such as defensiveness, and that major sin of discourse—being just plain wrong because of being poorly grounded. Both the often sketchy data and the importance of the issues recommend much more inquiry than has occurred; and, along the way, directions toward further research will be mentioned. But these pages will try to make the promised case: that the possibilities of worthwhile talk about art are good, but that the practice of talk is often bad; and that education does not do nearly as much as it could do to help.

What Can Be Said?

One worry over talk about art asks whether such talk can say anything worth saying. Artistic experience unfolds in so rich a way that words seem little equipped to represent it. This general concern conceals both some false and some real issues.

Popular attitude teaches that the trouble with words is their parched perspective on emotionally rich material. The critic's account renders little of the feel of a work. But this concern mixes up different functions of language. Expression is one thing, assertion quite another. Talk may offer true claims about a work in the driest of manners, or push outrageous nonsense with panache. Further, expressive language may match the work discussed, or merely make its own display: A review may radiate enthusiasm about works not enthusiastic, or project gloom about works hardly gloomy. And talk about art can be too passionate as well as not passionate enough. How many reviews brim more with conviction than cogency?

So, not only is all critical discourse not dry, but criticizing discourse for being dry overlooks its significant assertive, rather than expressive, function. This hardly condones dry or florid styles, but it does warn against visiting the sins of style on content. The student who complains the loudest about how studied the lecture is, *may* be the one who has missed what a lecture says, wherein its richness lies.

Such particular grumbles seem offspring of the odd generality that talk should somehow remake the experience discussed. Just why talk about art should do that is hard to see, since talk about other matters does not. Perhaps the language of poets and novelists goes furthest toward recreating experience, but even so we have little trouble sorting literary from real-world experience. Words are often blamed for being too crude and categorical to capture experience. But, as far as talk about art is concerned, the problem relates little to the limits of language as such and rather involves general canons of equivalence for works of art. Certainly, no one wants an interpretation in place of a poem, an analysis instead of the symphony, a formal dissection instead of the painting. But not even a dance, poem, or sonata, composed in response to a painting, could take the place of the original—though it may earn regard in its own right. As Howard Gardner has emphasized (1971), untranslatability—not only into words but into any other symbolic system—is a hallmark of the artistic. To expect words to provide full substitutes for an artistic experience, or for any other experience in all its subtlety, asks for something symbolic renderings hardly ever do.

If not insisting that talk remake experience, at least one might ask that talk adequately describe works of art and our experience of them. Perhaps in principle such is usually not possible, given the fundamental syntactic differences between language and other symbolic forms that Goodman has noted (1968). But, in any case, art and our experience of it are so full and varied, so real and substantial, so shaded from explicit to tacit, that any discourse of normal length can hardly hope to render a full account.

But does this imply that language never can make significant statements about art? That goes too far. Surely most critics, artists, and audiences think that sometimes some people make such statements. Nor would overweighting this failure of thoroughness match practice elsewhere. No one asks that physics (if mathematical symbology may be added to language here) describe the universe in detail instead of formulating sound theories about it.

The real concern seems different: If talk about art can only describe a small part of an intricate reality, how can such talk assist our experience of art? The answer rests in the way language interacts with experience. As many writers have stressed (e. g., Ecker, 1967; Goodman, 1968, page 262; Ziff, 1964), language adopts a sort of pointing function, which guides our senses to recognize things not apprehended before. Thus with the Oldenburg, "a couple embracing" in itself carries little information. But it leads the eye to look and find. Then the pattern surfaces in all its particular anatomy of part and contour. In general, one person may perceive something highly complex, utter a few words, and lead another to apprehend the same complexity, which was far from fully explicit in the words.

The same worry might reappear in new guise. Perhaps certain important areas of aesthetic experience forbid talk altogether, for lack of suitable vocabulary. But, if so, at least other areas allow fruitful discourse. And is it so? Of course, a developed vocabulary considerably assists discussion; but language seems barred in no obvious way from commenting on anything from structure to salience, affect to authenticity. Where single words do not provide, more elaborate statement, metaphoric usage, and new definition can extend the reach of language. In all, notions that language can't hope to discuss or guide our experience of art simply seem misfounded, perhaps through their construing the sins of bad talk as limits of language in general.

What Is Said?

But this optimism may mask some real problems. What usefully can be said is not necessarily what *is* said. Language likely will shape the practice if not the possibilities of talk. That which invites ready words and handy phrases will come to the fore; that which proves more subtle and strains language further will fall back, even if fundamentally more important.

In part, this is a problem of facility with the existing resources of language. Like talk about automobile engines or baseball, talk about art involves its own vocabulary and customs, its own tacit categorization of the important and less important. Simple lack of such sophistication marks one way that talk about art can fall short. Brent Wilson has conducted several studies investigating this concern.

An initial study (summarized in Wilson, 1974) found minimal differences in talk about art across primary- and secondary-school students with more cumulative training in the arts. Disappointingly, talk centered around literal characteristics of paintings. A further study (Wilson, 1972) examined critical appraisals of a painting by high-school students with zero, one, and three years in an elective art program. Students with three years of art training made significantly more frequent use of "organistic" and "contextualistic" reasons in support of judgments than did students with zero years. These terms referred respectively to criteria of unity, coherence, cohesiveness, complexity, and of intensity and vividness. Wilson (1974) later concluded that the differences were due less to the training than to the self-selection of the students entering the art program. To my mind, Wilson's own data table (1972) suggests more a continuously developing sophistication. Whatever the case, the study documents definite differences in reason-giving.

Another investigation by Wilson (1970) examined remarks on *Guernica* by three groups: art teachers, art historians and critics, and college students with no artistic training. The art teachers noted sensory qualities like shape and color more frequently than did the other two groups. As in other findings, the students emphasized the literal contents of the painting in contrast with the art teachers and the historians and critics. The latter groups commented on the work's symbolic meaning; but, for the most part, only the critics and art historians related the work to its time and social context. A different study (Wilson, 1966) explored whether deliberate and focused verbal training could broaden the critical categories students used. The effort induced statistically significant increases in remarks on relationships in paintings, aspects of sensory quality and formal structure, and symbolic significance.

Such investigations are fundamentally comparative, documenting broader versus narrower repertoires in talk about art. They leave open whether even conventionally sophisticated talk reaches as far as it might. Custom as well as linguistic convenience conditions what talk is about. In *With Respect to Readers*, Walter Slatoff (1970) reviews the conventions guiding contemporary critical practice in literature. He argues that many "personal" dimensions important to our experience of art are edited from written and classroom discussion. Yet they seem no more recondite than the "proper" subjects of critical discourse.

Also, beliefs about what can be said govern what is usually discussed. But efforts that challenge conventional belief disclose its limitations. For example, David Ecker (1973) has found children to be engaged by and able to discuss central issues of aesthetics. For a further instance, popular attitude holds that the subtle processes of creating art allow little inspection or explanation. Yet Patrick (1935, 1937) conducted process-tracing experiments of artists commenting as they worked. Reitman (1965) studied musical composition in like manner. Over the past several years, I have been investigating the creative processes of poets and artists with verbal reporting techniques (Perkins, 1977a). If rightly done, the approach surprises subjects with how much is accessible. One remarked to the effect: "Good God! I never knew I thought so much!" Such studies suggest that professional and student artists could share and compare their working patterns in ways much more intimate than even apprenticeship provides.

In general, the ramparts of popular belief, conventional practice, and linguistic convenience will not give way without deliberate challenge. Among other things, this calls for focused inquiry into just what opportunities are being missed. The present comments barely point a direction. At first, such exploration needs no more methodology than simple attention to what is, and might be, discussed. Creative boundary-breaking is important in talk about art, as well as in art itself.

How Much Is Said?

Examining critical repertoires still misses how detailed and comprehensive particular discussions are; and, further, what opportunities for talk occur—for instance, do student artists have sufficient access to criticism? The larger commerce of conversation that joins artist to audience to critic and peer to peer invites investigation.

Some small progress comes from my own study of twenty amateur and professional poets. Principally concerned with process tracing, the study also interviewed subjects about criticism and critical feedback. Some questions dealt with access to critical readings. Subjects received criticism on about three-quarters of their output, from an average of four different critics—peers or superiors. But the mean figures misrepresent the individual circumstances. Where six of the amateur poets showed almost all their work, one showed almost none, and three fell in between. Five professionals sought critiques of almost all their work, three rarely sought criticism, and two fell in between. The number of people usually commenting on a given work also varied widely. In denial of the popular image—the artist pursuing his private vision—most subjects maintained contact with the critical perspectives of others. But, at the same time, some proved isolated; these were not necessarily the "best" nor the "worst" poets.

The reasons for variation were several. Almost universally, the poets acknowledged the value of sound criticism. Some professionals felt they had sufficient craft not to need frequent feedback. Many subjects found good criticism hard to come by, though many of these sought any available criticism just the same. Thus, the present results also denied everyday notions of artists' antagonism toward criticism and doubt concerning the value of criticism.

Other interview questions examined how detailed critical feedback proved, when received. This varied widely, ranging from brief global remarks to an intensive "going over." Four of the ten amateurs reported almost never getting more than sketchy comments. Giving intensive commentary was the routine practice of only two professionals. Making detailed comments on several particular points was more characteristic. Informal discussions with some of the amateurs revealed that a really close examination of a poem with a teacher was a valued event—and one in somewhat short supply.

What people *do* often speaks more precisely than what they *say*. Each subject was asked to critique a poem given him as he would for someone requesting a reading. A professional poet provided a six-stanza, fifty-line poem. In the version used, the second and fifth stanzas were revised to be bizarre and obscure, and poetic devices were stripped from the third and sixth to make them flat. However, no blatant pattern showed.

Analysis disclosed that subjects averaged only 8.75 focused remarks (that is, exclusive of comments on the whole poem). The minimum was two and the maximum seventeen. Remarks addressed from one to five lines at once, with a mean of 2.6. For a fifty-line poem, such criticism could not be called detailed. Also, individual comments proved quite brief. This was not so fine-grained as the criticism most subjects claimed to give. The discrepancy invites *in vivo* study of critical feedback.

Subjects' remarks were categorized according to their critical concerns (meaning, rhyme, meter, metaphor, and several others) and according to any critical principle they invoked (unity, clarity, veracity, and several others). Where some subjects always gave reasons for judgments, others rarely did so. Pooled over all subjects, the comments revealed the manner in which the poem had been "rigged," as reflected in the principles criticizing various parts of the poem. But again, some individual critiques mirrored this markedly and others hardly at all. Subjects in the course of their critiques invoked as few as one principle or concern and as many as six or nine, respectively.

Related issues echo in Brent Wilson's (1972) study of high-school students with zero, one, and three years in an elective art program. He noted that over half the statements made by students with no art training lacked judgmental criteria, even though justification was constantly urged. Wilson recorded disappointment that even the art students mustered only an average of 10.9 sentences in support of their evaluations, and one-third of these lacked criteria.

In the study of poets, more detailed and comprehensive criticism proved correlated neither with professionalism versus amateurism, nor with the better poets versus the worse poets, as independently judged by professional poets. This may reflect the crudeness of the measures. On the other hand, it lends weight to the notion that good performers are not necessarily the best teachers, while allowing no comfort to the notion that the best critics are the worst artists.

Finding criticism often sparse, these results still allowed that comments might prove to the point. Perhaps each subject noted the same and most salient features of the poem. This was measured by testing whether subjects mentioned similar principles and concerns in association with the same lines of the poem. The results are best described by comparing one "average" subject with another. Tabulations revealed that sixty-five percent of the one subject's remarks could concern the same line as the other. Also, thirty-one percent would address the same line with the same poetic concern. Only thirteen percent would address the same line in terms of the same critical principle. In fact these small figures still overestimate the commonality. Remarks classified into the same concern or principle did not always make the same point; and, as already noted, many remarks spanned several lines at once, but subjects were credited with a common remark if their comments overlapped at all.

In another examination of "critical overlap," three professional poets were asked for close critiques of a poem. Another professional provided the poem, though this fact and the poet's name were concealed. Again, a careful examination of the comments revealed minimal overlap. Of a total of forty-nine remarks made, twenty-two concerned the same locale (word, line, or phrase) as some other remark. Only twelve comments noted the same property (e.g., nice sound play, an ambiguous word) as some other remark. Only nineteen comments evaluated the same locale with the same valence.

Some examples from the criticisms may illustrate how such divergence occurs. All three critics applauded the first line, but one characterized it as "weird, strong, surrealistic"; another noted that it "draws in the reader right away, and echoes a tradition (for beginning poems in a certain way)"; the third, that one abstract word and another concrete word in the line made for a nice opening. The critics may have been reacting to the same poetic strength in the line, but certainly formulated their approval somewhat differently. In other cases, contrary evaluations of the same concern occurred—a line with an "awkward sound" versus "the sound qualities work well." In still others, remarks addressed entirely different aspects of lines. For example, according to one critic a line dramatized an effect, not just said it; another felt the line a letdown, less surprising and more sententious; and the third thought it interesting but mismatched with the other images. Elsewhere, I have described like problems with discussion of a painting (Perkins, 1977b).

These examples have concerned criticism of works "small" and "portable" in a way that films, plays, and concerts are not. When the morning paper discusses the "large" work attended the night before, further problems can bother. Very often, remarks are so summative and/or vague as to forbid any easy check against the work, or worse, one's memory of it. If *Hamlet* occasionally was awkward, exactly when; if the violins seemed shaky, just where and in what way? Of course, the newspaper critic has little space to make a case, and if one sees him or her simply as judging and recommending, one need only learn whom to trust. But precision does not demand that much space, and if one hopes that criticism will be a guide to the work, the lack of clear reasons addressing well-localized parts serves but poorly.

In sum, the present results find critical feedback generally valued. But at least some individuals work largely isolated from criticism, deliberately or by circumstance. Critical feedback and criticism in general is not very focused, detailed, or wide-ranging in the considerations invoked. Different individuals highlight and overlook rather different features of works. All these results point up problems, not with the possibility but the practice of talk about art. An examination of twenty poets hardly allows the sure and comprehensive conclusion that broader studies could provide. But at least the findings outline a disturbing if partial picture.

Kinds of Confirmation

The foregoing pages have examined the range and richness, the frequency and forcefulness of talk about art. But they have deferred one fundamental problem: Are particular claims right or wrong, true or false? However sophisticated the language and subtle the proposed distinctions, talk that speaks falsely manages nothing but mischief. But for "truth" even to make sense, claims about works of art must permit tests of validity. For talk about art to be meaningful in any objective manner, claims must somehow allow a match with the work and discover confirmation or denial in it. On just this matter misgivings often feed. Against what standards or reasons can we test value judgments, for instance?

So venerable a problem can hardly be vanquished here. But at least a certain viewpoint will be offered. This calls for a detour concerning how we, in fact, try to confirm claims about works of art. First, word is not work—perception not labeling, nor labeling perception. For instance, one may see the clothespin as a kiss without a vocal or subvocal utterance; or one may know without seeing, by being told. This still allows perception to be considered a form of encoding or categorizing; such is a good way to understand it. But perception and verbal labeling are distinct experiences. Indeed, evidence exists that they are handled by different parts of the brain (Gardner, 1975). The general point seems so completely obvious and commonly held as hardly to need mention. But some people seem to worry over talk about art because they think that such talk is being put forth as constituting the whole experience of the work. They may be reassured that labeling something and perceiving something as "x" are distinct.

If word and experience are not one, how are they matched? A difference between two modes of matching, "analytic" and "synthetic," will help here. To confirm that Oldenburg's *Clothespin* doubles as an embrace, one only need see it that way. True, one may look for a bit before the pattern slips into place. But once discovered, it is seen suddenly whole. In this synthetic mode of confirmation, one affirms that "x properly describes y" simply by perceiving that it does.

In analytic confirmation, reasons are found. The claim that "x describes y" depends on points arguing to that effect—points themselves claimed about "x" and "y," and themselves subject to synthetic or analytic confirmation. Hardly emergent as a whole, the force of analytic confirmation accumulates piecemeal.

Much talk about art is meaningful, if not confirmable, without being matched to the work. But some claims require confirmation to be understood adequately. Of course, matters of degree are involved. "Hamlet forgot his first line" seems clear enough. But was "a stiff Hamlet" stiff in gesture, speech, demeanor? With the performance at hand this might be obvious; without it, or further explanation, some ambiguity bothers. Finally, "Hamlet delivered his lines as though trimming a suburban hedge" might be obscure without, but both clear and remarkably precise with, the performance at hand. The effort to confirm the remark interprets it as well, as the relevant perceptual *gestalt* appears. Such context-dependent usages allow unusual or subtle distinctions not well provided for in context-free discourse. It is a risky game, but sometimes a fruitful one.

Now some quick caveats are due before all this is taken too seriously. The analytic-synthetic contrast hardly marks a dichotomy; one can find experiences that fall in between—for instance, perceptual *gestalts* that mature moment by moment until complete (Julesz, 1974). Confirmation can occur by other than synthetic or analytic means—for example, by authority or from memory—which sources constitute indirect evidence for the claim. Nor is the distinction any analysis of truth. Rather, it concerns how grounds for belief are found, and one may have good grounds for what actually is false, or poor grounds for what actually is true. Analytic versus synthetic does not amount to language *versus* perception, because we often perceive properties of language in a rapid and *gestalt* manner, as in reading poetry or in recognizing grammatical errors as simply "sounding wrong." Neither is subjective certainty involved. Though some perceptions are compelling, others are vague, and perception can be notoriously inaccurate; too often the testimony of witnesses testifies more to the frailties of perception than to the facts of events (Buckout, 1974). Again, where some analytic arguments are feeble, others are devastatingly thorough.

Synthetic-analytic does not even stake out necessarily differing kinds of grounds. For instance, the eye synthetically seeing the *Clothespin* as a kiss must in some sense test the reality of that image; that test must involve some accumulation of evidence for and against, albeit unconscious. In another paper (Perkins, 1975a), I have explored how such covert processes might function and the sorts of evidence they might employ. But their being rapid and covert, rather than extended and deliberate, does not mean they amount to an epistemologically different mode of support.

Not epistemology, but phenomenology distinguishes analytic from synthetic. The experiences are distinct, though they may shade one into the other. Accordingly, they yield different apprehensions of a work of art. The embrace, if seen leg by leg, arm by arm, and with the right connections, would be just as much confirmed as the same seen whole. But the accent of the experience would be wholly altered. Just this difference makes not only whether, but how, a claim about a work is confirmed important to our experience of the work.

Meaning and Matching

Now the testability of claims about works of art can again be considered. Monroe Beardsley (1958, 1970) argues sturdily for the testability of evaluative and interpretive statements. He emphasizes that one may request and receive reasons for judgments; that everyday discourse proceeds as though such reasons were relevant; that terms like "good" or "bad," in contrast with "like" or "dislike," behave linguistically as though they were, or hoped to be, objective claims; that some purported cases of interpretive indeterminacy are not so indeterminate as suggested. In these and like ways, he builds the case that talk about art can be evaluated for its validity; or at least, much of it can. The present discussion will stand on the "much of it can." There is no need to argue that all talk about art is testable. The objectivity of talk about art can be rescued by matching claims against the work and one another to sift out the objectively meaningful parts. This stand depends on unraveling several misconceptions.

Critical disagreement defines the fundamental problem with talk about art. Sometimes blamed are the lack of definitions for terms like "good" or the lack of standards for value judgments or the validity of interpretations. Such doubts imply what might be called an "analytic-rule-based" notion of confirmation. Claims are established by reason-giving ultimately grounded in explicit and general standards. But this account misdescribes how talk actually proceeds. We do not usually require explicit standards to justify our labeling practices. We just label synthetically. For example, we worry little as to what definitions or standards govern which objects are properly called "chairs." In fact, devising a good definition of "chair" poses a formidable challenge. We easily sort the grammatical from the ungrammatical, yet linguistics has only recently and partially charted the governing rules. If lack of overt standards causes little disagreement in these cases, why should it do so in talk about art?

Then, if disagreement, not lack of explicit standards, points to the real problem, perhaps explicit standards at least propose a solution.

This hope observes that disagreement fosters a shift to an analytic mode of confirmation—the giving of reasons that invoke various standards and depend on various definitions. If only the *right* definitions and standards were settled, particular disagreements could be resolved. Thus dictionaries, legal codes, and grammars hope to formalize correct manners of spelling, behaving morally, and speaking grammatically.

One can debate their degrees of success. But, in any case, our understanding of aesthetics has not managed even that much. What terms like "good" mean has been the subject of continuous debate (Beardsley, 1958; Kennick, 1964). No one has yet put forth standards for evaluating works of art that can be applied in a mechanical manner, like dictionary spellings (Weitz, 1962). In fact, the use of analytic confirmation in talk about art perhaps misleadingly encourages such hopes. True, reason-giving invokes standards. But the standards are often terribly context-bound, rather than general. For instance, realistic portrayal of a figure may be perceived to be relevant in one painting, but not in another, because of the way the paintings are painted. Its relevance is apprehended synthetically in much the same way that the figure is perceived: What "looks right" in one case does not in another. Of course, the perception may be mistaken, but this does not deny its prompting the judgment.

But neither frequent disagreement nor lack of explicit and general standards are sure signs of disaster. All depends on what we make of the disagreements, how we interpret them. For instance, such claims as "smoking causes cancer," or "television violence encourages real-world violence," though hotly debated, are not dismissed as meaningless. Rather, paucity of evidence and emotional commitment encourage disagreement. One can easily promote an argument over whether the tree that falls in the deserted forest makes a noise. But then one can note that any resolution depends on what "noise" means in this odd context, without doubting its everyday serviceability. I may say the day is very warm, and you that it is hot—without feeling compelled to delete such vague phrases from our speech. We confess the fuzzy boundaries while preserving the clear-cut cases.

The same perspective applies to talk about art. What we make of disagreements is crucial. Perhaps one party has missed a consideration, overweighted the evidence, perceived a misleading *gestalt*. Perhaps generally meaningful terms are being used in contexts where their application is borderline. Perhaps alternative interpretations or perceptions are equally supported by the work. In this case, the "reality" of the situation is the ambiguity of the work; apprehending it as it is calls for acknowledging that ambiguity.

On the other hand, disagreements may be attributed to fundamental differences in talk and belief, forbidding any synthesis. For instance, if two parties hold different standards but both insist that their standards are objective, then this is a failure to construct a common reality. When such cases arise rarely, talk is not seriously threatened. When they arise often, talk can become a swamp of misdirection.

But Beardsley becomes important here through his rebuttals of others' arguments that certain kinds of claims about art are generically nonobjective. This denied, talk about the most evasive aspects of art promises a salvageable core. The strategy is matching—matching claim to work and meanings with one another. Where accounts hoped to be objective conflict, this invites interpretation as an error of one party, or ambiguity of the work. Where such resolutions fail, the accounts must be recognized as subjective. None of this forbids talk of the subjective; indeed, art, if any area of human commitment, urges such exploration. Rather, it asks that discourse work to clarify the objective or subjective status of claims. This sorting is a natural part of discourse, and apt here is the term "dialectics," meaning any method of argument that systematically weighs real or apparent contradictions with a view to resolution. Thus we refine our objectivity piecemeal and in context, not presume it all beforehand. The later discussion of critical dialogue will probe this process further.

Being Wrong

Promising a "salvageable core" of objective talk about art, the foregoing conclusions leave open just how much might be saved. On the one hand, perhaps most critical disagreements reflect unresolvable issues. Nothing remains but to refrain from discussing such issues as though they were objective. On the other hand, perhaps most reflect problems with the grounding of one or another claim. They allow a more satisfying resolution—one or the other party was simply wrong.

Then how often are different sorts of claims mistakenly confirmed? Certainly subtle matters of value and interpretation might encourage error, but not, one would hope, straightforward matters of content. But due warning comes I. A. Richard's *Practical Criticism* (1929). Richards gathered essays from college English students reacting to poems of varying quality, with authorship concealed. His book recounts the numerous and dismaying ways that the students misconceived the poems. Summarizing the problems (page 12), he notes:

> The most disturbing and impressive fact brought out by this experiment is that a large proportion of average-to-good (and in some cases, certainly, devoted) readers of poetry frequently and repeatedly *fail to understand it*, both as a statement and as an expression. They fail to make out its prose sense, its plain, overt meaning, as a set of ordinary, intelligible, English sentences, taken quite apart from any further poetic significance.

Of course, sometimes students merely admitted confusion, and this does not amount to a false claim about the poem. But very often, as with "poem 3," students attributed their own confusion to the poem instead. Frequently, for "poem 5," students advanced incorrect interpretations. In many other respects, Richards' work offers a grim guide to the ways critical accounts can go wrong.

If students encounter problems, so may critics and even schools of criticism. Weitz (1962) takes to task several classic critics of Shakespeare for appraisal without argument, contradictory standards, indefensible standards, and other problems. The psychoanalytic perspective has become notorious for all too easy application. Most any scene or story offers good hunting grounds for male and female symbols, but what evidence suffices for saying that some proposed symbol really, psychologically functions that way in the story? Just as there seem some cases of valid insight, in others the game goes all too far. How easy it is to defend one's favorite theory by chosen chapter and verse! In *The Pooh Perplex* (1965), Crews satirizes various schools of criticism by visiting their excesses one by one on Milne's *Winnie the Pooh*. His artifices demonstrate how readily absurd cases are made.

These problems of analytic confirmation have little to do with art specifically. They seem epidemic in everyday human thought. The popularity of such books as *The Secret Life of Plants* (Tompkins and Bird, 1972) and *Chariots of the Gods?* (Von Däniken, 1968) attest to a public not only with a taste for the exotic, but with little sense of what constitutes sound argument. One prominent pitfall concerns noticing or selecting only points confirming a position (Wason and Johnson-Laird, 1972); people tend not to seek out disconfirming instances, especially if already disposed to the conclusion. For a disconcerting example, studies suggest that a large segment of the population does not perceive the popular television series *All In the Family* as a satire, nor Archie Bunker as a satirical figure (Gross, 1975).

Reasons are already at hand to think that the missing of salient considerations is a severe problem in the arts. Earlier evidence argued that individual apprehensions are likely to be very partial, noting differing aspects of works of art. Richards' *Practical Criticism* documents many mistakes that might be attributed to overlooking; for example, cases where students simply miss formal structures like the sonnet, or advance readings of a poem inconsistent with the text.

Such lapses address particular works of art. But similar problems trouble talk about art that deals with general principles of criticism, arts education, or the nature of artistic understanding. Here again, Beardsley's (1958) rebuttals of naive positions on the meaning of terms like "good" apply. Elsewhere, I have reviewed some popular notions about the arts and arts education and pointed out how many can be questioned simply on the basis of common experience (Perkins, 1977b). Elliot Eisner (1974) has listed myths about arts education, some of which survive despite obvious objections. Such examples caution again that theories and beliefs, once formed, take on a vitality of their own and become partly detached from the exacting governance of logic and evidence.

One might hope that such problems would concern only analytic confirmation. But no such thing is true. For instance, in *Chariots of the Gods?*, Von Däniken (1968) claims that various ancient works of art suggest visitations by alien astronauts. Interpretation with a vengeance! Among the evidence is a temple drawing that looks like an astronaut in a rocket, and drawings from Italy and the Sahara that look like men wearing space helmets. Von Däniken is right at least in this; to some degree, his examples do "look like" these things. The confirmation, such as it is, is synthetic. But, of course, he has picked his few resemblances from the entire world of ancient art. And how otherwise would they "look" if we knew how else to read them, what authentic cultural perspective to wear? In general, how a work "looks" may sometimes mislead quite as much as any analytic argument, because how a work "looks" depends on how it is "looked at."

Whatever the human failings, art itself often aggravates the problem. Where people may grant too much weight to evidence, works of art may tantalize by offering borderline evidence. Consider the representational forms that often surface in abstract works—here a head, there a limb, and so on. Did the artist conceal a representation in his or her abstraction, or is one reading into the picture as one might into summer clouds? Similar issues arise in analytic confirmation, where works may tease with a mix of encouraging and contrary signs. In this sophisticated ear, the puzzle becomes compounded once over. Who knows but that the artist designed his or her work to offer just that disconcerting hint of pattern?

This would not matter if talk about art reflected the ambiguity of grounds. But neither critics nor laypeople deal much in qualified claims. Somehow, where evidence is tentative, statement shifts toward the absolute. Habits of discourse are needed that acknowledge rather than hide the uncertainties of confirmation.

So far, the discussion has stressed difficulties that could be met better simply by trying. But sometimes failure of confirmation may reflect perceptual limitations remediable only by extended experience. The musician points to the subtle counterpoint of the oboes, but the novice can't distinguish them from the clarinets; the expert on Oriental scrolls praises the elegance of the faces, but all Orientals look alike, and so on.

This problem is more complex than it may seem. What one can perceive is no simple matter of what one can perceptually test, given a sample and the question: "Is this an x?" The experienced eye may recognize in isolation what the novice eye can only acknowledge in comparison: the grace of an icon, for instance, seen alone or beside another. Then there is the problem of finding. The novice poet may verify forced rhymes when pointed out, but can he or she scan through the poem and find them without assistance? Beyond that is discovery without search: a drama critic recognizes an allusion in a play, a poet notes a forced rhyme, a painter sees the individual palette of another, without ever asking themselves about such matters.

These phenomena belong not only to the arts, but to perception and cognition in general. Simon and Chase (1973) discuss the importance of spontaneous pattern recognition in master-level chess. Elsewhere, I consider "noticing" in relation to mathematics education (Perkins, 1975b). Always the point is the same. Skillful performance depends in large part on perceptual automatization, so that significant features are simply noticed rather than sought, or found when scanned for rather than only when focused on, or recognized when focused on rather than only in a context of contrasting cases. This is the ladder perceptiveness climbs as sensitivity develops. Where one stands on that ladder influences whether one synthetically confirms a claim, or doubts or denies it for failure to find support.

Collectively, these points survey many ways to err in talk about art. They provide many ways to interpret disagreements as resulting from one or the other party being wrong, rather than from any lack of objective grounds. Obviously, such interpretation will not always be possible. But at least the present discussion proposes that simply being wrong happens much more often than is supposed.

Critical Dialogue and Dialectics

If, at the root, talk about art is not so troublesome as it seems, why at the surface does talk about art seem so problematic as it does? Critical dialogue provides one major means of constructing an aesthetic reality. Parties discuss their descriptive, interpretive, and evaluative claims, in effect testing their perceptions against the minds and senses of one another. The exchange of claim and confirmation or disconfirmation ought to sort the idiosyncratic from the objective, the limited from the comprehensive.

Yet, very often, perhaps even usually, matters don't work out this way. Discussion enters a spiral of assertion and counterassertion, rehearsal of the same points with minor variations. Discussants all the more conclude that aesthetic response forbids sharing, and talk about art wastes time. But such a conclusion presumes that the dialogue functions effectively, so that the persistent puzzlement of one person at another's viewpoint reflects inevitable distance. Just this presumption invites challenge. Here, informal observation must point directions toward more methodical research yet to be attempted. Over the past couple of years, I have attended to everyday critical dialogues. At least three problems apparently raise needless barriers to a meeting of minds.

First and most simply, people talk past one another. One may say, "I was impressed by the acting," where another answers, "But look, the plot makes no sense at all." One has given a point favoring, the other criticizing the work, and certainly accumulating such points contributes to a comprehensive appraisal. But the second has not indicated whether or not he agrees with the initial remark. Very often, exchanges "for" and "against" take little heed in determining which judgments both parties acknowledge.

Another problem concerns the distinction between what one "likes" and what one thinks "good" (cf. Beardsley, 1958; Ecker, 1967). Here is a dialogue reconstructed from a recent experience. "So you think this painting is the better one." "Yes." "Well, do you really think it's a better painting, or do you simply prefer it?" "Oh, I see. I'm not sure. I guess I don't really want to claim it's better, though I know I like it better." In another case, a person had held that quality was merely a matter of preference. Casually, though, he spoke of the "best" painting of two. Challenged as above, he concluded, "I mean it. I don't really want to say than I just prefer this one. I want to say this one is better—in general terms, not just in my terms." His own tacit understanding of what "good" and "like" meant upset, at least in this particular case, his stand on the subjectivity of value judgments.

Such occurrences remind us that "goodness" allows for debate, where "liking" does not. Conversation often moves casually between "like" and "good," but the distinction is crucial, because seeming disagreements may vanish if one or the other party does not mean to stand on a claim of goodness. Psychologically, the matter becomes more complicated. If I say I like this and you say you don't, there is a certain challenge, if not a necessary disagreement. This is all the more reason why dialogue would do well to consider calmly what claims really want to be made.

The third problem deals with the structure of attempts at analytic confirmation. Suppose, to support his conclusion that a work is bad, one party says, "The ending is terribly ambiguous." The comment collapses two points: "The ending is, in fact, ambiguous"; and "being ambiguous detracts from the work." In this case, one point makes an observation about the work, the other attaches value to the observation. A simple denial of the overt comment will never clarify which of the two tacit claims is problematic. Or, if a debate does ensue, only one claim may be pursued where both are debatable: Perhaps the ending is not actually ambiguous—or perhaps its ambiguity is itself a significant statement. Sorting out such matters requires respecting the several things often said in the same words.

These points about dialogue amount to a recipe for improvement, a formula for critical dialectics that takes as a guide the logic of dialogue itself: (1) answer all claims; (2) be sure claims are general and not simply personal, if they are to be considered as disagreed with; and (3) expand disagreements into reasons for the respective claims and reduce the original disagreement to disagreements about the reasons.

Then dialogue might proceed like this. Con: "The work has a terribly ambiguous ending." Pro: "I don't go along with that." Con: "Do you deny that the ending is ambiguous, or do you deny that the ambiguity is bad?" Pro: "Maybe both. I'm not sure. Can you give me reasons?" Con: "Okay. I see the ending as ambiguous because it could fit either of two interpretations [which he explains]." Pro: "I agree that the first interpretation is possible, but I disagree that the second interpretation fits." Con: "Well, what are your reasons?" And so on. Claims expand into reasons, which are themselves claims; and each reason, wherever there is disagreement, in turn expands into more reasons. When the parties agree on one of these claims, that particular branch of the debate is resolved.

But when does this ever end? When both parties synthetically (or by convention, etc.) confirm or disconfirm a claim, that one branch of the debate is settled. When they do not, but also cannot expand the argument analytically—offer reasons for their stands—that branch of the debate has "stalled." The only way the dialogue can fail to progress on an issue is by arriving at a stall. If the parties can continue to give reasons, the dialogue can always continue.

Not only whether, but where stalls occur is crucial. If a stall concerns a nonevaluative claim—such as that the ending is ambiguous—issues of value have vanished. The debate has come down to questions that *ought* to be objectively resolvable. If they are not, this simply speaks to the general problem of objectivity in perceiving and interpreting the world, not to the special problem of objectivity in value judgments that so bedevils the arts.

Given a stall, further tactics still apply. The disagreement can be tested in ways other than reason-giving. Each party can attempt to "try on" the other's viewpoint, to grope for the aesthetic apprehension the other possesses. Often apparent disagreements arise from ambiguities or alternative *gestalts*. Going outside the work, the parties can test their claims against other like examples. Going outside their own dialogue, they can test their claims against the judgments of other individuals. One result of such maneuvers may be a decision that the stall is fundamental, has no objective resolution. If a foundation cannot be found either in reasons or public consensus, there seem few other options. Such a decision means that the particular point can be discounted as bearing on the larger issue under discussion, presuming the parties persist in trying to construct a common aesthetic reality.

Thus, in a way, the whole issue of the objective testability of descriptions, evaluations, and interpretations depends on stalls and what can be done about them. If carefully conducted dialogue always encounters fundamental stalls along all branches, little hope of objective judgment is likely. If dialogue only stalls fundamentally along a few branches, which can simply be pruned while preserving the larger issue, then discourse remains substantive.

All this may seem both idealistic and not much fun. Some caveats are overdue. In the first place, I have invited students to try this procedure in a course I teach. It *is* an interesting experience, at least for an hour. In class discussion afterwards, the students reported several payoffs. Some agreements grew from initial disagreement. The dialogue procedure forced extended and close contact with the works, where sometimes important features were noticed only late in the game. At the same time, a few problems emerged: (1) one can lose track of the whole as the dialogue moves to details; (2) the debate can become too theoretical, not always staying close to the work; (3) apparent agreement on a claim may conceal divergent perceptions.

Whatever the problems, ample opportunities invite exploring dialogue formats further. Toulmin's *The Uses of Argument* offers an analysis of the structure of argument more elaborate than the present sketch and possibly useful in guiding dialogue more closely. Feldman's (1972) suggestion that talk about art proceed from description to formal analysis to interpretation to judgment defines another dimension for organizing discourse. Meux (1974) outlines a model of evaluating that allows pinpointing various errors and that might provide a frame within which evaluations could proceed. Oliver and Shaver (1966) extensively discuss problems of evaluative and other discourse in classroom discussion of public issues. With all this, there is no suggestion that everyone all the time attend to techniques of dialogue. Rather, good tactics provide when the concern urges the effort.

So far, problems of agreement have been emphasized. But decision is not the only fruit of debate. Certainly, if debate merely runs in circles, little is gained. But if debate bares the roots of disagreement and tests the objectivity or subjectivity of perspectives, then at least mutual understanding may result. For example, two people may find they can fleetingly obtain one another's perceptual *gestalt,* though the original perception of each remains dominant. People may agree on the relevance of a standard, though for one it applies with more weight to a particular case. These amount to ways of understanding a disagreement without resolving it. Nelson Goodman (1968, page 262) has quipped, "works of art are not racehorses, and picking a winner is not the primary goal." Rather, the aim is insight. It is just this potential of critical dialectics to synthesize disagreements into a more comprehensive understanding of the work that promises so much.

Talk and the Tender Self

Talk about art is more than a discourse of machines; cold logic and a cold eye. Human speech will mirror emotion as well as mind. Enthusiasm, commitment, playfulness are precious. But vulnerability also undermines the benefits of talk. Attention to three dimensions of this problem may earn dividends: censorship, where the speaker protects the listener against the speaker's thoughts; defense, where the listener protects himself; and distancing strategies—tactics the listener adopts to make way around his own defenses and to extract the objective value of the message.

Censoring cuts two ways. It guards against insult and eases discourse. But it reduces the flow of information. Such considerations affect ordinary dialogue on the merits and meanings of works, but especially affect critical feedback, where one party offers another a critique of his or her work. Now criticism itself can be sound and insightful, or ill-founded and superficial. Again, some would argue that even sound criticism rarely serves the artist well (e. g., Beittel, 1972, pages 237-241). But neither of these issues is the present concern. At least, so far as criticism is sound and useful to the artist, its good use depends on being delivered to the artist.

How much information loss does censorship cause? The bare beginnings of an answer come from the study of twenty poets discussed earlier. Subjects were asked about their frankness. What did they do in responding to a request to criticize a poem they disliked? It proved possible to sort answers into five categories: lie, say nothing, only praise the positive, comment with tact, comment candidly. The first three approaches deliver hardly any information at all. Tact at least allows negative points to be made tenderly. Since in assimilating criticism people will have problems that tact might ease, whether tact or candor is the best communicational strategy becomes a puzzling question.

In fact, tact proved the most popular answer, offered by ten of the twenty subjects. Five others avowed one of the three noninformative strategies, two acknowledging outright lies. The five remaining opted for candor. Also, about half the poets reported more frankness with friends. These figures hardly offer any grim picture of communications breakdown. On the other hand, not only is the sample small, but answers may be biased toward candidness. Studies examining real contexts of criticism would be valuable here.

Reciprocal to censorship is defense, the effort of the criticized party to protect himself. Defense must be distinguished from good judgment about the value of received criticisms. Quite properly, the recipient sorts out what seems sound or unsound in a critique. However, defensive maneuvers block objective consideration of the criticism in the first place. For several reasons, defense troubles artistic endeavors more so than many other kinds. The arts often involve personally revelatory statement; excellence seems particularly cherished, so that it is almost an insult to call an artist competent; commitment often runs remarkably high. At the same time, the problems of objectivity discussed earlier all too easily allow self-deception—the natural consequence of successful defense. Where the physicist or mathematician cannot readily fool himself that a problem is solved when indeed it isn't, the artist can easily suppose more success than he or she has earned. In part, this may be necessary illusion—the fiction that keeps commitment alive. But, at any rate, the present concern is with the anatomy, not the propriety, of defense.

Subjects in the poetry study reported how they reacted to feedback and how useful they found it. Defensiveness was ranked on a seven-point scale running from totally closed through ambivalent through totally open. Typical "open" remarks were (slightly para-phrased): "I'm very receptive to criticism. Given my different cultural background, I need criticism in a helpful style." And, "I want to meet criticism as head-on as I can. I want critics to be as involved in a work as I have been." "Closed" remarks included: "I get annoyed with comments like 'too simple'—I aim for simplicity, and 'too mushy'—that's what I strive for. Good comments are gratifying in that I've succeeded in sharing inner thoughts." And, "I'm very defensive due to my desire to please people. I don't like a sense of failure in this." Four of the amateur subjects, though only one of the professionals, were classified as at least slightly closed. Six subjects were ambivalent.

Classification overlooks the complexities of how defensiveness is accomplished. One means is a "defensive posture"—and attitude or position individuals adopt that provides excuses for dismissing criticism. Among those defenses that have been observed are: "Only the expert is good enough to criticize me." "I'm doing something so avant-garde, you have no perspective on it." "I'm just writing for myself." "I want to be judged by my own standards." Sometimes such positions may be legitimate rather than defensive. Some people may indeed just write for themselves, or innovate so much that cogent criticism is hard to come by. More often than not, though, one may suspect protective functions.

In critical dialogue as well, defensive postures guard one's own evaluation or interpretation of a work against others' opinions. For instance, one may hold that standards are all relative anyhow, or that one's role as audience member is simply to make the work one's own in whatever way one pleases. As emphasized earlier, many real problems with talk about art mistakenly nurture such attitudes. But these attitudes provide defensive postures, and this encourages them as well.

Such postures confirm again that man is the rationalizing, if not always the rational, animal. But defense amounts to more than having excuses to dismiss criticism; sound advice may go unheeded for many other reasons. The strain of hearing criticism might block synthetic confirmation of the claims, which would occur if another were the party criticized. But without personal confirmation, the criticism will likely not be taken to heart. The sense of threat may discourage a continuing dialogue that could clarify points and puzzle out solutions. The whole dynamic of facing criticism deserves more understanding than has accrued to date.

One welcome complication of that dynamic is that many adopt tactics to disarm their own defenses. In the poetry study, twelve of the twenty poets mentioned distancing tactics such as getting a third view, letting criticism rest and considering it later, reflecting on the criticism. Another distancing strategy takes the attitude that critical feedback is not judgment but merely data about another's response. It must be respected as data and sifted to determine which remarks point up problems in the work and which problems in the critic's apprehension.

In general, it seems plausible that defensiveness troubles enough novices in the arts to merit special study and particular educational strategies. Defensive postures can be understood for what they are and distancing tactics learned just as is any matter of technique. Perhaps censorship is fundamentally less of a problem, and one that would subside as defensiveness became better controlled. But none of this should conceal what seems one of the most difficult issues in talk about art: How much defensiveness and censoring are necessary evils, guarding the artist against unreasonable despair, and protecting the uniqueness of his or her vision?

This Much and More

So much talk about talk about art deserves a reprise, a pullback from the trees for a look at the forest. First of all, opportunities for research are plentiful. Despite some tentative answers, many results drew on small samples; others with larger samples still only addressed one art form. Some remarks depended wholly on informal observation. Often, further research could look to the phenomena themselves rather than to what subjects avow about them. Even if all present conclusions were well enough founded, much remains of more ground-breaking sort—for instance systematic investigation of alternative dialogue structures, or formats for feedback, or the problems of assimilating feedback. The previous pages have mentioned several research directions, and a casual eye can easily find as many more implicit.

The central question has been the adequacy of talk about art, as it could be and is practiced. For the first, many popular attitudes hold that talk cannot say what one ought to say about art. These pages have answered that significant assertion is possible, however dry the expression—and that it need not be dry; that talk should not be asked to recreate experiences or comprehensively describe them, but that talk need observe no obvious limitations in what it discusses; and, talk can guide our experience of works of art by directing attention to crucial features.

Other doubts challenged the logical foundations of talk about art. Here, the fundamental problem was argued to be critical disagreement in descriptions, evaluations, or interpretations. Explicit standards and definitions offered no likely resolution. But no sort of talk seemed generically meaningless. An aesthetic reality could be constructed through discussion and dialogue, by recognizing the many everyday causes of disagreement and by sifting idiosyncratic from shared apprehensions. In art as elsewhere, this process of dialectics refined a reality as it proceeded, rather than in advance. The process did not at all bar talk of subjective matters, which were very important in the arts, but only aimed to clarify whether claims had objective or subjective grounds and intent.

Such optimism about what talk could do gained perverse encouragement from pessimism about what talk did do. Disagreements that might prove fundamental often seemed matters of one party being mistaken for mundane reasons. Dialogue that might construct an aesthetic reality seemed subject to varied lapses—one party not answering another's point, claims with objective and subjective intent not distinguished, disagreements not pursued back into reasons. In addition, people without academic training lacked conventional sophistication in talk about art, attending mostly to the literal contents of works and offering fewer arguments than others. But conventional sophistication little addressed some important dimensions of artistic experience. Discussion of works usually proved unfocused, brief, and idiosyncratic rather than comprehensive in the features highlighted. Censorship and defensiveness further hindered good communications, though they were somewhat allayed by distancing strategies. These many problems both allowed room for much better talk about art and explained why everyday experience sometimes mistakenly suggests talk to be hopeless.

The reasons talk so often goes awry constitute no great mystery. Art is subtle, the demands of good talk substantial, and doing less always easier than doing more. Everyday beliefs about talk and about the arts in general discourage fruitful effort. Simple lack of sophistication about talk at its best and the difficulties of talk deprive people of a remedial understanding. Other problems reflect the limits of the individual perceiver in discriminating and noticing spontaneously what is significant. Finally, naiveté concerning sufficiency of evidence is a bother here as throughout human affairs.

These reasons urge the remedies of education. The very doubts about talk mark one problem to be faced. Schooling can meet this head-on, offering an explicit perspective on the nature and possibility of talk about art. Second, education can offer understanding of the practical problems—those of comprehensiveness, talking past one another, and so on. Simple awareness may go some way toward disarming them. Third, education can convey specific techniques—dialogue formats, distancing strategies, and so forth. All three of these points echo the same theme: Currently, arts education talks about art in plenty, but without confronting sufficiently the problems of such talk.

All this may sound too much as though better rhetoric were the aim of arts education. Indeed, talk deserves some attention. Critics, directors, professors talk for professional reasons. Scholarly discussion of art has its own value apart from the experience of art itself, just as in other disciplines. For instance, the historian hardly analyzes Napoleon's campaigns to put us inside his skin. But one principal reason for talk about art is the service often done our experience of art—the ways talk may enlighten, enrich, and expand it. Likewise, many misgivings wonder what mischief talk may do to experience.

There this essay, if exhausting, has not been exhaustive. It has addressed only difficulties of talk in communicating true and significant claims. It has argued that much talk about art is not very sound as talk. Of course, this bears powerfully on the adequacy of talk as a guide to experience. True, clear and comprehensive discourse promises a sounder guide than its opposite. So many and persistent are the problems that a good portion of doubt may be allayed right there. It is no fault of talk that some talk is bad; better talk may serve the experience of art more as we hope.

Nevertheless, other difficulties may hinder that service. For instance, what falls flatter than a joke explained? This common circumstance shows how little sound explanation sometimes does. Of course, the account has not destroyed the experience—offered just because someone failed to "get" the joke, it found no experience to destroy. Yet neither did explanation trigger a genuine response. The fact is that personal discovery often means much to our confrontation with art. Being told, even if personal confirmation follows, does not always stand in for finding out for oneself. Thus, reviewers wisely conceal surprise endings or the culprit's identity.

This one example will have to speak for a variety of problems that make effective talk about art more than a matter of cogency. Exploring them must await another occasion. Nevertheless, I think good cheer is in order. Talk about art may serve not only the work at hand, but the ones to follow, by priming the mind and eye for later discoveries. And if talk that deflates is real, it is far from universal. A point made often does remake a work in an interesting and involving way. No doubt discovering the double reality of the Oldenburg work for oneself offers more of a kick. But the visual organization snaps compellingly into place no matter what the cue. We can certainly feel optimistic, so long as words can find a kiss in a clothespin.

Boston, Massachusetts
May 1976

BIBLIOGRAPHY

Beardsley, M. C. *Aesthetics: Problems in the Philosophy of Criticism.* New York: Harcourt, Brace, & World, 1958.

Beardsley, M. C. *The Possibility of Criticism.* Detroit: Wayne State University Press, 1970.

Beittel, K. *Mind and Context in the Art of Drawing: An Empirical and Speculative Account of the Drawing Process and the Drawing Series and of the Contexts in which They Occur.* New York: Holt, Rinehart and Winston, 1972.

Buckhout, R. "Eyewitness Testimony." *Scientific American,* Vol. 231, No. 6 (1974), pages 23-31.

Crews, F. C. *The Pooh Perplex.* New York: E. P. Dutton & Co., 1965.

Von Däniken, E. *Chariots of the Gods?,* trans. M. Heron. New York: Bantam Books, 1968.

Ecker, D. W. "Justifying Aesthetic Judgments." *Art Education,* Vol. 20, No. 5 (1967), pages 5-8.

Ecker, D. W. "Analyzing Children's Talk About Art." *Journal of Aesthetic Education,* Vol. 7 (1973), pages 58-73.

Eisner, E. W. "The Mythology of Art Education." *Curriculum Theory Network,* Vol. 4, Nos. 2-3 (1974), pages 89-100.

Feldman, E. B. *Varieties of Visual Experience: Art as Image and Idea.* New York: Harry N. Abrams, Inc., 1972.

Gardner, H. "Problem-solving in the Arts and Sciences." *The Journal of Aesthetic Education,* Vol. 5, No. 1 (1971), pages 93-113.

Gardner, H. *The Shattered Mind: The Person After Brain Damage.* New York: Alfred A. Knopf, 1975.

Goodman, N. *Languages of Art*. New York: Bobbs-Merrill, 1968.

Gross, L. "Do the Bigots Miss the Message?" *TV Guide*, No. 11 (1975), pages 14-18.

Julesz, B. "Cooperative Phenomena in Binocular Depth Perception." *American Scientist*, Vol. 62, No. 1 (1974), pages 32-43.

Kennick, W. E., ed. *Art and Philosophy: Readings in Aesthetics*. New York: St. Martin's Press, 1964.

Meux, M. "Teaching the Act of Evaluating." *Journal of Aesthetic Education*, Vol. 8, No. 1 (1974), pages 85-105.

Oliver, D. W., and J. P. Shaver. *Teaching Public Issues in the High School*. Boston: Houghton Mifflin, 1966.

Patrick, C. "Creative Thought in Poets." *Archives of Psychology*, ed. R. Woodworth, Vol. 178. New York: 1935.

Patrick, C. "Creative Thought in Artists." *Journal of Psychology*, Vol. 4, (1937), pages 35-73.

Perkins, D. "Caricature and Recognition." *Studies in the Anthropology of Visual Communication*, Vol. 2, No. 1 (Spring 1975a).

Perkins, D. "Noticing: An Aspect of Skill." *Conference on Basic Mathematical Skills and Learning*, Vol. 1: Contributed Position Papers. Washington, D.C.: National Institute of Education, 1975b.

Perkins, D. "A Better Word: Studies of Poetry Editing." *The Arts and Cognition*, eds. D. Perkins and B. Leondar. Baltimore: John Hopkins University Press, (1977a).

Perkins, D. "Theory in Arts Education: The Pound of Feathers and The Pound of Lead." *Journal of Aesthetic Education* (1977b, in press).

Reitman, W. *Cognition and Thought: An Information-processing Approach*. New York: Wiley, 1965.

Richards, I. A. *Practical Criticism: A Study of Literary Judgment*. New York: Harcourt, Brace, & World, 1929.

Simon, H. A., and Chase, W. G. "Skill in Chess." *American Scientist*, Vol. 61 (July-August 1973), pages 394-403.

Slatoff, W. J. *With Respect to Readers: Dimensions of Literary Response*. Ithaca, New York: Cornell University Press, 1970.

Tompkins, P., and C. Bird. *The Secret Life of Plants*. New York: Avon Books, 1973.

Toulmin, S. E. *The Uses of Argument*. Cambridge, England: Cambridge University Press, 1958.

Walker Art Center. *Oldenburg: Six Themes*. Minneapolis: The Walker Art Center, 1975.

Wason, P. C., and P. N. Johnson-Laird. *Psychology of Reasoning: Structure and Content*. Cambridge, Massachusetts: Harvard University Press, 1972.

Weitz, M. "Reasons in Criticism." *Journal of Aesthetics and Art Criticism*, Vol. 20, No. 4 (1962), pages 429-437.

Wilson, B. G. "An Experimental Study Designed to Alter Fifth and Sixth Grade Students' Perception of Paintings." *Studies in Art Education*, Vol. 8, No. 1 (1966), pages 33-42.

Wilson, B. "The Relationships Among Art Teachers', Art Critics' and Historians', and Non-art-trained Individuals' Statements about *Guernica*." *Studies in Art Education*, Vol. 12, No. 1 (1970), pages 31-39.

Wilson, B. "The Relationship between Years of Art Training and the Use of Aesthetic Judgmental Criteria among High School Students." *Studies in Art Education*, Vol. 13, No. 2 (1972), pages 34-43.

Wilson, B. "One View of the Past and Future of Research in Aesthetic Education." *Journal of Aesthetic Education*, Vol. 8, No. 3 (1974), pages 59-67.

Ziff, Paul. "Reasons in Art Criticism." *Art and Philosophy: Reading in Aesthetics*, ed. W. E. Kennick. New York: St. Martin's Press, 1964.

Ralph A. Smith and C. M. Smith

The Artworld and Aesthetic Skills:
A Context for Research and Development

Any effort to set an agenda for research and development in aesthetic education must rest on a conception of the enterprise in question. Accordingly, this paper presents a direction for aesthetic education that (a) is defensible educationally speaking and (b) takes into account the larger context of aesthetic instruction. That context is the cultural life of the nation, or to borrow a term from contemporary aesthetic discourse—the artworld.[1] Such a project, it will be seen, entails taking a careful look at some current realities in the artworld and in education.

The Artworld and Policy Considerations

It will be useful to think of the artworld under two aspects: the abstract and concrete. Abstractly, the artworld is one of the domains of value—of aesthetic value, to be precise. What follows proceeds on the unargued assumption that the aesthetic domain is intrinsically worthwhile and ranks high in the hierarchy of values (though one should be on guard against the overzealous who tout the aesthetic as a panacea for all educational and social ills).

Concretely, the artworld can be identified as a sector of society. As such it has a number of components, some clearly established within its territory, others springing up along its flexible boundaries. These constituent parts can be conveniently categorized as artists, artworks, audiences (or the art public), and what has been called "aesthetic auxiliaries."[2] Only the last item requires some explanation. Aesthetic auxiliaries are the personnel, including volunteer workers, of what is variously known as the cultural establishment, the cultural complex, or the cultural services field. This, in turn, is composed of all the institutions, departments, councils, committees, foundations and the like that in some way or other serve the arts, as well as museums and galleries; theatrical, opera, and ballet companies; conservatories, arts academies, and colleges of art; and a host of others.

Whether this congeries can be directed by a general policy, and

RALPH A. SMITH is Professor of Cultural and Educational Policy at the University of Illinois at Urbana-Champaign. He is Editor, and C. M. SMITH is Associate Editor of The Journal of Aesthetic Education.

whether national guidelines are even desirable in a society such as ours, are questions to which this paper fortunately need not address itself. But, while there is no overall policy for the artworld, there are more than enough policies within it that are reflected in the programs, statements of objectives, declarations of purposes, and directives of the various institutions. Critical observers of this vast complex have concluded that such policies are often ill-conceived individually, at cross-purposes collectively, and generally devoid of theory from any perspective.[3]

It would be futile to try to frame a philosophical justification for what is being done in the artworld as it is now constituted. Yet it should, in principle, be possible to achieve a minimal consensus among those in the artworld, especially among persons responsible for shaping policy. This agreement is conceivable because it involves no loss of independence of action, commits no one to anything not already being done, and has a generally ennobling effect; but, most importantly, it would provide a conceptual handle on the artworld. It goes something like this: All members of the artworld, in their many different ways, ultimately contribute to the preservation and enhancement of aesthetic value and hence to the promotion of the aesthetic well-being of society. Some of the terms introduced will now be expanded on.

Let us begin with "aesthetic value." It will not do to leave the vague impression that aesthetic value resides somewhere in the artworld or is diffused throughout it. What is wanted is a firm grasp of what aesthetic value is and how each component of the artworld (artists, artworks, audiences, aesthetic auxiliaries) is related to it. Artists, of course, create the very basis for aesthetic value because works of art are the principal loci of aesthetic value. But is must be understood that aesthetic value belongs to artworks only as potentiality that awaits actualization in human experience. Aesthetic value, then, is best thought of as a property of an object as well as a quality of the appreciating subject's experience. This view of aesthetic value is not without ramifications, of which three are mentioned: (1) In practical terms, it can help deliberations on how best to manage "aesthetic wealth," for artworks locked away in vaults and private collections and poorly attended performances represent so much unrealized value potential.[4] (2) In theoretical terms, a conception of aesthetic value as both potential and real may qualify as a simplified version of the capacity definition[5] of aesthetic value according to which the aesthetic value of an object is estimated by its capacity for engendering and sustaining aesthetic experiences of appreciable magnitude. (3) In societal terms, aesthetic value as herein defined both explains and justifies "aesthetic well-being" as a worthy policy objective. It can be done thusly: Society can have no more legitimate aim for its policies than improving the quality of experience of its members; aesthetic value is actualized in each instance in the experience of a percipient; when members of society have numerous occasions for experiencing high levels of aesthetic value, a general state of aesthetic well-being prevails;[6] consequently, "aesthetic well-being" refers to quality of experience and is therefore a defensible objective.

But let us return to the examination of the relationship to aesthetic value the constituents of the artworld maintain — and now also to aesthetic well-being. Artists and artworks have been considered; they furnish the fundamental *conditions* for aesthetic well-being, but seldom more. For, in a large and complex society, artists usually have to rely on others to bring artworks and the art public together. It is up to the cultural services field to create aesthetic *opportunities*, that is, occasions for aesthetic experiences. This is a difficult task and, because it contributes to aesthetic value, also a worthy one that allows members of the cultural establishment to retain a vestigial dignity throughout all the frenzied marketing, managing, collecting, and exhibiting activities that lend the artworld its appearance of a thriving, booming enterprise.

We have talked about conditions and opportunities for aesthetic well-being; what about its reality? Artists, artworks, and aesthetic auxiliaries have been discussed; what remains for audiences? Theoretically, as was already pointed out, audiences attending to works of art are actualizing aesthetic value in experience. In practice, however, it is questionable that very much of this is happening, and this despite gratifying statistical increases in recent years in the numbers of persons observed at cultural events. Consequently, the careful look at current realities advocated at the outset ought to fasten also on the state of the art public; some disturbing phenomena might be noticed. That persons are eager for art and expect something special from it is plain.[7] Yet the art public is also bewildered, bemused, seldom critical, and almost never outraged. The art public can thus be characterized as strangely docile in its acceptance of just about everything done in the name of art—or anti-art, for that matter. This bespeaks an inability to cope with aesthetic phenomena, an incapacity for aesthetic judgment, and perhaps even an indifference to what art is or should be. What one finds today, in short, is a large and eager audience for the arts, but not a *discerning* public. But such a public is required if a satisfactory level of aesthetic well-being is to be realized.[8]

Two things should now be clear. First, the aesthetic value capacity of an art object must be matched by the percipient's ability to actualize it. Aesthetic well-being is not assured by ushering large numbers of people into the presence of artworks; if these persons are not properly prepared for the experience, they will derive little benefit from it. This leads to the second point, namely, that the preparation of a discerning public for the arts is a task for aesthetic education in the public schools; no segment of the artworld itself is really adequate to it. (Museums and arts councils, for example, usually engage in educational activities of some sort or other, but they reach far too few persons for the desired impact.)

To sum up, it was claimed that the entire artworld as well as each of its member institutions receive their ultimate social justification from the role they can play in bringing about a satisfactory degree of aesthetic well-being. However, since their contributions to aesthetic well-being depend on the cooperation of a discerning public, they also have a vested interest in solid programs of aesthetic education. Therefore, no matter who frames an aesthetic or cultural policy, or for which cultural institution, they would do well to take cognizance of and plan support for aesthetic education. It seems a strong societal case for aesthetic education has been made.

Aesthetic Education and Some Theoretical Considerations

A *societal* demand for any kind of education does not always translate easily into a good *educational* justification. While it is generally agreed that public schools should make good citizens of students and thus prepare them to live in society, the particulars of such a mandate are in dispute. Citizenship in what society—as it now is or as it will be when students reach adulthood? In our defective or in a better society? If the latter, according to whose blueprint? Many thoughtful educators resist the entire notion that whenever society is found to need certain types of persons, the schools are automatically charged to produce them forthwith. These educators argue that the schools' first concern should always be with individuals and their needs, not with fitting persons, cog-like, into some pre-existent structure. Happily, this difficulty does not arise here; for, in the present argument for aesthetic education, social and personal benefits coincide. True, society needs a discerning public for its artworld, and it gets it from aesthetic education. But the discerning public is composed of individuals capable of participating in the aesthetic realm—a value realm. This means that the members of a discerning art public would have been taught ways of meeting one of the most important needs of each individual—how to enrich life through value experiences.

The real question for educational policy is not whether aesthetic education can be justified in terms of the needs of individual students, nor yet what its ends should be. Rather, the problem is how it is to be taught, by what methods and procedures. There are two, possibly three, requirements that an acceptable method for aesthetic education should fulfill: (1) It must be demonstrably related to projected outcomes. (This ought to go without saying but apparently does not; for, as those acquainted with the general nature of aesthetic education programs know, the connection between activities and outcomes is often nebulous.) (2) It must not rely on educationally suspect means. (In value education, this means anything that would tend to deprive students of the freedom of choice and critical inquiry, thus making their value perferences inauthentic.) (3) It should avoid embarrassing the profession and infuriating the tax-paying public. (This is another item that should not have to be mentioned but does, in view of the many inanities proposed and practiced under the rubric of the "aesthetic.")

How, then, to teach aesthetic education? The clue lies in the aesthetic value situation itself. The situation involves, as it develops, an artwork and a well-prepared percipient; or, to put it differently, an object with aesthetic value capacity and an individual with the capability to realize it. It only remains to give some specificity to that "capability." It consists, first of all, in knowing how to approach an artwork, what point of view to take toward it, what kind of interest to take in it, and what other sorts of interest to suspend or suppress. More importantly, it implies knowing which properties of the object to probe for aesthetic value and which to ignore, and how and in what sequence to do all of this. In the aesthetic situation, one may say, individuals—though in a dispassionate and contemplative frame of mind—are perceptually very active; they are engaged in the *act* of appreciation (apprehending plus prizing). Individuals perform certain critical/perceptual operations on the object—in short, they practice a *skill*. Therefore, it can now be proposed that the proper method for aesthetic education is *teaching the basic skills of aesthetic appreciation.*

Aesthetic Appreciation and Skills

It would be overly optimistic to expect the idea of teaching basic skills in aesthetic education to be greeted with universal enthusiasm. Many strongly held convictions about the nature of art and aesthetic experience cannot be accommodated easily to something as pedestrian in its connotations as the concept of a skill.[9] The concluding portion of this section will attempt to indicate how a skills approach to aesthetic education could be used to counteract one of the most culturally and educationally damaging beliefs about art.

But other matters have to be addressed first. Among them is the understandable concern that the insertion of skills into the aesthetic situation might denature aesthetic experience, deprive it of most of its spontaneity and pleasure. Apprehensions on that score are easily allayed since it was never intended to *reduce* aesthetic experience to the exercise of a skill. Aesthetic experience is a value experience and, as such, includes prizing and savoring on the part of the subject. What has been insisted on is that aesthetic gratification, which can be immensely satisfying, differs from direct sensuous pleasures in that it *presupposes* a skill; its full measure is simply unavailable to the untutored. Consequently, while there may be a bit less immediacy, there will be more joy.

Secondly, one has to deal with those who would disparage skills. True, a skill is not an art or a science, but neither is it purely a case of physical dexterity. There are mental and perceptual skills that can be highly sophisticated. What is more, skills are not taught simply by imparting them. Harold Osborne, for example, who has described a skill as "a cultivated capacity for performance of a sort which involves following a set of rules," also says that skills depend a good deal on latent knowledge that cannot be completely specified, and that a practitioner follows more rules than he is conscious of or could ever make explicit.[10] There is more to a skill than meets the eye and not everything about it can be taught.

But enough can be, and this fact marks the singular advantage of conceiving of aesthetic appreciation in terms of skills. To elaborate, it is usual to think of a skill as something acquired; it is different from a natural bent or knack and from a habit (although all three may make a difference in the performance of a skill). The presence of rules establishes a presumption of teachability. If the skills needed for aesthetic appreciation can be analyzed into rules, steps, and procedures, it also becomes more likely that they are skills requiring teaching. Furthermore, there is a reasonable expectation that these skills can be taught by methods that would meet the first of the above-mentioned requirements for acceptability, that is, a clear-cut connection between classroom activities and overall objectives. Some suggestions for research in this direction will occupy the fourth section of this paper.

Once such methods have come to hand, another advantage of a skills approach to aesthetic education may make itself felt: improved teacher confidence. Educators who see themselves as engaged in teaching basic skills according to rules are generally better able to assess student progress and meet challenges to the legitimacy of what they are doing than teachers charged with, say, "making students more aesthetically sensitive and truly human" or "giving the students a feeling for beauty."

Aesthetic skills have still more to recommend them. Not only can they be taught, they can be taught to practically anyone with unimpaired sensory equipment. Students will not all become equally skillful, but more of them will probably be reached by a skill-oriented program than by a performance-based one in the arts and aesthetic education. At least an emphasis on appreciative as opposed to creative and performatory skills would ensure a greater carry-over into the adult lives of students. It will, in other words, make schooling more effective for more individuals; while relatively few persons have the talent for becoming artists, appreciable numbers are joining the art public.

The notion of aesthetic skills is also helpful for clarifying the previously mentioned second requirement for an acceptable method for aesthetic education. It was stated that aesthetic education should avoid "educationally suspect" means in reaching its goals. This was intended to refer to all those ways of teaching that might make authentic value choices difficult, if not impossible, for the student. Conditioning and indoctrination come readily to mind, but one also wonders about preachment and exhortation, as well as the ceaseless propagandizing for art some teachers indulge in. All these means could easily have the effect of inclining persons to attend cultural events because the feel they ought to rather than from a genuine desire for aesthetic experience. Whether these are perceived as being serious problems depends very much on how teachers interpret their authority. But, serious or trivial, these difficulties cannot arise with a skills approach. While conditioning may be difficult to undo, habit hard to shake, and dispositions troublesome to erase, skills can simply be permitted to die from neglect. And this is a choice individuals ought to be free to make. (It is also an option most persons exercise more than once in their lives with respect to skills they find unrewarding to keep up.) Aesthetic education will have done all it should attempt to do for students when students can demonstrate acquaintance with the aesthetic domain and facility in aesthetic skills; when, in other words, students know where to look for aesthetic value and how to realize it. It is strictly an individual decision whether or not, in later adult life, time is spent in aesthetic pursuits. Chances are, though, a decision favoring aesthetic experiences will be made. A program to endow students with the skills of aesthetic appreciation can be expected to recruit new members for the art public simply because it helps remove the greatest barrier between persons and artworks: the feeling of inadequacy, incompetence, or embarrassed ignorance about art.

As claimed at the beginning of this section, certain currently popular ideas about art would prove inhospitable to an understanding of aesthetic appreciation that depends on skills. An effort will now be made to show how the approach to aesthetic education sketched thus far could help educators deal with one of these contemporary tendencies, viz., the retreat from aesthetic judgment, also known as "nonjudgmentalism." Its genesis, various manifestations, and especially the brand of aesthetic theory that supports it are beyond the scope of this paper. But the possible consequences of nonjudgmentalism for aesthetic education, its objectives as well as its day-to-day conduct, should not be ignored.

It is safe to say that nonjudgmentalism accepts the proposition that there are not, in fact cannot be, any absolute standards—and not even very good proximate ones—on which to base aesthetic judgments. Since aesthetic judgments cannot be rationally defended, they are arbitrary in the sense of being expressions of purely personal, subjective perferences or likings. Responsible criticism in the arts (nonjudgmental criticism) should therefore describe but not evaluate. If people insist on making judgments, they must understand, and must make clear to others, that they are not estimating how good or poor a work is, but are telling the world how much they like or dislike it; in other words, they would be making statements about themselves and their feelings rather than about the art object.

This outlook poses dilemmas for the teacher of aesthetic education. For example, what kinds of artwork should be exhibited to students? If nothing can be definitely established as aesthetically superior, the distinction between "high" and "popular" art is pure snobbery. Can artworks even be said to be "better" than other artifacts or natural objects? Does not the teacher's selection of an object for display represent an attempt to impose the teacher's preference on students, since it cannot be more than a reflection of the teacher's taste?

Questions such as these and the mentality they betray force a choice

CHART OF AESTHETIC SKILLS AND CONCEPTS

1. Skills	2. Concepts	3. Anticipated Difficulties — inherent in concepts. Students may have problems in:	4. Anticipated Difficulties — based on misconceptions. Students may reflect (though they need not articulate) the belief:
1.1 discerning and describing the components of a visual aesthetic object	2.1 the visual field (or picture plane) 2.11 elementary areas (partless patches) 2.111 shape 2.112 size 2.113 position 2.114 color quality 2.1141 hue 2.1142 lightness/darkness 2.1143 saturation 2.12 complexes (clusters of elements) 2.13 line 2.131 line-area 2.132 boundary line 2.133 broken line 2.14 figure and mass 2.15 depth 2.16 movement	3.1 3.11 Coping with the inadequacy of discursive language to the task of describing perceptual qualities. 3.12 Realizing that so-called dependent qualities of elements (a cool color, an assertive line) are as phenomenally objective, i.e., part of the visual field, as basic qualities (e.g., a blue color, a thick line). 3.13 Learning to accept the fact that although tertiary qualities (those belonging to complexes) cannot be located in the elements and are unpredictable in their emergence from them, they are not subjective, emotional, affective — in short, are not contributed by the percipient.	4. 4.1 4.11 That analysis and detailed description of a visual aesthetic object is misguided because, as the whole is more than its parts, analysis can reveal nothing significant about the aesthetic object and may even be destructive. 4.12 That visual designs are exemplars of a nondiscursive language that speaks directly to our feelings and can be dealt with only on their own (affective, nondiscursive) terms.
1.2 discerning and describing relations among components of the visual aesthetic object	2.2 form (the total web of relations) 2.21 structure 2.22 texture } style 2.23 types of relations 2.231 dual relations 2.2311 similar ...	3.2 3.21 Continuing to overcome the problems identified in 3.11 and 3.12, above, since the task is still one of isolating (relations) and describing in terms of dependent as well as emergent properties (an uneasy balance, a bold structure). 3.22 Achieving some uniform ...	4.2 4.21 That a genuine dichotomy exists between form (here taken to mean the abstract elements of a work) and subject, meaning that 4.211 only the formal properties are the truly important ones (as borne out by the development of contemporary art toward abstractness and a concomitant ...

subject matter, where it does occur, should be disregarded.

...zzy in usage ... form is sometimes taken to mean shape or geometric pattern or the work seen abstractly; "texture" may refer to tactile or surface properties; "style" has many different meanings, etc.

...from distribution of elements) 2.2322 equilibrium/disequilibrium (created by implied movement) 2.2323 harmony		
1.3 interpreting a visual work of art		
2.3	3.3	4.3
2.31 characterization of overall quality (mood, attitude, tone)	3.31 Understanding that even nonrepresentational works of art usually have a definite overall quality (e.g., eeriness, joyousness)	4.31 That the interpretation of a work of art constitutes an invitation to being "creative" or "imaginative," inventing stories and calling forth associated ideas (notions often implanted in the elementary grades).
2.32 representation	3.311 that is not to be confused with the percipient's reaction to the work	4.32 That the task of interpretation always involves discovery of what the work "has to say to us," i.e., some message couched in propositional form.
2.321 depiction object	3.312 and not properly called its "meaning."	
2.322 portrayal object		
2.323 subject (action or scene portrayed or depicted)		
2.324 abstraction and distortion	3.32 Finding a work inaccessible due to unfamiliar subject or symbolism.	
2.325 symbolism		
2.33 content (relation of design to subject)	3.33 Perceiving the subtle relationships between subject and design — their congruence or incongruence — from which content emerges.	
1.4 assessing the aesthetic worth of visual works of art		
2.4	3.4	4.4
2.41 valuing (prizing, liking)	3.41 Coming to recognize the difference between liking (prizing, valuing) a work of art and assessing (judging, estimating) its aesthetic value.	4.41 That "nonjudgmentalism" is the only defensible attitude to take toward works of art; attempts at evaluation are therefore invidious.
2.42 evaluating		
2.421 critical reasons	3.42 Accepting the requirement to support aesthetic judgments with relevant reasons.	4.42 That pervasive relativism proves the impossibility of any standards in art; attempts at evaluation are therefore futile.
2.4211 genetic reasons		
2.4212 affective reasons		
2.4213 objective reasons		
2.422 criteria (standards, canons)	3.43 Differentiating between acceptable and unacceptable reasons.	4.43 That aesthetic judgments (especially when made by teachers) amount to an effort to impose personal (subjective, indefensible) values on others.
2.4221 unity		
2.4222 complexity		
2.4223 intensity of quality	3.44 Appreciating the peculiar logic of the criteria or standards on which aesthetic judgments may be based.	
2.423 evaluating reasoning		
2.4231 merits		
2.4232 defects		
2.424 judgments		

on aesthetic educators. The easy alternative is to join the retreat from judgment. But then aesthetic education would have to give up any pretense of promoting aesthetic well-being by educating individuals to discernment (which should certainly include ability to separate the good from the inferior), a characteristic so badly needed in the art public today. The more difficult alternative, that of pleading the case of aesthetic evaluation, can be made to appear more manageable by recalling what aesthetic skills are to be taught for: the actualization in experience of the aesthetic value an object *possesses* as a capacity. Aesthetic value, depending on an object's perceptual qualities and their arrangement, is in that sense objective, not a product of the subject's whims or feelings. Furthermore, since value is actualized in a critical/ perceptual performance employing skills, experiencing subjects should, in principle, be able to communicate their value determination and the way they reached it to others who also have the skill.[11] It is quite possible for people with the appropriate skills (for perception as well as for aesthetic discourse) to reach substantial consensus on such matters, and to do it in a way that makes it more than agreeing to like the same thing. Thus, the value that is in the object as potential is realized in experiences that are by no means condemned to being purely private and unsharable. In sum, teachers have no reason to fear that they may be corrupting students through the imposition of values that actually are no more than private, subjective, esoteric, and therefore indefensible preferences.

If they wished, teachers could justify the choice of classics or masterpieces by reference to what is required for teaching a skill. A skill is taught by guided practice, but also through performances by the teacher for purposes of demonstration. One of the objectives of such demonstrations is to acquaint students with the full scope of the skill, with the level to which they can hope to perfect it. But a demonstration of a high level of aesthetic skill demands an aesthetic object that brings the entire range of that skill into play. Such an object would most likely be a masterpiece of art, an acknowledged classic—complex, many-layered, subtle, and a great challenge to the percipient's skills.

Toward Proposals for Research

In the conduct of aesthetic education, the skills of appreciation are perceptual/*critical*. While the main objective is to enable students to perceive and judge aesthetic qualities correctly, the only way of teaching and testing for such perceptual skills is through critical discourse. Obviously, what was referred to as guided practice and demonstration would involve teachers and students in talk about artworks. Critical discourse reflects perceptual skills acquired when relevant critical concepts are properly applied to aesthetic objects. This is why the attached chart lists both skills and concepts.[12]

With regard to the chart, the following must be noted: (1) For illustrative purposes, it is limited to the visual arts; a task for research would be to determine the major concepts and skills in other art forms and to find out how much analogy exists between the different sets of skills. (The ideal would be maximum transfer without distorting the uniqueness of each art form.) (2) It is clearly not intended for use with very young students; how difficult adolescents, for whom it was more or less designed, would find the concepts and skills is another item for research to establish. (A great danger in any research of this kind is claiming too much for student accomplishment; children beating a drum in time have not necessarily "learned the concept of rhythm in music.") (3) The "anticipated difficulties"[13] are more or less educated guesses at this point. Again, research will help refine or replace them.

Urbana, Illinois
May 1976

FOOTNOTES

[1]Arthur Danto, "The Artworld," *Journal of Philosophy,* Vol. 61, No. 19 (October 15, 1964), pages 571-84. Danto speaks of an artworld as part of the ambience of response to art. Such a sense implies a knowledge of art's history and theory and extensive aesthetic experience. This sense of an art world fits well with some uses by educational theorists of Michael Polanyi's work. See, for example, H. S. Broudy's "On 'Knowing With'," *Philosophy of Education,* Proceedings of the Philosophy of Education Society, ed. H. B. Dunkel (Edwardsville, Illinois: Philosophy of Education Society, 1970). That is, it might be said that one "knows with" a sense of an artworld. Or, as Polanyi might say, a sense of an artworld consists of subsidiaries that bear on the focal meaning of a work of art. See Michael Polanyi and Harry Prosch, *Meaning* (Chicago: University of Chicago Press, 1975).

[2]The term, along with some other notions, is taken from Monroe C. Beardsley's, "Aesthetic Welfare, Aesthetic Justice, and Educational Policy," *Journal of Aesthetic Education,* Vol. 7, No. 4 (October 1973), pages 49-61. For purposes of this paper his analysis has been simplified and, in some instances, the terminology modified.

[3]This judgment may appear too dogmatic, but a persuasive defense of it is made by Jacques Barzun in *The Use and Abuse of Art* (Princeton, New Jersey: Princeton University Press, 1975). Originally presented as the A. W. Mellon Lectures in the Fine Arts, 1973, at the National Gallery of Art, Washington, D.C.

[4]Beardsley, "Aesthetic Welfare, Aesthetic Justice, and Educational Policy," page 52.

[5]Monroe C. Beardsley, "The Aesthetic Point of View," *Perspectives in Education, Religion, and the Arts,* eds. H. E. Kiefer and M. K. Munitz (Albany: State University of New York Press, 1970), pages 219-37.

[6]That is to say, at any given moment the state of aesthetic well-being within a society is a function of the number of aesthetic experiences being had and their magnitudes.

[7]Jacques Barzun, "The Rise of Art as Religion," Chapter 2, *The Use and Abuse of Art.*

[8]Shakespeare's audiences, we are reminded, helped to make Shakespeare great.

[9]For example, the discussion of skill learning in the *Second Handbook of Research of Teaching,* ed. R. M. W. Travers (Chicago: Rand McNally & Co., 1973), is devoted entirely to the study of physical movements in controlled laboratory experiments.

[10]Much of the discussion of appreciation as a skill is taken from Harold Osborne's *The Art of Appreciation* (New York: Oxford University Press, 1970).

[11]Osborne writes: "When the capacity for appreciating works of art is brought under the heading of connoisseurship ... as a category of skill, this is tantamount to denying that it is merely an expression of personal preference, a matter of individual likes and dislikes. . . . For that is a cognitive skill, purporting to apprehend and discriminate qualities residing in the object of attention, qualities which can be recognized and tested by others who have the skill." *The Art of Appreciation*, page 15.

[12]The classification of skills and concepts is taken, in large, from Monroe C. Beardsley's *Aesthetics: Problems in the Philosophy of Criticism* (New York: Harcourt, Brace and World, 1958).

[13]For further conceptions of art held by children, see Howard Gardner, Ellen Winner, and Mary Kircher, "Children's Conceptions of the Arts," *Journal of Aesthetic Education*, Vol. 9, No. 3 (July 1975), pages 60-77. Also Michael J. Parsons, "A Suggestion Concerning the Development of Aesthetic Experience in Children," *Journal of Aesthetics and Art Criticism*, Vol. 34, No. 3 (Spring 1976), pages 305-14.

Kathryn Bloom

Research and Development Needs for Comprehensive Programs in the Arts in Education at the Precollegiate Level

The recommendations made in this paper are based on nine years of experience as director of the JDR 3rd Fund's Arts in Education Program, working in school systems and with school representatives, and four year's experience working with representatives of state education departments. The focus of this work is the establishment of comprehensive arts in education programs that make all the arts integral to the general, or basic, education of all students in entire school districts, kindergarten through twelfth grade.

Arts in education programs do not attempt to define the arts in new ways. Instead, they build upon the values of the arts as they have been honored traditionally. Neither are arts in education programs cost-cutting devices that enable school districts and state education departments to deliver mandated instruction in the arts without the necessity of providing programs and specialist faculty members in these fields. Rather, professionals with particular expertise in the arts, both within the schools and at the community level, are considered essential to maintaining the quality of teaching and learning in the various fields of the arts and in arts-related instruction.

Arts in education programs operate from a much broader framework than the usual attempts to improve the status of the arts in the schools. They address the much more important question of determining how learning in all of the arts can improve the quality of education for all young people. These programs succeed when persons responsible for the overall content of educational programs and persons with experience and training in the arts agree on common goals and work cooperatively to accomplish them.

Prior to the work I presently am doing, I spent five years in the U. S. Office of Education as director of the newly created Arts and Humanities Program. There, for the first time, federal funds were allocated to support research and development in the arts and humanities. Responsibilities included the establishment of a national

KATHRYN BLOOM *is Director of the Arts in Education Program of the JDR 3rd Fund.*

constituency for the arts and humanities, which was done essentially through the support of a large number of developmental conferences that focused national attention on a great variety of educational needs. A second responsibility involved the encouragement and support of research that could address itself to all aspects of all fields of the arts and humanities in the public schools, in higher education, and at the community level in connection with educational programs carried on by arts institutions. There were a number of important outcomes, including the assistance given jointly with other agencies to establish CEMREL's Aesthetic Education Program.

Ten years ago, it was considered important, especially by those of us with strong commitments to the arts, for the arts to be part of general education in the elementary and secondary schools. We knew, however, that this was an idea and an aspiration, not a reality. During the five years I was in the U. S. Office of Education, proposals that would explore the feasibility of making the arts part of general education were a priority for the Arts and Humanities Program. Only two proposals, received during the fifth year, attempted to address this need, and neither could be supported by U.S.O.E. because they requested operating funds rather than funds for development based in research.

In the intervening years, interest in the concept of the arts in general education has continued to expand and has become a reality in school districts and state education departments. Several program administered by other agencies have goals and objectives that are similar or complementary to those held by the JDR 3rd Fund. They include CEMREL's Aesthetic Education Program; the Artists-in-Schools Program of the National Endowment for the Arts; and the Alliance for Arts Education (AAE), supported jointly by the U. S. Office of Education and the John F. Kennedy Center for the Performing Arts. AAE, through its capability to make small grants for planning and implementing comprehensive arts in education programs, is spurring interest in such programs nationally at the state and local levels.

What Is Meant by Comprehensive Arts in Education Programs?

For decades the arts in education have had many eloquent spokesmen. Numerous persuasive statements have been made regarding the values of the arts and the reasons why they should occupy an important role in the elementary and secondary schools. Until fairly recently, however, practices in the schools have not changed. The problem has been that while arguments may be convincing, an important element has been missing: the interest, commitment, and willingness by school people to work through a complex process, on a trial-and-error basis, to determine whether an idea can be translated into reality. And, once that formidable task has been accomplished, to determine whether the arts are actually as important as we believe they are in the education and life of all students in the schools.

Since its establishment nine years ago, the JDR 3rd Fund's Arts in

Education Program has worked cooperatively with carefully selected projects in school districts and state education departments to determine how the arts can be infused most effectively into total educational programs at the local and state levels. This has involved testing and refining the concept that the arts can and should be integral to every child's education; developing an acceptable rationale;[1] identifying characteristics of successful arts in education programs; evolving processes of change that enable school systems and state education departments to establish and maintain such programs; and attempting to determine the most effective means for evaluating the outcomes.

People who make decisions about school systems — school board members, administrators, supervisors, teachers, students, and parents who vote on tax levies — are the products of schools that are very similar to most schools today. For the majority of these individuals, pervasive experience and involvement in the arts as part of their own education has been limited or missing. If the role of the arts is to be changed, educational decision-makers must have a rationale that explains, not only the values of the arts for their own sake; but, equally important, how these subjects help meet broad educational goals and assist in improving the quality of education for every child.

Programs that are considered "special," or peripheral, to the main goals of education occupy a tenuous position, even in the best of times. During periods of financial stringency, their mortality rate is very high. Therefore, a useful rationale must begin with the role and function of the arts in the education of every student, rather than attempting to convince educators that they should improve the status of the arts in education.

Once a rationale is accepted and a priority established for the arts in education, questions arise as to how the content of instruction changes. In the development of such programs by the Fund, it was recognized from the beginning that "more of the same" — adding more specialists, more equipment and supplies, and more opportunities for cultural enrichment — would not be an answer. Rather, it was necessary to initiate a wider variety of teaching approaches that would enable all students to enhance their own personal understanding and enjoyment of the arts; and, at the same time, to improve their motivation to learn.

In considering the main characteristics of successful programs, one of the most effective approaches used grew out of the awareness that the arts are not created, nor do they exist, in a vacuum. They are part and parcel of society and life. Therefore, they do not need to be taught in isolation. Building on relationships that exist between science or history or reading and one or more of the arts can expand and strengthen learning in all these subjects. Interdisciplinary teaching is not a new idea. In fact, it is a hidden curriculum for the arts in many schools. However, it usually happens almost by accident and in isolated situations, as the result of personal interests and initiatives of individual teachers or principals. When this approach is consciously built upon and used systematically in all the elementary schools in a district, important changes can be observed almost immediately.

School administrators and teachers discover that, as children become involved in the arts as part of the total pattern of classroom teaching, attitudes and motivation toward other subjects of study may improve. Higher levels of motivation may help children learn "the basics" — reading, writing, and mathematics — more readily. Schools and classrooms become more humane and attractive environments for learning. Of major significance, the arts are increasingly seen as useful tools for living; a means for providing young people with a broader range of choices about the environment in which they live, the life-style they develop, and the way they spend their leisure time.

A second approach used in arts in education projects in school districts is providing continuing support for existing music and art programs, and gradually adding learning opportunities in other art forms such as theater, dance, environmental design, filmmaking, photography, and the literary arts. This approach may appear paradoxical, considering the peripheral role of the arts in most schools. However, as comprehensive programs demonstrate how the arts contribute significantly to every child's education, attitudes of school board members and administrators change and the arts begin to be viewed as legitimate subjects of study for their own intrinsic sake. Further, these positive attitudes are reinforced by the interests of students and their parents. For example, when the first pilot project for the arts in general education was started in the University City, Missouri, Public Schools in 1968, about thirty percent of the high-school population elected one or more classes in art or music. Last year, approximately seventy percent of the high-school students took courses in the arts, and the number of arts specialists in the school system has increased accordingly.

The third approach is to draw fully on community resources in the arts — artists and arts organizations such as music, theater, and dance groups; museums and art centers — as part of the total educational program. The services that can be provided through these community resources, however, are not used as "cultural enrichment" or entertainment. Artists and representatives of arts organizations work closely and collaboratively with school administrators and teachers in order that the services provided will be related functionally to the broader educational program of the school system, and will be appropriate to the interests and needs of all children, not just the talented ones.

A fourth approach that is emerging in the arts in education programs differs from the first three in that it is not designed to reach all children in a school system. Instead, it involves special programs for students with special needs — the handicapped, the talented, the gifted — and provides alternative learning opportunities.

If these approaches — interdisciplinary studies, support of the arts for their own intrinsic value, use of community resources in the arts, and special programs for special students — can be developed in concert, and if they include all the arts, and if they are designed to reach students at all grade levels from kindergarten through high school, a comprehensive arts in education program can be the outcome.

Once a framework has been established for changing the content of instruction, a plan is needed that provides for orderly and comprehensive change in the educational program and learning environment. Arts in education programs are complex undertakings that take time to implement. Effecting change in many school systems appears to take place almost by accident, and usually begins with the tried-and-true approaches of curriculum development and teacher training. In my experience, the curriculum development/teacher training model can work successfully under certain conditions, given sufficient time and strong, imaginative leadership at administrative levels. In large school systems with commitment to total school change and development and a more elaborate administrative and organizational structure, it is more difficult to implement effectively.

An alternate approach to educational change is currently being used in six school systems — New York City, Seattle, Minneapolis, Winston-Salem, Little Rock, and Hartford. This approach is an outgrowth of planning for "All the Arts for All the Children," a joint venture of the New York City Public Schools and the JDR 3rd Fund. It drew upon the previous experience of the Fund and the sophistication of the school system in accomplishing educational change in a district comprised of more than one million students and nine hundred schools.

The plan was based on the belief that a significant portion of the school system could, eventually, be changed most effectively through identification of individual demonstration schools that were believed to be the most effective units for change. Each demonstration school would have a team comprised of teachers, parents, specialists in the arts, and the principal, who would be the team leader. They would be responsible for identifying, designing, and implementing ways that all the arts could be incorporated most effectively into the school's total educational program.

Following the identification of demonstration schools, the next step would be the formation of a network among them to provide for communication and mutual support. In addition, functional working relationships would be established between the individual schools, their community districts, and the central board of education. Activities of the schools, the network, the school system, and the community would be coordinated by a project management team composed of representatives from the school system and the JDR 3rd Fund.

The six school systems mentioned above are at various stages of development; and the way the plan is being adapted to the characteristics of the individual districts looks more like a theme with variations than the use of a set formula. The work being done in these sites is considerably strengthened by the fact that the six school districts have formed themselves into a network known as the League of Cities for the Arts in Education, which is coordinated by the Fund.

Beginning four years ago, the Fund began working with the Pennsylvania Department of Education on a plan that evolved into the establishment of the arts in basic education as a departmental priority, and a highly successful state-wide comprehensive arts in education program was developed. This was followed by cooperative arrangements with state education departments in Arizona, California, Indiana, Massachusetts, Michigan, New York, Oklahoma, and Washington.

State-wide programs have several main points of emphasis: First, developing and establishing a state-wide plan that takes into account how various organizational units in the department, the state arts agency, and the state legislature can support the work to be done, both with finances and with human resources.

Second, drawing upon the capabilities of state educational and arts associations (school boards, chief school officers, parent-teacher organizations, state art agencies, art and music associations) to provide *organized* support for the program.

Third, providing support from categorical funds (according to established criteria) to enable school systems to plan, implement, and evaluate comprehensive arts in education programs.

Fourth, disseminating information regarding successful demonstration projects to assist school districts with their planning.

And, fifth, identifying professionals with leadership capabilities who can be trained to provide consulting assistance as needed by schools districts.

In May 1975, an organizational meeting of teams from each of these state departments was held, including chief state school officers (or their representatives). The result was the formation of the Ad Hoc Coalition of States for the Arts in Education, which is coordinated by the JDR 3rd Fund.

The Present Status of Comprehensive Plans and Programs for the Arts in Education

As was mentioned earlier, it was considered important by the Fund to work initially with a small number of carefully selected pilot projects. As these projects matured, they have been considered successful, as evidenced by the continuing endorsement and support of boards of education and school administrators. These were the projects that could actually be seen in operation, and that yielded the knowledge and understanding which made it possible to design programs to meet the needs of more complex systems, such as large urban school districts.

When the earlier projects were established, substantial grants were made by the Fund since these school systems were being invited to involve themselves with an idea that had never been tried before. However, the grants decreased in size over a several-year period. The school districts also made impressive commitments through the reallocation of existing resources and, at the end of grant periods, absorbed costs of the programs into their budgets. In the more recent comprehensive programs that have started in districts comprising the League of Cities some outside funds have been available—from the Junior League in Seattle, and from a local foundation and the Junior League in Little Rock—but the major financial commitments in all six sites have been made from the regular operating budgets of the school systems.

In the usual procedures of allocating resources—whether for educational planning, curriculum development, teacher training, or determining total budgetary requirements for school systems — these comprehensive arts in education programs receive equal treatment and are considered comparable in importance to such well-established subject areas as mathematics, science, language arts, and social studies. The fact that such commitments are being made is surprising, especially in view of the financial problems being faced at the state and local levels, and the increasingly strong movement "back to basics" taking place in schools nationally. Since the arts traditionally have been considered peripheral to the main business of education, such commitments are the strongest possible evidence that attitudes regarding the values of the arts in education are undergoing striking changes at decision-making levels.

Since it was established, the Fund's Arts in Education Program has operated with a budget of five hundred thousand dollars a year to use for grant-making and administrative costs. Since the school districts and state education departments have made decisions to allocate funds from their own budgets for operating costs, financial assistance from the Fund is given largely for dissemination purposes — underwriting support for network meetings and providing special-consultant expertise. Funds from other sources such as local foundations, community service orgranizations such as Junior Leagues, and state and local arts agencies have been provided to school districts to assist with developmental work with the projects and to help with the provision of services to school systems by arts institutions. Securing adequate funding for research and evaluation continues to be a problem.

The progress made (and problems encountered) in the earlier projects, as well as in the second generation of programs being carried on by the school districts that comprise the League of Cities, has potential national significance as demonstrations for other school systems that wish to make similar commitments.

Additionally, demonstration projects can help school districts and state education departments to assure the authenticity and quality of comprehensive arts in education programs, and help to avoid the mistake of doing the same old thing described in different language one more time.

The fact that this paper was to be written was an agenda item for discussion at meetings of the League of Cities and the Ad Hoc Coalition of the States. The views expressed here do not formally represent the views of either network or of the individual districts and state education departments. However, suggestions made have been incorporated into the recommendations. A lively interest was expressed regarding the conference on research in the arts and aesthetic education, as well as an obvious willingness to be involved in the research that may be undertaken as a result of the Aspen Conference — such as performing aspects of the research, field testing developmental products, and serving as primary dissemination networks for the fruits of the research projects.

Overall Research and Evaluation Questions for the Arts in Education

In my opinion, the major question is: How can the National Institute of Education be persuaded to examine the educational implications of a concept and a process designed to make all the arts integral to the education of every child in the schools, with a view toward allocating funds for the research, evaluation, and dissemination needs of these programs?

If for no other reason, the size of the school population presently being affected argues that this should be done. For example, the four largest states are members of the Ad Hoc Coalition, and the nine states in the Coalition contain between forty and forty-five percent of the total school population in the United States. Add to that the students affected by the League of Cities, the Aesthetic Education Program, the Artists-in-Schools Program, and the Alliance for Arts Education, and the total numbers must be impressive.

A second major research question is: How do we learn to ask the right questions, and get *accurate answers,* so that research priorities for the arts in education (as well as education in a larger perspective) can be identified? This is not a new question, but it seems to me that efforts to find solutions have been minimal.

The underlying problem, of course, is that too few educational researchers understand how schools operate, how priorities are established, how professional educators perceive their own problems, and how they attempt to solve them. School professionals, on the other hand, are well aware of the need for research and evaluation, but this awareness is often at an intuitive rather than at a clearly articulated level. In addition, they often do not understand the vocabulary or methods of educational research. There is a major need for educational researchers to work directly and intensively with school people to help them express research and evaluation needs precisely, if the results of research are to be of value to those responsible for educating young people.

There is a factor in this problem than needs to be noted, since it continually gets in the way of effective communication between educational researchers and school people; that is, the conscious (or unconscious) attitude that schools accomplish little nationally and are on the verge of collapse, either from inept leadership, ineffective educational programs, financial pressures, or a combination of these elements. Similar views, as we all know, are held by many persons representing public and private foundations and arts institutions who are attempting to do something about (as distinguished from working with) schools. In my view, school systems like other institutions, range from excellent to awful, with the majority in between. To quote Dr. Edythe Gaines, Superintendent of the Hartford Public Schools: "If educational research is to yield results that will be important to the schools, a marriage of inconvenience may have to be tolerated."

A third major, and overarching, research question is concerned with the need to determine ways to evaluate the effectiveness of the process and content of arts in education programs. It is easy enough to document a particular project, describe outcomes and draw conclusions about educational value. It is also possible to evaluate arts in education programs in terms of artistic quality, as illustrated by the College Entrance Examination Board's Advanced Placement Program in Studio Art. If, however, the major focus of a program is on the learning of creative and artistic processes (rather than products) and their values in the general education of every student, we are confronting the realities of evaluating covert or inferred learning, which is a nightmare.

From the beginning of our work with arts in education programs, we have operated from the belief that planning, developing, and implementing programs is an evolutionary, inductive process in which midcourse corrections can be made as needed. We also believe that the evaluation of projects is an inherent part of this evolution, and that the evaluator or evaluation team should be a major resource to those who are carrying on the project's development and operation, as well as being responsible for assessing the educational outcomes.

The following is a description of the main characteristics of evaluation that are considered important. These characteristics were the basis of the evaluation of the first pilot project in University City, Missouri, carried on by CEMREL, Inc., which, in turn, established the general pattern of evaluation used in other programs the Fund has worked with. This approach is perhaps best characterized by what Professor Robert Stake describes as "responsive evaluation," in that it attends to what programs and people are actually concerned with and doing in relation to stated goals and objectives. In my introduction to Dr. Stake's book, *Evaluating the Arts in Education: A Responsive Approach*, I summarized concerns as follows:

As school systems were identified, and planning progressed for the pilot projects, an evaluation component was built into each plan which was expected to be of value both to the school districts and to the JDR 3rd Fund. We believed that the evaluation should include the documentation of each project to determine what had actually taken place. There should be an ongoing assessment of each project to determine what was working and what was not, and whether a project was accomplishing its objectives. The assessment was also expected to provide feedback to those concerned with administering and implementing the project in order that mid-course corrections could be made promptly. It was expected that evaluation reports would be written in clearly understandable language, and that these reports would be useful to persons who make decisions about school systems and the directions to take with the arts in general education.[2]

There are widely divergent attitudes regarding the validity or feasibility of responsive evaluation, which perhaps are inappropriate for discussion in this paper. Nevertheless, recent experience indicates that this approach may turn out to be the most effective approach in assessing arts in education programs; and, in my view, it requires further exploration.

More specific recommendations regarding research needs I perceive grow out of the fact that the JDR 3rd Fund's Arts in Education Program is directed toward one major goal, and that the work done during nine years has been continuous and sequential in relation to the goal of making all of the arts integral to the education of all children.

Specific Research Needs for Comprehensive Arts in Education Programs

What difference does experience in a comprehensive arts in education program from kindergarten through high school make to individual students, compared with those who have not had such exposure? Does a child learn more effectively, not only with respect to the arts but in other subjects as well, if the arts are infused into the total learning process? Those of us with commitments to the arts are convinced that the arts are a powerful motivating force for all learning since they are directly related to a universal need for personal, creative expression. However, educational decision-makers must have more than our faith to go on if they are to continue their commitments to the arts in education in the face of financial crises and the increasingly widespread demand for more proficiency in basic skills. One attempt to find answers to this questions resulted in the paper, *The Arts in Education and Basic Skills.* The paper concludes:

> It is clear that arts in education programs in these school systems are considered valuable components in the total pattern of teaching and learning, and that student and teacher experiences are richer when the arts are integral to the life of individual schools. As noted before, it is not possible to attribute gains in general learning directly to the arts on a one-to-one, cause and effect basis. However, it is evident that the reports of school district administrators, principals and teachers converge with similar observations regarding the positive contributions of arts in education programs, and that achievement levels in basic skills hold firm or improve. This appears to indicate the arts in general education programs are of benefit to individual students, and help to serve the broader educational priorities of school systems.[3]

One member of the Steering Committee of the Ad Hoc Coalition of States viewed the question of arts in education and basic skills in relation to research needs in the area of "Arts and Competencies." Dr. Vivienne Anderson, Assistant Commissioner for General Education and Curricular Services, New York State Education Department, wrote as follows:

As you know, competencies have blossomed to the forefront of the news in the world of education. The State of Oregon mandated a switch to competency-based high school graduation requirements. California instituted a set of "competency-based equivalency tests" which awards students meeting those minimum standards an automatic high school diploma. Last month, the New York State Board of Regents mandated a set of Basic Competency Tests in reading, mathematics, science, social studies and writing/language skills that must be passed as prerequisite for high school graduation starting in June 1979.

As competencies become an integral part of instruction and evaluation systems, it is critical that serious consideration be given to the role of the arts. There are two areas of research that are needed in terms of arts and competencies:

• *Arts as Learning Opportunities.* Schools moving towards Competency Based Education will define a broad set of learner outcomes that are needed by students when they leave school. These outcomes will certainly include a large number of affective- and psychomotor-based objectives. The role of Arts in Education is essential in a school providing instruction in these areas. Research is needed on instructional strategies aimed at these types of objectives which utilize the full learning potential of the arts. In addition, the role of the arts as a tool for evaluating student competency in the affective domain remains almost totally unexplored.

• *Definition of Arts Competencies.* It is extremely important that we begin to explicitly define the competencies we want students to possess in the wide spectrum of arts disciplines. These definitions will differ from previous attempts to articulate behavioral objectives in the arts, since they will be focused on the roles arts play in our everyday lives. Research should have the goal of developing a process which can be utilized by a district in selecting its own competencies and establishing methods of certifying student mastery of those competencies.

Any research project into Arts in Education which ignores these issues misses the chance to provide the products, processes and data that will be needed by districts as they deal with the "competency" movement.

A second specific research priority is an examination of the process model for school change and development being used in the school districts comprising the League of Cities for the Arts in Education. As was described earlier, this model draws heavily on the basic concept of total school development identified by the Learning Cooperative of New York City Public Schools. The model also profits from the work done by other authorities on school change, especially the research done by Dean John Goodlad, Research Director of I/D/E/A, in connection with the League of Cooperating Schools in Southern California. The process model being developed by the League of Cities for the Arts in Education is the first attempt, to my knowledge, to combine this concept of school change and reorganization with the subject matter of instruction.

We know from experience that this approach requires extensive prior planning in order for implementation to take place. Progress made indicates that the long-term payoff may be very substantial, and therefore, the work underway in the six school districts deserves careful attention and evaluation.

A third specific research need is to develop approaches to leadership training of professionals in the arts and in education who can act in a consultant capacity to school districts and state departments that wish to develop arts in education programs. Aside from the staff on the JDR 3rd Fund and a few other professionals, the persons who have had firsthand experience with comprehensive arts in education programs over any period of time are staff members of school districts and state education departments. The Fund can work with a limited number of programs at the state and local levels, and can use available financial resources as constructively as possible to continue to gain experience and understanding and to assist these school districts and state education departments to further develop and refine their programs. Additionally, information regarding these demonstration programs can be made generally available through the two networks, the Ad Hoc Coalition of States and the League of Cities for the Arts in Education. However, it is not appropriate or desirable for a private foundation to assume consulting responsibilities on a broad scale. The amount of time that persons in school districts and state departments can give to consultation is limited.

While some written materials are available to those who wish to develop arts in education programs, there is a real need for a large pool of talent to work directly with program planners and developers. Probably the most successful approach to providing this resource would be to identify persons in higher education and, perhaps, in intermediate units in the states, and try out several alternative approaches to leadership training to determine what works most effectively.

New York, New York
June 1976

FOOTNOTES

[1]Kathryn Bloom and Jane Remer, "A Rationale for the Arts in Education," *Journal of the National Association of Elementary School Principals* (January/February 1976). See addendum below.

[2]Kathryn Bloom, "Introduction," *Evaluating the Arts in Education: A Responsive Approach*, ed. Robert Stake. (Columbus, Ohio: Charles E. Merrill Publishing Company, 1975), pages 3-11.

[3]Kathryn Bloom, "The Arts in Education and Basic Skills." This paper is the result of an inquiry sent in Jaunary 1975, to persons responsible for arts in education projects with which the JDR 3rd Fund has worked over a period of time. The inquiry was designed to clarify the relationship of the arts in education projects to achievement levels in the basic skills. The respondents were in agreement that achievement levels were maintained or improved. The complete text is available on request from the Arts in Education Program of the JDR 3rd Fund, 50 Rockefeller Plaza, New York, NY 10020.

Addendum

Many educators, as well as persons directly concerned with the arts, share the conviction that the arts are a means for expressing and interpreting human behavior and experience. It follows, therefore, that the education of children is incomplete if the arts are not part of the daily teaching and learning process. Arts in education programs are designed to make all of the arts integral to the general, or basic, education of every child in entire school systems. Work with these programs demonstrates that changes take place in schools so that they become humane environments where the arts are valued as tools for learning as well as for their own intrinsic sake. Experience further indicates that the arts are useful to educators in meeting some of their main goals — that is, providing a great variety of educational opportunities, distinguished by quality, for all children.

The following are specific ways the arts can contribute to the general, or basic, education of every child:

1. The arts provide a medium for personal expression, a deep need experienced by children and adults alike. Children's involvement in the arts can be a strong motivating force for improved communication through speaking and writing as well as through drawing or singing.
2. The arts focus attention and energy on personal observation and self-awareness. The arts can make children and adults more aware of their environment and help them develop a stronger sense of themselves and a greater confidence in their own abilities. Through increased self-knowledge, children are more likely to be able to command and integrate their mental, physical, and emotional faculties and to cope with the world around them.
3. The arts are a universal human phenomenon and means of communication. Involvement in them, both as participant and observer, can promote a deeper understanding and acceptance of the similarities and differences among races, religions, and cultural traditions.
4. The arts involve the elements of sound, movement, color, mass, energy, space, line, shape, and language. These elements, singly or in combination, are common to the concepts underlying many subjects in the curriculum. For example, exploring solutions to problems in mathematics and science through the arts can increase the understanding of the process and the value of both.
5. The arts embody and chronicle the cultural, aesthetic, and social development of humankind. Through the arts, children can become more aware of their own cultural heritage in a broad historical context. Arts institutions, cultural organizations, and artists have a vital role to play in the education of children, both in schools and in the community.

6. The arts are a tangible expression of human creativity, and, as such, reflect a person's perceptions of his or her world. Through the arts, children and adults can become more aware of their own creative and human potential.

7. The various fields of the arts offer a wide range of career choices to young people. Arts in education programs provide opportunities for student to explore the possibility of becoming professional actors, dancers, musicians, painters, photographers, architects, or teachers. There are also many lesser-known opportunities in arts-related technical areas such as lighting engineer, costumer in a theater, or specialist in designing and installing exhibitions in museums. Other opportunities lie in administrative and educational work in arts organizations such as museums, performing-arts groups, and arts councils.

8. The arts can contribute substantially to special education. Educational programs emphasizing the arts and the creative process are being developed for students with learning disabilities such as retardation and various handicaps. These programs are conceived as alternative approaches to learning for youngsters who may have problems in adjusting to more traditional classroom situations. The infusion of the arts into the general education of all children also encourages the identification of talented youngsters whose special abilities may otherwise go unnoticed or unrecognized.

9. The arts, as a means for personal and creative involvement by children and teachers, are a source of pleasure and mental stimulation. Learning as a pleasant, rewarding activity is a new experience for many young people and can be very important in encouraging positive attitudes toward schooling.

10. The arts are useful tools for everyday living. An understanding of the arts provides people with a broader range of choices about the environment in which they live, the life-style they develop, and the way they spend their leisure time.

Anne Taylor

Needed:
Aesthetic Learning Environments

Background

For years, our children have been closeted in sterile, monochromatic classroom-boxes that house antiquated desks, tables, and inadequate storage systems. There has been little or no relationship between classroom or playground architecture and what is to be learned by children. Environmental aesthetics as a means of learning has not been a design determinant for architects, nor a consideration for the teacher whose own visual literacy may be wanting from lack of training. The teacher talks of shapes, dimensions, spaces, objects, sounds, colors, and places, but he or she is limited to one-dimensional illustrations on the printed page, the blackboard, or a sheet of drawing paper. Today's classrooms are more pragmatic but not more aesthetic than the classrooms of a generation ago. In other words, although schools today provide more visual aids, equipment, and chairs placed around circular tables than their previous counterparts, children are still essentially learning from pieces of paper. Cognitivist learning theory has documented that stimulating environments, which in themselves can teach children and encourage them to use all their faculties, are the only viable options for learning. School environments, however, fall backward toward a dying system as passive arenas for learning rather than forward to an emerging, new, highly technological society. Most architects, educators, and school-users are aware that our educational systems are not equipped to cope with today's, much less tomorrow's, problems — an active adult life in the twenty-first century.

The relatively untapped potential of school environments as learning tools for children has been largely ignored by architects, educators, and parents. The concepts and the configuration of the physical space for learning activities remain relatively unchanged. The teacher, in the role of environmental manager, has yet to be fully and successfully developed.

ANNE TAYLOR is Associate Dean of the Graduate School, Associate Professor of Art Education, and Associate Professor in the School of Architecture and Planning at The University of New Mexico.

The ineffectiveness of present social and physical school environments is reflected, not only in the boredom and apathy of students, but
in their increased violence towards school buildings. The incidence of
school vandalism has become a major national problem and represents a
signficant drain on educational resources. Too often, the architectural
response to the increasing hostility towards schools has been to design
them more and more like prison structures with chain-link fences,
heavy doors, and windowless classrooms. These accouterments have
little to do with creative learning, and are, in fact, detrimental in that
they do not act as a support system for creative learning. Sensory
deprivation exists. Visual perception and aesthetic judgmental decisions
are impossible. The social environment of the school does not provide
release for the child's frustration and hostility, for if the child selects a
destructive channel, he or she is dismissed from the system. Therefore
the student directs this aggression towards the physical environment
wherein he or she spends a major portion of his or her non-adult life.

Added to this concern for learning environments is the concern for
the present state of the ecological environment, and the deterioration of
natural and man-made resources such as air, water, land, and the spaces
in urban areas. Research in these areas has pointed up the lack of
sensitivity people have to their surroundings. Exploration of environmental systems that support these kinds of learning have been examined
by such people as Harold Cohen (1969), whose work in the design of
schools as related to the behavioral sciences has been labeled "educational ecology." In the context of this paper, Cohen's work could be
"educational aesthetics." New models of teaching, such as simulation
models, conceive of the learning and the teaching environment
as a single system. For example, planetariums or the simulated
environments of Disneyland involve people. Such systems demand total
participation through as many channels of communication as possible
(Burnham, 1969). Today's student, whose psyche is being programmed
for tempo, information, and relevance by his electronic environment, is
still being processed in classrooms of another day (McLuhan, 1969).

In the past, educators have tried to improve the quality of education
by recommending the purchase of newly designed textbooks and
teaching materials, by sending teachers back to summer school, or by
holding in-service workshops to "tool up" for better teaching. Sensitivity training and the study of group dynamics have helped teachers in
changing the emotional climate of the classroom. Nonetheless, all these
efforts have not been effective in stopping the increase of student
violence towards the physical environment of the school. This is
because, despite new training, new textbooks and greater teacher
sensitivity, classrooms remain approximately the same everywhere —
colorless, textureless, and sometimes even windowless. Efforts of
educational development laboratories and publishers to develop new
instructional materials and delivery systems have not affected the
architectural settings for learning that remain passive and often

unsuited for the intended educational activities. Further, these changes have not addressed themselves to the crucial issue of the physical learning environment as a support system for education. Thus, there is an obvious need for a parallel effort in the research and development of the physical environment that correlates with the efforts of the present educational research centers and development laboratories in the design of instructional systems, especially in the area of arts and aesthetics.

For the past five years, this researcher has been studying the effects of aesthetically well-designed environments on the learning behavior of children. A conceptual system to use in designing learning environments and evaluation instruments was created to measure the effects of environment on children's productive and appreciative behaviors in art (Taylor, 1971). Subsequent work has led to measuring the overall aesthetic quality of children's creative work, oral language development (bilingual children), concept formation, visual perception, the basic skill areas, and the ability to make critical aesthetic judgments. Descriptive data collected have shown that learning environments designed to meet curricular needs have had a marked effect on teachers (Taylor, 1972). Participatory design techniques (utilizing teacher input), increased teacher awareness of excellence in design, and increased teacher ability to use an environment with built-in tasks as a learning tool have also been investigated (Taylor, 1975).

These environments, although prototypical and experimental in nature, were designed from a matrix of information constructed from subject-matter disciplines and based on the curricular, cultural, community, and aesthetic needs of children, teachers, administrators, and parents. The developmental needs of children and others were extrapolated through a democratic, participatory design process. The preliminary research information has convinced this researcher that educators have overlooked one of the greatest potential sources for multi-sensory and interdisciplinary learning — that of the well-designed and well-built environment. But, aside from the Taylor studies, the body of research on the effects of the physical environment on behavior and learning of children is small. Most work has been done with mental patients, prison inmates, animals, or with complex weapons and aerospace systems (Proshansky, et al., 1970; Cooper and Moore, 1976). Little work has been done with children.

Before looking ahead to the major research questions possible within this base of aesthetics, it is necessary to examine the synthesis of disciplines that gives impetus to this researcher's work. Perhaps the two most important premises on which this work is based are the following:

1. The environment can be a work of art in and of itself;
2. The environment influences and affects art learning behavior as well as other learning behaviors, and therefore can be designed, engineered, and provisioned to act as a learning tool in and of itself. (Crucial to this premise is the development of a conceptual base from which design determinants are derived. This base is the

curriculum and the learning objectives within are developmental levels for the learner.)

Traditionally, Western civilization has placed art off by itself. Many people therefore may ask: What does the design of the learning environment have to do with art, art education, or even aesthetics? As an infant field, man and environment systems have had to borrow from several fields of study and disciplines in order to define and establish a rationale for the importance of environmental design in the field of education.

Art Discipline

The research in this paper is based on a pragmatic and holistic definition of art. Several events have influenced this researcher's position. Having lived in the Southwest for the past sixteen years, she has come to realize and respect the man and environment systems inherent in Native American culture. Art is not an occupation or preoccupation for an elite producer or appreciator, but a way of life and an integral part of survival as well as celebration. In this way, art becomes a holistic part of a total living space. Intrinsic to the work of this designer/researcher is the decision to remove art from the hallowed walls of galleries and museums and to place it in the everyday lives of children, who are the future art audiences and the shapers of future environmental systems.

Some trends during the past five years have substantiated this decision. Artists have been acting on their environment in strange ways. Kaprow melted ice blocks on street corners. Oppenheimer jumped on a tractor and plowed up 200 acres in geometric patterns. Cristo draped a canyon for $200,000, and stretched miles of cloth fence across the landscape and into the sea. Steel I-beams are assembled at the Whitney Museum into structures not quite as beautiful in functional context as those an engineer might put together. All this is called "environmental art." Though these are certainly novel statements, this author would urge that the creative energy of these artists needs to be used to contribute to settings where future generations of art appreciators are sitting in some of the most neglected and sterile settings in this country today — the average school, playground and classroom. Their skills could put sculpture on the playground and graphics on walls in barren hallways; the products of their artistic efforts could become a part of the total architectural setting.

In this context then, art is considered to be more than painting or sculpture. Art objects include those everyday items and realia that make up the lives of everyday people — forks, spoons, knives, clothes, furniture, landscape design, perhaps even food preparation. These items and how they are designed and used enhance the quality of life. This approach takes art out of the exclusive realm of drawing, painting, sculpture, and decorative design, and makes art inclusive of everything that is part of a way of life. Those responsible for art education have too often failed to extend the fine arts into the ongoing, everyday lives of students. Hence, elitism in the arts is perpetuated by those who really should know better.

Systems Aesthetic

Borrowing from art, aesthetics, anthropology, human growth and development, environmental psychology, and systems analysis, the learning environment is considered to be an aesthetic system for learning because it is conceptualized as a well-designed art form. The total setting is systematically and carefully based on learning objectives. In Burnham's (1969) words, "the systems aesthetic of the total learning environment must be attacked not by a single solution, but on a multi-leveled, interdisciplinary basis." In this case, sculptors and artists can span a number of problems that have been the traditional domain of architects, civil engineers, or cultural anthropologists. In her own work, the author used the synergism of a design team. The concept of perceiving the environment as a systematically designed art form is a legitimate extension of McLuhan's remark about pop art when he announced that the entire environment was ready to become a work of art (McLuhan, 1969). This researcher also believes aesthetic education can not be accomplished in isolation. Multi-sensory and interdisciplinary understanding of the world around him or her can only deepen a student's aesthetic internalization. To build a design program, a systematic analysis of the educational curriculum is made to extrapolate concepts from each discipline at a given developmental stage. This is the basis for an interdisciplinary matrix of design determinants which, when built into the setting, becomes a systematic support for learning.

Developmental Psychology and Learning Theory: The Basis for Curriculum and Design

For experimental purposes, an organized curriculum system has been developed around which to provision the experimental settings with objects, things, events, and architectural systems. For young children, design determinants are based on concept formation. Cognitive meanings take several forms in the brain and have different potentials for decision-making processes or behaviors. Sensory percepts become concepts. Concept formation in young children can be accomplished by a variety of means: curriculum prescription, teacher prescription, child interest, and physical environmental stimuli. In traditional classrooms, for the most part, the former two are the only options. A number of learning opportunities can be woven into the structure of the school so that architecture becomes an active, three-dimensional textbook or teaching tool rather than a passive space housing "things." To maximize growth in intellectual development, the school and classroom should be a rich, multi-sensory environment with changing stimuli. The design of both school building and classroom should enhance, reinforce, and stimulate the individual interests of the child and play up his or her cognitive style. Cybernetic synthesis becomes the child's way of organizing input into his or her brain; percepts from media and materials organized to resemble or parallel the thinking process become concepts. The richer the environment, the greater the learning; "the more a child sees and hears, the more he wants to see and hear" (Piaget, 1964). Rate of growth then is in part a function of environmental opportunity, circumstance, and the ability to manipulate and do something about and within that environment. Humans are able to adapt to their surroundings because they inherit a mode of invariant intellectual functioning. Good pedagogy in any subject-matter area involves presenting children with situations in which they experiment, try out things, hypothesize, manipulate objects, pose questions, solve problems, and seek their own answers and values. This kind of growth occurs if the learners are physically and actively involved with the environmental inputs they are receiving.

Borrowing from many areas of study, one envisions classrooms and playgrounds as living museums, studios, and laboratories for "hands-on" learning. Learning materials include good children's literature, music, photographs, paintings, found objects, toys, games, creative materials, and natural materials systematically and hierarchically assembled, based on themes or concepts of known interest to children, perhaps retrievable by computer from resource centers. Should it not be possible for present and future learning environments to include communication centers, autotelic typewriters, printing presses, teletype machines, computers, art studios open and available at all times, music areas, dance studios, creative dramatics theatres in operation every day, and cooking-science areas? Part of the learning process for students can be maintenance of and care for the equipment and the school itself. Playgrounds have a great deal of potential as learning tools, but they are used least for this purpose. Trees, grass, earth mounds, flowers, gardens, greenhouses can be developed by sculptors, architects, and engineers to help children develop skills from movement education to ecological involvement in landscape design. (See examples of aesthetic systems for learning following this paper.)

Teaching methodology in this kind of environment will necessitate an opportunistic approach to using the well-provisioned environment. The teacher must become an environmental manager. A pattern of teaching that includes questioning strategies has been developed by this researcher to help the teacher through in-context communicative experiences (as opposed to terminal tests) in assessing the child's expressive (as opposed to receptive) development. This system offers a form of teacher diagnostic procedures and techniques to serve as an alternative to formal standardized testing. These techniques involve divergent and convergent teaching strategies, and intensive communicative experiences that act as reciprocating in-context feedback and assessment procedures.

The Model for Curricular and Environmental Design

It has been noted that the organization of the brain, like the organization of the real world, is not compartmentalized into subject-matter disciplines. More immediately relevant than this logical argument based on neurophysiological evidence, however, is the psychological argument regarding how cognitive structure is believed to be organized and how new material is incorporated and retained in it. One cognitive theorist (Ausubel, 1963 and 1968) argues that optimal learning and retention occur when the pattern of conceptual acquisition parallels the organization of structure itself. The postulated way that knowledge is represented, organized, and stored in the human cognitive system is based on a hierarchy wherein the more inclusive ideas occupy a position at the apex and subsume progressively less-inclusive and more highly differentiated propositions, concepts, and factual data. That is, at all age levels and at all levels of cognitive sophistication, new concepts and propositions are not randomly incorporated and stored, but are subsumed under a more inclusive, established idea as an example, extension, elaboration, modification, or qualification of it. Furthermore, the interactional product of the new idea and the established idea is hypothesized as being greater and more complex than either of the components.

Because concepts are organized hierarchically and inclusively, rather than randomly and in isolated form, the longevity of lesser ideas is at first increased; and then, with the passage of time, decreased, since meaning can be adequately represented by the ideational systems that subsume them. Despite this eventual memorial loss, however, the subsuming features make it possible to reconstruct information in a very economical and unburdensome manner, if necessary.

Other educational-research trends also support the principle that hierarchical organization of concepts produces optimal learning and transfer. An emphasis on fundamental concepts enhances memory, since details can be reconstructed when needed; facilitates transfer, since something will be seen as a specific instance of a more general case; and narrows the gap between advanced and elementary knowledge, with the consequence that material taught in the elementary grades is less likely to be "out of date." Further, once a hierarchical matrix of concepts is developed, these concepts can be translated directly into environmental design as design determinants, thus supporting the psychological argument for learning articulated above.

Figure 1 demonstrates how curriculum is articulated by the educator for the architectural designer in order to give him or her a conceptual basis for designing the learning environment, in addition to examining functional determinants of building structures and the anthropomorphic needs of children. An understanding of pedagogical theory on the part of the architectural designer is crucial to the building of well-planned learning environments. It is crucial, therefore, that the educator

Figure 1

A CURRICULUM MODEL FOR ENVIRONMENTAL DESIGN

There are two givens: The child and the environment.

Traditionally, the environment or world has been broken down into subject-matter disciplines taught to children as discrete material. This model puts disciplines back together and teaches the universe through concepts and themes.

AN ORGANIZING SYSTEM FOR
INTERDISCIPLINARY AND MULTI-CULTURAL LEARNING

The **context** cultural, symbolic: *The Where and When*	The curriculum develops and the environment is provisioned or utilized around concepts or themes that can be culturally determined. Could even be taught through fantasy. (Caves, trees, families, corn)

	Math	Science	Lang. Arts	Art	Music	P.E.	Social & Personal Growth	Soc. Stud.

The **content** of education: *The What*	form and shape fig./ground discrimination balance sym-bol-ism of color

science of color   color line form space texture   emotional equilibrium

balance ———————— balance

The **skills** needed by children for knowledge acquisition: *The How*	Perceptual interaction with environment Naming (beginning of language and concept formation) Classifying, sorting

Wondering
Remembering
Action on objects
Creative problem-solving

Scientific method
Self-expression, art production

Valuing — (aesthetic education methodology)

Context, content, and the skills needed are arranged in a hierarchy from simple to complex. What evolves is an interdisciplinary matrix of learning materials organized around theme or concept. Themes and concepts evolve from simple to complex also. This program can be developed for any age level.

A new model of teacher training is necessary to help teachers become more opportunistic in their use of the environment, and to pick up on the interest of children to help them gain traditional skills and to foster their art learning behavior. Further, teachers need a background or repertoire of materials from literature, poetry, music, art, history, architecture, drama, anthropology, and so forth, in order to help the students explore themes, concepts, and multicultural learning in depth. This too necessitates a new type of teacher training across disciplines.

also understand building design so that the designer and educator can work together as an effective team to produce the most functional and effective learning environment.

Figure 2 is an example of the planning document used by the designer/educator team to articulate and to plan a conceptual base for designing educational settings. Later evaluation of the effectiveness of the environment is possible if items and designs within it actually teach the subject matter they are intended for. (One inventory page is used for each document.)

Figure 2

PLANNING DOCUMENT FOR EACH THEME OR CONCEPT
USED BY DESIGNER/EDUCATOR TEAM

CONCEPT OR THEME

Developmental Skill Taught	Discipline: Where Concept is Found	Inventory of Concrete or Abstract Materials	Teaching Strategies (convergent divergent discovery learning)	Environmental Support System

Developmental levels: Preschool, K-2, 3-5, 6-8, 9-12

Research Question

The major research question in environmental design is: What are the effects of the physical setting and curriculum on the aesthetic development of children at the major developmental levels, based on child development and learning theory? There are variables that will be controlled or manipulated within this question; for instance, those that might or might not foster visual perception, aesthetic development, and so on. Described below are some of the variables within the question. Some research found in each case is also discussed.

Physical Environment Variables

What are the effects of specific physical variables such as scale size, proxemics, and private spaces on art learning behavior of children at all levels?

For example, the variable of the windowless classroom is most significant. How do windowless classrooms affect visual acuity? Does visual relief have any effect on aesthetic development of children: What are the physiological effects and how does this relate to aesthetics?

Poulton (1970) found that "visual landscaping" and management attempts to reduce dehumanizing in industrial environments decreased absenteeism and attrition rates. There is controversy over windowless classrooms — an unstudied architectural solution to climate control and window breakage because of vandalism. Ott (1975) points out the physiological need for natural light and the detrimental effects of fluorescent lights on hyperactive children. Some teachers have complained that working in windowless schools with no perceivable referent in the natural world is as non-informative about weather patterns and nature as working in a mine. Many do not like being closeted for up to eight hours a day.

A French geologist, Michel Siffre (1975), was the recent subject of extensive research designed to determine man's ability to endure long periods of total isolation. He spent six months alone in an experimentally rigged underground cave to measure the psychological and physiological effects that confinement has on the subject. The results indicated that confinement, or isolation, or both, contributed to a grave deterioration of Siffre's mental and manual dexterity. This cave was, in effect, a windowless environment, albeit combined with the factor of isolation. This environment had dramatic effects on an adult subject; and many questions can be engendered from this study, such as: the effects of isolation in a windowed environment, the effects on males as opposed to females; and the effects on the aged as opposed to the effects on children. Perhaps, also, some of the same detrimental effects could occur over long-range exposure to windowless environments.

Windowless classrooms may be affecting proper eye development. The human eye, on the average, develops from a state of farsightedness at birth to a normal adult state known as emmetropia. The most critical time for the development of the eye occurs from the age of eight until adulthood. Paul W. Seagers, a school building consultant and professor of education, reports that eye fatigue can be reduced and aid to the development of the eyes in adolescent students can be provided by occasionally glancing about or looking out-of-doors during close work (Seagers, 1963). Thus, windowed rooms can provide a source of benefit in insuring the proper physiological development of the eye. Aesthetic considerations of windowless classrooms have remained unstudied.

Curriculum Variables

What systems approach to curriculum design can be further developed across disciplines to synthesize concepts based on child interest that also can be hierarchically articulated and successfully used as design determinants for the environmental designer?

If, as in the curriculum design model in *Figure 1*, such elements of design are infused into the curriculum at a conceptual level and on an inter-disciplinary basis, how does this method of learning affect the following:

    a. the overall aesthetic quality of student's self-expression?

    b. the ability to make critical aesthetic judgments? Are there new ways to assess this?

    c. communication skills that might be related to visual perception? What is the relationship between creative manipulation of the environment and perception and reading skills?

ROLES OF TEACHERS/PARENTS/ADULTS IN THE CURRICULUM. There is a need to train teachers in the opportunistic use of the built and natural environment as a creative teaching tool.

What competencies will environmental designers need to (a) design aesthetically pleasing and functional learning environments based on user needs in educational settings? (b) work in participatory design situations with users to help them make their own environments more responsive to their own needs and management? (c) involve artists, architects, engineers, landscape designers, parents, and educators in a team approach to design solutions for education? (d) acquire knowledge of technological advances, such as holography, and adapt them to the learning environment?

Cultural-Community Variables

In her work in New Mexico and Arizona, the author found that optimal planning for schools took place when community members met with school administrators, teachers, janitors, children, and environmental planners. In some cases, parents, when asked what they would like their schools to exemplify, were devoid of answers. No one had ever asked for their opinions. Further, parents' ideas about priorities for schools are based on their own experiences, which usually have been traditional, structured, and limited. For the most part they want their children to read, write, negotiate math, and be disciplined. It is true these are important goals, but perhaps in the context of new alternatives and new learning environments that reach for the future instead of dipping into the past, parents could make better choices about schools if such choices were offered to them.

SCHOOLS AS COMMUNITY CENTERS. The concept of schools as community centers is a viable one. Schools are often built on the most valuable pieces of real estate in the neighborhood. In some rural areas, the land surrounding the school is limitless. Closing the school at 3:30 p.m. and for three months in the summer is a waste of valuable resources. Providing a dynamic learning environment where people help people, where schools may be open 18-24 hours a day, where young children can stay in a well-run day-care center, where parents and community members can use art studios, photography equipment, musical instruments, and weaving looms, and where the playground has been transformed into a public park, is a relatively new concept. A challenge in community problem-solving is to achieve effective utilization of human, physical, and financial resources for both individual needs and improvement of the total community. Community education provides an opportunity for people to work together to achieve community education and self-improvement. As citizens become involved in the decision-making process, a climate of mutual respect, acceptance, and understanding of differences often develops, which can result in improved community-school relationships. Through cooperation and communication, the schools will truly become community schools operated in partnership with civic, business, and lay leaders as well as community, state, and federal agencies. When the schools discard their hands-off approach and offer lifelong learning and enrichment opportunities in education, recreation, as well as social and related cultural services, with programs and learning experiences coordinated and developed for citizens of all ages, the schools will then become viable institutions for all.

RURAL SCHOOLS. The folk high schools of Denmark have been designed especially for rural people. The folk high school starts where other forms of schooling stop. In these schools, fellowship arises from a common concern about a subject or problem such as raising and shearing sheep, producing wool, weaving, and so forth. Community members are encouraged to help in the schools. Students receive subsidies from the State for a stay at the folk school.

IMPLICATIONS FOR RURAL AND INDIAN RESERVATION SCHOOLS. Schools attended by Native American students throughout the United States have been designed, built, and parentally administered by the Bureau of Indian Affairs. These schools, for the most part, have been and are irrelevant to the needs of the people they serve. Not only are curriculum and material Anglo-oriented, but school facilities are sterile, outdated, and institutional. If one accepts the rationale that the learning environment should reflect what is to be taught, the message to the Indian child is acculturation, not acceptance of cultural pluralism. Observations made by this researcher during visits to reservation schools have demonstrated settings that are passive and extremely traditional. Boarding facilities, in most cases, consist of pre-World War steel bunk beds lined up in straight rows in an empty room. Privacy or personal space is nonexistent. Children mill around, apparently without much to do, displaying mental and emotional apathy. This observer noticed that a majority of free time is spent watching television. In many cases there are no well-developed arts programs in the schools, especially at the elementary level. Boarding schools lack arts facilities, hobby shops, science experience centers, and other activity areas to stimulate children's creativity. Well-provisioned libraries are closed during the evenings and on weekends. Playgrounds are barren, and children have no experience with growing things, either plants or animals.

The school has divorced them from their culture. A considerable percentage of the Civil Service staff seems ignorant of cultural determinants and of methods by which they can be incorporated into the curriculum and lives of Indian children. Though there is new material and equipment, much of it is unused. There is an abundance of learning packages and teaching machines. Behavior modification used in some classrooms promotes competitiveness—an anachronism to an Indian child brought up in a cooperative community. The learning environment does not seem to reflect or act as a support system for what is to be learned.

NEW CONCEPTS FOR INDIAN SCHOOLS. Even if boarding schools were to be abandoned in favor of day schools and children were bussed to centers up to fifty miles away, new alternatives and options for educating their children must be presented to Indian school boards and officials. It is *not* enough to update or replace an architectural setting. Even though it is updated, it can still be passive and traditional. Indian communities need to think through and be presented with options for change that truly involve the community and meet the cultural and aesthetic needs of their children. If communities decide to bus children to rural centers, then perhaps a new kind of bus needs to be designed to stimulate children and provide a learning experience. If boarding schools are transformed into day schools, then perhaps they would be more viable as community centers involving the arts and aesthetics and value system of the Native American culture. The Native American schools, much like schools all over the United States, need to be rehabilitated and re-utilized. However, the task should not be handled solely by one architect. Present planning guidelines initiated from the outside-in for Indian schools are inadequate for the needs of communities whose lives and value systems are very different from the mainstream of American life. The articulation of functional determinants and square-footage needs is not enough. The *context* for learning *content* (the subject-matter disciplines) of curriculum needs to be articulated. The context or cultural systems then determine design constraints for schools that will serve that cultural system. Perhaps an Indian School should not look like a school. Besides present equipment, it might have corrals and animal pens, gardens, art studios, looms, ceramic equipment, and be placed on a site symbolic of or congruent with tribal customs and meaning. Colors and graphics within the school might be culturally meaningful also.

The process of designing new settings should be a synergistic effort among architects, curriculum coordinators, community artists, cultural specialists, parents, children, and other community planners. This process, heretofore unutilized, is a necessary and important prerequisite to the design, construction, or modification of any learning environment, especially those that reflect a unique aesthetic way of life.

Aesthetic Development Variables

Further research is needed to determine the variables related to aesthetic judgment and ways to measure them at the various developmental levels; i.e., visual perception areas such as part-whole, attending, and scanning.

THE COMMUNICATION VARIABLES: CONCEPT LABELING OF JUDGMENT PROCESSES. (Critical language) If children are surrounded by aesthetic stimuli in the learning environment, will they have greater understanding of art forms and concepts? Will stages of appreciation and understanding be accelerated? If a child is exposed to macro-scale geometric form and has a concrete mathematical understanding of it, will he or she better understand an op art painting? Will the child's aesthetic vocabulary be increased, enabling him or her to make critical aesthetic judgments?

The rationale for conducting research in this area is based on evidence that blatantly demonstrates the sterility and institutionalism of existing school environments (Taylor, 1971, 1972). Not only are future generations trapped in these unaesthetic, prison-like structures, but the designers, who already know this, continue to base design parameters on minimal input from users. What information they do use in design decisions is apt to reflect adult conceptions of what children find, or should find, attractive, satisfying, and necessary. A conceptual base, therefore, which has as its organization a curriculum of interdisciplinary concepts planned to move from simple to complex illustrations of fundamental concepts or representative ideas from subject-matter disciplines, from lesser to greater precision of analysis in the intellectual processes involved, and from limited to broad application of concepts needs to be incorporated into environmental design for learning. (See *Figures 1* and *2*.) A conceptual base for design coupled with greater sensitivity to human needs not only humanizes the environment but acts as a more efficient learning tool.

Related Research

A preliminary attempt has been made to integrate disparate bodies of literature on the effects of environment on learning and behavior. Preliminary evidence collected has shown the effectiveness of well-designed environments on learning and behavior. (Taylor, 1971, 1972, 1975; Rolfe, 1971; Sommers, 1959, 1962, 1973; Dennis and Fants, 1972; Sale, 1970; Srivaslava and Peel, 1968; Tizard, 1969; Proctor, 1966; Karmel, 1965; Maslow and Mintz, 1956; Deutsch, 1968; Coates, 1975; Moore and Cooper, 1976; Moore and Wong, 1976).

In three separate studies, Taylor (1971, 1972, 1975) found specific evidence on environmental effects. In the first study, the treatment consisted of an environment based on the elements of design and corresponding teaching strategies. The samples included twenty children each, in experimental and control groups, the latter group receiving a traditional kindergarten setting. The duration of the study was a period of eight weeks (sixteen sessions). Results indicated that children receiving the treatment in a systematically designed environment, as measured by the Overall Aesthetic Quality Rating Scale, the

Brouch Tempera Rating Scale, and a Concept Formation Test, showed significant gains in areas of art work (overall aesthetic quality) and concept formation. There was significant gain at different levels of abstraction in the concept formation of the subjects as compared to the control group.

In a replication study using four-year-olds, lower socioeconomic children showed significant gains in the Goodenough "Draw-a-Man" test, the overall aesthetic quality of art products, the move from parallel to integrated play, and a rapid increase in subjects' oral language production, as measured by the SWCEL Test of Oral English.

Using seventy subjects, a recent experiment assessed the effects (after a six-month period) of two renovated classrooms, a hallway area, and an adjacent outside/landscaped area. It was found that the most significant effects the environment had on fifty-five children in the experimental group were visual perception skills as measured by the MacGregor Perception Index, and creative flexibility, originality, and elaboration as measured by the Torrance Test of Creativity. Anecdotal data demonstrated that the environment had a marked effect on the teachers. Nonparticipant observation techniques were employed to make observations. It was discovered that designers need to train teachers to make maximum use of the environment as an opportunistic teaching tool. Further, Taylor (1971) found that four-year-olds could learn basic art concepts in varying degrees of abstractness, color, line, form, space, texture and balance.

Spatial learning and relationships were studied by Blaut, McCleary and Blaut (1970). They found children could read aerial photographs at the age of five and could use aerial photos to learn map reading as symbolic language (Muir and Blaut, 1970). Reseachers speculated that this was a way to learn a language in graphic form. One could also speculate that this skill could be enhanced on macro scale by building different levels in schools to give younger children visual perspective application in classroom and playground environments. The environment needs to be studied in this way as a support system to learning. Presently, it is a missing link in the educational process.

Societal Implications

Research related to the question will place an emphasis on the need for long-neglected environmental evaluation. Post-construction evaluation budgets are nonexistent. Until social scientists and society-at-large admit that they have a moral obligation to do applied research, it will go on being assumed that most designed environments fulfill the designer's objectives, and that those objectives are in keeping with the needs of the users. Thus, well-worn design clichés are repeated and mistakes go unrecognized — or, at least, unpublicized. Public or governmental support for research and development in this area is needed to foster more sensitive and aesthetic design awareness and implementation in education.

Ideally, environmental evaluation should be a continuous process employing a battery of simple, interrelated techniques that bring the designer/researcher into systematic personal contact with the users of their habitat. Unfortunately, especially in the area of school design, this kind of research is also relatively sparse. Furthermore, what little research there is has been largely ignored by public officials and designers. More is known about the behavioral needs of some species of wild animals in their natural habitats than is known about children in theirs. Many influential decision-makers who have the ultimate say in environments used and inhabited by children are convinced that they know what is right; therefore, they have no reason to encourage empirical research, for there is nothing to question. Further, children's behavior seems nonproductive to most and therefore is relegated to a low position in societal and budgetary values.

To accomplish environmental evaluation, new techniques for collecting data in prototype environments need to be developed. Such techniques include cognitive- and behavioral-mapping collection processes, time-lapse film photography, analysis of diagrammatic traffic patterns, and the use of metrics for formative and summative evaluation.

Summary

The time has come for applying new ways to educate children. Further research in the area of aesthetic learning environments will provide some futuristic ways to redesign our school settings and the way children are educated. Helped by the current debate on children's rights, the child-environment field is beginning to come of age on a political level. The International Playground Association (IPA) and Childhood City, a component of the Environmental Design Research Association, have been concerning themselves exclusively with the value of good environmental design for children. According to Moore and Cooper (1976), the movement is more advanced in Scandinavia and the United Kingdom that in the United States. Why is it so difficult to implement environmental research? The answer to this question is, in part, the problem in the attempts that have been made to establish programs of environmental design. Cost effectiveness is more important to policymakers than the quality of person-to-environment relations. Research is often too technical or too academic for design decision-makers; or, conversely, it is so oversimplified that it lacks operational applicability and credibility. Public awareness of good design for children needs to be increased by funding; with the effects of good design on children researched and the findings published.

The development implications for this researcher include the need for further research and trained staff in the schools to facilitate design and redelineation of spaces as determined by the needs of children and teachers. A recent decision by the National Endowment for the Arts to fund an architects-in-the-schools project points up one agency's recognition of the need for this kind of expertise in the schools. From experience, this designer/researcher has found, once enacted from the outside, newly designed environments, including wall graphics, remain unchanged and fall into disrepair without enthusiastic support from the presence of on-site aestheticians. Teachers have suggested that they are so unused to doing anything to or for the school environment that they do not even "see" what needs to be or can be done to make it a dynamic, as opposed to static, learning space. Nor do they see the student making alternative choices or manipulating the structural components of the environment.

Hence, it is essential to train, in an emerging new role for architects, designers, or educators—people who can move into the schools to help these teachers and children redesign dying educational environments for twenty-first—century aesthetic living.

Albuquerque, New Mexico
June 1976

Examples of Aesthetic Systems for Learning

A Solar-Energy Greenhouse

A solar-energy greenhouse on a school playground has a number of interdisciplinary opportunities. Listed below are some educational benefits to be derived from a greenhouse.

A. Cultural Education
   1. Sensitivity of man to living things
   2. Geographical facts relating to plants
   3. Cultural products from plants—woven baskets, cactus jelly, color extrusion for dyes, herbs as medicine
B. Sensory, Perceptual, and Conceptual Development
   1. Humidity and dryness
   2. The feeling of graininess and sandiness
   3. Color nuances of green, from gray-green to yellow-green, and other colors
   4. Touching and labeling plants
   5. Shape discrimination and labeling
   6. Flower-smelling experiences
   7. Feeling solar energy
C. Language Arts Learning
   1. Vocabulary development
   2. Descriptive terminology for green, texture, shape, botanical names
   3. Other specialized terminology—metamorphosis, photosynthesis, succulent as opposed to cactus, plant parts, keeping records and diaries of metamorphosis
   4. Reading thermometers, barometers

5. Relating events in chronological sequence

D. Math Learning

1. Reading thermometers, barometers
2. Time durations: a day, a month; and space durations: an inch, a foot
3. Geometrical terminology, using nature as a tool
4. Basic probabilities from Mendelian genetics

E. Science Learning

1. Solar energy systems
2. Categorizing plants, biological classification system
3. Experimenting with growing conditions and observing results
4. Labeling the parts of a plant
5. Breathing and drinking CO_2
6. Composting and recycling garbage from food centers to add to soil
7. How plants sustain animal life
8. Climatology and the survival of plants when it is cold
9. Fundamental Mendelian genetics
10. Plant reproduction
11. Hydroponics

F. Social Studies Learning

1. Products from plants and how they sustain man
2. The geography of growing things; seasonal change and its effects
3. Questioning a gardener who visits the class

G. Health and Safety Learning

1. Eating of plants; poisonous plants
2. Nutritional experience and instruction
3. Proper use and care of tools

H. Interpersonal Relationships

1. Care and concern based on the responsibility for maintaining life outside of oneself
2. Forming a collection
3. Pride in seeing plants grow to fruition
4. Developing sensitivity to man's harmony with nature

I. Creative Aesthetic Experiences

1. Showing children the ease of growing plants in contradistinction to use of plastic plants
2. Motivation for design and observation
3. Aesthetics of growing things; decorating with plants
4. Landscaping; planning parks and gardens
5. Processing and use of dried flowers
6. Showing children use of nature as motivation for artists

Educational Graphics

Paint is an architectural membrane, easily changed and inexpensive. The tedium of one color can be altered by educational graphics that have meaning and foster visual literacy. Quite often, graphics are used by architects to make a setting colorful or "pretty." If the designer understands educational objectives, the graphic artist can foster a number of sensory learnings through this aesthetic medium. An artist might design a graphic that helps a child discriminate between figure and ground. A "whale" graphic might help the child learn about scale. Among such learnings are the following:

1. Visual perception learnings
   a. figure/ground discrimination
   b. embedded figure discrimination
   c. rotating shape
   d. proximity
   e. size and shape constancy
2. Color learning
   a. primary
   b. secondary
   c. hues
3. Mathematical learning
   a. shape discrimination including conics, spirals, and triangles
   b. spatial recognition of mathematical patterns
   c. polyhedra patterns
   d. golden section, fibonacci numbers and related grid drawings
   e. the effect of scale
   f. modular forms
4. Science learning
   a. physics of color
   b. patterns of growth (tree branching, soap bubbles, crystal grains)
5. Music and rhythm — design a graphic to use for dancing or playing rhythmic patterns

BIBLIOGRAPHY

Alexander, Christopher, et al. *Pattern Language.* London: Oxford University Press, 1976.

Ausabel, D. P. *Educational Psychology: A Cognitive View.* New York: Holt, Rinehart and Winston, 1968.

Burnham, J. "Modern Art As a Teaching Machine." *Art Education,* Vol. 22 (November 1969), pages 27-28.

Coates, Gary, ed. *Alternative Learning Environments, 1975.* Chicago: University of Chicago Press, 1975.

Cohen, H. "Learning Simulation." *Art Education,* Vol. 22, No. 3 (1969), page 24.

Cooper, Clare. *Easter Hill Village: Some Social Implications of Design.* New York: Free Press, 1975.

Cooper, Clare, and Robin Moore. "Children and Their Environments, A Review of the Research, and a Discussion of Why the Findings Have Largely Been Ignored." *Journal of Architectural Education,* Vol. XXIX, No. 4. Washington: 1976.

Dennis, Frank, and B. Fants. "Complexity-Simplicity, Creativity, Intelligence and Other Correlates." *Journal of Psychology,* Vol. 67 (1967), pages 331-334.

Deutsch, C. "Effects of Environmental Deprivation on Basic Psychological Processes." *Art Education Journal*, National Art Education Association, Vol. 22, No. 1 (January 1968), pages 16-18.

Drew, Clifford. "Research on the Psychological-Behavioral Effects of the Physical Environment." *Review of Educational Research*, Vol. 41, No. 5 (1971).

Hall, Edward. *The Hidden Dimension*. Garden City, New York: Doubleday, 1966.

Hall, Edward. *Beyond Culture*. Garden City, New York: Doubleday, 1976.

Karmel, L. J. "Effects of Windowless Classroom Environment on High School Students." *Perceptual and Motor Skills*, Vol. 20 (1965), pages 277-278.

McLuhan, M. *Understanding Media*. New York: McGraw-Hill, 1964.

Maslow, A. H., and N. L. Mintz. "Effects of Esthetic Surrounding: I. Initial Effects of Three Esthetic Conditions Upon Perceiving 'Energy' and 'Well Being' in Faces." *Journal of Psychology*, Vol. 41 (1956), pages 247-254.

Montessori, Maria. *The Montessori Method*. New York: Frederick Stokes, 1912.

Moore, Robin, and Herb Wong. *Curricularscapes*. San Francisco: Chevron, 1976.

Ott, John. *Health and Light, The Effects of Natural and Artificial Light on Man and Other Living Things*. Greenwich, England: Devin-Adair, 1973.

Piaget, Jean, and Barbel Inhelder. *The Psychology of the Child*. New York: Basic Books, 1970.

Poulton, E. C. *Environment and Human Efficiency*. Springfield, Illinois: Charles Thomas, 1970.

Proctor, R. L. "An investigation of mental hospital nursing station design on aspects of human behavior." Topeka, Kansas: The Environmental Research Foundation, 1966.

Proshansky, Harold M., et al., eds. *Environmental Psychology: Man and His Physical Setting*. New York: Holt, Rinehart and Winston, 1970.

Rolfe, Howard. "Observable Differences in Space Use of Learning Situations in Small and Large Classrooms." Ph.D. Diss., Berkeley, 1971.

Romney, Brian. "The Effects of Windowless Classrooms on 7th and 8th Graders." Unpublished Master's Thesis, Albuquerque, 1976.

Seagers, Paul. *Light Vision and Learning*. New York: Indiana University Better Light Better Sight Bureau, 1963.

Siffre, Michael. "Six Months Alone in a Cave." *National Geographic*, Vol. 147 (1975), pages 426-435.

Sommer, R. *Personal Space*. Englewood Cliffs, New Jersey: Prentice-Hall, 1969.

———. "Room Density and User Satisfaction," *Environment and Behavior*, Vol. 3, No. 4 (1971).

———. *Tight Spaces*. Englewood Cliffs, New Jersey: Prentice-Hall, 1975.

Srivastava, R. K., and L. R. Good. "Pattern of group interaction in three architecturally different psychiatric treatment environments." Topeka, Kansas: The Environmental Research Foundation, 1968.

Strivastava, R. K., and T. S. Peel. "Human movement as a function of color stimulation." Topeka, Kansas: The Environmental Research Foundation, 1968.

Taylor, Anne. "The Effects of Selected Stimuli on the Art Products, Concept Formation, and Aesthetic Judgmental Decisions of Four- and Five-Year-Old Children." Tempe: Arizona State University, February 1971.

———. "The Effects of Certain Selected Stimuli on the Oral Language Proficiency, Art Products, Concept Formation, and Creativity of Four-Year-Old Non-English–speaking Children." Albuquerque: Southwestern Educational Laboratory, 1971.

————, and Vlastos, Wrona. "Justification for the Use of Prepared Environments in a Communication Arts Program." Albuquerque: SWCEL, 1972.

————. "The Effects of a Prototype Environment on the Behavior and Learning of Children." Albuquerque: Albuquerque Public Schools, 1975.

————. *School Zone: Learning Environments for Children.* New York: Van Nostrand Reinhold, 1975.

Tizard, B. "Observations of overactive imbecile children in controlled and uncontrolled environments, II Experimental Studies." *American Journal of Mental Deficiency,* 1969.

Willems, E., and Harold Raush. *Naturalistic Viewpoints and Psychological Research.* New York: Holt, Rinehart and Winston, 1969.

George Anselevicius

Man-Made Environment, Visual Pollution and Controls

A widely held belief of the twentieth century is the need for government to exercise ever more controls for the benefit of the people. Thus, it becomes ever more important to understand (1) if these controls merely deal with symptoms, and (2) what effect such controls may have.

As an architect—a profession with a base of humanist concerns—I can only hope that we are not overwhelmed by the game of numbers and quantitative issues at the expense of quality and spirit. These issues are interlocked. Finally, it is the quality of life we are in search of. This quality is something not too easily dealt with in our world, which, for good and sufficient reasons perhaps, is concerned with and wedded to materialism across most of the political spectrum. Strangely (or perhaps logically), it is in the United States, where, despite many problems and frustrations, youth and others young-at-heart are finding possessions and quantities not as fulfilling as they had hoped. There is a search for a life-style of individuality, yet with community sensuousness and love. With it goes a partial rejection of the technological world of numbers and statistics and its attendant alienation and mechanization of man and woman.

Part of this search includes a concern with the physical environment, the buildings, spaces, and towns we experience around us. The need of the many has to be fulfilled; but the solutions often degenerate into brutal, industrialized, scaleless, and bureaucratic patterns. Thus, the search is for a more satisfying and non-exploitative linkage between the built environment and nature, as well as for quality and spirit in the built environment itself. I want to quote Albert Eide Parr, writing in *Industrial Design*:

> It is a role of design as of all the arts, to keep our society from becoming too sensible for its own good, to defend us against the scientific dehumanization of our man-made environment, and to supply the surprises and perceptual values that judgmental engineering would ignore or destroy, the features that can never be

GEORGE ANSELEVICIUS *holds the SUNY Chair of Architecture at the School of Architecture and Environmental Design, State University of New York at Buffalo.*

included in the precalculations of a product from its components, its circumstances and its functions.

We are now involved in important tasks of quantifying data on water, air, and soil pollution, but I am also sure that more difficult questions deal with acceptable thresholds (clearly a matter of quality), and perhaps with such difficult but important issues as the social and political actions necessary to combat pollution—the same two issues of quality and of control that I will discuss in relation to the visual environment.

Thus, when we come to aesthetic and visual pollution in cities and the countryside, we are dealing with deeply relevant issues, especially because they are subjective and thus very human. As Henry Millon, Professor of Architecture at M.I.T., said in *The Historian and the City:*

But as historians of, if you will allow me, "urbitecture" we are still left with our most difficult assignment, which is the assessment of the visual character of the environment and in what this particular visual character resides — in other words, what it is that forms the environment itself, and how the walls, the surfaces themselves, are modulated, articulated to give a specific character to the city, to define the space or the group of spaces of the city. Then beyond that lies the most difficult thing of all, the value judgment on the quality of this environment. This judgment will certainly include the factors previously mentioned, but also will include a final assessment of the relative quality on a scale of good to bad of the physical, visual environment that has been created. This is yet to be done for any city anywhere, and it may well be a task that should be left to an historian of "urbitecture," if ever one should come up. But even through we do not have one at this moment, if one did come along, he would certainly have to develop a new analytical technique. We simply have not developed any technique for this kind of problem, and I believe this new historian would have to develop a whole new critical vocabulary.

Some may perhaps say that such questions are idle speculation and not of high priority at a moment when social and political crisis surrounds us. In a world in which people are killing each other and where children are starving, questions dealing with visual qualities of life could be suspect; yet, in many primitive (or what we call primitive) societies, which were and are surely less affluent than ours, the mystery and magic of the visual world was and is an inherent ingredient of the culture. This is missing today in our world and thus leaves us poorer for it.

Perhaps it is because I am an architect that I find questions of quantifying problems within the existing environment less of a challenge than helping to create a new man-made physical environment of visual quality and, hopefully, of social vitality and opportunity. Clearly, the aesthetic quality of the environment is a broader issue than just its visual aspect (for instance, people object to being captives of Muzak in many public situations), but I will stay with the visual world, although it cannot easily be isolated from all other senses.

Let me try and define visual pollution in the man-made or built environment. (Perhaps the word "define" is too absolute and scientific; "discuss" may be preferable.) I believe there are two aspects to visual pollution: (1) physical decay and blight; and (2) juxtaposition of incompatible elements.

It may seem that one does not have to talk too much about physical blight and decay. Surely peeling paint is peeling paint is peeling paint — it is blight and thus visual pollution. Yet avantgarde photographers glory in photographs of peeling paint and often prefer these and photographs of slums to photographs of freshly painted suburban houses (which they may photograph for satirical or social reasons). Why? Because peeling paint is visually dynamic, active, and produces rich, accidental, and varied patterns and forms. This makes it clear that seeing alone is not enough when we talk about visual pollution. To photographers and young children, peeling paint is exciting because they isolate it from its social meaning. Everything is beautiful under a microscope or from an airplane for those who cannot read the clues. To find peeling paint beautiful can be attacked as "art for art's sake"; but this, too, is inappropriate because the ability to see beauty unburdened by associations means a mind open to visual experiences. However, those that live in slums and those that search for a better and more equitable world cannot isolate themselves from their experiences. To them, peeling paint implies neglect, perhaps hopelessness. Therefore, blight and decay are visual pollution in social terms.

To give an example: In the past, a plume of smoke from a factory or a railroad implied hope and progress and therefore beauty. We can see it in many drawings and paintings of the past. Today a plume of smoke is a symbol of danger, such as the visual pollution of smog produced by automobiles. Our cities are filled with decay, blight, and neglect. (Unfortunately, the vitality of slums is often visually and even socially preferable to the many visually and socially bureaucratic housing projects that have replaced them.)

Visual pollution in terms of the decay and blight of the man-made environment is often the result of alienation, greed, hatred, shortage of resources, outmoded political structures, increasing populations, and so on; and is, therefore, clearly linked to the social and political organization of society.

Wolf von Eckhardt, an architectural critic in the United States, states that it was easier to pursue beauty and harmony in the eighteenth century than it is today because there was a universally accepted style then. It was also easier because there was no confusion between beauty and morality; beauty was its own moral justification. True, but how comforting it must have been to have such absolute beliefs — so useful for one's mental health because they compartmentalized concerns into neat packages—something not easily done today.

The second aspect of visual pollution, "the juxtaposition of incompatible elements," is much more subjective and difficult, and is heavily burdened with philosophical and cultural overloads. This means that we must try and understand such questions as: What elements are incompatible? Who says so? And why is it so?

In some cases, we may be able to identify this juxtaposition as hazardous — an overload of visual information at a critical stage of decision-making, such as obstruction of signs needed by the motorist; one kind of information polluting other information, such as flashing red, yellow, and green advertising signs interfering visually with traffic signals. How much visual chaos produces exhaustion and stress? Not enough is known to answer that question accurately, because most statements are personal and subjective.

Even more complex questions arise when we deal with aesthetic preferences in the juxtaposition of elements. Surely "beauty is in the eye of the beholder." Visual pollution will have to be identified as it relates to a person or a group based on specific cultural value systems and economic interests. Let us take some typically American examples of conflict:

1. Should a new hotel in a historical preservation area be camouflaged to look as if it were part of the past? This is a conflict between a conservationist view and a creative view, with governmental economic concerns for tourist income playing a part.

2. Should high-rise apartments block a view of great importance and quality? This is a conflict between real-estate values and humanist ecological concerns.

3. Should there be legislation against signs such as we are seen on many hamburger stands or even more gloriously in Las Vegas? Or do such signs give vitality and joy to the environment? This is a conflict between an elitist and a populist view. (There have been defections from the elitist camp.)

It is not always the good people versus the exploiters who are the combatants in these conflicts, but people with different sets of values generally controlled by experience, education, and self-interest. As usual, someone always wants to control the environment visually. I, too, often have such feelings, but it is dangerous to be carried away by abstract concepts of beauty, order, and design that do not allow for some dirt, conflict, and ambiguity.

There are many points of view. Theo Crosby in *City Sense* states: "It follows that the nature of the work of artist, architect and planner is fundamentally linked by problems of time, scale and complexity into a coherent hierarcy of responsibility for visual order." (This is proper and eloquent statement, as long as it speaks to individuals, and their responsibility for their actions; but it becomes much more difficult when applied to institutional controls.) Or S. Sadovsky, a Soviet architect, in an article in *The Ideal Communist City* states: "The real revolution comes with planning a unified urban environment." Finally, Gordon Cullen, who is not quite as sure about controls as Sadovsky, says in *Townscape:*

> There is an attitude of mind which recoils from the systemization of aesthetics, believing that the bird on the wing can never be the same when caught. There is another attitude which inclines to the view that unless you define your notes and establish a musical grammar you will never be able to play a tune — even a simple tune — let alone Mozart. This seems to be self-evident.

What is self-evident to me is that in planning and architecture there are always direct rules or implied rules. It is merely a matter of whether you like these rules or do not like them. For example, in some societies the rules help to maximize visual exploitation of consumers. The result is Las Vegas: exciting visual cacophony or visual chaos — take your choice. In another society this is forbidden, naturally producing a very different environment, or, as Cullen will have it, on the one hand cobbles and conservation, on the other outrage and visual pollution. Most societies develop compromises.

There have been some artists and architects worried about the conflict between populist and elitist views in terms of aesthetics who have worked hard to build bridges. The results are supergraphics, pop art, light and environmental sculpture — results in most cases influenced by commercial and advertising forces. A search for sources in vernacular architecture to help us in our creative tasks, and a belief that contradictions and ambiguities can have dynamic qualities are also with us, with Robert Venturi as an imaginative and persuasive spokesman. With this goes a deeper questioning of the more simplistic views of the intellectual functionalist revolution of the thirties, with its puritan ethic.

But finally, one has to ask the question: What is to be done? The operational response must be on two levels:

1. The individual involved in creating the physical environment must be educated to search for sensitivity in a world now only too often controlled by super-janitors and super-accountants. This is a tough task for us educators. It is not easy to establish a course on sensitivity, but it is possible to establish an ambience wherein sensitivity can be encouraged and will grow. But such studies may be of greater importance for our clients — those who make basic decisions, and those who control.

2. The institutional response generally deals with controls. The following ones are in effect in various countries:
   a. limitation of architectural style, height, material, and so on, due to forces of conformity;
   b. sign controls, due to forces of safety and order and conformity;
   c. setbacks and placement of buildings sometimes due to forces of safety, but generally due to forces of conformity;

  d. preservation of historic areas due to romantic and economic
     forces and conformity;
  e. all other zoning controls naturally affecting the visual aspect of
     the environment (but they are generally not written with this
     specific concern in mind);
  f. controls that mean each project must be evaluated and passed
     by groups consisting variously of politicans, professionals, and
     other citizens. While this is a much more flexible and open-
     ended system, it depends very much on the quality and self-
     interest of those evaluating the projects.

All these controls have been written mostly to keep the *status quo*
and to encourage conformity. Controls are supported by many groups
who are fearful of change and also want to safeguard what they believe
to be "good taste," "beauty," and "art." This implies a deep misun-
derstanding of what beauty and art are. There is no necessary link between them. Art, in my view, heightens the experience of a moment in
life and is not here just to support good manners, however pleasant that
may be, but also to provoke radical and disconcerting questions.

Such controls as those stated above are now generally administrated
by the dead hand of bureaucracy, and it is obvious that I am generally
opposed to them. What kind of controls should there be? Let me say that
these answers cannot be universal; my experiences deal mainly with the
United States.) Controls should do the following:

  1. minimize blight and decay (mainly economic controls);
  2. encourage visual identity and character, but not uniformity;
  3. help develop a city with choices and opportunities for both
     populist and elitist views and experiences;
  4. develop strong visual controls as they affect safety and provide
     necessary information essential to the well-being of citizens;
  5. protect a unique visual and cultural past, not by making such en-
     vironments into museums but into a part of a creative present;
  6. respect unique land forms and unique natural experiences, with-
     out romantic notions that an urbanizing world can remain the
     world of our childhood dreams.

Obviously, I am against controls that impose superficial conformity —
controls that inhibit personal or commercial vitality with the dead hand
of "good taste."

Walter Lippmann, the political critic, writes in the *Method of Freedom*: "It is in the countless realms of privacy that civilization is carried
on. Were it not for these ultimate reserves of private habit, energy and
adaptability the failures of the rulers of men would long since have
proved to be irreparable." This can also speak to us as architects and
designers, warning us not to exclude the potential self-expression and
even the idiosyncrasies of those for whom we design.

It is clear to me that in a complex industrial society the larger patterns or the infrastructure of cities — such as highway networks, sewer
systems—must be carefully and democratically planned and controlled,

but that the maximum amount of aesthetic freedom be possible in the infill of these patterns, as long as they do not endanger the safety and health of the population. My views are obviously relative; I am generally opposed to absolutes. It is my belief that there are too many who confuse uniformity and conformity with beauty while I am searching for freedom, variety, and vitality.

Boston, Massachusetts
June 1976

A View by George Anselevicius

Architecture/Arts/Aesthetics

Architecture used to be known as "the Mother of the Arts," a phrase not heard for a long time. As a matter of fact it would now sound rather funny and pretentious. When sculpture and painting stopped playing a part in the making of public buildings, many of the symbolic messages and much imagery were eliminated. Concern shifted to social needs, such as the housing of people, the filling of their material wants, and preoccupation with art *per se* became almost suspect.

This is clearly expressed both by forces on the left and on the right (my definition) who are pressuring the architectural profession and the schools, whose traditional concerns since Vitruvius have been with "commodity," "firmness," and "delight." From the left the "advocates" are calling architects "elitist"—too much concerned with their own aesthetic values and egos and not enough with the underprivileged, the socio-political environment, low technology (do-it-yourself power to the people); and from the right the "managers" are also calling architects "elitist" for different reasons—not enough concerned with cost/time, efficiency, high technology, social engineering, and so on. The advocates speaking for the users and the managers for the providers, both attack architects for their over-concern with elitist, aesthetic/spatial value systems.

Now what about these aesthetic/spatial values? Originally, aesthetic concerns in architecture came from two sources:
1. the pride of craftsmanship; the ability to make things well; and to make things appropriate and elegant within available means;
2. the response to mystical, magical, religious forces; a search for support and truth, expressed significantly in eternal geometric ordering systems.

Both these forces can be seen in contemporary efforts, as in Mies Van der Rohe's "God is in the details," and in Le Corbusier's use of a geometric proportioning system "the Modulor," based on the golden section. However, increased rates of change, scientific concepts of uncertainty, and indeterminacy have replaced classical aesthetic concepts of perfection (static) with new ones searching for a growth-morphology   **359**

(dynamic); e.g., the Venus de Milo (the static symbol of beauty and perfection) versus the beauty and open-ended quality of cellular structures
under the microscope (always complete and never complete).

Thus, man created in the image of God (perfect, absolute) searching
for the perfect proportions and forms is not a fashionable view today —
but, rather, pragmatic individuals or groups searching for ever-changing
and adaptable patterns and forms, hopefully with the help of psychological and behavioral insight.

This has led to some scholarship and research and thus to a number
of people involved in these activities. Unfortunately, there is a gap between researchers, who are often involved in knowing more and more
about less and less (a reductive approach), and practicing professionals
whose training and vision are holistic and synthetic. Stronger links and
connections will have to be made between the two groups.

Let us then look at these areas of contemporary concern and study as
they relate to aesthetics in architecture.

1. *Psychological/behavioral insights linked to physical space/form.*
   For instance: If self-expression is of importance, what kind of
   spaces are most responsive? Should people be able to affect their
   environment with their own aesthetic preferences; or, if older
   people have to move, is familiarity with their new environment
   more important than the aesthetic/spatial preference of the architects? In this whole area, the insights of psychologists—
   Eriksen, Maslow, etc.—and of behavioral scientists—Sommer,
   Hall, Perrin, etc.—become important.

2. *Cultural/semiotic insights linked to physical space/form.* This is
   a search for symbolic messages, metaphors, images. Reasons and
   sources for such concerns and studies are many, and among them
   are:
   a. attacks on elitist cultural/aesthetic attitudes (Gans, Venturi,
      etc.);
   b. attacks on the influence of the Bauhaus in the United States, its
      puritan ethic, and, according to some (Geoffrey Scott, etc.), a
      false link between morality and art (words like "memory,"
      "mystery," "magic" are replacing words like "function," "ra-
      tionality," "industrialization");
   c. the search for ethnic roots, concern for the past, keeping the
      important physical environment of the past intact — not merely
      important aesthetic monuments, but the ambience of neighbor-
      hoods;
   d. interest in such philosophers as Levi-Strauss, Chomsky, and
      Karl Popper.

3. *Political/economic forces linked to physical space/form.* Here are
   probably some of the most difficult and emotion-laden questions,
   as they challenge the political *status quo;* e.g., Dewey in *Art as
   Experience:* "As long as art is the beauty parlor of civilization,
   neither art nor civilization are secure"; and "character (of physical

space) is determined by the economic system in which land is used and kept out of use for the sake of gain." In contrast to this view, Venturi's honoring Las Vegas as an important American achievement, as well as J. B. Jackson's earlier attempt to see "strip" developments along our highways as something to be looked at with an open mind and eye rather than dismissed by elitist aesthetes, opens the whole question of the physical expression in response to the economic system, the power of the market and of marketing, and their aesthetic consequences.

The problems architects face with some of this research is that they have a tendency to search for innovation, to be didactic, and, in common with many creators, to be ego-oriented — thus seeing some of such studies and research as interfering with their creative effort. This has much to do with their education as architects, which places high value on being a creative artist rather than on serving social needs. I believe that the conflict between these two attitudes should be faced and discussed, and a proper balance sought.

The concern with the aesthetic environment is obviously not a purely professional concern. It is a part of society's responsibility: individuals, communities, businesses, corporations, and government — the architects' clients. Government, with its powers of controlling the environment directly or indirectly, must be involved in a search for quality, as I have stated previously in *Man-made Environment, Visual Pollution and Controls*. Architects must be able to advise government as to public policy in such matters, above and beyond their narrower responsibilities as professionals, although their work may be more effective than many words.

As to the education of young people, including those who may wish to become architects, public education must identify, discuss, and experiment with aesthetic issues in comprehensive terms. Many architectural schools do not any longer choose students because they can draw well and/or have done well in art; they are searching for well-educated, balanced, intelligent men and women. What kind of education they should have had is a basic issue for us all.

Boston, Massachusetts
June 1976

John W. Cataldo

Major Research Questions:
To Form New Alliances*

The inevitable acceleration of technology has created a need to form new alliances and to develop strategies of response in which change and collaboration with technology are part of the learning processes.

Until a more experimental approach is taken with non-traditional learning modes in art and education, only a few will derive personal or aesthetic meanings from today's transformative technology, related art processes, or any future of art.

A positive reorientation of art with technology for younger generations may be centered in the careful matching of human functions and purposes with technical functions and future uses.

Strategies for Establishing Alliances

I suggest using the following strategies as a means for establishing alliances that will enable us to assimilate the high-energy technologies into our art programs and learning processes. (These will be the headings for the sections of this paper.)

    I. The Alliance of Ancient Impulses with Contemporary Art Processes

    II. The Alliance of Contemporary Art Forms and Processes with Technology

    III. The Alliance of Television Technology with Learning and Art Processes

I. The Alliance of Ancient Impulses with Contemporary Art Processes

Loren Eisely has said that "we are all looking for something of extraordinary importance whose nature we have forgotten." The anonymous artists of the walls and streets of antiquity celebrated the mundane, the ordinary, and the familiar. The ancient makers who constructed pyramids and mile-long earth paths at one level of perspective "for the gods to see" at another angle of vision, and the artists who painted the low ceilings of cave homes and inscribed the walls of canyons understood their intimate correspondence to nature and to the "absolute"

JOHN W. CATALDO is Dean of the Massachusetts College of Art.

 *Based on a paper titled "The New Alliances for Art and Technology."

elements of earth, air, fire, and water as sources for inspiration and subject matter. In the *Shape of Time,* Kubler raises a concern

> that radical artistic innovations or innovators may not appear with the frequency we have come to expect in past centuries. We and our descendants may choose to resolve such ancient incomplete kinds of forms, whenever we need them. If we are inhabiting "a finite world of limited possibilities with only some remaining exploration, adventure and discovery," then the relation of the future to the past world will alter radically. (George Kubler, *The Shape of Time:* Remarks on the History of Things [New York: Yale University Press, 1962].)

Contemporary artists are searching for deeper, natural, redemptive, creative resources and energies to overcome that sense of dislocation and disjunctive purpose in twentieth-century culture. In anticipating outcomes for the future, they have been forced to look backward and inward. In ancient societies, the past had relevance, and people had an intimate place and correspondence with nature — one that made the organic cycles of decomposition and renewal a basis for ritual and ceremony. Lowery Burgess, a process artist and an associate professor on the Massachusetts College of Art faculty, exercises a poetic art within which "a person can find the relationship of their own heartbeat in a time and space framework"; and he talks about the central energy of all art emanating from three areas: (1) the sacred dance-drama, which was related to astronomical phenomena and distances; (2) natural earth processes such as generative seasonal cycles; and (3) the resources of past art as present possibility in human time and as a human continuum for man as a species on earth. In one of his representative probes, D. L. Burgess, in September of 1974, buried twelve holographic plates in a desert valley called Kushkak (perpendicular to the valley of Bamijan) in Afghanistan at an angle of our galaxy at sunrise during the month that each plate is valid.

In the seventies, we are noticing an intriguing and increasing commitment by the artist and scientist towards humanistic, cosmic, and aesthetic involvement. Young artists like Robert Morgan say that they are interested in process works as a means for showing space as a culture and not as an object, and that harmony occurs when certain biospatial patterns exist according to physical law. At that point of harmony, Morgan says, he experiences an extension of his "inner processes." Apparently, our stresses today come not only from the separation of humans from nature but from the gross classification of nature as an object — exterior to man, hostile to man, and to be regarded as a marketable commodity.

Stresses and dualisms between ceremony and science were not uncommon in ancient cultures, for the preColumbian cosmos is described as a mixture of light and dark, blood and flowers. While drenching altars with human hearts, the Mayans, as superb astronomers, also had calculated the length of the solar year with a precision unmatched until the last century; they had developed a true form of writing, the concept of zero, and the decimal system. Yet, it is precisely in this dualism between ceremony and scientific thought that we may search out current solutions. Schelling says that the first principle of a philosophical system of science is the "search for polarity and dualism throughout all nature." Our current dualism and disconnectedness may be in the failure to mediate our past with an anticipated future, through remembrance and examination of an historical process that recognizes art forms as the appropriate mediator between natural, supernatural, social, and technical phenomena.

Current research places a special value on prime works of art and their role in aesthetic education. The energy impulses contained in art images form part of a continuing nonverbal discourse and establish an intriguing hypothesis for identifying a new relationship between iconic theory and learning theory; that is, to seek out and identify the many levels of non-discursive communication operating in the formation and conception of art objects and operating between peoples, and also to seek out within the deep mechanisms of the human mind, preconscious patterns, analogs, icons, and representations. The study of visual images (iconology) and the study of form or structure (morphology) are both prevalent in our century, and contemporary artists and designers have been using with increasing frequency these and similar descriptive phrases to describe their artworks and processes.

The words and images that we use transform a biological source or relationship into a social one. Yet dilemmas arise when words, used in single and sequential form, do not express those unconscious impulses or desires that are analogically or intuitively sensed. As artists and educators, we are being forced again and again to examine the historical role of the arts as an interface with the present; and we are forced to examine that there are certain current ideas, feelings, and contents in the arts that can be caught and revealed only through structuring time, and that are authorized only by past experiences.

We are returned again to first sources when Nathaniel Champlin says that aesthetic sources and methods are found "in the streets"; and that the most inclusive character and definition, if not the ultimate test of a civilization, is the way of life found in the streets and in the natural environment, as it was once found in caves and in the deep valleys by an earlier people.

The idea of the environment as a structural extension of the premise of the art work itself (where work and environment modify each other) is an historical, anthropological, and recollected natural model of the art process, and provides the soundest basis for past and future art works and processes. As Max Reinhardt says:

> the next revolution will see the return again of natural brute, expressionistic, collage, assemblage, "merz," "pop," happening, unconscious, accidental, poetic, dramatic, "song and dance," every-day theatre and environment, to the entertainment field and

junk-yard, to the folk places, and the lower depths where it all
came from in the first place.

For rituals are conjunctive, and they construct and reinforce organic relationships while maintaining a social equilibrium. Levi-Strauss tells of
the Gahuku-Gama of New Guinea who "have learned the game of foot-
ball but, in their interpretation, will play, several days running, as many
matches as are necessary for both sides to reach the same score. This is
treating a game as a ritual." (Claude Levi-Strauss, *The Savage Mind*,
[Chicago: University of Chicago Press, 1962], pages 30-31.)

It is an intriguing thesis that recent art forms and environmental
statements-as-process take the place that was filled, historically, by
representations and objects as art forms. Real materials and phenomena
are used in "fire" or "ice" statements; earth, air, water, fire have now
become and are the phenomenal media, content, aesthetic statement and
promise. In effect, they constitute comtemporary media and art equiva-
lents of ancient concerns. The physical and natural phenomena used by
the ancients remain rooted in our human nature; for these phenomena
are immediately bound up with emotions that exercise our senses in
ways we cannot ignore. The primitive artist allowed original and
painted forms to crumble away. Even today, the Dahomeyan artists of
Africa are interested only in the dialogue-process of creation and see no
point in preserving the objects, while the Asmat tribe of New Guinea
use their ceremonial forms once and throw them away after use. In
similar ways to process-works, the ancients incorporated motion and
time in equal measure to their seasonal work and ceremonial rituals.
And, in similar ways, the works of the contemporary process artist is
fugitive—appearing, happening, resolving, and dissolving. Both the
primitive and contemporary process-artists function within value systems far removed from the historically recent notion of art as a highly
marketable and permanent commodity that continues to increase in
saleable value in future time.

II. The Alliance of Contemporary Art Forms and Processes with Technology

Herbert Marcuse declares that "the history of thought is a history of
changing conceptual structures"; and, since the Renaissance, the artist
has gradually moved from a perspective representation as the focus of
his or her images, to transformative and collaborative art processes that
are centered in the deep mechanisms and sensorium of the human
mind. A survey of the historic evolution of art forms reveals the reflected view of a specific cultural or social order at a special entry point
in time.

Historically, we have witnessed the following aesthetic viewpoints:
(1) the magical imagery of the icon's role in the church-state society; (2)
classicism and its perceptive landscapes as stage settings; (3) genre and
folklore with its street and field vitalities, as well as heroic myth figures;
(4) the abstract ordering of space and time (divorced from human con-

cerns and actions); (5) a new edge of aesthetic consciousness for art processes and interacting systems that make a collaborative effort towards matching different levels of human needs and technical functions. At this point in time, our developing culture contains discrepancies and contradictions and stressful dualities best exemplified in the apparent dualism between art and technology. Hugo Bettelheim says "that modern man is haunted by machines and is unable to overcome his fear of technology because of its awesome capability and potential to alter human-organic growth." This haunted view of technology, when carried to unacceptable extremes, recalls Samuel Butler's story of the mystical Erewhonians who decreed the destruction of all machines back to a "prescribed date in their history, after which no further technological progress was to be allowed." Now, with a careful matching of technical functions with human purposes, we may get over our atavistic fear. We apparently have overemphasized, overused, and overstated new forms of technology in obsessive ways, and prematurely condemned them without fully exercising their functional or aesthetic potential. The real problem is linked to a disproportionately smaller group making technological decisions that are shaping our future living environments, and the slow assimilation of technology into our formal learning programs.

Scientific and art processes share similar mental operations that differ not so much in kind, even syntax, but in the different types of phenomena to which they are applied; e.g., perception, observation, imagination, impulse and drive, descriptive research, intuition, probability, and predictability. These are only a few modes of inquiry in scientific and aesthetic research that vary as much as human personality does. Apparently, scientists recognize that the future pace and success of science and technology are becoming more dependent upon interactions with the social system, and less on scientific discovery, (J. Forrester, 1967). And Burnham cites the transition from an "object-oriented to a systems-oriented culture . . . not things, but the way things are done."

When Stan Van Der Beek, at a conference dealing with visual media and technology, presented "some ideas of particular interest to current filmmakers," he listed the following: (1) simultaneous images and compressions; (2) discontinuous visual information; (3) episodic structures; (4) loop film; and (5) film as a reflection or a visual equivalent of mental processes and operations (such as the dream). The nomenclature and taxonomy of art and science have become mutually applicable to descriptions of visual technologies, mechanisms, and processes. Technological resources of the Massachusetts Institute of Technology were used by Nicholas Negroponte in 1970 to develop a classic experiment entitled "Seek." Negroponte made a very disquieting commentary about the current disjunctive consequences of a mechanical ordering of an organic living movement. The "Seek" statement included a group of live gerbils, and about five hundred wooden blocks arranged in a glass case. The gerbils, by their natural movement, "instructed" a small sensor-effecting computer to rearrange the environment of blocks in a structural pattern more suitable to their movement patterns. The feedback system enabled the "users" to influence the computer to model and reshape a different and preferred organic living environment.

Such an awareness of dualism and dysfunction will permit future artists and engineers to establish an affirmative humanistic reorientation with technology and mass media, and prevent a deepening crisis. Eventually, technology and mass media will become subject to, and subject of, an improved social and aesthetic research. Richard Loveless's work with the "New Place" in Tampa is an excellent and successful example of the city-wide use of video as a popular communiciation art form and social mediator — one that reduced the wide discrepancies existing between social levels in the city of Tampa, and allowed the young members of a new ethnic community to broadcast their social concerns and express their cultural style throughout the community. A positive reorientation of art with media and technology for younger learners may very well be centered in the careful matching of human purposes with selected future uses of technology's hardware.

The physicist's approach can be compared to an interactive dialogue-process with nature and the scientific process. And both the scientific and art processes require an equal measure of conceptual and physical ordering.

The ordering of vast amounts of accessible materials—visual impressions, available experiences, messages, dualisms, the increasing complexity of ideas — confronts every scientist and designer, and requires the same intentional mental processes and operations for resolution. The kind of phenomena each chooses to examine is the critical variant; the analytical process itself is not the variant. For example, how would the scientist and the artist separately respond to da Vinci's observation of a common phenomena when he said, "The air, as soon as there is light, is filled with innumerable images"?

Buckminister Fuller, in his efforts to develop an effective strategy for thinking "our way through to understanding what our human function in the universe might be . . . confronted with a vast amount of materials and experiences" found that he "always tried to make a basic division and subdivision of the universe (or problem) until an understandable, relevant and very *local level* in the universe was reached."

Today, the engineer (according to Jay Forrester) is less dependent on scientific discovery than he or she is concerned with human organization and interaction with the social system. The engineer in this role is described by Forrester as the "enterprise-engineer"; and as such is, like the artist, a mediator for the convertability of concepts through a structuring and facturing process that responds to human needs and purposes.

Conceptual structures in art and in the physical sciences have moved closer to human purposes, furthering the distance from metric systems while searching for the deeper mechanisms and structures of intuition.

The degree to which the relationship of science to technology in art has increased is apparent in the arts curricula of the public and private colleges of art. Curricula dealing with functional aesthetics are prevalent, moving well in advance of those past movements identified in the main with architectural (metrical) outcomes, such as De Styl, the Bauhaus, and Constructivism. A random sampling of catalogs of major art institutions included the following offerings: Snow Platforms; Rain Locations; Sectional Analysis (prismic forms, sections, and human scale); 2500 Problem (materials and gathering); and Process-Determinant of Structure (individual and collaborative problems).

The development from architectural, or metric, influence to the process-transformation movement of the seventies derived from the bio-technologies of space technology and achievements, such as life-support systems, non-lineal program plotting, and computer processing of vast information banks and inputs. The contemporary artist in America responded almost immediately to the new influences of space explorations through the use of documentary film, *cinema verité* sound and video works that reflected a new aesthetic consciousness directly attributible to new space technologies.

The public, meanwhile, was receiving instantly documented real experiences, images, and happenings of an unprecedented "foot-on-the-moon" order. A public of roughly 80 million was witnessing the history-making processes of the world in real time, through the medium of television technology. And a nation of people was interlinked with a visual medium serving as mediator between spatial situations, astronauts, and audience. The wider public has since internalized the visual medium to such an extent that even the cool Andy Warhol spoke of feeling "very much a part of my time, of my culture, as much a part of it as rockets and television. . . ."

III. The Alliance of Television Technology with Learning and Art Processes

"We are on the edge of a new consciousness which includes television as a central technology." (Marshall McLuhan) Since 1945, our society and people have been symbiotically involved to an unprecedented degree with the processing of visual information and data. The involvement of Americans in the processing of visual information is astronomical; e.g., ownership of 6.5 million (8mm) cameras; an increase from 100,000 black-and-white TV sets in 1945, to 150 million black-and-white and color TV sets in 1972; 4½ hours daily of television viewing time per family; not to mention color slides, self-developing film, 35 mm cameras, postcard mania, and poster graphics collections. By age eighteen, an American will have seen a minimum of twenty films for every book read, and have experienced a minimum of 15,000 hours of television viewing. That's 4,000 more hours than was accumulated in high school itself.

This accumulation of experiences and learning is happening mostly outside the schools, colleges, and universities. And, in large part, the collegial environment has not played a significant role in shaping television programs for learning-in-the-arts purposes. For contrast, we might look at the educational uses of TV by the major networks, the medical profession, the government, and the Public Broadcasting System.

According to Norman Cousins, "more than 200 public TV stations now serve the American people with a wide variety of cultural, informational and entertainment programs." Cousins, pointing to the "Open University" of Great Britain, recommends "a full college course on public television during prime time." By 1969, the U. S. Government had invested more than 2.5 billion in research with instructional technology (Molmar).

I am only now beginning to understand fully what McLuhan means when he says that "anything that alters a sensory threshold alters the outlook and experience of a whole society . . . it is the new technological environment indeed that influences shifts to new sensory and political levels." In addition to the altering of this generation's sensory threshold, we find the following shiftings occuring, such as (1) the superceding by the younger generation of the "idea of reason" with the "idea of happiness" as a desirable objective for living; (2) the persistent and gradual transition from a "working" to a "learning" society; and (3) a new, current angle of vision that has displaced the conventional view of the earth as a segmented marketable commodity to an holistic, global ecological system and process-art form.

Video broadcasting as an image-producing medium has accelerated and expanded the potential for new levels of image patterning and visual transformations that are at once multi-sensuous and multi-dimensional, and that provide the basis for a new iconic learning. Unlike film, television is a real-time medium—one that accommodates a careful pacing of information content. For, coupled to television's "live" (real-time) capability and immediate recall of any point of visual content, we now have the engineering capability, through synthesizers, to transform and modify visual content into discrete graphic elements, and, to do it at any specific point or at any preferred accommodating rate. Currently, there is no single visual technology that can process and transform or feed back visual images as rapidly, as extensively, or as effectively as a video color synthesizer.

Color synthesizers have created new levels of possibility for an iconic visual imagery and syntax that have altered sensory thresholds; and they have not only redefined the roles for artist, engineer, graphic designer, and educator but have influenced a redirection of each—from an individualistic or metric posture towards a new collaborative necessity between these fields and social research. The first collaboration, according to Buckminister Fuller, will call for visual designers to reduce and order overwhelming numbers of visual impressions within a preselected time-space condition. For, without a reduction and selective process, we may develop, by the sheer force of the information mass, a nonproductive, mindless relation to a compelling, an obsessive visual medium. And, thereby, we will surrender the creative and educational potential the medium holds for art and learning experiences.

Video is a unique, nondiscursive, visual communication mode that advances constituents of a message (or configuration) simultaneously—shaping images that must be comprehensively grasped in one holistic act of perception. Film, with all of its innovative capabilities, is still a lineal-unit medium, advancing by unit frames from a point to a middle and a conclusion. It follows, in the main, a literary serial mode, and can be selected for use by a designer for its special metric pace and link with literature and mathematics. Video, in turn, does not compete with film or print media; nor does it displace any medium. It provides another expressive communication option that can combine and transform visual images from real or artificial sources into unprecedented visual statements. In the *Basic Training of Pavlo Hummel,* Al Pacino uses a typewriter, a pencil, and a pen in the same message and describes these mixed media as "cool." No communication medium displaces any other, yet the preference for using a single medium to shape and communicate a message persists, even though the message content may be diverse, accelerated, or decelerated in pace; increased or decreased in stress; and offered on several levels of meaning and interpretation.

Our attitudes as artists and educators remain relatively fixed and resistant to exercising the new video technology for visual learning purposes. Research for educational uses of visual media for affective learning is gaining support, and is reflected by Elliot Eisner's salient statement from *Media, Expression and the Arts:* "new forms of art evoke new forms of experience, inform us about the qualitative aspects of life, and reawaken our awareness of the old." He further notes, "the unique consequences of non-discursive media for facilitating human understanding"; and he concludes, "so long as our educational means and ends are conceived and dominated by verbal performance we will harbor only a crippled conception of human potentiality."

The evidence that people learn from viewing television and film is described by Hoban as "overwhelming." He further states that not only is conceptual and visual learning advanced, but voluntary related reading and social awareness are advanced as well.

We are beginning to evaluate in a systematic way television processes and their effects; not only television's ability to convey images and information but to create out of its unique characteristics genuine aesthetic statements and models for social interaction. I am willing to speculate that such characteristics of video may be parallel to the description of the human mind as a continuous, fluctuating, cybernetic process and mediator between the inner self and the outer world. Perhaps for this reason only, children, adults — highly intelligent people—are literally spellbound by the image-making properties of television. Only recently, Chomsky, the generative semanticist, developed a theory of linguistics that took off from his vision of a "complex universe within the mind, governed by myriad rules and prohibitions and yet infinite in its creative potential." *(New York Times* Book Section, December 3, 1972).

Media and the New Technocracy as Learning Environment

The pervasive effects of the technological environment upon the human sensorium are obvious in the aesthetic revolutions of contemporary arts and architecture. New visual forms and images directly attributed to the new technocracy are rapidly assimilated by the artist and graphic designer, and have immediate effect upon the mental operations and aesthetic outcomes of studio performance. Artworks are not only described as canvasses and sculpture but as environments and systems as well.

The instruments of our technology produce images and forms supportive of marketing and functional concerns; yet, when placed in an aesthetic field and correspondence, they assume a new value for illuminating and clarifying the human condition and purpose in contemporary living.

Documented and analyzed through the dissemination media, the social revolution is, in immediate and universal ways, reinforcing the interrelationship and simultaneous developments of the aesthetic with social and technological conditions and status.

Computers, new alloys, light and dissemination media have upset programs of art and forced the redefinition of traditional arts disciplines. In turn, our current visually literate students have lived in symbiotic ways with the instruments and forms of the new technocracy since birth, and they will require and expect new learning resources and arts environments so as to interact with and humanize the technological advance.

The new arts tradition deals with unprecedented ideas and reveals a search for appropriate processes and formative media. Collaboration with existent or emergent technology has accelerated, and fine arts programs and institutions are beginning to combine their arts curricula with technical sources. Divergent conceptual intentions require different and variable physical space for interaction; and future learners in art will interact within the institution, society, or the technocracy as is required for the resolution of the aesthetic encounter.

The new arts curricula are inseparable from the youth generation and its preferred life-style and purposes. Film, television, electronic media, sound synthesizers are used extensively in the every-day-and-night youth environment, while they are only gradually (however skeptically) introduced into arts programs of higher education. Students (when they are outside of academic institutions) and/or youth in the social environment have entered into an enthusiastic social and aesthetic correspondence with the new sounds, forms, and visual configurations of the new media environment.

Nontraditional media and concepts have yet to become the principal base for arts programs in higher education, although they have the potential for being the change-agent for re-creating a humanistic tradition and role for the arts in a systems-oriented technocracy.

The widespread acceptance of the video medium and experience has advanced the expectations for unprecedented visual images and forms. Designers and educators are expressing delight in the unexpected developments for improved visual learning and communication.

New Concepts of Learning Environments

Special arts programs of recognized achievement typically function as in-depth workshops within traditionally defined disciplines. The impacted programs continue to service and preserve the traditional and romantic aspects of the arts as we have known them. However, the recent turn to nontraditional curricula and comprehensive arts environments for learning anticipate the next development for arts programs by:

1. accommodating the self-governed life and world of the artist, in that, supportive resources (human and technological) are available as needed; and
2. retaining the nature of traditional studio programs while, however, the current developments are accelerating towards a collaborative correspondence with the technocracy and social research.

Emphasis in the arts is now located in conceptual and issue-centered objectives. Developing the students' ability to conceptualize ideas and transform them into objects requires an intimate collaboration between artists, educators, and technologists; in that, the means for forming and evaluating art works are accessible in the social, academic, technological and media environments. In new definitions for the arts, we can project that components of a learning environment in the arts include the following:

1. *comprehensive arts programs* - art studio, dance and movement, theatre and happenings, film, video and visual communications, music and sonics, dialogue-process models, the new technologies;
2. *psychological studies* - human behavior from birth to death, as well as a study of the psychology of form;
3. *linguistic structure and conceptualism* - a study of verbal and nonverbal modes of communication, as well as the simultaneous and comparative study of divergent cultures, languages, and forms such as English, French, and Chinese.
4. *ecology* - patterns of human interactions from historical, psychological, sociological, anthropological viewpoints;
5. *world and space ecology* - man's position on earth and in space;
6. *research and development* - continual search and development of strategies for new learning modes and environments.

Conceptual concerns in arts environments would be approached for resolution through the media and operations of light, time, space, motion, systems analysis, dialogue-process, and a participatory learning and participatory aesthetics between situations and people.

When television education was compared with conventional teaching by Chu and Schramm (1967), their findings demonstrated that instructional TV can be used more easily and effectively with primary- and secondary-school students than with college students. And Levien found (1972) that after employing films, computers, and programmed instruction, few faculty members had the combined interests and expertise in subject matter, media development, and learning theory that the design of the high-quality material required. *(The Fourth Revolution: Instructional Technology in Higher Education,* [A Report and Recommendations by the Carnegie Commission on Higher Education, June 1972].)

The obvious value and increased future use of the television medium in learning situations will require, in the initial stages, a heavier dependency upon "outside" professional agencies and specialists. *The Fourth Revolution* in education involves the development of learning systems based on existing sophisticated technologies already far in advance of the emerging nontraditional learning and arts curricula and the emerging group of dedicated techno-process artists.

Boston, Massachusetts
May 1976

Stanley S. Madeja

Structuring a Research Agenda for the Arts and Aesthetics

Introduction

Looking back on the last decade of research in the arts and aesthetics, its dominant characteristic has been the selection of research questions by individual researchers and the absence of large-scale efforts to solve significant problems reaching across the various disciplines and areas of study. There are a few exceptions to this generalization, particularly the Arts and Humanities Program of the Office of Education. Created in 1962, it set the major research and development priorities for the sixties in five areas: the role of perceptual learning in the arts, the role of the arts in general education, investigation of the place of environmental design in general education, development of training programs, and the relationship of the arts to education for the disadvantaged. This was the first time a government agency defined priorities for research and development in the arts and aesthetics. Yet, the Arts and Humanities Program had a very short tenure and is already a program for the historian to report on; unfortunately, no direct support for research in the field has been forthcoming in recent years. The priorities were established, but no support was provided over a long enough period to have any significant effects.

Another characteristic of the Arts and Humanities Program was the funding of individual researchers whose products related broadly to problems in the arts or aesthetics, but had no direct relationship to one another. Consequently, while the results of the program and the studies held up individually, there were many gaps; and, taken together, they did not answer the larger questions posed by the research priorities.

One program initiated by the Arts and Humanities Program that did receive long-term support was the Aesthetic Education Program. It was continued by CEMREL, Inc., and will be completed this year, meeting the long-term objectives set in 1968. These were to design an aesthetic education curriculum for kindergarten through sixth grade using multi-media approaches to instruction, and to design within that

STANLEY S. MADEJA *is Vice-President of CEMREL, Inc., and Director of CEMREL's Aesthetic Education Program.*

curriculum a modular system of instructional units that could be manipulated by the student or the teacher in the school into a curriculum reflecting their values and choices; to develop a teacher-education program that would accompany the curriculum and facilitate the installation of the Aesthetic Education Program in the schools; to sensitize the field in the arts and education and also in the federal government to the importance of aesthetic education for every student; and to gain a broad base of support and install the Program in as many schools in the United States as possible.

The Aesthetic Education Program has met these objectives in part because it has benefited from eight years of continuing support from the Office of Education and the National Institute of Education. The Program is a good example of what can result from a long-term, directed research and development program in one problem area.

What I am suggesting as an agenda of research and development over the next decade is that we select a few problems for research, concentrating our efforts on these larger topics, so as to solve problems in these specific areas before moving on to others. Such an agenda parallels the ways significant advances in medicine have been made. For example, polio was a major medical crisis in the forties and fifties. Jonas Salk made the major breakthrough in this area, but he was not the only one working on the problem—researchers all over the world contributed to the effort. The same design is being used in research on heart disease and cancer. Although we are not operating under the same crisis conditions, the strategy of organizing research and development efforts to solve fewer but larger problems is the design that can be applied to a research agenda for the future in arts and aesthetics.

I am recommending that we select a number of major topics for investigation; and, in this paper, I am outlining two areas that I feel could be major fields for research: evaluation in the arts and aesthetics; and the relationship of the arts and aesthetics to technology.

Research in Evaluation and the Arts

A fertile area for research and development in the arts lies in evaluation. This is not to say that evaluation in the arts is a wasteland. To the contrary, if there is any area of research in the arts that has some history, it is the area of measurement. We can trace interest in developing tests and assessment in the arts to the very beginnings of measurement in education.

During the early part of this century, the emphasis on scientific methods in research became very influential in many areas of education. The arts were no exception, and devices for measuring the artistic product were designed. Some of the earliest attempts were in the visual arts, rating the drawings of children. The scales, as they were termed, were attempts to standardize evaluation and set up criteria for judgment at various levels on the assumption that the drawings could be categorized. Thorndike, in 1913, was one of the first to develop such a scale; its purpose was the measurement of achievement in drawing. Kline and Carey (1922), Tiebout (1936), and McCarthy (1942) followed with development of their own scales for the purpose of measuring art achievement. A significant test measuring general intelligence through the use of drawings was the *Goodenough Draw-A-Man Scale*, developed in 1926; later revised by Harris (1963).[1]

Tests measuring visual artistic aptitude and appreciation can trace their history back through the work of McAdory (1929), Christian and Karwoski (1929), Meir and Seashore (1929), Meir (1940), Burt (1933), and Graves (1946). Even with this long interest in testing and measurement in the visual arts, there has not been a comprehensive long-term study that has resulted in evaluation techniques for aesthetic learning in one or more of the arts.

In addition, assessment techniques in one or more of the arts have not been developed that are applicable for general use in schools, especially at the elementary level. Only recently have we seen the development of art and music tests, such as those developed by the National Assessment Program, having some applicability to larger audiences. These tests are for high-school students, however, and are still in the developmental cycle.

It is an axiom in education that the content of the tests to some extent determines the content of the curricula. Graduate-school exams have an effect on undergraduate courses of study, and college entrance exams determine high-school curriculum. What is taught in elementary school reflects testing programs at the high-school level, while elementary-school testing programs affect elementary-grade-level curricula. The absence of tests in aesthetics or the arts has had an effect on whether or not the arts and related subjects with aesthetic content are taught in the public schools. In my opinion, there is a very great need for a concentration of research efforts on the development of instruments that can describe and diagnose the aesthetic accomplishments of the student at each level of instruction. The development of such instruments will have an effect on the presence of the arts in the curriculum.

Evaluation in schools has two major purposes: One is to determine the effectiveness of the instructional program and all its components. The second purpose is to assess students' progress and to diagnose their problems. In the following examples, I have tried to describe one approach that is applicable to each function; descriptive methodology as an approach to program evaluation in the arts and as a diagnostic instrument for recording student progress in arts criticism.

Descriptive Techniques as a Methodology for Arts Program Evaluation

The major need in arts and aesthetics evaluation is for new methodologies that are in character with the nature of the phenomena studied in arts and aesthetics programs. One of the mistakes made by many past evaluation or research studies in the arts was to draw methodology only from the psychometricians and their very quantitative techniques, and to ignore the more humanistic methodologies of the anthropologist and sociologist. It became evident in our work in the Aesthetic Education Program at CEMREL—especially during the early stages of designing activities and materials for students—that very precise quantitative techniques were not at all appropriate in classroom settings. This led us of necessity to discover or identify new methods to record what happens to students and teachers in the classroom when arts activities were being taught. One of our first attempts was an evaluation of the Arts in General Education Project (AGE) conducted by Davis, Thuernau, and Hall.[2] For this project, a team approach to evaluation was used to look at a new arts program throughout an entire school system.

The evaluation team was concerned with four areas:

1. a detailed description of the progress of the AGE Project;
2. identification and isolation of factors contributing to success or failure of the AGE Project;
3. development of methods and instruments for evaluating the arts instructional units; and
4. small experimental and descriptive studies related to specific problems.

The areas of evaluation and the activities actually engaged in are summarized in *Figure 1*.

It should be noted that the evaluation of the Arts in General Education Project developed methods and techniques for assessing student activities and instructional units in the classroom, as well as for monitoring the overall progress of the Project. The techniques originally designed and tested in actual classrooms in the AGE evaluation were used later in the Aesthetic Education Program evaluation.

The evaluation process that evolved for use by the Aesthetic Education Program is based on the use of trained observers who carry out an exhaustive observational monitoring of an entire set of instructional materials from beginning to end. This information, fed back to the development staff, serves as a basis for revision and further trials of the materials before they are considered for publication. In this stage, the materials must meet three major review criteria: First, they must be in keeping with the overall goals of the Program; second, there must be evidence that, in the hands of a competent teacher, the materials can be successfully implemented without aid beyond that given in the teacher's guide; and, third, the materials must meet certain short-term objectives, demonstrated by measurable differences between students who have studied the materials and those who have not.

Hall and Thuernau (1975)[3] have documented these methods in their summary of the formative evaluation procedures of the Aesthetic Education Program. They show the relationship between the evaluation techniques and the development of instructional materials in a classroom setting.

Figure 1

ACTIVITIES IN FOUR AREAS OF FORMATIVE EVALUATION
ARTS IN GENERAL EDUCATION PROJECT

Areas of Evaluation	Activities	
	YEAR ONE	YEAR TWO
Detailed description of Project progress	Periodic progress reports of AGE and evaluation staff	Periodic progress reports
		Accounting of student/ teacher involvement
	Accounting of student/ teacher involvement with Project arts activities	Accounting of number of students enrolled in formal, existing art programs in district
Identification and isolation of factors contributing to the success or failure of the Project	Interviews with planners, principals, and teachers	Secondary-school survey of arts experiences, needs, and desires
		Teachers' reactions to Hubbard-Rouse materials
Development of methods and instruments for evaluating the units	Development of instruments for instructional units	Systematic observation of units
	Data collection for unit revisions	
Descriptive and experimental studies	*Data collection for*	*Data collection for*
	Experimental Kindergarten	Experimental Kindergarten
	Space Place	Space Place
	Artists' performances	
	Powell Hall — elementary	

A number of other studies were conducted that contributed to some definitions clarifying this methodology over time. Smith and Geoffrey (1968)[4] investigated the classroom form and its social structure, and developed a methodology termed "classroom ethnography" calling for direct observation of classroom instruction on a pre-selected topic by a trained observer who did not become a participant in the instructional process. Later, Stake[5] developed a methodology for classroom observation he terms "response evaluation," having some of the same characteristics. Response evaluation in Stake's definition "is an alternative, an old alternative, based on what people do naturally to evaluate things they observe and react to." He goes on to say that this alternative has been avoided in district, state, and federal planning documents and regulations because it is subjective and poorly suited to formal contracts. He defines an educational evaluation as response evaluation if it orients more directly to program activities than to program intents, if it responds to audience requirements for information, and if the different value-perspectives present are referred to in reporting the success or failure of the program.

Smith and Schumacher[6] used observation techniques on a very large scale in an evaluation of the Aesthetic Education Program in Pennsylvania. The direct observation of arts activities in the classroom and the documentation of these observations in varied settings were demonstrated as viable. As summarized in their report, the methodology used was "participant observation," as defined by Malenowski, Whyte, and Becker, et al. The process model used for designing the study was the one previously proposed by Smith and Geoffrey. The essence of the model was to bring educational theory together with educational practice through field research in classroom ethnography. The study was the second by CEMREL that made use of controlled observation techniques for project evaluation; but this one was on a larger scale and involved classrooms situated across an entire state rather than localized in one school system.

It should also be noted that, in 1971, the National Art Education Association (NAEA) had a preconference training program, which featured participant observation as a research methodology. NAEA also devoted an entire issue of their research journal to the topic.[7] In addition, the JDR 3rd Fund has recently supported seminars on the topic of descriptive research at the American Educational Research Association. These efforts resulted in the Stake book on the topic.

Observation techniques as a research methodology have some distinct advantages for evaluation in the arts: They are characteristic of a more humanistic and less mechanistic approach to describing the phenomena; they are compatible with the diversity of the arts experience (which tends to be non-linear), since observation reports are more descriptive of a non-linear process or event; they are based on primary data, student work, rather than on secondary data, student performance on a test; and they provide concrete examples of the actual experience while taking a neutral stance as to the worth or value of the experience.

On the other hand, there are some distinct disadvantages and shortcomings to the techniques of descriptive evaluation: The methods are non-standardized, therefore subject to the criticism of bias and non-objectivity; they are subject to personal interpretation, so observers have to be trained; and the generalizability of the data is suspect because of the collection methods.

There are pros and cons about every new methodology. However, the point is that these techniques seem to have some very positive attributes when used as assessment devices for the aesthetic experience. They give the researcher another method of documenting and evaluating a problem. The development of new methodology applicable to aesthetic phenomena is of primary importance to arts evaluation, and it is particularly important that the arts take on this responsibility.

Controlled observation of classroom activities is an evolving area of measurement that shows promise for the arts and aesthetics. The major research and development need here is to adapt the methodology for large-scale use on both school and classroom levels, providing the school with a method of analyzing its own program and the teacher with methods appropriate to the classroom. We need observation techniques that are directly applicable to the teaching of aesthetic content in the classroom, and that give the observer a method for perceiving the aesthetic experience. What I am suggesting is not the adoption of another methodology for the arts but the creation of new observation techniques directly applicable to the arts.

Developing a Diagnostic Instrument for Student Progress in the Arts

For the purpose of illustrating how instruments may be developed to diagnose student progress in the visual arts and in the broader area of aesthetic judgments, let me describe the process I used to develop an instrument for teachers to use in analyzing the responses of elementary-school students to works of art.

In some of my own work on visual perception and on student ability to describe and analyze a painting, I have come to the conclusion that it is possible to categorize students' responses to art and to provide some means for assessing their level of expertise. My interest was in how students perceive the work of art and how they respond to that work. Early investigation led me to the work of Arnheim and his analysis of the perceptual process as it relates to works of art:

It is in works of art, for example, in paintings, that one can observe how the sense of vision uses its power of organization to the utmost. When an artist chooses a given site for one of his landscapes he not only selects and rearranges what he finds in nature; he must reorganize the whole visible matter to fit any order discovered, invented, purified by him. And just as the invention and elaboration of such an image is a long and often toilsome process, so the perceiving of a work of art is not accomplished suddenly. More typically, the observer starts from somewhere, tries to orient himself as to the main skeleton of the work, looks for the accents, experiments with a tentative framework in order to see whether it fits the total content, and so on. When the exploration is successful, the work is seen to repose comfortably in a congenial structure, which illuminates the work's meaning to the observer.[8]

Perceiving the object in this way goes beyond merely looking at an object, as perception implies some intellectual process. Arnheim makes it quite clear that the perceptual process involved in "seeing" a work of art is a cognitive function of human intellect.

Work such as Arnheim's led me to believe that categorization of responses using varying levels of visual perception would be possible. Analyzing Arnheim's work, I defined five levels of perceptual learning that are applicable to the visual arts and that make up a continuum of visual learning:[9] They are observation, description of visual relationships, selectivity, generalization of form, and abstraction. The first four of these were used in the development of the diagnostic instrument.

The first level of perceptual learning is *observation:* the recognition of the object or event and a consciousness of various types of visual stimuli. The *description of visual relationships,* the second level, concerns the ability to select and generalize visually, in and out of the object's context—an ability that Arnheim characterizes as the apprehension of relationships between the whole of the visual field and some item within it. Piaget concurs in this characterization and adds that the establishment of relationships is one of the principal cognitive mechanisms. In perception, such mental operations function within the so-called "rules of grouping by similarity" (e.g., shape, color, movement) described by *gestalt* psychologists.

At the third level, *selectivity,* the process is similar to the method used by a photographer to select parts from the whole using a camera's viewfinder. Selectivity is concerned with the cognitive function of recognition, and the ordering and simplification of visual phenomena. The ability to pick out the dominant characteristics of a painting, such as line, texture, or color, is an example of selectivity. Selectivity, thus, is a part of direct perception, as perception is selective by its very nature. For the artist, the selection of visual phenomena from any natural or man-made environment is the source of information for aesthetic judgments. This is sometimes called the "artistic eye."

The fourth level, *generalization of form,* is the ability to synthesize visual principles. At this level, an individual will be able to analyze visual phenomena and make a verbal statement about them. Generalization of form also requires the individual to take apparently unrelated visual phenomena and interrelate the parts into a generalizable whole. The ability to talk about or explain the work of art in its totality and to generalize about its content distinguishes this level from the others.

These four levels of visual learning were the categories I used to develop a continuum describing the student's perception of the art object. *Figure 2* shows a general description of the four levels, matched with a checklist for assessing and categorizing verbal and visual responses of the student.

The process of developing this instrument has several key elements that are generally applicable to the development of more complex diagnostic instruments: (1) existing research was used as the theoretical base (Arnheim's work in visual concept formation); (2) the instrument was designed to be applicable to the teaching of art; and (3) the content was related to the school, the teacher, and the student. These three steps are necessary to the development of evaluation devices in the arts and aesthetics that will be of use in the schools.

Figure 2

Characteristics of Student Responses	Check List
Observation:	**Observation:**
1. Simple recognition that the object exists and is in some way categorized by the student: "This is a painting."	1. The student can categorize the work as a painting, sculpture, drawing, etc.
2. A description of the subject matter in a factual manner with some mention of the formal properties of the work: "This painting is of a ranch in the southwestern part of the United States."	2. The student can describe the subject matter and list its formal properties.
Related to this is recognition of parts of the subject matter of the art object: "There are green trees, cattle, a horse, a ranch house, and ranchers in the painting."	3. The student can describe the parts of the subject matter of the work of art.
3. Recognition of the visual qualities of the art object that the subject matter conveys: "The painter was able to establish strong feeling of depth in this watercolor by the use of contrasting colors."	4. The student identifies the visual qualities that the subject of the work of art conveys.
Description of Visual Relationships:	**Description of Visual Relationships:**
1. A description of the visual relationship between one or more of the formal qualities within a work of art: "The shapes used in the painting are square. The artist created a controlled geometric pattern within the square." Here the relationship between shape and texture is established and mention is made of how they relate to one another in the art object.	1. The student is able to describe the relationships among the formal qualities of a work of art.
2. A description of the relationship between the work of art and its context or setting. This is based on the ability to comprehend the relationship between the whole of the visual field and some object within it: "The sculpture in the courtyard has a relationship to the structure because of the use of circular forms that are similar to those used throughout the building."	2. The student is able to determine the relationship between the work of art and the setting it is placed in.
3. A description of the parts of the work and how they contribute to the whole work. This is the ability to establish the relationship between one or more of the art elements within the work and the whole work: "The use of line within Rouault's painting of *The Seated Clown* unifies the variety of colors used."	3. The student can describe the relationship between the whole work of art and the dominant art elements within it.

Selectivity:

1. Selection of parts of the work that can be considered dominant, or distinctive qualities of a work of art: "The use of color by Turner made his paintings much different from those of his contemporaries"; or "Moore's method of creating positive and negative space within his sculpture makes the form unique."

2. Ordering the importance of parts of the work based on criteria and rationale: "Color in this painting acts as an accent and is not as important a unifying element as the thick black lines." A relationship is established between the elements in the work, and a judgment is made about their importance to the overall composition.

Selectivity:

1. The student is able to select and identify the dominant and distinctive qualities of a work of art.

2. The student is able to select the important parts of a work of art based on his or her own criteria or those of the scholar.

3. The student is able to order the elements of a work of art according to their importance to the total composition.

Generalization of Form:

1. Recognition and description of the synthesis of visual elements as they form the whole work of art. It implies the ability to take unrelated visual phenomena, interrelate the parts, and then develop a rationale for their synthesis. The rationale may be based on recognition of the style of the work; the period or school in which it was created; or a combination of techniques, style, and period, as in this description by Jean Leymarie of Rembrandt's *The Night Watch:* "With its amazing tensions and complex lines of force, this picture is a summing-up of Rembrandt's Baroque aspirations as defined by himself: to employ the (maximum) of movement, movement of the most natural kind."

Generalization of Form:

1. The student can combine or synthesize the visual elements in the whole work of art and state reasons for this synthesis.

2. The student can recognize and give reasons for the synthesis of visual elements.

Research Needs in Evaluation of the Arts and Aesthetics

I am not advocating adoption of a single rigid measure or methodology for aesthetics and/or the arts, but I am arguing that we should be striving towards some techniques for assessing aesthetic competencies that will solidify the place of the arts and aesthetic education in the school curricula. Instruments providing meaningful information to school boards, administrators, and teachers on student aesthetic accomplishments will be of great use in both program and student evaluations. Producing this kind of information in the arts calls for development of assessment techniques that may be as completely different from the formats of standard tests as the observation techniques described earlier are from traditional observation techniques.

There has been a great deal of criticism of standardized testing at the elementary, secondary, and college levels. We have available a new technology—video and audio recording devices, for example—that could be used as the means for sophisticated and economical testing. We already have tests, such as the Strong Vocational Inventory, the

Sixteen PF, and the Kuder Preference Test, that give profiles of attitudes and interests, rather than a single score. If resources and talent were allocated to the task, instruments to determine strengths and weaknesses in the aesthetic domain could be designed as part of the assessment program of the school. The instruments could assess student accomplishments and abilities in such categories as arts appreciation; visual, oral, kinetic, tactile, and olfactory organization and planning; visual, oral, kinetic, tactile, and olfactory memory and reproduction; arts vocabulary, arts techniques and history; conscious and unconscious interest in aesthetic phenomena; and attitudes towards aesthetics and the arts.

We may not like the problem of test dependency in education; and the inadequacies of existing testing programs should be corrected. But the fact that the testing program now being used in the schools has some shortcomings should not preclude continued work to develop testing in the aesthetic domain. I am convinced that, if this could be accomplished, the results would be additional respectability and credibility for the arts-in-the-schools program, and smoother entry of the arts into the general education program.

Research in the Arts and Technology

The other major topic that I feel is ripe for investigation is the relationship of art and aesthetics to technology. Certainly the ballooning possibilities for utilizing our rapidly expanding audio and visual media should not be overlooked by arts researchers.

The great difference between education in this century—even this quarter-century—and the last century is technology. The telegraph, telephone, radio, television, audio and video recording devices are now a part of everyday life. The schools possess a technology ranging from audio and visual equipment and devices, such as tape recorders and record players, to very complex computerized learning systems with retrieval capabilities rivaling those of large corporate enterprises. School libraries have broadened their function to include becoming media centers, providing not only books but films, filmstrips, slides, video and audio cassettes, and in the most advanced centers, dial-access retrieval of information. The character of instructional materials has changed from simple-format single texts to multi-media educational resources. A network of audiovisual delivery systems, including television stations devoted exclusively to educational enterprises, has been established. Thanks to the acceleration of the transportation system and other technological advances during this century, we now have at our command educational devices and techniques that are applicable to the student at practically every level.

Industry has brought the technology to a mass audience and made it accessible to everyone. We only have to think of the omnipresence of the television set, which was priced twenty years ago at about three times what it sells for today. (There are more households now with TV than with bathtubs.) The radio, which at one time was a very expensive item occupying a place of honor in the family living room, is now a personal possession of many young people. The hand calculator, selling a short time ago for well over $200, is now about $10 and in use in elementary classrooms. The technology of the media is now available to a mass market at a price it can afford, and this has implications for the schools. Radios, cameras, tape recorders, hand calculators can now be considered everyday educational resources.

This same technology has changed the nature of art forms, with significant implications for the arts and aesthetics. Technological advances have made available to the artist a whole repertory of new devices and techniques to be used as possible expressive means and materials. In the sound medium, for example, new methods of amplification and improved fidelity in recording have transformed a musical performance into something that could be termed multi-track magic. Recordings once made on one track now have the potential of combining some twenty-four or more tracks onto a single tape or disc. Amplification devices and electronic manipulation have given the composer a whole new sound repertory, even creating new instruments like the sound synthesizer. In video, electronic editing, the generating of images by computers, and the video synthesizer allow the artist to create images and effects never before possible.

Theatre also has capitalized on the new technology, utilizing the new sound and visual techniques in stage productions. Multi-media devices are integrated into a total theatrical experience. The recent Broadway play *Indians* is a good example of media utilization in theatre. Because of the advances in sound systems, lighting, structural design, and projection systems, the whole "look" of theatrical productions has changed. All of this has, in turn, affected play-writing and stage-directing, which now can capitalize on technical possibilites never before available in stage productions. Similar transformations have taken place in dance. Alwin Nikolais's Dance Theatre was the first to make use of the media in a dance score twenty years ago, and now electronic sounds and images are commonplace.

Film is the art form of this century and has made such rapid technological advances that it is hard to compare filmmaking in the seventies to what it was in the twenties. We have only to view Stanley Kubrick's *2001: A Space Odyssey,* a masterpiece of the new film technology, to see the advances in this area over the last fifty years. The cinematographer is a new artist created by the technology of this century.

It is obvious that the majority of schools are at least twenty years behind in their utilization of the existing technology. This may be the case because of the cost and the sophistication needed by the user group to obtain and use these new techniques. However, it need not always be so. Educational processes using the new technology can go beyond the school, if need be, and into the home through the mass media. A new concept is emerging—something I term "entertainment education"—that was pioneered by Walt Disney and is now an ever-expanding enterprise in this country. The school may play a part in this process, but it may be that the classroom will become only one component of a larger educational effort encompassing the mass media, home-based educational programs, and community out-of-school programs.

Research is needed to bring together three things that seem somewhat disparate at this point: the new technology, the artist who creates with the technology, and education. The potential of the technology and the excitement of the artistic possibilites are evident; how they can be brought to bear on educational problems in the arts and other areas seems to me a major new avenue for research.

What are some areas of research that can bring the technology, the artists, and education closer together? It is appropriate that we investigate how to do this, since, when this technology gives artists new horizons for creation, it also opens up ways for research to explore aesthetic decision-making and aesthetic judgments. Little has been done to utilize our present technological capability to design settings where we can study the visual, oral, and kinetic aesthetic choices that students and others make.

Kenneth Beittel's work in the area of visual concept formation as exemplified by drawing[10] is one example of the type of setting that might be designed. Beittel's work was concerned only with the drawing medium in the visual arts field. There needs to be an expansion of his work to include all the sense modalities and all the media available beyond photography. We have at hand recording devices capable of documenting visual, aural, and kinetic responses simultaneously and providing "instant replay." We can record, play back, analyze and discuss arts activities, and feed the results back into the system immediately without any significant time-lapse. "Instant replay" is a tool for arts education that has never been explored—no matter what its usefulness to the physical education department is. It has tremendous potential for analysis of the creative process, evaluation in the arts, and description and interpretation of aesthetic judgment.

Creating a Laboratory for the Study of Aesthetic Perception

What I see as a possibility for research in the arts and aesthetics is the creation of a new kind of facility—a facility that would have the capability of recording all the responses by every sensory mode: what we see, hear, touch, feel, or smell—a "sense laboratory" for the investigation of aesthetic perception. The laboratory would be designed so that we could carry on experiments and basic research in the arts and education utilizing the technological base we now have available as the data-collecting and analyzing mechanism. The primary purpose of developing a laboratory like this would be to study, in a setting where actions and reactions could be recorded for further research and analysis, how people actually make aesthetic judgments and what criteria they apply. This laboratory is envisioned somewhat like the setting the United States Navy used during World War II in studying visual perception, where various kinds of problems were designed for subjects to solve while the subjects were, in turn, studied throughout the problem-solving process. Such a facility would also permit observations never really possible before to take place in a controlled environment.

One of the problems such a laboratory might investigate is the whole process of visual concept formation. What are the steps leading to the final form an individual creates visually? Is there a pattern to this process or is it a random operation? Is it a linear or a non-linear process? What is the relationship of visual concept formation to basic cognitive functions? What are the aesthetic decision-making functions?

These questions could be investigated using a video synthesizer. A small video synthesizer designed for individual use would give the subject techniques for creating images on a screen. These images could be recorded as they are made, providing a visual record of concept formation. For example, four lines of varying thicknesses appear on the screen. The subject has electronic control of the lines and the ability to create various relationships among them. The subject's manipulation of these lines is recorded and the problem-solving process documented. A record of the subject's performance of the task is videotaped. Some instruction intervenes, and the subject repeats the task. Again a visual record is made, and the first tape is compared to the second. The question is asked: "Is there any improvement in the subject's ability to form a visual concept after instruction?"

This is akin to what artists are now doing with video synthesizers in such places as the Channel 13 Experimental Television Laboratory, directed by David Loxton. Here artists are given a number of ways of manipulating and controlling images, and they actually create forms on the screen that are transferred onto a videotape, forming a statement for a mass audience. The same kind of techniques could be applied to audio. A sound synthesizer controlled by the subject would provide for organizing sounds into compositions. The choices made and the sequences developed would be related to the subject's aural concept formation. Again the process would be recorded, preserved on tape for immediate playback, and analysis would be made either by the subject or by the researcher.

Arranging Sounds with Magnetic Tapes—a set of materials developed by CEMREL's Aesthetic Education Program—contains some activities appropriate for investigation as examples of a problem-solving approach to aural concept formation. A sound problem-solving situation was created that gives the student the opportunity to compose and arrange sounds at varying levels of complexity, the composer-arranger being the model. The student in each case has, in a sound library, twenty taped environmental sounds that can be arranged in different sequences through splicing sections of tape. Two sample problems are described below. The activities are for upper-elementary children.

Here is where you begin to use the sounds as a real arranger-composer would. The team will choose four sounds and arrange them into a theme. A theme is the main sound idea in a sound composition. Repeat your theme three times until your holding board is filled to slot 12. Decide how long you want each sound to last. Then make each sound last the same amount of time whenever you repeat your theme.

Listen carefully to all the sounds in the Sound Library when your teacher plays the information-narration tape again. To arrange a theme, you have to think about how the sounds sound by themselves, and how they sound next to other sounds. Decide if you want to use all fast sounds, or some fast and some slow; some high and some low, or all low; sounds that are steady and even, or sounds that are not. Whichever ones you choose, try to imagine how they will make your listeners feel. That is one of the things a composer thinks about when he or she is working.

A more advanced problem:

Arrange a three-sound theme again. Change the order and the lengths of the sounds when you repeat them. Put in silent pauses, or rests, where you think they're needed. But this time compose a sound to perform during some of the rests, instead of leaving them all silent. You can clap, sing, read, play rhythm instruments, or do anything else you can think of. In order to make this work, you have to place yourself "inside" the composition. Think about what you compose in relation to the rest of the arrangement. Does it fit in? Does it tie together? What comes before it and what follows it?

These are creative problems of increasing difficulty that have multiple solutions but also a defined set of parameters to follow.

Investigations of aural and visual concept formation are only two possible research areas for a laboratory of this kind. It could also contain settings such as those John Cataldo described at the 1965 NAEA Conference ("The Uses of Newer Media in Art Education") as

the creation of a multi-media coordinating studio involving a visual resource library and a composing studio in which images can be brought together and placed in juxtaposition. The project is one that grows out of his work in graphic communications. The purpose of the instrument is to enable students to draw upon a vast store of imagery as a resource for their own creative solutions. Visual information (organized under three major categories; cognitive, what we know; perceptual, what we see; and psychological, what we feel) would be placed in a storage retrieval unit. These images would be drawn from museums and galleries, as well as other sources of visual information (our mass media, photographs, films, etc.). The images would also be categorized within large thematic headings: people at play, death, trees, conflict, celebration, etc. A key problem in the teaching of art is that of helping students to deal with multiple possibilities instead of linear stereotyped solutions. Students need to be helped to see the poetic and imaginative aspects of ideas; they need to learn to tolerate the ambiguity of multiple possibilities.[11]

The Aesthetics of the Media

Another major area for investigation lying outside the study of the aesthetic response and visual, aural, and kinetic concept formation is the aesthetics of the technology and what it provides. What are the aesthetic qualities of the media that affect us so immediately? In a recent attempt at television programming, I found little interest on the part of the television industry in the aesthetics of the medium that they create and we all live with. When we were producing a program about the arts in everyday living, one of the subjects I thought most appropriate for inclusion was the aesthetics of the medium itself. Yet no one on the production team was willing to deal with it. Nevertheless, the questions are still there.

What *is* the aesthetic of television? Is it Laurence Olivier doing a scene from *Hamlet*? Is it a visual artist creating a video sequence using a synthesizer? Is it a well-written, well-directed situation comedy? Is it Leonard Bernstein conducting the New York Philharmonic? Or is it a one-minute commercial? Any of these, or all of them, could be part of the aesthetics of television. No investigation or research has yet tackled the question. This medium probably affects all of us more directly than any other single piece of the technology available today, and we still do not know its effect on our aesthetic values; nor do we know what aesthetic values it really promotes or defines for viewers; nor do we know all we could about how to present what we do want to promote. The aesthetics of the mass media is vital to all of us, as it affects us directly at every age and in every setting.

I have touched on only a few topics for research that a laboratory might investigate, but I feel they are important ones for "basic research" in the arts. Let me now state them more concisely as areas for investigation:

1. The nature of the aesthetic response in all the sensory modes—the oral, the kinetic, the tactile, the visual, and the olfactory;

2. The utilization of the new technology and the media as devices to record a variety of aesthetic responses, and their applicability to the collection of data on the formulations of aesthetic judgments;

3. The nature and aesthetic properties of the media themselves— concentrating first on television, then on other mass media such as recordings, radio, and film; and then leading to an investigation of presentation techniques for using the media in the school. This should answer the question: How can teacher and student use the media aesthetically to enhance their handling of information in the classroom?

One note of caution in doing research with and about the media technology is that the technology may become the subject matter rather than the problems that need to be researched. Any facility or media device should be created for solving significant problems in the field. The media technology should serve and should suggest things to the researchers, not the opposite. We have no need for a giant gadget box for researchers.

Summary

I have tried in this paper to review two areas that pose problems broad enough to be the focus of a research effort: evaluation in the arts and aesthetics, and the relationship of the arts and aesthetics to technology. Both areas have implications for the aesthetic development of the individual and for the arts and aesthetics as basic education. The question really becomes one of allocation of resources to these efforts. The strategy is simply to take on fewer and larger problems selected on the basis of national priorities and limitations of resources and expertise. To do this, three things are required: first, federal and private agencies who provide support must include the arts and aesthetics in their priorities for research and development; second, the field must set topic areas for research that will receive support; and third, both the support agencies and the arts field must respond to the aesthetic needs of schools. At this time, a target research agenda should be prepared, supported, and coordinated at the national level. This is our primary need in education in the arts and aesthetics.

St. Louis, Missouri
June 1976

FOOTNOTES

[1] For a complete review, see Madeline Kintner, *Measurement of Artistic Abilities* (New York: Carnegie Foundation, Psychological Corporation, 1933); Dale B. Harris, *Children's Drawings as Measures of Intellectual Maturity* (New York: Harcourt, Brace and World, Inc., 1963).

[2] Donald Jack Davis, Patricia K. Thuernau, Alletta Hudgens, and Betty W. Hall, *Final Report, the Arts in General Education Project Evaluation Component: Review of Formative Evaluation Activities, 1969-1971*, Vol. 1 (St. Louis, Missouri: CEMREL, Inc., 1969-1971); Stanley S. Madeja, *All the Arts for Every Child* (New York: The JDR 3rd Fund, Inc., 1973).

[3] Betty Hall, and Patricia Thuernau, "Formative Evaluation in the Aesthetic Education Program," *Council for Research in Music Education*, Bulletin No. 43 (Summer 1975).

[4] L. M. Smith, and W. Geoffrey, *The Complexities of an Urban Classroom* (New York: Holt, Rinehart and Winston, 1968).

[5] Robert Stake, ed., *Evaluating the Arts in Education* (Columbus, Ohio: Charles E. Merrill Publishing Co., 1975), page 14.

[6] Louis M. Smith, and Sally Schumacher, *Extended Pilot Trials of the Aesthetic Education Program: A Qualitative Description, Analysis, and Evaluation* (St. Louis, Missouri: CEMREL, Inc., 1972).

[7] *Studies in Art Education* (Spring 1972).

[8]Rudolf Arnheim, *Visual Thinking* (Berkeley, California: University of California Press, 1969), page 13.

[9]Stanley S. Madeja, "Early Education in the Visual Arts," *Art for the Preprimary Child,* ed. Hilda P. Lewis (National Art Education Association, 1972), pages 110-127.

[10]Kenneth Beittel, "Manipulation of Learning Set and Feedback in the Teaching of Drawing," *Studies in Art Education,* Vol. 10 (Fall 1968), pages 17-32.

[11]Reported in *Final Report of the Uses of Newer Media in Art Education Project,* NDEA Project No. 5-16-027, Vincent Lanier, Project Director (National Art Education Association, August 1966), pages 61-62.

Samella Lewis

Art and Aesthetics
(A Minority Report)

Introduction

In discussing the issue of art and minority groups in the United States, it is not possible for any one member of any of these groups to respond to the needs of all in a manner that would be satisfactory for all. Wherein minority groups may share or hold in common a number of situations and experiences, they each remain distinct, and nurture cultural characteristics that have been passed on from generation to generation.

A sense of "oneness" or "commonness" of minorities is actually interpreted in that fashion from the perspective of the dominant culture. Unfortunately, the attitude of "for us" and "for them" still prevails. Therefore, the cultural strengths of so many minorities go unused, to the detriment of the total society. The energy of many minority peoples is turned upon themselves for lack of a meaningful outlet; while the majority culture suffers because its energy is spent perpetuating a controlling position.

Of course, my statements refer to my experience as an artist, art historian, and educator of African-American heritage in the United States today; and I will elaborate on my experiences and the experiences of the African-American people, primarily.

As I look ahead from my own base in the arts, I see clearly that *one of the major research issues concerning minority groups is the development of a strong research base concerned with the major contributions of non-European cultures to the art cultures of the world.* Research has to be undertaken documenting the contributions of non-European cultures to the art cultures of the world in order to provide an accurate baseline of information to develop the complete history of the arts for this generation and future generations.

In this regard, that members of minority groups act as the principal researchers of their respective cultures is an absolute necessity. This leadership is of the utmost importance because experience has proven

SAMELLA LEWIS *is Professor of Art History at Scripps College.*

that, unless one has a full understanding of what it means to live as a minority-race person in a white-oriented culture such as the United States, then the capacity for interpretation of that culture is extremely limited. Misinterpretations and misconceptions based upon a superficial knowledge currently form the basis of interpretations of minority life — the sensibilities and the sensitivities.

If research questions in art and aesthetics are going to be of significant value, they must come from minority peoples who are concerned and interested in actively participating in the clarification, documentation, and dissemination of cultural experiences that have contributed to the whole civilization. The direction of research pertaining to minority peoples must be based on substance that is of vital importance to those within the culture, and not statistics tabulated to prove to outsiders that the investigation being made is valid, or that those investigated represent what is considered to be the acceptable norm. Frequently, real substance grows out of uniqueness and differences between individuals; and it is those differences that, when comprehended and nurtured, make important contributions to the whole society.

The Role of Art: A Minority Perspective

In the early period of the settlement of this country, art was used primarily to glorify wealth. Objects of art were imported from England that clearly defined class distinctions; and indentured servants were brought in who could reproduce these artifacts. Some of the indentured servants functioned as artisans who fashioned the jewelry, clothing, wigs, and other decorative items that were in demand by the upper class, who coveted these objects of wealth and prestige.

After the Revolutionary War, art was used to glorify the actions of those whose deeds were recognized as worthy of distinction. With this, we witness the proliferation of the limited view of history, and — as evidenced by those paintings still in existence — the making of America by white men only. The documented history reveals that Native Americans, Blacks, women, and all groups other than white males, had little or nothing to do with the founding of this country. There were no "founding mothers" or "founding Blacks." In written and pictorial history, the women who participated were there only to assist the men, while the Blacks were invisible. Native Americans were depicted at first as kind and cooperative; but, later, as they protected their property, inhibiting progress of the newcomers, they began to be depicted as savages. Indeed, art became the visual instrument that these images were transmitted through.

Throughout the first century of European settlement of this country, art continued to be regarded as a sign of affluence. Art collections became a natural part of the great houses of wealth, while at the same time establishing the owners as the taste-makers for the nation. Our museums were founded by and under the guidance and control of these wealthy contributors, who viewed themselves as representing the highest level of aesthetics available in the nation. They naturally sought to use their wealth, power, and prestige to aid in fostering the kind of artworks or artifacts they had personally chosen to be the arts of the nation they were instrumental in founding. The museums and storehouses used today as public institutions, supported by public funds, grew out of these beginnings.

Originally, when all peoples of non-European cultures were either being ignored or degraded artistically, or made to integrate their talents to produce the acceptable image, museums and storehouses were essentially used as annexes of "major" private collections. Although this still would seem to be an apt description of museums as they exist in this country, a review of the purpose of a public museum is in order.

Public museums should be institutions where all cultural groups are represented equitably. Of course, our museums would need to (1) conduct adequate research into non-European cultures of the past to clarify the data base they should have been founded upon, and, concurrently, (2) review the values these institutions were founded upon in order to incorporate all members of the society. An occasional exhibition separate from works and shows considered to be "mainstream" and/or of the "masters" is not acceptable.

Black Art: A Case in Point

Reverence for life and zest for living may be the common threads held by the survivors of the Middle Passage — and their most valuable gift to posterity. Expressed as folktales, music, and dance during the bleak years when there were neither tools, leisure, nor demand for craft products, this feeling survived. Where conditions permitted, it began to be expressed in the graphic arts. Then, when the opportunity for artistic expression returned, sculpture and painting in the New World were divorced from the religious context, and the artist no longer functioned in a socially sanctioned framework with a firm set of artistic guidelines transmitted through the apprentice tradition. The artist learned skills where he or she could — or developed his or her own, if necessary. Now, substituting for a central theme that was religious, we have instead the driving necessity of establishing a place of honor in a hostile culture for the artistic expression of the many descendants of that tough band of survivors who were brought to this country in chains. They left the appurtenances of a culture behind, but salvaged the most essential ingredient — the will to live and to love. It is the expression of this spirit, in diverse ways, and in diverse media, that we deal with now in appraising the black artist.

The late Alain Locke, former professor of philosophy at Howard University, and a leading scholar on black art, believed slavery to be one of the experiences most damaging to the creativity of black Americans. According to Locke, slavery not only physically transplanted Africans, but also cut them off sharply from their cultural roots.

In participating in the work force of the colonies, a few Blacks were able to use skills of their former crafts. However, most were relegated to the fields and were forced to communicate with each other through secret methods—some of which involved the arts. While slavery most certainly inhibited their creativity, it did not destroy it. Utilitarian pottery, dolls, bone carvings, staffs, baskets, and gravestones are items found among the various types of slave art forms. The lack of opportunities to concentrate on the creation of art objects caused a serious loss of technique for slave artisans. This reduced to a minimum the opportunities for Blacks to continue to create those fine works of art that were basic to their African tradition.

During the period of slavery, black artisans were required to produce works primarily for the use of the white slaveholders. As the nation progressed and demands for craftsmen increased, slaveholders had little choice but to use Blacks in craft positions that had been reserved for whites. The skills of slaves were used in building and furniture construction, woodcutting and engraving artistry, gold and silver smithing, cabinetmaking, printing, and portrait painting.

During the latter part of the eighteenth century, the Rev. G. W. Hobbs of Baltimore established himself as the official artist of the Methodist Episcopal Church. He is identified as the first known black artist in the United States to execute a portrait of another black person. The subject of his early pastel portrait, completed in 1785, was a former slave, Richard Allen.

Unlike artist/churchman Hobbs, other black artists such as Joshua Johnston of Baltimore spent their time capturing the likenesses of members of wealthy slave-holding families. Later, artists such as Robert S. Duncanson and Edward M. Bannister painted landscapes and seascapes, while Edmonia Lewis and Henry O. Tanner used black subjects in their works.

Following the tradition of European art, white artists of the eighteenth and nineteenth centuries were working within their cultural milieu. There was not only security in the knowledge of materials used, but familiarity with the style of the period, and, of course, the subject matter. Black artists who desired any recognition as artists were forced to encompass the prevailing European style as their own, for it was represented as the leading and only direction of the time. This limited view of art encouraged non-white artists to set aside the ideas and customs of their own cultural heritage.

During this time, Blacks were not completely ignored by white artists as the subject matter of their works. They were depicted as benevolent "darkies," or buffoons and "coons."

It was not until the 1920s that black art really began to flourish. A sense of cultural identity and awareness was evident in the arts. Although the Abolitionist movement had offered some opportunities for the projection of self-image for black artists, it was not until the period of the Harlem Renaissance that this came to fruition.

Through the efforts of Alain Locke, W. E. B. DuBois, Marcus Garvey, and numerous other notable black figures during this period, black artists and writers were encouraged to look towards Africa for resources. Those who accepted the charge produced art genres that depicted black people involved in their day-to-day experiences. Working in collaboration with writers, and in the presence of creative musicians, artists were able to gain a fuller sense of the collective force of ceremonies and celebrations that have contributed so much to black creativity.

The periods of the 1930s and 1940s reflect similar directions in the styles practiced by most artists in the United States. They included a realistic, regionalist style; an abstract, Cubist style influenced by African art; and a dramatic, mural style wherein the major influences can be traced to the Revolutionary artists of Mexico. The genre/regionalist art was a major factor in the social and economic reconstruction of the nation following the period of the Great Depression. The nature of the subject matter and the financial support given to individual artists through the W. P. A. enabled numerous minority artists to open studios for the first time and to express themselves on a more personal basis.

Those artists who were influenced philosophically and content-wise by the Revolutionary mural art of Mexico became the subject of great concern to government authorities. This concern led to a lessening of opportunities and a general boycotting by museums and galleries of artists whose works were labeled as propaganda.

The 1950s and 60s witnessed a clear break from the traditional directions in art in the United States. The rigid standards of traditional European art were all but abandoned, and subsequent styles were developed based on tendencies and characteristics of art in non-European cultures. In spite of the fact that the styles that developed were related to and meaningful for minority artists in the United States, the opportunities to participate significantly in the social and economic program were limited.

Today, avenues of approval through exhibits and other forms of distribution continue to be in the hands of a coterie of people whose approval is necessary before works are suitable for public consumption.

Conclusion

It can be said that art results from a deep-rooted urge to modify, to introduce order into experiences, and to reflect personal interpretation of emotional and intellectual experiences. Art covers a range of activities as wide as the basic experiences of life itself. The desire to re-create and share these experiences with others is there because they are emotionally significant and intellectually meaningful.

This ordering of experiences follows principles that can be found in nature and in human desires — principles suggesting that ideas and emotions be filled into some unified design or plan of action. Consequently, a work of art becomes a whole experience that reflects a unity of effort. To organize experience in this way, to incorporate into it order and design demands a logical procedure or plan of action that will aid in insuring that feelings and thoughts become intelligible. The strength of art, therefore, lies in the structure that derives from an inner desire to impart to the world an order which, in varying degrees, is present in all activities.

Is there some possibility that thinking people might find in art ethical values that have been overlooked? Art is the process of intelligence by which humans turn creative products into statements of their condition. It offers the means for individuals to conceptualize ideas and render them comprehensible. It is an important carrier of civilization and, in addition, serves as an antenna capable of guiding individuals and keeping them in touch with the undercurrents of their times.

Art can satisfy a felt need for activities that confirm people as individuals. It provides opportunities to deal with feelings and emotions, where individuals can place their experiences into value relationships and where necessary feelings of importance and uniqueness can be sustained. One of the basic issues that divides the world today revolves around the importance of the individual. The arts are one of the few remaining areas that offer the individual the potential to remain an effective and controlling agent. The works of contemporary artists seem to reflect the necessary right of each person to individuality. It is important to recognize that each person is unique; and that this uniqueness, when seen in relationship, can become an asset. An enormous potential resides in the use of the arts as a means of developing understanding among peoples of the world.

What can be done, *now,* at this juncture in history — especially within the field of education — to explore the possibilities of the arts to assist all peoples (i.e., minorities, women, children, *and* men) to express creatively their uniqueness?

Research that relates the children, the arts, and education, might be approached as follows: Does the use of open, reinforcing experiences in the arts (i.e., the exploration of media and of self through the use of media) assist in the young child's transition from the home and/or familiar environment to the learning environment of a public-school setting? Does the literal or symbolical exploration of self through the use of media assist the student in the process of learning the more academically oriented subjects? Describe the process whereby this happens. What qualities would one enumerate as necessary for a teacher in such a setting? If this research proves positive and fruitful, how can it be reinforced and promoted within the total public-school setting?

The above research should be considered in the light of developing a more complete education for each individual from the time he or she enters school to completion. This research is suggested because a more humanistic philosophy, combined with clear, responsible thinking and planning, is essential for survival.

And what of those citizens — Asians, Blacks, Latinos, and women (adults now) — who find themselves in an environment that has denied them full representation in the artistic tradition, and which for the most part has inhibited their creative expression? Assistance is needed to work with the institutions (i.e., local and national governments, museums, local education institutions, etc.) created by people with limited vision, to expand the possibilities for all citizens to participate in the restructuring of a more equitable and creative system.

A review of the development of the arts in America is helpful in showing us how we reached our present position, as well as showing us possible inroads available or pitfalls inherent in the situation. According to our history, this country was founded principally by people of European ancestry, and it is natural that they should attempt to preserve their art forms and cultural heritage. Problems arise in our democracy when the European heritage is continually imposed upon other members of the society — some of whom were already here; others who came freely and willingly to seek a life where freedom of expression, within bounds agreed to by all, could be practiced; and still others who were brought in chains. All, however, chose to remain to contribute and participate further in the development of this country.

Minority peoples are asking, not unjustly, for fuller representation in the arts of America. History has proven that this is difficult to obtain. How this representation, which gives support culturally, spiritually, and economically, is to be accomplished remains unresolved and unanswered. In view of the artistic climate that has existed for so long in the United States, how is it possible to make the necessary changes that will permit any major degree of participation on the part of minorities within this system where the lines are so clearly drawn? Is it possible to make the necessary changes in the educational system that would bring about any meaningful participation in the arts by larger numbers of groups and individuals?

The rationale for conducting research over the next ten years on any one of the issues raised herein is to induce some measure of change and to slow down a dependency upon a system that is based on limited vision and indoctrination. Unless real changes are made in our system of education through the arts and humanities, it will be impossible to think of art as a meaningful aspect in the lives of Americans.

In the current crunch for funds, school systems throughout the nation have reduced services to the bare essentials. Concern with aesthetics through art, music, and dance is not included; and the number of teacher specialists in those fields has been reduced drastically. There is no rationale for conducting research over the next ten years on any one or more of the issues raised in this paper unless we are serious about support for the findings — support in the form of money for research, money for implementation.

Some research related to these questions has already been done. However, because the results are sometimes counter to established beliefs, findings have been set aside to drift away and be forgotten. Those persons who advocate change are seldom heard. They seem drowned out by the ongoing momentum of "business as usual."

Claremont, California
May 1976

BIBLIOGRAPHY

Davidson, Basil. *The African Past.* New York: Grosset and Dunlap, 1967.

DuBois, W. E. B. *The Supression of the African Slave Trade.* New York: Schocken Books, 1967.

Franklin, John Hope. *From Slavery to Freedom.* New York: Vintage Books, 1967.

Lewis, Samella. *ART: African America.* New York: Harcourt Brace Jovanovich, 1976.

Locke, Alain, ed. *The Negro in Art.* New York: Hacker Art Books, 1968.

Porter, James A. *Modern Negro Art.* New York: Arno Press and the New York Times, 1969.

Porter, James A. "The Transcultural Affinities of African Negro Art." *Africa Seen by American Negroes,* ed. John Davis. Paris: Presence Africaine, 1958.

Lionel Landry

The Arts in Multicultural Education:
The Case for Asia

I

The purpose of the traditional art teacher in imparting the usual Western art syllabus has lain somewhere between teaching a skill or a métier and inculcating art "appreciation." More adventuresome teachers have sharpened student perceptions of such things as volume, space, color, rhythm, sound and timbre, and the quality of movement; and the most successful have been able to get away from the "All right, children, now let's do art" approach and to introduce their subject in an almost subliminal way.

Whatever the purpose and method, however, the objectives of aesthetic education have generally remained quite squarely in the aesthetic realm. Study of the Asian arts has also tended to remain on a purely aesthetic plane — even in those few institutions that have had the imagination to approach it at all.

This could well represent an opportunity missed. Valid though the painting and sculpture, the decorative arts, and the literary media of Asia may be as purveyors of aesthetic delight, they can yield far more than a purely aesthetic awareness of the forms and processes of the world or a heightened response to an aesthetic experience. The Asian arts can and should be made to reveal something of the quality of Asian life itself; aesthetic education can be a vital ally to social studies and humanities curricula.

To put it differently, aesthetic education can also have a purpose outside the world of aesthetics — at least where Asia's aesthetic canons are concerned — and the same could be said, of course, of those of pre-Columbian America, of the American Indian today, and of Africa's cultures. Multicultural education, in other words, can almost ideally be conveyed through the arts.

One can enunciate three assumptions in regard to Asia's great aesthetic experience:

    1. The arts of Asia are a crystallization of the values of the Asian
       society concerned and an expression of them;

LIONEL LANDRY *is Executive Vice-President of The Asia Society.*

2. Study of the Asian arts can yield perceptions of aesthetic worth and perceptions of the value system of the people who created them;

3. The arts of Asia are very much involved with ethics and norms of interpersonal behavior.

Though much research remains to be done, experimental projects in the St. Louis area have shown that the Asian arts can and *do* communicate to fifth-grade students something not only of the aesthetic but also of the social values of an "exotic" culture like, for instance, that of Japan. A plan devising new teaching approaches and materials for this purpose has been devised by CEMREL, Inc., in association with The Asia Society, tested in the St. Louis area public schools, and found to be effective.

In terms of pure aesthetics, the experiment dealt with the basic Japanese canons of asymmetry, respect for the inherent nature of materials, and economy of means in execution. (These reflect such traditional traits of Japan's culture as observation and love of nature, the Shinto reverence for indwelling spirits of materials, and the graceful austerities of the Zen heritage.) The materials and methods were designed and tested among children in three distinct socioeconomic environments in the St. Louis area. The children's experience was described by evaluators as surprisingly profound; lasting cognitive and affective impressions appear to have been created in all three groups. A prototype learning unit is now ready for production and distribution.*

Early plans are now being made for a similar approach to another Asian culture through the arts, that of Java, utilizing "hands-on" materials associated with the shadow-puppet theater. Also in the planning stage is a project to design mathematics/geometry-teaching methods and materials utilizing the basic design concepts of Islamic decorative arts. This is expected to promote an understanding of the principles of Islamic two-dimensional design, which will also provide an insight into the actual philosophical and ethical world view of the Muslims, not to mention angles, chords, radii, and even such advanced concepts as rotational symmetry.

The objective — devising methods and materials in the field of aesthetics that also reveal something of the socio-cultural backgrounds of Asian art forms — can be achieved. There is much investigation left to be done, however. Research is needed that would center on such topics as these:

1. Identification of specific aspects of Asian civilizations lending themselves to multimedia, multidisciplinary, manipulative materials and methods of introducing Asian systems of values and belief, as the aesthetic canons of Asia's arts reveal them;

---

*Inquiries about the instructional unit on Japan should be addressed to Aesthetic Education Program, CEMREL, Inc., 3120 59th Street, St. Louis, MO 63139.

2. Grade levels at which specific intellectual, social, or metaphysical aspects of Asian cultures can be handled by pupils within an aesthetic education framework;

3. Identification of types or combinations of learning materials that enrich perceptions on the affective as well as the cognitive levels, that can best transmit to the teacher and the student a vivid sense of participation in Asian life — an experience at the farthest possible remove from reading "about" Asia among the dry typographical bones of an idea on a printed page.

There are answers to such problems. Some already have been found and successfully put to the test. A great many more problems need to be solved; but the fact that solutions are now possible should give impetus to a great deal more searching — and to the quest for research funds.

II

At this point someone is sure to ask, "Why encumber concepts of asymmetry with biology as the Japanese see it, or purely aesthetic ideas with the notions of the lives and loves of the Javanese?" The answer is that they cannot in fact be separated; just as in Western art, for most of our history, aesthetic notions could not be separated from religion, philosophy, or secular concepts upholding or challenging traditional social structures. Fra Angelico was a religious artist whose vision concentrated on a blissful Heaven. Leonardo da Vinci, while not forswearing the Divine, focused on mankind and the exciting potentialities of the human mind. Daumier challenged the rising nineteenth-century bourgeois-industrial values and beliefs of Europe, just as Fragonard had earlier enshrined in his painting the delicate pleasures of an idealized aristocracy. Art for art's sake is a recent, and perhaps sterile, phenomenon.

And why Asia? Why don't we explore our own Western traditions and aesthetics as Chartres embodies them, or as Goya or Picasso, Palestrina or Webern, John Singleton Copley or Jackson Pollack expressed them? The answer is that Western masterpieces are brought, by the mass media and mass education, into a common ken impossible to foresee a century ago. At station breaks, the background "logo" of a commerical television channel in New York features scenes from El Greco and other European masters. The news weeklies and even the daily press now carry art news as featured stories. One hundred and fifty years ago, you had to be wealthy — and preferably an English milord — to visit Chartres or marvel at the Acropolis. A surprising lot of people today know about the Elgin Marbles (though few have learned their pronunciation), and Picasso is a household word.

Western art, in other words, is familiar. The values it celebrates are, at least in the shadowy recesses of the collective memory, not unfamiliar or novel to people in the Western world, including Americans.

Why Asia? There are important reasons. For all our military involvement in Asia over the last generation, Asia remains as resolutely a *terra incognita* in the American mind as Lapland. Its art, though incomparably rich and sophisticated, matters so little in the West that the successful BBC/Lord Clark television feature series called "Civilisation" focused entirely on the arts of the Mediterranean and Europe. The implication for Asia's civilizations is clear: They simply do not exist.

In the orthodox view of archaeology and art history, "civilisation" is uniquely something that lies to the West of the Tigris and Euphrates Rivers. The magic of the unknown bronze-caster who makes a Siva, Lord of the Dance, is not less than the magic of Cellini. But "civilisation," in this view, holds no place for the dancing Siva, for the Buddhas of Gandhara, or the architectural refinements of the Katsura Detached Villa and its exquisitely thoughtful gardens in Kyoto. The challenge to Mont Saint-Michel of the great temples of Pagān and Angkor remains unheard and unanswered.

Why Asia?

Within a very few years Asians will make up two thirds of the world's population.

Only the Pacific Ocean, reduced by supersonic air travel to a thin ribbon of water, will throw up a physical barrier to Asia. In terms of flight time, Seattle and Tokyo will be almost contiguous.

Yet the psychological gulf remains immense. Ease of physical transport will bring not only continents but ideas into virtual contact, perhaps into actual collision. Previous understanding will be the solvent; knowledge may make peaceful what otherwise can only be a painful confrontation. We cannot, except at our great peril, overlook two thirds of humankind today and still expect a peaceful world for our own children.

Our children, however, are seldom being reached with any effectiveness on matters Asian; and, when they are, one can take little satisfaction at the quality and amount of what they are taught. The Ford Foundation recently funded an evaluation, by The Asia Society, of the Asian content in the most commonly used textbooks (K-12) to be found in schools across the country.* A few series and individual titles fared well at the hands of the specialists who judged them. Most, however, could do with revision and many were deemed inadmissible.

The information offered by most of the textbooks runs the gamut from the patronizing to the false, via stereotypes of Asian poverty, backwardness, mechanical ineptitude, superstition, squalor, and oppression. Asian efforts at modernization are portrayed in laudatory terms, one suspects, principally because these authors assume that Asians should, ideally, become very much like us.

An almost all-pervasive feature of the books studies is a lack of affective immediacy in their treatment of life in Asia. The height of an Indian dam, the length of the Yangtze, or figures on the population of

---

*The volume reporting this study, titled *Asia in American Textbooks: An Evaluation*, was published in March 1976, by The Asia Society, Inc., 112 East 64th Street, New York, NY 10021.

Tokyo cannot even hint at the underlying outlooks of Indians, Chinese, or Japanese — nor can data on demographic growth, gross national product, or the quickening pace of technological advancement. The noblest and most moving aspects of Asian life are not presented in text or illustration at all; or, when they are, they are sanitized both by the author's basic unfamiliarity and by the need to be "objective." Hardly any thought is given to understanding how Asians perceive their universe; or what they think is good, beautiful, and useful in their own terms.

The joy of perfected movement in the work of a Chinese calligrapher or painter of scrolls is scarcely ever mentioned. Passages from Asia's literatures, great and immediate purveyors of affective insights, hardly ever appear. The tremendous symbolization in Siva's cosmic dance, captured in bronze, remains untapped. The arts and humanities, powerful instruments for comprehension of Asian life, are not normally even a modest ally to the social studies teacher; and Asia remains, at best, an object of unimpassioned cognition.

The Ford Foundation/Asia Society textbook report suggests the need for a sweeping revision of the way our children's schoolbooks represent Asia. But even the best textbooks have limitations where Asian cultures are concerned. Pictures of Hindu temples will not necessarily open a view into the vastness of Hinduism's fundamental concepts; and some of the basic concepts of Chinese art — and life — might be learned more appropriately, for instance, on a kitchen counter than on a printed page.

Chinese cuisine is a high art, intimately related to a highly particular Taoist view of the universe. Use of the knife and the flame are very special. Chicken, mushrooms, nuts, pork, green vegetables, all require a special approach to slicing and cutting — an approach based on a keen understanding of texture, grain, body, and resistance.

The knife must be handled in *wu wei,* that is, in accord with the inherent way of things, with the forces of nature itself, as these are part of the Taoist universe. The story of T'ing the Butcher is a superb example of working *with* nature, of letting nature help develop the skill at hand. T'ing's knife always followed the "empty" spaces between sinews or between bones and sockets, so that it met with no resistance and never needed honing. Man's way, when at one with the Way of the universe and not at cross-purposes, is effortless and brings a kinesthetic thrill of a very special nature. That the concept finds one of its expressions in China's cookery is perhaps not to be wondered at.

The fact is that, in traditional Chinese aesthetics, T'ing the Butcher and the Confucian scholar-painter both felt the ultimate creative pleasure, the joy of perfected movement. Shoulder, arms, hands, torso were trained so that one swing of the knife or one stroke of the brush was a thing of beauty and effectiveness in itself. In the painter this one movement of the body and the arm, with the ink-brush as its extension, when perfected, could bring into the painting a life-force, called *ch'i* by the Chinese, which gave life to the painting itself. Training was first for the managing of *wu wei*, or acting in consonance with the forces of nature. Perfection of movement could only come afterward, and both were needed if *ch'i* were to come into the painting, or the perfect calligraphy, or the perfectly executed platter of food — no matter how modest — or the basic movements of *t'ai-chi-ch'uan* — perfected movement for its own sake and itself an aesthetic affair.

Such attitudes are deeply rooted in Chinese culture. All the other great cultures of Asia have distinctive outlooks, expressed and embodied in their arts perhaps as nowhere else.

Understanding — a real human understanding — of Asians, not just "Asia," is becoming an urgent need for Americans. Except in a few states with praiseworthy foresight, American education ignores Asia. And, where Asian cultures are the objects of study, the affective input of the aesthetic factor is generally neglected, potentially helpful though it is.

III

It is one thing to have the aesthetic canons of Asia as useful complements to the factual and objective presentations on Asia made in social studies. It is quite another to use these aesthetic canons as means in themselves in order to provide socio-cultural insights, or as keys to unlock not-so-mysterious doors into Asian world views.

What is involved here is not merely studying about these Asian world views as revealed in the arts in textbooks, although that would mean a considerable improvement in itself over what students must read now. What is involved is a multisensory, manipulative approach to an understanding of certain Asian aesthetic canons and their application through use of "hands-on" materials, as guided by audio and visual models and a student book, as well as by a teacher furnished with his or her own background and guidance texts.

The CEMREL/Asia Society project shows that such an approach can provide benefits not only in the aesthetic realm but in the social realm too. This having been demonstrated, one can take heart for the development of many similar teaching units on Asia, with the arts as the doorways to real social understanding.

America has extraordinary resources on which to draw in the design of such units as CEMREL's on Japan, mentioned earlier. First there are the scholars, the academic specialists in Asian affairs. In the United States, more than anywhere else on earth, the last thirty years have seen unparalleled intensification of scholarly investigation of Asia and Asian life. The membership of the Association for Asian Studies, the guild of professional Asianists in this country, now numbers more than 5,000. Expertise flourishes in dozens of disciplines and fields of study. No other country has a similar body of knowledge in its midst.

Until recently, however, the scholar has played a very small role in the broader areas of education. Some evaluators of the textbooks surveyed in the Ford Foundation/Asia Society study were shocked that their scholarly investigations were so little reflected in the works they examined. They expressed dismay at the long-bearded stereotypes dating from ages past that still were offered in educational materials. If one can generalize from their reaction, it is safe to say that the scholars will now quickly consent to being consulted by textbook authors and publishers alike, and by designers of multimedia teaching units. Certainly their active participation in improving general education on Asia would bring a vitally important national resource into play. The rise of a new scholarly discipline, "ethnosociology," already provides hope that we may pinpoint aspects of Asian cultural and aesthetic life susceptible to treatment in multimedia learning units.

There are also the great collections of the Asian visual arts. These dot the country. Boston, New York, Philadelphia, Washington, Cleveland, Chicago, Kansas City, Seattle, San Francisco, and Los Angeles have long had world-important collections of masterpieces of Asian art. Growing new collections are to be found elsewhere, too, as in Dallas. Taken together, these works outshine in variety and quality the Asian collections of any other nation by far, forming an incalculable reservoir of visual resources.

These treasures are available for designers and authors of new teaching materials, just as the scholars are there to be consulted on subject matter. And there exists the new methodology for translating Asian aesthetic concepts into physical "hands-on" learning materials, particularly in the trans-cultural field. Having isolated the topics or canons it wishes to treat, CEMREL devised the whole process whereby the idea was translated into material. As the process goes on, classroom participation is enlisted, not merely for testing and evaluation, but for the sake of co-creation by teacher and pupil. Ideas are tried out, thrown away, modified, and adopted as groups of children demonstrate the aptness or the inaptness of the ideas and materials presented. This goes on throughout the creative process, not merely once the prototype is ready for the more conventional tryout. All of which is to say that we now know how to prepare materials that use aesthetic education to provide insights into the life of Asia — where art, work, life, and the gods form one indivisible whole.

Publishers represent still another great resource. For all the faults about Asia one seems to lay at publishers' doors, their attitudes are no different from those of almost everyone else in our American culture. Their assumptions, conscious and unconscious, about American values and beliefs, and the extent of their knowledge of Asia, are in no way dissimilar to those of even the educated American public; and this obviously includes the teachers and curriculum developers, as well as the editors, newscasters, and filmmakers, who bring the Asia of the mass media before the public.

Most publishers are businesspeople with an eye to the bottom line of a balance sheet and another to the front row of stockholders' meetings. If it can be demonstrated to them that a reasonable demand exists for a new approach to teaching about Asia, and if their risk capital is sufficient, there is no reason to expect them not to put before the public as good a product as the public demands.

This brings us to the teacher, probably America's most underrated national resource. Pre-service training and general education have not, in the main, prepared our teachers to deal with the massive unfamiliarities of Asia, however pressing the need they feel to deal with it in their classrooms. Perhaps more than most, they sense the urgency of understanding the Asian people and of passing this understanding on to their pupils.

They know that David Carradine's *kung-fu* is suspect as authentic Asian experience; that the *samurai* performances of Toshiro Mifune are more nostalgia than history; and that the late shows with Warner Oland and others as Mr. Moto, or Luise Rainer as Pearl Buck's Olan, reflect an Orient that has been refracted several times away from reality. Yet the proof and the framework for proof are missing.

The textbook becomes the unavoidable crutch. And the textbook is the work of qualified educators, presumably people who know both how to teach *and* how to present Asia — and one takes the latter on a faith inspired by the former. So Asia's billions go on being represented to the children of the world's most powerful democracy by the highly limited and limiting perceptions of the authors, who often carry what is perceived as endorsement of Asian content in their degree from graduate schools of education.

How to break the circle? How to bring into concerted action the great resources the nation possesses?

The teacher in aesthetic education may hold the key.

IV

If one assumes the successful development of a new approach to teaching about Asia — one that works on an almost subliminal level, that leads the student step-by-step across both cognitive and affective terrain, that is based on a facet of a given Asian world view, that separates neither art nor Asia from the student's "real" world, and that has developed a valid teacher's guide as well as necessary audiovisual and "hands-on" materials; and, if one assumes its introduction into the classroom, then one can expect a number of interesting results. Some of these results could well be the following:

1. Attention to an Asian art and an Asian society without consciousness of a grinding trans-cultural shifting of gears;
2. "De-exoticizing" of Asian art canons and societies;
3. A conscious sharing of humanity *through*, not *despite*, the art of a "different" culture;
4. A gradual adoption into the students' own frame of reference the aesthetic canon — and often the ethical/social ideals — of the Asian society at hand;

5. A lowering, consequently, of the threshold of resistance to "foreign" and especially Asian concepts;
6. Ultimately, a heightened appreciation of aesthetic experience as such, and of concepts of skill-development, creativity, and discipline; and
7. Ultimately, also, on the social level, a lessening of bias and prejudice arising from unconscious assumptions in the society at large about Asia and Asians — or, on a positive note, a heightened awareness and appreciation of some of the fundamental outlooks of Asian civilizations as embodied *and practiced* in their arts.

Preliminary evidence that one may expect some or all these things to happen on a fifth-grade level was furnished in the testing that CEMREL conducted at the three St. Louis schools serving as centers of co-creation and testing. While results and reports varied a bit from school to school, and additional variables arose according to the drive and the perceptions of individual teachers using the materials, the critics who evaluated teacher and student response found a high general level of effectiveness.

The socioeconomic levels of the three test sites varied from the depressed to the affluent, adding yet another potential variable. On this latter score, however, no difference in the effectiveness of the materials and methods was perceived. This is of some importance, as culturally deprived inner-city students had been expected to have a less fully developed frame of reference for absorbing the new experiences than would the children of more wide-reading and travel-wise households in better economic situations. That this was not so yielded the greatest satisfaction in the testing and evaluation of the pilot materials.

There is no reason to foresee any failure in the replication elsewhere of the means, and the success, of these trials and tests done in St. Louis. The scenario laid down for the teacher's guidance, the student materials, and above all the high-quotient affective and manipulative elements provided throughout allow for flexibility and a good deal of adaptation to each learning situation within the overall scheme.

It might be well to add a note on teacher reactions. Most had never had contact with Japanese aesthetics and, beyond newspaper accounts and television screenings of Japanese films, had had little information, if any, on the nature of the Japanese outlook on life and nature. They shared, thus, the new insights of the students with as much intensity as the students themselves.

While the teachers were cognizant of the entire step-by-step scenario in advance, the students were not. Yet, as the teachers led them through the application of basic canons to the Japanese garden, the *tokonoma* (a place reserved for art display), ink-brush calligraphy, scroll painting, scroll making, the step-by-step creation of a symbolic teahouse, *ikebana* or flower arranging, ceramics, and as culmination the human and social interaction in the elaborate etiquette of the tea ceremony, the cumulative effect seemed as positive among the teachers as among the students.

Of necessity, there have to be makeshifts used in the actual materials at hand, and a Japanese person might agree in general or disagree in detail that some of the audiovisual elements utilized are helpful. This being said, there seemed to be no question of the authenticity of the *concepts* learned about Japanese aesthetics, Japanese views on nature and life, and the refinement that still is a characteristic of formal art and formal interpersonal relations in Japan — whatever the coarseness one may perceive in more comradely relationships there.

Teachers shared in the student's experience, despite the fact that they had *a priori* a picture of the total process and the students did not. The exercise was one of common discovery of pleasurable and satisfying knowledge about an "exotic" society that had shed its differences and revealed a glimpse of humankind's essential oneness.

V

The materials on Japan used in the process described above were brought to a prototype level and were tested in pilot programs. We now need funds to manufacture and distribute the finished teaching units in substantial numbers, not only to in-service and pre-service training programs, but to school systems. More especially, we need funding for investigative research on the aspects of other Asian cultures most likely to yield similar programs, be they on Java, the Islamic world, India, China, Viet Nam, or other Asian societies.

Funding — assuming eventually the successful manufacture and marketing of the Japanese materials — would also be required for the following:

1. Exploration, with cadres of academic and other experts, of various culture traits in a number of Asian civilizations, with a further view to seeing in what ways the aesthetics of a civilization can be conveyed to American students — and in what ways the aesthetics can also reflect for American children something of the realities of the social and ethical values of that civilization.

2. Identification by smaller specialist cadres of the art form to be adopted — drama, shadow-play, mask making, visual arts, decorative arts — as best illustrating basic aesthetic canons of a certain Asian culture; and recommendations on the manner of "translating" these canons into specific teaching scenarios and into methods and materials.

3. Translation of cadre recommendations into actual method and materials: pedagogical steps designed, textbooks written, visuals employed, audio components selected, teacher's guides developed — the whole being an editorial process.

4. Evaluation and co-creation of materials, as they are developed, in actual classroom situations, with editorial adjustments made in the light of successful or unsuccessful testing.

5. Preparation in prototype of materials devised and tested; package-design.

6. Manufacture, promotion, and distribution of the final product.

The range of funding needs would vary according to the number and expense of cadre meetings and of viable projects these would produce. It is not an exaggeration to say that at least a dozen Asian projects might be outlined, and probably a good many more.

Since standard unit costs could be anticipated for the writing, editing, testing, creation of prototype, and final distribution of each of the teaching units, these costs would have to be multiplied by the number of viable units the cadres might recommend and for which a total design would have to be devised and implemented.

The project process might be modest in the numbers of facets of Asian culture it interprets to Americans. Responding to the urgency of the need for trans-Pacific understandings, on the other hand, it might also be one of important dimensions.

This would be aesthetic-education-plus. The transcultural communication made possible would be an added bonus when joined to the underlying purposes of education for the arts: broadened and refined perceptions, heightened self-awareness, and human enrichment.

New York, New York
May 1976

Elliot W. Eisner

Thoughts on an Agenda for Research and Development in Arts Education

Conducting a broadly defined program of research is one of the vehicles a profession uses to keep itself intellectually alive. Through research, and the journals that serve as its teachers, new ideas are presented, examined, and revised, and the stimulus for inquiry into the problems of the field is made available to its members. Such inquiry is normally the result of the particular interests of individual scholars; and although there are styles of inquiry and fashionable programs that emerge from time to time within the profession, there has not been a national research agenda in arts education that might more rationally and systematically generate insights, if not answers, into the problems the field faces. Research in arts education is best characterized as a piecemeal approach: Whatever connections one makes across research projects are more the result of the reader's efforts at synthesis than of a plan intentionally designed to facilitate them.

While such an approach to the problems of the field has a great many virtues — problems change in educational practice, individual scholars may be interested in "offbeat" problems that eventually prove productive, different levels of schooling and different geographic and cultural areas have different needs — the identification and pursuit of the field's generic research needs through a funded research program over time is one important way to foster intellectual growth and to improve educational practice. Thus, the first task in building such a program is to identify the areas needing study and the kinds of problems within those areas that appear significant. What follows is my attempt to identify a few of the major research areas in arts education, to describe why I believe each of the areas to be important, and to identify a few of the problems within them in order to illustrate what might be undertaken.

Status Studies of the Arts in American Schools
Although it is one of the "easiest" types of projects that might be

---

ELLIOT W. EISNER *is Professor of Education and Art at Stanford University.*

conducted, studies of the status of the arts in American schools have been undertaken only rarely. I refer here to statistical descriptions of important dimensions of the field such as, but not limited to, the number of arts teachers working full-time in their fields in elementary and secondary schools and the trends over time regarding their employment. For example, we do not have reliable information in the field of art education about the number of art teachers in this country, nor do we know whether the figure has increased or decreased over the past decade. We do not know whether enrollment in the arts has changed significantly since, say, 1970, or whether students would elect more work in the arts at the secondary level if they had the opportunity.

The last study of a comprehensive nature was conducted by the National Education Association[1] in 1961, but the data that study provided are now fifteen years old and might not accurately represent the current situation. What is greatly needed is a bi-annual national survey of the arts in American schools that would provide the field with dependable status data on the educational health of the arts. Such data could include not only enrollment figures in the various arts, but trends in employment patterns, such as the availability of supervisory personnel in arts education; trend data on the types of curricula that are offered; workloads of arts teachers; criteria used for their employment; level of funds allocated to support arts programs; and the like. Such data could be analyzed by type of school district, region of country, state, and through other criteria that would provide pertinent information for national policy-making bearing upon arts education.

The development of such a survey could be constructed through the joint efforts of the major professional arts-education groups and, with the technical assistance of survey specialists (the National Opinion Research Center at the University of Chicago, for example), research could be undertaken, if funding was available. The information that such a survey could provide would help arts educators and educational policy-makers to locate trends, and could enable them to anticipate serious problems in the field. For example, in many school districts at the present time, arts teachers are being reassigned to other responsibilities within the school or school district and, in some cases, are being dismissed from their positions. At the same time, federal funds are being used to support artists in schools; which, in turn, creates the impression that the arts in American schools are growing and healthy. Just what *is* the current situation? Are artists in the schools replacing arts teachers? Are school districts reducing the number of arts teachers on their faculties? Is enrollment in the arts diminishing, remaining the same, or growing? Presently, there is no bank of nationally developed data that would allow one to answer these questions with confidence. Yet, surely the questions are important, and just as surely the data needed to answer them could be secured. At a minimum, arts educators ought to develop and implement a survey research program that would provide information that describes the basic parameters of the field.

Descriptive Studies of the Teaching of the Arts

Educational research, as it has typically been pursued, has attempted to isolate particular variables that influence specific forms of learning. The well-controlled experiment, usually modelled after an experiment in the physics laboratory, has historically represented the model of scientific rigor that educational scientists have attempted to emulate. While the well-designed experiment has its place in educational research, it is not the only mode for creating educationally relevant knowledge. We need, for example, to find out what goes on in classrooms where the arts are taught. We need to examine critically the forms of teaching students are exposed to, the types of content in the arts they come into contact with, and the kinds of environment all of this occurs in. To learn about the educational context and the quality of teaching and curriculum that are provided in schools, the first necessity is to be in schools in order to find out. What we do not have, either in general education or in arts education, are vivid portrayals of educational life as it is provided and experienced by teachers and students. What actually is taught in the name of the arts in the elementary schools of this country? What goes on in the teaching of music for adolescents? What is the general quality of the visual arts that children in schools create? Have competency-based orientations in education influenced the teaching of the arts? What consequences, if any, has the accountability movement had upon curriculum and teaching methods in the arts, and in what ways has it influenced evaluation practices?

Questions such as these could serve as general foci for what I refer to as "educational criticism."[2] In general, educational critics do for educational practice what art critics do for the arts: They attempt to create a vivid description, interpretation, and evaluation of what they encounter so that others not possessing the critic's level of connoissuership might also see what has transpired. Educational critics write educational criticism; they supplement such criticism with photographs, slides, recordings, videotapes. They attempt to create an understanding of the character and quality of educational life.

In some respects, all of us have impressions of what goes on in the arts in the schools; but often these impressions are from the distant past, and things often change. Even more often, our current experience in the public schools is very brief and yields information that might not adequately represent—and, at times, perhaps distorts—the reality being experienced by the students and teachers in whom we are interested. The creation of educational criticism could—if appropriately planned in a variety of schools, fields, and locales—enhance our understanding of the character of arts education now being provided in schools.

It could be that, through such criticism, what we now believe to be the major problems facing arts education might change. For example, in what ways, if at all, does the allocation of time within elementary and secondary schools influence what can be taught and learned in the arts? What is the level of artistic sensitivity and understanding that arts teachers reveal in their teaching? If, as some sociologists claim, the behavior of individuals is dominantly influenced by the social and organizational structure in which they function, then significant change in arts education might require a change in the structure of schooling itself. If, however, it was found that the majority of arts teachers are basically uninformed about the arts and and insensitive to their most important qualities, then other kinds of changes would be necessary for strengthening arts education. What I therefore envision is the creation of a descriptively rich series of educational criticisms dealing with the character and quality of arts education as it is provided in American schools. Such a series should be useful in creating generalized forms of understanding based upon what now transpires in schools. Such criticism would enable readers to get a feel for educational practice, because telling educational criticism is constituted in a fashion that allows the reader to participate vicariously in the situation being described—something that scientific forms of descriptions, typically reductionistic and abstracted into quantity, seldom succeed in doing. In sum, the availability of educational criticisms of arts education would help us understand what is now provided in its name in schools.

Development and Assessment of New Curriculum Materials and Pedagogical Approaches to Arts Education

At the present time, there are two federally funded curriculum-development programs in arts education in the United States: one at CEMREL, Inc., and the other at SWRL Educational Laboratory. CEM-REL's program is aimed at aesthetic education at the elementary and secondary level, and SWRL's program is geared to the art and music education of children at the primary grade level. Two programs in a nation of this size cannot possibly generate and test the curricular possibilities that might be developed for arts education. Furthermore, there has been a tendency among the federally funded laboratories and research and development centers to be preoccupied with development and dissemination, rather than with theory-building or with rigorously testing the materials they develop. This tendency to develop and market, to cultivate a positive image, and to develop a strong political lobby is, of course, due to the need to compete for federal funds in order to have the resources to keep staff employed and to maintain expensive physical plants. The cost of overhead and the need for resources to survive has, in my view, limited the amount of risk and exploratory activity that should characterize the work of national educational laboratories. It has also limited the type of curriculum-evaluation work that could serve the intellectual and practical needs of the field.

Laboratories, like art studios, should be places where people can feel free to "fail." Laboratories should be places that work at the forefront of knowledge in developmental activity. They should contribute to the field not only those materials and ideas that have been demonstrated to be successful, but also share with the field insights into the variety of its other efforts that did not work. Alas, the fiscal and political climate in Washington has made such a disposition difficult to achieve. Hence, one can understand why organizations do what they do. At the same time, the field needs fresh, imaginative approaches to curriculum development; approaches that not only will result in new forms of pedagogically useful material, but in new insights into and understanding of why certain forms of material are effective or not effective. For example, recent research into brain physiology has indicated that the right and left hemispheres perform particular functions in human consciousness and expression. It has also been suggested by students of the brain that the use or exercise of, say, right hemisphere operations prior to their crystallization during adolescence is important in maintaining cognitive elasticity. At the same time, the ability to draw upon the right hemisphere as a source of artistic conception and expression appears to be very great indeed. One could develop curriculum materials and activities derived from the implications of brain research that would intentionally attempt to strengthen the child's capacity to engage in modes of thinking that are analogical, metaphorical, synthetic, appositional, in order to increase his or her ability to appreciate and create in the arts. Such a curriculum-development program, stimulated by and derived from research on hemispheric specialization, could prove to be extraordinarily important; and, if rigorously evaluated, would yield to the field new insights into how such modes of thinking could be encouraged in a variety of the arts.

Another example of curriculum-development work that could be conducted deals with the related arts. In the literature, at the present time, there is much discussion of the virtues of "related arts," "unified arts," "allied arts," "trans-disciplinary arts," "aesthetic education," and the like. Yet there are few well-articulated models of what these notions mean conceptually, and how they would, in fact, function in the classroom. Is "unified arts" the same as "aesthetic education"? Is "related arts" like "trans-disciplinary arts," or are there significant differences? What are the assumed benefits of any of these notions? On what theoretical grounds are these assumptions made? If funding were available, individual curriculum-development groups could develop such approaches by articulating their meaning in terms more precise than those that now exist and could develop, implement, and test their effectiveness.

At present, there is, for all practical purposes, a virtual monopoly on federal funds for curriculum development. I believe this is not healthy for the field of arts education. A nation as large and as wealthy as ours should be able to support a score of programs in curriculum development in arts education. Furthermore, I believe such programs should not be funded for more than a five-year period, except under extremely unusual circumstances. Such a condition would, I believe, have two important consequences: First, it would encourage a level of productivity that might now be absent because of a tendency to perseverate in the development of curriculum materials. Second, it would encourage developers to take appropriate risks in development, since they would be aware of the fact that there was virtually no prospect for a lifetime of federally funded support for work in the development field. Such a realization should help encourage autonomy and a greater sense of intellectual adventure and professional candor. As it is now, laboratories and research and development centers feel compelled to politick, to persuade, to cultivate people and bureaucracies; in short, to do what must be done to keep funds flowing from Washington. More diversity, more autonomy, more courage to take risks and to be willing to fail, but to learn from failure would, in the long run, be far more productive for arts education. The support of such diverse efforts is sorely needed.

Development of New Approaches to the Evaluation of Artistic Learning and Experience

Evaluation has two important functions in education. One of these is to provide information useful for improving the quality of educational practice. The other is to provide information to the community to enable it to understand what has been accomplished in education and why. At the present time, the major thrust of educational evaluation has been directed to the task of demonstrating "educational payoff." "Being held accountable" has come to mean "demonstrating effectiveness." There is a host of problems with the ways educational accountability has been conceived and practiced, more than it would be appropriate to discuss here. Yet, two kinds of problems are sufficiently important to mention now. One is the tendency to expect educational development to be reducible to quantity, and the other is the impact such an expectation has upon what is emphasized in the curriculum. The former tendency results in a type of reductionism that often distorts our understanding of what has, in fact, occurred: Numbers or quantification cannot reveal most of what transpires in a classroom and they have great limitations in helping us to appreciate much of what is learned or experienced, particularly in the arts. The tendency to reduce evaluation to quantification encourages teachers and administrators to emphasize in the curriculum what can be counted and measured—thus the paradox of the evaluation procedures influencing, if not determining, the priorities within educational programs.

What we very badly need is the creation of forms of evaluation that will not do violence to our most highly cherished educational aspirations in the arts.[3] We need to develop procedures and forms of reporting that capture and convey to people who might not themselves be sophisticated in the arts what types of achievements and experience children have secured. In the field of music, when skilled performance is an aim, one might, for example, use taped sections of music played over time to illustrate and interpret to parents how individual children have learned to tone a phrase, to sustain a rhythm, or to alter a pitch.

Through comparison and contrast, supported by an educational interpretation of what has occurred, parents would be in a far better position to understand what types of learning have been fostered by an effective program in musical performance.

Similarly, we need to develop means of identifying, assessing, and presenting processes employed in visual performance. What now transpires in virtually all school districts in the country is the display of the best work produced in a classroom or school. What parents see on school walls are the products produced by individual children. What they don't see and what they don't understand are what these products represent. Children's art work is now displayed in a manner comparable to hanging a show at the New York Metropolitan Museum or the Art Institute of Chicago. What we need to do first is to have work collected over time from the same child and to identify, through the analysis of that work, the profile of learning that it represents. Then, through such an analysis, we need to provide an educational interpretation, visually as well as verbally, of what such learning means and what the relationship is between the types of artistic problems encountered and the kind of intellectual processes used and developed. Furthermore, we could supplement such an analysis with time-lapse photography of work in progress or create time-lapse film or videotape in order to illustrate and interpret the relationships between the process and its consequences as found in the work.[4]

At the present time, we have few actual models for such disclosure, but that does not mean that they could not be created. The thrust of these remarks points in two directions. First, we need to develop evaluation procedures that locate in the work and in the process that created it the kind of thinking that was going on and how the problem encountered by the student elicited such thinking. Second, once having identified such processes, we need to be able to interpret their meaning and educational significance to parents and teachers so that they can come to appreciate the value of work in the arts. In the latter area, we should be able to use nonverbal as well as verbal (oral or written) forms of reporting. Such an approach to evaluation not only would provide materials that were theoretically generative, they would also serve as potent tools for the educational edification of administrators, teachers, and parents.

The creation of new approaches to the evaluation of artistic learning and experience could have some important political consequences. At the present time, over 2,400 tests are listed in *Tests in Print*.[5] But of these, only thirty-five are in the arts. The paucity of tests and other modes of evaluation has forced arts educators either to not evaluate formally what students learn or experience, or to use tests or procedures that might be inappropriate to their aims. I frequently receive requests from art educators throughout the country for permission to use the *Eisner Art Information* and the *Eisner Art Attitude Inventories* to evaluate the effectiveness of projects for which these instruments are clearly inappropriate. The fact of the matter is that there are few standardized instruments available; and, when arts educators are obliged to use "objective" means to evaluate, they use what they can get. Such a practice can, of course, lead to disastrous results since what was, in fact, achieved may not show up on standardized instruments.

At the same time, school districts in many states are required to administer tests in reading, writing, and mathematics on an annual basis. The public is informed about the progress students make on these instruments. The absence of tests in the arts (and I am not advocating the use of standardized tests in the arts, but using tests for purposes of illustration) leaves the arts educationally vulnerable, since there is no adequate way at present to demonstrate strength or weakness in the arts within school districts or to explain to the community why the level of performance is what it is. The availability of telling forms of evaluation in the arts could function not only as a potent educational vehicle but also could have a strong positive impact on the educational values that the community holds.

Studies of the Non-artistic Consequences of Work in the Arts

To what extent, if any, does work in the arts develop forms of cognition that affect competencies in areas outside of the arts? If the arts are taught and experienced aesthetically, does such experience influence one's ability to deal with "non-artistic" problems? Does the type of sensory awareness and intellectual flexibility that programs in the arts attempt to foster increase the child's ability to read or to do mathematics effectively? Questions such as these have been raised from time to time within the field, particularly when arts educators have been pressed to justify the teaching of the arts in schools where reading scores are down. By directing attention to the possible ways that arts education fosters the development of processes used in other modes of academic work, two benefits might result. First, if it were, in fact, demonstrated that work in the arts makes an important contribution to the acquisition of reading skills, for example, a stronger political case could be made for having the arts in the school curriculum. At present, national educational priorities place reading and mathematics quite high; and, when budget decisions are made, programs that are not considered central to the school's major purposes are often given low priority or are excised. If one could demonstrate that work in the arts is instrumental in achieving the educational priorities that people now hold, the case for arts education could be strengthened.

There is, of course, potential liability in justifying arts education programs *primarily* on this basis; namely, it could lead people to believe that the arts cannot be justified adequately on their own terms. This, of course, needs to be avoided. Ideally, one would not need an instrumental justification for teaching the arts in the schools, and I am not proposing that such a justification should be central to arguments for the arts in the school curriculum. Yet, if the arts do, in fact, develop intellectual processes that are useful in other fields, I not only would have no objection to such information being made available, I would urge arts educators to use such information actively in pointing out the benefits derived from work in the arts. Indeed, several of those individuals doing basic research on hemispheric specialization in the brain have themselves pointed out that the arts have an important contribution to make to the development of human intelligence and, by implication, that such development plays an important role in forms of learning used outside the arts.

The second potential benefit that might come from research on the non-artistic consequences of work in the arts is essentially theoretical. The question itself is interesting. Just what is the array of cognitive style, human sensitivity, intellectual flexibility, and metaphorical modes of thought that work in the arts might generate? What forms of arts teaching and arts experience are related to or instrumental in such processes? And what does the ability to use such processes mean for work in history, the sciences, and mechanical forms of problem-solving? Aptitudes, as Glazer[7] recently suggested, might be usefully conceived of, not as the product of human thought and action, but rather as the processes that are used to create such thought and action. It may well be the case that such processes can be fostered through the kinds of problem-solving that work in the arts stimulates and develops.

One further caveat must be entered here when one talks about the contributions of the arts to non-artistic forms of human action. That caveat deals with the fact that the arts can be taught and experienced themselves in non-artistic ways. This seems to be something of a paradox, but only until we recognize that we use the term "art" in different ways: (a) the arts refer to a certain classification of subject matters—painting, dance, music, filmmaking, and the like; and (b) they also refer to a certain quality of experience. It is the case that, given the former conception, the arts can be taught and experienced *in*artistically and that, given the latter concept, the sciences and other so-called *non*-artistic fields can be taught and experienced artistically. What I am referring to with respect to the non-artistic consequences of work in the arts is to be determined by studying arts programs in the first sense (a above), taught and experienced in the second sense (b above). Research into the arts could, and I believe should, investigate their psychological spinoffs.

Developmental-Experimental Studies of Artistic Learning

Traditionally, developmental research has been aimed at describing and explaining the patterns and processes of human development as they unfold over the course of the human life cycle. Such research has attempted to describe what is and to explain why it has occurred. Schools, however, are institutions intended to facilitate a process—

education—and are not simply places for development to unfold naturally. Schools are institutions created to influence development, to cultivate and shape human possibility.[8] Schooling is a cultural artifact guided by social values. What we seek to determine through research concerns not only what is, but what might be—thus, the hyphen in the subtitle of this section: "developmental-experimental." What we seek is the creation of experimental programs that can be used within a developmental framework that will adumbrate the possibilities that educational programs in schools might seek to attain. What are the limits of a seven-year-old's perception of the expressive qualities found in architecture, dance, or painting? Can a program that systematically encourages children to translate ideas, images, and feelings from one expressive modality to another have important consequences at a later stage of human development? Do age-graded expectations place artificial ceilings on learning; and how could such a question be tested within the arts? How do exploratory modes of thinking develop among children and what effects do schooling have upon such thought? Would programs that emphasize the sensory aspects of experience instead of emphasizing rule-governed forms of learning in the early grades tend to foster a richer, more imaginative mode of intellectual life? Questions such as these, when put into a developmental framework, could be used for the creation of potentially significant experimental educational programs. Although, currently, the most influential developmental theory tends to focus upon the so-called cognitive aspects of behavior, this need not be the case. By positing new images of development— images that honor what the arts might generate—a wider view of human potential might be created and a wider scope for schooling encouraged.

The point here is that our views of children—views that now emphasize cognitive development—have an important influence on what we consider important in the conduct of education. Different images of developmental virtue lead us to prize different educational ends. We badly need to be able to conceptualize the developmental aspects of thought and action in the arts in a form that has as much intellectual significance as Piaget's conceptions of the child's cognitive development.

Developmental-experimental research in arts education might profitably address itself to the relationship between forms of early socialization and preferred modes of thinking among children. What impact does the children's home environment have upon their attitudes towards the arts and the forms of thinking they can engage in? To what extent are the arts stereotyped, and where and when do children learn them? What consequences does such stereotyping have upon performance in the arts and in career aspirations? How do we convey to children what is considered masculine and feminine behavior, and how are the arts regarded in the socialization process? Finally, if the arts are stereotyped, what kinds of educational programs might be created to de-associate them from sexual bias?

The Impact of Social Institutions on the Educational Significance of the Arts in the Schools

Schools do not function in a social vacuum. Their mission, their priorities, and their structure are influenced by a host of social forces they have little or no control over. The creation of an oil embargo by a sheikdom on the other side of the globe has educational consequences felt in the Peorias of the United States. Sputniks I and II circling the earth become the final impetus for ushering in a new era in science and mathematics education in American schools. These are dramatic events, the ones that we notice; but there are a variety of other events—events that become institutionalized, that affect the quality and character of arts education in American schools. Take, for example, the Scholastic Achievement Tests that are given annually to almost 2 million students leaving secondary schools who wish admission to colleges and universities throughout the country. The SAT test is aimed at measuring the student's ability in verbal and mathematical performance. Abilities in the arts simply do not count. What impact does the use of such a test have upon students? How does it affect the secondary-school cur- riculum? What effect does it have upon high-school guidance coun- selors from whom students receive advice about what they should study? In what ways does such a test influence the public's view of what counts as "quality education"? What is the interaction between high-school graduation requirements and the existence and use of the SAT?

Take, as another example, the priorities established by the National Institute of Education. At present, at least one of those priorities is represented by the program dealing with "basic skills." How do the monies allocated through this program affect the public's views of the significance of the arts in the schools? What is implied by "basic skills"? And how were these terms determined? What are basic skills? Does imagination count? Is personal initiative basic? How basic is curiosity and the love of learning? I raise these questions not to appear glib or clever but because I believe that educational values impacting the arts are conveyed in subtle ways and that arts educators would do well to study how these influences affect arts programs in the schools. What would a White House Conference devoted to the theme "The Arts in the Schools and Society" mean to arts programs serving the 50 million students in the nation's schools?

I believe one of our very important research needs in arts education resides in the study of the ways that social institutions outside the schools affect arts programs inside the school. We need to recognize that the school has established an ecological balance with the community and the nation it is a part of. It functions as it does because social factors shape its configuration and influence its aims. What we need to learn is how that influence occurs and what might be done to shift the balance so that the environment of the school and the values that animate it are hospitable to the arts. This is no small task, but one that must be undertaken. At present, the sociology of the arts in American education is an unstudied area, but one we can neglect at the cost of vitiating our more specific, molecular efforts to strengthen arts education in American schools.

Stanford, California
June 1976

FOOTNOTES

[1] *Music and Art in the Public Schools,* Research Monograph, 1963-M3 (Washington, D.C.: National Art Education Association, 1963).

[2] Elliot W. Eisner, "The Perceptive Eye: Toward a Reformation of Educational Evaluation," Invited Address, Division B, American Educational Research Association Convention, Washington, D.C., February 1975. Also see "Educational Connoisseurship and Educational Criticism: Their Forms and Functions in Educational Evaluation," *Journal of Aesthetic Education,* Bicentennial Issue (1976, in press).

[3] Elliot W. Eisner, "Toward a More Adequate Conception of Evaluation in the Arts," *Art Education* (October 1974).

[4] The earlier works of Kenneth Beittel are illustrative of some of the possibilities of time-lapse photographs for describing the "arting" process; particularly his work on spontaneous, academic, and deliberate strategies in painting and drawing.

[5] Oscar K. Buros, ed., *Tests in Print,* Vol. 2 (Highland Park, New Jersey: The Gryphon Press, 1974).

[6] Elliot W. Eisner, "The Development of Information and Attitudes Towards Art at the Secondary and College Level," *Studies in Art Education,* Vol. 8, No. 1 (Autumn 1965).

[7] Robert Glazer, "The New Aptitudes," Presidential Address, American Educational Research Association, 1973.

[8] Although I recognize that some educational critics believe that schools limit more than they expand human possibility, their intention, I would argue, is positive.

Conference Participants
Aspen, Colorado, June 22-25, 1976

George Anselevicius
SUNY Chair of Architecture
School of Architecture and
  Environmental Design
State University of New York at Buffalo

Adam Aronson
Chairman of the Board
Mark Twain Bancshares

Judith Aronson
Director
Project Development and Aesthetic
  Education
Webster College
St. Louis, Missouri

Anne Bartley
Director
Department of Arkansas Natural and
  Cultural Heritage

Judith Bauer
Supervisor
Instructional Specialists Program
Michigan State Department of
  Education

Thomas P. Bergin
Dean
Center for Continuing Education
University of Notre Dame
Representing the National
  Endowment for the Arts

Kathryn Bloom
Director
Arts in Education Program
The JDR 3rd Fund

Dorothy Brooks
Fine Arts Specialist
Michigan State Department of
  Education

Harry S. Broudy
Professor of Philosophy and
  Education Emeritus
College of Education
University of Illinois at
  Urbana-Champaign

Herbert J. Burgart
Dean
School of the Arts
Virginia Commonwealth University

John Cataldo
Dean
Massachusetts College of Art

Richard Colwell
Professor of Music Education
School of Music
University of Illinois at
  Urbana-Champaign

Richard Courtney
Professor of Arts and Education
Department of Curriculum
Ontario Institute for Studies
  in Education, Toronto, Canada

Donald W. Crawford
Professor and Chairman
Department of Philosophy
University of Wisconsin

Diana Crump
Trustee
Memphis Academy of Arts
Brooks Memorial Art Gallery

D. Jack Davis
Professor and Chairman
Department of Art
North Texas State University
Senior Editor
Studies in Art Education

Charles M. Dorn
Professor and Head
Department of Creative Arts
Purdue University

David Ecker
Professor
Art Education Department
New York University

Elliot Eisner
Professor of Education and Art
Department of Art
Stanford University

Martin Engel
Advisor for Arts and Humanities
National Institute of Education

Arthur Wells Foshay
Professor of Education Emeritus
Teachers College
Columbia University

425

Mary Frates
Oklahoma City Arts Council

Jane Garmey
Assistant to the President
WNET/Channel 13, New York

Roland Gelatt
Arts Editor
Saturday Review

Peggy Gonder
Reporter
Education U.S.A.

Dwaine Greer
Program Area Coordinator, Fine Arts
SWRL Educational Research and
  Development

Alma Hawkins
Professor and Chairman
Department of Dance
University of California at
  Los Angeles

Harlan Hoffa
Head
Division of Art and Music Education
Pennsylvania State University

Samuel Hope
Executive Director
National Association of Schools
  of Music

Harold Horowitz
Director of Research
National Endowment for the Arts

Albert Hurwitz
Supervisor of Art
Newton, Massachusetts, Public
  Schools

Morgan Johnson
Research Coordinator
Western States Arts Foundation,
  Denver

Lonna Jones
Education Program Specialist
Arts and Humanities
United States Office of Education

Francis Keppel
Director
Program on Education
Aspen Institute for Humanistic
  Studies

Chelsea Kesselheim
Reporter
Christian Science Monitor

Gerard Knieter
Professor and Chairman
Department of Music Education
Temple University
Representing the Music Educators
  National Conference

Sarah Knight
Data Analyst for Art
National Assessment, Denver

Mary Ann Koenig
Founding Director
Aspen Foundation for the Arts

Lionel Landry
Executive Vice-President
The Asia Society

Gil Lazier
Professor of Theatre
Director of the Graduate Program
The Florida State University

Charles Leonhard
Professor of Music
School of Music
University of Illinois at
  Urbana-Champaign

Hilda Lewis
Professor of Education
San Francisco State University

Samella Lewis
Professor of Art History
Scripps College
Claremont, California

Stanley S. Madeja
Vice-President
CEMREL, Inc.
Director
Aesthetic Education Program

John Mahlmann
Executive Director
National Art Education Association

Sue Marsh
Administrative Assistant
CEMREL, Inc.

Gerry J. Martin
National Executive Director
Young Audiences, Inc.

Clyde McGeary
Senior Program Advisor
Pennsylvania State Department of
  Education

John Merriam
Trustee
Aspen Institute for Humanistic Studies

Nadine Meyers
Associate Director
Aesthetic Education Program
CEMREL, Inc.

Mary Ella Montague
Past President
National Dance Association

Bradley G. Morison
President
Arts Development Associates, Inc.,
    Minneapolis

Jack Morrison
Executive Director
American Theatre Association

Richard Munson
Assistant Professor of Fine Arts
University of Northern Colorado

Nancy Pelz-Paget
Assistant Director
Aspen Institute for Humanistic Studies

David Perkins
Co-Director
Project Zero
Harvard University

Wade Robinson
President
CEMREL, Inc.

David Rockefeller, Jr.
Chairman
Arts, Education, and Americans Panel
Chairman
Associated Councils of the Arts

Forbes Rogers
Executive Director
Alliance for Arts Education
John F. Kennedy Center

George S. Rosborough, Jr.
President of the Board
St. Louis Art Museum

Bernard Rosenblatt
Associate Director
Aesthetic Education Program
CEMREL, Inc.

Mary Runge
Secretarial Supervisor
CEMREL, Inc.

Mark Schubart
Director of Education
Lincoln Center for the Performing
    Arts

Larry Schultz
Coordinator, Visual Arts
Jefferson County Public Schools
Lakewood, Colorado

Joseph Slater
Chairman
Aspen Institute for Humanistic
    Studies

Sara Smilansky
Professor of Child Psychology
Tel-Aviv University
Fellow
National Institute of Education

Barbara Smith
Art Instructor
Aspen High School

Fred Smith
Principal
Aspen Middle School

Ralph A. Smith
Professor of Cultural and
    Educational Policy
University of Illinois at
    Urbana-Champaign
Editor
The Journal of Aesthetic Education

Verna Smith
Director of Public Information
CEMREL, Inc.

Wallace Smith
Assistant Principal for Instruction
Evanston, Illinois, Township
    High School

A. B. Spellman
Consultant
Author
Lecturer in Afro-American
    Studies
Harvard University
Representing the National Endowment
    for the Arts

Anne Straus
National Board of Directors
Young Audiences, Inc.

Christine A. Sturges
CTAA Program Chairman
1976 American Theatre Association
    Convention

Willem J. H. B. Sandberg
Director
Municipal Museum of Amsterdam
The Netherlands

Jacqueline Sunderland
Director
Center for the Arts and the Aging

Anne Taylor
Associate Dean, Graduate School
Associate Professor, Art Education
Associate Professor, School of
    Architecture and Planning
University of New Mexico

Raymond W. Thompson
Coordinator
Arts and Sciences Division
Seattle Public Schools

David Warren
Acting Director of Education
Bureau of Indian Affairs
United States Department of the
    Interior

Morris Weitz
Professor of Philosophy
Brandeis University

Joseph Wheeler
Executive Director
CENTRUM
Representing the Western States
    Arts Foundation

Margaret Bush Wilson
Chairman of the Board
National Association for the
    Advancement of Colored People

Larry Winegar
Art Resource Teacher
Jefferson County Public Schools
    Lakewood, Colorado

Jean Wolff
Elementary Teacher
Clayton, Missouri, Public Schools

Tom Wolff
Toy Designer
Pitkin County Toy Company

Lin Wright
Assistant Professor
Department of Theatre
Arizona State University

CONTRIBUTORS: DID NOT ATTEND CONFERENCE

Linda Fosburg
Consultant
Associated Councils of the Arts

Howard Gardner
Co-Director
Project Zero
Harvard University

Harold Hodgkinson
Director
National Institute of Education

Eugene Kaelin
Chairman
Department of Philosophy
The Florida State University

Christiana M. Smith
Associate Editor
The Journal of Aesthetic Education

Seminar Panelists

Seminar 1

Chairperson
Nancy Pelz-Paget
Assistant Director
Aspen Institute for Humanistic
  Studies

Panel
George Anselevicius
SUNY Chair of Architecture
School of Architecture and
  Environmental Design
State University of New York
  at Buffalo
John Cataldo
Dean
Massachusetts College of Art
Sara Smilansky
Professor of Child Psychology
Tel-Aviv University
Fellow
National Institute of Education
Anne Taylor
Associate Dean
Graduate School
University of New Mexico
David Warren
Acting Director of Education
Bureau of Indian Affairs
United States Department
  of the Interior
Morris Weitz
Professor of Philosophy
Brandeis University

Seminar 2

Chairperson
Herbert J. Burgart
Dean
School of the Arts
Virginia Commonwealth Univer-
  sity

Panel
Arthur Wells Foshay
Professor of Education Emeritus
Teachers College
Columbia University
Alma Hawkins
Professor and Chairman
Department of Dance
University of California
  at Los Angeles
Harold Horowitz
Director of Research
National Endowment for the Arts
Gil Lazier
Professor of Theater
Director of the Graduate Program
The Florida State University
David Perkins
Co-Director
Project Zero
Harvard University
Mark Schubart
Director of Education
Lincoln Center for the Performing
  Arts

Seminar 3

Chairperson
John J. Mahlmann
Executive Director
National Art Education Association

Panel
Kathryn Bloom
Director
Arts in Education Program
The JDR 3rd Fund

Harry Broudy
Professor of Philosophy and Education Emeritus
University of Illinois at
Urbana-Champaign

Richard Colwell
Professor of Music Education
University of Illinois at
Urbana-Champaign

Elliot Eisner
Professor of Education and Art
Stanford University

Lionel Landry
Executive Vice-President
The Asia Society

A. B. Spellman
Consultant
Author
Lecturer in Afro-American
Studies
Harvard University

Seminar 4

Chairperson
Jack Morrison
Executive Director
American Theatre Association

Panel
David Ecker
Professor
Art Education Department
New York University

Martin Engel
Advisor for Arts and Humanities
National Institute of Education

Harlan Hoffa
Head
Division of Art and Music Education
Pennsylvania State University

Charles Leonhard
Professor of Music
University of Illinois at
Urbana-Champaign

Samella Lewis
Professor of Art History
Scripps College

Ralph A. Smith
Professor of Cultural and
Educational Policy
University of Illinois at
Urbana-Champaign